THE CRAFT OF COOKING

The Craft of Cooking

A DIGEST OF THE HOWS AND WHYS
OF COOKERY

Margaret Paterson

MACDONALD AND JANE'S
LONDON

FIRST PUBLISHED IN 1978 BY
MACDONALD AND JANE'S PUBLISHERS LIMITED,
PAULTON HOUSE,
8 SHEPHERDESS WALK, LONDON, N.1

ILLUSTRATIONS BY WENDY JONES

ISBN 0 354 04086 3

PHOTOTYPESET BY TRADESPOOLS LTD
FROME, SOMERSET
AND PRINTED AND BOUND IN GREAT BRITAIN
BY BILLING AND SONS LTD, LONDON, GUILDFORD
AND WORCESTER

Contents

	Acknowledgements	vii
	Introduction	ix
1	The Dilemma of Kitchen Equipment	1
2	Terms and Techniques	30
3	Ingredients	62
4	Pastry	98
5	Eggs and Egg Dishes	106
6	Hors-d'oeuvres	115
7	Soups	123
8	Savoury Sauces	129
9	Vegetables, Pasta and Rice	140
10	Salads, Salad Components and Salad Dressings	157
11	Fish	165
12	Meat	179
13	Poultry and Game	198
14	Sweets and Puddings	223
15	Dessert Sauces	239
16	Breads, Continental Breads and Scones	243
17	Cakes	250
18	Cake Icings and Fillings	260
19	Beverages	268
20	Miscellaneous	273
	Bibliography	277
	Index	279

Acknowledgements

My greatest thanks are to Mrs Joyce Westcott (née Arnison) who first taught me to cook, passing on both her knowledge and her infectious enthusiasm. She has given me a lifetime of happiness and interest.

I would also like to thank Mrs Margot Mayes, Mrs Vivienne Hines and Miss Marjorie Stone who taught me in later years, after we moved south to live.

I could not and would not have written this book without the encouragement, kindness and help of my husband Pat, Walter Parrish (of Walter Parrish International Ltd) and my sister Barbara Elliot.

I am also grateful to the librarians at Winchester County Library for their unfailing and willing help.

Please note that where quantities are given in this book in spoonfuls, I am assuming you'll be using traditional average-sized spoons from your kitchen drawer, not the measuring spoons in a set, which are smaller.

Introduction

Beware! If it's a recipe book you are looking for, *The Craft of Cooking* is not for you. This book aims to be *different*: by helping you to make the best of your *own* recipe books, also your equipment and your money. Whether you like or dislike cooking, my main purpose is to help you to enjoy it more, and to eat better.

When I was once bewailing the lack of practical guidance in so many recipe books, a cookery expert commented: 'cook books can't tell you everything you need to know about a recipe – that's why people should have lessons.' This book aims to fill those gaps, by providing the knowledge which most recipe books must take for granted. It is not intended for experts, who will know much more about cooking than I do, but for the enthusiast who wants to learn more about English and French cooking. If, for instance, you find some kinds of fish tasteless, your soufflés are a disaster, your meringues 'weep', or your melting chocolate turns to rock, let's hope I can help you to discover why.

Scores of books give recipes for things like pea soup, sausage rolls or fish cakes, but they don't tell you why one type of ingredient may be preferable to a marginally different one; advise a suitable piece of equipment for a particular task, or give you the ABC of *how* to do it. If I can then help you to make all the basic dishes, of which most others (many also here) are an elaboration, it should be easy to put together the combination of your skills and knowledge to use any reliable recipe book with success.

Couldn't we enjoy cooking more if we knew *why* we should do things in a particular way? Wouldn't we for instance remember to stir boiled rice with a two-pronged fork if we knew it becomes a solid mass when we use a spoon? Wouldn't we cook better and make more of our housekeeping money if we knew *all* the whys and wherefores?

This is a reading and reference book. For good measure, you'll find hundreds of hints, snatches of history, the origin of some familiar names and words, and some ways to help you beat fatigue in the kitchen.

Most of all, I hope you're going to love cooking as I do and enjoy years of good eating.

Margaret Paterson
1 September 1977

1

THE DILEMMA OF KITCHEN EQUIPMENT

And dilemma it is, with so much to choose from. Some items are ideal, some expensive and impractical, some more practical and *less* expensive. Just as a pretty face may be no criterion of anything but looks, so it may be with equipment, which one should never judge by its appearance.

Your needs may not be mine, nor mine yours: some folks like a working kitchen, others a dining-kitchen; some will enjoy making and eating the sort of dishes which others wouldn't even consider; some can afford the luxuries, others must improvise when it's possible, as I'll try to show how.

If I can highlight some of the advantages, warn you about some of the snags, or simply bring a useful piece of equipment to your notice, that's all I aim to do. In addition, I've included certain things like a pancake pan only because I refer to them through the book.

You'll cook better, eat better, save time and will *enjoy* cooking more if you have the right tool for the job. Having worked in numerous well-equipped colleges over several years, I have had the opportunity to see and use a wide range of kitchen equipment. The opinions I express, therefore, although personal, are based on outside experience as well as on the good, bad or indifferent things I have been fortunate or unfortunate enough to buy myself.

Bags

PAPER ICING BAGS. Cost nothing to make and eliminate the need for one of those expensive, difficult-to-manipulate and rather useless icing syringes. It's not much trouble to make several bags at a time if you ever have 10 minutes to spare, then they're ready for use when you want them. Although not re-useable, they're efficient as well as economical. A 10″ (25 cm) square of greaseproof paper must be accurate, so that you can cut it into two identical triangles and make them, one at a time, in the same way:

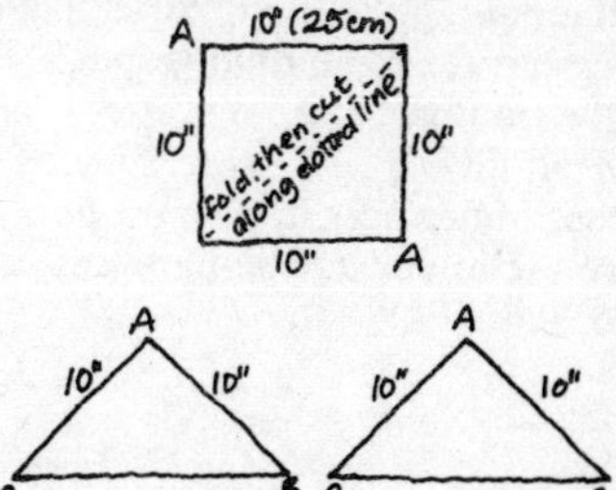

(1) Fold square in half and cut along diagonal line, as illustrated.
(2) Hold the triangle up in front of you with the right-angle A at the top, held between thumb and first finger of left hand.

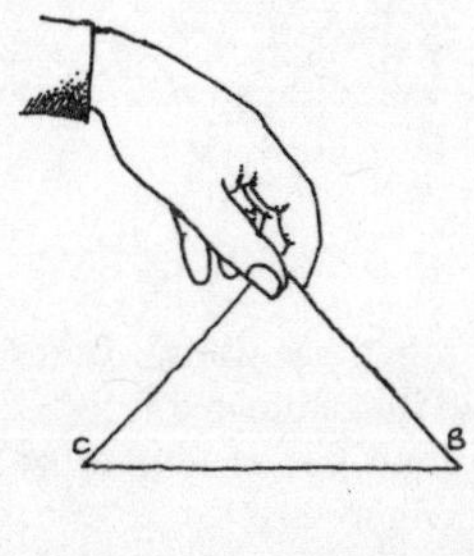

(3) Now bring the point B to the point A, turning it so that the *underside* of the paper at point B faces you, giving a single thickness cornet.

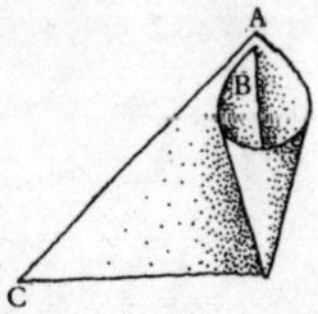

(4) Bring point C round front of cornet and up round back to join points A and B precisely, giving now a double thickness cornet. The bottom of cornet, D, see below, should be a sharp point.

(5) Fold down the points A, B and C, to hold them tightly together and to hold cornet in shape.

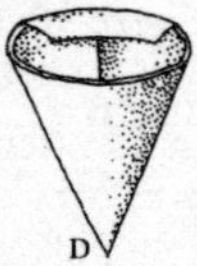

(6) Cut off tiny tip at D if to use for writing (or if without any tubes) or cut off *about* $\frac{1}{4}''$ (6 mm) to let point of chosen tube come right through. Drop tube into bag.

(7) Half fill bag with prepared icing, fold front of bag over it, then the back, and press icing down to bottom, see illustrations

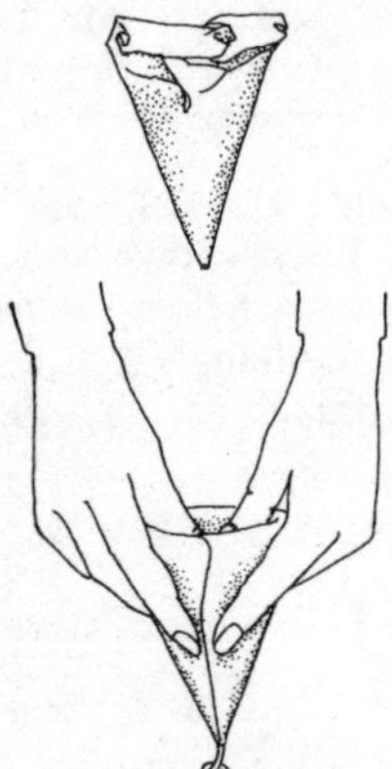

(8) Put filled bag inside other (empty) bag and fold *it* down too.

(9) Hold and use as illustrated.

PIPING BAGS. Made of nylon, these come in graded sizes. If you can rise to only one, choose a medium-sized bag, but for bulky things like meringue mixture or choux pastry, a larger (14″ or 36 cm in length) will save time. You may also want a smaller one. Unlike twill bags, you can wash, dry and re-use nylon as soon as you like. See also *Paper Icing bags*, above.

POLYTHENE BAGS. Much cheaper if you're *able* to buy them in bulk, and also lucky enough to live somewhere near a shop like 'Transatlantic Plastics', who sell odd sizes, numbers and thicknesses in 2 lb (say 1 K) or 6 lb (say 3 K) packs, their surplus from large orders. The bags are perfect, but it's a blind buy so your luck and your selection may be better sometimes than others. A pack may last you for months or even years, according to use and care.

★ For the freezer heavy-weight bags are *best*, and essential for things like meat, poultry or game, to prevent freezer burn (see page 41) and consequent loss of flavour from the food: remember, the bag is usually the only barrier between food and freezer. Thinner bags will become brittle at freezer temperatures and will eventually split, leaving the food exposed. If the bags are thin, use one inside another, but even then preferably not for poultry etc. Foods in bags large enough to tie in a knot at the neck are easy enough to open blindfold, and eliminate the need for wire ties which often pierce other packs.
★ Three or four really large strong bags will save rummaging and electricity, and prevent your freezer from becoming a jumble: you can then lift out a whole bagful at a time, sorting it at leisure. It's ideal to have coloured bags if you can buy them – red for meats, blue for fish, green for vegetables and another colour for fruits. Freezers with several baskets are naturally easier still, or you can buy baskets individually.

Bain-Marie

Sounds slightly daunting but need only be a roasting tin half-filled with hot water, and any small strong pans with lids (or foil) to cover them.

★ The water should be 'shivering' – slightly cooler than simmering – when using the bain-marie as a double saucepan for the thickening of tricky sauces likely to curdle if put over direct heat.
★ It should be even cooler when used to keep this sort of sauce hot, and cooler still for sauces of the Hollandaise family. It's fatal to try and keep these hot either in the oven or in a pan over direct heat, because they'll curdle.
★ Small pans are best because there's room for more of them and because the sauce will be deeper, with a smaller surface over which skin can form.
★ With simmering water, a bain-marie is splendid too when a large household strains a small cooker, because you can keep 3 or 4 pans of food hot over just one burner.

Baking Sheets

These should always be sold with a cooker, I think. They must *fit* because you'll waste oven space if they're too small, and the hot air can't circulate properly if they're too large: you'll probably feel it's *your* fault when foods burn or cook unevenly.

★ Good quality sheets are vital, otherwise foods will burn on the bottom. The heavy aluminium baking sheets are excellent, added to which you can see when they're dirty.
★ There are two main types:
(1) Those with four shallow sides – the safest to hold pie-dishes, casseroles, large cakes or puddings etc, and therefore the best for general use.

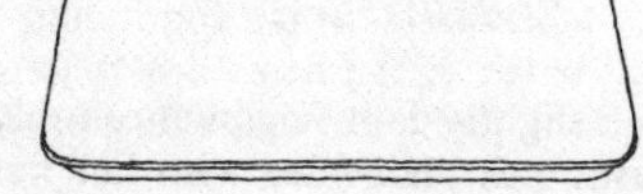

(2) Those with one end turned up. Pastry and scones slide off easily when you want them to, but so just as easily can casseroles or anything else. In addition, spilt liquids are not contained, and some foods spread over the edges as they cook.

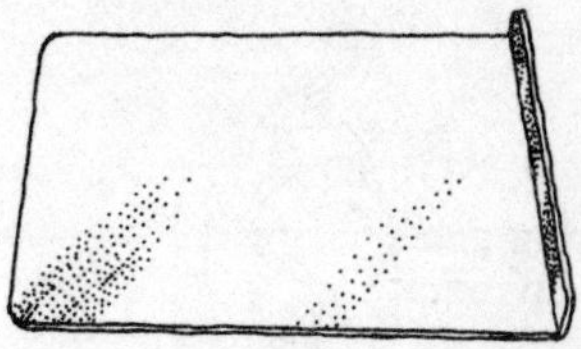

★ Why, you may ask, should at least 2 baking sheets be part and parcel of every cooker? Because:
(1) They're vital for safety, to lift dishes in and out of the oven and to give protection from burns and scalds.
(2) Without them, you can't make successfully such things as pastry, scones, dinner rolls, biscuits etc.
(3) They save individual handling of dishes and foods, so saving your time and also cutting down heat loss, which may spoil some dishes and certainly wastes fuel.
(4) They save work, by protecting both oven and shelves from spills.
★ To save labour and to make full and proper use of a hot oven when you want to, you need as many baking sheets as you have oven shelves, plus one for the 'floor'. For good measure, if you're bulk baking for the freezer, you'll perhaps even be glad of one or two more than that.

Ballers

Known also as ball-scoops, these are for making balls of the flesh of fruits or vegetables, often as a garnish, e.g. melon, potato, cucumber. They are made in

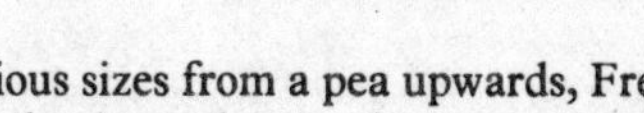

various sizes from a pea upwards, French ones having a sharper, better cutting edge than British, which are double-ended, and cheaper.

★ It's easy to make half a ball but more difficult to make a complete one: hold thumb under back of scoop as illustrated, press hard into vegetable or fruit and twist wrist right round. Use a baller also to hollow out such fruits as apples or small melons, to serve 'stuffed'.

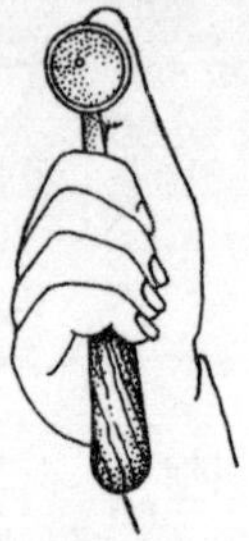

Baskets

BLANCHING BASKET. For the quick boiling of vegetables before freezing. Shops which fail to stock them or have possibly run short may try to persuade you that a chip basket or salad basket serves the same purpose. Some designs are unsuitable however, because small things

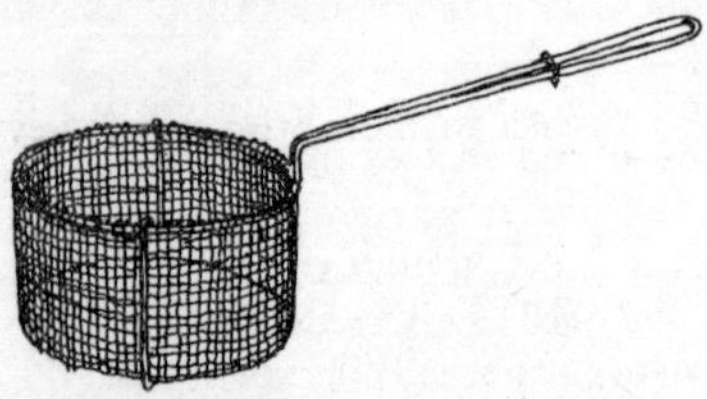

like peas or sliced beans dive straight through the gaps. You'd be better to use a nylon wine-straining bag if you have one, which is quite practical anyway. If you grow and freeze lots of vegetables, you'll save both fuel and labour by buying a large-size basket.

CHIP BASKET. See *Deep fat pan*, page 18.

GARLIC BASKET. May be an extravagance to buy for oneself but is possibly a very welcome present for the friend who enjoys cooking. It stores garlic as it *should* be stored, so if hung in the right place, where it's airy and convenient, your garlic will keep in good condition too. In appearance, it's like a miniature salad basket.

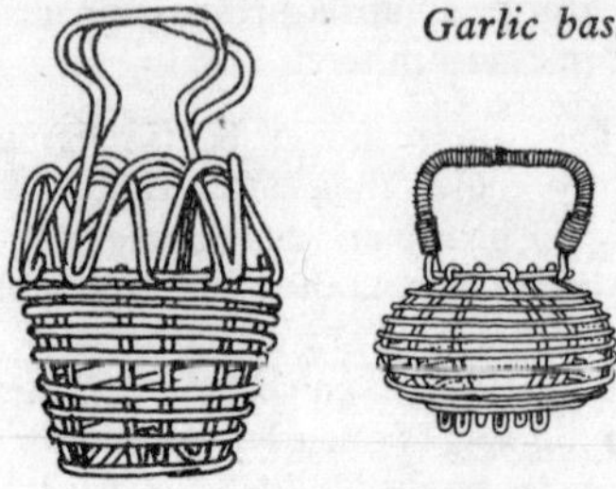

Garlic baskets

SALAD BASKET. Dries lettuce and other plants efficiently, and without bruising. Dryers which spin the lettuce dry by centrifugal force don't soak the kitchen, but are pricey compared with others – fine for anyone without a garden.

★ If short of space, you may like a collapsible basket? They're usually more costly, and some designs more fiddling than the simple but practical wire basket illustrated.

★ If without, just gather up the lettuce in a clean tea-towel, then swing it to and fro.

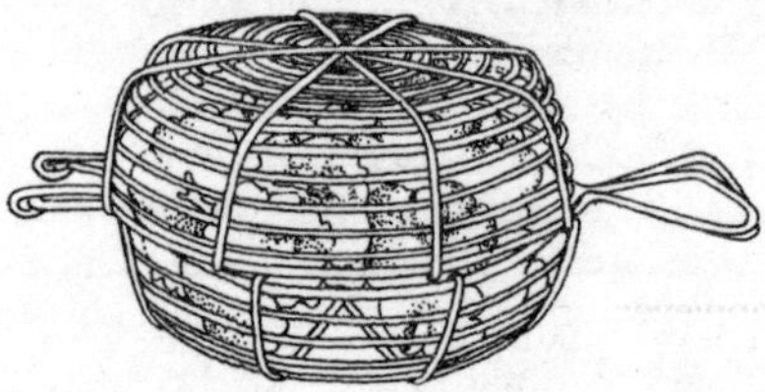

Bean Slicer

The Zipp is well named because it's efficient and quick, also easily washed up – and inexpensive.

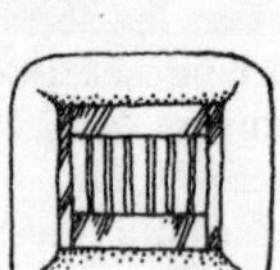

Bin

A pedal bin may be impossible to house if your kitchen units form a continuous line and all reach to the floor, otherwise it is ideal. In it, guest flies can't dine on your rubbish, pets can't poke about and even the strongest smells are contained. For good measure, there's nothing unsightly to look at and, with both hands either sticky or full, you can still open the lid – with your foot.

Blender

See *Liquidizer*, page 15.

Boards

WOODEN CHOPPING BOARDS. Will warp gradually if too thin or of poor quality, making it impossible to chop herbs, vegetables and so on properly. A once-in-a-lifetime buy, it pays to buy a good, thick one *about* 14″ × 9″ (36 × 23 cm) say of sycamore or utile (a hardwood), which can if necessary double as breadboard or cheeseboard as well. You can use it for anything and foods don't slip about as they do on melamine.

MELAMINE CHOPPING BOARDS. Both decorative and handy. Herbs don't stain, nor does the smell of onions or garlic penetrate, but it's best to use the 'wrong' side for chopping, to avoid wearing away the design on the colourful side. Knives, however, are blunted more quickly by melamine than by a wooden board.

WOODEN PASTRY BOARD. An asset if you can afford and house one. It keeps cooler than a formica table top, and flour dusted over it is distributed more evenly, making it easier to roll pastry well. Often made of sycamore.

★ For a very small household, you *might* manage with a board 18″ × 12″ (46 × 30 cm), otherwise go for one 20″ × 14″ (51 × 36 cm) or better still 24″ × 18″ (61 × 46 cm).

Bowls

COPPER BOWL. Ideal for whisking egg whites if you're lucky enough to have one. You might find one cheaply, as I did, on a market antique stall. A useful household size is 10″ (25 cm) in diameter. See also *Whisking*, page 60.

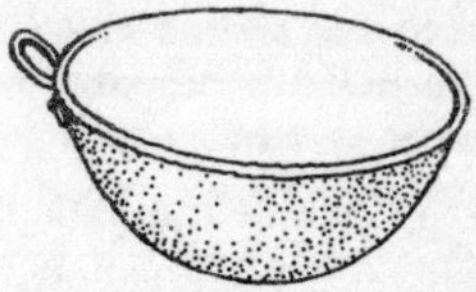

MIXING BOWLS. Much wider at the top than pudding basins (see illustrations below), to allow room for your hands to move about freely when doing things like rubbing fat into flour, beating a sponge mixture, or whisking egg whites etc. This

Pudding basin

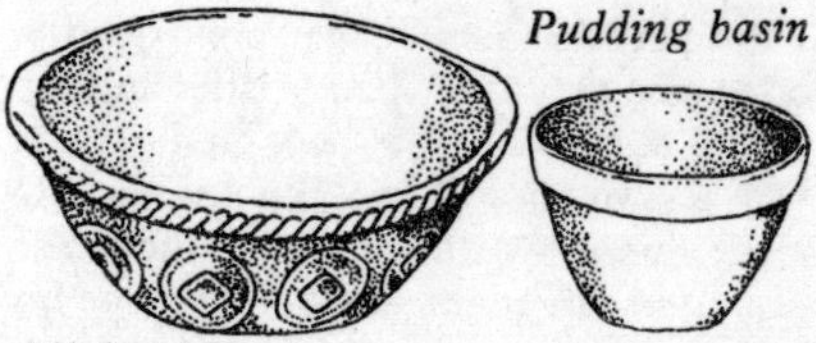

Mixing bowl

means you can entangle more air in the mixture than you could in a pudding basin so you'll make *lighter* pastry, sponges, meringues and so on.

★ They may be old-fashioned but I think it's difficult to beat the thick china bowls illustrated, glazed inside and out: they don't wobble about; you can use any and every utensil in them with ease; they're good for mixing pastry or bread-making; will withstand considerable heat; 'nest' perfectly for easy handling and minimum storage space, and with care will survive years of punishing use. Pyrex-type bowls would be my second choice; stainless steel, aluminium and plastic bringing up the rear.

★ You need at *least* three, say $9\frac{1}{2}$″, $10\frac{1}{2}$″ and 12″ (24, 27 and 30 cm) in diameter.

★ Aluminium bowls may give a greyish cast to such foods as whisked egg white, royal icing or ice cream.

PLASTIC WASHING-UP BOWLS. As light as a feather when empty and have a huge capacity, so may sometimes be useful for certain stages of some jam or wine-making. Keep one specially for the purpose, of course.

WOODEN SALAD BOWL. Should be large enough to turn over the contents easily in the dressing. Small individual ones look lovely on a table and are perfect to use when you serve a salad with hot food. Look out for them if you're abroad – they're much cheaper than here.

★ To keep it shiny and feed the wood, occasionally rub a wooden bowl inside and out with a tissue dipped in salad oil – and keep your bowl well clear of a dishwasher; otherwise it will dry out and crack.

Brushes

Pastry brushes should be of good quality, otherwise they shed their bristles and can be just as maddening as poor quality paint brushes: you need a small compact one to glaze a narrow strip of pastry without also egging its cut edges, and a bigger one for brushing fat quickly over the larger areas of a baking sheet or cake tin etc.

Cake Tray

A tray or rack allows hot cakes and bread etc. to cool without sweating, and pastry to become crisp as air circulates around. Round ones may be cheaper than, and are just as spacious as, rectangular, especially if the latter has 'sides'. You can't do without if you bake much.

★ You may need a cake tray too sometimes for cake icing, or for coating foods such as cold cooked fish with aspic jelly or chaudfroid sauce, with a dish or large bowl underneath to collect the drips.
★ The rack in a grill pan will substitute for very small amounts.

Cherry Stoner

This does a fiddling job quickly and well (it also serves for olives). It's worth having if you use a lot of either fruit. The design illustrated below is the one I like best.

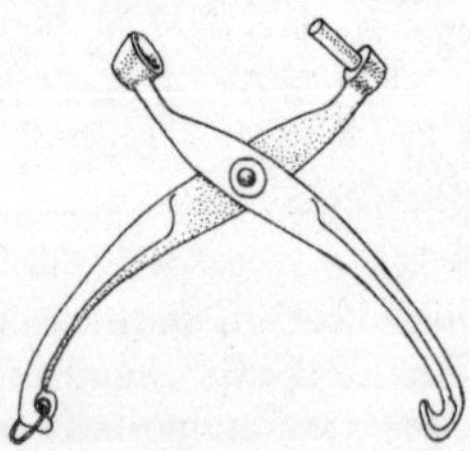

Cloths

DISH CLOTHS. Become positively antisocial if they aren't washed, and preferably boiled too, regularly.

On a non-polished work surface or in the sink, a wet dish cloth keeps a mixing bowl steady and cuts down the noise if spread underneath it when beating a mixture, kneading a dough etc.

OVEN CLOTHS. Not nearly as 'costly' as a burn or scald. The type illustrated below is practical, safe and one of the least expensive (but do make sure you buy the top-quality heat-proof make because there are also some dangerously thin ones on the market): it's quick and easy to slip your hands in or out of; long enough to hold a baking sheet or large casserole (even when grabbed in a hurry); both hands are protected from scalds or burns, and it's easy to keep clean.

★ Amazing it is how some people never think of *washing* an oven cloth: these, if white, can join the weekly wash, but coloured ones may not be dye-fast.

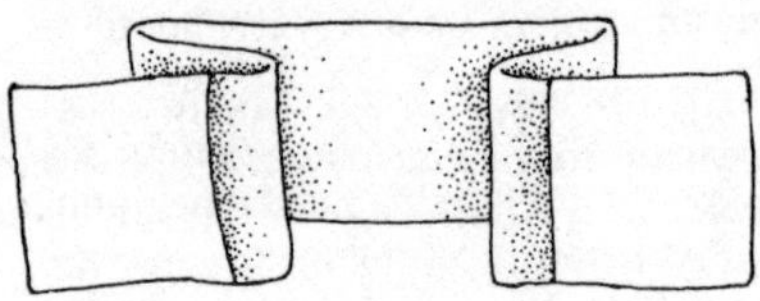

Cocotte

French for casserole. Foods cooked and served in them are described as 'en cocotte' or 'en casserole'. Ramekin is the English word for an individual cocotte: ramekins don't have lids, and are used for such dishes as Oeufs en Cocotte and individual savoury soufflés. They may be

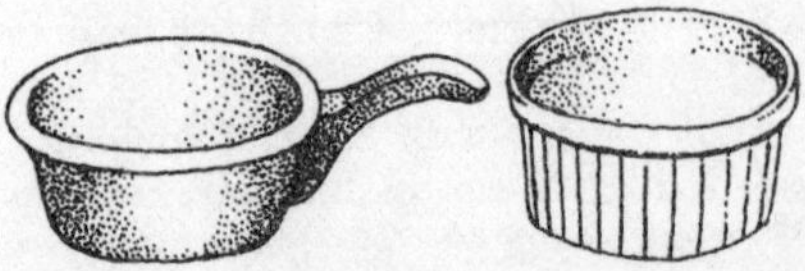

made of ovenproof china or glass, pottery, fine porcelain or sometimes of metal.

Colander

One of these is essential, to avoid serving sodden vegetables. If you drain off the water with a pan's lid, you're not really giving your vegetables a fair chance. You may need a colander as well to 'refresh' vegetables under a running cold tap (see page 54).

Cookers

PRESSURE COOKER. Something people seem to swear by or swear at. Be quite convinced you need one and will trouble to read all the instructions before you take the plunge and buy. A pressure cooker is designed to harness the steam which in an ordinary saucepan escapes and is wasted. The sealing in of this steam and the consequent build-up of pressure causes a rise in temperature. It is this high heat, coupled with the fact that the pressure generated in the cooker actually drives the heat into and through the food, which explains the rapid cooking action of even normally slow-cooking foods like tough meat or cereals etc.

★ Even if you don't like vegetables, fruit or say a beef steak and kidney pudding cooked in a pressure cooker, it certainly scores in *some* ways. Here are a few:

(1) It can save up to hours of cooking when making things like stock, steamed puddings, marmalade or chutney. This cuts down on fuel costs, and also on your time.
(2) It's a way of saving on the weekly cost of meat because cheaper cuts of meat cook in a shorter time.
(3) A meal can be on the table long before it would be *cooked* in the traditional way.
(4) Many frozen foods can be cooked or reheated straight from the freezer, cutting substantially the time otherwise involved.

COOKERS. Very much a matter of personal preference, so I'm keeping quiet about my own, but when buying a new or secondhand one, there are many factors to consider: we all think about the *type* we want – gas, electric, solid fuel or oil – as well as the cost, colour and size for a particular space in the kitchen, but what about some of these details:

(1) In relation to the size of your family and to the amount of entertaining you may do, is the oven large enough and are there enough burners or hot-plates? A cooker with a small oven can't be a long-term economy if you cook much.
(2) Would a split-level unit suit you better or fit better into limited space?
(3) Is the hob easy to clean? Some are a nightmare, others child's play. One with a spillage tray may save a lot of work.
(4) Do you dread cleaning your oven? If so, some gas and electric ones never need it.
(5) Do you want warmth from your cooker, and with that somewhere to dry and air clothes? If so, a 'solid fuel' type of cooker is your answer, but think of the disadvantages as well as the many advantages.
(6) Is there a good and efficient grill, large enough for your needs? If not, you'll miss some of the finest dishes imaginable.
(7) Could small children, if any, turn on the taps or meddle with the control panel?
(8) Would you be better with a built-in hob, with counter space on each side? There are no sides to clean, and no dust can gather underneath.
(9) If an electric cooker, is there a thermostatically controlled hot-plate? This is no luxury, but a near necessity for anyone using deep fat who hasn't got a similarly controlled deep-fat pan. I may have a bee in my bonnet about this but if you've ever seen deep fat go on fire, you'll know why.
(10) Have you considered a convection (fan-assisted) oven? I haven't used one myself but those who have one seem to swear by it – and I'm certainly sold on the idea. Although slightly more expensive initially than its counterpart with elements, the advantages are real;

especially that of having even heat throughout the oven. It's worth enquiring about, but here, meanwhile, are some of the assets:

(a) It cooks about 8 mins. faster in the hour than a conventional oven because the heat is absolutely constant. It also heats up about 5 mins. faster, so is slightly more economical on electricity.

(b) The oven is wider because there are no space-taking elements at each side – and no elements to wear out.

(c) Roast meat neither spits nor shrinks quite so much.

(11) Do you want an oven with an inner glass door and a light inside, to have a peep at what's going on without letting in cold air?

(12) Might a cooker with double oven suit you better; the smaller for restricted use, the larger for when the family is at home?

(13) Is automatic control important to you?

(14) Do you want a rôtisserie? Some people wouldn't be without, because the food is so succulent. Enquire about running costs though. See also page 21 (rôtisserie).

(15) Will the smallest saucepans stand steadily on the burners?

(16) Is there anywhere to warm the plates, without actually cooking them?

(17) Are baking sheets provided and included in the price? If not, you'll have to buy them separately. See *Baking Sheets*, page 3.

Cups

American measuring cups save a lot of calculations and muddles if you ever want to use an American recipe. A nest of four is quite inexpensive, lasts indefinitely with care, and is available in many good kitchen shops. A set consists of:

$\frac{1}{4}$ cup (approx. 2 fluid ozs or 65 ml)
$\frac{1}{3}$ cup (scant 3 fluid ozs or 85 ml)
$\frac{1}{2}$ cup (approx. 4 fluid ozs or 125 ml)
1 cup (approx. 8 fluid ozs or 250 ml)

Cutters

PARSLEY CUTTERS. A Mouli-Parsmint, for instance, is useful if you've no idea how to chop parsley otherwise (see page 35), but for sheer speed, efficiency, results and easy washing-up, you can't easily beat the simplest pair of things, a sharp knife and a chopping board. Why waste money and drawer space on *this* kind of gadget?

PASTRY OR SCONE CUTTERS. Must have a sharp edge, otherwise they 'drag' pastry edges, and so prevent the pastry from rising properly. Plain cutters are normally used for savoury things, fluted for sweet, then there's no confusion at the table, in larder or freezer.

Dishes

CASSEROLE DISHES. Exist in so many shapes, sizes, types and materials, and so much depends on your taste that it's impossible to say what's the best choice. You may want a colourful oven-to-table dish, a shallow wide one to fit easily into a smallish oven, or perhaps the earthenware pot-au-feu type with its narrow neck, and from which consequently, there's less evaporation of liquid? Alternatively there are the lead-weight Le Creuset vitreous-enamelled cast iron casseroles, the pyrex type of dish if you want something really simple, or the sophisticated colourful enamelled steel or cast aluminium dish which you can put on top of the cooker *or* in the oven. You name it, some shops have got it – at a price.

★ Whatever you have, it's easier to keep most of them spick-and-span if you remember to grease them before use. See also *Cocotte*, page 6.

FLUTED GRATIN OR BAKING DISH. Made of ovenproof china, they are perfect for *those* purposes but not so good for a flan – a metal flan ring (see page 10) produces crisper pastry because it's a better conductor of heat than china.

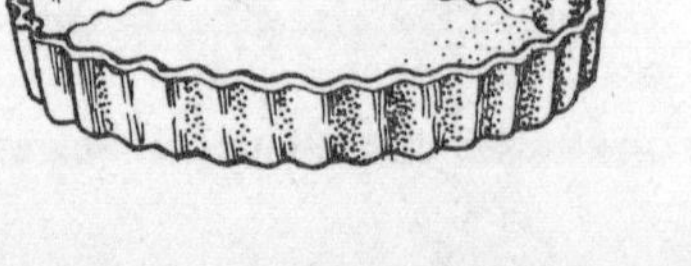

Should your flan pastry have a hole in it, or shrink badly at one side however, (when liquid could escape) then you're safer with this dish than with a mere flan ring!

SOUFFLÉ DISHES.They vary enormously. The thin, fluted, white, ovenproof, porcelain French type are the ideal kind for a hot baked soufflé because, *being* so thin, the heat penetrates the mixture almost as soon as you put it in the oven, which helps it to rise well. *I* prefer the wide shallow shape to the narrower deeper, because a soufflé firms up better in the middle when the mixture isn't so deep – but you may prefer a soufflé that *is* slightly moist in the centre?

★ French soufflé dishes come in litre sizes and you'll possibly want at least two: say 1 × 750 ml (scant 1¼ pts) and 1 × 1 L (approx. 1 pt 12 fl ozs) for a household of four: 1 × 500 ml (scant 1 pt) and 1 × 750 ml (scant 1¼ pts) if for only two people. It's a bonus to have some individual ones as well, see *Cocottes*, page 6.

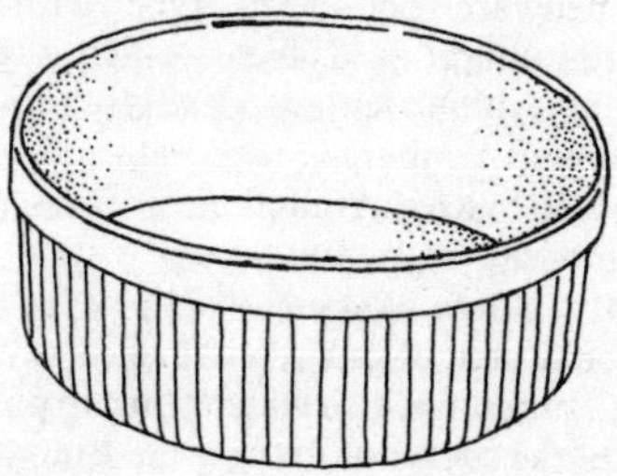

★ English fireproof china soufflé dishes are so thick by comparison that, using them, you can't hope to bake an equally good soufflé. If necessary though, if without a soufflé dish at all, improvise with any ovenproof dish of similar size and depth.

★ For pâtés and terrines, if you haven't got a proper terrine, a *deep* soufflé dish is best, while for cold soufflés a wider shallow one seems to set the sweet off better.

Dough Hook

This attachment, on a mixer, saves a lot of energy and does the job well, but the *average* domestic machine will only 'knead' smallish quantities of dough. It's of no help when baking a large batch of something for the freezer.

Doyleys

These can kill several birds with one stone:

(1) They make an attractive background to set off food, like a frame round a picture.

(2) They absorb excess fat from fried foods such as croûtons, fried fish, fritters or chipped potatoes.

(3) They prevent foods and dishes sliding about on their serving plate.

★ Fancy doyleys are used for cakes and all *sweet* dishes, but plain ones for savoury, to indicate the nature of the food, particularly of pastry, scones or sandwiches etc. Then of course there are gold, silver or Christmas doyleys for any *special* occasion. Many things look less attractive without.

Dredgers

FLOUR DREDGER. One of these, or a coarse strainer, is essential if you want to make light pastry or scones. Without, you can't (with your hand) distribute the flour *evenly and thinly* over the surface of a pastry board: excess flour gets rolled into the dough which, when baked, is spoiled.

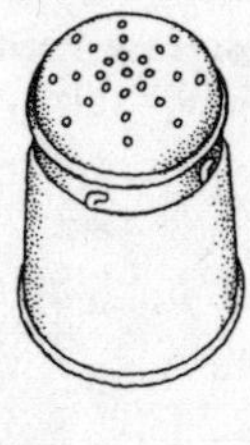

★ A flour dredger has larger holes than a sugar dredger (or caster, see below).

SUGAR DREDGER. Used to sprinkle either caster or icing sugar over the surface of something like a fruit pie, shortbread or a plain sandwich cake.

Improvise with a small fine-mesh strainer if without the real thing.

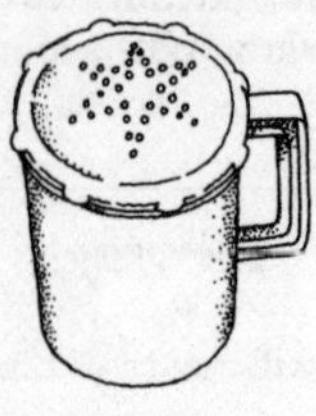

Egg Utensils

EGG CODDLERS. Like deep egg-cups, with a tight-fitting lid. They're easy for those who dislike the messiness of an egg in its shell. See also page 109.

EGG POACHERS. Would be better called 'egg steamers'. Poaching is done *in* water, not over it, and the steamed egg is a tougher and less digestible egg than the poached.

EGG POACHING RINGS. Like miniature metal flan rings. Shallower than a scone cutter, so that water can flow over the top, they help to control the antics of the egg white. I have some made of aluminium, others of tin, but the latter tends to stick to the cooked egg. Go for aluminium.

EGG PRICKER. Has a needle on a spring. One type looks like this.

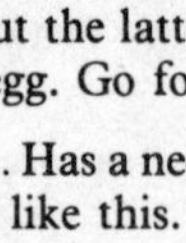

★ Prick egg at the blunt end, where there's air: the shell won't then crack because the trapped air now has an escape when, due to the heat of the water, it expands. See also page 106.

EGG SEPARATORS. Come in various designs. They are useful for the handicapped, for those who often buy or use cracked eggs – or for anyone with ten thumbs!

★ The snag about a separator is that when you want to get the clinging 'bobbles' (called the chalazae) off the yolk, you can't. You need the sharp edge

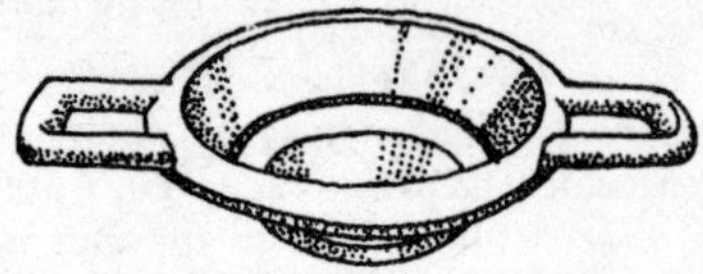

of the egg shell for that. (The chalazae are one cause of curdling, see page 107.)

EGG STANDS. One in your kitchen should ensure that at least some eggs are always at room temperature if you want to boil any or make a 'creamed mixture', see page 107. Eggs keep longer too if stored point downwards, see page 106.

Fish Slices

These should be flexible enough to slide *flat* along the bottom of a small frying pan, and long enough to hold a fillet of fish without breaking it; not stiff, small or square, like so many on the market.

★ One costly model fools the buyer even more – the 'blade' is solid, so you can't drain the food on it. Why can't *all* manufacturers realize it's the functional end of a utensil that matters, not the beautiful handle?

Do buy

Flan Rings

Metal rings, and frames used in conjunction with a baking sheet make much better flans than a flan-shaped, fluted, ovenproof china gratin dish (see page 8). This is because metal is a better conductor of heat, so the underneath and sides of the pastry bake more crisply. A plain ring is meant for savoury dishes, fluted for sweet, then there's no chance of getting them mixed on the table, in your larder or freezer. I'm a glutton for frames of all shapes and sizes: round, square or rectangular – the big ones are excellent for large numbers.

For 4 ozs (100 g) pastry (or for shortbread) you need a 7″ (18 cm) ring.

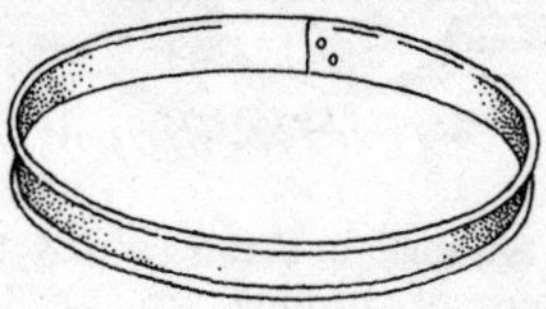

Foil

One of the most indispensable modern inventions. Unlike polythene, it keeps out light, which makes fatty foods go rancid and hastens the deterioration of many others. This explains why saltless butter and some kinds of margarine and cheese are sold in foil wrappers. The one great snag is that you can't *see* what's in or under foil.

★ Its qualities are extraordinary: it gives food neither smell nor taste; it's waterproof, malleable (marvellous for the freezer the way it fits so closely and tightly to anything wrapped in it), non-absorbent, non-inflammable, non-perishable and impervious to grease. It won't let food smells or flavour out, light or air *in*. It conducts heat quickly and evenly.

★ As long as you use the 'heavy-duty' quality, and seal foods in it properly (covering them finally with a polythene bag to prevent foil being torn), they will be almost immune to dehydration even after weeks in a freezer.

★ As well as cooking food in it, its uses are legion. Here are just three you *may* not have thought of:

(1) Use a strip to protect the rim of your best ovenware dishes when under a fiercely hot grill.

(2) Use instead of greaseproof paper as a 'collar' round the top of a soufflé dish (see page 235).

(3) Interleave sliced cold meat, chops, fillets, sandwiches etc. with a strip of foil before putting in freezer; to simplify taking out a limited quantity later.

Fork

A two-pronged meat fork, rather like a carving fork, is better for stirring boiled long grain rice than a conventional fork or a spoon, either of which tend to turn the separate grains into a solid mass.

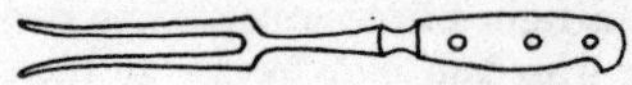

Freezer

A deep freeze is surely the most revolutionary piece of kitchen equipment of our time. It is quite amazing that for generations we have preserved in sugar, vinegar and salt; by drying, smoking and various other methods, but we failed to think out the simplest and most obvious of them all: preserving foods in their natural state in freezing conditions.

★ A freezer can be as valuable to someone living alone as to a family, to the old as to the young, to townsfolk as to countryfolk and to the woman who dislikes cooking as much as to the born cook. If you can't afford or lack the space to accommodate one that's final, but those who resist change or are unaware of a freezer's boundless help can have no idea of what they're missing in terms of convenience, economy, time saved, increased variety of food, and the new interest and dimension it gives to cooking.

★ To make the best of a freezer doesn't in my opinion mean filling it with a carcase, or even a quarter carcase, of meat and commercially prepared, expensive frozen foods; but to use it more as an ice-cold larder-cum-storecupboard where the life of everything is extended: a wide range of raw ingredients like meat, fish, poultry, fruit, vegetables and yeast as well as partly prepared foods like pastry, breadcrumbs, fruit rinds and juices, fruit purées etc. enable you to make all kinds of recipes at almost any time.

★ If you live alone and eat very little bread for instance, why not freeze half the loaf when you buy it, or freeze half a cake when you've baked it? Whatever the size of your household, you can have ready or put there as leftovers, prepared foods such as cooked cold meat, cakes, cake fillings, puddings, cold sweets etc, and the only thing a freezer asks of you is to defrost it occasionally – about twice yearly for a chest type, three or four times for an upright, or when the frost build-up exceeds 3/16″ (½ cm) thick.

★ Choosing a freezer needs knowledge – more than you *may* have – so there are advantages in buying from a freezer specialist, where you'll see a wide range and get professional advice; rather than from a general electric shop where the choice may be strictly limited and the advice even more so. Besides all the obvious considerations like size of family, amount of entertaining you do, money and space available, and the type you prefer (chest or upright), it's worth having a good dose of 'think' before you buy. The *capacity* is all-important and will depend on how you plan to use a freezer:

(1) What basically do you want it for?
  (a) To save you shopping: three weeks out of four, or seven out of eight?
  (b) For carcase meat, or will you only be buying smallish pieces of meat?
  (c) To preserve your garden produce? Could you perhaps *grow* more if you could freeze more?
  (d) To hold bread galore and space-taking packs of commercially prepared foods like ice cream?
  (e) To save you work in the summer? Do you for instance *enjoy* bottling and making jams, or would you be thankful almost to throw some of your fruit into the freezer?
  (f) To have a constant supply of home-made goodies which you'll be able to bake in bulk?

(2) Are you Mrs Method or Mrs Higilty Pigilty, thrifty or wasteful? Have you time on your hands, or not, to use it to its greatest purpose, also to pack things neatly in the minimum of space?

(3) The fuller a freezer, the less its running costs as a rule, but beware of over-filling it. What price your back if you have to *lift* out heavy baskets, and have you contemplated the problems of an arctic bran-tub?

It may be difficult before you have a freezer to understand why a small one won't do. It's just as baffling a year or two later, when you're experienced, to know why one was so short-sighted.

Fruit Decorator

Helps you to cut things like lemons, oranges, cucumber or courgettes attractively. Pare off the peel in strips longwise down the fruit, to give a striped appearance, then slice the fruit. Alternatively, for a salad, you could use a sharp-pronged fork on a cucumber or courgettes. See below:

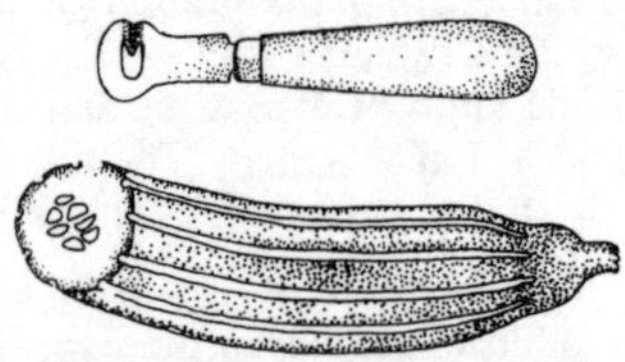

Funnels

METAL JAM FUNNEL. An absolute godsend when you come to fill jars with the piping hot jam because you can do so without handling them, as well as without waste or mess. It fits perfectly inside a 1 lb

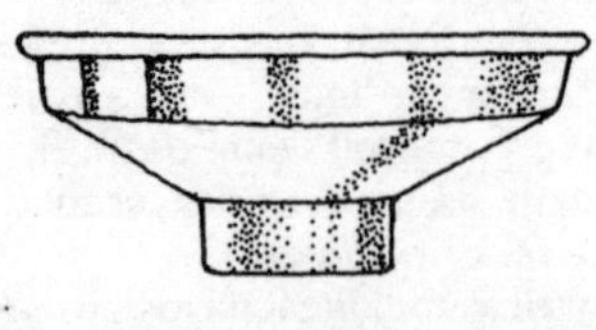

(450 g) jar. Use also to transfer dry ingredients like coffee, rice or lentils to a storage jar.

PIE FUNNELS. Shouldn't be necessary in a fruit pie because the fruit should be deep enough to support the pastry, which will 'set' (and therefore 'stay put') before the fruit cooks and shrinks. If there isn't enough fruit to do this, it's going to be a somewhat mean and miserable sort of pie.

★ You can't do without a funnel for a *meat* pie of course, (2 for a large pie), because it's this, not the meat, which supports the pastry. Otherwise the pastry will collapse into the middle before it can set.

Garlic Basket

See *Basket, Garlic*, page 4.

Garlic Press

This is handy if you use much garlic, and will last a lifetime. Though quick and easy to use, it's bothersome to wash clean. The garlic, with all its volatile oil released, is more pungent than when crushed with a knife, see page 73.

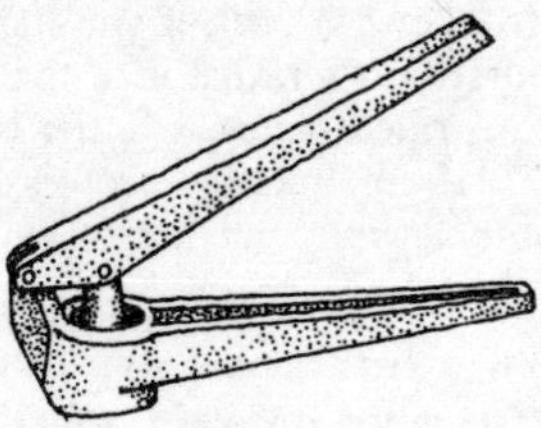

Girdles

They are usually made of cast iron or heavy aluminium. They may be square, with a frying pan type of handle, or round

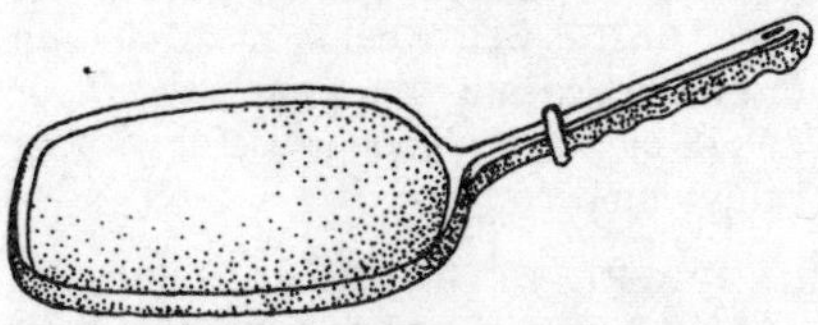

with a similar or half-hoop handle spanning the top: these are a curse to store unless the handle drops down. Unlike a frying pan containing fat, a girdle is just greased, so it pays to buy a good one which will stand up to the heat without burning the food.

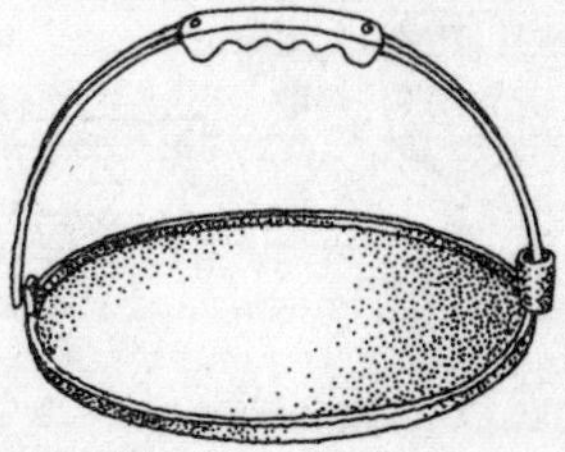

★ You can't really 'make do' with a frying pan: many aren't strong enough, and its high sides make it difficult if not impossible to turn some kinds of scone over. A galettière (pancake pan, page 18) is better. *Griddle* is just another name for a girdle. Some cookers have one built in.

Graters

They are of all shapes and sizes, some easy to handle, others not. The coarser ones are for grating carrots, onions and potatoes etc rather than for cheese or suet, which would be guaranteed to give indigestion if so roughly prepared. A circular one, or a conical-shaped grater as illustrated below, is practical to use and

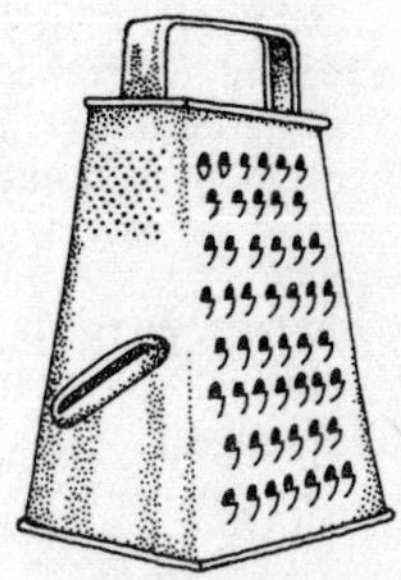

has several shredding sizes: things like lemon rind or nutmeg on the finest part; cheese or suet on the next; vegetables on the coarsest.

MOULI-GRATER. It grates cheese, suet, nuts or chocolate finely, and in a trice – also efficiently and without cut fingers. You only have to put in the food, turn a handle and – lo and behold! This is a gadget I couldn't be without, though the plastic type breaks more easily than the metal. See illustration overleaf.

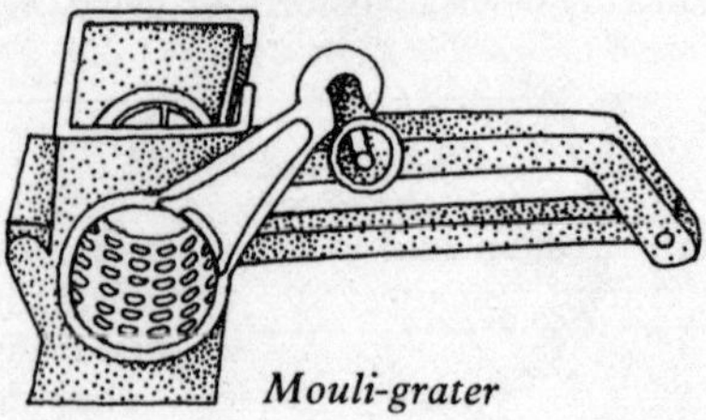

Mouli-grater

NUTMEG GRATER. Ensures a strong fresh spicy flavour, 100% nutmeg, but is it really worth the initial cost, and then the bother of using and washing it up when ground nutmeg is itself spicy and so temptingly convenient?

Hatpins

Are just the thing for decorating cakes, sweets and moulds, the bottoms of which are awkward to reach with your fingers! Use one to place the decoration, and a second to slide the decoration off the point. This is an easy way to handle sticky things like glacé cherries or angelica.

★ Use hatpins also to prick bubbles in royal icing before they set; to clear the point of an icing tube if a lump obstructs it while you're icing; to break icing off the tube when doing trellis-work, or to 'pull' the colours together when 'marbling'.

Icing Bags

See *Bags, Icing*, page 1.

Icing Tubes

See *Tubes, Icing*, page 27.

Kettles

Electric kettles, which switch off automatically, or others which whistle when they boil, ensure the best cup of tea – because over-boiled water is flat. Although the electric one may be initially fairly costly, it's a long-term saving on fuel.

Knives

Knives are an important part of any kitchen's equipment, though I can't cover them all here. Basically, they should be comfortable to hold, easy to use and, when possible, made for the particular job. Above all, a knife which is supposed to be sharp should *be* sharp, because a blunt one wastes time, bruises vegetables, makes cutting up food hard work and drags pastry edges, which may prevent a pastry from rising properly. If you can't sharpen them yourself on a steel, (see page 46), it's worth buying a knife sharpener. Apart from some specialized knives, the professionals tend to buy steel in preference to stainless steel, because they're sharper.

BREAD OR SLICING KNIFE. One of these is basic to the good cutting of bread – unless you have an electric saw-knife.

FILLETING KNIFE. Makes it much easier to fillet fish well, if you like to do this yourself. It's rather like the cook's knife illustrated below, but the blade – about 7″ (18 cm) is a good size – is thinner and more flexible, so that it will bend enough to take fillets off the bone.

FRENCH COOK'S KNIFE. With its handle designed to keep your fingers tucked away, and with its curved steel blade, this knife makes it quick and easy to slice or chop vegetables, or to chop herbs

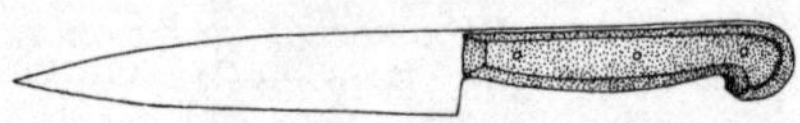

(see page 35) and nuts in the professional way. Use it as well to cut up meat, chicken or even a delicate cake. One with a 7″ or 8″ (18 or 20 cm) blade is useful without being cumbersome.

GRAPEFRUIT KNIFE. Has no substitute, and is essential to prepare the fruit properly and without waste. If left-handed, be sure to buy one serrated down *both* sides.

PALLET (OR PALETTE) KNIFE. One of the most necessary of all specialized knives: use it to clean foods off the sides and bottoms of basins and pans (excepting

non-stick); for turning and lifting pieces of fried food; for lifting or turning over flat things like pancakes or drop scones; for spreading things like cake mixture in its tin, or for icing work.

★ Because it's often easier to find a bad pallet knife than a good, one can't help wondering if some manufacturers find that an elegant handle is a better selling point than a perfect, forged blade? When *pressed* on a flat surface, a good pallet knife should bend gradually and evenly towards the handle, like this:

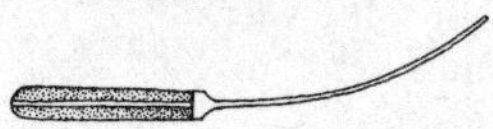

If it bends in only one place, like this:

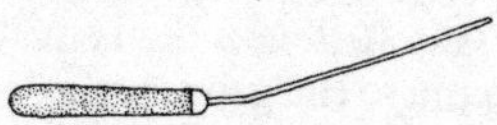

there's no point in buying it at all. Take professional advice in a professional shop if you're uncertain how to choose.

★ Made in various lengths, a 6½″ (16½ cm) blade is a good all-purpose sized knife.

SAW KNIFE. Fine, small, stainless steel, it is especially good for tomatoes or citrus fruits; whether to slice them thinly or just to cut in half. There isn't then the need for a tomato knife, which may be unsuitable for anything else.

VEGETABLE KNIFE. One with a 3″ (7½ cm) blade gives you complete control when scraping potatoes or old carrots because the blade becomes like a short extension of your hand. Perhaps you've got a 'sharpened-away' relic though to serve the same purpose, and from which no one can part you?

Larding Needle

These are of different thicknesses, pronged (or with a clip) at the 'eye' end, for piercing and larding with strips of fat,

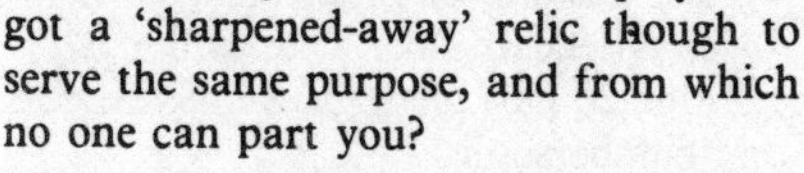

lean cuts of meat, poultry or game. See page 46.

Liquidizer

Turns tedium into pleasure, effort into relaxation, minutes into seconds, oily liquids into emulsions and of course many solids into liquids or purées. They do things you cannot do by hand, and better than you *can* do by hand.

★ Be careful what you buy: it's no exaggeration to say I've found *some* makes more trouble than they're worth, while others are too small or too limited by their power to be of real value. Those with a single high-speed motor are for instance unsuitable for making mayonnaise, which requires a slowish speed.

★ The big Kenwood liquidizer – adjustable through a range of speeds – is worth its weight in gold and indeed deserves a gold medal for being one of the best ever kitchen gadgets. It is reliable, strong, a good and sensible size, easy to handle and wash up, and 100% efficient with the minimum of human effort. I'd sell anything but our cat to replace ours if necessary!

★ If you're thinking of buying a liquidizer though, why not consult the magazine *Which?* It's worth remembering too that the prices of electrical goods are highly competitive, so it pays to shop around.

Measures

Measures ensure accuracy about liquid quantities, which can often make just that difference between good and disappointing results: this is because the texture of a dish will frequently depend on the correct consistency of the mixture.

★ You need a pint measure, marked at 2-fluid oz intervals (500 ml measure, marked at 50 ml intervals), and if possible a quart (or litre) measure in addition, for things like stock or milk. If you haven't got anything for the smallest quantities, why not buy a medicine glass from the chemist? They are marked at 5 ml intervals.

For measuring spoons, see *Spoons, Measuring*, page 24.

Mills

PEPPER MILL. A gadget for which there's no real substitute, if you like freshly ground black pepper. In constant use then, it is ideal if you can afford it, to have one mill by the cooker and another for the table. See also *Pepper*, page 85.

VEGETABLE MILL. Does most things a sieve will do, excluding breadcrumbs – but in a fraction of the time. The Moulin-Légumes illustrated below, particularly the larger size, makes purées in a jiffy: wonderful for such things as potatoes, spinach, apples or blackberries. A bonus too – it's as quick and easy to wash up as to use.

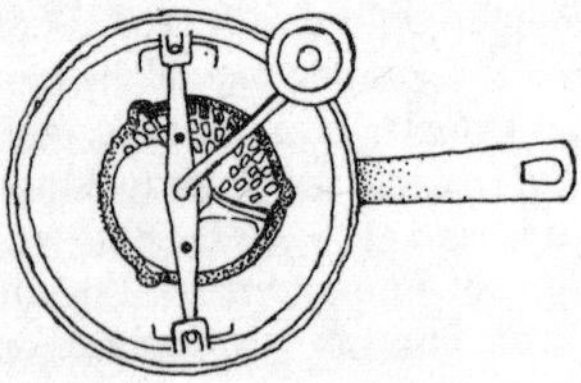

Mincer

One of the old-fashioned types, as illustrated below, is as efficient as they come: there's nothing to go wrong with it, you can't hurt your fingers and it doesn't need power. Beware of one snag though: have you a good sturdy table, or unit with a 'lip' to which you can screw it, otherwise you may not even be able to use it?

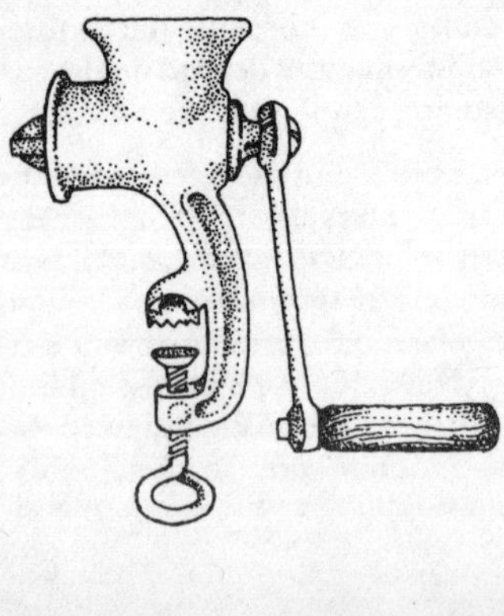

Mixer

An electric mixer, if you get a really good one, is a sort of mechanical kitchen maid who is always standing by, ready and willing to do the heaviest slogging whenever you ask. It may have its limitations, but who and what hasn't? It might be worth consulting *Which?* to see the pros and cons of different makes before you buy.

★ Some people scorn them, but (*given a good make*) have you given your mixer a fair chance? For a 'creamed mixture', did you really cream the butter and sugar until soft as cream, beat in the *whisked* eggs gradually and fold in the sieved flour with a tablespoon? Have you cut game chips or marmalade oranges in the slicer, kneaded a dough with the hook, whisked six egg whites whilst you were getting on with something else? It will do all these things and a whole lot more. With some makes, a liquidizer can be used on the same motor.

★ Being really greedy, one also needs an electric hand-mixer, for jobs the fixed model can't do: like beating egg and other mixtures over hot water.

★ There's a need for both.

Moulds

CHARLOTTE MOULDS. Plain, deep, copper or tin moulds with sloping sides. They're used for things like Charlotte Russe, fruit charlottes, Crème Caramel or

a steamed soufflé. When turned upside down, the wide top makes a wide firm base, which reduces the risk of the shape (or whatever it is) collapsing.

★ Some have handles and some also have a lid, depending upon purpose: it's better to have a lid for Crème Caramel for instance, to protect it properly during cooking, but you wouldn't need a lid for Charlotte Russe.

A 4″ (10 cm) mould holds $\frac{3}{4}$ pt (375 ml)
A $5\frac{1}{2}$″ (14 cm) mould holds $1\frac{3}{4}$ pts (875 ml)

DARIOL MOULDS. 'Castle Pudding' tins.

HINGED RAISED PIE MOULD. Ideal if you can afford one and enjoy making hot water crust pastry. Alternatively, you can manage with a loose-bottom oval mould, or at no cost at all make tiny individual ones with cartridge paper or very fine card: use each as if it were a metal flan ring, rolling and moulding the pastry to fit inside. (Remove card when pastry is about

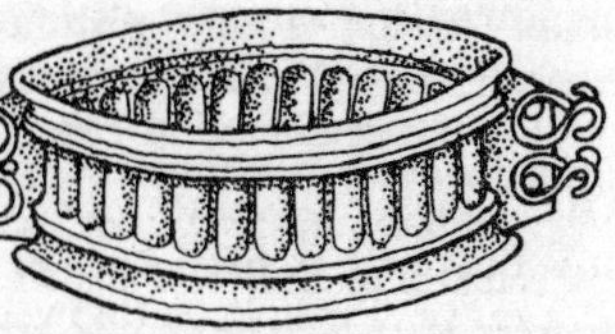

half cooked, glazing it now to make nice and brown). This is how to make it: (Use 4 ozs or 100 g pastry for each case and lid).

(1) Cut a strip of fine card 14″ (36 cm) long × $1\frac{1}{2}$″ (4 cm) wide.
(2) Make it into a 'flan ring' 4″ (10 cm) in diameter and join overlapping ends at 'top' with 2 paper clips.
(3) Stand it on a baking sheet before moulding pastry inside.

JELLY MOULDS. Not as easy to choose as one might expect: it is sometimes difficult to visualise what a 'shape' will look like when turned out. If you select something very plain, don't be surprised if whatever comes out of it looks plain! If you're lucky enough to have a tin-lined *copper* mould, that's the one to use: it will revel in showing off its craftmanship. Easily unmoulded too, I know of nothing to compare with them for sheer beauty of design.

★ *Aluminium* moulds are good, but *china* ones a nightmare to unmould. To avoid years of irritation and innumerable wrecked masterpieces, I'd 'throw it', as a Canadian friend of mine would say. I can't think why any manufacturer makes them, except to look at.

Oil Dropper

A special one, for making mayonnaise by hand, isn't necessary when you can improvise with any medium-sized bottle and a fitting cork: simply make a small groove down the opposite sides of the cork, one for air to get in so that the oil will drop out at the other.

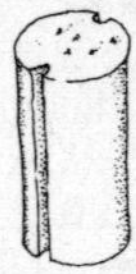

Pans

OVAL BAKING PANS. A type of baking tin with lid, made in various metals. Aluminium is good because it's strong, yet light in weight and easy to keep clean.

★ Meat steams rather than roasts in a covered tin so it's more suitable for braising than roasting if you haven't got a real braising pan. It is particularly good for cuts of meat which require longer, slower cooking. You can of course use it without its lid as a roasting tin. See also *Roasting*, page 54.

DEEP FAT PAN. Should be thick, strong and deep, otherwise the fat is liable to bubble over and catch fire. It should be large enough to meet family needs: this not only saves fuel and time, but ensures things can be served in crisp and perfect condition if you can fry whatever you're cooking in just one, or at the most two, batches.

★ A thermostatically controlled plug-in fryer is the safest if you haven't got a thermostatically controlled hot-plate on your cooker. Just in case you're unaware of it, this is because if fat is greatly overheated, it will burst into flame by itself (see page 45).

★ You can use the same fat repeatedly if strained regularly and the pan kept clean inside and out: you *may* be able to use it more than once without straining for something like chips, as long as you leave no floating morsels, but never after anything coated with batter or egg and breadcrumbs, because 'bits' or crumbs fall off and burn.

★ A frying (chip) basket should fit loosely inside the pan: choose one with a fairly close mesh, then you won't waste time fishing for the small things that slip through. (If you *don't* fish for them, they'll burn and make the fat bitter).

EGG POACHING PAN. See *Egg poachers*, page 10.

FRYING PANS. Should be thick, strong and, preferably, not too heavy because they're more difficult to handle. You need at least two or three, of different sizes, one of which I'd have non-stick, two with lids: then you can use them to sweat vegetables as well as fry and, if deep enough, to complete the cooking of some foods *after* frying.

★ If without a sauté pan, a *deep* frying pan is useful for poaching eggs, as well as for sautéing.

OMELET PAN. Possibly an unnecessary expense for the housewife who has a good quality non-stick frying pan of the right size and strong enough to withstand the heat required for omelets: perfect omelets almost slide out of them, you can rinse them in a second, and the only worry is that of spoiling the pan itself if too thin or greatly overheated.

★ Of the true omelet pans, I prefer non-stick or iron to the poor quality aluminium ones which many people buy, because *they're* apt to become inseparable friends with the omelet inside. To prevent rusting, keep an *iron* pan covered with a film of oil.

★ It is difficult to recommend a size without knowing your needs, so see page 111.

PANCAKE PAN. Must be strong to withstand the fierce heat needed for pancakes.

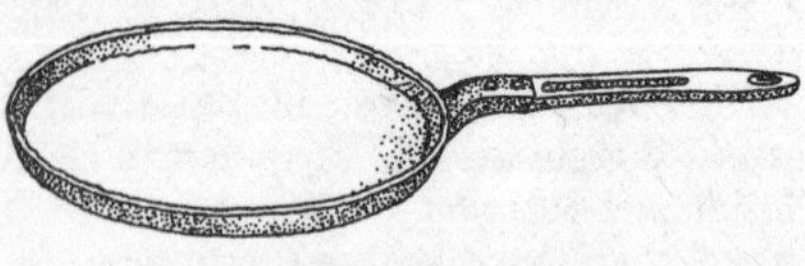

A good frying pan will often do, a smallish one (say about 8″ or 20 cm in diam.) being easier to cope with than a large. In fact I *prefer* my frying pan to a real pancake pan – or galettière, as above. Should you buy this Breton pancake pan, be sure to get the size you need because they're too costly to make a mistake about.

PRESERVING PAN. Really essential if you make much jam because like so many other pans, they're designed especially for their purpose: they allow the fast evaporation of liquid over a large surface so that the jam will reach setting point with the minimum of cooking, to have the best possible flavour and colour.

★ You may envy friends with a copper or brass jam pan but as they weigh a ton empty, what about laden? There's less risk of a slipped disc with a strong aluminium one. The acid in fruits keep it shiny, so it's dead easy to clean.

SAUCE PANS. Needn't break the bank but it does help to have a range of sizes and a range of metals, so that you've got the right one for the job. *Some* will double as a stewpan: good quality *aluminium* for instance is ideal for a caramel or for stewing fruit but a curse to clean after boiling vegetables or using with a steamer. Top-quality *enamel* pans are good for lots of things, including vegetables and steaming, but not so good as some other types for a stew or for sauce-making. *Non-stick* pans are perfect for sauces and green vegetables but not the kind in which to mash potatoes or make a caramel. *Stainless steel* are versatile but expensive: in the early ones, food tended to collect at the bottom of the pan where the heat was also concentrated, but today's top class stainless steel pan has no such imperfections. *Enamelled* pans have the great advantage of being decorative, many of them 'oven-to-table', which saves washing up too. There are others as well.

★ Lids? By and large you're better to buy pans with them than without. You can always leave a lid off but can you always conjure one up?

★ Handles? These also need thought: some pans, especially the heavier types, have a small handle at each side instead of one long one: it's more difficult to drain water out of these without scalding yourself in the steam, but on the plus side they're compact, and some will go both in the oven *and* 'on top'.

SAUTÉ PANS. Have an extra-thick base, straight sides and are deeper than a frying pan: they are used for sautéing small steaks, liver, veal scallops or foods like chicken that are browned then sometimes covered to finish their cooking there. It's therefore better to have one with a lid than without.

★ A strong frying pan will frequently do instead but there may be *some* dishes you want to make, and can't.
★ Sauté pans are made in tinned copper, cast aluminium, stainless steel etc, and in various sizes.

Pepper Mill

See *Mill, pepper*, page 16.

Potato Masher

One with a *round* head is an impractical design because, unlike an oval-headed masher which fits snugly into the contours of a pan, you can't get at the potato round the sides. What about the handle? Some, like the first one illustrated below, are round-ended and comfortable to press on with the palm of your hand, others painful – makes one wonder if some designers have ever themselves *tried* mashing a big panful of potatoes?

Do buy

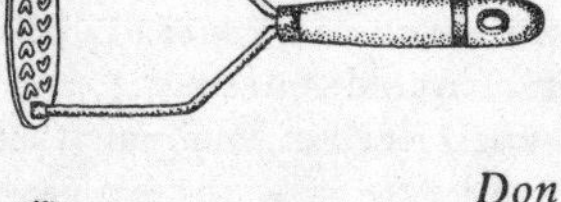

Don't buy

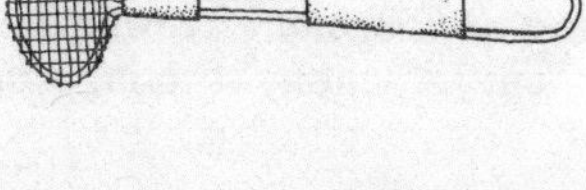

Potato Peeler

Unless you're a wizard at peeling thinly, a peeler is better than a knife because it takes off the minimum of skin, around which there's goodness. If necessary, you can buy a left-handed one.

★ The Skyline 'Speed' (or Miracle) peeler is excellent for potatoes which are just too difficult to scrape, and for old carrots or other thin skinned vegetables. Use it too to take the strings off runner beans in a flash. Hold and use it as a pen-knife rather than as a conventional peeler.

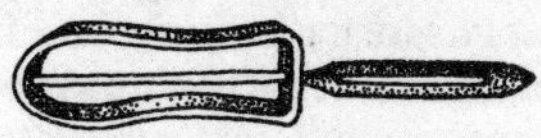

Ramekins

Are individual cocottes, see page 6.

Recipes

Recipes on filing cards are useful because:

(a) You can add to them indefinitely without overflowing from say, *Cakes* into *Soups*, as one is apt to do in a book.
(b) By using dividers, you can have as many sections as you like, in the order you like.
(c) You can re-write or tear up any recipe you want to alter or don't want to make again.
(d) If you acquire new tips about a recipe, there's usually space to add them.
(e) If kept in alphabetical or some kind of order, it is easy to find quickly what you want.
(f) There's no book to close up on you just as your fingers are stuck up with dough.
(g) A card takes up no space on your table if propped up against the wall, or say, the pepper pot. With three or four plastic covers to keep recipes clean while in use, they won't get splashed either.

★ 6 × 4″ (15 × 10 cm) cards give plenty of room for long or short recipes unless your writing is giant-sized, and a filing box keeps them clean and orderly. For easy finding, I like to have the name of the dish and any tips on the front, the recipe on the back: that way there's seldom need to turn a card over once your hands are messy.

★ How do you cope with friends' and magazine recipes without ransacking a drawer to find the one you want? One way is to have a number of large strong envelopes, labelled Soups, Starters, Fish etc etc – and one for Miscellaneous.

Refrigerator

This is not just for keeping food fresh or cool: anyone without can't possibly have the same success as anybody with, because a refrigerator extends even the best cooks' skills. Here's why:

(1) Salad foods such as lettuce, watercress or cabbage are crisper and more delicious after being chilled an hour or two. Even slightly *limp* lettuce may revive.

(2) Pastry is easier to manipulate when fat is firmed up between rollings, and will rise better and be lighter because trapped *chilled* air expands more than warmer air when heated.

(3) If chilled, Yorkshire pudding batter, whose raising agent is 'air', will also rise better when cooked – again because cold air will expand more than warm.

(4) One's range of dishes is widened: including making ice cream, masking a mould, setting layers of fruit or fish in a jelly, making dishes containing gelatine on a hot day.

(5) Fat-free stock is guaranteed, because most fats will go solid enough by the next day to lift off.

(6) Constant supply of ice cubes to help cool a mixture quickly if necessary, or to use in iced drinks of all kinds.

(7) Nutrients are better retained because enzyme action is slowed down. This is important for something like a green vegetable, which you may occasionally have to prepare in advance of a meal.

★ Some foods keep better in one part of a refrigerator than another, *sometimes* in one particular type of wrapping rather than another: for instance, because the coldest part is nearest the ice box, foods like lettuce which would be affected by frost outdoors are just as likely to suffer if put near the ice box. Some foods are better to *live* in the refrigerator, others should be there only temporarily.

★ To prevent the drying out of solid foods, the evaporation of liquids, and smells passing from one food to another, it is best to keep *most* things closely covered: foil, a polythene bag, a plastic (elasticated) pudding basin cover or a container with lid will meet almost every need. Be sure, though, to leave enough space between foods for the cold air to circulate – it's asking for trouble to pile things up on top of each other.

Here are a few do's and dont's which may help:

BACON RASHERS. Keep unwrapped rather than wrapped, in a polythene (or similar) container with lid.

BREADCRUMBS, FRESH WHITE. Will keep for days if not weeks in a polythene bag in coldest part of cabinet.

CHEESES. Wrapped in foil or polythene, should be taken out of refrigerator at least an hour or two before serving, otherwise they'll lack flavour. *Soft* cheeses, like Camembert, Brie or Dolcelatte will suffer in texture permanently if refrigerated so are better in a cold larder.

CHIVES. See *Herbs*.

CREAM. Keep low down in cabinet, otherwise it may go thick and icy.

EGGS IN SHELL. Are usually better in a cold larder than refrigerator, with a few in the kitchen *at room temperature* (see page 107). Refrigerating is wise for reserves, or when on holiday, to keep fresh longer.

EGG, (WHOLE, BUT MIXED UP). Keep in small covered container.

Egg whites. Keep in small polythene container with lid.

Egg yolk. Either mix with 1 teasp cold water or cover lightly with water if whole. Prevent drying out by covering with foil.

FATS. Won't suffer in the coldest part. If short of space, white cooking fats will keep for weeks *without* refrigerating.

FISH. Cover well with foil to prevent smell passing to other foods.

FRUIT JUICES. Have more flavour when served chilled.

HERBS. Keep well in a salad box or polythene bag well away from coldest part of cabinet. They'll keep fresh longer here than in a jug of water in the kitchen.

LEFTOVERS. As long as they're covered, will go in almost any part of the cabinet.

LEMONS OR ORANGES. If refrigerated, retain their natural oils and keep both fresher and longer, in a polythene bag away from the coldest part. (Foil is unsuitable as wrapping, because acid affects it). Refrigerated fruits don't produce so much juice: you'll get more out of them if they're at room temperature when squeezed. Surplus juice keeps well in a tiny bottle, or almost indefinitely if you freeze it as ice cubes.

LETTUCE AND OTHER SALAD PLANTS. Keep best in the compartment or box often provided – otherwise a *thick* polythene bag, well away from ice box.

MEAT. Joints will, *if necessary*, keep three or four days if covered loosely with foil or waxed paper, and placed low down in cabinet: remove an hour or two before roasting, for best flavour. Other meats, cover with foil or waxed paper.

MILK. Should live in the refrigerator – or don't your family like *drinking* it chilled?

MUSHROOMS. Keep well in a heavy-duty (never thin) polythene bag in least cold part of refrigerator. Wipe as you need and use them, not before.

PARSLEY. See *Herbs*.

STOCK. Is always handy to have, both in liquid form and as ice cubes, if you have a spare ice tray?

TONIC WATER. This and bitter lemon etc make better drinks when served chilled. Many people won't thank you for a 'warm' gin. Any space inside the door for these?

VEGETABLES. Prepared green vegetables (and some others) will keep fresher and longer refrigerated than if exposed to light and air outside it, even if only for half an hour. Wrap in foil or polythene and put in lower part of cabinet.

Rolling Pin

This can affect your pastry for better or for worse. With the 'handle' type, there's a tendency to put too much weight and pressure on the sides of the pastry, not enough in the middle, so the pastry rises unevenly. In addition, as some have as much handle as 'pin', you may only be able to roll a doll-sized piece of pastry.

★ What price the gaily coloured china ones? Being designed to roll (!), they don't even make a practical ornament, never mind a practical rolling pin.

★ A long, no-fuss rolling pin made of beech, as illustrated below, is the least expensive and also the best for the job. Unless you make very large quantities of pastry, a good average size is 16″ (40 cm) long and about 5½″-6″ (14-15 cm) in circumference.

Rôtisserie

This, or *spit roaster*, as it's alternatively known, is the modern way to cook an old-fashioned roast. Then it cooked over *direct* heat, instead of, as today, in indirect heat in a closed oven. The great advantages of a spit are the flavour, succulence and tenderness of the food, because the initial intense heat seals in the juices – many of which, in oven roasting, escape into the tin. Once the juices are trapped, slower cooking starts because the heat has to penetrate and cook the inside without overcooking the outside.

★ Birds need brushing with oil or melted fat first, their fat being under the skin, but there's no need to baste – unless you want additional flavour – because they and meat are self-basting on the rotating spit.

★ 'Accompaniments' are one of the disadvantages of spit-roasting: roast potatoes and Yorkshire pudding for instance can't exactly join the beef on the spit so, with an oven on as well, it can be extravagant on fuel – and is.

★ Gravy? If enough fat and juices don't drip into the pan below, you'll have to use another, appropriate, fat to make the roux, then finish with really good stock. Otherwise you could serve a savoury butter (see page 131).

★ Some rôtisseries are fiddling to operate and much more difficult to keep clean than others. This may explain why some people say 'I wouldn't be without a rôtisserie', while others vow 'I'd never have another'. *Caveat emptor!* 'Easy clean' spits are what they claim to be, others may be a curse. If tempted to protect the surrounds with foil, it *could* be dangerous except in the drip pan – better be safe than sorry.

Scales

★ Those which weigh small as well as large quantities accurately are essential for *constant* success: I fear those who pride themselves in never weighing or measuring anything, can't realize how much *better* they'd cook, and eat, if they did.

★ Balance scales are ideal if you haven't a cash or space problem, when wall scales with a dial may be Hobson's Choice. It pays to know just what you want. What about capacity – 2 lbs (say 1 K), 4 lbs (say 2 K), or larger? Do you like the type with a scoop for easy pouring and frequent washing, or do you prefer weighing ingredients on paper on a *flat* pan?

★ Some of the main advantages of balance scales are:

(1) They're accurate enough to weigh ¼ oz or 5 g precisely.

(2) They are generally more spacious than others for weighing bulky ingredients like flour or cornflakes.

(3) You can use them almost blindfold: the correct weight is when the two sides are perfectly balanced. (If old scales don't balance precisely when *empty*, correct by adding the exact weight of plasticine to the 'light' half, then stick the piece underneath).

★ To know more about scales, why not consult the magazine *Which?* At least you'll learn the snags of some types and makes, the advantages of others.

★ Should you lose any of your smallest weights, these coins will make an almost exact temporary substitute if you get stuck:

2p (2 × 1p or 1 × 2p) = ¼ oz
1½p (1p + ½p) = 5 g
3p (3 × 1p or 2p + 1p) = 10 g
45p (4 × 10p + 1 × 5p) = 50 g

Scissors

Are as basic as knives and forks. You need a pair strong enough to do the tough jobs, but also pointed enough to do the precise – like taking the core out of a lamb's kidney, or cutting the tightly tied string on a trussed bird.

Scissors, dipped in hot water, are good for cutting glacé fruits or marshmallows.

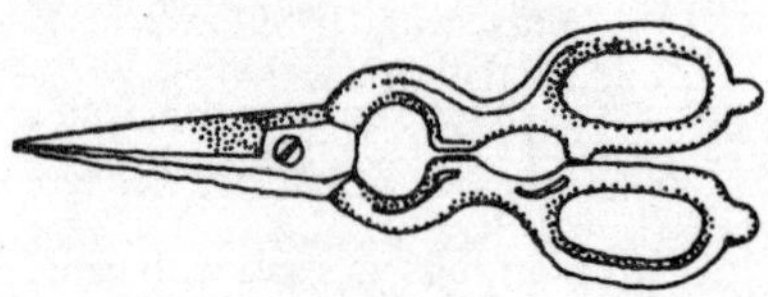

Sieves

One is essential if you haven't got a liquidizer or vegetable mill – and may often be in use even if you have.

A large sieve 10″ or 12″ (25 or 30 cm) in diameter is more practical than a small, unless you are without a large mixing bowl to stand it on.

A WIRE SIEVE. Used for things like vegetable purées, soup making, fresh white breadcrumbs, or to sieve golden breadcrumbs.

A HAIR OR NYLON SIEVE. Very fine versions of a wire sieve, useful especially for a seedless purée like raspberries or blackberries (which they won't flavour or discolour) as well as for a fine purée of vegetables etc. More of a luxury than necessity.

Sink

The kitchen sink is a good working height for those of *us* who are not of 'standard' height, to work at standard-height kitchen units and tables! I use the sink when:

(1) Rubbing fat into flour: you can lift your hands well above the bowl, trapping lots of air.
(2) Kneading a bread dough in a mixing bowl: it is less tiring than at table level.
(3) Whipping cream: it is easier, and if you're over-enthusiastic with the whisk, it couldn't matter less.
(4) Whisking eggs and sugar over near-boiling water. The strain is reduced, and a scald unlikely.

Skewers

Skewers' many functions do not include getting knots out of string, which is a good way to lose an eye. Besides using them for meat, game, poultry or even fish, stainless steel skewers can have a varied role. For example:

(1) For bacon rolls, to serve with game or poultry. It is as easy to handle 12 rolls as one.
(2) To use food colouring sparingly, not glaringly: dip skewer in bottle, shaking off a drop or two into whatever you are colouring.
(3) To test – with a very fine skewer – if a fruit cake is cooked.
(4) To blanch the leaves of say, tarragon, if you find it too strong fresh. (You'll need a very short skewer, to fit easily in a small pan).
(5) To garnish, with a straight line of chopped parsley (see page 77).

BROCHETTE. The French name for a skewer.

SHISH. The Turkish name for a skewer – kebab on a skewer. These skewers are flat, long and arrow-headed, to pierce the meat easily. Food doesn't slip about when turned over, as it does on round or butchers' skewers and, because they are so long, they're easier to handle when very hot.

★ The important quality of metal skewers – and the reason why wooden ones are unsuitable – is that they conduct heat through the centre of the meat, cooking it from the inside at the same time as it's being grilled *outside*. If you like kebabs, they're a good investment.

Spatulas

FLEXIBLE METAL SPATULA. Popular with some people for folding whisked egg white into a mixture, or for folding sugar into egg white. I personally prefer a tablespoon.

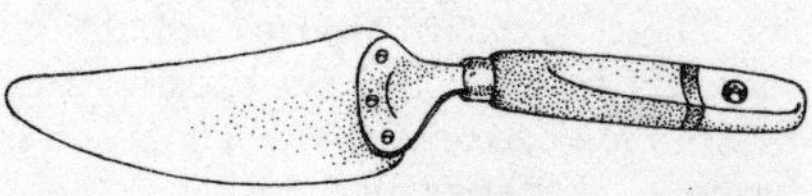

PLASTIC OR RUBBER SPATULAS. Marvellous for cleaning out bowls, basins, dishes and pans – even non-stick pans: good if you're slimming as it leaves nothing to lick! Plastic is cheaper than rubber.

WOODEN SPATULAS. Sometimes more practical than wooden spoons, particularly for stirring sauces, creaming potato etc. They are easily scraped off on the edge of a pan as well.

Spike-Murphy

This, of course, takes its name from the slang reference to a potato as a Murphy,

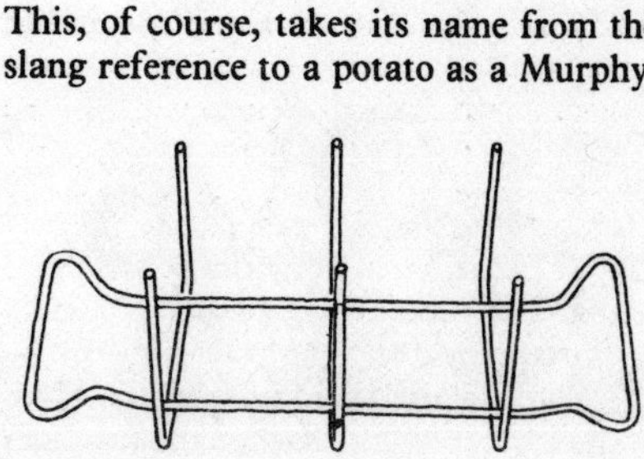

because for the Irish, the humble spud was at one time their staple diet.

★ This 'gadget' is a pronged stand for baking jacket potatoes: they cook more quickly and evenly than lying on a baking sheet because the metal prongs conduct heat through the centre of each potato. You can buy them for 4 or 6 potatoes.

Spoons

MEASURING SPOONS. Those which come in sets, made according to British Standard Institution specifications, must be one of the most controversial subjects in British cookery because they're a different measure from the *average*-sized spoons most of us have in our kitchen drawer. The standard tablespoon for instance holds 3 teasps, whereas your own may hold 4? Many of us don't have a set anyway, and many who do, don't use it.

★ These standard spoons would be incorrect for any *old* recipe book, written before 1964 and not revised. Today, some authors, magazine writers and many manufacturers base their recipes on them, but others don't. Some colleges and schools use them; many certainly do not, as I'm aware from evidence. How are we supposed to know who uses what, and when we follow a new recipe, which sized spoon should *we* use? You might as well ask if a pint measure holds a pint!

★ Using the *standard* spoon, there are 3 level tablesps flour or 2 level tablesps sugar (icing excepted) to the oz (25 g) (levelling the spoon off with a knife). Using your *own* spoons, it would pay you just once to check whether 1 oz (25 g) flour is 2, 2½ or 3 level tablesps, then you'll know for all time.

★ There's also a set of metric spoons but I'm not going to confuse you any more. *Quantities given in this book are based on the assumption that you'll be using traditional spoons from your kitchen drawer*. See also *Spoonfuls*, page 58.

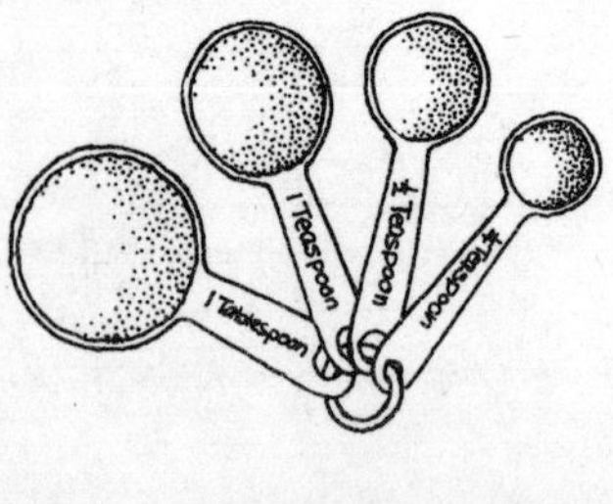

METAL TABLESPOONS. These are used variously:

(1) To fold whisked egg white or sieved flour into a light mixture because a wooden spoon, with its thick edges, would squash out some of the air just beaten in, spoiling the lightness of things like cakes or soufflés.
(2) For fried onions and similar pungent foods: a wooden spoon picks up and holds the flavour, passing it afterwards to delicately flavoured foods such as cream.
(3) To stir a syrup, because a metal spoon is free of smell and ensures a clear syrup with a pure taste.
(4) To turn over grilled meat, because a fork pierces it, delicious juices escape into the grill pan below and, with them, some of the flavour. You'll need *two* spoons for this, or grill tongs if you have them.

★ Table and other metal spoons are *not* used for dishes containing wine or vinegar because of the reaction to the metal and the possibility of spoiling the flavour.

WOODEN SPOONS. More practical than metal spoons for many jobs because they are more comfortable to hold and don't transmit heat. Also, being flatter, it is easier to beat thoroughly things like mashed potatoes, or butter and sugar. It pays to buy good quality because those with a rough unfinished surface absorb flavours from strong foods. A long spoon sticking out over the edge of a small pan can be dangerous: a small spoon will disappear in a large panful of soup, so it is important to have at least three or four of different lengths.

Steamer

An adaptable one to fit on more than one size of pan, makes it easy to handle steamed foods, and gives you wider scope than steaming direct in a pan. The lid must fit tightly and the steamer itself must fit the pan snugly, otherwise there won't be enough trapped steam to cook the food properly.

Storage Jars

These are the best way to keep dry ingredients in good condition. If not in an airtight container, sugars for instance will go lumpy, dried fruits will really deserve their name, and nuts will lose their freshness.

★ Glass jars aren't decorative but they're practical: you can *see* when the jar is getting empty and you can see too if you've stored sugar in the rice jar!

★ They are less expensive than many and you can name them with labels of your own choice.

Strainers

Are made in various materials and many different sizes. At least one – say about 5″ ($12\frac{1}{2}$ cm) in diameter – is essential and it is *better* to have more. It depends what you're doing as to which you should use:

(1) A tiny fine mesh aluminium one is useful for straining pips out of fruit juices, or even to strain tea.

(2) A medium-sized wire strainer is essential to sieve dry ingredients together and – if this is your only one – for anything that needs straining.

(3) A largish-sized wire or nylon strainer is practical for bulky things like boiled rice or pasta.

(4) A conical strainer is the ideal type to use for clean pouring into a jug or sauceboat – useful for other liquids too of course.

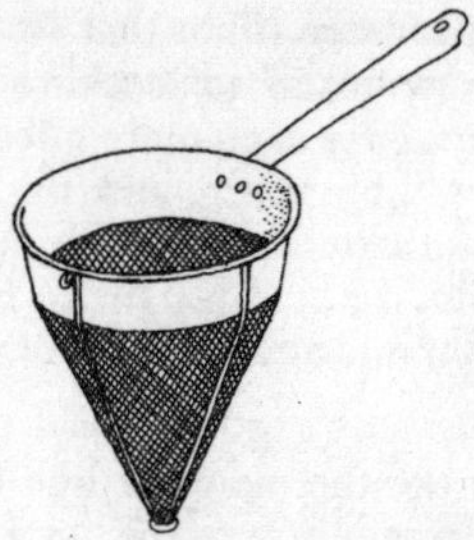

Terrine

Used of course to cook terrine or pâté and takes its name from the Latin *terrineus*, 'made of earth', which explains why *most* of them are made of glazed earthenware. Nowadays they're also made of ovenproof porcelain or vitreous-enamelled cast-iron.

★ Oval, round or rectangular in shape, all of them are fairly deep but it isn't essen-

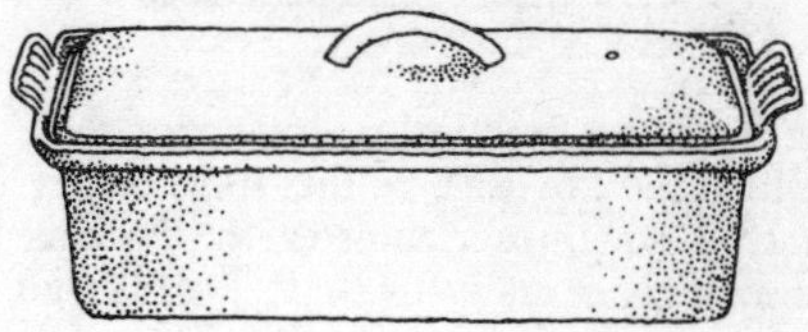

tial to have one – just a pleasant luxury: providing a dish is deep enough, you can cook pâté in a soufflé dish, casserole, foil freezer tray or even a bread tin, using foil and a lid to cover.

★ To *serve* it direct from the dish, you should have the real thing.

Thermometer

MEAT THERMOMETER. Especially helpful *if* you ever roast joints of meat

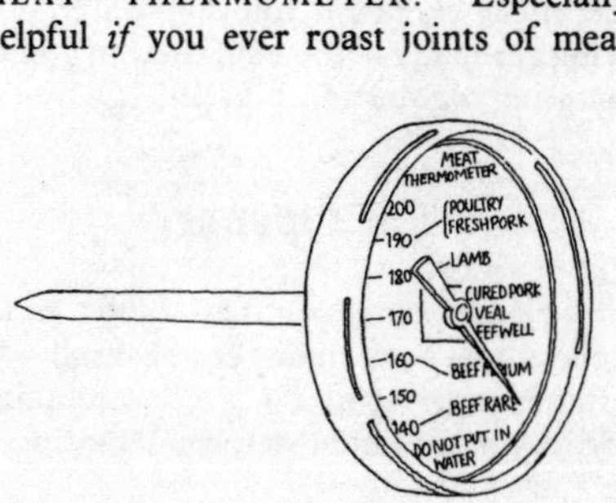

while still frozen – not that I personally ever *choose* to do so: cooking times of frozen meat are even more affected than fresh meat by shape and thickness so without a thermometer it is difficult to be sure a joint is just as you like it. It's useful for poultry and any 'fresh' joint as well of course.

★ Stick the thermometer into the meat 10-15 mins before the end of the calculated cooking time: a pointer on the dial indicates the condition of the meat, e.g. whether beef is rare, medium or well done.

SUGAR AND DEEP FAT THERMOMETER. Prevents guesswork. Successful cooking is sometimes a matter of doing the right thing at the right time at the right heat.

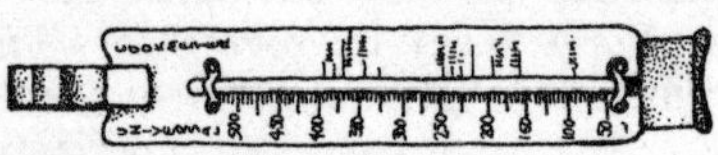

★ The most practical thermometer is one which you can use for either sugar *or* deep fat. A sugar thermometer for instance may register only to 420°F, 216°C, and might break if used for deep fat, while others may register up to 525°F, 273°C.
★ With care, a thermometer will last a lifetime: to avoid severe contrast in temperature and danger of breaking, stand it beside the cooker in a large pan or heavy jug of *hot* water before putting into or taking out of a hot liquid. Alternatively, allow it to heat with the contents of the pan, particularly deep fat, when a wet thermometer would cause spluttering.
★ If in doubt about the accuracy of a thermometer, put it into hot water and bring gradually to the boil, checking thermometer registers 212°F, 100°C.

Tin Opener

This piece of equipment has a busy time in some homes and is indispensible in all – or would you never follow a recipe containing things like anchovies, condensed milk or tinned tomatoes?

★ A *good* wall-type opener is quick and efficient, easy to use and doesn't play hide and seek: surely the best long-term investment of the lot? Think before you fix it though, choosing a practical position before drilling holes in your nice wall.

Tins

BREAD TINS. Not vital for success but are extra-strong, as well as giving that professional appearance to the bread. If without, a stoneware dripping jar (straight-sided, no neck), a good quality rectangular cake tin or even a clay plant-pot all make interesting loaves. Failing any of these, you can always make a cottage loaf or 'cob' on a baking sheet.

CAKE TINS. Good quality tins are a long-term investment because how a cake bakes will to some extent depend on its tin. Aluminium are high on my shopping list, non-stick only the French: rightly or wrongly, I think the outside of a cake made in most non-stick tins is less good than those made in others. Gingerbread will bake in a roasting tin but I'd suggest these tins are basic for anyone with a family:

- 2 × 7″ (18 cm) or 1 × 8″ ($21\frac{1}{2}$ cm) sandwich cake tins
- 1 × $6\frac{1}{2}$″ ($16\frac{1}{2}$ cm) ordinary cake tin
- 1 × 8″ (20 cm) ordinary cake tin
- 1 or 2 sets bun tins
- 1 Swiss roll tin

and I myself wouldn't be without these too:

3 moule à manqué tins, 7″, 8″ and 9″. (18, 20 and 23 cm) top diam. (see below).
1 × 9″ (23 cm) cake tin for a larger fruit cake.

MOULE À MANQUÉ. May be plain or fluted, round or square, but always with

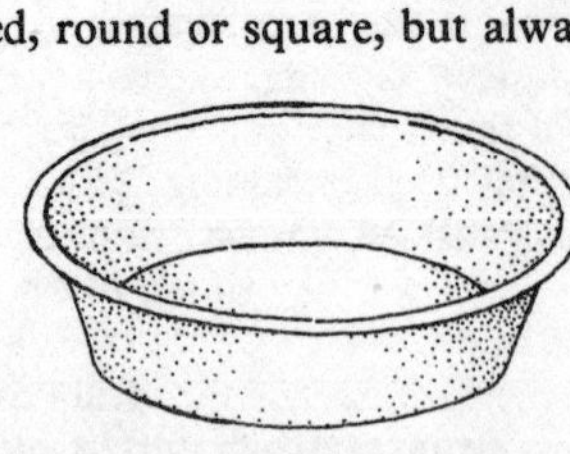

sloping sides. Cakes and sweets turn out easily and the former are child's play to ice because the sides slope outwards when the cake is turned out.

★ Use a large plain one (at least 9″ or 23 cm) for gâteaux, and one or two smaller tins are useful for other cakes or for a wider range of dishes like a steamed soufflé, Crème Caramel, 'Upside Down' or other puddings.

TART TIN. One with a removable base is excellent for a flan – more expensive, but easier to use than a fluted flan ring if

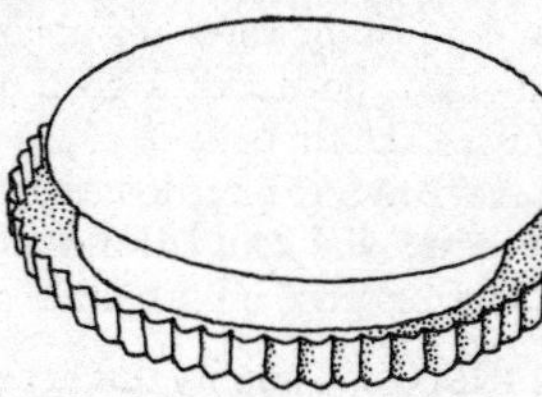

you've never used either before. They're made in various sizes from about 4″ (10 cm) in diameter upwards: ideal for individual flans or, if large, for a party.

YORKSHIRE PUDDING TIN. Should be the correct size for the quantity of batter used, if you want a really perfect 'Yorkshire'. For $\frac{1}{2}$ pt (250 ml) batter, use a tin as illustrated below about 10″ × 7″ × 1$\frac{1}{4}$″ deep (25$\frac{1}{2}$ × 18 × 3 cm deep). This is much better than a roasting tin, which may be larger and is certainly deeper.

★ Alternatively, why not use individual Yorkshire Pudding tins?

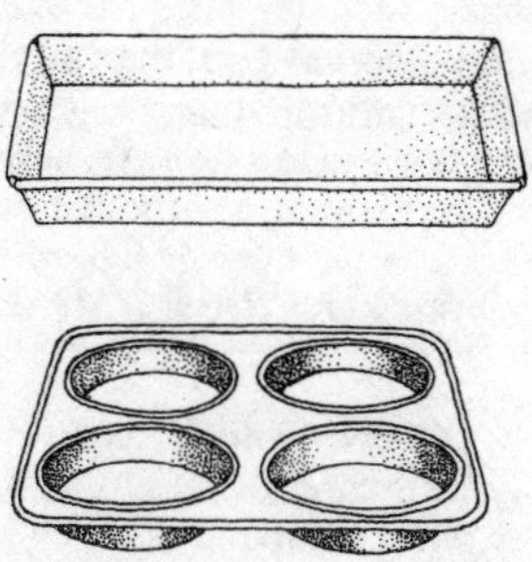

Trussing Needle

This is essential if you like or have to draw and truss your own birds. If you can do them properly there are several advantages over the oven-ready bird: you can pull the sinews out of the legs, sew in stuffings and make sure the bird will rest steadily on the dish when carved.

★ You *may* want a lesson in drawing and trussing, the technique being difficult to grasp from a book. See page 201.

Tubes

ICING TUBES. May be made in metal or plastic. Plastic are much cheaper and less easily damaged but, due to the nature of plastic, you don't get the range of beautiful shapes available in metal. Choose these carefully when you buy. I don't know whether it's because of careless customers or shop assistants, but too many are faulty in *some* shops. Treat them with kid gloves to prevent damage, because the slightest imperfection produces a blurred result.

★ Fussy about all my equipment, I'm a real crank about metal tubes! They're not things to bury amongst the washing up, or to leave someone else to dry. Wash them under a warm tap the moment you've finished icing and, if necessary, soak rather than poke before drying in a warm place and putting carefully away.

★ Although a professional may have a complete assortment of over a hundred tubes, those of us less ambitious can accomplish quite a lot with a few simple ones:

(a) *No. 1 writing tube*, to make thin lines, fine stems, scrolls, stamens on large flowers, and particularly for fine writing on a cake.

(b) *No. 2 writing tube*, for bolder writing than the above, for thicker lines and for the centres of certain flowers etc.

(c) One or two '*open star*' *tubes* – easy for a beginner – to pipe stars, scrolls, border designs, floral sprays etc.

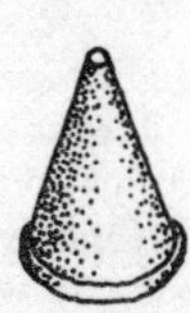

(a)

(c)

(d) One or two '*closed star*' tubes, say a six-point and an eight-point star, to pipe stars, shells, lettering or a bold border etc.

(*d*)

MERINGUE TUBES. A larger edition of an icing tube, in metal or plastic – the type you need to pipe things like Duchess

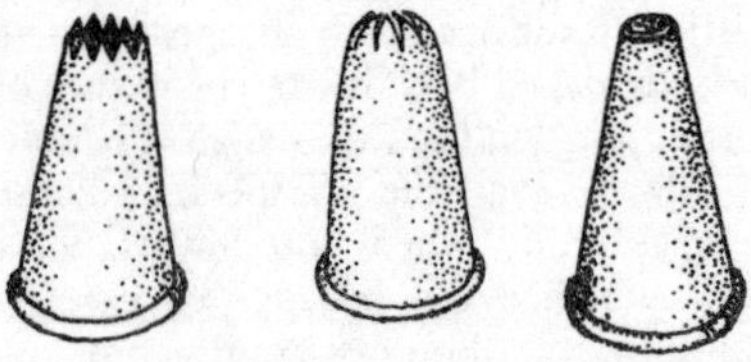

potatoes, large stars of whipped cream, certain Petits Fours, butter cream fillings on cakes, or of course meringues and anything similar.

★ You could get by with three: one 'star' tube, one 'rope' and one plain $\frac{1}{2}''$ tube ($1\frac{1}{4}$ cm), the plain one for a limited number of things like éclairs or macaroons.

Tweezers

Are invaluable if you're decorating a cake with something like silver balls or mimosa. You can put them precisely where you want.

Vegetable Mill

See *Mills*, page 16.

Weights

See *Scales* page 22.

Whisks

Are of all shapes and sizes and for all sorts of purposes. The serious cook will want several different types. Here are some of the well known:

BALLOON WHISKS. Generally acknowledged to be the best for egg whites, giving greater volume than most others and consequently making lighter dishes. The 10″ or 12″ (25 or 30 cm) size is manageable and efficient for 6 egg whites but a 9″ (23 cm) whisk may be more generally useful. Modern stainless steel whisks are light and so easy to handle compared with the heavy, old type. If difficult to track down, try a catering equipment shop. (See the yellow pages of a telephone directory).

COIL-RIM WHISKS. The Skyline version is *my* favourite. If I could only have one

whisk, this efficient, inexpensive, nearly all-purpose design would be my choice.

ELECTRIC HAND-MIXER. Invaluable for whisking eggs and sugar (or other mixtures) over a pan of hot water. Also to whisk mixtures into which a hot syrup is poured from a height, e.g. Crème au Beurre Mousseline, American Frosted icing.

ELECTRIC (FIXED) WHISK. Not in the same class as the best hand-whisk, producing a dense mass of egg white rather than a light fluffy one – so you can't make such feather-light mixtures with it. It is also less good than an electric hand-whisk, which can be circulated round the bowl to incorporate more air. I wouldn't be without one though because at times one is too busy or too exhausted to use anything else. See also *Mixer*, page 16.

'MAGIC SPOON'. Small, spoon-shaped, and may be used in turn as fork, wooden spoon or whisk. Though not well known like the others, it's good for whisking a tiny quantity of cream or egg white, or for

sauce-making. Called 'La cuillère magique', it is sold by some of the specialized kitchen shops. It is 8¼″ (21 cm) in length.

ROTARY WHISKS. Seem to be one of the most popular of the lot though it's difficult to know why – perhaps because they're so easy to use or because they're expensive, and people think they *must* be good! You can't *compare* results with

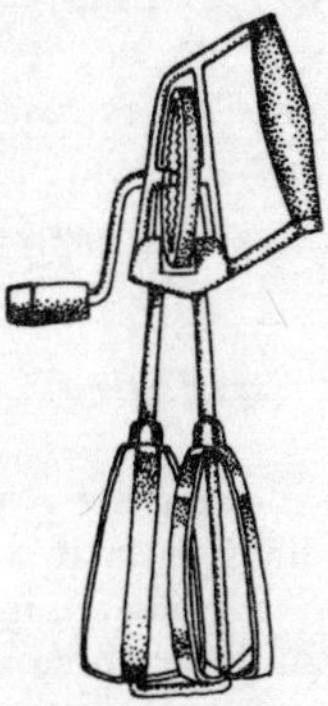

those of a balloon or coil-rim whisk, which give far greater volume and much lighter egg white, cream etc. Besides being inefficient, you need both hands, which is sometimes impossible, and sometimes – over boiling water for instance – dangerous.

WHIPPER OR BATTER WHIP. Of strictly limited use. Although some people use one for everything, I personally wouldn't use it for anything because, due to its structure, you can't incorporate as

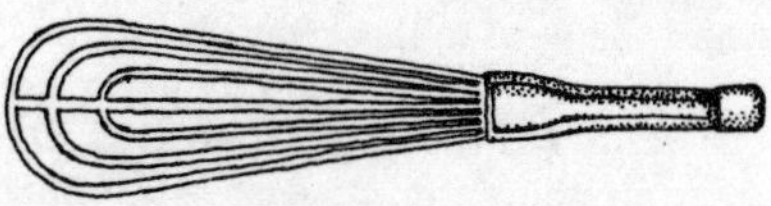

much air with it as with many other whisks. You could use a wooden spoon for a batter, otherwise I can think of little for which a coil-rim whisk wouldn't be better.

WIRE WHISKS. Good for whipping cream as well as for beating eggs, dried soups and – lumpy sauces! Use also for sauce-making, to whisk hot liquid into the roux. They are made in various sizes from about 7½″ (19 cm) upwards; a simplified form of the balloon whisk.

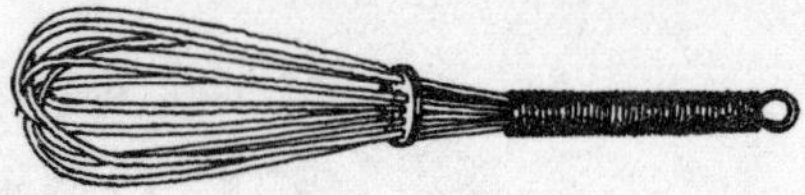

Zester

More efficient than anything else for scraping the zest off citrus fruits. See also *Zest*, page 61.

2

TERMS AND TECHNIQUES

A kiddie can ride a bicycle if he's taught; an adult may still be walking if never taught – and so it is with cooking: there's no real magic in it but you'll get there faster if you're skilled, whether rolling pastry, chopping parsley, whisking egg whites, or folding them, when correctly whisked, into another mixture.

If your creamed mixtures will curdle, you're afraid to use deep fat, you're not sure why some foods are blanched or others are given names like '*à* la lyonnaise' or '*à la diable*', I hope you may find the answer here.

Agitating

Is just what it sounds like – gently jerking a saucepan 'up and down' and 'round and about', to make sure that the contents are moved about enough to cook evenly without being stirred. When agitating a *frying* pan, the movement is a backward and forward slide.

Al Dente

Is an Italian term meaning, literally, 'to the tooth', i.e. with a little bite, slightly crunchy. It is used to describe foods, particularly rice, pasta and certain vegetables, which should be cooked until firm to the bite, but not soft.

Antipasto

'Before the pasta', this is the Italian name for *hors d'oeuvres* or appetizers.

Baking

Baking and roasting are really the same thing these days, even if we do seem a little crazy to talk of baked ham, but roast beef, lamb and everything else. Baking, the term we apply mostly to cakes, pastry and so on, if of course cooking in a current of air by dry heat.

★ When recipes give oven temperatures, the hottest part of a preheated oven is implied unless otherwise stated – that's the top of *most* ovens. This is the reason why bread, pastry and things like scones and small cakes which need a hot oven are best cooked at the top: it is also why fruit cakes and meringues etc which need a much cooler oven are best baked at or near the bottom. (Some modern ovens have an even temperature throughout, see page 7, *Cookers*).

Baking Blind

Means baking 'empty', like flan cases which are baked first, and filled later.

★ A double layer of tissue paper filled with haricot beans (preferably), dried cherry stones or split peas, is softer and damages the pastry less than greaseproof paper. Crumpled-up foil can be used alone, quickly and easily, but I don't like it because it's apt to spoil your carefully fluted flan.

Barding

A way of protecting lean meat and the breast of dry birds with slices of fat – often preferably pork fat – before braising or roasting, to keep the meat juicy and tasty. The fat – bacon fat if you *like* – needs tying on, otherwise it falls off when it cooks and shrivels.

Barquettes

Are boat-shaped tartlet shells, very tedious to cut if you don't know how, easy when you do:

(1) Line up several boat-shaped tins close enough to each other just to touch:

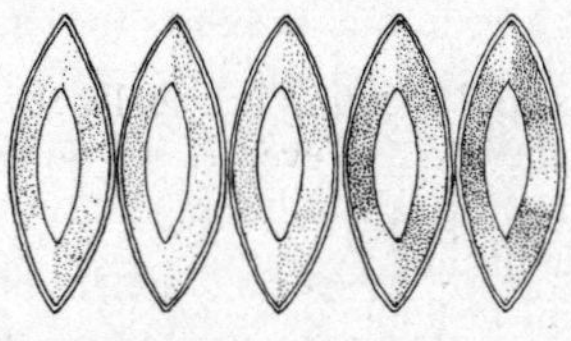

(2) Lay the rolled out pastry on top of them – a strip wide and long enough to cover the whole line.

(3) Roll carefully from one end to the other with a rolling pin, to cut out each boat on the sharp edges of its tin. Place pastry neatly inside.

Batter

Comes from the French word *battre*, to beat. Batters such as Yorkshire pudding and pancake are lighter made with half milk and half water instead of all milk.

★ A batter will rise better if it is chilled in the refrigerator rather than used at room temperature, because cold air expands more than warm air – and there's no other raising agent.

Beurre Manié

This sounds more elaborate than the simple butter and flour mixture it is, used to thicken sauces, soups or the liquor from cooked foods. It's useful too if, by mistake, you make a soup or sauce too thin: just work together with a fork equal quantities of butter and flour, drop small balls of it one at a time into the sauce or soup, and whisk it continually with a wire whisk to blend it in rapidly. Then boil the liquid for a minute or so, to burst the starch grains in the flour and so thicken the liquid.

★ If a dish contains fish or meat, blend in the beurre manié by gently shaking and turning the pan, otherwise you may end up with fish purée!

Bind

To bind is to add egg, flour, potato flour or cornflour etc to a liquid to thicken it, *or* to hold a mixture of foods together with egg, melted fat, mayonnaise or other sauces. Fish cakes, for instance, if made without egg, will disintegrate when fried, but those made *with* egg will stay whole because the egg coagulates when heated, binding the mixture together.

Blanching

Involves using boiling water in various ways for various purposes:

(1) *To remove fruit skins*, by covering fruit for a given time with boiling water, sometimes aside from the heat; eg tomatoes 10 seconds, peaches 1 min, almonds 1–2 mins if boiled, or 3–4 mins aside from the heat, stirred well.

(2) *To cook or partly cook a food* prior to cooking by another method, by putting food into boiling water for a limited time, eg potatoes before roasting or sautéing, cauliflower flowerets before making fritters, sweet peppers before stuffing.

(3) *To have a cooked vegetable ready to serve*, see *Refreshing*, 3, page 54.

(4) *To remove the strong flavour and smell of some foods, also to make some of them more digestible*, by bringing to the boil in cold water and then discarding water, eg tripe, *or* by plunging into boiling water and boiling for a limited

time, eg sweet peppers, celery, onions, turnips.

(5) *To clean and remove saltiness*, by bringing food to the boil in cold water, then discarding water, eg salt pork, smoked bacon joint.

(6) *To make firm before cooking*, by bringing to the boil in cold water before plunging into more cold water, eg sweetbreads.

(7) *To prevent deterioration of foods in deep freeze*, by plunging into deep, fast-boiling water for a limited time before 'refreshing' and sealing in containers, eg numerous vegetables.

Blending

Has various meanings. It may mean mixing things together in a liquidizer or blender, or variously combining different ingredients or mixtures smoothly together.

★ A basic rule in cookery is that mixtures should be of a similar consistency if they are to blend successfully together: neither whisked egg white nor over-whipped cream for instance will combine properly with a mixture which is much more liquid than they are. This explains why a cold sweet recipe often directs that a mixture should be showing signs of setting before adding whisked whites.

★ *Dry ingredients* blend best if sieved together. If using a spoon, the back of a tablespoon does in seconds what the tip of a teaspoon may take much longer to do.

★ *To blend a liquid into sieved flour and other dry ingredients*, make a well in the middle of the flour, pour liquid into it – not too much at a time as a rule – and gradually draw in all the surrounding flour by stirring in an increasingly larger circle. If a very small amount of flour, as for flour and water thickening, it's quicker and easier to use a fork than a wooden spoon, see below:

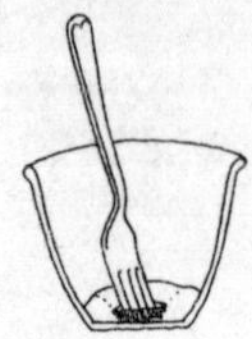

Adding water to flour for thickening

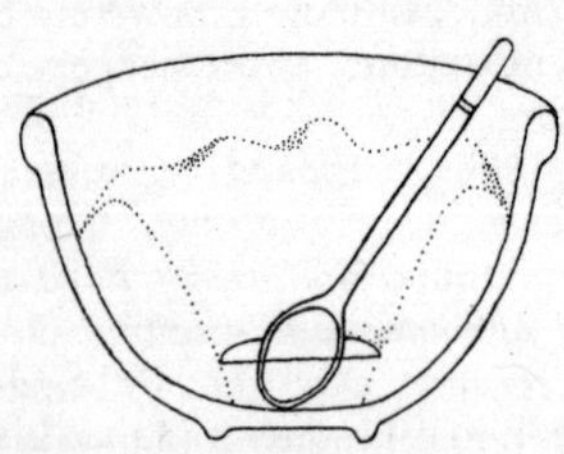

Adding egg and milk to flour for Yorkshire pudding

Boiling

Doesn't always mean exactly what the word implies. Water, if boiling, is turbulent on the surface with bubbles breaking all over it, but meat and fowl harden, and fish breaks up and becomes watery if boiled like this throughout the cooking time. This is why boiled beef, for instance, is actually boiled for only 5 mins, then simmered for remaining time; and why stews are *simmered*, the liquid showing only the slightest movement on the surface.

★ Most foods, including vegetables, are tenderized in a given time by boiling slowly in a covered pan, bubbles breaking gently all over the surface.

★ Rice and jam, which boil fast, are of course cooked without a lid, because they would boil over if covered.

★ Liquids to be 'reduced' are also boiled fast and uncovered, otherwise they'd take ages to evaporate. See *Reducing*, page 54.

Boning

Boning a bird is a tedious and rather difficult process until you know the ropes – or should I say the bones – and is one of those jobs I'm happy to watch someone else do! You need a short sharp knife to *scrape* the flesh off the bones rather than cut it off, to avoid piercing the skin. It's quicker and easier to do too if the bird is 'drawn' *after* it is boned. The drumstick bones are sometimes left in, to keep a bird a better and more realistic shape when stuffed. See also page 201.

Bouillon

Is the French term for stocks or broths, from *bouillir*, to boil.

★ Bouillon or stock is, of course, used as a basis for soups and sauces, and bouillon cubes are just well seasoned stock cubes.

Bouquets Garnis

Are exorbitant to buy, and not nearly as good as a fresh one made from herbs in your garden, or even partly from dried herbs in your store-cupboard. It surprises me that even people with a garden will buy them, when basically all you need are three herbs – ½ bayleaf, a spray of thyme, 3 or 4 sprigs of parsley – and a small square of clean cloth about the size of a baby's handkerchief; easily cut, several at a time, from a piece of old cotton sheet.

★ Be sure to include the parsley stalks, because they carry more flavour than the leaf: simply roll the herbs up in the cloth, knotting the ends tightly.
★ Vary as you like by adding other herbs, a clove of garlic, or the odd spice.
★ Adjust the proportion of herbs to the nature of the dish, but use thyme and bayleaf sparingly because they're strong, and may dominate rather than improve the flavour of your dish.
★ Use a bouquet garni in soups, sauces and stews, but be sure to remove it before serving the dish – or before liquidizing soup. If you're likely to forget, tie it with thread to the pan handle.

Braising

The French equivalent of English pot-roasting; a combination of a type of stewing, and roasting. It is a good way to cook choice cuts of very lean meat, cheaper cuts of meat, elderly game or poultry, whole fish and certain vegetables. Meat, particularly beef or anything tough, is often marinated first to tenderize and flavour it.
Generally speaking, these are the how's and why's:

THE PAN. A French braising pan is ideal, otherwise use a cast-iron casserole, or other dish or pan which has a tight-fitting lid and in which you can both fry the meat over direct heat and then cook it in the oven. If the lid doesn't fit tightly, flavouring juices will escape.

MEATS. Are fried for a minute or two in very hot fat – ends as well as both sides of a joint – to seal in the juices. (This is a vital part of successful braising.) The meat afterwards cooks (in steam) on a bed of vegetables in a small amount of liquid, with seasoning and other flavourings.

VEGETABLES. Act as a base for the meat to stand on, and to flavour the meat and cooking liquid (used later for the sauce), not themselves to be *served*. To prevent them going mushy during cooking, slice onion thickly, carrots longways in half, cut a leek in half, and a celery stem into pieces. The prepared vegetables are then fried (after frying and removing meat) for just a few minutes, to flavour them and to absorb the fat. See also *Mirepoix*, page 52.

LIQUID. Wine, stock, cider, or whatever the recipe calls for, is added and heated to simmering point before placing meat on top. There should be just enough to cover the vegetables, baste and keep the meat moist, and finally to use in an accompanying sauce.

THE OVEN. Should be slowish, about gas 3, 325°F, 165°C. This all-round heat is better than direct heat under a pan on top of cooker because the meat cooks more evenly. Cooking time is *about* 25 per cent longer than for roasting. Finally the heat is for a short time increased and the pan lid removed, to 'roast' the meat.

★ If too extravagant to heat your oven for a very small bird or piece of meat, cook it over direct heat but turn the meat over occasionally, to cook evenly.

Breakfast

Means 'break fast', and that's what the whole family needs after a gap of 10–12 hours or more since the last meal. The blood sugar and other blood nutrients will have fallen to base level, so if you start off the day empty, it's like trying to start an engine without fuel.

★ If you want your children to do their best at school – and what parent doesn't? – the first step is yours. Give them a proper breakfast because without, it is more difficult to concentrate. Besides, nearly all of us look better, feel better and work more efficiently when we have, literally, broken our fast.

Broiling

Is the American term for grilling. A broiler for instance is a chicken young enough to be grilled, hence its name.

Calorie

Is simply a measurement of heat or energy which the body can obtain from a given amount of food. If the body takes in more calories than needed or used, then the surplus is stored as fat. The principle of wise slimming is therefore to reduce the intake of calories and force the body to use up its excess store of fat.

★ Foods like green vegetables, radishes, cucumber, gherkins, celery and unsweetened fruit juices are very low in calories, so some of these may be useful for snacks and nibbling, if nibble you feel you must. On the other hand, if you feel like feasting on a bag of peanuts, you may think again when you know each nut means 5 calories down the hatch. Below, in case you're interested, are just a few more foods:

Canapé

French for a sofa or settee – something to sit on. That's what canapés are: small 'platforms' on which sit tasty cocktail snacks, hors-d'oeuvres or savouries. They may be shapes of pastry, or of buttered, fried or toasted bread.

★ Fried bread canapés to be served cold are better fried in oil than butter because it doesn't congeal when cold; and if you want a filling to sit on top without falling off, make a hollow in the middle of each while they're still hot: using the end of the handle of a wooden spoon, press down the middle in up-and-down movements.

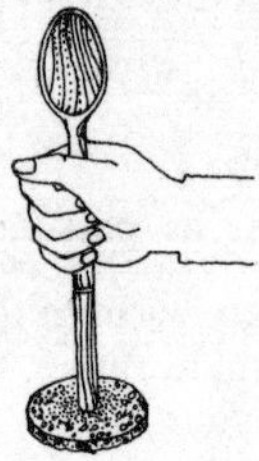

Food	*Quantity*	*Calories*
Biscuits	on average, each	50
Bread, small loaf	3 thin slices	100
Butter	½ oz (say 15 g)	100
Cheese, Cheddar	1 oz (25 g)	100
Chocolates	average, each	50
Cream, double	1 tablesp	100
Eggs, boiled or poached	each	100
Eggs, fried	each	200
Jams	1 rounded tablesp	100
Milk, fresh	1 small tumblerful	100
Pork chops, lean	average, each	200
Potatoes, chipped	6, average size	100
Potatoes, boiled or jacket	medium size	100
Sherry or vermouth	small glass	100
Spirits	1 'nip'	100
Sugar	¾ oz (say 20 g)	100
Tea	without milk or sugar	nil

Carving

Said to be one of the least understood of the arts of the table, and I can believe it. Earlier generations thought skilful carving so essential that it was looked upon as an indispensable part of a well-born man's education. Nowadays, with large joints of meat so expensive, and with so much cut-up meat sold by supermarkets, many young people lack any real opportunity to learn. Some of course are luckier.

★ To make the best of any joint or fowl, you shouldn't underestimate the value of good carving: you'll get more and better servings from the meat, it will be more tender and will have better flavour. Bad carving wastes and spoils good food.
★ To carve well, you need two things especially: a really sharp carving knife and some knowledge about anatomy. As a general principle, nearly all meat is carved *across* the grain, because this shortens the meat fibres, making each slice more tender. Leg of lamb or mutton is the exception: it can be carved either parallel to *or* at right angles to the bone.
★ The slices should be as large and of as even thickness as possible, some meats being carved thicker than others to provide their perfect flavour:
★ *Lamb and mutton* (and as a general rule *venison*, depending on the cut) are sliced $\frac{1}{8}''$ – $\frac{1}{2}''$ (3 mm – $1\frac{1}{4}$ cm) thick, thicker than *beef* or *veal* which are sliced thinly, at the most $\frac{1}{8}''$ (3 mm). Though it depends on the cut, *pork* is generally sliced as beef. *All cooked meat* should be cut thinly and evenly.
Duck (page 207) and *goose*, because of their different structure, are carved quite differently from a bird like *chicken or pheasant*. A small *turkey* may be carved like chicken but a large bird is carved differently because the limbs also must be carved, being too large to eat whole (see page 221.

Chalazae

Plural of *chalaza*. The chalazae are the two 'threads' which hold an egg yolk in the middle of the white, so preventing the yolk being broken easily. See *Eggs*, page 107.

Chambré

Means at 'at room temperature', the temperature at which red wines are served, and to which they are brought gradually, over a period of hours, from cellar temperature.

Chopping

Can take various forms according to the food in question. Onions (page 148), jelly (page 45), chives and parsley for instance all require a different technique.

★ You only need a sharp knife – preferably a French cook's knife (page 14) – and a chopping board for herbs, for *most* of which the action is basically the same as for mint or parsley.

CHIVES. As if to defy what I've just said, these are 'chopped' easily and quickly with scissors: bunch several tightly together, break bunch in half to shorten, and then cut across finely with sharp scissors.

MINT. Pile several leaves up on top of each other, roll them tightly together (like a magazine for the post) and slice finely first one way, then the other, before sprinkling lightly with a pinch of granulated sugar to make them easier to chop. Now hold your knife at both ends: using the heel of the knife to chop, hold the point down on the board with the left hand and move the right hand in rapid up-and-down movements, and at the same time backwards and forwards in an arc-like direction. Scrape the mint continually into a heap again with the knife, chopping it until very fine.

PARSLEY. For best flavour and to make an attractive garnish, parsley should be very *finely* chopped. Bunch the washed, dried parsley heads tightly together on the chopping board with your left-hand thumb and finger tips. Keeping the point of the knife firmly on the board, move the right hand up and down to cut parsley, and at the same time backwards and forwards in an arc-like direction. All the time, still with your thumb and finger tips, keep the parsley bunched until in much smaller pieces. Now change your grip and hold the knife at both ends as for mint above, and continue as for mint.

Clarifying

Is of course to purify. For particular dishes where colour and flavour are important, salted *butter* may need clarifying before you fry with it because, due to the salt, it burns more readily at frying temperatures than saltless butter.

★ It is usually cheaper as well as easier however to *buy* saltless butter because clarifying is wasteful – you'll end up with only about 3 ozs (75 g) clarified butter from 4 ozs (100 g) salted.

MARGARINE. May need clarifying for frying, should you particularly prefer it to oil or a cooking fat, because the milk products in it burn at high temperatures.

DRIPPING. Needs clarifying for deep fat frying especially, because the impurities in it burn at high temperatures. It also of course keeps longer when purified. See *Dripping*.

Coating

Coating foods evenly with sauce is easy if you start at one end of one side, and pour

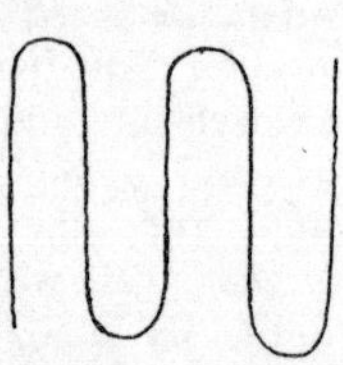

the sauce rather quickly over the food in up-and-down lines.

★ For coating foods which are to be fried, see *Frying*, deep fat and shallow, pages 41 and 42.

Concasser

French term meaning to chop roughly or to break up by pounding in a mortar: tomato concassé for instance is the roughly chopped up flesh of a tomato which has been peeled, seeded and juiced. You may need it like this for a garnish, or as an omelet filling.

Consistencies

Play a much more important part in cookery than many people realize, because it is frequently upon just this that the success or failure of a dish depends. Knowing the right consistency – what a mixture should look like or feel like – is one of the main skills of a good cook, and something most of us can only learn by experience.

★ Over-thick soups and sauces are just as unappealing as runny. The latter take longer to adjust but the remedies are all there – beurre manié, egg yolks and cream, flour and water thickening, arrowroot, cornflour or potato flour – whichever is appropriate.

★ Cold sweets, especially creamy ones, ice creams, puddings, cakes, scones, pastry and doughs etc are affected for better or worse by the amount of liquid used, or by the amount of beating, whisking, whipping or kneading done to acquire the right consistency at each stage.

★ Mixtures won't combine successfully if of different consistencies: flour and water thickening for example will only blend properly with a liquid if it is liquid itself, and *half*-whipped cream blends more evenly with cold dessert mixtures than fully whipped cream, because the latter is much stiffer than the mixture itself.

★ *Coating consistency* usually implies a sauce just thick enough to coat the back of a wooden spoon smoothly.

★ *Dropping consistency* would be better described as flicking consistency because it implies a mixture which can be *flicked* off a spoon, not one which is soft enough to drop off without help.

★ If you want to know any more about consistencies, see *Blending*, also *Ribbon, To the*, pages 32 and 54.

Court Bouillon

An aromatic liquid used *mostly* to poach whole or large pieces of fish; to give flavour they would lack if simply poached in water. It may contain wine, lemon juice or vinegar, sliced onion and carrot, herbs and spices, garlic, salt etc. As its name implies, it's a type of bouillon (or stock).

★ Here is a simple recipe, to be prepared in advance and set aside ready to use:

- 4 pts (2 L) water
- 1 lb (450 g) carrots, sliced
- 2 medium-sized onions or 3 shallots, sliced
- 1 bayleaf
- 3 or 4 sprigs parsley, washed
- 1 sprig thyme
- 1½ ozs (40 g) cooking salt
- ¼ pt (125 ml) wine vinegar or cider vinegar
- 12 peppercorns

Method. Put everything except the peppercorns into a saucepan, bring slowly to the boil and simmer 1 hr. Add peppercorns 10 mins before end of cooking. Strain and cool.

★ It's a pity to waste the liquid from the cooked fish. Strained, it will easily keep a week in the refrigerator, or will freeze well, as ice cubes. Then you can use it to cook more fish, or you could make a tasty sauce with it.

To Cream

To cream is to soften or beat a mixture until it has the consistency of whipped cream. Creaming generally means beating a fat by itself, or with sugar, to trap air and to make the fat or mixture smooth and fluffy enough to blend easily with other ingredients.

★ Caster sugar blends with fat better than granulated, because it is finer, smoother and more like the fat in texture. That's why a 'creamed' cake made with caster has a more even texture than one made with granulated.

★ When creaming fat and sugar, the sugar won't fly about so much if you cream the fat by itself first.

★ It saves time and energy – and you'll probably end up with a better cake – if your butter or margarine is soft; which either means thinking in advance, to have the fat at warm-room temperature, or using a soft type of margarine. When soft, it is then just a matter of minutes to cream it with the sugar as above. Only when they are completely blended, will they accept the gradually added whisked eggs without the mixture curdling. (As long as the eggs are warm, and the fat and sugar are properly creamed, as many as a dozen eggs can be added to a pound (450 g) of fat without the mixture curdling).

★ If a mixture looks like curdling – curdled, it will make a heavy cake – beat in a spoonful or so of the measured, sieved flour. This may correct it.

★ Be sure to clean down the sides of the mixing bowl, and the wooden spoon (or beater) from time to time, otherwise there'll be lumps of unblended mixture. See also *Cakes, creamed mixtures*, page 251.

Crescents

Usually made of fried bread or puff pastry, and used as a garnish. Cut quickly with a plain scone cutter, like this:

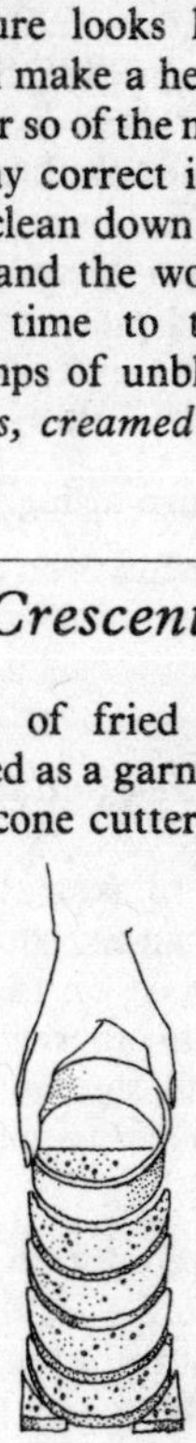

To Crush Garlic

See page 73.

Decorating

See *Garnishing*, page 43.

Deglaze

To deglaze is to add liquid – wine, stock, lemon juice, water or cream – to a roasting tin or pan in which food has been roasted or sautéd. Scrape into the liquid all the tasty particles and juices sticking to the bottom and sides of the pan, then use this as the perfect complement to the food.

Dégorger

A French word which we can't exactly translate in culinary terms, but it means 'to clear' or 'to purify'. Sweetbreads for instance are soaked in cold water to remove impurities like blood; aubergines, courgettes and cucumbers are sliced, put in a colander, sprinkled with salt, covered with a weighted plate and left to stand about an hour, to make them less watery and bitter. Dry them afterwards if necessary, in a clean cloth. (A cucumber salad for example is less watery and bitter if the cucumber has been dégorgéd before the dressing is poured over.)

Degrease

To degrease is to skim the fat off foods such as stock, sauces, soups and gravies. Fat floating about on the top of any of these can spoil an otherwise lovely dish, so skim it off with soft absorbent kitchen paper or with paper tissues if you haven't anything else.

★ Better still, refrigerate stock overnight and lift the fat off in a sheet the next day. Whatever you want it for, you then know it is fat-free. (*Most* fats solidify.)

★A quick way to degrease a hot liquid is to put a piece of butter muslin in a colander or a large strainer, fill it with ice cubes and pour the liquid over them into a bowl below.

Dicing

See *Slicing and Dicing*, page 57.

Dredging

Similar to dusting, but implies a heavy coating instead of a light sprinkling.

Dusting

Dusting foods, cake tins or pastry board etc with sugar or flour implies a light sprinkling, not a coating. Too much can easily spoil the consistency, flavour and/or appearance of whatever it is you're making or doing.

Entrée

Literally the 'entry' to a meal; a dish served before the main course. Complete in itself, it is all served on one dish, usually with a sauce, and artistically garnished with flavourful, colourful vegetables etc.

★ Dishes which in days gone by were served only as entrées, are frequently served nowadays as the main course. There's no need to say why.

Faggot of Herbs

The English term for a bouquet garni, but now seldom heard of.

Farce

Just another word for stuffing, used to give foods extra flavour, to correct fattiness (say of goose or pork) or dryness (say of turkey), to make food go further, or sometimes to make a main dish out of a minor ingredient, eg Dolmas.

★ While we English, by and large, are adventurous if we stuff veal or plaice with forcemeat, or loin of pork with sage and onion stuffing, the French use a vast variety of stuffings to bring new life to all kinds of food. They bring a fresh dimension to eating so why not search through your recipe books, and stuff the next five chickens you cook in five different new ways?

Fats

Saturated and *Polyunsaturated* fats are words often used in the same breath as cholesterol. Medical research has shown that many people who have suffered from heart attacks have a high level of certain types of fat in their bloodstream, including the fat-related substance, cholesterol. On a long term basis, the cholesterol level in the blood can be lowered by avoiding foods high in saturated fatty acids and using foods high in polyunsaturated fatty acids instead.

★ All the different fats we find in foods contain these substances called fatty acids, which are of two main types:

(1) *Saturated fats* are the fats which contain a high proportion of saturated fatty acids *and are usually solid at room temperature.* (Some vegetable oils are exceptions, eg coconut oil and groundnut oil, which solidify when refrigerated.) Foods of animal origin and some other foods contain saturated fats. All hard margarines, like Stork and Echo for instance, contain saturated fats. In fact the very process of hardening the fat in the manufacture of margarine from vegetable oils involves the 'saturation' of the fat. The physical and chemical changes taking place during hardening mean that the fatty acids are converted to the saturated form. See chart.

MAZOLA'S GUIDE TO FOODS CONTAINING FAT AND CHOLESTEROL

Foods high in 'saturated fat' and/or cholesterol	*Foods high in 'polyunsaturated fat' and low in cholesterol*
butter milk yoghourt cream hard cheeses, eg Cheddar, Stilton	
'fat' meat, eg pork, sausages, duck, goose	
	oily fish, eg herring, tuna
dripping lard hard margarines white cooking fats coconut oil suet	corn oil, eg Mazola sunflower seed oil cotton seed oil safflower seed oil 'polyunsaturated margarine', eg Flora, Sainsbury's Special Super Soft
coconut cashew nuts	most nuts, eg almonds, walnuts
egg yolk (particularly rich in cholesterol)	
chocolate	
baked goods made with butter, margarine or egg yolks, eg pastry, cakes, biscuits	baked goods made with corn oil and without egg yolks

(2) *Polyunsaturated fats* are the fats which contain a high proportion of polyunsaturated fatty acids which *are liquid at room temperature* – and are often called oils rather than fats. Oils usually come from vegetable sources: corn oil and other seed oils such as sunflower or cotton seed oil. See chart.

Fécule

Particularly implies potato flour – *fecula* is a very fine flour usually extracted from potatoes – but is sometimes loosely interpreted to mean other starches like arrowroot, rice flour or cornflour. Fécule is used to bind and thicken soups and sauces.

Flambé

Means 'in flames', and indicates the flaming of brandy or other spirits, used to flavour foods.

★ Warm the spirit or liqueur first in a spoon, soup ladle or very small pan, otherwise it probably won't ignite.
★ The *reason* for flaming is to burn away the alchohol and concentrate the flavour, which will permeate the food.

Fleurons

Small shapes of puff pastry, usually crescents, used as a garnish. It isn't worth making pastry specially, because they take so little – better to cut a strip off some partly thawed frozen puff pastry, and pop the rest back into the freezer. See Crescents, page 37.

Flour, Seasoned

Flour mixed with a generous amount of salt and pepper, used to coat fish, meat, poultry etc. It gives flavour, protects foods from heat when frying, makes egg and breadcrumbs adhere better to foods, or it acts as a slight thickening in stews etc.

★ To give seasoned flour more pep, there's nothing to stop you adding a hint of cayenne, ground mace or nutmeg.

Folding

Quite different from stirring, and is the customary term used to describe quite a complicated skill which many recipe books take for granted, but which many of us may not know how to do.

★ You may be adding sieved flour to beaten eggs and sugar, whisked egg whites to a soufflé, or sugar to whisked egg whites: whichever it is, the movement is always the same. It's best to use a tablespoon or metal spatula because, unlike a wooden spoon, these have a thin sharp edge which will cut through the ingredients without expelling any of the air just beaten in. That's why it is sometimes called 'cutting' in the egg whites.

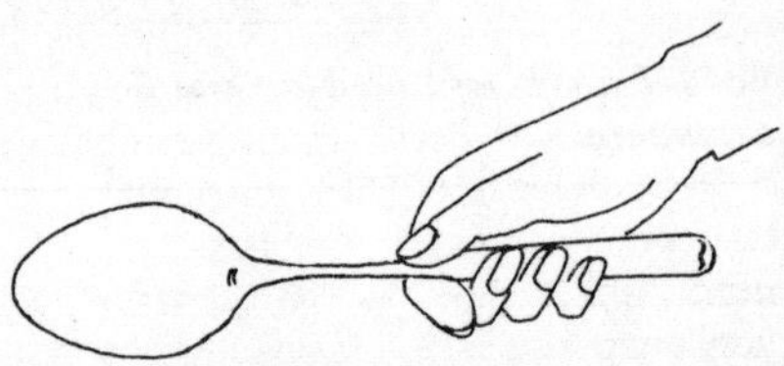

★ Hold the spoon so that its sharp edge cuts down through the mixture. Instead of going round and round as when stirring, stir once round the outside, then bring the spoon sharply through the middle, towards you, turning it 'bowl' upwards and lifting it right out. Continue doing this until the two mixtures are blended.
★ The mixture at the bottom of the mixing bowl is thus brought up over the egg whites, flour or whatever it is, which is literally folded inside.

1 Start

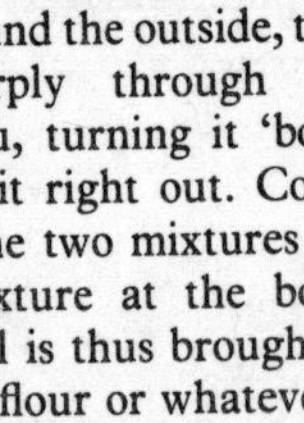

2 Lift spoon out

★ It is easier to incorporate whisked egg white evenly into a mixture if you first fold in one large spoonful of it. The mixture then more readily accepts the remainder.

Freezer Burn

The name given to foods which become dried by surface evaporation. The tissues of such foods as meat and poultry for instance develop dry white patches, and the foods become tough and spongy through dehydration. Not even the best of cooks can recapture a food's original flavour and texture once this has happened. All sorts of things can cause freezer burn: air in the packages, foil torn or too thin, polythene bags either too thin or perhaps pierced, seals broken. See also *Water*, page 95.

Freezing

The ideal way to preserve many foods because it simply arrests their life cycle and holds them in their natural state until you are ready to use them at the moment of *your* choice. The nutrients are unaltered, and apart from watery foods such as fruit and vegetables whose texture changes, freezing changes neither the structure nor the flavour of food to any significant degree.

★ Excepting those foods which can be cooked while still frozen, the golden rule is *freeze quickly, thaw slowly*. Jill McWilliam in her book *Freezing* explains why:

> All foods have an interior cell structure which can be destroyed if freezing is done too slowly. As food freezes, ice crystals form within the structure – the faster the food is frozen, the smaller the crystal formation, keeping the interior structure intact as far as possible. Slow freezing produces large ice crystals which destroy the structure both internally and externally. Foods with a high water content such as strawberries, cucumbers etc never freeze very successfully as even the tiniest crystal formation breaks down the very delicate structure. On thawing they go rather soft and mushy but can be utilized in dishes, or for cooking, as the flavour is unchanged. Food frozen slowly is disappointing in texture and flavour, but of more importance is the loss of nutrients when defrosting or cooking. The correct use of the fast-freeze device is important.

OPEN FREEZING Means freezing foods as they are, uncovered, for a short time, until firm enough to seal in a polythene bag or other container without damaging or squashing.

★ You may, for instance, have some butterfly cakes or 'nests' of duchess potato you want to pile into one bag, or a gâteau piped with crème au beurre. Twenty to thirty mins is usually all they'll need to firm up.

Frying, Deep Fat

The greatest danger in the home for anyone who is either careless, or unaware that fat will burst into flame spontaneously at very high temperatures, even without being anywhere near a flame. Besides the fires I've known of, a neighbouring family lost their whole home within the space of an hour or two, because the mother left the kitchen while the fat was heating. Do, for your own and your family's safety:

(1) Use a *thermostatically controlled* hot plate or plugged-in fat pan if you can. Failing this, use a thermometer. (See *Ignition temperature*, page 45.)
(2) Keep a rug or heavy blanket handy. This is a fire to *smother* – never one to throw water over.

THE PAN. See *Pans, deep fat*, page 17.

THE FAT. Should be of best quality for best results. The more refined it is, the higher will be its smoke point:

★ Oils. Mazola is a highly refined corn oil, or you can use a good 'vegetable' oil, or sunflower oil. Olive oil is unsuitable because, quite apart from its cost, its smoke point is too low.

★ Pure lard or white cooking fat of top quality also give excellent results.

★ Dripping can only be used if you clarify it, otherwise its impurities cause it to break down at high temperatures.

Have the pan $\frac{1}{3}$ to $\frac{1}{2}$ full. If deeper, the fat may bubble up and boil over when you lower food into it. If too shallow, floating foods can't float, and others – like Scotch eggs for instance – will spoil if not completely submerged.

COATING. Foods need coating with *something* – egg and breadcrumbs, batter or pastry – before frying in deep fat, to:

(1) Protect them from the intense heat.
(2) Prevent certain foods disintegrating, when watery ones might make the fat bubble over.
(3) Prevent flavour and juices escaping into the fat – which spoil both food and fat.
(4) Give flavour, colour and a crisp texture.

★ Dry thoroughly any wet foods like chips, to prevent the fat spluttering and bubbling over.

FRYING TEMPERATURES. Vary from about 340° – 400°F (170° – 204°C) according to the food in question. (A thermostatically controlled hot plate on the cooker should be set slightly above the recommended temperature for the fat, because without a lid on the pan, there is considerable heat loss.) Pre-cooked foods such as fish cakes are fried in hotter fat than raw foods, which have to be *cooked* at the same time as being crisped outside.

★ If the fat is too hot, the outside of foods will brown and burn before the inside is cooked: if too cold, the food will absorb the fat, becoming greasy and indigestible. In addition some coatings may burst. It's important to avoid over-filling the pan with food too, otherwise the fat's temperature will drop too low.

★ Reheat fat before frying a second batch of food, to bring back to the required temperature.

★ Oil only smokes when it is too hot to use. If *any* fat becomes too hot, turn off the source of heat at once, and leave the pan to cool: more lard or cool oil, as the case may be, will lower the temperature immediately.

FRYING BASKET. Not used for foods coated in batter because the batter may stick to the wire, exposing the raw surfaces of the food, which the fat then penetrates. Foods such as doughnuts, aigrettes and parsley aren't fried in a basket either, because they'll stick to it.

Sweet and savoury foods can follow each other in the same fat because, providing each is properly coated, and the fat hot enough, no flavour or juices will pass into it.

★ Drain all foods on absorbent kitchen paper, to make sure they aren't fatty and indigestible.

★ Avoid covering fried foods with a lid while keeping them hot, because the trapped steam will make them go soft.

★ Heat fat after use, until all bubbling stops, to drive off any water, which would hasten decomposition.

★ Strain fat through butter muslin after use, to remove even the smallest crumbs, which if left in, may cause decomposition and will burn when next the fat is heated. Thus darkened it will give anything fried in it a bad colour and a bitter flavour.

Frying, Shallow

Isn't as tasty a way of cooking as deep fat frying, and foods like fish are more likely to break up because they aren't sealed by the fat in the same way, and because they need extra handling.

★ Coat foods with such things as egg and breadcrumbs, seasoned flour or seasoned oatmeal to protect them from the intense heat, as well as to give flavour, colour and a crisp texture.

★ Butter gives foods a heavenly flavour but it burns easily unless saltless or clarified. Adding a dessertspoon oil to 2 ozs (50g) butter allows it to reach a higher temperature without burning.

★ Preheat the fat, of whatever kind, to seal the surface of the food and prevent flavourful juices escaping into it. If not hot enough, the food will absorb the fat, making it greasy, indigestible and in some cases soft instead of crisp.

★ Avoid overfilling a frying pan, first because it cools the fat too much and secondly because, without air space between each piece of food, things will steam rather than fry and will consequently be soft instead of crisp.

★ As with deep fat, avoid covering fried foods with a lid, because they'll go soft in the trapped steam.

Fumet

The liquid left from cooked fish, meat or game, boiled down rapidly to a syrupy consistency, for addition in concentrated form to the accompanying sauce.

Garnishing

Implies savoury foods, 'decorating' sweet. Both should make a dish look more attractive and will almost invariably add extra, complementary, flavour. Some provide contrasting texture to the food with which they are served, while others add moistness to a dry one or richness to a plain. Some on the other hand *counteract* richness. While their purpose is therefore varied, their presence is always pleasing if carefully and thoughtfully carried out.

★ Many classic dishes are so called because of their garnish (see page 48), but it's often up to your own imagination to provide that final touch which makes the difference between dishes which look dull and uninteresting, or alternatively tempting – sometimes even a work of art.

★ Here are some examples of what one food can do for another:

ASPIC JELLY. Used to coat things like cold salmon cutlets or certain cocktail snacks, secures the position of a garnish like hard-boiled egg or green pepper, gives flavour and a glistening appearance, and prevents the food itself becoming dry.

BUTTER, SAVOURY. Such as Maître d'hôtel (see pages 131 and 133) gives an enticing appearance, flavour, moisture and richness to grilled foods like fish, steaks or lamb's liver.

CAYENNE PEPPER. This or paprika give colour and flavour to lots of savoury dishes, like egg mayonnaise or a cheese savoury.

CREAM, SOURED. Adds a dash of colour to the centre of a plateful of beetroot soup.

CROÛTONS. Look nice, taste nice and give both richness and a crisp texture to a vegetable purée soup (see page 126).

CUCUMBER. Finely sliced and perhaps decorated with a fruit decorator, cucumber makes lots of cold dishes look colourful and complements the flavour of salmon particularly.

EGGS. Hard-boiled, and sliced, quartered or cut into shapes with aspic cutters, eggs often give a lovely splash of colour. Used to glaze, egg gives a shiny appearance and may help a garnish like poppy seed to stick to dinner rolls or a milk twist.

FLEURONS. These or small shapes of fried bread or toast look attractive, give flavour and a crisp texture to a dish without 'bite', like mince.

HERBS. Especially the brightly coloured ones like chives or parsley (page 77), which flavour also combines well with other foods, can be used to garnish almost anything, whether egg dishes, cheese, soups, vegetables, fish, meat or poultry.

LEMON BUTTERFLIES. And/or lemon quarters look lovely, give additional flavour and counteract the richness of foods like fried fish. See page 79.

MUSHROOMS. Cooked, give flavour more than anything else to many meat or fish dishes. See page 147.

NUTS. Whether chopped, grated or flaked, they give crunchiness to soft foods like fish. If browned (in the oven, under the grill or by frying), they also contribute enormously to the flavour of a dish. Delicious too with fried chicken or with curry.

ONIONS. Cooked pickling onions are mainly to give flavour to meat dishes. Batter-dipped rings of a larger onion will give richness and a crisp texture in addition.

PEAS. It goes without saying that they cheer up many a dull looking dish. Because of their perfect yet rather mild flavour, they're a good partner with many kinds of food.

POTATO STRAWS. Look enticing, add richness, flavour and a crisp texture when accompanying something like grilled steak or fried fish.

TOMATOES. Look bright and cheerful whenever they're used, besides adding flavour to many savoury dishes. Make tiny ones yourself from larger (see page 155), for a particular purpose like replacing the stalk of a stuffed green pepper. Tomato quarters, juiced and seeded, make a better garnish than slices, which tend to disintegrate and make a dish watery.

VEGETABLES. Cooked and diced (page 57), they give colour, flavour and food value to many dishes, especially if a mixture of, say, carrot, turnip, peas and celery.

Gas Flames

Are hottest at the tips, so if they're licking up the sides of a pan you're wasting gas, not getting as much heat as you may think.

Glaze

GLAZE, MEAT. See page 274.

GLAZE FOR PASTRY, ROLLS ETC. Use egg yolk if you can spare it, mixing with it a pinch of salt and a teasp cold water, which make it easier to brush on and gives better results than whole egg.

★ Glaze sweet pastries with egg white if you like, sprinkling them with caster or icing sugar before baking.

★ Use milk if you can't spare egg – though it's not as good.

Goulash

Comes from the Hungarian national dish, *Goulasch*, generally a kind of beef stew made with diced onions and seasoned with Hungarian paprika.

Gratiner

Means to brown the top of a dish under the grill, or in a hot oven, after sprinkling it with breadcrumbs and melted butter, or with grated cheese – and perhaps breadcrumbs too.

Grilling

Is suitable for only best cuts of meat because only they will cook so quickly and yet so perfectly under such intense heat. Other foods grill deliciously too of course – like small whole fish, fish steaks, lamb's or calf's liver, lamb's kidneys, bacon, sausages and certain vegetables.

★ Slash the fat round beef or gammon steaks, or the fat of bacon rashers before grilling, otherwise the meat curls up and cooks unevenly because the fat sizzles and shrinks faster than the lean.

★ Score whole fish two or three times across the top thick part, to allow the heat to penetrate to the middle, and to let out some of the surface fat so that it will cook crisply.

★Salt on grilled meat? Some people say you shouldn't use it because it draws out the flavouring juices and hardens the meat. *I'll* settle for salt and flavour – the meat will still be juicy unless overcooked.

★ Brush the surfaces of the food with oil or melted fat, to keep moist and prevent charring.

★ Preheat the grill, making it red-hot before you start, in order to seal in the juices, which would otherwise escape into and evaporate in the grill pan. By first grilling meat fast for just one minute on each side, the sealed in juices then rapidly evaporate on its own surfaces, giving grilled meat its characteristically delicious flavour.

★ Turn meat over with tongs or two tablespoons, and fish with two fish slices or a fish slice and a pallet knife. If you pierce meat by using a fork, some of the juices will escape.

★ The time foods take to grill depends on their type and thickness, the maximum heat of the grill, the distance between food and grill, and upon your own taste – whether you like meat rare, medium or well done.

Hands!

There are times when you're cooking, when two hands just aren't enough, as when making mayonnaise in a basin: with a large tea-towel folded diagonally as below, and tied firmly round the top of the basin, you can then twist the ends together and grip them between your body and the table, leaving both hands free to work; the basin held steadily in front of you.

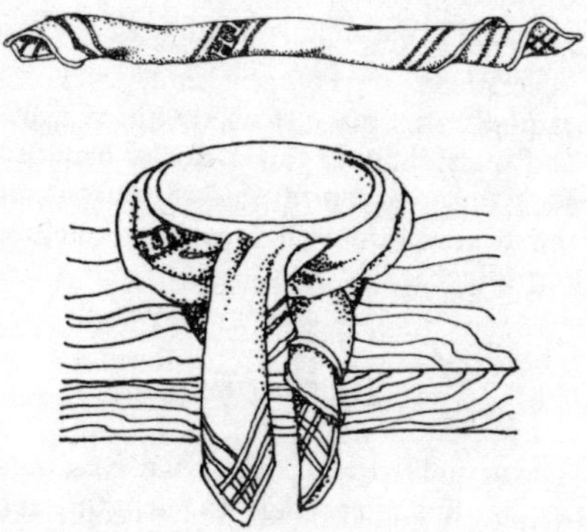

Ice Cubes

Can speed things up when mixtures are slow to cool or set, especially in hot weather. Decorated moulds and cooling mixtures will respond quickly if surrounded by ice in a larger bowl.

★ Make ice cubes in advance and transfer them to the freezer when a large party is likely to be a strain on a smallish refrigerator. Set a mint or borage leaf, a maraschino cherry or a sliver of lemon peel in some of them if you like.
★ Use an ice cube tray to freeze and store such things as stocks, lemon juice, orange juice, chopped fresh herbs, court bouillon, meat glaze or cream.

Ignition Temperature

Is that at which oils and fats burst into flame spontaneously, without any flame being applied. Beware therefore when deep fat frying. This temperature varies according to the type of fat – oil, lard, cooking fat, clarified dripping – and even to particular types and brands of oil. The more refined each oil or fat is, the better, because the higher the ignition temperature will be. *Most* ignite between 685°F and 800°F (365°C and 425°C).

Jelly

TO CHOP JELLY. Requires a spot of know-how. Whether 'aspic' or 'sweet', it won't sparkle if you either finger it or chop it too small. Make it stiff, either with rather less liquid or rather more gelatine than usual. Chop the jelly on wet greaseproof paper with a long wetted knife, then it won't stick to either. Hold the knife by each end, cutting *coarsely* in up-and-down movements. Use to decorate (aspic for a savoury dish, sweet for jellies, creams etc). It will make a dish go further besides dressing it up.

TO DECORATE WITH JELLY. To decorate the bottom of a mould is easy when you know the ropes but the most exotic dish can look amateurish if you don't. Here's some help:

(1) Have the jelly cool but still liquid, so that it can find its own level yet not melt anything already set. If necessary, *keep* it liquid by warming its basin in a larger one of warm water.
(2) Set a thin layer of jelly in the bottom of your chosen mould, using ice cubes in very hot weather or to speed things up if you're in a hurry.
(3) Whether cherries, angelica, grapes, banana, peas, prawns, cooked carrot, chives or whatever, pierce each in turn with a hatpin (or very fine skewer), dip it in the liquid jelly and place where you want it, sliding it off the first hatpin with a second. Put in refrigerator and leave to set, otherwise the decorations will float when you add more jelly.
(4) *Spoon* a little more liquid jelly over the decorations, just to cover, and now leave *this* to set. (If poured from a jug, the decorations may be dislodged by the force of the jelly's fall.)

Now add your mixture and leave *it* to set.

Kneading

Is very difficult to learn effectively from a book. If I were you, I'd have just one lesson from an expert. Many people find it difficult to learn even after *seeing* how to do it. You need actually to *do* it.

Knife Sharpening

To sharpen correctly is all-important in the care of knives. Skilful sharpening before use will keep the blade razor-edged. Sharp blades should be honed (sharpened) with a fine steel; a coarse steel only when knives are really blunt.

★ Hold the steel firm, as illustrated, and draw the knife blade down it: ensure that the full length of the blade is sharpened by drawing the knife from hilt to tip down the full length of the steel on both edges, as shown in figs 1 and 2 below:

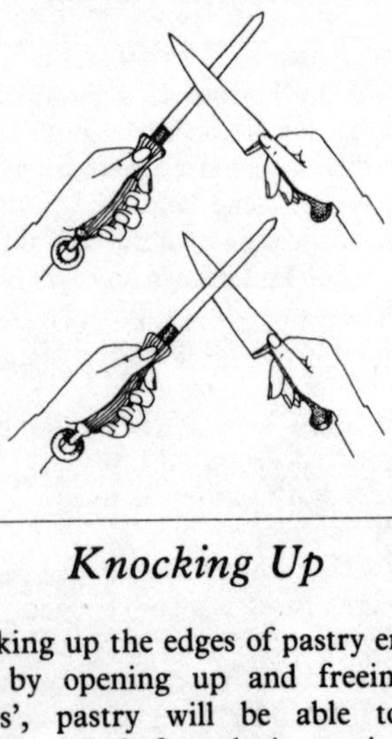

Knocking Up

Knocking up the edges of pastry ensures that, by opening up and freeing the 'layers', pastry will be able to rise properly: just before glazing a pie, plate pie, sausage rolls or whatever, work your way all round the cut edges with the sharp edge of a knife blade, tilted slightly backwards (see illustration). It's a matter of almost brushing the blade lightly against the edges in an upward movement, from the lower part of the edge to the upper. Steady the pastry with the fingers of the other hand and turn the pie round gradually as you work, so that you're always knocking up the edge furthest away from you.

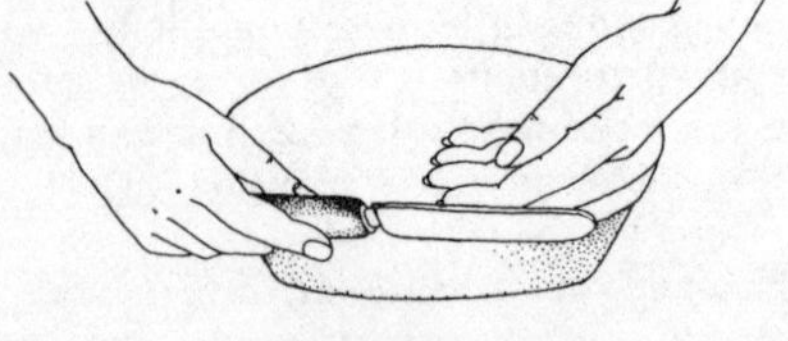

Larding

A way of giving some fat (before roasting) to very lean joints of meat, and 'dry' types of poultry or game, to make them moist and juicy. Thread thin strips of firm dry pork fat or bacon fat into the surface of the meat or bird with a special needle, see *Larding needle.*

Lardoons

The actual strips of pork or bacon fat used in larding, varying in length and thickness, according to the meat for which you need them.

Lemon Butterflies

An attractive and quickly made garnish, used largely for fish or veal. Use the lemon as it is, or decorate it first with a fruit decorator. To make, see page 79.

Liaison

May be a roux, flour and water, fécule, beurre manié, egg yolk, or egg yolk and cream – any of them used as a thickening or binding for soups, sauces and other liquids.

Lining a Cake Tin

Lining a cake tin properly is particularly important when you want a well-shaped fruit cake. Tins sometimes have to be lined for other cakes as well:

SQUARE OR RECTANGULAR TINS. Shallow or deep.

(1) Grease tin, preferably by brushing with a pure fat such as melted lard or white cooking fat.

(2) Stand tin on a sheet of greaseproof paper, ABCD, at least the size of the tin plus the depth, plus about 1″ (2½ cm) for stand above. Mark round the tin with a pencil. See illustration.

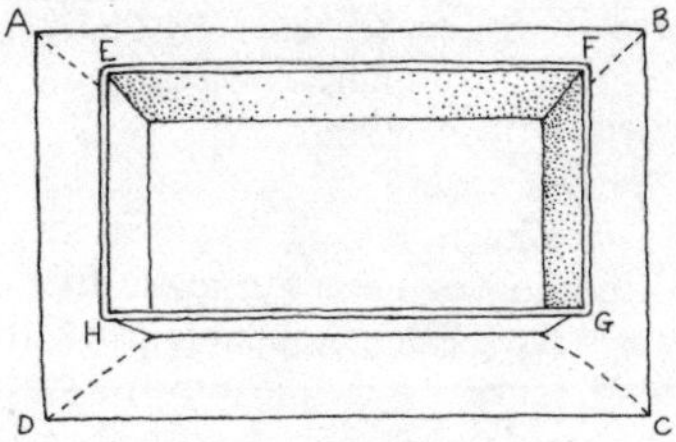

(3) Cut diagonally, accurately, from A to E, B to F, C to G and D to H.

(4) Fit paper in tin, the pencilled lines precisely along its bottom edges. Overlap paper at corners, cutting off the points if they get in the way.

(5) Brush all surfaces with fat again.

ROUND TINS. To line bottom only.

(1) Grease tin with fat, as square tin.

(2) Stand tin on piece of greaseproof paper, mark round with a pencil and then cut just inside the line. Fit disc precisely in bottom of tin.

(3) Brush all surfaces with fat again.

(4) Dust out lightly with flour, giving tin a sharp knock, upside down, to remove any surplus.

ROUND TINS, TO LINE FULLY. Use more than one layer for a rich fruit cake.

(1) Grease tin with fat, as square tin.

(2) Stand tin on a doubled sheet of greaseproof paper, to make *two* discs, as above. Fit one of these in bottom of tin.

(3) Cut a strip of greaseproof at least 2″ (5 cm) longer than the circumference, and 1–1½″ (2½–4 cm) wider than the depth of the tin, Fig 1 below.

(4) Fold over a good ½″ (about 1½ cm) of the paper along the whole length, Fig 2.

(5) Open out the fold and cut slanting lines through the narrow piece, exactly to the fold line, Fig 3.

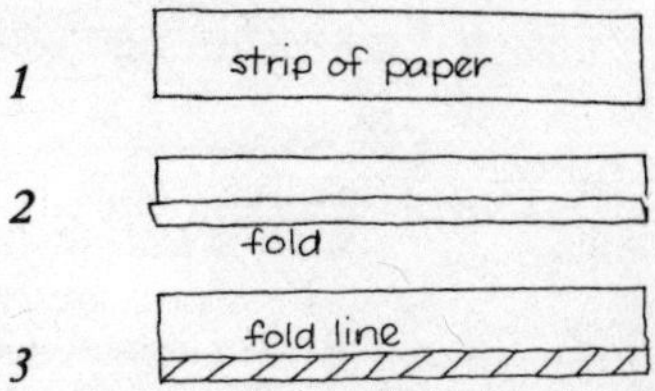

(6) Fit paper into tin, the narrow slashed strip fitting round bottom.

(7) Fit second disc in bottom to cover and hold down all slashed edges.

(8) Brush all surfaces with fat again.

ROUND TINS TO LINE BOTTOM QUICKLY. Put a small *square* of greased greaseproof paper on the bottom of the greased tin. As long as ⅔ of the base is covered, the cake should turn out easily. (Cut several squares of paper while while you're about it, then they're handy in a drawer when you want one.)

Macerating

Like marinating, but concerns fruit instead of meat and fish. It is as simple to macerate as to breathe, and yet the result is delectable enough for any dinner.

★ Ripe, fresh fruits are flavoured and softened by caster sugar sprinkled over, together with a liqueur in which they are soaked for a limited time, according to the kind of fruit: use both liqueur and sugar 'to taste', (approx ½–1 tablesp liqueur per serving).

★ *Cover* fruits like bananas, pears or peaches (which discolour easily) while they are soaking, and don't leave too long – bananas and pears about half an hour, peaches about an hour.

★ Use two wooden spoons to turn fruit over once or twice in the 'syrup', to make sure the liqueur permeates it completely.

★ Serve the fruits just as they are, preferably with Crème Chantilly, cream or Crème Anglaise etc.

★ Use macerated fruits also to make fritters, see *Fritters*.

★ Some good combinations are:

Fruit	*Preparation*	*Liqueur (+ sugar)*
Apricots	Skin, cut in half, stone	Kirsch or apricot brandy
Bananas	Slice thickly, diagonally	Rum
Cherries	Stone	Kirsch or cherry brandy
Figs	Peel and quarter	Cognac
Nectarines	As peaches, below	As peaches
Oranges	Cut off rind and pith in spiral. From between skins, ease out segments of flesh. Remove pips	Curaçao, rum or Grand Marnier
Peaches	Peel and cut in halves, quarters or slices	Peach brandy, Cognac, rum or Cointreau
Pears	Peel and cut in halves, quarters or slices	Cognac, Kirsch, rum, Calvados or, best of all, Poire William
Pineapple	Peel, slice, remove core and cut as liked	Kirsch or rum
Plums	Skin, cut in half, stone	Kirsch, Cognac, rum or Quetsch
Raspberries		Cointreau or Cognac
Strawberries	Hull	Kirsch or Grand Marnier

Marinating

Means soaking meat, fish or game and sometimes vegetables, in a highly seasoned liquid – a marinade. It can transform cheaper cuts of meat into the luxury class. Marinating flavours foods, tenderizes tough meat, gives moisture to dry meat, or helps to preserve meat or game which you may have to keep a day or two longer than desirable.

★ A marinade may be cooked or uncooked, simple (like French dressing for salad vegetables or lemon juice for fish), or complicated, with up to a score of ingredients, as for venison. Marinating may take half an hour or several days, according to size and texture of the food, and whether it is hot or cold weather.

★ A cooked marinade works more quickly than an uncooked, even though the ingredients may be identical, because cooking brings out their aroma and flavour. The ingredients may include wine, vinegar, brandy, oil (preferably olive oil), onion, garlic, carrot, herbs and spices. To cook a marinade, fry the vegetables lightly in the oil to bring out their flavour, then add the other ingredients and simmer for half an hour. Use cold because, if hot, it would amongst other things encourage rather than discourage the growth of bacteria.

★ Use a roasting tin or similar deep dish for large joints of meat, or for venison, so that you can baste and turn it over from time to time, as necessary.

★ After the food is marinated, add the strained liquid, if you like, to an accompanying sauce, freezing any surplus as ice cubes, and transferring them to the freezer for use another time.

Menu

A restaurant menu can be a teaser if you have no idea what's what and are too shy or embarrassed to ask the waiter – though you needn't be. When food is served, doesn't another diner's choice sometimes look twice as good as ours, and don't we occasionally regret a choice we would never knowingly have made?

★ Given that a certain name implies a particular method of preparation, or certain foods (either cooked in the dish, as a garnish, or perhaps with an accompanying sauce), you should be spared disappointment. By being informed, you'll for instance be able quietly to ignore Florentine if you don't care for spinach, steer clear of Marinière or Nantua if shellfish bring you out in a rash, or make a mental bee-line for Provençale if you're a garlic and tomato fan. Here are some well known names, but first 'à la carte' and 'table d'hôte'.

À LA CARTE. The type of menu on which each dish is individually priced. Because special dishes are cooked to order, they're always more expensive than a set meal, where cooking, serving and choice are restricted to a few dishes.

TABLE d' HÔTE. French for 'the table of the host' – or landlord – and is a set luncheon or dinner menu at a fixed price.

Restaurant Menus

Name	*Method of Preparation or Principal Components*	*Comments*
Bonne Femme	Cooked in some homely way, which often includes potatoes. As in Poularde à la bonne femme.	
Bourgignonne	Red wine, mushrooms and tiny onions. As in Boeuf à la bourgignonne.	
Brochette	The food is cooked and served on a skewer. As in Brochettes de sole à la duxelles.	Brochette is French for skewer.
Chasseur	White wine, mushrooms and shallots. As in Tournedos chasseur.	
Darne	A thick slice of a large fish; poached, grilled, braised or sautéd. As in Darne de saumon à l'ancienne	
Daube	A kind of stew, of meat, poultry or game. As in Boeuf en daube	The meat has usually been marinated and is cooked in the same marinade.
Diable	To cook by grilling with mustard: to devil it. As in Poulets grillés à la diable.	Diable is French for devil.
Duxelles	A mixture containing mushrooms and shallots. As in Pommes de terre farcies à la duxelles.	The name is thought to have originated where the dish was first created, in the household of the Marquis d'Uxelles.
Fines Herbes	Chopped fresh herbs, especially chervil, chives, parsley and tarragon, together. As in Omelette aux fines herbes.	
Florentine	Spinach, and mornay sauce. As in Sole à la florentine.	Usually fish or egg dishes.
Forestière	Morels, diced potatoes fried in butter. As in Entrecôte à la forestière.	Morels are an edible fungus. In practice, in English cookery, mushrooms are used instead.

Grecque	Dish should be of Greek origin in the method of preparation. As in Concombre à la grecque.	In practice, the name is often given to dishes of French origin.
Hollandaise	'Hollandaise', the rich sauce made with egg yolks and butter. As in Fonds d'artichauts à la hollandaise.	Served with eggs, fish or vegetables.
Hongroise	Paprika flavoured cream sauce. As in Soufflé à la hongroise.	
Indienne	Curry. As in Hachis de boeuf à l'indienne.	
Italienne	Finely diced or chopped mushrooms. As in Oeufs à l'italienne.	The name is also given to a method of preparing pasta.
Jardinière	Neatly cut, separately cooked vegetables, as garnish. As in Escalopes de veau à la jardinière.	
Julienne	Garnish of vegetables cut in thin strips, especially carrot, turnip, celery and leek. As in Consommé Julienne.	May also apply to any foodstuff which is shredded, e.g. julienne of mushrooms, julienne of chicken breast.
Lyonnaise	Onions. As in Tripe à la lyonnaise.	
Marinière	Shellfish, especially mussels. As in Homard à la marinière.	Fish dishes only. Loosely translated means 'fishwife style'.
Ménagère	A 'household' dish – something simply made. As in Crème au beurre à la ménagère	Ménagère is French for housewife or housekeeper.
Meunière	Fish fried in butter, served with lemon juice and chopped parsley. As in Raie à la meunière.	Fish only (see also page 174).
Milanaise	Food is dipped in egg and breadcrumbs (often mixed with grated Parmesan cheese). As in Côtes de porc à la milanaise.	May also imply a method of preparing macaroni.
Nantua	Crayfish tails or a covering of crayfish purée. As in Potage velouté de volaille à la nantua.	

Niçoise	Tomatoes and garlic, also often anchovy fillets and black olives. As in Salade niçoise.	
Normande	Mainly for fish braised in white wine, or may sometimes imply cider and/or calvados As in Sole à la normande.	Used also for small cuts of meat, chicken or winged game, prepared quite differently. This often also includes cream.
Paupiettes	Thin slices of meat, or fillets of fish, stuffed and rolled up into cork-shaped parcels. As in Paupiettes de veau à la grecque.	Beef olives are paupiettes.
Polonaise	Hard-boiled egg yolk and chopped parsley. As in Chou-fleur à la polonaise.	
Provençale	Tomatoes and garlic. As in Courgettes à la provençale.	
Ragoût	A stew, of fish, meat, fowl or vegetables. As in Ragoût de champignons.	Regoût is French for stew.
Saint-Germain	Fresh green peas, usually as a garnish. As in Tournedos Saint-Germain.	May also describe a thick soup made with peas.
Soubise	A purée of onion and rice, or an onion sauce. As in Côtelettes d'agneau soubise.	
Suprême	Implies the best part – breast of fowl or game, or a choice piece of fish. As in Suprêmes de faisan.	Suprême may also describe a rich, white, creamy sauce.

Menu Planning

Is an important part of a housewife's work, whether she's arranging family or special-occasion meals. Subconsciously you probably think about most of these things anyway but here are the main points to consider:

(1) For whom is the meal? Young children; ravenous adolescents; over-fed business men or a ladies' lunch?

(2) How much time and money can you spare to make the meal?

(3) The need for 'balanced' meals – that means being sure that sometime during each day you serve all the nutrients.

(4) People's likes and dislikes. It's not really fair to give your friends shellfish, hare or curry as a main course, unless you know they like and can eat it. If you don't know them well enough to ring up and ask, it's kindest to choose something else.

(5) Variety of texture. Supposing you want to serve soup, fish and then a caramel custard, do think of making croûtons to go with the soup, chips or sauté potatoes to go with the fish, or

perhaps meringues to go with the soft sweet.

(6) Variety of flavour. Avoid serving, say, mushrooms, tomatoes or a milk sauce in more than one course.

(7) Variety of colour. Use green vegetables to cheer up a brown or white dish, and avoid following, say, gammon with strawberries.

(8) The capacity of your cooker, both hot-plates and oven.

(9) The weather. Chilled soup is lovely in July but probably not in December.

(10) Variety of cooking *methods*. Avoid overdoing the frying, the boiling or the stewing for instance.

(11) It isn't wise to mix homely and elaborate courses at the same dinner party. If you start off in Ritz style, that's the standard you're setting for the whole meal.

Metric Quantities and Measurements

Those given in this book are as follows: 1 oz = 25 g (although in fact 8 ozs = 225 g and 1 lb = 450 g)
For convenience, when exact quantities are unnecessary, as for vegetables, they may be rounded up to 'say 500 g' or 'say 1 K'.
$\frac{1}{4}$ pt = 125 ml (although in fact $\frac{1}{4}$ pt is 1 tablesp more than 125 ml)

Mirepoix

A cooked mixture of coarsely diced vegetables, bacon and herbs. Its purpose is to give flavour and it is used mainly as the foundation on which meat, fish or fowl are braised. If the vegetables are diced smaller, it is sometimes used as a garnish for cutlets or for a fish dish. It should consist of such vegetables as carrot, onion, celery and leek, in quantities balanced so that no one flavour predominates.

Mocha or Moka

Always implies a coffee flavour, taking its name from a variety of coffee bean grown in Mocha (Yemen).

Nutrients

They are all vital to good health. They are:

Proteins	Minerals
Fats	Vitamins
Carbohydrates	Water

Roughage also is essential, although strictly speaking it isn't a nutrient.

Oven Temperatures

On gas cookers, temperatures vary slightly in their numbering according to make, but in the majority, number '4' corresponds to 350°F and each number up or down represents 25°F *more*, or *less* – ie 350°F = gas 4, 375°F = gas 5, and 325°F = gas 3.

★ Oven temperatures throughout this book are based on these figures, *approximate* equivalent temperatures being given also in degrees Celsius (Centigrade).

Speaking generally, a
slow oven is gas 2, 300°F, 150°C
mod oven is gas 4, 350°F, 175°C
hot oven is gas 6, 400°F, 205°C
very hot oven is gas 8, 450°F, 230°C.

★ Celsius, the scale in general use in Europe, and called after its Swedish inventor, Anders Celsius, is to replace the unit which we have called Centigrade. The reason for changing is to avoid confusion with a unit (in some other countries) having the same name, but used to denote fractions of a right angle.

Panada

A very thick sauce. The base of a savoury soufflé, a panada is also used to bind croquettes and similar mixtures.

Parboil

Just as it sounds: to partly cook by

boiling, prior to completing the cooking by another method, see *Blanching*.

Pare

Simply another word for peel – to remove the outer skin from fruit and vegetables. Strips of lemon or orange peel are best taken off with a potato peeler, to take the minimum of bitter pith with the rind.

Pinch

A pinch of any dry ingredient is the amount which you can pick up between your thumb and forefinger. In fact, a pinch of salt, as so often called for, is frequently totally inadequate to bring out the flavour of a food.

Piping

Piping attractively and successfully comes only as a result of practice as a rule: an excellent way to acquire this is with hot sieved potato. You can pipe it over and over again, either to improve your skill, or to plan a design; using something like an inverted breadboard as a dummy 'flan' or 'cake'.

★ Piping is a difficult skill to learn from a book. It would pay dividends to have just one lesson if you've never had one.

Piping Bags

Are most easily filled like this, a cuff turned over at the top, leaving both hands free to work. Only three-quarters fill the bag, then turn back the cuff and close bag up.

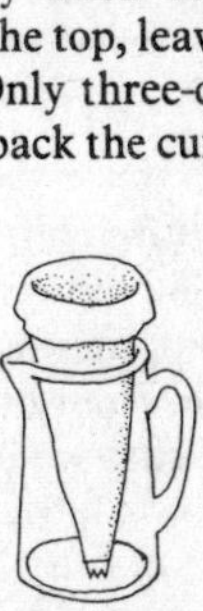

Pockets of air need to be pressed out with a pallet knife before piping, otherwise it is difficult, if not impossible, to pipe an unbroken chain.

Poaching

Is done in 'shivering' – barely simmering – water (see page 57). Only delicate foods such as eggs and fish will cook at such low temperatures, consequently this method of cookery is restricted.

Point

A point of garlic or of cayenne, is the minute quantity which can be held on the point of a knife.

Proving a Dough

The second raising of a yeast dough, see page 244.

Proving a Girdle

Proving a warmed girdle or iron omelet pan, implies cleaning it with salt and rubbing it with soft paper instead of washing it with water. This prevents rust forming, and ensures that scones or omelets will not stick.

Purées

Fruit or vegetable purées are made in seconds in a liquidizer. Failing this, a vegetable mill is usually quicker than a sieve, but seedy fruits may still need sieving.

Raising Agents

May be chemical or otherwise. These are they:

(1) Baking powder, see page 63

(2) Bicarbonate of soda with cream of tartar or another acid, see *Bicarbonate of soda*, page 63.

(3) Bicarbonate of soda alone, in certain circumstances, see *Bicarb* again.

(4) Yeast, see page 96.
(5) Air, see page 62.

Réchauffés

Dishes made up from cold cooked fish, meat, game or poultry, these will be tough and indigestible if the meat is re-cooked rather than reheated. Cold foods usually lack flavour and nourishment when reheated, so these are introduced by using such things as onions, herbs, spices, batter, egg and breadcrumb coating, or by accompanying sauces.

★ All flavourings are precooked, because quick reheating allows no time for raw ingredients to cook.

Reducing

Boiling a liquid down rapidly in an uncovered pan, to thicken the consistency and concentrate the flavour in a very *small* amount of liquid. This is an important step in the making of many delicious sauces. Any salt you add will also become concentrated, so go lightly with that until after the liquid is reduced.

Refreshing

Is *making* vegetables go cold, instead of *letting* them do so, by running cold water through, or plunging them straight into deep cold water for 2 or 3 minutes – or long enough to cool them – after they've been blanched (or boiled) and drained. This abruptly halts their cooking, consequently they don't lose any of their colour, flavour, texture or nutrients, as they do if just left around simply to cool. In this country we don't seem aware of the advantages and *convenience* of refreshing, on occasions such as these:

(1) When you're *serving* vegetables cold, as in salads, eg asparagus, peas, sweet pepper, sweetcorn, cauliflower sprigs, French beans.
(2) When you've blanched vegetables for some particular reason, page 31.
(3) When for some reason you don't want to serve a vegetable immediately, but you want it to be *nearly* cooked, so that you can serve it within a few minutes:
(a) You're going out, and want to serve the meal a few minutes after you return.
(b) The vegetable is in the pan when a telephone call comes, asking you to delay the meal.
(c) Meal time is uncertain. As cook-hostess, you can't spend too long in the kitchen.

Rendered Fat

Is fat melted down from pieces of fat cooked either in the oven or on top of the cooker until the dripping runs freely and the pieces of fat are shrunken and golden. It needs straining through butter muslin, otherwise the tiny particles will burn when the fat is heated and used.

To the Ribbon

The term used to describe the consistency of eggs and sugar whisked until a ribbon-like trail forms on the surface of the mixture when you trail some back into it off the whisk. Only if the mixture is thick and fluffy enough to support this 'ribbon' will it support the other ingredients to be folded in.

★ You can beat the eggs and sugar quickly and easily with an electric hand-whisk over very hot but not boiling water, or less quickly with a good hand-whisk. Alternatively you can manage without water if you use a fixed electric beater – but *I* prefer the result when the eggs are warmed.

Roasting

Strictly speaking, roasting is cooking in a current of air in front of or over a fierce glowing heat. What we today term roast meat is in fact baked, because it is cooked in a current of air by dry (or radiant) heat in an enclosed oven. The rôtisserie (page 21) is the modern return to true roasting.

★ Roasting is traditional for cooking *tender* joints of meat, poultry or game: they are too large and too thick to be grilled. Some people like to set their joint or bird on a wire meat stand in the roasting tin. Others prefer to set it on a bed of roasting vegetables (say a peeled onion and/or a large carrot cut into three or four thick slices), because when these caramelize as they do during cooking, they give a delicious flavour to the gravy.
★ Initially, roast meats need a preheated hot oven to seal the outside surfaces. The flavouring juices will then be kept *in*, instead of escaping into the tin, with the result that the meat will be moister, will have more flavour and will shrink less.
★ Cooking a joint or bird in a roasting bag or baking pan (page 17) produces different results from using an open roasting tin: when, with the heat of the oven, the juices in meat or fowl turn to steam, the steam is trapped, so this food is cooked by moist rather than by dry heat – which isn't really roasting. Even though you remove the covering towards the end of cooking, you can't for instance expect a chicken to become crisp and golden as it is after roasting in an open tin throughout its cooking time. Your oven will be clean and meat will shrink less, but it's unlikely it will taste as good and the texture will be less firm.
★See also individual meats and birds.

POT ROASTING. A simpler but less good version of *Braising*, see page 33.

Rolling Pastry

Is quite an art. The aim is to elongate the dough, away from you, not simply to enlarge it by squashing! With a cool dough, and with pastry board and rolling pin lightly floured, the dough shouldn't readily stick to either.

★ Hold the rolling pin (page 21) *lightly* at each end, fingers over the top, and the thumb ends almost pointing towards each other along the pin. In this position, you can roll it and then pick it up, repeatedly.

★ Roll the pin sharply yet lightly forwards, until under upper part of hand, then roll it backwards and lift it up. Continue like this, lifting pin up after each short forward and backward roll, until the dough is the size, shape and thickness you want. See also page 99.

Roux

Can be made with butter, margarine, dripping or oil, depending upon the purpose for which it's needed. There are three kinds:

(1) *A white roux*, used for white sauces and soups, when a white colour is important. Make with butter, margarine or oil – preferably butter, for its flavour – and cook it 2 or 3 mins. For perfection, use clarified or saltless butter, so that you can cook the roux a minute or two longer, to give extra flavour without also colouring it.

(2) *A blond roux*, used ideally for velouté and piquant sauces. Use butter rather than margarine because margarine doesn't colour so well, and burns more readily if overheated. Cook this a few minutes longer than a white roux, until pale straw colour.

(3) *A brown roux*, used for brown sauces and soups. Make it with dripping, oil, saltless butter or clarified butter. (With salted butter, the sediment will burn during the long cooking, giving the sauce a bitter flavour.) With beef dripping, the roux will go brown more easily than with oil or clarified butter, but delicately flavoured dishes sometimes call for a particular fat. Cook a brown roux about 15 mins., or until a golden nut-brown colour.

★ Equal quantities of fat and flour are normally used, but those who guess rather than weigh their ingredients, are better to have a tiny bit too much fat than too little. (Too *much* fat can cause a greasy sauce, but at the same time it is difficult to incorporate the liquid when a roux is too solid.)
★ A roux seems so straightforward and easy to make, yet it isn't. If the fat gets too hot, either because you *heat* it instead of just melting it, or because you don't set the pan aside from the

heat while stirring in the flour, the starch in the flour will turn into tiny pellets which you can't get rid of. In addition, the flour will lose some of its thickening properties.

★ If tempted to dodge *cooking* the roux, do have second thoughts, otherwise your sauce won't be anything to write home about. This is why:

(1) Cooking the roux gives a sauce or soup extra flavour.

(2) Cooking the flour at this stage prevents the sauce having a floury taste, and also prepares the flour to absorb the liquid; as a result of which the liquid will thicken more readily when it comes to the boil. (As laundry starch bursts when boiling water is poured onto it, so the starch grains in flour burst, thickening the liquid when it boils.)

(3) You can't make a blond or brown roux *without* cooking it.

★ A roux is cooked over *low* heat and stirred at regular intervals, to prevent the flour burning. *If* it burns, it not only gives the sauce a nasty taste, but may prevent it thickening properly as well.

★ Liquid is added to a roux aside from the heat because it is easier to incorporate that way. If you want to prepare a sauce in advance – leaving it ready just to boil up later when required – stir in the cold liquid gradually, with a wooden spoon. To add a nearly-*boiling* liquid to a roux, whisk it in all at once with a wire whisk, as soon as the roux has stopped bubbling.

★ You can make a roux hours before needed, if you want to – even the day before: melt it again slowly when ready for it, but be careful not to leave any congealed on the spoon, or you'll probably end up with a lumpy sauce.

Salpicon

A preparation of one or more diced ingredients, bound together with a flavourful sauce. There are endless varieties. Use them to fill such things as vol-au-vent cases, bouchées, tartlets or croustades.

Sauté

From the French '*sauter*' – to jump (some foods jump about when fried). Small pieces of fish, meat poultry or game – liver, kidneys, tournedos, salmon, chicken etc – are browned initially in a small quantity of preheated very hot fat in a sauté pan, or very strong frying pan, to seal in the juices.

★ Ideally you should use either a mixture of butter and olive oil (the oil allowing the butter to reach a higher temperature without burning), or saltless or clarified butter.

★You can cook the food completely, in which case lower the heat after browning, or you can just brown it prior to cooking in another way. Some vegetables are sautéd in hot butter from start to finish. Others are blanched first.

★ Be sure the food is quite dry and the pan not overcrowded, otherwise the food will steam, not brown.

Use the juices left in the pan to make a sauce, see *Deglaze*.

Savoury

Served as the last course at dinner, this is intended to clean the palate after the sweet, before serving port.

Scalding

Means either bringing a liquid to *just* below boiling point, or pouring boiling water onto a food, like blanching.

Scraping

Scraping cut or chopped-up food off a chopping board into a pan or bowl, isn't just a combination of good aim and luck when you have the board overlapping the front of the table, hold the pan or bowl underneath it, and guide the food into it with a knife.

Searing

Is browning meat quickly under high heat, or in hot fat, to seal in the juices. If the fat isn't hot enough, the juices will escape into it – and with them, flavour.

Seasoning

The name we give to salt, pepper and other dry ground spices when we add them to food during cooking. If added at table, we call them condiments! This word comes from the Latin condire, to season or pickle. See also *Salt*, page 88, and *Pepper*, page 85.

Shivering

An even lower temperature than simmering; no bubbles on the surface, 180°–190°F, 82°–88°C. This is 'poaching' temperature.

Simmering

Is boiling *very* slowly in a covered pan on top of the cooker or in a covered dish in a very slow oven, the liquid showing only the slightest movement on the surface. Simmering temperature is around 200°–210°F, 93°–99°C.

Sitting Down

Sitting down to cook, wash up, dry up and iron is a technique worth cultivating because it greatly reduces physical strain, especially for a busy, pregnant or ageing housewife.

★ Like becoming accustomed to a thimble or rubber gloves, what at first seems impossible, soon becomes natural, even essential. A high stool – and some determination initially – are about all the average-height (or taller) woman needs. Many sink units have an unshelved cupboard underneath, with sliding door. With your feet in the cupboard, you can work completely at ease – there are few jobs you can't do easily, and just as well.

Slaking

Is blending a small amount of liquid with a thickening agent such as arrowroot, potato flour, cornflour or custard powder, prior to thickening soups, sauces or gravies with it.

Slicing and Dicing

Is an art, especially to do fast, evenly and without cutting your fingers. Given ten minutes, a chef will probably cut almost as many pounds of vegetables as most of us could cut ounces. It's worth watching if ever you have the chance – a case of 'practice makes perfect'.

★ To acquire this professional technique needs time, patience and maybe weeks of practice. The art is to keep the tip of the blade on the chopping board, raising and lowering the knife handle to slice as you feed the vegetables under the blade. The *amateur's* way of cutting potato chips or diced vegetables is simpler:

(1) Using a sharp knife (preferably a French cook's knife, page 14) gripped as illustrated, and keeping the finger tips of your left hand all the time tucked *under*, slice off thinly the rounded sides of a potato (or carrot or turnip) to make a more-or-less rectangular block.

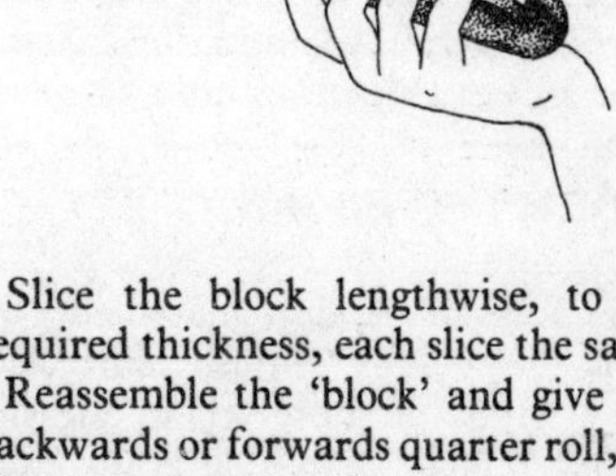

(2) Slice the block lengthwise, to the required thickness, each slice the same.
(3) Reassemble the 'block' and give it a backwards or forwards quarter roll, the slices now lying neatly piled up on top of each other.
(4) Control them, still as one block, with your thumb at end of potato nearest to you, small finger at far end, and your

remaining three fingers on top, tips turned under. Then the slices can't slide about and you can't cut yourself, see illustration:

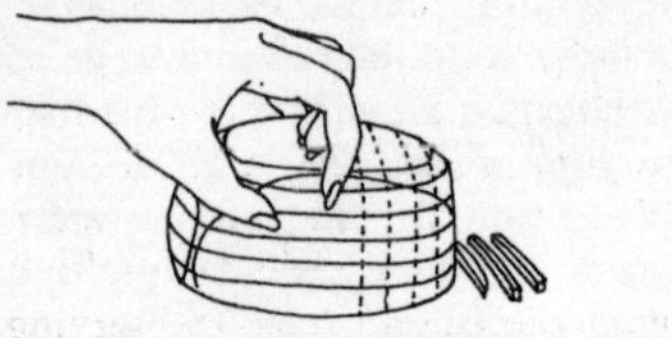

(5) Slice the potato the same thickness as before, this time into chips.

(6) *To cut dice* (for which you'll need thinner slices than for chips), give the block a quarter turn and slice *across* the 'chips', again the same thickness and with the same grip as before, to produce even-sized cubes.

Smoke Point

The temperature at which oils and fats begin to break down and give off a blue vapour. The temperature varies according to the type of fat, and the more refined it is, the higher the smoke point will be. Pure lard, for instance, has a high smoke point, while olive oil and unclarified dripping both have low smoke points. This explains why these two fats are unsuitable for deep fat frying, where the *lowest* temperature ever required is higher than their smoke point.

Soufflé

Comes from the French *souffler*, to blow up. The mixture is blown up by the air whisked into the eggs. See also *Savoury Soufflés*, page 113, and *Cold Soufflés*, page 235.

Spoonfuls

Spoonfuls of a dry ingredient mean rounded spoonfuls in this country, unless you use one of those sets of measuring spoons (which are used level) or unless a recipe book tells you otherwise.

1 teaspoon means as much above the 'bowl' as in it, not a heaped or mounded one.

$\frac{1}{2}$ *teaspoon* means a teaspoon levelled off with a knife.

$\frac{1}{4}$ *teaspoon* means half a *level* teaspoon.

$\frac{1}{8}$ *teaspoon* means quarter of a level teaspoon.

See also page 24.

★ *A liquid spoonful* means a *full* spoonful, not about $\frac{3}{4}$ or $\frac{7}{8}$ of it! Especially when a recipe calls for 3 or 4 spoonfuls of an ingredient, that imbalance can make the difference between the perfection or otherwise of certainly some dishes, if not many.

Steaming

Is cooking by the vapour from boiling water, which must be kept boiling just hard enough for steam to escape continually; except for egg dishes when the water should just simmer. The lid must fit the steamer tightly, and the steamer must fit the pan, to prevent too *much* steam escaping.

★ Allow steamed foods about half as long again as boiled. There's less danger of overcooking, and of foods breaking up, because they're cooking more slowly.

★ Not all foods steam as well as they boil, however, green vegetables especially.

Stewing

Is long slow cooking in a small quantity of liquid in a covered vessel, either in the oven or in a pan on top of the cooker. A close-fitting lid is essential, to prevent evaporation.

★ It's an economical method of cookery

because it utilizes cheaper, tougher kinds of food.

★ See also *Stews*, page 196.

Stuffings

See *Farce*, page 38.

Sweating

Plays an important part in the tenderizing of vegetables, especially of finely sliced onions before other ingredients are added. They are softened without being browned, by being partly cooked in fat, usually butter or oil, in a strong *covered* frying pan or saucepan over low heat.

Talmouse

Implies a kind of cheese tartlet, served as an hors d'oeuvre or savoury.

Tasting

Is a 'must' if you want to be a good cook. No sauce or soup should go to table without, nor should anything else you can easily sample. All your efforts may be wasted if you fail to taste, perfection often depending on it.

★ If it breaks your slimming rules, be strong-minded and taste without swallowing.

Toasting

Toasting thinly sliced or frozen sliced bread is neither difficult nor impossible. The bread won't curl up at the corners and burn, if you first grill each side until dried out but not coloured. Toasting in this way draws the moisture *evenly* out of both sides, helping the bread to stay flat when then toasted in the usual way.

Unmoulding

Unmoulding creams and jellies etc can be tricky if you don't know how. A few drops of water smeared over the serving dish will make it easier to slide and centre the mould if it falls slightly to one side. Dip the mould for a few moments (not seconds) up to the rim in a large bowlful of water almost as hot as your hand can bear, to break the seal without also melting the jelly. Now use the tips of your fingers to loosen the top of the mould round the edges. Place the serving dish upside down on top, so that you can invert them both together, and then give a few firm shakes to release the jelly. If they refuse to part company, go back to the hot water stage.

★ Some people prefer to invert a mould over their flattened palm, carefully withdrawn as the mould slides out onto the dish.

★ Hold thick china moulds longer in the hot water than copper or aluminium. See *moulds*.

Vandyking

Is a way of garnishing and can refer to various things, including the edges of fruits, like this one:

It is attractive but time-taking, earning its name from the small pointed beard made famous by Van Dyck, the painter. The points must be fairly even if not to look amateurish.

GRAPEFRUIT. It's quicker to use scissors than a small stainless steel saw-knife but you may ruin your scissors in the process.

Cut just deep enough to show up, but not so deep that juice will run out. I like to do it when the fruit is empty, see page 118.

TOMATOES. Are done while whole, preferably with the tip of a small vegetable knife: hold fruit up in front of you in left

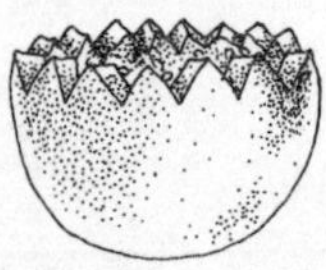

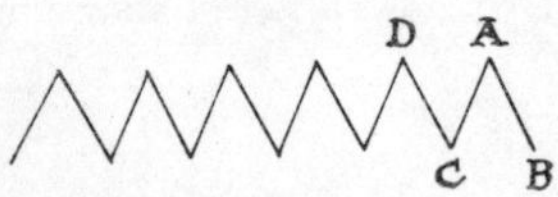

hand, and work round in a circle until the ends meet.

(1) Stick the knife point in the middle and make a small gash AB.
(2) Turn point downwards and make the next gash CA to meet the first at A. The next gash is from D to C – and so on.
(3) When circle is complete and ends meet – you hope – slip knife into middle of fruit to cut through the core, then ease and gently pull the two halves apart.

APPLES. Are easily done with a small pair of scissors after the fruits are hollowed out, before stuffing. Do the edge of the lid as well, dipping the cut edges in lemon juice to prevent discolouration.

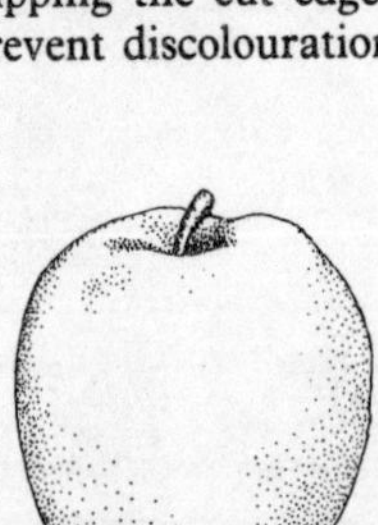

Whisking

Whisking egg whites successfully depends largely upon three things – the freshness of the eggs, your own skill and the type of whisk you use. Upon effective whisking and prompt, correct folding, depends the lightness and the volume of whatever you are making.

★ The tiniest trace of egg yolk, or a greasy or damp bowl or whisk, will spoil perfect results.

★ An aluminium bowl may give white of egg a grey cast, but an unlined copper bowl is ideal if you're lucky enough to have one. The slight acidity of the copper apparently acts as a stabilizer to the whisked whites, and consequently gives a greater volume of firm 'snow'. As not many of us *have* a copper bowl, the best substitute is a small pinch of cream of tartar per egg white, added soon after starting to whisk, when the whites look foamy.

★ Whether whisking by hand or with an electric whisk, you get the best results by whisking slowly at first, increasing gradually to a moderate speed when the whites start to foam.

★ If you whisk egg whites properly, they should be about 7 or 8 times their original volume, but just *how* stiffly you should whisk them depends upon what you want them for. You can easily *over*-whisk them, making them difficult to incorporate into a mixture.

★ These are the different stages to which recipes may tell us to whisk them:

(1) *Stiff*: as you need egg whites for such things as soufflés and mousses. Whisk just until you can safely turn the bowl upside down, when the white is still rather frothy.

(2) *Like cotton-wool* is self-explanatory and it's quite a lot stiffer than *stiff*! This is the way you need them at the half-way stage for meringues, before you add the first of the sugar.

(3) *Rocky* is much stiffer still, when the whites are shiny like satin, and as you need them for meringues, meringue toppings and for decorating. If you're whisking by hand, it may take you 5 mins hard work between the cotton-wool and rocky stages, but only if you've whisked whites really stiff like this will they support the sugar when you fold it in, and keep a perfect shape when piped.

Zest

Is the outer part of the skin of citrus fruits – lemons, oranges, limes and grapefruit. It contains the essential oil of the fruit, and is used to flavour such things as creams, whipped cream, ices, butter creams and custards. All the bitter pith is left on the fruit.

★ Scrape it off with a *zester* or remove it by rubbing a serrated knife up and down against the fruit.

★ You can also take zest off with sugar lumps, rubbing them one at a time up and down against the fruit. When impregnated, crush them, and allow to dissolve in the mixture.

★ Some graters have an extremely fine section which *may* act as a zester.

3
INGREDIENTS

Successful cooking and the enjoyment you may have from it often depends on oddly varied scraps of knowledge so I'm not going to apologize for the hotch-potch of facts you'll find here.

There are some well-known and some little-known bits of information about the best-known as well as the not-so-well-known ingredients. I just hope that by filling in some of the missing pieces in the cookery jig-saw, they'll stimulate your interest and bring greater success to your results.

Agar Agar

The Malayan word for a species of red algae and is used primarily to mean the trade product made from that particular algae or seaweed. The vegetarian's equivalent of gelatine – and hideously expensive – it is the oddest stuff to use, and is unlike gelatine in every way, except that both gel when combined with liquid.

★ A little goes a long way, because agar has enormous gelling power – though this is destroyed if it is heated with even a small amount of anything acid.

★ You must boil to dissolve it, and it forms a firm jelly without refrigeration, setting some mixtures even before they're cool. It makes a more chewy jelly than one made with gelatine.

Air

The intangible ingredient which every good cook incorporates into things she makes, by sieving flour and other dry ingredients, by whisking egg whites, by whipping cream, or by folding and rolling pastry. Without it there would be no soufflés, sponge cakes, or even pastry as we know it, because air is their *only* raising agent.

★ A cupful of flour for instance becomes $1\frac{1}{4}$ cupfuls when sieved, and egg whites will, if correctly whisked, multiply their volume by 7 or 8 times.

★ The tiny particles of trapped air expand when heated. The colder it is the more it will expand, which explains why cool pastry and chilled Yorkshire Pudding batter rise better than when at room temperature.

Almond Essence

This may seem unnecessary when a recipe already contains ground almonds, but it brings out the flavour of the almonds.

Angelica

Candied angelica is the stem or leaf stems of the angelica plant. See also *Herbs*, page 76.

★ When using angelica to decorate, thick slices or chunks look clumsy, so wash it under the hot tap (to make it pliable), dry it, then cut into long thin slices. Now it's easy to cut these slices, with the minimum of waste, into several leaves or whatever shape you want, as below:

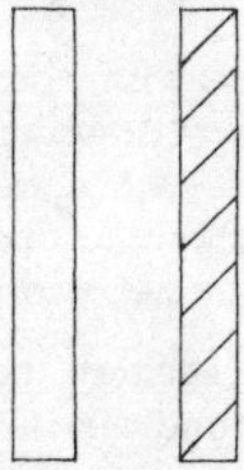

Arrowroot

Comes from the roots and rhizomes of a tropical plant, taking its name from the American Indian word for flour-root, *araruta*.

★ Its great advantages over cornflour are that it is tasteless and it gives a clear finish when used to thicken certain soups, gravies, fruit syrups and fruit sauces. Used to glaze a fruit flan for instance, where cornflour would obscure the fruit and give a distinctive flavour, arrowroot simply makes the fruit shine.
★ Slake it (blend with a little liquid) before using – 2 level teasps to $\frac{1}{4}$ pt (125 ml) fruit syrup. Unlike cornflour which needs cooking to get rid of its raw taste, arrowroot is ready to use as soon as it clears and thickens.
★ If you overheat (boil or nearly boil) the liquid before pouring onto the slaked arrowroot, it *won't* clear and thicken properly.
★ Grocers don't usually sell arrowroot – it's a chemist's item.

Aspic

Ready-made aspic lacks that home-made flavour, but is useful when you only want a small quantity, or when its 'bought' flavour will be masked by others which are stronger. See also page 116.

Baking Powder

Made from bicarbonate of soda and a mild acid. When moist and warm, these chemicals react and give off carbon dioxide, causing foods to rise.

Bicarbonate of Soda

Will also combine with acids other than cream of tartar to act as a raising agent. This is why vinegar may figure in a simple fruit cake recipe which omits baking powder, and why you can make scones with bicarbonate of soda and sour milk. The strength of these acids is not constant however, so they are not as reliable as the pure chemicals.

★ Bicarbonate of soda used alone with plain flour will give off carbon dioxide when wet and warm, but it leaves sodium carbonate (washing soda) as a residue, which not only has an unpleasant taste but makes mixtures brown. When this strong flavour can be disguised therefore by other strong flavours such as mixed spice, ground ginger or black treacle, and when a brown colour is *wanted*, as in gingerbread or soda cake, bicarbonate of soda used alone with plain flour is *better* than other raising agents.
★ Use bicarbonate of soda in the proportion of 2 parts cream of tartar to 1 part bicarb., otherwise the bicarb. will dominate, spoiling both the flavour and colour of whatever you're making.
★ Bicarb. should always be *sieved* with other dry ingredients because any tiny lumps of it cannot unite with the acid.

Bread

Keeps fresher and remains good longer if in a polythene bag in the bread bin; longer still in the refrigerator. If you have a deep freeze, you can have fresh bread continually, by putting part of a new loaf straight into it.

★ Sliced bread can be fried while still frozen, and even thinly sliced can be toasted without curling up, if you dry out both sides before toasting either until golden, see page 59.
★ Soft bread and rolls freeze perfectly for months, but the crusts of *crusty* loaves and rolls soon shell off.
★ You can rejuvenate a loaf of bread by wrapping it in foil and cooking, direct

from the freezer, in a hot oven, gas 6, 400°F, 205°C for about ¾ hr. Hot, crisp and new again, it needs eating quickly, because it soon dries out. See also page 243.

Breadcrumbs

DRIED WHITE BREADCRUMBS. A 'must' for perfect results when coating delicately flavoured foods, such as fish, with egg and breadcrumbs. If crumbs are golden before you fry food, they will be too dark, if not burnt, by the time it's cooked.

★ Dry fresh white breadcrumbs thoroughly, without colouring, in a very cool oven, then sieve and store them in an airtight jar. They'll keep for months – it's moisture which makes bread go mouldy.
★ 4 level tablesps dried breadcrumbs weigh 1 oz (25 g).

FRESH BREADCRUMBS. Will keep for months sealed in a polythene bag in the freezer, or for a long time in the refrigerator, so it's worth while making a quantity while your're about it.

★ Sieve them for special things, such as coating foods with egg and breadcrumbs, but for less important purposes such as stuffings, bread sauce, or a Queen of Puddings, you can easily make crumbs in a liquidizer.
★ If you haven't got a sieve or a liquidizer, you can crumble stale bread between your hands, if the worst comes to the worst.
★ 4-5 level tablesps fresh breadcrumbs weigh 1 oz (25 g).

FRIED BREADCRUMBS. See page 210.

GOLDEN BREADCRUMBS. Also known as *Raspings*. Made from oven-dried bread crusts etc, they are sieved and used to sprinkle over dishes cooked 'au gratin', to coat the fat of cooked ham, or they're lovely fried, to serve with roast game. They'll keep almost indefinitely in an airtight jar.

BOUGHT BREADCRUMBS. They're a sham. You must be very short of time to use *them*!

Butter

Butter is the fat with which I most love to cook. Mainly because of its flavour, I would usually rather use the cheapest butter than the most expensive margarine – providing I could afford it.

★ In French cookery, butter, eggs, oil, cream, cheese and wine are all considered essentials, but in England the true qualities of butter seem often to be neither realized nor understood. There isn't another fat to compare with it for many purposes, as far as *I'm* concerned. If you fry, sauté or otherwise cook in butter such foods as eggs, vegetables or small pieces of fish or meat, they seem to taste twice as good as those cooked in other fats. Cakes made with butter both taste better and keep fresh longer than those made with margarine.
★ When you fry or sauté with butter, it needs to be *hot*, the condition of the foam indicating the right moment to start cooking: as the butter melts, there is no foam and nothing would brown in it. As it heats, the liquids in the butter begin to evaporate, making it foam. It is as the foam subsides – when the liquids have almost evaporated – that you should begin to cook. If you fail to catch this moment, the butter starts to change colour. The hotter it becomes, the darker brown it turns, until at 278°F, 137°C, it burns.
★ Salted butter – that's most kinds of butter – goes brown and burns at a lower temperature than saltless butter, discolouring food cooked in it. This is why some recipes call for saltless or clarified butter (butter from which you've removed the salt) when a good colour and flavour really matter (see page 36).
★ If you're frying foods such as chicken, which need longish cooking, add 1 dessertsp oil to 2 ozs (50 g) butter. The oil allows the butter to reach a higher temperature without burning.
★ Avoid sprinkling salt over foods while they're frying in butter, because salt makes them stick to the pan. Foods fried in saltless butter won't stick as they do in salted.
★ Butter congeals on fried or roasted

foods served cold, unlike cooking oil (and some white cooking fats). It therefore pays to fry or roast in oil those foods which you *intend* to serve cold.

★ Because softish butter is easier to cream than when hard, it is also easier to beat more air into it. The chances are, therefore, that you'll make a lighter cake if your butter is nice and soft to start with. Firm butter is better than soft however for things like pastry which require manipulation. Some brands of butter are basically slightly firmer than others.

★ 'Melt' butter means melt, not *heat* butter as a rule. It's wise to stand a pan over minimum heat, because if you overheat butter, it 'separates' and goes oily, and won't amalgamate with other ingredients properly, spoiling things like Genoese Pastry. If you overheat *saltless* butter, it loses its fresh flavour into the bargain.

★ Saltless butter keeps 6–8 months in the freezer, salted 3–4, but it's hardly worth storing in bulk unless you can buy it cheaply, because it keeps so well in the refrigerator (useful in an emergency of course).

Buttermilk

The liquid remaining after butter has been churned from cream.

Canned Foods

Let's face it, canned foods are often radically different from the original because unlike freezing, preservation or canning alters their nature. It's sometimes hard to remember that canned peaches once smelt and tasted of the sun, that salmon tasted of the sea, or that peas came out of crisp green pods. Whilst we'd undoubtedly find catering more difficult if deprived of canned foods, many families would surely feed better with fewer?

★ If you can be bothered to 'date' cans before storing, you'll bless your discipline later. Though it will give no indication of time spent on a shop shelf before finding their way to your larder, it's a reminder of their purchase date, to use them in rotation.

★ Canned foods and vegetables are harvested in their prime and immediately prepared and canned. The majority are cooked foods which can be eaten straight from the can or used in various recipes. Once the can has been opened and only part contents used, Metal Box say it's perfectly in order to cover and put it in the refrigerator, using as you would cooked food. Fruits, fruit juices and evaporated milk are the exceptions and should be 'decanted' when opened, otherwise they tend to alter slightly in flavour.

★ All blown or leaking cans should be discarded, the former distinguishable by bulged ends. Small dents on the body of a can are not significant, but cans with severe dents affecting the end seams should not be stored; which is why a supermarket will usually sell them at a reduction.

★ The length of time a product will keep after manufacture depends both on the conditions under which it is stored and the type of packaging materials used.

★ Metal Box's list below gives times of keeping during which the product will remain in good condition if stored in a cool, dry place – but never in a freezer. It doesn't mean that after the times stated the foods will be inedible, but certain changes in colour, texture, aroma or flavour will start to occur. However, any products with a storage life of *less than one year* should be used within the year.

Product	*Storage life in good condition*
Cocoa and drinking chocolate	1 year
Coffee, instant	1 year
Cornflour	1 year
Custard powder	1 year
Drinks, carbonated	6–12 months
Fish in oil	Up to 5 years
Fish in tomato sauce	1 year
Fruits (most fruits)	1–2 years
prunes and rhubarb	9 months
Fruit juices	1 year
Hams, pasteurised, over 2 lbs (If pasteurised, it will be stated on the label)	Keep refrigerated and use in 6 months

Product	*Storage life in good condition*
Ham, sterilised, 2 lbs and under	2–3 years
Jams and marmalades	1–2 years
Meats, solid – see also Hams, above	Up to 5 years
Milk in cans	1 year
Milk, dried, skimmed and full cream	9–12 months
Pasta foods in sauce	2 years
Soups	2 years
Vegetables	2 years

Capers

The pickled, bottled flower-buds of the caper-bush, which grows wild (and is also cultivated) around the Mediterranean particularly, hence the frequent use of capers in sauces and for flavouring in Provençal cookery.

★ While the English by and large may not find much use for them beyond boiled mutton or tartare sauce, some love their piquancy with fish, meat or poultry, and others will eat them with almost anything.
★ Capers *aren't* the same thing as pickled nasturtium seeds.

Carmine

Made from the dried bodies of female cochineal insects, after they've been fertilized, but before the complete development of the eggs.

See also *Food Colourings*, page 73.

Cayenne Pepper

Not in fact a pepper, but a very hot powder ground from the dried seeds and pods of red chillies. Its colour soon fades, so buy a microscopic quantity at a time.

Cereals

Strictly speaking, cereals are cultivated grasses and their seeds or grain. These include wheat, oats, barley, rye, rice and maize, the word cereal being derived from Ceres, the goddess of the harvest.

★ Wheat is known to have been used as human food for at least 6,000, possibly 10,000 years. The ability to farm cereals, of which wheat was apparently the first, is probably one of the chief causes which led man to live in communities rather than to live a wandering life, hunting and herding cattle and other animals. When man discovered cereals, he found a food which could be grown in quantity during the warmer months of the year, and stored successfully through the colder. You could even say that with the discovery of cultivating wheat and other cereals, civilization began. They are the most important of all food plants. We eat more cereal food than any other.
★ See also *Gluten*.

Cheese

Cheese is almost as old as time, records going back to at least 4,000 BC. David was delivering cheese to Saul's camp at the time of his battle with Goliath. Cheeses travelled with the armies of Caesar. Marco Polo returned from his travels with reports of cheeses as made in the East. Its discovery was undoubtedly an accident; a simple matter of milk curdling.

★ Cheese isn't just made from cow's and goat's milk. Depending on the part of the world, it may be made of ewe's milk, yak, lama or even reindeer milk. Not only does cheese differ according to type and quality of the milk, but also according to the seasons and the mineral salts in the pasture land on which the animals have fed; the *way* a cheese is made; and the skill of the cheese-maker.
★ On average, cheese contains $\frac{1}{3}$ protein, $\frac{1}{3}$ fat and $\frac{1}{3}$ water – but, unlike milk, contains no carbohydrates. This is because in cheese making, the milk sugar (lactose) is converted into lactic acid. It's mainly because of this concentration of fat that cheese is difficult to digest unless properly cooked – yet it would seem so simple that one couldn't go wrong. It's sometimes the *cook's* fault that people can't eat cooked

cheese so here are a few tips just in case you want them:

(1) *Always* grate cheese very finely, to melt quickly and completely in a mixture. See *Mouli grater*, page 13.

(2) Add cheese to a sauce *after removing pan from heat*, so that it isn't in fact cooked at all. Providing the sauce is boiling hot and the cheese finely grated, it will melt without being heated.

(3) Add mustard, vinegar or a piquant sauce to cheese mixtures, to stimulate the digestive juices as well as to give flavour. Accompanying a cheese dish with a dressed salad serves the same purpose – say a green salad, tomato or even cucumber salad. As cheese is salted in manufacture, use *salt* sparingly.

(4) Always use a *preheated red-hot grill*, to brown cheese rather than cook it through. If you cook it slowly, it becomes leathery and indigestible. If the food is *too* close to the grill, however, it may go black in patches.

(5) Reheated cheese dishes are only for those with an iron constitution.

(6) Use the right kind of cheese. Soft cheeses are unsuitable because you can't grate them like hard and, if even only slightly over-mature, they irritate the digestive system.

★ *Cheddar* is probably the best of the English cheeses for cooking because it's flavourful without being acid, and is also hard enough to grate finely.

★ *Parmesan* and *Gruyère* – or *Emmenthal* – are often used together, the Parmesan for its flavour, the other for its creaminess. Another advantage of a dryish cheese like Gruyère is that it is less inclined than many others to become oily in hot mixtures. (Emmenthal has larger holes than the true Gruyère).

★ Cheese and red wine are natural partners, so cheese is always welcome *somewhere* in a dinner menu.

★ Refrigerating and freezing spoils the texture of *soft* cheeses, so it's better to buy little and often.

★ Most cheeses will keep fresh and moist longer when wrapped in foil than in other wrappings, because both light and air are excluded.

★ Mouldy cheese is quite edible once you've cut off the mould – cheese mould isn't harmful, so there's no need to waste any *more* of the cheese.

★ A catering pack of Parmesan cheese is a cheap way to buy if you can store most of it in the freezer, keeping a little in the refrigerator for general use. Freshly grated Parmesan naturally has more flavour than ready-grated.

★ See also *Cheeseboard*, page 273.

Cherries

Glacé cherries which are preserved in a very thick syrup should, for a cake, be washed in *hot* water, dried in a cloth and lightly dusted with a little of the weighed flour: otherwise, due to their weight, they'll probably sink before the cake mixture 'sets' and can support them.

★ For decorating, cherries are daintier, just as colourful, and much nicer to eat when cut in small pieces.

★ Glacé cherries are incorrect for grapefruit because they have the wrong flavour and texture. You need *Maraschino* for these.

Chocolate

As we all know, chocolate starts life as cocoa beans, but *cocoa butter*, the fat present in the beans, isn't so well understood. It is quite hard at ordinary room temperatures but melts at just below body temperature – which explains why chocolate melts so easily on a hot day. This enables chocolate to be used for bars, or as a coating for sweets and biscuits, where it remains solid until you eat it – when it at once softens.

★ Chocolate is broadly defined as 'cooking' or 'dessert'. The latter may be plain or milk chocolate:

COOKING CHOCOLATE. Typically but not necessarily, cooking chocolate contains a softer fat in place of the cocoa butter, so that it can be used for icing cakes etc. The 'snap' of a dessert chocolate makes it difficult to cut through the icing on a cake for instance, and without special cooling facilities a dessert-type chocolate sets with a dull, greyish, irregular appearance. The main advantage of this cooking chocolate therefore lies in its softer texture and its appearance – so this is the type to use when these factors are important.

DESSERT CHOCOLATES.
(1) *Plain*. A variety such as Menier or Bournville, contains no other fat except cocoa butter, and is the best to use when flavour really matters, as it certainly does if you're making anything special like a chocolate soufflé, a fine sauce, chocolate crème au beurre, chocolate fudge or truffles etc. It is made from cocoa beans selected to have the desired flavours, and roasted to bring out those flavours to the extent required. Often a blend of cocoa bean from several different countries will be used.

(2) *Milk*. A variety such as Cadbury's Dairy Milk Chocolate tends to be softer than plain chocolate because butter-fat (present in the milk), which replaces *some* of the cocoa butter, is softer than cocoa butter, which is the *only* fat in plain chocolate. Milk chocolate is usually less good for cooking than plain because it contains less cocoa, and therefore doesn't give such a strong chocolate flavour. There is also the danger that the milk will break down when the chocolate is heated, see point 2 below.

★ The hardening or 'scrambling' of chocolate when overheated is usually due to too rapid heating and can result from:

(1) Caramelization of the sugar.
(2) Breakdown of the milk, in the case of milk chocolate – which is one reason why so many recipes call for *plain* chocolate.
(3) Condensed steam getting into the chocolate, such as can happen when one uses a double saucepan.

★ You can't 'unscramble' it if caused by 1 or 2 above, so the only remedy is to start again – if remedy you can call it. Unless you've got the patience of Job, I wouldn't bother to try and recover it from 3 either. It requires long-continued stirring and gentle warming.

★ Chocolate *is* tricky to melt without liquid. The vital thing is to do it really slowly in a thick china basin and to be sure that the water over which you're melting it is neither actually boiling, nor deep enough to touch the bottom of the basin. It's sometimes easier, depending on how you are going to use it, to melt a small quantity on a plate, resting on top of a pan containing 'shivering' water.

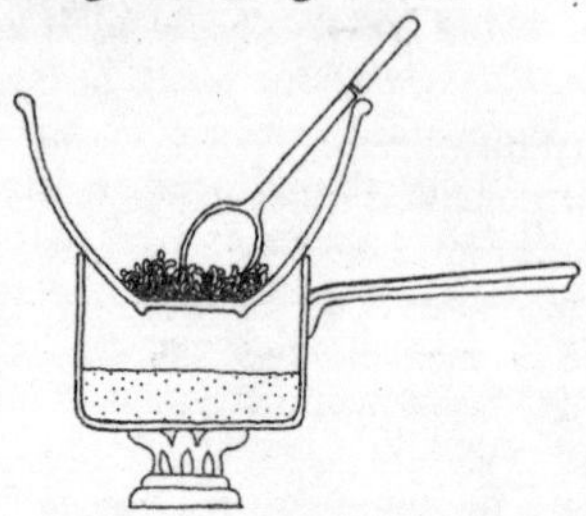

★ A Mouli grater grates chocolate quickly – more quickly than shredding it with a sharp knife.

★ Chocolate flavoured cold sweets have more flavour when served at room temperature than chilled, from the refrigerator.

DRINKING CHOCOLATE. This is cocoa with sugar. It is not recommended as a substitute for either cocoa or chocolate in cooking, except as a coating, say for truffles.

Cider

Made from special apples, sweet and sour, the varieties of which, differentiated by cultivation, have given a reputation to certain localities in which cider is produced; like Somerset in England, or Normandy in France. In general, cider is made with about $\frac{1}{3}$ sweet apples and $\frac{2}{3}$ sour.

★ For cooking, cider teams up in flavour with and counteracts the richness of pork, gammon and bacon in just the same way as apple does. Use some as part of the liquid when braising or boiling gammon for instance.

Cinnamon

Comes from the bark of the cinnamon tree. It gives character and a lovely flavour to certain cakes, puddings and meat dishes, as well as to hot wine punch.

★ 1 level teasp ground cinnamon sieved with ½ lb (225 g) flour makes delicious spicy pastry for a baked jam roll, an apple pie, apple dumplings or mince pies. See also *Cinnamon sugar*, page 93.

Citric Acid

A sharp-flavoured crystalline acid, made from lemons and other citrus fruits. If a lemonade recipe includes citric acid, don't imagine it's unimportant, because it helps to give a concentrated flavour without using too many lemons.

Citron

A variety of the true lemon, originating in the Himalayan region. Like an overgrown lemon with a knobbly skin, it is used *mainly* for candied peel.

Cloves

Used infrequently in many households, but these dried unopened buds of the clove tree give flavour and fragrance to soups and sauces, as well as to the well-worn favourites: bread sauce, cooked apple and hot wine punches.

★ Pop one into a bouquet garni sometimes, or into the milk for a béchamel sauce. They're one of the most lovely of all spices – almost magical in effect.

Cocoa

See page 268.

Coconut

Desiccated coconut, browned in a slow oven or toasted lightly under a grill, makes a quick and delicious accompaniment to curry. Turn it over with a fork, to brown evenly.

You can colour coconut for a cake decoration in the same way as sugar, see page 267.

Coffee

COFFEE ESSENCE. 'Camp', for example, gives concentrated flavour to a soufflé, sauce, cake, or to crème au beurre etc, any of which would be spoilt by the wateriness of real coffee.

INSTANT COFFEE POWDER OR GRANULES. Can *sometimes* be used to give coffee flavour, making it with a *very* small quantity of boiling water to concentrate the flavour in the minimum of liquid. It's also useful when for instance a recipe calls for spongecakes dipped in coffee-flavoured milk.

★ See also page 268.

Cooking Fats

Those of good quality are 100 per cent pure fat and made with refined oils which aim to be colourless, flavourless and odourless. They keep well, even without refrigerating, so there's certainly no need to deep-freeze them.

★ They are good for deep-fat frying, and though more expensive than lard, are less expensive than a good oil.

★ The cost of a cooking fat is usually determined by the oils used. All are fully refined but some sources that can be used are cheaper than others, and a greater proportion of these cheaper oils are present in the cheaper brands. Spry, Cookeen and White Cap for instance are made from a blend of oils which can include animal, marine and vegetable oils. Trex, once purely vegetable oil, may now include marine as well as vegetable oils. Hi-Fry is a pure *beef* cooking fat, which claims to be easily digested, quick to melt, slow to burn, and to be virtually smokeless and odourless in use. I can't say I find it odourless.

★ Spry, Cookeen, Trex and White Cap can be used at all times in place of lard, over which they have certain advantages:

(1) They don't smell, as lard does, when frying.
(2) Refrigerated or at room temperature, some brands – Spry, Cookeen and Trex

for instance – are easier to rub into flour than lard of similar temperature. This is because they're slightly aerated.

(3) Cooking oils and some white fats do not congeal on fried or roast foods when served cold, because they solidify at a lower temperature, and so the fat or oil is more thoroughly drained onto absorbent kitchen paper.

★ See also *Lard*, page 78.

Cornflour

Milled from maize, it isn't nearly as good a thickening as potato flour, which is extensively used in France and other European countries. Cornflour needs more cooking, makes a cloudy sauce (unlike arrowroot) and – more important still – has a distinctive flavour, which may dominate a delicately flavoured dish.

★ One part cornflour to four parts plain flour, makes light sponge cakes, because cornflour contains no gluten. It therefore lowers the overall gluten content, when you want a light, soft mixture. If using regularly, it's easiest to blend a *quantity* of flour and cornflour while you're about it, sieving them together twice, before storing as other flours, ready for use.

Cream

Cream comes in three different thicknesses, double, whipping and single. Sometimes one has particular advantages over another, sometimes they are interchangeable. It's also quite easy to make cream in a liquidizer or cream machine, but its use is limited, see page 273.

DOUBLE CREAM. Good for vegetables, and usually best for a cream dressing, a gâteau or for anything which would be spoilt by the wateriness of thinner cream, such as meringues, brandy snaps or éclairs. This is also the cream for piping and decorating.

WHIPPING CREAM. Not in all the shops, but you can make it by mixing equal quantities of double and single cream. It's both better and cheaper than double cream when cream has to be *half*-whipped, as for a cold soufflé, a mousse or ice cream. This is because it is less easily over-whipped, and gives dishes a smooth light texture.

★ You can whip it quite thick enough to serve separately with a sweet – it makes lovely Crème Chantilly for instance – but not thick enough to pipe well.

SINGLE CREAM. Ideal for vegetables and for many soups and sauces, and for anything which has to be thinned down with cream.

★ As long as you're not a weight-watcher, and have a deep purse, it's just the thing for Quiche Lorraine or, used instead of milk, switches a down-to-earth dish like egg custard into the luxury class.

HALF-WHIPPED CREAM. Should be thick enough to leave a trail, which sinks fairly quickly without trace, when dropped from the whisk back into the cream.

★ When adding half-whipped cream to a mixture, if you whip it to roughly the same consistency as that mixture, it will blend perfectly without forming snowflakes, as it does if too stiff. Be sure the mixture is cold though when you add the cream, otherwise cream will lose its stiffness and thin out.

WHIPPED CREAM. Should be light, airy and about doubled in volume – so I beseech you to avoid using a rotary whisk! A coil-rim whisk will give you more, and *better* whipped cream, see page 28.

★ If whipping cream for decoration, whip it just thick enough to stand in light peaks.

★ If you *over*-whip cream, you'll end up with a small quantity of buttery cream instead of a large quantity of airy cream. Should double cream look buttery in hot weather, stir in a tablespoon of milk before trying to whip it.

FROZEN CREAM. Useful for cooking but few makes are as good as fresh. They don't hold air in the same way when whipped, so you get neither the texture nor the volume. Some bought frozen creams are slow to thaw and troublesome to saw, if you only want a little.

Kerrygold's 'fresh frozen pieces' are excellent. A few 'ice cubes' of cream in the freezer can be handy for soups, sauces and emergencies.

LONG LIFE REAL DAIRY CREAM. If you can buy it, this makes an excellent emergency store.

SOURED CREAM. Gives a subtle piquancy in unlikely places; particularly if stirred at the last minute into sautéd vegetables, vegetable soups, or into some bland sauces. When adding it to soups and sauces, stir a little of the hot liquid into the cream before adding the cream to, and heating it with the remainder. Soured cream doesn't separate.

★ You can use soured cream too to replace some or all of the oil in a salad dressing. See also *Cream, sour*, page 239.

Cream of Tartar

A purified form of the deposit from fermented wine. It is used in the proportions of two parts C of T to one part bicarbonate of soda, so that the flavour of the latter won't dominate, or make a cake or scones too brown.

★ You can sometimes substitute other acids for cream of tartar, such as sour milk, buttermilk, vinegar or lemon juice, see *Bicarbonate of soda*, page 63.
★ A small pinch of cream of tartar acts as a stabilizer to egg whites when whisking, see page 60.
★ Cream of tartar acts as a deterrent to the crystallization of the sugar – when a recipe calls for it in a syrup heated to a high temperature.

Curry Powder

The powders we *buy* consist of a combination of many spices, seeds and herbs, while those people who make their own will use special combinations to go with various dishes – which sometimes call for mild seasonings, and other times for hotter.

★ Traditional basic spices include turmeric (for its flavour and colour), chillies, ginger, cloves and poppy seeds.
★ It pays to buy the best, and use it while fresh.

Custard Powder

Like cornflour and cornflakes, it is made from maize (corn).

Dried Fruits

CURRANTS. Take their name from Corinth, from where they originated – raisins de Corinthe. They are of course very small, seedless, sweet dried grapes.

DATES. From the date palm, are rich and nourishing. For thousands of years they have provided food for tribesmen in the deserts of Arabia. One bunch can weigh as much as 30 lbs ($13\frac{1}{2}$ K) or more.

PRUNES. Dried plums with a particularly high sugar content, and firm flesh.

RAISINS. A special variety of grape, dried in the sun or by artificial heat, to crystallize their sugar, and so preserve them. Besides being full of goodness, they are valuable in cookery for their flavour and texture.

SULTANAS. Also a special variety of grape, similar to raisins; seedless, golden-yellow and very sweet. The Americans call them seedless white raisins.

Dripping

Must be the downfall of many an English housewife, who pours any kind of fat, whatever has been fried or roasted in it, into a jar labelled *Dripping*. This awful mixture, possibly strong with age, is used to cook anything and everything from eggs to game. Full of impurities, which irritate the digestive system – often guaranteed to *cause* indigestion – it spoils the true flavour of anything cooked in it, unless first clarified.

★ Beef dripping is of course the right fat

to use for roast beef or something like a beef stew; pork dripping for pork and gammon etc., but each needs a jar of its own, and should be used soon.

★ Chicken fat has a fine flavour. When using chicken stock, you can use this fat to sweat the vegetables for a soup, or to make a roux for a sauce, if the flavour isn't too strong for the dish concerned. It has a semi-liquid consistency; never solidifies.

★ The 'jelly' under the solidified dripping from roast meat keeps well, sealed from the air, but if you freeze it as ice cubes and pop it in the freezer, it makes an excellent home-made stock cube when you want one.

★ Dripping must be clarified for deep fat frying, because the impurities in it burn at high temperatures, giving food a bitter taste and a bad colour.

★ You can also use clarified dripping for a plain luncheon cake.

Eggs

See pages 106 to 108.

Flour

White flour should always be sieved for things like pastry, cakes or scones, however fine it is. Sieving traps air, blends together dry ingredients and gets rid of even the smallest lumps in any of them.

★ Water absorption depends on the type of, or mixture of wheats, so of course flours vary in the amount of liquid they'll absorb. This explains why recipes can't always give precise quantities, and why it is such an advantage for a cook to know what a mixture or dough should look or feel like, at different stages of its making.

WHITE PLAIN FLOUR. Has dozens more uses than self-raising, and is the one to use unless a recipe directs otherwise. With the addition of various raising agents, you can use it to make almost anything.

WHITE OR BROWN SELF-RAISING FLOUR. Is plain flour with a raising agent (bicarbonate of soda plus an acid) added, so it has limited uses. Its raising agent often conflicts with others which you may want or have to use, giving inferior results in various ways.

★ White self-raising flour is fine for things like a sponge pudding or a sandwich cake, but it has too much raising agent for rich cakes with a high egg content, and not enough for scones. It's not impossible to make a yeast dough with it, but bread very quickly goes dry.

★ The advantages of self-raising flour seem to be few, as far as *I* can see: it's convenient; you can't forget to add the raising agent; it isn't essential to cook immediately certain cakes or puddings made with it.

★ These plain and self-raising flours which we use are *soft household flours* produced from our own 'winter wheat', which is sown in the autumn and harvested the following summer. Soft flour has a lower gluten content than 'strong' so makes poorer bread, but better and lighter pastry and cakes.

★ Even though it has less gluten, soft flour makes excellent bread, and is cheaper than 'strong' because so much of the wheat is grown here. There's no need to fear that without strong flour in the house, you can't make good bread.

STRONG FLOUR. Rich in gluten so makes the *best* bread, and you can't make real croissants or perfect puff pastry without. It is made mainly from 'spring wheat', which is grown in cold climates like North America, Canada or Russia, where winter wheat can't be sown because it would be frozen in the ground. They sow it in the spring, and harvest it in the late summer. We are trying to grow it here, but can't rely on any quantity because we don't usually have enough sun in the spring and summer months for it to grow fast enough.

100 PER CENT STONEGROUND WHOLEMEAL OR WHOLEWHEAT FLOUR. Flour such as Allinson or Prewett, is the whole of the wheat grain, without separation, ground between stones. It contains all the natural richness of the wheat and is, healthwise, the most valuable of all flours. It provides a balance

of nutriments to give staying power, and helps to prevent constipation. At the same time, it is a lower calorie flour than white or brown.

ROLLER MILLED WHOLEMEAL. A similar flour, but during milling the wheat constituents are separated by the roller and have to be mixed together again at the end of the process, to make the meal up to 100 per cent extraction.

WHEATMEAL OR BROWN FLOUR. Terms used to describe flours which are *not* Wholemeal. The rate of extraction can vary, but officially 'shall contain not less than 0.6 per cent of fibre calculated by dry weight'. (Wholemeal or wholewheat contains about 1.8 per cent.)

Food Colourings

Edible food colourings will last for years so it's common sense to buy good quality. Essential for much cake decorating and confectionery, they'll also cheer up the dullest things if used discreetly: as usually only a drop or two is needed, you can avoid some hideous results by dipping the point of a skewer into the bottle, shaking the dye off into whatever you want to colour.

★ A drop of colour for instance will buck up junket or a milk shake. A dash of green added to the syrup glaze will spotlight the pears in a flan. A drop of yellow makes cream look extra rich for meringues and takes away the all-white look at the same time.

★ Coloured milk may tempt children to drink it, especially if you give them straws as well. For a small–children's party, you could even let them choose the colour they want, mixing it as they watch. You just need imagination. See also *Carmine*, page 66.

Garlic

A member of the lily family, the bulbs varying very much in size, as do the number and size of their cloves. French or Italian garlic is easily brought home from a holiday, storing well in a dry airy place. Grown in a warmer climate, either is much better than English.

★ You can use just as much or as little garlic as you like, but one clove, a segment of the head, is often enough. Its strong smell and flavour are weakened by blanching, but you can also use it so subtly that you may find friends claiming to dislike it while unwittingly enjoying it! Add a crushed clove for instance to a bouquet garni for certain dishes, to give an elusive and lovely flavour; or put a cut-up clove on top of a roast, or on beef or gammon steaks before grilling them.

★ Fried garlic tends to be bitter and pungent. Some people prefer to add it to onions and other foods *after* they've been fried.

★ The reason why garlic hangs around for hours after we eat it is because it is expelled through the *lungs*.

★ Garlic is *crushed* either in a garlic press (page 13) or with a sharp, round-ended knife. To crush with a knife: pull a 'clove' off the 'head', remove its outer skin, slice very finely, sprinkle with salt and then squash it in up-and-down movements with the end of the knife until soft and mushy.

Gelatine

A material extracted from the bones and tissues of animals.

★ Gelatine is a tasteless, odourless, transparent, brittle solid, very faint yellow in colour.

★ According to Davis Gelatine Ltd. 'The introduction of jelly into England undoubtedly took place from the observation that when using bones to make soup, the liquid gelled and by gradual clarification, a reasonably clear jelly could be obtained. Mention is made in the household chronicles of Charles II that His Majesty delighted in "jelleys made of the juices of fat capons, rich wines and ye finyst of herbes". It was not until the early part of the nineteenth century that gelatine manufacture emerged as an industry.'

★ ***When milk is heated with gelatine*** or gelatine is added to hot milk, the separation of milk solids takes place and a curdled appearance results. It is not a true curdle because the milk, or custard as the case may be, is perfectly sweet. For *Milk Jelly*, see page 231.

★ Although you *can* use up to 1 oz (25 g) of gelatine without soaking it first, it is better to soak it. Soaked, it goes into solution more rapidly than unsoaked, owing to the solution occurring from the outer and inner surfaces, whereas if gelatine is put in hot water before soaking, swelling is retarded to a certain degree and solution takes place from the outer surface only.

★ Sprinkle powdered gelatine over the liquid so that the granules can easily absorb it, swelling and softening quickly. If you do it the other way round – and pour the liquid over a little heap of granules – the liquid can't penetrate them so easily.

★ Perhaps the safest way to dissolve gelatine – soaked or unsoaked – is in a basin over a pan of hot water, though I personally prefer to dissolve it over very low heat in a small saucepan. If you use a metal spoon to stir it, you can see when it's dissolved and ready to use because there'll be no sign of granules on the spoon.

★ Avoid boiling gelatine at all costs, unless a recipe calls for it, because this reduces its setting power. When it *is* necessary almost to boil it, say for a cleared jelly, a higher proportion of gelatine than usual is used, to counteract its loss in strength.

★ When adding dissolved gelatine to a partly cooled mixture in a cold basin, pour it slowly from a height into the middle of the mixture. It may go ropy if you don't do it carefully, whisking to blend it at once.

★ The strength of a jelly is influenced by its temperature, so it may not set in hot weather unless you use more gelatine or less liquid. For most purposes ½ oz (say 15 g) gelatine will set 1 pt (generous 500 ml) liquid.

★ A smaller proportion of gelatine can be used for small individual moulds or when serving a mixture in the dish in which it is set. A larger proportion is needed for a very large mould, or when things like shellfish or fruit have to be supported in it.

★ Raw pineapple contains an enzyme which liquifies gelatine mixtures, so be sure to cook it before putting in jelly, or in any mixture containing gelatine.

★ Gelatine dissolved in sherry or Madeira gives subtlety to a sweet like a chocolate soufflé.

★ Gelatine is a protein food. As it also helps the digestion of foods with which it is combined and is itself so nutritious and easily digested, it's ideal for old people, invalids or children. The blandness and monotony of a semi-liquid diet for instance can be livened up by using gelatine and flavourings to alter the consistency and flavour of things like milk, cream, eggs or fruit juices.

FREEZING GELATINE DISHES. With the exception of ice cream, all should first be allowed to set in a cool place. Close cover them while thawing, to prevent condensation forming, causing the jelly to liquify. Generally speaking, gelatine dishes which are *water* based and are of a predominantly jelly nature, are unsuitable for freezing. When thawed, the dish loses its jelly-like composition.

★ In ice cream, gelatine prevents the formation of coarse crystals and helps to stabilize the mixture.

Ginger

ROOT GINGER. Is the root of a tropical plant – and looks like it! Tied in a piece of cloth so that you can remove it after cooking the jam, chutney, home-made wine or whatever it is you're making, it is used solely for its flavour.

★ Bruise it first with a hammer, to release its strength, preferably enclosing it in a

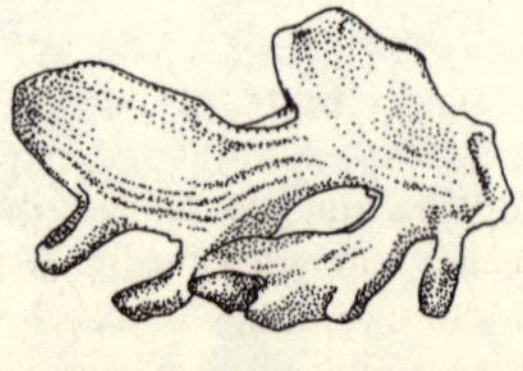

scrap of cloth to control and prevent it flying about. This is more a work-bench job than kitchen table because it's very hard.

STEM GINGER. Is the type bottled in syrup. Have you tried it chopped, and served with some of its syrup over vanilla ice cream, with a dessert apple, or to make a kind of Ginger Cream? Stirred into Crème Chantilly, it makes a quick, heavenly and ridiculously easy sweet.

Glucose

Liquid glucose, like cream of tartar, acts as a deterrent to the crystallization of the sugar in syrups heated to a high temperature, the amount used depending upon the purpose for which the syrup is required. Stir it in after the sugar has dissolved, but before the syrup comes to the boil.

★ If you can't get glucose out of its jar, run your fingers under cold water and *pull* it out.

★ You can easily measure a level spoonful if you first heat the spoon.

Gluten

Being, so to speak, the invisible part of an ingredient, gluten deserves mention because it is a key factor in the choice of flour for bread, *puff* pastry and croissants on the one hand, and cakes, scones and all other kinds of pastry on the other. It is thanks to the gluten in wheat – and so in flour – that it forms a paste, and makes an elastic dough when mixed with water. If rice, oats, barley or maize contained any gluten, we could make a paste and a *type* of bread with them too – but they don't.

★ If you've never seen gluten, and if you have time, energy and interest simultaneously, to do a short experiment to 'isolate' the gluten from some flour, it might just help you to make better bread and pastry, because you'll understand the *need* for gluten, and also *why* bread has to be kneaded, and pastry rolled and re-rolled.

★ Here's what to do: mix about 3 rounded tablesps flour – preferably strong flour, because there's more gluten in it – to a stiffish dough with water, and leave it to soak in cold water for ½ hr. Now squeeze and press it under slow-running cold water until all the starch is washed out. You'll be left with the gluten which looks rather like chewing gum in colour, texture and elasticity. If you then bake this wet gluten, you'll find that the steam and air inside blow it up like a balloon. On further baking the gluten sets to a light crisp sponge, like a slimming roll. This dry gluten is the 'skeleton' which supports the body of the loaf, cake or pudding.

★ When a wheat flour dough is heated, the gluten in the dough is blown up into balloons in the same way.

Grapes

Basically of four main types, each one being superior to another for the purposes for which they are grown: wine, dried fruits (raisins etc), the table and fresh grape juice.

Gravy Browning

A good make of gravy browning is indispensable for colouring gravies and sauces – unless you have loads of time on your hands, to brown a roux to perfection. Caramel based, you can make it at home if you have a recipe.

Grenadine

A cordial made from pomegranates, but they don't come from the Grenadines! A very little adds colour and flavour to long cool drinks.

Gum Arabic

Comes from acacia trees. The yellowish or reddish fragments are soluble in water, and if left long enough, acquire a viscous consistency. It is an important ingredient in the art of confectionery, for jujubes, marshmallows etc. Buy it at the chemist's. See also page 266.

Herbs

Used carefully, to bring out the flavour of a dish, herbs can add a subtle fragrance and character unlike anything else. By and large, we aren't adventurous with herbs in English cooking, but just to see the herb stall in the market place in Nice is to scent some of the magic of French cooking; the very memory of it is nostalgic. It is fascinating to see – and smell – such a stall, but it isn't *surprising* when one stops to think about it, because most of the aromatic herbs originate from the Mediterranean. Herbs have been used for centuries for their flavouring, health-giving, preservative and magical qualities.

★ If you *could* always buy fresh herbs, it would still be difficult to match freshly picked home-grown. Even in a smallish garden, you can grow quite a selection, because you don't need serried rows. A plant or two, of many of them, is probably all you'll want to meet a family's needs.
★ The very thought of fresh lemon juice is enough to make some of us flinch, yet mixed with sugar, or blended in a sauce, lemon is mellowed. So it is with certain herbs, which are much harsher raw than when prepared and blended in the right proportions in a cooked dish. If you overdo something like sage or thyme for instance, you can put people off that herb for life.

PRESERVATION. I much prefer frozen herbs to dried, because freezing doesn't alter their flavour to any degree. If washed and dried thoroughly, they'll keep through the winter without even blanching: chop them, and either make into little foil parcels, or freeze with a little water in ice cubes. Alternatively, tie the herbs in small bunches, interleaved with foil or polythene for convenience, and store in a rigid container. Make up bouquet garnis, single herbs or what-you-like.

ANGELICA. 'The angelic herb' or 'herb of the angels' – is so called because of its medicinal properties. Angelica was supposed to have finally dispelled the plague, and protected all those who used it. Angelica is grown mainly for its beauty, but the leaves may be used to flavour a sweet sauce or a wine drink. See also page 62, *Candied Angelica*.

BASIL. Sweet basil, much used in Mediterranean cookery, is the natural and classic partner of any tomato dish – soups, sauces, salads, omelets etc.

★ Dried basil has a completely different and much less attractive flavour than fresh.

BAY. The bay leaf is one of the three basic components of a bouquet garni. Use bay to flavour marinades, a court bouillon, stock, soups, sauces, fish and casseroles, not to mention sweet dishes like stewed prunes and egg custards.

★ Why not grow a bay tree if you haven't got one, to have bay leaves as handy as parsley?
★ Dried bay leaves are much cheaper at a chain-store grocer than in a clever little pack from a specialized kitchen shop.

BORAGE. You have probably met it in a Pimms, but have you ever used it in a salad? The leaves must be *very* finely chopped, because they're hairy.

CARAWAY. Seeds fresh from your own plants have a stronger and more lasting flavour than bought. They can go into all sorts of things if you like them, but aren't things to give to the unsuspecting guest.

★ In Sweden you can meet caraway in almost anything, even in vanilla ice cream. Have you tried it with cabbage, in brown bread, potato soup, cucumber salad, beetroot salad, apple pie or a cheese spread?

CHERVIL. A more important herb in French and Italian cooking than in English. With its delicate aniseed flavour, it is a herb which demands to be eaten fresh, like chives, not used in dishes which require long cooking. Use it in chilled soups, salads, sauces, or with eggs, cheese or beef.

CHIVES. Are a 'must' if you like a subtle

hint of onion. If we didn't have a garden, I'd *have* to grow chives in a pot, because they pep up the blandest of dishes, as well as the more tasty: macaroni and other cheese dishes, scrambled eggs, omelets, soups, sauces, potatoes, and of course sautéd vegetables and salads.

★ Cooking spoils and alters their flavour, so bunch and chop them finely with scissors, and then stir into whatever you're making at the very last minute.
★ In your garden, break off at the bottom any stems on which buds form, otherwise they harden, shortening the life of the plant as well.

DILL. The herb for fish dishes, and for potatoes or a cucumber salad. Though a member of the parsley family, it isn't used nearly as much in England as in Sweden for instance, where you're almost lucky to escape from it. Dill water, the cure for babies' wind, is made from its seeds.

FENNEL. Florence fennel, with its flavour of anise, is traditionally used – like dill – to flavour and garnish fish. Chop and use it in salads too, try it instead of parsley to make a sauce, or use in a marinade.

★ Fennel leads a double life, because it is both a herb and vegetable, see page 146.

MARJORAM. Sweet marjoram is worth trying with pork if you don't care for sage. Use it also of course in other meat dishes as well as in omelets, a green salad, or with fish or tomatoes.

★ Add marjoram sometimes to a bouquet garni, for a hint of something different in soups or sauces.

MINT. Probably brought to Britain by the Romans, who used it a lot in their cooking. Of the many kinds of mint grown, there is: *Spearmint* which is ideal for sauces, jellies, salads and cool drinks, and *Peppermint* which is, of course, the species from which oil of peppermint is distilled.

★ To chop mint, see page 35.
★ Better still, pound the chopped leaves to release even more flavour. (Do this in a basin, with the end of a rolling pin if necessary).
★ Finely chopped mint makes a welcome change from parsley with new potatoes or green peas.
★ Mint vinegar is a good way of introducing mint to a salad; or it makes an extra-minty sauce.
★A mint leaf set in an ice cube gives a pleasant tang to a cool summer drink, and *looks* lovely and cool too. Do several at a time, and pop them in the freezer.

OREGANO. A wild marjoram. Stronger than sweet marjoram, it needs using with discretion. It's a great favourite in Italian cookery.

PARSLEY. The stalks are even more important in a bouquet garni than the leaf, because they carry more of the flavour.

★ Parsley is used by many to camouflage rather than to garnish a dish, as if something *had* to be hidden! Tiny pieces give just as much colour, and don't have a strong flavour.
★ If you want to garnish a dish perfectly (or in advance) with finely chopped parsley, it is easy to sprinkle, and won't lose its colour so quickly if you gather it up in a corner of fine cloth, hold it under a cold tap for a minute or so, and then twist it tightly, to squeeze dry.
★ To chop parsley, see page 35.
★ A decorative straight line of parsley looks tidier and is quicker than a random zig-zag:
(1) Make a furrow on the surface of the food with a skewer.
(2) Wash the skewer, and while it's still wet, dip it in the chopped parsley.
(3) Lay the skewer back in the furrow, and lift it out – leaving the parsley behind.
★ Parsley fried in deep fat makes a tasty and crisp garnish with savoury fritters or fried fish. Be sure to dry it very well before frying, then turn off the heat – after everything else is fried – and fry it without a basket (otherwise it gets entangled).
★ *Parsley wine* is an easy, delicious and inexpensive way to give character to a simple casserole, or to quite a lot of other dishes. Sweetish, but with a good cooking flavour, you may be surprised how versatile it is. I'd never be without it, and

it's quite easy to make, as long as you sow a big bed of parsley. See page 96.

SAVORY. With its faint suggestion of sage, savory is the classic herb with broad beans – in fact it's good with any kind of bean. If you grow it between the rows of broad beans, they shouldn't be troubled with black-fly.

TARRAGON. One of the great herbs. It is very pungent fresh, but if you thread the leaves onto a fine, short skewer, and blanch them 30 seconds, they'll have a milder flavour.

★ Tarragon is the classic partner with chicken, and is an essential flavouring in Sauce Béarnaise or Sauce Verte.
★ Tarragon vinegar is a good way of introducing the flavour to salads, sauces and savoury dishes – easily made with fresh tarragon and white wine vinegar, see page 95.
★ Tarragon butter (butter, tarragon, seasoning and lemon juice) is delicious with grilled fish, chicken or steaks, or to enrich certain sauces.

THYME. One of the three basic components of a bouquet garni: essential to flavour soups and sauces. Thyme goes with poultry, meat, game and vegetables, and is especially good with rich foods like shellfish or pork.

Honey

Before the days of sugar, honey was the main sweet food of ancient times. Its flavour, aroma, quality and consistency vary according to the type of flavours most widespread in the region where it is gathered. Some of the finest French honey for instance is that of Narbonne, which owes its distinctive flavour to the nectar of the rosemary flower. In Greece, where it is more widely used than in English cookery, the prized honey is that of Hymethus. I myself often think nostalgically of the honey gathered from the Northumberland moors, in which you can almost smell the very heather from which it is collected.

★ Honey is a rich and concentrated food, high in calories and slightly laxative. While it is generally more readily digested than sugar, and its effect in cooking is very similar, its flavour is more distinctive than *most* types of sugar. Because it so easily dominates the flavour of other ingredients, honey's use in cookery is therefore much more limited. It is for example sometimes used as the 'sweetness' in a sweet-sour sauce, to glaze some kinds of meat after roasting, and to make certain spiced cakes, biscuits and breads.
★ Honey is easiest to measure in a hot tablespoon, 1 level spoonful equalling approx 1 oz. (25 g).

Horseradish

Hardly justifies taking up garden space when its uses are so limited and its need therefore so small. The root, rather like a huge brown carrot, white inside, has a sharp and piquant flavour and a very penetrating smell. All parts of the horseradish which grow *above* the ground are said to be poisonous so don't try eating the top! You can use horseradish grated, as a condiment, to serve with boiled or cold meat; to make a savoury butter, good with grilled steaks; or of course to make horseradish sauce to serve particularly with roast beef. You may find it easier to buy grated, in a bottle, than fresh.

Kirsch

Distilled from ripe fermented wild cherries, it is an ideal flavouring to combine with lots of fruits – apricots, cherries, plums, pears, pineapple or strawberries. Use it to flavour the syrup glaze for a cherry flan, in a sweet custard sauce, in crème au beurre or particularly to macerate fruits, see page 47. You don't always have to put *sherry* or *rum* in a trifle either – why not try different liqueurs as a change?

Lard

The melted, clarified fat from the inside of a pig. Because top quality lard is a pure, almost flavourless fat, it is excellent for both shallow and deep-fat frying – has a high smoke point – and ideal for certain kinds of pastry and breads. Its one drawback, from the cook's angle, is its unpleasant smell when heated for frying. It is cheaper than the best white cooking fats as a rule, and in my opinion gives better results, particularly in pastry and bread.

★ Unlike butter and margarine, lard contains no water or curd. It bears no comparison of course with the lovely flavour of butter for shallow frying, but it has no complications and is hot enough for frying when a smoky haze starts to float above it. For general use, it is infinitely preferable to dripping, which may have a strong flavour of its own, besides making anything fried in it indigestible.

★ It pays to buy first quality lard for deep-fat frying. It's a false economy to buy cheaper because top quality gives the best results and can be used and re-used over and over again.

★ Lard or cooking fat alone makes lovely *light* pastry or scones, but as both fats are virtually flavourless, so, it goes without saying, must be the pastry or scones. The reason why lard and margarine (or butter) are so often used together therefore is to have the lightness of the lard and the flavour of the other.

★ Because it is pure, melted lard is ideal for brushing and greasing cake tins, bread tins and pudding basins etc. before dusting out with flour. Only cakes with a high sugar content (like a Genoese sponge or gingerbread) or fruit cakes which require long cooking then need usually to be in a lined tin – unless it's a poor quality tin.

★ See also *Cooking fats*, page 69.

Lemons

Owe much of their powerful aroma and flavour to the zest, the *outer* part of the skin or rind.

LEMON RIND. Thinly pared with a potato peeler, rind contains less of the bitter pith than when grated. This explains why *pared* rind is so often used to flavour liquids, and why grated rind is unsuitable. In large pieces, you can also remove it from some liquids without straining.

★ Any surplus thinly pared peel needn't be wasted. Freeze it in ice cubes, to use in drinks another time.

★ *Grated* rind contains both zest and pith. Finely grated lemon rind, as so often called for in recipes, is therefore less bitter than coarsely grated rind, giving a finer flavour to whatever you're making.

LEMON QUARTERS. Served especially with fish, are cut lengthwise from the fruit, so that when you squeeze one, you direct the juice downward over the food, not everywhere else!

LEMON JUICE. Usually added to dishes after they are cooked, whenever it's possible to do so, to avoid loss of Vitamin C.

★ If you squeeze a refrigerated lemon, you won't get much juice out of it – better to let it reach room temperature first.

★ Lemon juice does numerous other things besides giving flavour:

(1) Added to fruit while it's stewing, it prevents the fruit breaking up or losing shape. Allow 1 teasp to $\frac{1}{4}$pt (125 ml) syrup – but omit it if you *want* a purée.

(2) It keeps boiled rice, poached fish or poached eggs a good colour. Add a spoonful to the cooking water if you want to.

(3) It can replace vinegar in salad dressings.

(4) By counteracting the richness of foods, lemon juice helps digestion, whether in a salad dressing, hollandaise sauce or with fried fish etc.

(5) It delays the discoloration of certain fruits and vegetables: for example, sprinkle some lightly over sliced banana, or add a tablespoonful of it to both steeping and cooking water for Jerusalem artichokes.

(6) It provides the pectin lacking in strawberries used for jam. Allow the juice of 1 lemon per lb (450 g) of fruit.

LEMON BUTTERFLIES. To make as a garnish:

(1) If you have a fruit decorator (page

12) and the time, 'stripe' the lemon before cutting it in half, crosswise.

(2) With a stainless steel saw knife (preferably), cut fairly thinly as many slices as you need, starting at the 'cut' end of each half lemon.

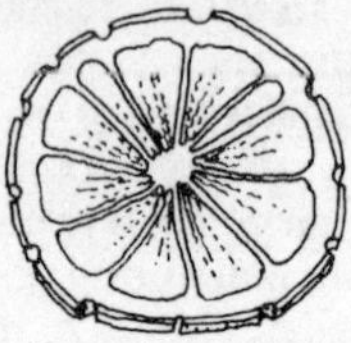

(3) Cut each slice in half, to make two butterflies.

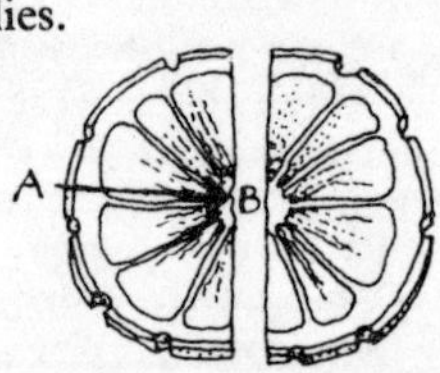

(4) Cut the rind, only, at point A, hold one end in each hand and gently open up the half slice to form the butterfly. Avoid cutting or breaking it at centre.

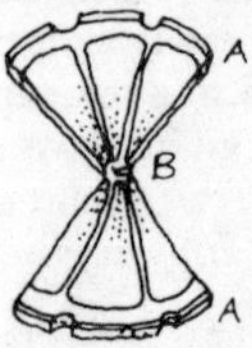

(5) Place on the food and garnish centre of butterfly with a minute piece of parsley, for extra colour.

TO FREEZE LEMONS. Whole, they don't freeze well. Because so watery, they go soft when thawed, making them difficult to *squeeze* – much better to freeze rind and juice separately: for convenience later, put the rind of each half lemon in a tiny polythene bag, then put them all together in one large bag for easy finding in the freezer. Freeze the juice as ice cubes, say $\frac{1}{4}$ lemon to a cube, keeping a few handy in the refrigerator if you like, in the ice tray.

★ Bought and prepared when lemons are plentiful, perhaps from a market stall, there should be no need ever to cut a whole one for a spoonful of juice. If you're doing several, de-rind them all, then just divide up the rind equally into separate bags.

Lentils

See page 86.

Limes

Look like very small green lemons. Although mostly about half the size, they are much sharper, containing about $\frac{1}{3}$ more citric acid than the average-sized lemon. Just because they're small therefore, don't imagine you'll need twice as many limes as you would lemons to flavour things with their juice.

★ Lime juice is a cordial made from the much sweetened juice of the fruit.

Mace

Mace, the outer layer of the nutmeg, is fragile and rather beautiful; almost like starched unbleached lace. It has a slight hint of both nutmeg and cinnamon. Buy it whole or ground, to flavour sauces, marinades and sweet or savoury egg or milk dishes.

★ Have you ever tried adding $\frac{1}{2}$ level teasp ground mace to $\frac{1}{4}$ pt (125 ml) whipped cream?

Margarine

Varies widely in quality, flavour, texture and cost. The best brands are a very superior fat, and although they lack the flavour of butter, essential to some dishes, they do have the odd advantage over it. The cost is usually determined by the oils and fats used. All the oils used are fully refined, but some sources that can be used are cheaper than others, and a greater proportion of these cheaper oils are present in the cheaper brands.

★ Edible *vegetable* oils are the more expensive variety. They cost more than marine oils and animal fats, so products made only with vegetable oils, such as Blue Band and Flora margarines, are the more expensive brands.

★ The difference between a soft and hard margarine is that the soft product contains a higher proportion of oils which are liquid at room temperature than the harder wrappered products. A hard margarine makes pastry easier to manipulate and gives better results than the soft, but the soft is of course ideal for creaming, because it's so easy to beat until light and fluffy – even direct from the refrigerator – trapping air as you do so. Van den Berghs, Britain's biggest domestic margarine producer, claim that under standardized conditions, margarine is easier to cream and has greater creaming power than butter – that is, it can hold more air.

★ Margarine contains more Vit D than butter, and from a dietetic point of view, some people prefer it. There's approximately the same amount of water in butter as in margarine, the water content of the latter being controlled at not more than 16 per cent of the product.

Milk

Easily digested if you sip, eat some food with, or use it in cooking, but if gulped down, it forms one difficult-to-digest clot inside you.

★ It boils at 196° F, 91° C, a lower temperature than water, at 212° F, 100° C.

★ You can prevent hot milk from changing its flavour, and a skin from forming on top, by heating it *fast* in a *covered* pan – but don't forget it!

★ A liquidizer makes hot milk drinks deliciously frothy – skin and all – and milk shakes are a wonderful way of encouraging children who don't like milk, to take it. This is important because milk contains every type of nutrient and is the most complete single food we know. Make sure the milkman doesn't leave it on your door-step in sunlight though, because it loses up to ⅔ of its vitamin B content within 2 hours.

DRIED MILK. Makes good milk puddings, as long as you roughly double the quantity of butter or margarine used with fresh milk. The chief nutritional difference between dried and fresh milk is the lack of fat, and the fat-soluble vitamins A and D in dried milk. Some types of dried milk, eg St Ivel, now have vegetable fat added.

LONG LIFE MILK. See *Ultra-heat treated milk*.

HOMOGENISED MILK. Smooth and creamy because the milk and cream are so completely emulsified that the fat *stays* suspended evenly throughout the milk, instead of rising to the top and forming a cream line. I buy more of this than anything else now, it's so good on cereals, in milk puddings and for any milk-based sauce.

★ Homogenised milk freezes better than pasteurised because the cream and milk don't separate. Beware of freezing milk in a bottle though: put in a plastic container, with room to expand.

PASTEURISED MILK. The favourite of most housewives, whether the rich, creamy Channel Island kind, or the milk from cows of more ordinary breeds. The milk is heated to a temperature (162° F, 72° C) which kills harmful bacteria, without destroying any of the nutrients.

STERILISED MILK. Homogenised, bottled, and then heated to an even higher temperature, so that it remains fit for consumption for at *least* seven days without refrigeration – as long as it isn't opened. Despite having rather a 'cooked' flavour, it is all right for cooking.

UTRA-HEAT TREATED MILK (UHT). 'Long Life', for instance, is homogenised milk heated to 270° F, 132° C for just one second, which explains why it keeps perfectly (unopened) for several months without even being refrigerated.

★ Because the milk and cream are emulsified, it gives sauces a creamy smooth texture you don't get with pasteurised milk – ideal for a custard sauce for instance, or to make yoghourt, see page 236.

★ This kind of milk is a splendid larder stand-by when short of milk for cooking – who isn't sometimes? Two or three cartons on the shelf seem just as necessary as spare fats, flour or sugar.

Molasses

The thick non-crystallizable dark syrup which drains from raw sugar during manufacture; the thickest kind of treacle.

Mustard

Strongest when absolutely fresh, so dry mustard gives a dish more flavour than 'tired' made mustard. Some recipes call for one, some for the other, but a spoonful of made mustard is more than a spoonful of dry.

★ Mustard helps the digestion of rich dishes, especially cooked cheese, so it has more importance than simply its flavour.
★ French mustard, with its piquant flavour, makes much tastier Mustard Butter than English mustard.

MUSTARD SEED. Makes a 'hot' and unusual garnish for some savoury dishes. If you've never tasted it before, do bite a seed, to understand why they need to be used with restraint.

Nutmeg

This, the seed inside the membrane of mace, is a versatile flavouring. It goes well with minced meat – beefburgers, meat balls, or a cottage pie etc. – or is equally at home sprinkled lightly into cream soups, cauliflower sauce, spinach, milk puddings or custards.

Nuts

Often have to be shredded, flaked or chopped, and it is important to do whichever a recipe says because the flavour, texture and appearance of a dish will to some extent depend upon this.

★ Nuts tend to go rancid because of the very high proportion of fat in them. They'll keep longer in an airtight jar in the refrigerator if you have room for them, or longer still in the freezer.
★ It's unwise to give tiny children nuts, because they can easily cause choking.
★ See also *Nuts, devilled* and *salted*, page 274.

ALMONDS. Can be skinned either by boiling them for just a minute or two, or by covering with boiling water, stirring and leaving to soak 3–4 minutes. If you then put them into cold water, you can easily 'pinch' the skins off. If you have to flake or shred almonds after blanching, they're easier to do while still hot and soft, because they go brittle when cold and dry.

(1) You can *flake* them quickly with a potato peeler or small vegetable knife, paring off the *side* of the nut.

(2) It is easiest to *shred* them if you split each through the middle, and then cut finely longways.

★ *Ground almonds* can be made in a liquidizer from chopped or flaked blanched almonds – not too many at a time. If ground almonds are used in a fruit cake, their purpose is to help to keep it moist, as well as to give flavour. Using almond essence with ground almonds in a cake helps to bring out the flavour of the almonds. It isn't an unnecessary extravagance.
★ *Almond nibs*, if one can buy them, save a lot of time when you need almonds for decorations or texture. Brown them lightly in a slow oven to bring out their true nutty flavour.

BRAZILS. Have the distinction of christening a nation – so called after the gigantic native brasil tree. The nuts as we buy them are really only *parts* of a huge nut. Inside a massive woody seed vessel at least ½″ (1¼ cm) thick and nearly as big as a man's head, are four divisions. In each of those divisions fit, rather like the segments of an orange, a number of the triangular nuts we call Brazils. The fruits fall to the ground when ripe, often from as high as 100 ft up.

HAZEL-NUTS. Rich in oil, they are *delicious* in cookery and for this reason often used in confectionery as well as in things like cakes and sweets. The cob and filbert are simply *cultivated* varieties of the hazel, the filbert having a very full husk which completely conceals the nut, and the cob being much larger than an ordinary hazel-nut.

★ *To skin hazel-nuts*, spread them out on a baking sheet, put in a hot oven for a few minutes and then rub together in a clean cloth to flake off the skins. To get rid of any lingering fine shavings, shake the nuts over a sieve or in a strainer.

PEANUTS. Are of course the same thing as groundnuts and monkey-nuts. Nutritional as they are, and eaten raw or roasted (or as groundnut oil, below, or as peanut butter), they have a rather dominant flavour which limits *their* use in cookery more than for instance almonds, walnuts or hazel-nuts.

PISTACHIO NUTS. Have a sweet and pleasant flavour, for which they are mainly used. If very fresh, very green and very finely chopped after blanching (like almonds), they are also very decorative on something like a lemon soufflé or meringues which need something simple but colourful to dress them up. Alternatively, you can thinly slice a blanched pistachio and arrange the pieces like clover leaves, with stalks cut from another nut. (Place them with 2 hatpins, see page 14.)

★ Pistachio nuts grow in pairs inside a thin husk about the size of an olive, brown-reddish in colour.

Oatmeal

Oatmeal, bread and ale were for centuries the three great dietary staples of the British Isles. It is hard to believe today, when one cannot even buy oatmeal in many parts of the country, that oatmeal porridge was at one time celebrated as the national dish. It was used then – as it no doubt is still by some people – as basic nourishment, and to sustain. It was used to thicken, coat and make foods go further, never mind to give comfort and warmth. It offers a balance of protein and carbohydrate, with a whopping bonus of Vitamin B and iron, not to mention other essential minerals.

Oil

Often the best substitute for butter, especially for frying, and has one great advantage over most other fats – it doesn't congeal on fried or roast foods served cold.

★ The flavour of an oil is to some extent dependent on the refining process. The more highly refined the oil is, the less flavour and odour it will have – that's why it pays to buy a good one. The level of refining is set by a manufacturer's specifications, so of course even the same types of oil can and do vary.

★ You can use oil to make cakes, scones, pastry and roux-based sauces if you want to. Mazola, for one, will send you recipes should you want them, but I don't think you can beat butter for a *cake* – the flavour is better, and the texture lighter.

★ A dessertsp oil used with 2 ozs (50 g) butter when frying, allows the butter to reach a higher temperature before it burns.

★ If you want to make an egg go further when coating foods with egg and breadcrumbs, mix a dessertsp oil with it.

★ Give your wooden kitchen and dining room possessions an occasional rub with a tissue lightly soaked in oil, to feed the wood and keep them shiny – salad bowl and servers, cheeseboard, breadboard, butter dishes, sugar bowl, toast rack or what-have-you. They all like a face-lift.

CORN OIL. Comes from the germ of the maize kernel – and it takes approx 56 lbs ($25\frac{1}{2}$ k) of maize to produce 32 fluid ozs (approx 925 ml) of a top quality oil like Mazola – no wonder it is so expensive.

★ You can use good quality corn oil for anything and everything – shallow or deep fat frying, marinades, roux based sauces, pastry or cakes, some people actively *preferring* it to olive oil in mayonnaise and salad dressings, because it is 'lighter' and flavourless.

★ The shelf life of an unopened bottle of pure corn oil is about 12 months, in practice probably quite a lot longer.

GROUNDNUT OIL. Comes from groundnuts, which we know better as peanuts (see page 83) or monkey-nuts, They are the oily edible seeds of a trailing plant, ripening underground in very brittle pods – hence their name.

★ See also *Vegetable oils*, to follow.

OLIVE OIL. Has been used for thousands of years. As early as 2500 BC in Crete, forests were felled to make room for olive groves. Trade in 'liquid gold' as they called it, formed the basis for much of Greece's maritime and imperial expansion. The Romans grew even richer by planting huge orchards throughout their empire. In the ancient world, the olive was the richest source of their necessary oil. It flavoured and cooked Mediterranean man's food, lit his lamps, formed the base of medicines and was the ritual liquid used for anointing priests and kings.
★ Olive oils, like wines, vary according to the country and area of origin, as well as from season to season, Spanish oils tending to be heavier and more fruity than French or Italian – which is one reason why Spanish food tends to be heavier than French. Among all fats though, olive oil is closest in chemical composition to the fat in mother's milk, making it the most easily digested of all fats and oils. Its high content of unsaturated fat means no cholesterol.
★ Olive oil is used mainly in mayonnaise, dressings, marinades and for shallow frying where its own strong flavour can safely dominate. If you find it too strong and 'heavy' why not try a good corn oil instead? *It* is flavourless.
★ Olive oil is unsuitable for deep fat frying because – quite apart from its cost – it has too low a 'smoke point'. This is approx 280°F, 138°C, whereas most foods are fried at temperatures between 340°–380°F, 170°–193°C.
★ If olive oil goes cloudy when very cold, just stand the bottle in a jug of hot water until it clears again.
★ If olive oil 'goes off', its rancid taste is a traumatic experience, so it isn't necessarily an economy to buy it in a 5 litre or even a litre tin. (A good wine merchant is usually a reliable source of supply.)

SOYA OIL. From the soya bean, this is one of the cheapest oils on the market. It has rather a marked 'back taste', a flavour always associated with soya which is difficult to diffuse even in refining. This explains why it is somewhat unsuitable for sale as a pure oil but often forms part of blended cooking oils.

SUNFLOWER OIL. Is being used more and more, and is good for deep fat frying as well as for shallow, because it has a fairly high smoke point. Use it in salad dressings and baked products too, as long as you don't dislike its flavour.

VEGETABLE OILS. Usually a blend of various oils chosen by the manufacturer and may include sunflower, groundnut, soya and rapeseed but not *usually* corn because of its high price. Blended oils aren't necessarily highly refined as this would add to their cost. For some, the usage is restricted largely to frying, as their back taste would be unacceptable in cakes and pastries.

Olives

Used mainly for their oil, olives grow in hundreds of varieties in the great olive-producing countries like Spain (with some 200 million trees), Italy (with 185 million), France and Greece. Generally speaking, green olives are the unripe fruit, black the ripened, but there are emerald olives, purple olives, thick black juicy olives – some very small, others lush as plums. A tree is probably 15–20 years old before it produces a paying crop but some still bear fruit 400–500 years later. (The average age of today's Mediterranean olive trees is 200 years.) Not surprisingly, olives figure often in Mediterranean cookery – in salads, stuffings, sauces, as an essential ingredient in the garnish for many dishes, pickled etc. Here we are much more conservative in our use of them.

★ If you buy olives loose, they keep best in a jar, covered with olive oil. See also *Olive oil*, above.

Orange Flower Water

Doesn't sound nearly as fragrant as

orange *blossom* water, its other name. No wonder it's used in almond paste, in pastry-making and confectionery. Buy it at a chemist's.

Oranges

Like lemons, oranges owe much of their aroma and flavour to the zest, the *outer* part of the skin or rind. Like lemons also, the rind when thinly pared with a potato peeler, contains less of the bitter pith than *grated* rind. This explains why pared rind is often more suitable to flavour a liquid than grated. In large pieces, it's also easier to remove from the liquid without straining.

★ For the rind's finest flavour, an orange must be fresh and shiny looking, not dry and dull – when the natural oils in it have dried out. It is these which *contain* the flavour and aroma.

★ Grated rind will contain less pith and give a finer flavour if you use a really fine grater, and the juice is, when possible, better added to a dish after it is cooked rather than before, to avoid loss of Vitamin C.

TO FREEZE ORANGES. See *Lemons*, page 80.

TO MAKE ORANGE-FLAVOURED CREAM. Rub a cube of sugar up and down all over an orange, then break up the sugar and add to cream.

TO CUT AN ORANGE INTO SLICES WITHOUT RIND OR PITH.

(1) Cut off each end of orange just deep enough to expose the flesh.
(2) Hold fruit up in front of you, and with a small stainless steel saw knife (preferably), and with a sawing action, cut the peel off in a continuous spiral – again just deep enough to expose flesh.
(3) Slice the orange across thinly or thickly, as required by recipe.

TO CUT AN ORANGE (OR GRAPEFRUIT) INTO SEGMENTS:

(1) Peel as above, for slicing.
(2) Using a pointed knife, ease back the dividing 'skins' to release the flesh.

Paprika

Hungarian for a sweet pepper, from which it is ground. It lacks the heat of cayenne, but has a slightly pungent taste and is an important seasoning in the Hungarian national dish, *goulash*. Use it to garnish cheese canapés, grilled fish and other savoury dishes, or to flavour sauces and meat dishes. It soon loses its colour and flavour, so buy in minute quantity at a time.

Parisian Essence

A fine quality gravy browning.

Pasta

Latin name for a paste. Made from strong flour and probably invented about 6,000 years ago by the Chinese, pastas include spaghetti, macaroni, vermicelli, noodles, lasagne, tagliatelle, ravioli, canneloni – and a whole host more if you enjoy Italian food (over 100 different kinds are produced now in *this* country). *Verdi*, of course implies a pasta is green; coloured by the addition of spinach to the dough.

★ See also page 149.

Pepper

Varies widely in quality, flavour and colour, the best being pure, the cheaper containing additives.

★ Black pepper, which is more spicy than white, loses its flavour during cooking, which explains why it is usually added to a dish just before serving, and also at table, from a mill.

Peppercorns

BLACK. The unripe green berries of the tropical climbing pepper shrub, which turn black when dried. Use them loose when a liquid is to be strained, otherwise tie with other spices and herbs as required, in a small bag.

★ For a really hot, spicy flavour and some 'bite', crush some with a rolling pin, then press or roll them into the surface of meat before grilling it.
★ Stored in an airtight jar, they keep indefinitely.

WHITE PEPPERCORNS. Come from the same shrub as black peppercorns, but the berries are riper when picked, and the outer husk is removed.
★ Use them particularly to flavour special white sauces or soups, which colour would be spoilt by using ground pepper.
★ It is of course from these peppercorns that white table pepper is ground. It is less pungent and less aromatic than black.

Poppy Seed

Not exactly a modern idea. It was known to the Egyptians more than 35 centuries ago.

★ To give a thoroughly professional finish to your efforts, sprinkle poppy seed lightly over the top of dinner rolls and milk twists etc after glazing – just before popping them in the oven.
★ Poppy seed is usually a Health Food Shop buy.

Porridge Oats

Will keep indefinitely in an airtight container away from any contamination, according to a producer. Although there used to be a tendency for them to go rancid, because of enzyme action, the big millers don't expect it to happen nowadays, with modern processing.

★ Quaker oats make smoother porridge than Scott's, due to different processing, but if you *prefer* a slightly rougher porridge and use the former, sprinkle the oats into *boiling* liquid instead of adding to cold.

Potato Flour

A powdery-fine flour prepared from cooked, dried and ground potatoes, it is both expensive and difficult to buy in England. Why, when it knocks spots off cornflour, and when we normally grow and eat enough potatoes to come out of our ears?

★ This is the thickening particularly intended when a recipe calls for *fécule*.
★ Slake it, and use as arrowroot, using 2 level teasps to thicken ½ pt (250 ml) thin liquid. It is flavourless.

Pulses

Include dried peas, beans and lentils which are the seeds formed in the pods of leguminous plants. The term is sometimes extended to include the seeds of other leguminous plants such as the soya bean and peanut. They are important to vegetarians because of their protein.

★ Cover beans or split peas with boiling water, and soak 12–24 hrs, to soften them. Lentils don't need soaking – they'll cook in simmering soup in about 20 mins.

Raspings

Golden breadcrumbs, the word meaning, literally, scrapings or gratings. See page 64.

Ratafia

A liqueur or cordial distilled from almonds, peaches, apricots or plums etc and flavoured also with the crushed kernels of the fruit. This is why ratafia essence is so full of flavour, and so often used instead of almond essence. To quote *Larousse Gastronomique*, 'All home-made liqueurs are made by steeping fruit and other basic ingredients in alcohol or spirits. . . Liqueurs made in this way are often called ratafias.'

RATAFIA BISCUITS. Sweet biscuits flavoured with ratafia – hardly surprising if they don't all get as far as the trifle!

Rennet

An extract from, or preparation of, the

inner membrane of the stomach of the sucking calf.

★ When rennet is used to make junket, the milk is warmed to blood heat, since this is the temperature at which rennin – a substance in our stomachs which makes milk clot – is accustomed to working in our stomachs, and those of calves.

Rice

Known to have been cultivated in China as long ago as 5000 BC and in different countries for century after century, rice has meant life for millions, the only source of food for many. Though there are said to be 7,000 different types – and all rice-eating peoples have different ideas about how it should be cooked – the rice we buy in England is *mainly* of two kinds: long grain and short grain. Various other kinds are available of course, some only if you're prepared to hunt for them.

★ Rice will keep indefinitely as long as it's dry.

LONG GRAIN RICE. The long thin grain variety which originally came only from Patna, is used for things like curries, salads or kedgeree, which require the grains to be kept separate.

★ Some think that because it is more expensive than short grain, it will make a better rice pudding. It won't, however, because it doesn't absorb the milk, nor does it go so creamy.
★ To cook rice, see page 154.
★ Long grain rice like 'Uncle Ben's', is a high quality rice with grains that remain separate when cooked, but it takes longer to cook than the above. Follow directions on packet.

SHORT GRAIN 'PUDDING RICE'. The variety needed for rice puddings and other sweet dishes, because it absorbs the milk well, is very white, and goes creamy when cooked. If you can't buy Italian rice for risotto, short grain is better than long grain, because it absorbs the stock better.

BROWN RICE. The whole unpolished grain, with only the husk removed. It is eaten by peoples whose principal nourishment is rice, because it's a vital source of the Vitamin B complex – which we in the West can get from other foods in our diet, namely brown bread, eggs, milk, cheese and so on.

★ Brown rice has a stronger flavour than polished, so is served with things like steaks, stews, game or roast duck. Use it too in stuffings, or substitute it for polished rice where its brown colour doesn't matter.
★ As it's about twice the price of long grain polished rice, and takes at least four times as long to cook, I myself can't see any reason to buy it unless you enjoy its unusual flavour – which some people really do – or live on a rather special diet.

ITALIAN RICE. A thick stubby grain with a hard central core; the correct kind for risotto, page 154. It is very absorbent, absorbing at *least* twice its volume of liquid (ie 1 cup rice, 2 cups liquid). It becomes creamy during long slow cooking (25–30 mins), but at the same time manages to retain a little 'bite'.

Rice Flour

Rice flour, if you can buy it, is milled rice ground into flour. It is slightly finer than ground rice, which like cornflour is sometimes used with plain flour to vary the flavour and texture of a cake: in shortbread for instance, to keep it flat and give it a close texture.

Rice Paper

Used especially for macaroons, is made from the pith of a Formosan tree.

★ Have you ever thought of using it as place names for a birthday tea? It's a novelty for children to be able to *eat* their names, even if it doesn't taste all that good! Pipe names in icing sugar on a sheet of it, and cut (with pinking scissors for a decorative edge) into 'cards'.

Rum

Originates from cane sugar, hence the

rums of Jamaica and Guyana (formerly British Guiana), the 'home' of Demerara sugar.

★ As long as you accept that the flavours are different, you can usually substitute cognac for rum, or vice versa, in cookery.

Saffron

Is an appalling price, but hardly surprising when one considers that it takes thousands of the orange-red stigmas of the saffron crocus to make one oz (25 g). The stigmas contain a volatile oil and a colouring substance, which give the familiar musty flavour and 'saffron' colour to rice or anything else in which they're cooked. Use it with restraint: you only need about 9–12 stigmas for $\frac{1}{2}$ lb (225 g) rice, a tiny pinch of sugar making them easier to pound. Mix with a spoonful or two of stock or water from whatever dish the saffron is to flavour, soak until the liquid is bright orange and then strain it in.

★ A native of Southern Europe, saffron was at one time extensively cultivated in England, particularly at Saffron Walden.

Sago

The starchy pith of certain kinds of palm, particularly of Malaysia. Our word comes from the Malay word, *sagu*. It is used for cooking as a liaison element, often also to prepare thick or thin soups and dishes recommended for special diets.

Salt

A necessity of life itself, the most important seasoning in the world. Precious enough once to have been used as money in some parts of it, salt was the origin of our word *salary*: it comes from the Latin word *salarium*, 'money paid to a soldier in lieu of his allowance of salt' – soldier's pay.

★ There are two sorts of salt: sea salt, the purest, which is distilled from sea-water, and rock salt, the kind most of us use, which is found in the earth in crystalline form.

TABLE SALT. Refined to make it run easily, but it isn't the kind for cooking because it doesn't bring out the natural flavour of the food as cooking salt does.

COOKING SALT. Infinitely preferable to table salt for cooking because it's both purer and stronger, never mind less expensive. Salt is extraordinary stuff when you think about it because nothing tastes of anything without it, whether a succulent steak, fried fish, a cake, a milk pudding, scones, pastry or simply a plate of porridge. It's true magic is in bringing out the flavour of the food itself, when *cooked* with it. That's why you can never make up for a cook's shortcomings at the table.

★ Salt raises the boiling point of water (to 224°F, 106°C), therefore vegetables boiled with a good quantity of salt cook more quickly than when boiled without, and there is consequently less loss of Vitamin C. For the same reason, if you add salt to the water when boiling an egg – misguidedly thinking that because the water goes off the boil, the egg will boil more slowly and therefore won't crack – the water will in fact get hotter still! See *Egg pricker*, page 10.

Semolina

Made from hard wheats, rich in gluten. The grains are granulated into coarse particles, but not crushed enough to reduce them completely to flour. Some wheats of hot dry countries, such as France and Italy, are especially suitable for its preparation. It's used to make soups, puddings and various other dishes.

Soya Beans

One of the most important foods in the world. They form one of the major crops of America, having almost as much acreage as wheat. For 5,000 years they've been an important part of the diet of people in the Far East, especially China.

★ Containing about 40 per cent protein, and including all the essential amino acids except one, they are among the most valuable of all vegetable sources of protein – and also one of the most economical yet discovered.

★ To us, some of the most familiar products of soya beans are perhaps soy sauce and soya flour, while soya oil is widely used in cooking oils, salad dressings and margarine. The various textured vegetable proteins which are being used today, to extend the yield of wheat, are produced from soya beans.

Spices

Mostly of tropical origin and have been described as 'perfumes trapped in glass jars'. To enjoy their full aroma and flavour, buy in small quantities and store each in a small airtight container.

★ The spice trade was once the most profitable in the world. Although comparatively inexpensive today, especially at a shop like Boots where they are very simply packeted, spices were at one time worth their weight in gold. So precious was a cargo, that the loss of several hundred men on one voyage was not considered too high a price to pay.

★ Spices used in Indian cookery before the days of refrigerators were often chosen as much for their antiseptic and medicinal purposes as for their flavour. In curries etc their use was in fact of great importance.

★ See also individual spices.

Stock

One of those details a good cook really cares about. It is the very fabric of good gravies, soups and sauces, just as milk is the fabric of a milk pudding. Without it, there is neither 'body' nor flavour.

★ Anyone with a freezer can store stock in cubes, like ice, to have a constant supply. If pressed for space in the freezer, 'reduce' the stock; to concentrate it, see page 000. Concentrated, it can even be stored in the ice tray of a refrigerator.

★ Quite good stock comes from bones alone, but the best stock includes meat – raw or cooked beef or veal bones, with fat-free meat, or meat scraps; or the carcase of a bird, with scraps and giblets. Break up and cut up both bones and meat, to expose maximum surface, and so draw all the goodness out of them. Use a variety of vegetables – strong ones sparingly – to achieve the right balance of flavour, without any of them dominating. Put meat, bones and vegetables into *cold* water, bringing gradually to the boil. (Pouring boiling water over them doesn't draw out the flavour in the same way.)

★ Cloudy stock is unfortunately much easier to make than clear. Here's how to make it clear.

(1) Cut vegetables into largish chunks. Slices or small pieces go to pulp.

(2) Avoid using cooked vegetables, or starchy ones like potatoes. Besides making stock cloudy, they also tend to make it go sour quickly.

(3) Blanch raw veal bones – a knuckle bone makes lovely jellied stock – before using to make stock for a special white sauce or soup, otherwise there'll be masses of scum.

(4) Skim off any scum (impurities) when it forms, and then again occasionally during cooking.

(5) Always *simmer* stock. Boiling causes the scum to combine with any fat there may be.

★ If stock lacks flavour, *reduce* it, to concentrate its strength, see page 54.

★ Strain stock as soon as it is made, leaving it to cool uncovered, so that it will do so rapidly and keep fresh longer.

★ Whatever you want it for, you need fat-free stock. The easiest way to make sure of this is to refrigerate it overnight, because you can then *lift* the fat off it the next day. See also *Degrease*.

BROWN STOCK. Used for meat dishes where its strong flavour and dark colour will improve, but never dominate or spoil a dish. See beginning above.

FISH STOCK. Quite different from meat stock because it's made so quickly and, made with white fish, is fat free. If simmered *longer* than 20–30 mins it goes bitter.

★ Use it for anything fishy – soups, sauces and of course fish dishes – for special occasions making it with fresh fish (not oily), bones, trimmings and perhaps a little wine, or otherwise quite simply with the head (minus eyes), bones and trimmings of the fish you are cooking. (You need onion, salt and parsley stems as well, but not the leaves because they'd darken the stock.) You may be surprised, if you refrigerate it overnight, what good jellied stock it will make.

★ The important thing is not to leave the fish carcase and trimmings with the fishmonger. If nothing else, you're losing some very tasty soup.

★ Fish stock doesn't keep like meat stock. Use it quickly, or transfer it to the freezer as ice cubes.

WHITE STOCK. Made with veal or chicken, for use in these and any other dishes where a light colour and a delicate flavour are important. See beginning above.

STOCK CUBES. Useful for convenience and emergencies, but the stock may need degreasing.

Suet

PACKET SUET. Good for stuffings, emergencies, or if you're short of time, but its flavour doesn't compare with that of fresh suet. I'd *never* use it in anything that matters, like a Christmas pudding or mincemeat, and preferably not in a steak and kidney pudding either – not if you want the real thing.

FRESH SUET. Like cheese, this needs to be very finely grated or chopped, otherwise it's indigestible. Use a Mouli grater to do it easily and quickly.

★ If shredding and chopping suet, sprinkle a little flour over the top of it, to make it easier to do – it prevents the fat from sticking to the knife.

★ Render it down if you like and use it as required, or freeze it as it is, and grate it direct from freezer if you suddenly decide you want it.

Sugar

Has a long history, although only known in Britain for the last 900 years. According to Tate and Lyle, no one knows who first discovered sugar or began its cultivation, but Polynesian folklore suggests that it was first used in the South Pacific. The fame of sugar took some time to travel westwards from the Orient. People in Europe *heard* about it, but due to its primitive processing, there were no means of preserving it during long voyages. Only in the sixth century, when the cane was introduced into Persia, did sugar come within range of the Mediterranean countries. From Persia, in time, it reached Venice – then the great commercial centre of Rennaissance Europe – soon becoming a major article of Mediterranean trade. The first recorded shipment of a large quantity of sugar to arrive in this country was in 1319. At £20 a lb, nicknamed 'White Gold', only royalty and the nobility could afford it for the next 200 years or so, and even then it was something only for the well-off.

★ Through the Portuguese and the Spaniards, however, who were developing their Empires in the East and West Indies, cane sugar was planted and grown in such quantity that by the eighteenth century the West Indies were supplying the whole of the Western world. The boom of coffee houses in Charles II's reign added to sugar's popularity, and sales rose dramatically.

★ Sugar *beet* was first grown in England by a group of Quakers in 1832, as a protest against slave labour being used on the West Indian plantations, but it wasn't until the First World War, when necessity demanded it, that beet became an established crop in Britain.

★ It's lucky for mankind that of all the plants which contain sugar, two of them – cane and beet – contain so much that it is commercially worthwhile to extract it. Sugar is made from their juice. Here are some of its qualities:

(1) Stored in a dry place, sugar keeps well for years. In addition, it helps us to preserve all kinds of *other* foods – pre-

serves, confectionery, frozen fruits and simple things like cakes and icings.

(2) Sugar has a constant level of sweetness. Weight for weight, all refined sugars are equally sweet. The finer the sugar though, the more quickly it dissolves, which explains why icing sugar may *seem* sweeter than others when we add it to something like cream.

(3) We absorb sugar instantaneously, explaining why a sweetened hot drink is a better pick-me-up (especially when suffering from shock) than one without sugar.

(4) Sugar acts as an odour fixative, helping to preserve the balance of the aroma components of many delicate foodstuffs.

(5) In *low* concentration, sugar speeds the action of yeast, so bread doughs will rise faster with than without it.

(6) Sugar preserves the flavour, texture and shape of *frozen* soft fruits and berries: if you freeze them without, their liquid turns to particles of ice, which break up the structure of the fruit and make it disintegrate when thawed. *With* sugar, whether dry or in syrup form, the ice particles are prevented from forming. Don't however freeze fruit *immediately* after adding dry sugar. In a strong polythene bag, give them about $\frac{1}{2}$ hr together first, turning bag over at intervals to let the juices run, and to allow the sugar to penentrate all the fruit. If freezing in syrup, make it strong – about $1\frac{1}{4}$ lbs sugar to $1\frac{1}{2}$ pts water (say 500 g to 750 ml), boiling it about 5–7 mins, for extra concentration.

★ Varying types of sugar give varying flavours and textures to foods: some dishes can be made with several kinds, all producing a perfect yet slightly different finished product, as for example meringues. Other dishes may need one type in *preference* to another, as explained with each type of sugar below:

BROWN SUGARS.

(1) *Demerara* took its name and came originally only from the old colony of that name, now a part of Guyana. Today, it comes from various cane-sugar producing countries and although originally a raw sugar, may now also be a fully refined, mingled with molasses to give it a distinctive flavour.

★ Because of its syrupy flavour, Demerara is many people's chosen partner for coffee, porridge, cereals or grapefruit. It's also the ideal choice to caramelize on top of a sweet like Crème Brûlée.

★ Because of its coarse crystal, you can usually only use Demerara successfully in a cake or pudding when it can be dissolved and added in liquid form, as in gingerbread. Meringue shells are an exception.

★ 'London Demerara' is the first demerara to be produced from fully refined sugar in this country. Tate and Lyle called it by this name partly to distinguish it from the more traditional demeraras which are *not* fully refined. I myself find it flavourless.

(2) *Soft brown sugars* are sometimes called moist, soft, sugar pieces, or 'foot' sugars, one name perhaps being used in one part of the country rather than another. It is occasionally even called sand sugar, because it looks like damp sand.

★ The most important thing about brown sugar is the very individual flavour that it gives to cakes, puddings, biscuits, stewed fruits, chutneys and pickles, toffees and fudges, to sweet and sour sauces, and to bastes for hams.

★ Brown sugars may range in colour from a creamy golden beige to a warm dark brown, the degree of colour depending on how refined it is. As a rule, the darker the colour, the richer the flavour.

★ These soft brown sugars are so fine that they will cream and blend as well as caster sugar with fat, or can be used for 'rubbed in' as well as 'melted' mixtures – as long as the flavour is acceptable of course.

★ If you're caught without brown sugar at any time, try using a teasp black treacle with 4 ozs (100 g) white sugar.

★ Brown sugar makes an 'Oxford' type of marmalade. Cut the fruit slightly thicker than usual and substitute brown sugar for not more than 25 per cent of the white –

adding about 1 level dessertsp black treacle for every 3 lbs (say 1½ K) total sugar.

★ If brown sugar goes lumpy because not in an airtight jar, pop it in a large plastic bag and roll out the lumps with a rolling pin. If the sugar has gone *rocky*, it's better to use it in a recipe where it is dissolved. Alternatively, put it in a bowl, cover with a damp cloth and leave overnight.

(3) *Brown loaf sugar* is available for those who like a measured quantity in a cup of coffee.

WHITE SUGARS.

(1) *Caster sugar* has the smallest crystal of all boiled sugars. It is the best for creamed mixtures because it blends so smoothly with fat, consequently giving this type of cake an even and perfect texture. Use caster for whisked sponge mixtures as well.

★ Caster, or better still icing sugar, will sweeten a fresh fruit purée well because it dissolves more readily than granulated without heat – unless you make and sweeten the purée in a liquidizer, when granulated is just as good. Most recipes for meringues call for caster sugar, but perhaps surprisingly, you can also make meringues with other sugars – icing, demerara, and *lovely* ones with granulated.

★ Caster versus Castor? Tate and Lyle's reasons for preferring to call it Caster are as follows: 'A castor is defined in the dictionary as a trailing wheel. It seems likely that because late nineteenth century/early twentieth century versions of this fine sugar were milled from coarser granulated sugar by a wheel resembling a castor, the resulting sugar took its nomenclature and spelling from the machine that made it. Later and present-day finest grain sugar is produced by boiling sugar syrup to the required crystal size, and not by milling as previously. It has therefore lost its associations with a castor (wheel) and is now recognized as the type of sugar ideal for casting (ie sprinkling) from a caster (sprinkler).'

(2) *Coffee crystals* are the largest and slowest dissolving sugar crystals. They were originally intended for the coffee connoisseur who likes the first sips of his coffee to be bitter. As the crystals dissolved, so the coffee would gradually become sweeter. The custom then was to eat any remaining crystals with the spoon.

(3) *Cube sugar* has succeeded the sugar we used to call 'loaf' – pieces taken off the large loaf. Only brown loaf sugar is now sold.

★ Cube sugar is produced from selected granulated sugar which is moistened and moulded into neat shapes. This is obviously first choice therefore for all hot drinks, because you can add a measured quantity of sugar to each cup every time. Use cubes as well for picnics, and for crushing coarsely to sprinkle over cakes and tea-breads before baking them.

★ Many old caramel recipes call for loaf sugar because at one time that was the purest white sugar. Granulated and caster, being less pure, were therefore less suitable because impurities in sugar are one of the causes of it crystallizing. Nowadays icing, caster, granulated and cube are each as pure as the other, so you may just as well use granulated, which is cheapest.

(4) *Granulated sugar*, the main product of the normal refining process, is best used in recipes where the liquid content and cooking time are such that the crystals dissolve completely. While too coarse for 'creamed' mixtures, it blends easily with the fat for 'rubbed in' mixtures. Because it is as pure as, but considerably cheaper than, the other white sugars, this is the best one to use for syrups.

(5) *Icing sugar* wasn't even thought of until towards the end of the nineteenth century. It began as a by-product of loaf sugar – the sievings of the rough-shaped nibs that fell from the early form of cut cubes.

★ It is made nowadays by grinding sugar crystals to a fine powder. This is the ideal sugar for cold drinks, fresh fruit purées, whipped cream, icings, butter-cream fillings and uncooked sweets like truffles –

because it is so fine that it dissolves quickly, even without heat.

★ If ever you're short of caster sugar, icing is better than granulated for flan or French flan pastry, or for shortbread. Granulated tends to caramelize when these things are baked, giving a speckled appearance.

(6) *Preserving sugar* is specially designed for making jams, jellies, marmalades and preserves. As the slow-dissolving crystals don't settle in a dense layer at the bottom of the pan, it doesn't need so much stirring to prevent burning, so the final preserve is therefore clearer and brighter – important particularly for delicately coloured jellies such as apple or gooseberry, and for anyone seeking perfection.

★ Another plus about preserving sugar is that it produces very little froth when it dissolves. This means it needs less skimming than other sugars, so there's less waste of preserve, and less work into the bargain.

(7) *Vanilla sugar* is as easy to make as it is expensive to buy. Ideally, have two jars, one with caster sugar to use in sauces, cakes and desserts, the other with icing sugar to flavour whipped cream – because this dissolves most quickly and sweetens the cream immediately, making it *appear* sweeter than say, caster.

★ Be sure the vanilla pod is fresh when you buy it. Simply break it into pieces, then split and bury in up to 1 lb (say 500 g) of sugar in an airtight jar. Top up the jar when you use the sugar – or whenever you think about it – and you'll never be without vanilla sugar.

★ A pod will give flavour for months and months. There's no need to replace it until its aroma fades.

★ In just the same way, you can make *cinnamon sugar*, burying two broken up sticks of cinnamon in the sugar. It's delicious with almost any apple dish, or is an easy way to make *Cinnamon toast*, see page 275.

SUGAR HINTS, from Tate and Lyle:

(1) Sprinkle a spoonful of sugar over a chicken or duck before roasting, to help make the skin crisp.
(2) Rub a spoonful of sugar and a knob of fat into very dry or dirty hands. The fat softens them and the sugar draws out any ingrained dirt.
(3) A spoonful of sugar added to the water when cooking vegetables will improve their flavour, especially peas and carrots.
(4) A cube of sugar in your biscuit tin will help to keep the biscuits fresh and crisp.
(5) A spoonful of sugar or a cube added to the water in a vase of flowers will make them stay fresh longer.
(6) Three or four cubes of sugar put in a suitcase before storing it will help prevent odours.
(7) A spoonful of sugar sprinkled over tomatoes before grilling or frying will give them more flavour – because it caramelizes.
(8) A spoonful of sugar sprinkled over mint makes it easier to chop – *and* gives mint sauce a better flavour.

Syrup

Golden syrups vary in flavour and colour according to the different refineries. They are made from selected refinery liquor after the refined sugar has been crystallized.

★ Syrup won't leave a sticky trail if, when taking it out of the tin, you keep turning the spoon steadily over and over.

MEASURING HINTS.

(1) To obtain level measures, warm the syrup slightly in cold weather – perhaps just standing the tin in a warm place for a while.
(2) Rinse cups and spoons in very hot water first, so that you can scrape the syrup off cleanly, without waste.
(3) When accuracy is important, for recipes using syrup melted with other ingredients, weigh the empty pan first, then add the required amount of syrup to it. In other recipes, put a weighed cream carton or something onto the scales, and weigh into this.

Here are some easy measures for syrup – all used level:

One tablesp holds approx 1 oz (25 g) syrup by weight
$\frac{1}{4}$ pt measure (125 ml) holds 7 ozs (*about* 200 g) syrup by weight
$\frac{1}{4}$ pt measure + 1 tablesp holds 8 ozs (225 g) syrup by weight
$\frac{1}{2}$ pt measure (250 ml) holds 14 ozs (about 400 g) syrup by weight

Tabasco Sauce

Takes its name from a red pepper introduced into the United States from the state of Tabasco, Mexico. It's so hot that it takes only a few drops to give soups and gravies some zest.

Tapioca

Comes from the roots of a tropical shrub – it's not a cereal.

Tea

Can't be described as an ingredient, but see page 270.

Treacle

The thick syrupy substance which drains out of sugar in the process of refining – use it in baking and confectionery when you want its strong flavour.
★ See also *Syrup*, previous page.

Vanilla

VANILLA ESSENCE. The extract obtained from vanilla pods, usually added to a mixture *after* it is cooked, because it loses some of its flavour when cooked.

★ Use it in almost anything containing chocolate or cocoa, to flavour custards of almost any kind, in sweet sauces, cold sweets, certain puddings, cream, ice cream, certain cakes and cake fillings. In some dishes it is used in *addition* to another flavouring.

VANILLA PODS. The dried, rather liquorice-like pods of a Mexican orchid, which give the *true* flavour of vanilla. Use to make vanilla sugar (page 93), or break a piece off, split and drop it into heating milk; to flavour sauces, milk puddings or whatever you like within reason. If rinsed in warm water after use, dried carefully, and kept buried in sugar, you'll be able to use it several times before its aroma fades.

Vegetable Fats

They are expensive because vegetable *oils* are expensive, costing more than marine oils and animal fats. Products such as Blue Band and Flora margarines are therefore bound to reflect this in their price.

★ White cooking fats, thought by many people to be purely of vegetable origin, do in fact mostly contain other fats as well – unless they claim to be pure vegetable.
★ Tomor Margarine and Outline low fat spread are both completely free of milk products, and can therefore be used by strict vegetarians who wish to avoid the whey normally present in margarine.
★ See also *Oil*, page 83.

Vinegar

Takes its name from *vin* and *aigre*, meaning 'sharp wine', so let's hope this may remind you, if you are in doubt, that for *most* purposes wine vinegar – made by the fermentation of diluted wine – is better than malt or cider vinegar.

★ The difference in the flavour, quality, colour, price and most importantly in its use, naturally depends upon what vinegar is made of. Cheap vinegars taste harsh and spoil good food – better for furniture washing – but a selection of good vinegars can bring new life to your eating, and each is child's play to make, (see below). Some recipes may call for *mixed* vinegars, say a spoonful each of chilli, tarragon and wine. This is the way in which you can introduce flavours to something like aspic jelly without making it cloudy, or introduce them quickly and easily to whatever you are making.

★ If hard pressed on the housekeeping, you can stretch out the vinegar by topping up a half bottle with cold *boiled* water, before leaving it for 3 days. If not 100 per cent what it was, it's still surprisingly strong.

★ Vinegar is versatile stuff. Use:

(1) In marinades, to tenderize cheaper cuts of meat as well as to flavour.

(2) To give piquancy to rich foods. By stimulating the digestive juices – with a dressed salad for instance – the food is more *easily* digested.

(3) To soften and dissolve the smaller bones in fish, as soused herring.

(4) To wash strong-smelling meat, using a vinegar-soaked cloth.

(5) Instead of lemon juice in a savoury dish if you've run out of lemons, or want a change of flavour.

(6) To rinse out a jar still smelling of earlier contents.

GARLIC VINEGAR. Easy to make and gives instant flavour of garlic to a salad dressing or anything else. Bring $\frac{1}{2}$ pt (250 ml) white wine vinegar just to boiling point – this brings out the flavour of the garlic better than cold vinegar – and pour it onto 4 largish cloves of crushed garlic. Cover it as it cools because of vinegar fly, then bottle and store it 2–3 weeks before straining.

HERB VINEGARS. Usually best made with white wine vinegar so that you can use them for anything. It's generally just a matter of having about 1 pt (say 500 ml) of loosely packed leaves – basil, dill, fennel, mint, savory, tarragon, thyme – and covering them with, and soaking in, the same amount of vinegar. Cover the jar and leave 2–3 weeks, or long enough for the flavour to develop.

MALT VINEGAR. Used mainly for pickles and for some kinds of chutney, but it is *not* the vinegar for salad dressings. Malt vinegar doesn't cut through oil as wine vinegar does, so the oily taste dominates, spoiling both the salad and the food it accompanies. It's a pity to be miserly over using *wine* vinegar, because it only takes a spoonful or so to 'make' a dish – or the same amount of malt vinegar to spoil it. In fact if you use malt vinegar to make French dressing, it *isn't* French dressing – it's something quite quite different.

★ Distilled malt vinegar is the white one, the sort you need when brown malt vinegar would spoil the colour of something, like pickled pears.

WINE VINEGAR. Best for cooking, and also for salads, because unlike malt vinegar, it cuts through the oil in a dressing – so preventing the oil from dominating – and sharpens the taste. If you want to make the real thing, French dressing *must* be made with wine vinegar.

★ White and red wine vinegar are often interchangeable, but it naturally depends upon what you're making as to which you use. You'd spoil the colour of a cucumber salad, mayonnaise or white fish for instance by using red vinegar, but how monotonous food would be if we only had white? A green salad is *lovely* made with red.

★ High-class grocers or good wine merchants are usually a reliable source of supply.

Water

Keeps us alive – we can't live more than a few days without it in fact – about 1–1$\frac{1}{2}$ pts (say $\frac{1}{2}$–$\frac{3}{4}$ L) a day coming from 'solid' foods. Water is the medium in which the body's 1001 reactions occur.

★ It is in nearly every food we eat, roughly as follows:
40 per cent in bread
33 per cent in cheese
75 per cent in eggs (whole)
67 per cent in oily fish
80 per cent in white fish
70 per cent in meat
87 per cent in milk
And even more than this in some fruits and leafy vegetables; up to 97 per cent in lettuce.

★ It's because of water in foods that you need to pack them carefully and effectively before freezing. It is – hardly surprisingly – converted to ice within their cell structure, and if it isn't maintained there the foods dry out, losing both nutrients and flavour as they do so.

ICE-COLD WATER. Better than tap water to make pastry and batters rise well. The colder the trapped air, the more it will expand when heated.

SALT WATER. Boils at 224°F, 106°C, which explains why boiling water appears to go slightly off the boil when you add salt to it.

Wine

Used in cooking to give flavour to bland dishes, to bring out the flavour of a food with which it is cooked, to blend other flavours together, to give 'fullness', and sometimes – as in a marinade – to tenderize tough meat. To use wine is like waving a wand over even the simplest foods. It doesn't have to be the best, but it ought to be good, its flavour being what matters. Whether a good or a poor wine, that flavour will be stronger – for better or for worse – when a wine is 'reduced', to vaporize the alcohol and concentrate the flavour and fragrance, as it may be for say, a sauce: a good wine will do wonders, but a harsh one is more likely to predominate and spoil the sauce.

★ A lovely way to 'use up' a bottle of wine is in a savoury butter such as Beurre Bercy or Beurre Marchand de Vins, freezing the butter until you want it.

HOME-MADE WINES. Parsley and elderberry, for instance, can be wonderful in cooking if their flavour goes happily with whatever you're making. If you'd by-pass a recipe because you can't afford the wine, why not *try* one of these if you're a wine-maker? I make them specially.

★ The parsley wine recipe I like is in a Countrywise book *Home Made Country Wines*, the recipe using: 1 lb (450 g) parsley, 4 lbs (1.8 K) granulated sugar, 2 oranges, 2 lemons, 1 gal (4.5 L) water, ½ oz (15 g) bruised root ginger, ¾ oz (say 20 g) fresh (baker's) yeast.

FORTIFIED WINES, SPIRITS AND LIQUEURS. Used for their flavour, so they too have to be good if things are to *taste* good.

★ If a recipe calls for cognac, it's usually just a way of indicating a brandy of that quality. See also *Flambé*, page 40. See also *Macerating* if you like fruits soaked in liqueur.

Yeast

FRESH YEAST. Should have that lovely strong yeasty smell, should be a good even colour – no dark patches – and it should be in large pieces which crack rather than go crumbly. Stale yeast won't become liquid when mixed with a teasp sugar. A pinch of fresh yeast will dissolve quickly on your tongue.

★ Yeast's life depends upon temperature: it is dormant when frozen, flourishes in warmth, but is killed by too much heat. This explains why it can be deep frozen for months, why a warm dough rises faster than a cold, and why bread needs a hot oven to stop it rising through the roof.
★ If you have a freezer, fresh yeast is considerably cheaper by the lb (say 500 g) than in smaller quantities, because it is an easier and more economical way for a shopkeeper to sell it. It's a lot easier for you too because it's always there, fresh, when you want it. (Now metric, you may have to buy it by the kilo.)
★ Cut the yeast into equal-sized pieces *before* you freeze it – 8, 16, 32, according to the weight you generally use – and parcel each up before packing them into a freezer *container*, to protect well. When you want it, it acts more quickly if thawed for an hour or so first (say in a covered basin), because it doesn't cool down the liquid when mixed with it. Once again, you can't then cut it into pieces because it *liquifies* when thawed.
★ Given three things, *warmth*, *moisture* and *suitable food*, you can't stop yeast growing. The warmth I've mentioned above, the liquid is obvious, and its food is the sugars and other carbohydrates in the flour. This explains why there's no need always exactly to double the quantity of yeast in a recipe when you're using double the amount of flour – because the more

flour there is, the more food there is for the yeast cells to feed on and so multiply. For *bread*, the proportions required of yeast to flour are approximately as follows, but you can step up the yeast slightly to make a dough rise faster:

Imperial weights	*Metric*
$\frac{1}{2}$ oz yeast to $\frac{1}{2}$–1lb flour	15g yeast to $\frac{1}{4}$–$\frac{1}{2}$ K flour
1 oz yeast to 1–3lbs flour	30g yeast to $\frac{1}{2}$–1$\frac{1}{2}$ K flour
2 ozs yeast to 3–6 lbs flour	60g yeast to 1$\frac{1}{2}$–3 K flour

★ Dried fruit, eggs and extra sugar delay the action of yeast, slowing down fermentation, so a rich dough containing these, usually calls for a little more yeast than above and may also be made in a slightly different way from bread.
★ 'Creaming' (mixing) the yeast with sugar is a method we've said goodbye to, because it's now known that this inactivates some of the yeast cells, so slows down rather than speeds up fermentation. Just add the warm liquid to the yeast, and stir to dissolve it.

DRIED ACTIVE YEAST. This, such as Allinson,may not keep as long as frozen fresh yeast and is more expensive into the bargain, but some people like to use it and others for various reasons must. If kept *cool and dry* it will keep for very long periods, but will deteriorate if kept in warm, humid conditions. Buy it from a shop with rapid turnover if you can, then you know it will be fresh when you *buy* it. It's wiser to buy by the oz (25 g) pkt if you don't use much. Yeast in a tin will 'live' longer if you exclude air from it; either by putting it into a smaller tin as you use it, or by filling up the air space in its own tin.

★ Dried yeast is used differently from fresh, as follows:

(1) 1 oz (25 g) dried yeast equals 2 ozs (50 g) fresh.
(2) Dried needs slightly hotter liquid (110°F, 43°C) than fresh (about 85°F, 30°C) for good results.
(3) It is reconstituted by sprinkling it on top of warm liquid in which a teasp sugar has been dissolved. *It* needs sugar to activate it.
(4) It needs to stand for about 10 mins or until frothy in a warm place before you use it – and if it doesn't become frothy, it's dead. You'll have to forget about your bread-making.

Yoghourt

Dates back centuries, and probably originated in the Balkans. It's taken a long time to become popular here.

★ Have you tried adding a tablespoonful or two at the last minute to soups, sauces or sautéd vegetables, cooking it just long enough for the flavours to blend together?
★ Addicts can invest in a commercially-made yoghourt maker. To make it, see page 236.

4

PASTRY

General Information

Pastry would be flat as a board when cooked, if it wasn't for the particles of air trapped in the making. These expand when heated, and the cooler they are the more they expand, so the lighter the pastry. This explains why everything has to be cold – flour, fats, water (iced if possible), hands, and finally the dough itself. It's the main reason for sieving the flour, for using a large mixing bowl, for using a knife to mix it with, and for lifting your hands well above bowl when rubbing fat into flour. The success of all pastries *depends* on air – on trapping and retaining it.

★ The variety and texture of a pastry is determined by the proportions of flour, fat and water, and the way in which they are incorporated.

FLOUR. Use plain flour, because self-raising gives a spongy, cake-like texture. Apart from suet-crust pastry which is heavy, pastry neither needs nor wants the chemical raising agents present in self-raising flour, because *air* is pastry's raising agent. Strong flour, which contains more gluten, is used only for really rich pastries, soft household flour giving a better texture for all others.

FATS. Vary according to the kind of pastry being made. Butter (which gives the best flavour) or margarine provide the flavour and crispness of pastry, while lard or cooking fat provide the lightness. That's why a combination of the two is used in some pastries. Pastry made with lard or cooking fat alone may well be light as air, but it will also be utterly tasteless.

★ Cold butter or 'hard' margarines make better pastry than 'soft', and the pastry is easier to manipulate, but neither should be refrigerator-hard if to be rubbed into flour, because they won't blend properly. Ideally, they should be cold and firm.

WATER. Can be the cause of success or disaster in pastry-making, depending on whether you get the dough the right consistency or not. Some pastries are drier than others, eg shortcrust is drier than flan, but basically pastry should neither be too dry nor too wet, and certainly never sticky. If too wet it is difficult to handle, tough and hard when cooked. If too dry, it's also difficult to handle but for different reasons – some kinds of pastry crack, and others aren't pliable enough to roll successfully.

SALT. Is used in the proportion of 1 level teasp to $\frac{1}{2}$ lb (225 g) flour, in *all* kinds of pastry. Without it, you might as well eat straw.

LEMON JUICE. Is used in some kinds of pastry to give greater elasticity to the gluten, which makes the pastry rise better. It also slightly counteracts the richness. If called for in a recipe, results won't be as good if you omit it.

EGG YOLK. Makes pastry crisp, full of flavour, rich and golden when cooked, as for instance in flan, cheese, or French flan pastry. It also helps pastry to keep a 'sharp' shape, as round the edge of a flan.

HEAVY HANDLING OR OVER-HANDLING. Knocks the air out of pastry, so the more you can do with a knife, the less you'll have to use your hands. This is why it is better to cut the fat up into smallish pieces amongst the flour, before you start to *rub* it in. If it's either very hard or very soft, or if the proportion of fat to flour is high, it is more important than ever to do this.

★ It's important too that you should just lightly brush your finger tips and thumbs against each other when rubbing fat into flour, because *squashing* them together expels air. If you're one of those unfortunates with permanently hot hands, cut the fat extra small, and see if it's easier to use your palms instead of your fingers, just lightly brushing *them* against each other, with the flour and fat between.

ROLLING PASTRY. A floured pastry board may be old-fashioned, but it is still better than formica or melaware. This is because it keeps cooler, and also because you can't distribute flour evenly over formica – which makes it more difficult to roll the pastry well.

★ Use the minimum of flour on a board (sprinkled preferably from a flour dredger), otherwise a dough which was soft and perfect in the mixing bowl may become dry, heavy and difficult to roll – and then it won't rise well. The same sort of things will happen if you sprinkle the pastry itself with flour.

★ Pastry is rolled and folded – some kinds 5–7 times – for two main reasons; first to produce lots of wafer-thin layers of pastry, which give it its characteristic flaky texture; secondly to trap more air (see illustrations) and then to distribute it, together with the fats, throughout the pastry. If it is rolled *too* often, the fat simply mixes with the dough instead of remaining in layers.

★ If you're not sure how to roll, see page 55, because heavy rolling makes heavy pastry: the aim is to extend pastry in whatever direction you want, not to flatten by squashing it. Many people unconsciously put more pressure on the rolling pin with one hand than with the other, the would-be rectangle ending up either with a waist, or perhaps even worse – shapeless. To correct a waist, roll the pastry diagonally wherever it has narrowed. To avoid shapelessness, consciously roll more firmly with the weaker hand wherever the pastry is thicker. Unevenly rolled pastry will *rise* unevenly, the thinner parts perhaps burning before the thicker are cooked.

★ The usual way to fold a strip of pastry ABCD is like this, dividing it in your mind's eye into thirds, see dotted lines.

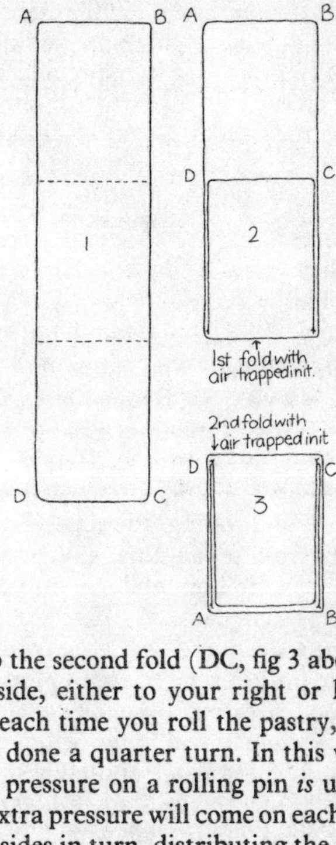

Keep the second fold (DC, fig 3 above) to one side, either to your right or left, so that each time you roll the pastry, it will have done a quarter turn. In this way, if your pressure on a rolling pin *is* uneven, the extra pressure will come on each of the four sides in turn, distributing the weight evenly in the end. If your memory is as bad as mine, it's probably best to make a habit of *always* turning the fold to the same side.

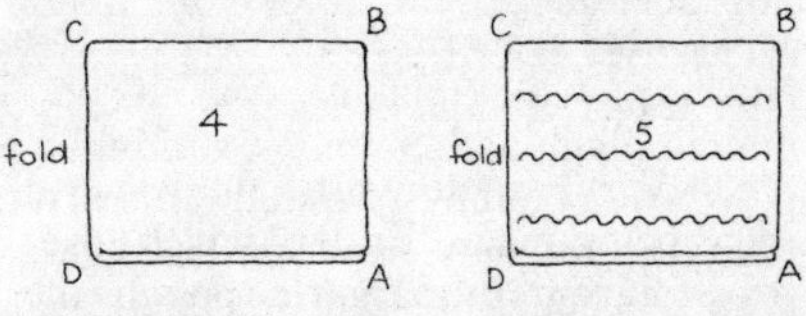

Before actually rolling out the pastry (fig 4), distribute the air trapped at folds by pressing down gently right across pastry (with your rolling pin) in about 3 places, see wavy lines, fig 5 – *then* start to roll.

★ Here are a few general tips:

(1) Some pastries are intended to rise more than others: there's a right or wrong thickness for them all – and the latter may easily spoil results.

(2) No pastry tolerates being turned over during rolling. This makes it tough.

(3) Roll pastry larger than required size, to allow for shrinkage *before* cooking. If you stretch it to fit a dish, it will inevitably shrink later – that's its nature.

★ It is better and easier to lift a large piece of rolled-out pastry over the rolling pin than with your hands, especially if it's thin. It is much less likely to tear or break, because the weight is evenly distributed over the length of the pin, and if you're lining a flan ring or covering a pie, it's easy to centre the pastry precisely above it.

RELAXING PASTRY. A period of 15–20 mins – in the refrigerator if possible – between rollings, and after the final rolling, is a vital but frequently *neglected* process in pastry-making, because there's no *apparent* reason for it. Here's why:

(1) It allows the gluten, stretched during mixing and rolling, to relax. If it *isn't* given time to do this, the pastry is difficult to roll out and will also shrink badly when cooked – like stretched elastic suddenly released. See *Gluten*.

(2) The fat has time to firm up, making the dough easier to handle.

(3) The pastry will rise better when cooked because, chilled in the refrigerator, the cold air in it expands more than warmer air would.

(4) After the final rolling, relaxing gives the pastry the opportunity to shrink on the board rather than on the pie, plate, or whatever.

★ To keep it moist and prevent it from cracking while relaxing, put it on a floured plate, and cover it with foil or a polythene bag. If pastry is refrigerated *too* long, the fat may have hardened more than the dough, so will break through when rolled – best then to leave it at room temperature for a while first.

CUTTING PASTRY. Use a sharp floured knife or cutter, to free the 'layers' and so allow it to rise properly. If either is blunt, or if you twist a cutter instead of making a clean cut, this drags and seals the edges.

★ The edges of pastry are 'knocked up', page 46, to help ensure they are open, allowing the pastry to rise perfectly when cooked.

GLAZING PASTRY. This needs care. If you brush any cut edge with egg, the egg coagulates immediately in the hot oven, causing a seal, which stops the pastry rising there – fatal for vol-au-vents and patties, and not very good for a pie or anything else. See also *Glaze*, page 44.

STEAM. Must escape, otherwise, sealed in, it makes the inside of pastry soggy. An 'escape' is usually made by making a hole in the middle of a meat pie, by slightly raising one corner of the pastry on a fruit pie, or by pricking the top of a plate-pie in 2 or 3 places with the prongs of a fork. The more water there is in a dish, the more steam there is, so obviously a meat pie needs a bigger outlet than a plate pie.

THE OVEN. It must be preheated and hot, and the richer the pastry the hotter the oven. This makes sure that the starch grains in the flour will burst and absorb the fat before it can melt and run out. (If you've ever found a baking sheet running with fat, it's probably because the oven was too low.) A hot oven also helps pastry to rise quickly, and form a crust which will hold its shape.

★ To allow a dish to cook inside, you can lower the heat or, once it has set, lower the position of some kinds of pastry in the oven.

★ A pastry like puff, with very high fat content, is baked on a *wetted* baking sheet. The moisture prevents the bottom of the pastry from browning too quickly, and consequently from burning in the necessarily very hot oven.

Cheese Pastry

A crisp, rich, savoury form of shortcrust pastry. If some of the cheese can be Parmesan, so much the better for the flavour

– and do remember a pinch of cayenne.

PROPORTIONS.
Half to equal quantities fat to flour
Half to equal quantities cheese to flour
2–4 egg yolks to each lb (450 g) flour.
If you use equal quantities fat and flour, the fat has to be very cool, and is easier 'cut' in with a knife than rubbed in. This is because so much fat tends, with warm fingers, to form a dough with the flour, even before you have added the water.

★ The fat should be either butter or margarine – never lard or cooking fat, because these would give the pastry the wrong texture.
★ Too much water makes cheese pastry tough, not short, so it's better to err on the dry side if in doubt. It may crack, and be difficult to roll and handle, but at least it will taste good.
★ A delicious melt-in-the-mouth cheese pastry (suitable for straws and canapés, but not for moulding because it cracks too easily) can be made by using equal quantities of flour, margarine, cheese and fresh breadcrumbs – salt and cayenne too – but no egg yolk or water. 2 ozs (50 g) of each ingredient makes quite a stack of straws. Rub or cut the fat into the flour and seasonings, then add the cheese and breadcrumbs, and knead it lightly to a dough. Rolled to $\frac{1}{4}''$ (6 mm) thick, straws take about 7–10 mins in a hot oven, gas 6, 400°F, 204°C.

Choux Pastry

As quick and easy to make as a sauce, for that's all it is; a very *thick* sauce (called a *panada*, see page 52) into which egg is beaten. Quite different from all other pastries, choux is the basic mixture to which various flavourings and other things can be added to make dishes like cheese aigrettes, quenelles or gnocchi. It's no bother to do and it widens your range of cooking in all sorts of ways.

PROPORTIONS. Opinions vary about the proportion of flour, butter and water used to one egg, but this is *my* favourite recipe, followed by *why* it's better to do one thing than another:

1 oz (25 g) butter
4 tablesps water
$1\frac{1}{2}$ ozs (40 g) plain flour
pinch of salt
1 egg
few drops vanilla essence, if for cakes

METHOD
(1) Melt butter, add water and bring to boil.
(2) Sieve flour and salt onto clean sheet of paper and when butter and water boil, stir in the flour all at once, still over the heat. Reduce heat to low and beat mixture until it leaves the sides of the pan clean, probably in seconds.
(3) Cool mixture two or three minutes, beat in half the lightly mixed egg (using wooden spoon still) and when amalgamated and quite smooth, add remainder, beating again until smooth.
(4) Leave to cool before using, and then pipe or use as required.
(5) If baking, bake in a hot oven on greased baking sheet, gas 7, 425°F, 220°C for $\frac{1}{4}$ hr, then lower to gas 4, 350°F, 175°C until crisp and golden, *probably* 25–35 mins altogether, according to whatever you're making. (After 20 mins, when the choux is 'set', puncture small things like éclairs with the point of a knife to let steam escape, or *slit* large puffs.) Cool on cake tray.
(6) Remove any uncooked part in the centre of puffs etc as soon as they're cool, slitting open with a sharp knife or a pair of scissors.

★ Why it's better to do one thing than another:
(1) Butter gives the best flavour. Neither oil nor margarine are a patch on it.
(2) With the flour and salt sieved onto paper, you can 'shoot' the whole lot *at once* into the boiling liquid.
(3) When the panada leaves the sides of the pan clean, this indicates the flour is cooked. If you *continue* to cook it beyond this stage, the choux won't rise properly and will have a heavy cake-like consistency.
(4) If you add the egg to the boiling mixture without allowing mixture to cool at all, the egg will cook *now*, which it mustn't. Then it won't be able to blow up the mixture when it's baked (or

otherwise cooked).

(5) The lightness of choux pastry depends on thorough beating of the mixture *after* the egg is added, to incorporate air.

(6) Choux, like other pastries and for the same reasons, is used cold (but not chilled) – unless otherwise specified. (Some cooks like to use it warm but I never think it makes such good pastry.)

(7) A preheated hot oven is essential to raise and 'set' choux, and if you take it *out* of the oven before it's firm to the touch, it will collapse.

(8) If you don't puncture (or slit) the nearly cooked choux, the trapped steam will make it go soggy when cold.

(9) Any uncooked centre, if not removed, will spread its dampness to the outside, which *should* be crisp, firm to the touch, and tender and dry to eat.

★ And here are a few more general tips:

(1) A filling shouldn't be added until the last possible minute because any moisture in it will make choux go sad.

(2) Deep fat, if used, should be 320–340°F, 160–171°C – not too hot. If much hotter, the outsides of the choux harden before the insides can expand, so the mixture can't rise – making cannon balls instead of featherweight puffs. The heat is increased slightly *during* cooking.

(3) For perfection, choux pastry should be no more than a few hours old. If you freeze things like éclairs or puff shells, bake them 3–4 mins in a hot oven, gas 7, 425°F, 220°C to thaw and crisp them just before using.

(4) Any left-over uncooked choux *will* keep, refrigerated, for a few days: put it in a basin, brush surface with oil and cover closely with foil to prevent a skin forming. Don't expect it to be quite so good though.

Flaky Pastry

Should rise more, and be lighter than shortcrust, because of all the air trapped during folding and rolling.

PROPORTIONS. Are $\frac{2}{3}$ fat to flour. You need 6 ozs (150 g) pastry for a 1$\frac{1}{2}$ pint (750 ml) pie-dish.

★ If you mix the lard and margarine together on a plate with a knife while they're at room temperature, then refrigerate them until firm, but not too hard, they'll be evenly distributed when you come to using them.

★ After rubbing in a quarter of the cooled fat, cut the rest into large sugar-lump-sized chunks. Like this, air will be trapped between them each time the pastry is folded over.

★ Most of the water is added at once, to prevent the dough getting a flaky appearance. It should be soft to the touch, without sticking to the fingers.

★ Seal the edges of the folded dough with the rolling pin, to *trap* the air. If you then press the dough in ridges 2 or 3 times with the rolling pin (see page 99), this distributes the air more evenly throughout, before re-rolling.

★ Keep the edges straight and the corners square, to ensure even thickness when folding, and avoid rolling over the ends of the pastry if you can, because this forces out the air.

★ Lay any 'trimmings' flat on top of each other, rather than kneading them into a lump. This keeps the pastry in layers.

Flan Pastry

Made with butter or margarine, never lard, then, (unlike shortcrust, which may become tough and hard) its crisp short texture isn't spoilt by a filling.

★ It's important not to make this dough too wet, otherwise the pastry *won't* be crisp. The amount of water needed may vary according to the size of the egg yolk.

QUANTITIES. For a 7″ (18 cm) flan ring, you'll need:

- 4 ozs (100 g) plain flour
- $\frac{1}{2}$ level teasp salt
- 2 ozs (50 g) butter or marg.
- 1 egg yolk
- 2–4 teasps cold water
- 1 level dessertsp caster sugar, for a sweet flan

★ Caster or icing sugar is used rather than granulated because granulated caramelizes during baking, so the flan ends up speckled. If you use too *much* sugar, it makes the pastry heavy.

French Flan Pastry

Also called *Pâté sucrée* or *Sugar pastry*, this makes the most delicious flans ever – but then I have a sweet tooth! Its crisp, short texture depends upon the careful blending of the right ingredients in an unusual way, as well as upon very light handling. It isn't too easy to make.

★ Butter gives a better flavour than margarine, but if it isn't fairly soft, it is difficult to blend with the yolks, sugar and flour.

PROPORTIONS. Some recipes call for 2 egg yolks to 4 oz (100 g) flour, or 1 yolk and 1 dessertsp water. Whether you use one, or two yolks, the texture is crisper and lighter without *any* water. 1 small whole egg can take the place of 2 yolks, but because of the wateriness of egg white, once again the pastry isn't as crisp.

★ Caster or icing sugar are used for the same reason as for flan pastry, but caster keeps the pastry a sharper shape than icing.

★ Work the dough just until smooth, shiny, pliable and soft. If over-worked, it tends to become a sticky mass, which is difficult to roll out without using extra flour, which spoils the texture.

★ Unlike most other pastries, it is very malleable, and easily patched if it breaks during rolling or moulding. It doesn't shrink in the same way either, so can be rolled to the exact size required.

★ Brush both baking sheet and flan ring with oil or melted lard, otherwise the pastry, because of its high sugar content, will stick.

Frozen Pastry

Can be thawed, made up into dishes, and refrozen. A 'filling' is often pre-cooked, but the pastry is usually better cooked fresh when you need it.

★ *Some* commercial frozen pastries are so good that a busy person would have to be a perfectionist *never* to use them. One particular make of puff pastry is probably better puff than the great majority of people can make anyway – and lots of people can't make it at all. I find it a must for the occasions when I haven't time to make it. You can't really compare it, though, with the *best* home-made puff, nor with rough puff or flaky pastry for such things as a meat pie or sausage rolls, because it isn't the right kind of pastry for them.

★ Left-over scraps of pastry, bought or home-made, are best made up into a dish if possible, but otherwise you can wrap them in foil and freeze, to use later.

★ When making your own pastry, if you have a freezer, it's not *much* extra trouble while you're busy with it, to make two or three times as much of *some* kinds as you need, lining two or three foil plates with it, instead of just one. A future 'quiche' or flan is about $\frac{3}{4}$ made when the 'case' is ready, while jam rolls and other simple dishes can be ready for the oven.

★ Some of the juice from stewed apple etc in plate pies, tends to seep into the pastry during freezing. Brushing the inner side of the pastry with egg white seals the surface and prevents this happening.

★ Frozen pastry must be allowed time to thaw enough to roll it evenly, otherwise it will rise unevenly. Like others however, it will rise better if chilled, than if at room temperature.

Hot Water Crust Pastry

Odd man out, as it sounds. Everything has to be warm instead of cold, otherwise it's almost impossible to manipulate. Few doughs are more quickly made.

QUANTITIES. You need 4 ozs (100 g) pastry for a small pie (see page 17) to serve 2, or 6 ozs (150 g) for a $1\frac{1}{4}$ pint (625 ml) oval loose-bottom tin, to serve 3, ie about 2 ozs (50 g) pastry per person. Proportions are $\frac{1}{3}$ fat to flour. Lard or cooking fat is the only fat which gives a raised pie (the kind like a bought pork pie) its characteristic texture.

★ You can't stop midstream to make the filling for a raised pie. This must be ready before you start to make the pastry, because the dough has to be rolled and moulded while still warm, before the lard has time to set, making it brittle and difficult to handle.

★ Use a wooden spoon to mix it – it's warmer than a knife – until cool enough to use your hands. The boiling lard and water partially cook the starch grains in the flour, forming this lovely-to-handle, warm, soft, pliable dough. (It's *quite* different from other doughs and rather greasy by comparison.) Knead it for just a few moments, until free of cracks and absolutely smooth.

★ Any pieces of pastry you cut off, say to make a lid or a second pie, should be kept warm in foil. Even then you need to work fairly quickly.

★ If you add an egg yolk, the dough cracks more easily, but the flavour is better and the pastry keeps fresh longer.

Puff Pastry

Called *Pâte Feuilletée* in French (pastry of leaves), because of the way it is folded and rolled so many times, to produce the infinite number of layers.

PROPORTIONS. Equal quantities of *butter* to flour. Margarine doesn't make good puff pastry. The texture of the butter is important because ideally it should be the same consistency as the dough, so that they will blend together evenly. If too soft, it keeps bursting through the dough when rolled, but if too stiff it won't distribute easily. The firmer they both are though, within reason, the more easily they will roll. If butter is too hard, press it with your hands in a floured cloth to make it more pliable.

★ Rubbing ⅛ of the butter into the flour makes the dough slightly easier to roll out, before enclosing the remaining ⅞.

★ You can't make real puff pastry without strong flour – it's a waste of time and materials with 'soft'. Only strong flour has the high gluten content needed to construct thin layers which won't collapse in the oven.

★ Rolling is done with quick short rolls, lightly but firmly backwards and forwards. If you *push* the rolling pin, the butter is likely to go sideways, and the pastry won't rise properly.

★ Relaxing between rollings is necessary for all the usual reasons (see page 100), and absolutely essential to keep this large amount of butter firm. Otherwise it will come through both top and bottom of dough, making it impossible to roll without using extra flour, which spoils it.

★ I find rolling and folding puff pastry seven times (in envelope form as illustrated on page 99), gives better results than rolling it four times in the 'double folded' method. The pastry is so thick the latter way that it's difficult to roll it evenly – and any unevenness is greatly exaggerated when *puff* pastry rises.

★ Good shaping when rolling – straight sides and square corners – is still more important with puff pastry than with flaky or rough puff, for the same reasons. It must be *rolled* evenly if to *rise* evenly.

★ The large amount of rolling toughens the gluten in the flour, and develops the strength of the pastry, counteracting the softening affect of so much fat.

★ A cutter dipped in boiling water gives the sharpest cut, and helps the pastry to rise best.

★ A vol-au-vent or patties are better turned upside down to cook, because the side which was uppermost when rolled, shrinks more than the side which was against the table – they'll be a better shape and less likely to topple over.

★ If one side of your oven happens to be hotter than the other – it shouldn't be, but sometimes is – the pastry at the hotter side rises more quickly than the other, giving yet another cause for toppling.

★ ½ lb (225 g) flour is the easiest quantity for most people to handle. It isn't easy to make a larger amount successfully at one time.

Rough Puff Pastry

A richer version of flaky.

PROPORTIONS. Are ¾ fat to flour. You need 6 ozs (150 g) pastry for a 1½ pint (750 ml) pie-dish.

★ Margarine and lard (or cooking fat) are

best mixed together on a plate with a knife while at room temperature, then refrigerated until firm, but not too hard. If you then toss walnut-sized lumps of the fat lightly in the flour, this makes the pastry easy to handle.

★ Add the water and lemon juice (see page 98) almost all at once – *all* at once if you're sure of the quantity, because this ensures an even texture.

★ Keep the edges and ends straight during rolling, and the corners square, to ensure even thickness when folding. After folding each time, seal the edges with the rolling pin to trap the air caught under the fold.

★ Rough puff is flakier than flaky as it happens. Because it's rolled more times, there are extra 'layers' to rise, with more air trapped in the by-going.

Shortcrust Pastry

Must be 'short' and light, but it won't be if you add too much water. 1 teasp to each oz (25 g) flour gives about the right consistency with *most* flours.

PROPORTIONS. Are half fat to flour, but of course you can make a richer melt-in-the-mouth version – *rich shortcrust pastry* – by using a higher proportion of fat to flour, and an egg yolk in place of some of the water. You need 4 ozs (100 g) shortcrust pastry for a 1 pint (500 ml) pie-dish.

★ If you shake the mixing bowl lightly after rubbing the fat into the flour, any remaining lumps will come to the surface. If the fat isn't properly rubbed in, the pastry may end up blistered.

★ Some famous cooks say that the water should be added by sprinkling all at once over the surface, to give an even texture and avoid blisters in the cooked pastry. I only know *my* shortcrust is better when I add it to a 'well' in the flour, because that way I can be sure not to make the dough too wet. I think it also distributes the water more evenly.

★ Once the dough has formed into a few large lumps, it's best to draw them together with your finger tips into one big ball, when the sides of the bowl should be quite clean. Then you can *feel* if the consistency is right.

★ Kneading shortcrust is quite different from kneading bread. It simply means drawing up the edges very lightly into the centre, to bring it to the required shape – round, square or rectangular – and to make a smooth even dough.

★ If you cut portions of dough off a batch of pastry to make different dishes, put the *cut* side uppermost on the board before kneading it to the required shape. It's easier to roll the pastry evenly this way, than when the pastry is cut side downwards.

★ *To roll a circle of pastry*, first knead the dough lightly into a round lump, then turn it upside down (smooth side up). Turn the pastry round little by little *each* time you roll – in other words avoid rolling it twice running in the same direction.

Suet Pastry

Needs self-raising flour, or baking powder with plain flour, because AIR isn't a strong enough raising agent when the fat is suet. The proportion of baking powder to flour is higher than for cakes, the pastry being hard and tough if too little is used. Using self-raising flour, there is less urgency to cook suet pastry as soon as it is made. It can easily wait an hour or so.

PROPORTIONS. Are $\frac{1}{3}$ – $\frac{1}{2}$ fat to flour, but $\frac{1}{4}$ of the flour can be replaced by fresh breadcrumbs if liked, to make extra-light pastry.

★ Fresh beef suet gives much more flavour than 'packet', but must be finely grated, as with a Mouli grater, to make it digestible. If coarse, you'll be able to see the undissolved lumps of suet in the cooked pastry – so you shouldn't be *surprised* to get indigestion!

★ A suet pudding – meat or sweet – will be very solid if not well protected from condensed steam during cooking. I don't know of anything quicker or more effective than covering it first with greased greaseproof paper – a butter wrapper is handy for this – and then with foil.

5

EGGS AND EGG DISHES

General Information

Eggs are packed with goodness, and worth understanding. They *look* so simple, and are such an everyday food that their complexities often go unnoticed. It is difficult to realize, because the shell hides an egg's changes, that they deteriorate if improperly stored, or with age, giving gradually worsening results when used to cook.

★ Because we don't know exactly when shop eggs were laid, although an egg box gives a good deal of information, anyone who has their own hens scores over every one else, qualitywise. Next best to having your own, if you can buy them, are fresh farm eggs: two fresh ones can be better than three, or even four older (or badly stored) eggs. It depends on what you're making.

STORAGE. *How* eggs are kept is of even more importance than their age. For instance, a week-old egg which has been kept in warm conditions is likely to be in a worse condition than a three-week-old egg which has been kept cool from point of lay to cooking.

★ It's on account of the air chamber (see below) that eggs are always stored point downwards, because they keep better when the yolk rests on the white, rather than on the air chamber. If the other way up, the yolk will in time press against, and stick to the shell; then soon goes bad.

STRUCTURE OF AN EGG.

★ *The shell* is not as elementary as it looks: it is porous so you should avoid storing eggs near strong-smelling foods like kippers or cheese. It also has an invisible protective coating, so if you wash an egg, you wash this off, shortening its life as you do so. If dirty, just wipe carefully, unless you're about to use it.

★ *An air chamber* at the *blunt* end increases in size as an egg deteriorates, either through age or bad storage conditions. When you boil an egg, the shell often cracks, as the air expands with the heat, so the staler the egg, the more likely it is to crack. It's easy to prevent a fresh egg cracking, by *giving* the expanded air an outlet: simply prick the egg at the blunt end with an egg pricker, see page 10. A thoroughly stale egg will actually float in a bowl of salted water, being so full of air.

★ *The egg white* is sometimes thin when an egg is fresh from the nest, most of it becoming thick and jelly-like by the next day. So it will remain for the next few days, then very gradually becomes thinner and more watery as the egg ages. This explains why, if you compare a fresh with a stale egg, each on a saucer, the former will be compact – with the yolk standing high, on the thick jellied white – while the older yolk will sink down amongst the spread-out, more runny white.

★ Before poaching or deep frying an egg, it pays, for reasons explained with each recipe, to examine it first.

A compact fresh egg. A runny, stale egg.

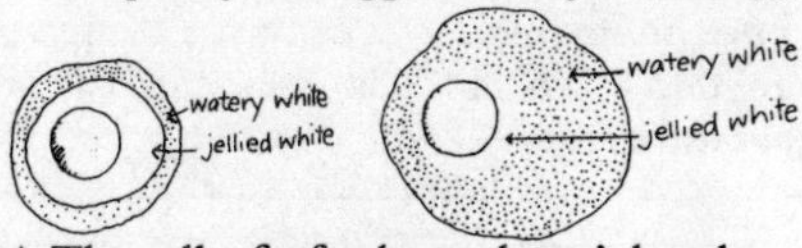

★ The yolk of a fresh egg doesn't break as easily as that of an older one when you drop an egg into a basin or pan. This is because the 'jelly' acts as a cushion for it to fall on.

★ Because of its glutinous nature, you can whisk egg white into a froth which is almost permanent. Fresh whites, correctly whisked, will increase their volume by 7 or 8 times – $\frac{1}{8}$ egg white, $\frac{7}{8}$ air – so is it surprising that something like a savoury soufflé will rise so magnificently without any other raising agent being added? If on the other hand you have oldish whites, is it any wonder that a soufflé may hardly rise at all?

★ *A membrane surrounding the yolk* is strong and firm when the yolk is fresh, but weakens as it ages. This is often why a yolk breaks when you 'separate' an egg – unless of course you're a bit careless.

★ *The yolk* is held and protected in the middle of the white by two 'threads' or bobbles, called the *chalazae*. To do their job, they cling so hard to it that you may actually have to break them off over the sharp edge of the shell, when you're separating the white from the yolk. They're a curse when it comes to cooking, because they are the main cause of curdling in cooked mixtures, and therefore the main reason for straining beaten raw eggs before making a custard or sauce.

COOKING.

★ *Eggs begin to coagulate* (set) at 140°F, 60°C – a temperature well below boiling point at 212°F, 100°C. Apart from omelets and fried eggs, great heat or long cooking make eggs hard and indigestible, which explains why they are 'boiled', poached or coddled at a temperature *below* boiling point, and why the best scrambled eggs are made over low heat. Most other kinds of food wouldn't cook at all at such a low temperature. It's not surprising then that such lightly cooked food is good for invalids, tiny children or old people.

★ Eggs are most easily digested – talking of people with a delicate tum – when the white is just set, and the yolk still liquid.

★ *Refrigerated eggs* are tricky to cook with because they crack easily when boiled – the colder the air is the more it expands – or curdle easily when added to creamed fat and sugar. It's better to keep most of them in the larder – and a few in the kitchen at room temperature, if you know you're going to be making a creamed cake or pudding.

★ If you aren't yet convinced that you will cook better with fresh than with ageless eggs – supposing you *could* get fresh ones – here are some more advantages:

(1) They have more flavour, which they pass on to any dish made with them.
(2) The yolk is more golden, so gives food a better colour.
(3) They make bigger and better omelets, lighter and bigger cakes, more and better meringues.

EGG WHITES. If eggs are fresh when you buy them, whites keep well in a covered container in the refrigerator for some time – you can even add to them day by day within reason. This is because they are virtually fatless – unlike the yolk – and contain 87 per cent water. You can also freeze them of course.

★ Egg whites can be used up in various ways besides meringues and meringue toppings:

(1) Meringues cuites, macaroons, coconut pyramids, royal icing, Crème au Beurre à la Meringue, fritters, or to make mashed potatoes lighter, or whipped cream go further, see page 239.
(2) To glaze sweet pastry – but they give no colour.
(3) To bind a mixture – but they give neither flavour nor colour.

EGG YOLKS. If eggs are fresh when you buy them, yolks will keep two or three days in the refrigerator. Either pop an odd one into an egg cup, lightly cover it with water and then with foil, *or* mix the yolk with one teaspoon water and cover closely with foil, to exclude air.

★ However you use up an egg yolk, it is always nutritious, and you never need wonder what to do with them. Here are some suggestions:

(1) Make a custard – baked, boiled or caramel. Whichever it is, it will be creamier, richer and better than when made with whole egg.
(2) Use yolk to glaze pastry, rolls or scones, etc, see page 44.
(3) Use for egg and breadcrumb coating – much better than whole egg.
(4) Bind a mixture, like fish cakes or beefburgers.
(5) Use as a liaison, to make soups and sauces thicker, richer and more creamy.
(6) Make mayonnaise or hollandaise sauce etc.
(7) Enrich creamed potatoes or shortcrust pastry. Make French flan pastry.
(8) Add an extra yolk to a ground rice or semolina pudding.
(9) Make French toast, see page 275.
(10) Make chocolate truffles.

★ Egg yolks are much less likely to cause curdling than the whites. This is the main reason why only yolks are used as a liaison in soups and sauces.
★ If you want egg yolk to form an emulsion with fat, as for mayonnaise, either liquidize it or beat it very hard with a whisk, to break it down to a condition when it will readily absorb the fat. It will take a minute or two by hand, or about 30 seconds in a liquidizer. The yolk will turn pale yellow.

EGG SHELLS. Are used in consommé and cleared jellies, because the impurities cling to them when the whites are whisked, heated and begin to coagulate.

★ Half an egg shell makes a much more efficient scoop than any utensil if you let a spot of yolk escape into the white when 'separating' an egg.

DEEP FREEZING. Eggs are one of the few things which don't deep-freeze successfully. This is because the contents expand like any other liquid, when frozen, and the shells crack. Worse still, eggs don't recover their natural state when thawed.

★ Two or three eggs mixed together – with a big pinch of salt to prevent coagulation – and stored in a covered container, are *more* successful, but even they have limited use. You can't use them for anything which calls for *whisked* or *beaten* egg.

Boiled Eggs

Aren't so ready to crack if you prick them at the blunt end to let the expanded air escape, see *Egg pricker*, page 10.

★ Eggs are 'boiled' – a misnomer – in *simmering* water over low heat, to prevent the white becoming tough and indigestible, as it does when an egg is boiled fast or for too long. By adding salt to the water, you make them boil faster, not slower, as many people seem to think (see page 88).
★ If you crack the shell at one end after an egg is boiled, this helps to halt further cooking if anyone is late for breakfast.
★ Use a frying basket when boiling several eggs if without a special holder, to lower into and take them out of the water all at the same time. Give them an extra minute or so too, because they'll cool down the water if in a small pan.
★ It evidently isn't *dangerous*, according to the British Egg Information Service, to use the boiled water for something else. If the shell's dirty, however, then things are of course different, so it may be this rather than anything else which has given rise to the opinion many people hold that such water was harmful. Apart from campers and others like them, anxious not to waste *any* really hot water, I can't see why anybody would want to? Used to make tea for instance, the water would be completely flat after such long boiling, so your 'cuppa' would be horrid.

Eggs en Cocotte

Simply eggs in ramekins. To make a quick light meal, it's more economical and usually quicker to cook them in $\frac{3}{4}''$ (2 cm) *simmering* water in a frying pan than in the oven:

★ Melt a good knob of butter in the ramekins, in the hot water, before sliding an egg into each. If you put another knob of butter on *top* of each as well, this helps

to keep the yolk moist, and avoids that hard skin forming.
★ 3–5 minutes is all they'll need to set the white without hardening the yolk, but the pan needs to be covered, to trap the heat.
★ Ring the changes by putting something tasty into the melted butter before you pop the egg into each ramekin – finely chopped fresh herbs, cooked chopped mushrooms, asparagus or shellfish etc.

Coddled Eggs

Look after themselves while you dress, or set the breakfast table.

★ They're just like boiled eggs except that you *cover* the pan, set it aside from the heat – to a warm place if possible – and forget about it for the next 7 or 8 minutes.
★ If you use an *Egg coddler* (page 10), the water has to be hot enough to penetrate the coddler, so they're usually simmered for about 7 mins rather than set aside from the heat – but instructions are usually given with them.

Easter Eggs

Are unique when dyed in the brown outer skins of onions, with a few coffee grounds, and a flower head or two as well, to vary the colours.

★ Prick each egg at blunt end, and wrap it – with coffee and flower – in the onion skins, inside a small square of white cloth. Parcel each up in a piece of newspaper, tie with thread and simmer them in a covered pan for 20 mins (25 if several) to dye well. Unwrap them when cooked, put straight into cold water and, to make them look nice, rub shiny with salad oil when cold. The colours can be so beautiful that it's worth overlooking the faint taste of onion and the rather tough egg. What matter if you never eat them, they're so ornamental – and just right for an Easter picnic.

Fried Egg

Will stay compact if you slide it off a saucer into a tilted pan, because the fat – if as hot as it ought to be – will set the white immediately. You need enough fat to baste the egg, so that it cooks top and bottom simultaneously. Fry an egg on one or both sides, as you like.

★ If you fry an egg in butter – if you never have, you've missed something – it shouldn't be quite as hot as lard, bacon dripping or oil, because butter burns at a lower temperature.

EGGS FRIED IN DEEP FAT. Are used mainly for an entrée, and should be almost egg-shaped if perfectly done. If you're anxious about doing them, use soft hard-boiled eggs instead, see *Oeufs mollets*, overleaf.

★ Deep fried eggs *CAN BE DANGEROUS* to cook – and *will* be if they're old and watery, because the hot fat may splutter and bubble over, just as if you'd poured water into it, not an egg.
★ The eggs *must* be very fresh, the yolk standing high on the jellied white (see illustration, page 107), so it's safest to examine each on a saucer first. You can only fry one at a time.

The egg will be oval, as it should be, if you slide it off the saucer, held close to the fat, into a whirlpool made by stirring the fat fast but carefully with a tablespoon. Keep it whirling until the white completely envelops the yolk – in a matter of seconds. The heat is so intense that each egg takes only about a minute.

Hard-boiled Eggs

Are surprisingly deceptive unless you know their idiosyncrasies:

(1) Prick them at blunt end, like boiled eggs, to prevent shells cracking.
(2) Put into boiling water, so that the yolk will set instantly in the *middle* of the white. If you bring them to the boil in cold or warm water, the yolk is gradually drawn to the side by the heat. A lop-sided yolk of course spoils Scotch, stuffed, or any sliced egg.
(3) 'Boil' the eggs 10 mins in simmering water, because they become tough and rubbery if boiled fast, or for too long.

(4) Put the eggs straight into cold water when boiled. This halts cooking at once, makes them easy to shell, and should prevent that unpleasant black rim forming round the yolk. The rim is due to a chemical change of the sulphur in the egg white and the iron in the yolk, but can also be caused by over-cooking, or by the egg being stale.

(5) Hard-boiled eggs are almost impossible to shell hot. If you want to *serve* them hot, the shells will come off more easily if you pop the boiled eggs into cold water for a few minutes first – you can always heat the eggs again by putting them into a basin of hot water for one minute.

(6) To shell an egg easily, give it a sharp knock, and then roll it gently between the palms of your hands, to crack and help the shell to come off in large pieces.

(7) Put shelled eggs straight into a basin of cold water, to keep them moist, if you want to prepare them in advance of a meal.

★ A vegetable mill chops several eggs in a trice.

★ Sieved hard-boiled yolk makes a gay garnish for a savoury dish, but it dries and discolours quickly.

Oeufs Mollets

These eggs – you can't really translate the name – can easily end up in the dog's dish, unless you know how to cope with painfully hot, squashy boiled eggs that need shelling.

★ Used particularly for egg entrées and as a substitute for 'deep fried' or poached eggs, they are a cross between a soft and a hard-boiled egg – the whites set and the yolks still just runny. It's important to try and choose eggs all of similar size, and put them all into the water at the same moment, because small eggs need exactly 5 minutes, 'medium' $5\frac{1}{2}$ and large, 6 minutes.

★ Instead of *trying* to shell them while agonizingly hot, pop them straight into a basin of cold water for a few minutes to set the white, and to make shelling possible. If you then tap them carefully all round with the back of a teaspoon or the blade of a large knife, the shell will come away better.

★ Put them straight into a basin of warm water if for a hot dish, or into cold if for a cold dish. This prevents the whites becoming tough, through being exposed to the air. If necessary, for a particular hot dish, put them into a bowl of *hot* water for one minute, when all of them are shelled.

★ If fragments of shell persistently cling to the white, it's usually quicker to wash off the bits than to pick them off.

Poached Eggs

Are tricky, and difficult to cook *successfully* unless the eggs are very fresh, with the yolk standing high on the thick jellied white (see illustration, page 107). Older or badly stored eggs are watery, and a watery white simply disintegrates when poached, drifting about in the water in uncontrollable wisps – unless you have a poaching ring to make things easier (see page 10).

★ Eggs aren't poached in a poaching pan, despite its misleading name – poaching is done *in*, not *over* water – and the easier if less professional way to do them is in a deep frying pan, or a sauté pan.

★ To cook them perfectly, the shivering (barely simmering) water should be deep enough to cover the eggs completely. If the water is too hot, the eggs will cook too fast and will be tough. If too cool, the white may not set. They need *about* 4 mins, to set the white lightly.

★ If you slide the egg very gently into the water, off a saucer held close to it, you can easily direct it into the poaching ring; or can control it at once with a wooden spoon, if loose in the water. Simply spoon the white gently over the yolk, until it sets, a few seconds later.

★ With a large frying pan, you can cook 3 or 4 eggs at the same time, but you may need to raise the heat slightly, to keep the water at shivering temperature.

★ It's easier to lift the cooked eggs out of the water in a draining spoon, than balanced on a fish slice.

★ If you're going away for the night, or

want a long lie-in next morning, you can if you like, poach your husband's breakfast egg the afternoon before: put it *straight* into a basin of cold water to halt its cooking, and all *he* need do, when he wants the egg, is put it into a basin of very hot water for one minute. If an egg is perfectly poached in the first place, it will still be almost perfect the next day – as long as it's left in the water.

★ Older eggs will sometimes poach better if first boiled 20 seconds. This usually makes the whites just firm enough to cling to the yolk.

Scrambled Eggs

Just don't have the same flavour made with margarine instead of butter. A creamy texture is their other important characteristic, so if you want them creamier still, use a dessertspoon of cream instead of milk per egg – or stir in a spoonful of cream at the last minute.

★ Scrambled eggs are best if cooked over very low heat, and stirred frequently, or better still constantly, if you can spare the time. If you cook them too fast, or overheat the eggs by leaving unstirred in the hot pan bottom, you'll end up with a leathery mass, not a soft creamy mixture which will almost pour out of the pan. Avoid overcooking too, because even while taking a plate out of the oven, they'll continue to cook in the hot pan.

★ Pep them up, by adding at the very last moment chopped chives, instant garlic powder, finely sliced chopped green peppers, or chopped anchovy fillets etc, and serve in bouchées, hollowed-out vegetables, or croustades, as a change from the time-worn hot-buttered toast.

Omelet, French

One of the most feeding meals you can put on the table within minutes of starting and no problem to make well, if you know the ropes. Serve the moment it's cooked, because it can become sad and leathery if kept hot. You'll enjoy it all the more for a light lunch if you serve some crisp rolls or crusty French bread and a dressed salad with it.

★ If not an omelet expert, you'll probably find it's easier to make two small omelets using 2 or 3 eggs each, than one 4 or 6 egg omelet, for two people. Small ones are often the lightest and best anyway.

PANS. To start with, you need the right-sized pan, because the eggs shouldn't be more than about ¼″ (6 mm) deep, otherwise they won't cook fast enough – they shouldn't be too shallow either. These are about the pan sizes required:

Bottom diameter				
7″ (18 cm)	for	2–3	large	eggs
8″ (20 cm)	,,	4	,,	,,
9″ (23 cm)	,,	6	,,	,,
10–11″ (25–28 cm)	,,	8	,,	,,

★ You should avoid washing an omelet pan – unless of course it's non-stick – because the eggs will stick more easily, especially if it gets rusty. Just clean it round with soft paper, or if necessary heat a sprinkling of salt in it *before* rubbing it out with the paper. See also *Pans, omelet*.

★ Lots of people have their own way of making omelets but these are the basic guidelines.

THE INGREDIENTS. Should be ready before you start to cook, because it's a one-minute operation when you do so.

★ *Butter* is best, giving an omelet its characteristic flavour, and preventing the eggs from sticking to the pan. Oil and margarine lack flavour, and margarine burns at high temperatures – unless clarified – *and* may make the eggs stick to the pan.

★ *The eggs* will make a better omelet if fresh and large. Just mix them lightly together with a fork, because they shouldn't be frothy.

★ *Water* – one dessertsp per egg – helps to make a light omelet. Milk on the other hand makes it heavy.

★ *Seasoning* is essential – plenty of it, to bring out the flavours.

★ *Flavourings* like finely grated cheese, chopped fresh herbs and finely sliced spring onions are simply mixed in with the raw eggs.

★ *Filling*, if any, mustn't be watery, and

should be in small proportion to the eggs. This is the way to ring the changes with omelets. Simple fillings, such as chopped mushrooms or tomato flesh, can be just lightly cooked in butter.

METHOD. From the time you mix the eggs until the omelet is on the plate, you only need one utensil – a fork. You can't easily give an omelet its characteristic formation with anything else.

★ The butter has to be very hot – likewise the heat under the pan. The right moment to add the eggs is when the butter's foam has almost subsided, and when the butter is on the point of colouring – but *just* before it does so.
★ Use the *side* of the fork, drawing it along the bottom of the pan, to draw the eggs from the sides to the centre, where they set, while liquid egg fills the gaps round the sides again. This is the movement which gives an omelet its almost 'veined' appearance.

★ An omelet should be moist, so will be better if you take it off the heat before the top is quite set. When folded, the undercooked part will be surrounded by the part which was on the hot pan bottom, which will quickly set it.

FOLDING AN OMELET. Shake the pan so that about $\frac{1}{3}$ of the omelet overhangs the edge *opposite* the handle. If in any other position, it's very difficult to turn out a perfectly shaped omelet.

★ Put the filling, if any, into this hollow, fold the overhanging piece back over it, and then envelope the filling with the remaining omelet in pan.
★ An omelet is traditionally kidney-shaped, taking this shape from the curves of the pan, in which it is now lying.
★ To turn an omelet out without doing contortions, put the pan down and change your grip, your thumb up the front of the handle, see illustration.

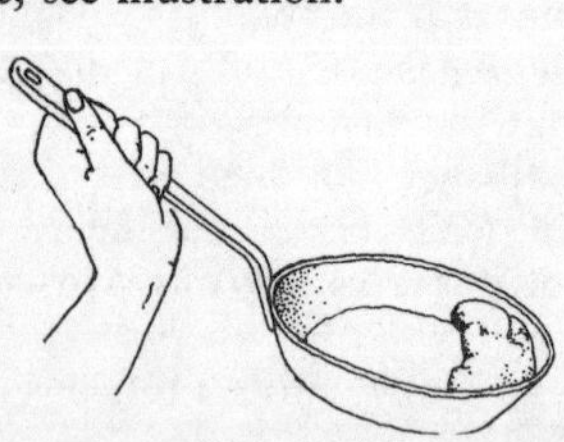

OMELET VARIATIONS. Vary omelets however you like. They're delicious filled even with such unlikely companions as fried onions and garlic croûtons (fried separately in butter). You can serve omelets *au gratin*, topped with whipped cream and a sprinkling of Parmesan cheese before grilling, or you can fill and coat them with a sauce, like Omelette à la florentine.

Omelet, Spanish

Is really made with finely sliced onion and chopped potatoes, which are fried in oil (preferably olive) and generously flavoured with garlic. In practice, people often make it with other cooked vegetables in place of the potatoes, it being a quick and tasty way of using up leftovers. It's a more solid affair than a French omelet and is served flat, cut into wedges, like a cake. (I'm afraid I like to fry the onion in butter, but that's not then a true Spanish omelet!)

Pipérade

This Basque speciality is neither quite French nor quite Spanish; neither quite an omelet nor quite scrambled eggs. It's a good recipe if you'd like it, briefly?

★ The quantities given serve 2 generously: in 2 tablesps olive oil sauté for a few minutes 1 small green de-seeded pepper and 1 small onion (both thinly sliced), 1 clove crushed garlic and 1 large tomato, previously skinned, seeded and chopped. Add 2 tablesps chopped ham, then simmer over lowest possible heat about 15–20 mins until vegs are tender. Stir in $\frac{1}{2}$–1 oz (15–25 g) butter, and when melted make very hot over increased heat. Pour in 4 lightly beaten seasoned eggs. Stir just two or three times, let the eggs set and serve very hot direct from the pan.

Scotch Eggs

Excellent with a salad for a picnic, or you can serve them hot or cold for a buffet lunch, or for a light lunch or suppery meal. Be sure to put the eggs into boiling water, to have the yolks in the middle of the whites (see page 109).

★ The sausage will crack if you flour the eggs too heavily – better just to dust them lightly.

★ Coat the eggs twice in egg and breadcrumbs for a perfect result. It's best to use *dried* breadcrumbs, not golden, because the latter would burn by the time the sausage is cooked.

★ The halved eggs won't stand up when served unless you flatten both ends of each egg after breadcrumbing.

★ The eggs will be firmer – and will fry better as a result – if you refrigerate them ¼ hr after coating.

★ The fat *must* be deep enough to cover the eggs completely, otherwise they'll burst. The temperature should be about 340°F, 170°C. If too cool, the sausage will burst and absorb the fat, or if too hot the crumbs will brown and burn before the sausage is cooked. Fry them without the basket, because the eggs will only stick to it, and the wire may break the egg and breadcrumb 'seal'.

★ If you're serving Scotch eggs on croûtes of fried bread, it's quickest to fry these in the deep fat too of course.

★ A fine stainless steel saw-knife makes it easy to cut Scotch eggs in half.

Soufflés, Savoury

Are either baked or steamed. Serve individual ones, if you possibly can, for an hors-d'oeuvre or savoury, using a large dish if the soufflé is for lunch or for a suppery meal.

★ Soufflés aren't really the feat which some fear, and others think they are – they're reasonably easy in fact. It may simplify things if you know there are two main parts:

(1) *The base*, a thick sauce called the *panada*. This carries the flavour, which may be something like finely grated cheese, vegetable purée, cooked mashed fish (not a watery tinned fish), minced or finely diced cooked chicken, or sweetbreads.

(2) *The egg whites*, holding the air which blows up the mixture and gives a soufflé its name. Large fresh eggs and skilful whisking to the correct stiffness, needless to say play a big part in the 'blowing'. If *over*-whisked, the whites are difficult to incorporate.

BAKED SOUFFLÉS. *The oven* must be preheated, because nothing much will happen to your soufflé if it isn't! Give it the oven to itself if you can, and be sure the temperature is right – ideally, *I* think, gas 5, 375°F, 190°C. If too hot, a top crust will form, which will stop the soufflé rising and prevent the inside cooking. If too cold, it won't rise properly either.

★ To rise perfectly, a soufflé should have heat simultaneously from top *and* bottom. If you put it in the middle of the oven, this avoids too much heat being concentrated on the top of the soufflé, and if you stand the dish on a hot baking sheet – pop one into the oven when you turn it on – this gives the instant *bottom* heat needed.

★ Don't be surprised to find your perfect soufflé has grown through the oven shelf above it – it *will*, if you don't raise or remove that shelf when you turn on the oven.

★ If you forget to preheat the oven, or if the telephone rings just at the wrong moment, cover the soufflé closely with an upturned mixing bowl. The mixture will 'hold' surprisingly well for 20 mins or more, providing the whites were properly whisked.

★ *The dish* is important, see *Soufflé dishes*. The size you need depends on the freshness of the eggs, and how well you whisk the whites, as well as on the quantities used. For a well risen soufflé, the uncooked mixture should come to within about ½″ (1–2 cm) of the top. The figures below are just a *guide*, because as I've said, so much depends on the eggs and the whisking:

2 large fresh eggs should well fill a 1 pt (500ml) dish

3 large fresh eggs should well fill a 1½ pt (750ml) dish

4 large fresh eggs should well fill a 2 pt (1L) dish

★ *The mixture* needs lots of seasoning, to avoid a soufflé being tasteless. (The whisked whites need flavouring just as much as the panada, so allow for them as well.)

★ Whisked egg whites can only raise a *light* mixture, so it's important to drain a vegetable purée well, before you add it. Soggy purée makes a soggy soufflé.

★ The panada to which the egg yolks have been added, should be just tepid when you fold in the whisked whites. If it's too hot, they'll start to cook before you can get the soufflé into the oven.

★ A soufflé should be firm when cooked, especially in the centre – unless of course you *like* it rather soft there? A slightly undercooked soufflé flops faster than ever once you take it out of the oven, but an *over*cooked one is hardly worth eating because, more than likely, it will be dry, tasteless and shrunken.

STEAMED SOUFFLÉS. Although basically the same as baked, there are some important differences:

(1) An oval or round (charlotte) tin mould is preferable to a cake tin because it has a wider top than base. When inverted, the wide part will be the bottom, so the soufflé is less likely to collapse. To ¾ fill it, you'll need about a 1½ pt (750 ml) tin for a 3 egg soufflé.
★ A band of doubled foil, or three-fold band of greaseproof paper to stand about 3″ (7½ cm) above top of tin is needed to support a steamed mixture when it rises: tie on tightly, otherwise mixture will run down the sides when it rises.
★ As a steamed soufflé is turned out, it's *wiser* to line bottom of tin, and essential to brush with oil or melted lard (or saltless butter) all inside surfaces, band included.

(2) A steamed soufflé is covered with greased paper or with foil to protect it from condensed steam during cooking.

(3) The base is usually *un*cooked; fish, liver, chicken or veal. Fish should be finely shredded, the others finely minced, then they're easy to sieve and will cook with the mixture. (You may find it quicker to pass the mixture through the sieve with your hand, rather than with a wooden spoon.)

(4) The pan must be full of steam (just as an oven must be preheated) before the soufflé is put in, then the most gentle steaming is essential: if the heat is too high, the soufflé will rise very rapidly like a blown-up balloon, then will collapse when that air is expelled. For good measure (or should I say bad measure?) a 'burst' soufflé is tough and close in texture.
★ Should you move the soufflé, or lift off steamer lid before the mixture has set, or should you *over*cook it, these are more causes for collapse. Reckon on about 40 mins – 1 hr to cook, firm to the touch in the centre. (When pierced with a skewer, the skewer should come out quite clean.)

(5) If you remove the 'band' and wait half a minute after taking soufflé out of steamer, this allows it time to shrink, so makes it easier to unmould. To unmould, allow the weight of the soufflé to pull it away from the sides of the mould, by moving it round very gently while slightly tipping it.

(6) It's best to hold an inverted dish over the top of a soufflé without actually touching it. Then carefully turn dish and soufflé over, allowing soufflé to slide out gently, holding the mould so that its weight doesn't press on the soufflé.

(7) A steamed soufflé needs a tasty sauce, otherwise it's both dry and uninteresting.

6

HORS-D'OEUVRES

General Information

Hors-d'oeuvre, translated, means 'outside the main work'; in this case before it. It should enliven one's appetite, never spoil it, so do be sure your hors-d'oeuvre *is* appetizing – fresh, light and attractive – and a carefully thought-out forerunner to the main course: try to choose something different in flavour, colour, richness and texture.

★ Hors-d'oeuvres fall into three groups, *Plain*, *Dressed* and *Mixed*. Although this chapter consists mainly of old favourites because these will give you the basics, you can be much more adventurous yourself, especially if prepared to explore the possibilities with fruits, salads and vegetables.

★ Here are some examples of each group. *Plain*: Asparagus, Globe Artichoke, Melon, Smoked Salmon, Whitebait. *Dressed*: Egg Mayonnaise, Prawn Cocktail, Ratatouille, Tomatoes in Aspic. *Mixed Hors-d'oeuvre* (Hors-d'oeuvres Variés): a selection of *at least* six, preferably eight different dishes (see page 119).

★ Ideally make and serve something like cheese soufflé or prawns in aspic in individual dishes rather than in a large one, so that everybody has a perfect and complete portion of their own, rather than an untidy helping. An attractively arranged individual hors-d'oeuvre, served directly on the plates, can in addition work wonders as table decoration.

★ You can *prepare* everything in advance for an hors-d'oeuvre, but it's best to assemble a dish at the last minute, especially if serving it chilled.

★ Serve thinly sliced and *generously* buttered fresh brown bread with those hors-d'oeuvres that need it. It's best crustless, cut into triangles or fingers; or you can roll up each slice like a baby Swiss roll. If you have one, use an electric saw-knife because rolls will crack unless the bread is very finely sliced.

Artichoke, Globe

Is a variety of thistle, cultivated for centuries in various parts of the world. Not many people seem to grow them in England, probably because ours don't compare in flavour with those grown in sunny climates; but they are decorative enough to grow in the flower rather than the kitchen garden, even if you never eat them! The hairy 'choke', or inedible part in the middle of the artichoke, would develop into a flower if allowed to grow.

★ Washed well under the cold tap, to flush out any grit, an artichoke will stand upright best if you trim the bottom with a sharp knife, rubbing the stalk with lemon juice, to prevent discoloration. Cutting the tips off the inner circle of leaves is to make the artichoke easier to eat.

★ Unlike most other vegetables, artichokes are cooked in water deep enough to well cover them, for anything from 20–45 minutes, according to variety, size, recipe or personal preference. A draining spoon is handy to lift them carefully out of pan, before turning upside down to drain.

★ In case you're not sure how to eat them, the edible parts are the *fond* (bottom) and the fleshy base of each leaf: detach each leaf separately by hand, dip its fleshy base in a butter sauce and draw off, between your teeth, the pulp.

Asparagus

If prepared and cooked properly, asparagus is one of the most heavenly of all vegetables, especially when eaten within an hour of picking.

★ There's a tender moist green stem inside each spear of asparagus, which lots of people never seem to find. You can eat the *whole* spear if, when preparing, you cut off all the lower, outer, hard skin; holding it as if sharpening a pencil, and cutting deep enough to bare that stem.

★ If you tie the spears in bundles near each end, either with cotton tape or string, this protects the tips during cooking, and also makes it easier to lift the bundles out of the boiling water without breaking the tips; a fork slipped under each tape.

★ If you have to prepare asparagus in advance, either refrigerate the bundles, standing them in a jug of shallow cold water, covered with a polythene bag, or wrap in foil, to exclude light and air. You'll need about 8–10 stems per person, according to their size.

★ Be sure not to boil asparagus too fast – the tips tend to break off.

★ *I* think it's difficult to improve on melted butter with asparagus, but you can, if you like, ring the changes with Beurre Noisette, Hollandaise, Maltaise or Mousseline Sauce (see Sauces).

★ *Cold asparagus* can be a mixed blessing if boiled and then *allowed* to go cold, instead of being *made* to go cold: 'refresh' it for one minute, to halt cooking, and to preserve its glorious colour and flavour (see page 54).

★ Tinned asparagus spears are tasty for a buffet meal, each one rolled in very thinly sliced new brown bread, spread generously with butter and home-made mayonnaise.

Aspic

The name of the pale coloured savoury jelly in which fish, meat, poultry and vegetables are often served. It is a classic garnish, used for some of the most sophisticated dishes because of its flavour, transparency, and ability to keep foods moist. In addition it makes a delicious savoury mould, or can be mixed with certain sauces to coat a huge variety of cooked foods served cold. If you just want a very small quantity as a glaze, or if its flavour will be masked by other stronger ones, you can easily get away with bought (to which you can add a little sherry to taste), otherwise it's much better to make your own. It is troublesome though because unless you're careful, it won't be crystal clear. Here, I'm afraid, are a lot of do's and don'ts:

(1) Have the pan, bowl and jelly bag scrupulously clean, never washing the bag in soapy water.

(2) Use absolutely fat-free stock (see *Degrease*, page 38).

(3) Cut the carrot and onion into largish pieces, then they won't break up.

(4) Peel the washed lemon very finely with a potato peeler, so avoiding the bitter pith you get with *grated* rind.

(5) Wipe the eggs before separating yolks from whites, and crushing the shells. All the impurities in the liquid (stock, water, vinegars and sherry) will cling to the shells like metal to a magnet when the mixture you're whisking becomes hot enough for the egg whites to coagulate. There's a snag though; if you don't stop whisking just before it reaches boiling point, the impurities will be released back into the liquid.

(6) Let the liquid go through the jelly bag without helping it, however tempted you are to press or squeeze, otherwise the jelly will be cloudy. Providing it is hot, it will go through, so *keep* it hot by standing a 'pyrex' type glass of very hot water in the middle of all the contents.

★ Here are a few *more* hints:

(1) An electric hand-mixer saves effort.
(2) If you boil the jelly bag just before using it, and also rinse the bowl out with hot water, they won't cool the liquid so fast – important if it has to go through the bag a second time.
(3) You can make a Heath Robinson contraption with a calico jelly bag and a large liquidizer 'jar': stand the jar (no other part of the liquidizer) in the clean hot mixing bowl, draping the jelly bag over the top.
(4) If you're surprised by the amount of gelatine in aspic, it's not a mistake. There *must* be extra, to allow for it losing strength when almost boiled. Besides, aspic is used slightly stiffer than a sweet jelly.
(5) Don't skip the 'soaking' time (about 10 mins) before pouring everything through the jelly bag: just as tea infuses in a tea-pot, so extra flavour is drawn out of *these* ingredients into the liquid.
(6) When using aspic as a glaze, it should be cold but *just* runny. Should it show signs of setting before you want it to, stand its basin in a pan of warm water.
(7) Use twice mayonnaise to aspic for *Aspic Mayonnaise*.
(8) Use twice 'sauce' to aspic for *Chaudfroid Sauce*.
(9) To chop aspic jelly, see page 45.

Avocado Pear

One of the most nourishing of all fruits, containing more protein than any other and up to 25 per cent oil. For good measure, it contains various minerals and boasts of Vitamins A, B, C, D and E – perfect for vegetarians.

★ An avocado should be soft without being mushy. If you've ever eaten one which *wasn't* ripe, you'll know what a totally different (and rather unpleasant) texture and flavour it has. Should you be wary of choosing them yourself, do buy from a reliable greengrocer.

★ To help them to ripen, wrap each fruit separately in several thicknesses of newspaper.

★ To prevent them becoming over-ripe, they'll store for a few days either in the salad compartment of the refrigerator or in a thick polythene bag on the floor of it.

★ A dressed avocado has more flavour if served chilled.

★ Freezing avocados whole is unsuccessful – better to freeze the purée: remove flesh from skin and mash to a pulp. Add 1 teasp lemon juice per fruit and season to taste.

Bouchées

If true to their name, bouchées are only a mouthful, the word coming from the French word *bouche*, mouth.

Broccoli, Purple Sprouting

This and *some* varieties of calabrese are almost as good as, and surprisingly like, asparagus if you cook, serve and eat it with your fingers in the same way, with melted butter or one of the sauces given with asparagus.

★ Allow about 6–8 ozs (say 150–200 g) per person, tie the sprigs together in bundles (the head, a finger's length of stalk and the smallest leaves), boil about 8–12 mins, drain well and serve piping hot. (Cut or slit thick stalks, as slender.)

Egg Mayonnaise

A quick and good prelude to various main dishes – it doesn't *have* to be dull. You can ring the changes by adding green herbs to the mayonnaise, by garnishing the coated eggs with capers and strips of drained anchovy fillets, or with shrimps or prawns etc. Alternatively, you can liquidize or finely chop asparagus spears or lobster before adding to the mayonnaise, while garnishes such as cayenne pepper, chopped chives, watercress, tomato quarters, or finely sliced cucumber or radishes will make a lovely colourful dish.

★ The eggs won't be tough if slightly undercooked: boil only 8 mins to make the white firm, but to leave the yolk still just moist (see page 109).

★ Served cut in half lengthwise and

arranged *round*-side up, they are easier to coat perfectly, look more professional when finished and take less mayonnaise.

Grapefruit

Their name comes from the way the fruit hang in 'grapes' or clusters. They may be as sweet and heavenly as the sweetest orange, or sour enough to make one's head spin, depending upon the climate in which they grow, their variety and state of maturity.

★ For an hors-d'oeuvre, they ought to be juicy, fleshy and properly prepared; which means knowing how to choose them – heavy for their size, firm and with a shiny skin – and having a grapefruit knife.
★ Cut just before eating if you want their full cargo of Vitamin C, or prepare at least a few hours before, to sweeten and mellow a sour one.
★ Eating a grapefruit should be neither a bath nor a battle. Here's one way of making it as easy as melon balls:

(1) Using an up-and-down sawing movement, cut all round between the flesh and skin of each half, sides first and then the bottom, taking care not to puncture skin at bottom, otherwise the juice will escape, then lift the whole lot out bodily onto a plate.
(2) Slip knife point between the segments and bitter white 'skins', easing out each piece of flesh until only core and skins remain.
(3) Replace segments in grapefruit just as they came out. (It may sound fiddling, but with practice only takes a minute or two altogether.)
(4) Garnish with a *maraschino* cherry, 'glacé' being wrong both in flavour and texture.

★ If you can stretch to it and serve it well chilled, a spoonful of liqueur such as Kirsch, Grand Marnier or Crème de Menthe, will give grapefruit some punch.
★ To freeze grapefruit, cut into segments (see *Orange segments*, page 85) and freeze in a strong, chilled syrup, or in dry sugar (page 91).

Melons

Belonging to the cucumber family, melons grow in warm and temperate countries and are of two distinct groups, *musk melons* and *water melons*.

MUSK. Those we know best are the *Cantaloup*, (named after the castle of Cantalupa near Rome, where it was developed in the seventeenth century) which is the round rough-skinned type with sweet flesh, varying in colour from a pinkish yellow to pale green; *Tiger melon*, which is similar to the cantaloup but has a smooth skin. They are both a good choice for an hors-d'oeuvre; *Charentais*, a small melon which has a delicious flavour and deep orange flesh; *Honey-dew*, which is sweet and fragrant, with greenish flesh not unlike a water melon. Use for hors-d'oeuvre, desserts and pickles.

WATER MELONS. They are smooth-skinned and very juicy, but their pink flesh has less flavour than musk melons.

★ Have you ever travelled through Provençe at 'melon time', the perfumed air even penetrating your car as you pass these road-side stalls? If only one could bottle it! Melons usually aren't *so* good in England, but carefully selected – the skin should 'give' a little when pressed at the stem end – and served chilled, the flavour can still be delicious. Could many things look more tempting and decorative on a dinner table than sliced honey-dew melon prepared quickly in the following way: cut flesh from skin, slice it in about finger-width pieces and arrange in zig-zag pattern, with a maraschino cherry and a crescent of orange on a cocktail stick to give a splash of colour.

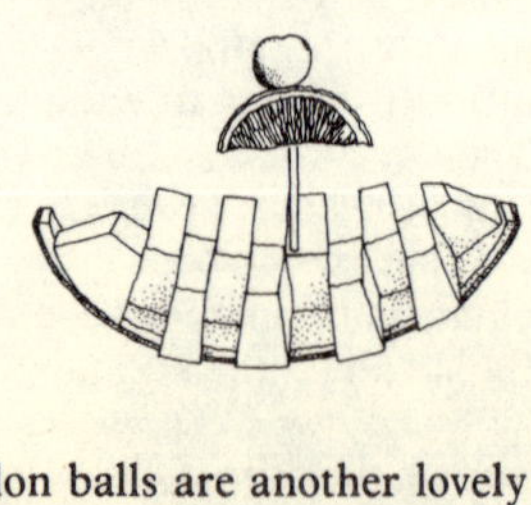

★ Melon balls are another lovely way to serve melon, will cheer anyone up and aren't much bother to make because the flesh is so soft (see page 3). If sprinkled with caster sugar and soaked about half an hour in a little port (failing which, madeira, marsala, sherry or kirsch), you can serve them in glasses as a fruit cocktail or, if made from a tiny melon, put them back in the skin. (If without a baller, cut the flesh into smallish even-sized dice.)

★ Do you like ground ginger with melon? It won't catch in your throat if you moisten it well in the melon juice before popping each piece into your mouth.

★ Melons are too watery to freeze successfully whole but that doesn't mean you can't freeze them at all. Slice the flesh, cut it into dice or make into balls as above and freeze either in dry sugar (see page 91) or in a strong chilled syrup, using 1 lb (450 g) sugar to 2 pts (1 L) water.

Mixed Hors-d'oeuvre

A dish one seldom seems to meet in people's homes, though I never know quite why. It's expensive and *can* be time-consuming, but doesn't have to be complicated – just carefully chosen, fresh, well seasoned and nicely arranged. It's supposed to be an appetizer, not an appetite killer – with at *least* 6 dishes – so serve rich foods in moderation.

★ If there are 6 dishes, it is usual to have two meat (one can be egg), two fish, and two (or more) others which can all be vegetable if you like: aim to serve something bland like rice salad or a salad of cooked vegetables; something raw like a salad of mushrooms, cucumber or tomatoes; and something salt like anchovy fillets or salt herring.

★ Piquancy is introduced with various kinds of dressings – mayonnaise, oil and vinegar, or cream dressing – while thinly sliced brown bread and butter rounds everything off.

Niçoise, Salade

See *Salads*, page 162.

Pâté or Terrine

Nowadays both names apply to the same thing when it is cooked and served cold. *Pâté en Croûte* is moulded in a pastry case and served hot or cold.

★ Fowl or game pâtés are usually made basically with pork, veal and the chosen game, the proportions of each depending on the richness or otherwise of the game. Hare for instance, which is dry, needs a higher proportion of fat pork than domestic duck, which is fatty.

★*Pâté Maison*, despite its name, isn't necessarily the speciality of a restaurant: you may find the same thing called *Terrine de Campagne, Terrine du Chef*, or in this country, *Pork and Liver Pâté*. Whichever the name, it is usually made basically from pork belly, lean veal and pig's liver.

★ To make a successful pâté requires a certain amount of know-how, so here are some tips:

THE INGREDIENTS. Providing the flavours blend and the final texture of the pâté is right, you can vary the proportions of meat and seasonings according to your own taste. The correct proportion of *fat* meat is the important thing, because with too little, the pâté will be dry.

★ For pâté to have the right texture, mince the meats finely together, twice. Warned in advance, your regular butcher (even possibly a supermarket) will probably be willing to do it for you.

★ Marinating the meats in wine, spices and seasonings for 2–3 hrs before cooking, makes the pâté more tasty because the flavours penetrate the meats better. Marinating (overnight) also tenderizes tough game.

★ The right kind of *firm* pork fat plays an important role, and comes from the belly or from the back of a fat pig (hog) next to the skin. When cut into dice, it is these wee squares of fat which are characteristic of a home-made pâté and, unlike fats from other parts of the animal, this particular fat doesn't disintegrate when cooked. In addition, it helps to keep the pâté moist and gives it a smooth light texture. Again, ask your butcher in advance, otherwise he may not have any.

★ Brandy helps pâté to keep well, in addition to giving flavour.

★ Breadcrumbs, if used, are to give a firm texture.

★ If you use bacon rashers instead of thinly spread-out pork fat to line the terrine, they should be very fatty and preferably not 'smoked', because the flavour is too strong.

COOKING. You'll need a $2\frac{1}{2}$ pt ($1\frac{1}{2}$ L) terrine (see page 25) for $2\frac{1}{2}$ lbs (generous 1 kilo) meat. If you use two smaller terrines for that quantity instead of one large, you'll need more fat to line them because there's a bigger surface to cover.

★ Avoid over-cooking. Pâté is cooked when it begins to leave the sides of the dish, and when the surrounding juices are clear yellow, not pink. Cooking time is determined by the *depth* and *shape* of the terrine, not the surface area. A narrow rectangular shape for instance will cook faster than a round or oval shape.

COOLING. When pâté is cooked, you'll save a mess if you stand the terrine on a large plate, to catch any overflow of fat and juices.

★ Compressing the pâté properly as it cools plays an important part in it acquiring the right texture. After removing lid, cover pâté with foil or greaseproof paper, then a *close-fitting* pan, pie-dish, casserole or plate. Into or on this put a 3–4 lb (say $1\frac{1}{2}$–2 kilo) weight. Allowed to cool completely in this way, preferably overnight, at room temperature, there'll be no air spaces in the meat, so the pâté will be easier to slice and serve as well as good to eat.

SERVING. Pâté is often served in its dish. If sliced in advance for a party, it *looks* untouched, but at the same time makes it easy to lift pieces out. Otherwise unmould and serve it on a dish, or directly onto plates.

★ Do remember to serve something of contrasting crisp texture with pâté, like Melba toast, fresh crusty rolls or French bread.

FREEZING OR REFRIGERATING? You can freeze pâté if you don't mind spoiling the texture slightly, but it's much better sealed and refrigerated. If you want to keep it more than a few days, unmould it when cold, wipe the meat jelly off the surfaces and it will keep well for some time: return it to the terrine then, and seal it with barely melted pure lard. (If too hot, the lard may penetrate the pâté.) Alternatively, you can unmould the pâté, wrap it in greaseproof paper and seal completely in foil.

Prawns in Aspic

Look mouth-watering if you're willing to spend some time on them, and make individually in dariols. If not, the quickest way is to three-quarters fill a plain mould with liquid aspic (page 116), adding the prawns, seasonings and anything else as the jelly begins to set.

★ After garnishing dariols or a large mould (see page 45), be sure to allow each alternate layer of prawns and aspic to set before adding the next, otherwise the prawns will float, landing up on the bottom when unmoulded.

★ Everything will glisten if you set a 'film' of aspic on the bottom of the serving dish and use any remaining aspic chopped, as a garnish. (See *Jelly, to chop*, page 45, also *Prawns*, page 175).

Prawn Cocktail

Really *must* be served chilled, in chilled glasses, to have tip-top flavour. This is definitely an hors-d'oeuvre to be assembled at the last minute, otherwise the lettuce goes slimy and the whole thing looks unfresh. The mayonnaise-based sauce needs to be piquant and well seasoned. Numerous recipes contain curry powder and something like Worcester sauce, while others may be flavoured with things like soured cream, fresh cream, tomato purée, lemon juice etc. Here's a quick and very tasty example, to serve 6, which you can prepare and chill at least two days ahead of time:

★ Mix together $\frac{1}{4}$ pt (125 ml) each of mayonnaise and tinned tomato soup, $\frac{1}{2}$ level teasp curry powder, 1 teasp Worcester sauce, 1 teasp lemon juice, salt and pepper. Pass them through a strainer to blend properly, pour into a jug, cover with foil and chill in refrigerator until required. Shred the lettuce finely (with a stainless steel knife) for prawn cocktail, otherwise it's difficult to eat with a teaspoon and in addition looks clumsy. Serve each in a wineglass on a small plate, preferably on a small plain doyley, to steady the glass, and put the teaspoon beside each, rather than on the dinner table.

★ See also *Prawns*, page 175.

Ratatouille

A ragoût or stew of vegetables, ratatouille is one of the famous dishes of the Mediterranean, everything tasting of the sun.

★ Although there are various versions, they differ more in the quantity of the ingredients used than in their content – aubergines, sweet peppers, onions, tomatoes, courgettes and garlic being the principals.

★ Dégorgé the aubergines and courgettes to make them less watery and bitter. This concentrates their flavour too, and prevents the stew being runny.

★ Use olive oil to cook it in the traditional way, but if you don't like it or haven't got any, use another vegetable oil. Ratatouille isn't exactly the right dish for slimmers!

★ Be careful just to sweat the onions enough to soften without browning them, because browning spoils the colour, and changes the flavour of the dish.

★ Serve it hot or cold, today or tomorrow, when the flavour is even better. Reheat slowly if serving hot.

Shrimps, Potted

Are finest when made with the tiny brown shrimps – if you can buy, and have energy to peel them. No other local shellfish are said to match their flavour.

★ Warm the butter, shrimps, spices and a touch of lemon juice just enough for the shrimp flavour to permeate the butter, without at the same time allowing the butter to become hot enough to 'oil' and separate.

★ Youngs Seafoods, famous for their potted shrimps, say the flavour of the shrimps and spices comes through best when you serve them slightly warmed; just until the butter melts enough to lose its hardened state. Arrange on lettuce leaves and serve at once, or if you have a fondue pan, warm them at table if you like.

Smoked Fish

A wonderfully easy and delicious hors-d'oeuvre, as long as it's fresh and moist. This means removing the skin of a fish like mackerel or eel at the last minute. Serve the fish – or half a fish if large – direct on the plate with some 'greenery' for colour, and a wedge of lemon to counteract the richness as well as to give flavour. Don't forget the brown bread and butter, and the pepper mill.

★ Have you tried serving smoked mackerel or trout *warm*? Some people think this is the best way to eat them: simply wrap in foil and pop in a cool oven, gas 2, 300°F, 150°C, for about $\frac{1}{4}$ hr. Horseradish sauce gives piquancy too.

★ See also page 177.

Tomatoes, Stuffed

Good either cooked or raw as an hors-d'oeuvre. The latter are often spoilt by a stuffing becoming watery because the tomatoes themselves aren't prepared properly. This is the best way to draw all excess juices out of them:

(1) Slice off a shallow lid at end opposite to stalk, and with a teaspoon to help, gently squeeze out the seeds and juice without splitting at rim.
(2) Cut out flesh and core, keeping flesh for stuffing.
(3) Dégorgé: sprinkle salt inside and turn tomatoes upside down in a colander or

on absorbent kitchen paper, to drain. Leave 15–30 mins before stuffing.

★ Here are a few ideas for stuffings, each to include any chopped tomato flesh removed from inside, seasoning and chopped herbs of your choice, especially basil:
Mayonnaise and cold cooked 'refreshed' vegetables (see page 54);
Mayonnaise and shrimps or prawns;
Mayonnaise mixed with sardine, hard-boiled egg, few chopped capers, chives and a squeeze of lemon juice;
Curry mayonnaise (page 137), and cooked chicken;
Scrambled egg and chopped anchovies;
Taramasalata type of filling (smoked cod's roe, olive oil, lemon juice, chopped parsley, finely chopped shallot and seasoning).

Whitebait

So called from their former use as bait, these are said by some authorities to be the 'fry' or young of the herring or sprat, while others equally categorically say this has never been proved. Whatever they are or were, they are an inexpensive luxury at their price. It's *time* they take, not money. You need about 3 ozs (75 g) per person.

★ If not dried thoroughly, or if you try to toss too many at a time in the seasoned flour, the flour forms a paste and all stick together in a mass. The secret is to keep them separate.

★ Shake off any surplus flour before frying in hot deep fat, 380°F, 190°C, for a few mins until golden. For tip-top results, they need frying twice: reheat the fat and fry them another minute or two, to become crisp.

★ Garnish with fried or fresh parsley, and serve well drained, piping hot and with a wedge of lemon to counteract their richness. Don't forget the brown bread and butter as well.

★ Speed things up if you like by thawing frozen whitebait in cold water. Bought frozen, they're good value.

7
SOUPS

General Information

Soup. What a warming welcoming start to a meal on a cold wintry day, or alternatively what a lovely cooling start it can be to dinner in summer time. Whether the homely 'filler-upper' for a light lunch, or the opening to a formal dinner, nearly everyone enjoys a good home-made soup. Imaginatively garnished and served with something scrunchy like fried croûtons, crusty French bread, garlic bread, newly baked dinner rolls, or perhaps Melba toast, who *couldn't* feel cheered up?

★ When choosing a soup, there are other considerations besides the occasion, weather, cost and time you can spend on it. Your choice should also depend on the richness, flavour, colour, texture and bulkiness (or otherwise) of the following courses – because soup must harmonize with them all.

INGREDIENTS. A well flavoured soup starts with good ingredients:

★ *The stock* is the foundation of the whole thing: the more gelatinous it is from meat, bones, fish trimmings (for fish soup), or whatever it is made from, the better its flavour and the better the soup. It simply must be fat-free as well, because nobody wants soup floating with grease (see page 89).

★ *Vegetables, meat or fish* should be very fresh and in correct proportion to the amount of stock used. Vegetables should be finely diced, shredded or cut into julienne strips, to ensure quick cooking, good flavour and easy eating. Finely sliced onions, shallots, leeks etc are usually sweated until soft without being coloured, otherwise they may spoil the flavour and colour of a soup.

★ *Butter* makes twice as good a thickened soup as any other fat, so use it and not margarine. So little is needed that the difference, spread over 6–8 helpings, is enormous in flavour but marginal in cost.

★ *Herbs and garlic* should be used with subtlety. A bouquet garni, containing extra herbs for a particular soup – say basil for tomato, tarragon for chicken, or dill for fish – can make all the difference to a soup's final flavour.

★ *Salt,* plenty of it, is a 'must', and so usually is pepper – or peppercorns, if ground pepper is likely to spoil a soup's colour. Without enough salt to draw out the flavours, the most exotic soup is hardly worth eating.

★ *Cream and egg yolks* make the simplest soups luxurious. There's nothing to beat this liaison for a smooth, rich, creamy, bursting-with-flavour soup. Use about 3 yolks and $\frac{1}{4}$ pt (125ml) single cream to each 2 pts (say 1 generous litre) of soup. Be sure to add a little of the hot soup to the mixed yolks and cream before adding them to the soup. This way, the egg is gradually warmed, instead of suddenly scalded, then binding and making the soup creamy and delicious. If by mistake you now *boil* the soup, instead of just reheating it, the liaison will curdle unless the soup contains a starch thickening like potato flour or arrowroot. (You may be able to correct a curdled mixture by liquidizing it in small amounts.)

★ *Cream* by itself, stirred in at the last minute, gives soups a glorious flavour besides making them rich and smooth. It doesn't take much to transform a soup. Have you ever experimented with single cream to invent your own versions of chilled vegetable purée soups, like vichyssoise? You may be amazed at your success. Simply stir about $\frac{1}{4}$–$\frac{1}{2}$ pt (125–250 ml) cream into 2 pts (say 1 generous litre) soup, chill it until the last minute, and sprinkle in finely chopped fresh herbs just before you serve it. Cucumber, pea, celery, tomato etc are all lovely.

★ *Soured cream or yoghourt* stirred into a vegetable soup at the last minute makes it piquant.

★ *Savoury butters*, stirred in at the last moment, can enrich and flavour many soups. See page 131 for how to add.

★ *Sherry* can do miracles for many a soup based on meat stock, like oxtail or kidney – or even in something simple like pea soup. It only takes the odd spoonful to make family or guests inquisitive. Sherry, after all, is often drunk with soup, so it stands to reason it's good stirred into it at the last minute.

★ *Wine* is the making of some soups, especially white wine in fish soups.

OTHER NECESSITIES. There's more to making a good soup, however, than just good ingredients:

(1) It isn't practical to make a tiny quantity, because so much is lost through evaporation; better to make it for at least 6–8 while you're about it.

(2) Simmer soups slowly, to extract all the flavour and goodness from the ingredients.

(3) The right consistency is important. Thickened soups should be 'flowing', not thick – just thick enough for diced vegetables, if any, to be held in suspension. Adjust a soup before you serve it if necessary, adding a little cream or stock if too thick, or a liaison if too thin.

(4) Take care that a skin doesn't form on top, or you'll soon have lumpy soup if you stir it in. If you keep hot soup covered with a lid or foil, there'll he no evaporation from the surface, which is the cause of skin. (A liquidizer will of course cure it.)

(5) A liquidizer purées soups in a jiffy, the result being creamy, smooth and delicious. If you find the texture characterless for some kinds of soup, try sometimes using a vegetable mill instead.

(6) If soup is supposed to be hot, then piping-hot in hot plates it must be. If on the other hand it's cold, keep it chilled up to the last minute at the bottom of your refrigerator.

(7) Soup is intended to stimulate the appetite, to help you digest whatever is to follow; not to *kill* your appetite for the rest of the meal. It's a mistake to serve too much.

★ Soups, very broadly speaking, fall into two main groups: thick and thin. The former may be thickened in various ways; with a roux or a starch such as potato flour, arrowroot or cornflour; by the starchy purée of a vegetable like potato; or very often with a cream and egg yolk liaison. Some very rich soups may have a roux base *and* a final binding of yolk and cream.

THIN SOUPS. These consist of consommés, and also homely soups like broths. The latter have a relatively large amount of garnish cooked in them. They are served without being sieved or liquidized, so the garnish should be cut into neat, even-sized pieces.

THICKENED SOUPS. *Purées* made with a vegetable base such as lentils, cauliflower, pea or potato, are usually cooked in stock, or stock and milk. It may not be traditional but I prefer to thicken these soups with a roux (*when* flour thickened), the flour stirred into and cooked with the sweated onion rather than mixed to a liquid with stock, and added at the end. The well-cooked flour gives the soup more flavour, and in addition there's no last-minute thickening to bother with, or danger that if careless, the soup will go lumpy.

★ In case you'd like the *basic* recipe for a vegetable purée soup, here it is – to serve 6 generously:

1 medium-sized onion
1 oz (25g) butter or 3 dessertsps oil
1 oz (25g) flour
2 pts (generous litre) fat-free stock, or stock and milk
salt and pepper
1 lb (450g) prepared *fresh* vegetables or 4 ozs (100g) *pulse* vegetables
bouquet garni
croûtons, fried, to serve separately

(1) Sweat (fry over low heat with lid on) the *finely* sliced onion in the fat in a strong saucepan for about 10–15 mins until soft but not coloured, agitating pan occasionally.
(2) Remove pan from heat and stir in flour. Return to low heat again and cook this oniony roux 2–3 mins, stirring occasionally.
(3) Away from the heat again, add the stock, very gradually at first as for a sauce, stirring in each addition before adding more. Season generously with salt and pepper.
(4) Bring to the boil (over high heat now if you like), stirring continually. Add fairly thinly sliced or cut-up vegetables and bouquet garni and bring back to the boil.
(5) Reduce heat to minimum, cover with lid (beware of a milky soup boiling over) and simmer until vegetable is tender, usually about 10–20 mins, according to type, or to thickness sliced.
(6) Remove bouquet garni. Liquidize, sieve or put soup through vegetable mill, and then reheat.
(7) Taste, adjust seasoning if necessary and serve piping hot with fried croûtons.

★ And here are a few tips if of any help:

(1) The thicker you cut or slice a vegetable, the longer it will take to cook, and the poorer the flavour of the soup – just like any overcooked *vegetable*.
(2) You can vary the proportion of stock to milk as you like: cauliflower, courgette or mushroom soup, for instance, are good made with equal quantities stock and milk; potato soup with $\frac{3}{4}$ stock and $\frac{1}{4}$ milk; pea, split pea or lentil soup with $\frac{7}{8}$ stock and $\frac{1}{8}$ milk.
(3) If a vegetable purée soup contains something starchy like a large potato (this of *course* includes potato soup itself), it probably won't need a flour thickening if you're going to liquidize it – and this sort of soup freezes splendidly.
(4) Liquidized soups are blended better and are lighter and smoother than sieved – but you may *prefer* the different character of a soup which has been sieved or put through a vegetable mill?
(5) If a milky soup 'separates' after freezing, liquidize it. Made with homogenised or Long Life milk, it *won't* separate though.

CREAM SOUPS. By and large, these are basically a purée of vegetable, fish, shellfish or poultry thickened with a béchamel or velouté sauce. The soup is enriched at the last minute with cream, or in the case of a velouté, with a cream and egg yolk liaison, using 3 yolks and about $\frac{1}{4}$ pt (125 ml) single cream to 2 pts (generous litre) liquid. Béchamel and velouté differ in that the former is made with milk and the latter with the liquor in which was cooked the fish or poultry. (It would be silly *not* to use such liquid since it contains so much of the flavour of the main ingredient.) A *vegetable* velouté soup can be made with chicken stock.

★ A 'cream of vegetable soup' is the sophisticated version of a vegetable purée soup. Although differently made, its main advantages are that it is smoother, richer, has more 'body' and is much more tasty. This is mainly due to the milk (for a béchamel based soup) being previously flavoured (see page 138) and to the presence of the cream, or cream and egg yolks as the case may be.

Artichoke Soup

Is one of the best ways to enjoy Jerusalem artichokes, either as a purée soup (page 124), or as 'Cream of Artichoke'.

Asparagus Soup

Needs straining if liquidized, otherwise it is 'stringy'.

Beetroot Soup

Made of course with raw beetroot for the best flavour and colour. Peeled and diced or cut into thin strips, say together with a sliced potato, it doesn't matter how much the beetroots 'bleed', because they'll be flavouring the stock.

★ A blob of double or soured cream in the centre of each serving takes away the 'dead' look of beetroot soup, doing wonders for both looks and flavour.

★ *Borscht* (or various other spellings) is the famous beetroot soup of Russia and Poland. According to one author, 'there may well be as many versions of it as there are Russians'!

Bisque

The sort of soup it's less costly to dream about than eat nowadays – so dream about it I do. Made usually with lobster or crayfish, and with wine, brandy, spices and cream amongst other things, could anyone ever think up a more heavenly dish than this?

Bouillabaisse

There are all sorts of variations, but the real and authentic soup is one made within a small radius of Marseilles. It originated as a simple fisherman's soup, made from several varieties of the day's catch, or its unsaleable left-overs, cooked in water or perhaps white wine, and flavoured with many of those heavenly products of Provençe, such as olive oil, tomatoes, onions, garlic, parsley, bayleaf and saffron. The classic dish includes fish only found in the Mediterranean.

Cauliflower Soup

A 'purée' or cream soup very few people seem to make, yet it's quick and delicious. It is just as good made with home-grown frozen cauliflower as with fresh, so you can make it all year round if you like (see page 124).

Chowder

Often with a milk base, chowder is a thick feeding soup, frequently made basically with fresh fish or shellfish, or both. Bouillabaisse for instance is a chowder. The name is a corruption of *chaudière*, a large heavy pot or cauldron used by French country people and fishermen to make their regional soups and stews.

Cockie Leekie

Is just what it sounds like; a soup made basically from an old cock or hen, and leeks. At one time this was a favourite dish of the Scots – probably still is with many families.

Consommé

The French name for meat stock which has been enriched, concentrated and clarified. Beautiful as it is, how *many* people will appreciate all the work and expense involved? Innumerable versions as there are, it's never the sort of soup you can make in a hurry. Like aspic, it must end up sparkling, whether you want to serve it hot or jellied. For the latter, be sure to make the stock with something like a knuckle of veal, which will *make* it gel; and give the consommé 12–24 hrs to do so. Taste it for salt too – cold foods nearly always need extra. See also page 116, Aspic.

Croûtons

When fried, croûtons make a vegetable purée or cream soup absolutely tip-top. Unlike *toasted* croûtons, which hardly seem worth bothering with, they garnish and enrich the soup as well as giving it a crispness. The bread-dice should be dainty, not clumsy, so that you can sip them off the side of the soup spoon without appearing to make a meal of them!

★ You can't look after anything else while

frying croûtons. If not turned over continually, over lowish heat, they're more likely to burn than to colour evenly. Shoot them all at once off a sheet of paper into hot lard, oil, garlic butter or butter – preferably clarified or saltless, for a perfect golden colour.

★ Drained well, first on the draining spoon used to stir them, and then on absorbent paper, a plain doyley on the small serving plate will absorb any surplus fat and ensure they won't be indigestible – unless of course the fat was only semi-hot when you shot them into it.

★ Croûtons are best when freshly made. If you're going to have half a dozen other things to look after however when making the meal, fry them earlier in the day, reheating in a low oven while the plates are warming.

Fish Soups

Those such as bisques or bouillabaisse are the real thing, but you don't need a deep purse to enjoy some sumptuous fish*y* soups. Instead of using white stock in purée soups like potato, tomato or pea, why not use fish stock (page 89) made from the head, bones and trimmings of the sole, plaice, halibut, skate, trout or other white fish you bought for lunch or dinner? It's a real loss to waste so much flavour and goodness.

Garlic Soup

The very thought of it may appal you. If you've ever *boiled* garlic though, you'll know that it loses all its pungency, so it isn't overdoing things to use a whole 'head' of cloves in soup for six people. Even though you're a garlic-lover, you may be unable to define its flavour if you've never had this soup before.

Gazpacho

A speciality of Andalusia in Spain, it is an excellent hot-day forerunner to a rich main course.

★ Its delight is in all the fresh vegetables: cucumber, sweet peppers, tomatoes, garlic and Spanish onion. (You *could* use shallots but not the average English onion because it's too strong raw.)

★ Served well chilled, with ice cubes in each plate, the other ingredients are white bread, olive oil, wine vinegar (preferably red), seasoning and water.

Lentil Soup

It may sound plebeian, but can vie with the most luxurious when made with the best chicken or veal stock, and served with fried croûtons. There's no need to steep the lentils, which will be tender after 20 mins simmering.

Minestrone

Means a substantial *minestra*, the Italian word for a thick soup, which derives from the Latin *ministrare,* to serve. In the days when there were great distances between inns, travellers often found food and shelter in a monastery. The monks, ready to 'minister' to them at whatever hour they arrived, would serve them at once with a meat and vegetable soup, which was kept simmering for the purpose.

★ Minestrone in England usually contains no meat, as it does for the agricultural and manual workers of Northern Italy where it may be served as a one-course meal.

★ Made in the Italian way (but without meat), there should be just enough stock to float the large mixture of vegetables and pastas (or rice).

Mulligatawny

An Indian soup by origin. The name is a corruption of the Tamil *molegoo tunee,* 'pepper water'. It is made with a boiling fowl or breast of lamb cooked in water until tender – with garlic, onions, herbs, spices etc. Rice and slices of lime or lemon are usually served as a garnish along with the meat, sliced small.

Mushroom Soup

Has more character I think when you *chop* the mushrooms finely, rather than liquidize the soup. Alternatively, use a vegetable mill. Frozen mushrooms make excellent soup because freezing concentrates their flavour.

Onion Soup, French

Isn't the sort to choose if you're short of time. It's not that the soup is laborious to make, but rather that the actual cooking is so long. It will only have its characteristic flavour if the large quantity of finely sliced onions are first sweated (to soften them), and then fried in butter and oil over very low heat until deep golden colour. This may take 1–1¼ hrs, stirring frequently.

Pea Soup

Can be made almost in a flash if you use frozen peas and have a liquidizer. It's twice as good if you stir in a little sherry at the last minute – and three times as good if you add single cream as well!

Potato Soup

As you may find I've mentioned elsewhere, potato soup has lots of character and flavour made with *fish* stock for a change.

Vichyssoise

Comes in my 'Top 5' never mind 'Top 10'. Basically the most humble of purée soups – leek and potato – cream and chives are the making of it.

★ Here's the recipe, to serve 8. Make the soup at least several hours before you need it, preferably the day before, to serve it well chilled:

¾–1 lb (350–450 g) *white* of leek (to make sure the soup is white)
1 large onion
1 oz (25 g) butter or 3 dessertsps oil (butter for better flavour)
¾–1lb (350–450g) potatoes
2 pts (generous litre) fat-free chicken stock
salt and white pepper (black pepper will spoil the soup's colour)
½ pt (250 ml) single cream
2 tablesps chopped chives
Melba toast, to serve (see page 275)

(1) Sweat (see page 59) the prepared and finely sliced leeks and onion in the butter until soft but not coloured, agitating pan several times.
(2) Add peeled and thickly sliced potatoes, stock and seasoning, bring to the boil and simmer until tender, about 15–20 mins.
(3) Liquidize, sieve or put through finest cutter of a vegetable mill. Leave to cool, cover and chill at bottom of refrigerator.
(4) On the day you're going to eat it, stir in the chilled cream, and at the very last minute (for their finest flavour), stir in chopped chives. Taste before serving.

Watercress Soup

Rather good if you've never had it before, but the watercress must be really fresh, you should cut off the thick part of the stalks, and the soup *must* be sieved (even if liquidized), otherwise it's 'stringy'.

★ I like to add some thinly sliced potato when making watercress *purée* soup, to give it a little more 'body', but there's no need for it in 'Cream of Watercress' because this gets its body from cream, or a cream and egg yolk liaison.

8
SAVOURY SAUCES

General Information

Sauces tend to be an absent art in English cooking, often spoiling the most expensive dishes either by their dullness or by their complete absence. What a waste! With a little bit of extra know-how and trouble, a sauce-minded cook can transform the simplest dish into a remarkable one.

★ So many people seem to think a simple white sauce (maybe with cheese, parsley or mushrooms, etc added) meets every need. How characterless – and how boring! Some will even wash down the sink those heavenly juices stuck to the bottom of a frying pan or roasting tin rather than use them to make a sauce or delicious accompaniment to serve *with* the food.

★ Lots of even quite enthusiastic cooks don't appear to realize that sauces can give endless variety to simple everyday meals, are a splendid 'medium' for using up cooked foods, enhance flavour, can enrich plain foods, or make rich ones more digestible. There is in fact little better or much easier than a good sauce to uplift something otherwise rather tasteless.

★ A sauce may sometimes be in direct contrast to the dish it accompanies, subtly blending two flavours in one. If 'partners' are traditional, like pork and apple sauce, or lamb and mint sauce, there's generally a gastronomical as well as 'tasty' reason for serving them together.

★ The 'egg yolk and butter' sauces, like hollandaise, and the savoury butters come into their own when there aren't any 'trimmings' with which to make a sauce, as for instance with grilled meat or boiled vegetables.

★ Flavour is what matters most. Good stock scores over poor, butter over margarine, 'béchamel milk' (page 139) over ordinary milk, wine vinegar over malt, fresh herbs over dried.

★ Roux, liaisons and stock are discussed in earlier chapters, all playing their part in good sauce-making.

★ The right consistency follows close behind good flavour, because however good the sauce, you can ruin it by making it either too stodgy or too runny. It's child's play to adjust a thick sauce with extra stock, milk, or perhaps cream, but it's more bothersome to correct a thin one. This may involve using a liaison such as beurre manié, fécule, or egg yolk and cream, or it may be better to 'reduce' it by evaporation.

★ If a sauce thins out during cooking, this is caused by a chemical change in the flour used to make it, when a sauce cooks too long.

★ Lumpy sauces can often be corrected in a liquidizer. If without one of those marvellous gadgets, then you'll have to whisk the sauce vigorously (preferably with a balloon or wire whisk), or pass it through a sieve and simmer it a few minutes.

★ If a skin forms on top of a sauce kept hot, this is due to evaporation from the surface, and can be prevented in various ways:

(1) Float a film of stock over the top of brown sauces, or of white sauces made with stock, eg velouté based sauces.
(2) Float a film of milk or melted butter over white sauces made with milk.
(3) Cover a sauce closely with a disc of foil, or wet greaseproof paper, and then with the pan lid.

★ A bain-marie (page 2) is invaluable to keep sauces hot or warm, as necessary, especially sauces which 'separate' if overheated, like the egg yolk and butter ones.
★ Apart from a number of unrelated miscellaneous sauces such as apple, bread, horseradish, tomato etc., the classic French sauces largely belong to 6 definite groups. As long as you know how to make the basic or 'Mother Sauce' of each group therefore, you can make dozens of others without difficulty. The technique remains the same, while varied ingredients and trimmings are added or changed, to give a different flavoured sauce with a different name, suitable for all kinds of fish, meat, poultry or game. The *family tree* on page 132/3 shows how simple it in fact is.

Apple Sauce

Add a pinch of ground cinnamon, or some finely chopped chives or mint to make an interesting variation.

Béchamel Sauce

See page 138.

Bread Sauce

Tastes good if you flavour the milk first, by heating it slowly with the onion (stuck with cloves) and a small piece of bayleaf. When nearly boiling, and infused, take out the flavourings and add the breadcrumbs, butter and seasoning. To give the sauce extra last-minute flavour, add a spoonful of cream and a pinch of cayenne.

★ It's worth remembering that if you're over-generous with the breadcrumbs (failing to weigh them or measure the milk), simmer the sauce more than 3 or 4 mins, or keep it hot long after it's made, you'll end up with a poultice, not a sauce. You need 2 ozs (50 g) breadcrumbs to $\frac{1}{2}$ pt (250 ml) milk.

Brown Sauce

Can take either several hours to make, about an hour, or about 5 mins, (if you have some good stock at hand), according to the method. Demi-glace Sauce, itself based on a sauce base called an Espagnole, is the traditional 'Mother' of the brown sauces, but the Espagnole is such a performance, so specialized and so little used except by the professional that I'm only mentioning, not describing it.

★ A simple roux-based sauce is much quicker, or it's quicker still to thicken a really good brown stock with a starch such as potato flour, arrowroot, cornflour or rice flour.

ROUX-BASED BROWN SAUCE. *Brown stock* is necessary, for its strong flavour and basically dark colour. If the sauce is to be fat-free, the stock certainly has to be.

★ *The fat* can be oil, cooking fat or clarified dripping – or saltless or clarified butter if the sauce is accompanying something with a delicate flavour. If you use any old dripping, or unclarified salted butter, it may burn during the long cooking of the roux, spoiling both the colour and flavour of the sauce. See *Roux*.
★ *The vegetables* – onion, carrot, celery – should be finely diced, to extract all their flavour. If you sauté them gently in the fat before making the roux, the sauce will have much more flavour than it would have by adding them to the liquid later, *un*fried. After making and simmering the sauce as your recipe directs, you'll extract flavour from the vegetables if, when straining the sauce, you lightly press their juices out.
★ *A bouquet garni* simmered in the sauce gives subtle flavour. A herbless sauce is a characterless one.
★ The made sauce, degreased if necessary, can now of course be used just as it is, or you can use it as the base for the

brown sauces on Family Tree, page 132.
★ You may just as well make extra if you have a freezer, then it's there when you want it.

STARCH-THICKENED BROWN SAUCE. *The brown stock* should be tiptop as well as fat-free because this sauce is simply thickened stock, and is only good if the stock is good. See *Stock*.

★ *Starch thickening*. Potato flour or cornflour are generally used unless the sauce needs to be very clear, when arrowroot is better. A sauce made with cornflour needs to simmer a few minutes longer than one made with either of the other two thickenings, to cook it, as well as to thicken the sauce lightly.
★ If 2 or 3 tablesps port or Madeira are added for extra flavour, the sauce is simmered 2 or 3 minutes, to evaporate the alcohol.
★ As for a roux-based brown sauce, this sauce can form the base of the brown sauces on the family tree, page 132.

Butters, Savoury

One of the easiest yet most delicious ways of flavouring food that I can think of. I love having a selection of them in the freezer, to use in any of the ways described below.

★ Individual recipes, if necessary at all, may vary slightly, but basically all you have to do is cream some butter and seasoning together until soft enough to blend with the flavouring of your choice. This may include such things as crushed garlic, finely chopped herbs, French mustard, finely sliced shallot, cut-up shellfish, juiced and seeded tomato flesh, anchovies or wine (see Family Tree). You can use a *combination* of these flavours if you like; say mustard and parsley, or garlic and tomato. If you're in too much of a hurry to cream the butter properly, simply make sure it is soft and squash it on a chopping board with a round-ended knife, then blend the flavour with it; gradually if something moist like mustard. (A liquid flavouring such as wine, previously flavoured and reduced, needs blending in a bowl of course.)
★ Here are some ways to use them:

TO ADD FLAVOUR, RICHNESS AND MOISTURE TO GRILLED FISH, MEAT, POACHED EGGS ETC. Put a pat of chilled savoury butter on top of each piece of fish or meat just before taking it to table. The food must be hot enough to melt the butter before you eat it, so that its flavour is spread everywhere. Anyway, who wants to eat a lump of chilled butter?

★ The sort of butters you may want to use include anchovy (for fish dishes), Bercy, Colbert, herbs, horseradish, garlic, Maître d'hôtel, Marchand de vins, mustard, tarragon or tomato.

TO ENRICH SAUCES. Cut the *soft* savoury butter into small pieces, and stir it into the boiling hot sauce aside from the heat, just before serving it. If added over heat, or if the sauce is re-boiled, the butter will 'oil' and lose its flavour.

★ $\frac{1}{4}$–$\frac{1}{2}$ oz (say 10–15 g) butter will flavour $\frac{1}{2}$ pt (250 ml) of, say, simple white sauce. If the sauce then *has* to be kept hot, use a bain-marie.
★ Butters to use include anchovy (for a fish sauce), Bercy (white sauces), garlic, Marchand de vins (brown sauces), mustard, shallot, shellfish (shellfish sauces), tomato (white sauces) or tarragon.

TO ENRICH SOUPS. Add the savoury butter as for sauces, above. Butters to use include garlic, shallot, shellfish (bisques, and tinned or frozen shellfish soups), tarragon or tomato.

TO TOSS WITH BOILED VEGETABLES. Chive, garlic, mint, parsley or tomato butter are good with certain vegetables.

TO BASTE FISH, MEAT, TOMATOES OR MUSHROOMS ETC WHILE BAKING OR GRILLING. Butters to use include chive, garlic, mustard, tarragon – or anchovy butter for fish.

TO GARNISH APPETIZERS, COLD DISHES AND CANAPÉS. if you want to pipe a savoury butter, it will need sieving – and possibly also chilling slightly if too soft to use. If on the other hand you want

*Mother Sauces** (Indicating, unless obvious, the essential characteristic of different sauces)

	White	Brown
**Béchamel Sauce*	**Velouté Sauce*	**Brown Sauce*
ANCHOVY	ALLEMANDE (egg yolks and butter or cream)	BERCY (white wine and shallots)
AURORE (tomato)	AURORE (tomato)	BIGARADE (bitter orange)
CAPER	BERCY (white wine and shallots)	BOURGIGNONNE (red wine, mushroom and onions)
CARDINAL (lobster)	CHAUD-FROID, White (aspic or gelatine)	CHASSEUR (white wine, mushrooms and shallots
CRÈME (cream)	FENNEL (Allemande + fennel)	CHAUD-FROID, Brown (aspic or gelatine)
CURRY	HONGROISE (Suprême + paprika)	DIABLE (white wine, very peppery)
EGG	NORMANDE (white wine, for fish)	DUXELLES (mushrooms)
MORNAY (cheese)	PARISIENNE (another name for Allemande)	ITALIENNE (mushrooms, ham and herbs)
MUSTARD	POULETTE (Allemande + shallots and mushrooms)	LYONNAISE (onion, white wine)
POULETTE (shallots, mushrooms, egg yolks and cream)	RAVIGOTE (white wine, onions, herbs)	MADEIRA
RAVIGOTE (white wine, onions, herbs)	SUPRÊME (cream)	ORANGE
SOUBISE (onion purée)	TARRAGON	PIQUANTE (Diable + pickles and capers)
TARRAGON	VIN BLANC	POIVRADE (peppery)
		ROBERT (onions, mustard)
		TARRAGON
		VENISON (poivrade + red currant jelly and cream)

Egg yolk and butter Sauces	Egg yolk and oil Sauces	Oil and vinegar Sauces	Flavoured butters
**Hollandaise Sauce*	**Mayonnaise*	**French Dressing*	*(1) Savoury butters*
BÉARNAISE (white wine, shallots, tarragon)	AÏOLI (garlic)	ANCHOVY	ANCHOVY
CHORON (Béarnaise + tomato)	ANDALOUSE (tomato, sweet red pepper)	AURORE (tomato)	BERCY (white wine, shallots)
COLBERT (Béarnaise + meat glaze)	CARDINAL (lobster)	CREAM	COLBERT (tarragon, meat flavouring
MALTAISE (orange)	CHANTILLY (whipped cream)	MARSEILLAISE (garlic)	EGG YOLK
MOUSSELINE (whipped cream)	COLLIOURE (anchovies)	MINT	GARLIC
NOISETTE (browned butter)	CURRY	MUSTARD	HERB
PALOISE (Béarnaise, with mint instead of tarragon)	FINES HERBES (chervil, chives, parsley, tarragon)	RAVIGOTE (onion, herbs, capers)	HORSERADISH
VIN BLANC	INDIENNE (curry)		MAÎTRE D'HÔTEL (parsley, lemon juice)
	REMOULADE (anchovies, pickles, capers, herbs)		MARCHAND DE VINS (shallot butter with red wine
	TARTARE (pickles, capers, herbs)		MUSTARD
	VERTE (green herbs)		PAPRIKA
			SHALLOT
			SHELLFISH
			TARRAGON
			TOMATO
			(2) Hot butter Sauces
			BEURRE BLANC (shallots, wine)
			BEURRE AU CITRON (lemon)
			BEURRE NOIR (or NOISETTE) (browned butter)
			MELTED BUTTER

fancy shapes, spread it fairly thinly but evenly on a plate, refrigerate it until hard, then cut with a cutter dipped in boiling water.

★ Butters suitable for garnishing include anchovy, egg yolk, paprika, sardine, shellfish or tomato.

TO FILL HARD-BOILED EGGS OR TO USE AS A QUICK SANDWICH SPREAD. Butters to use include anchovy, egg yolk, sardine, shellfish or tomato.

Butter Sauces, Hot

Serve them with fish, chicken or turkey breasts, asparagus, sprouting broccoli, or poached or fried eggs. These are some of the quickest and easiest sauces.

★ The important thing is just to melt and warm the butter with the seasoning, not to overheat it – because it then 'oils' and loses flavour.

★ A few drops of lemon juice added at the last moment, help to counteract the richness..

BEURRE NOIR. This is really a misnomer because if allowed to become black, it will be burnt. See Family Tree, page 133.

★ A good beurre noir should be clear, unspeckled, and golden nut-brown; and needs to be made with clarified butter because the milk solids in ordinary butter turn black and bitter.

★ Use for certain egg dishes, calf's brains, fish (especially skate), chicken breasts and some vegetables.

Deglazing Sauce, Brown

An incredibly simple, useful, delicious and quickly made brown sauce using the coagulated juices left, after straining off any excess fat, from foods cooked in a roasting tin, sauté pan or frying pan. It's perfect with something like say, roast chicken or steaks.

★ All you need do is add wine or stock to the pan, scrape into and dissolve in it these tasty crispy bits, then 'reduce' the liquid until syrupy. If, aside from the heat, you then stir in a little softened, cut-up lump of *butter*, it will act as a slight liaison as well as flavouring and making the sauce creamy.

★ To make even better still, if the flavour goes well with the dish the sauce is accompanying, fry a little sliced shallot or spring onion in a spoonful of retained fat, before pouring the wine or stock into the pan.

Gravy

Originally this meant only the natural concentrated juices which come out of a roast. Nowadays the word is more loosely used, indicating in addition a sauce made from them. It's made in the tin in which the meat, poultry or game has been cooked, largely (if not of course sometimes entirely) from these juices extracted during cooking.

★ Serve *thick* gravy with a *stuffed* roast, thin with others, for the simple reason that these make the best partners when it comes to eating them.

★ It's quite tricky to make good gravy so here are a few tips:

(1) You need stock (made from the giblets, if a bird), a stock cube or vegetable cooking water, such as onion or potato.

(2) The sediment, meat juices and tasty crisp brown bits stuck to the tin and caught by the sieve when straining off the fat, are a gravy's essential flavourings. Without them, your gravy will be tasteless and characterless.

(3) Be sure to cook the roux (fat and flour) for 2 or 3 mins if you're using flour to thicken it, scraping into it with a metal spoon all those tasty bits stuck to the tin.

(4) Make sure a thick gravy is just thick, not coating consistency! Use 1 oz (25 g) flour and 1 tablesp of the fat to 1 pt (500 ml) stock.

(5) Taste your gravy, seasoning it generously with salt and pepper.

(6) Use a few drops of a good gravy browning to colour it if necessary. At all costs *avoid* using a flavoured gravy

powder, unless you like every gravy to taste of that and nothing else.

(7) Before serving in a sauce-boat, skim off any fat that rises to the surface.

Hollandaise Sauce

A 'warm' relation of mayonnaise, the difference being that hollandaise is a lemon-flavoured emulsion of *butter* and egg yolks, while mayonnaise is an emulsion of *oil* and egg yolks.

★ Simple flavourings like finely chopped herbs or purέed asparagus tips can be stirred into it, and the classic sauces on page 133 (see Family Tree), are only slight variations of this, the 'Mother Sauce' of its group.

★ Anyone can make it in a liquidizer, it's so easy, though the texture is *slightly* different from hand-made, which is slower and more chancy for a beginner.

★ However you make it, hollandaise is served lukewarm, preferably the moment it's made. If it has to be kept warm, but is in fact *heated*, it will thin out and curdle. It will 'hold' for some time in a sauceboat, standing in a pan of warm water – the water replaced as it cools – or in a pan in a bain-marie containing lukewarm water.

★ If too thick, thin it down with a tablespoon of cream or hot water, but it *is* a thick sauce.

MADE IN A LIQUIDIZER. *The butter* should be cut into small pieces and heated in a small saucepan until foaming hot, but not coloured. A smaller amount is used than when making the sauce by hand, because the emulsion becomes so thick that the cutters can't rotate. You can slowly beat in some extra butter later though, if you transfer the sauce to a bowl.

★ *The egg yolks* should be at room temperature, fresh, and free of all egg white, including chalazae, to avoid risk of curdling. Liquidize them with the strained lemon juice and seasoning at maximum speed for 30 seconds, to break down and so prepare them to absorb the butter.

★ With liquidizer at maximum speed, and the central cap removed, you can now pour in the hot butter, in a very thin steady stream – there's no need to add it drop by drop, as long as the yolks were well liquidized in the first place. (Beware of the mess if your liquidizer has no central cap, and you have to take the whole lid off.)

★ If the yolks and butter do fail to emulsify, pour the mixture into a jug and add it gradually to the liquidizer again, *very* slowly to start with. As the butter cools, it should begin to cream and will form itself into a thick sauce.

MADE BY HAND. There are numerous ways to do it but all must accomplish the same result, that of forcing egg yolks to absorb butter and hold it in creamy suspension.

★ *The egg yolks* should be fresh, at room temperature, and free of all the white, including chalazae, otherwise the sauce may curdle. The smaller the yolks, the less butter they will absorb, one yolk taking about 2–3 ozs (50–75 g) butter. It's easier to make a sauce with 2 or 3 yolks than just one, because there is more yolk to beat, initially.

★ If you beat the yolks with a small wire whisk for at *least* a minute, until thick in consistency and pale yellow in colour, they will absorb the butter much more readily. Beating them for a further ½–1 minute when the lemon juice is added, is an extra precaution worth taking.

★ For the yolks to thicken into a smooth cream, slow and *gradual* heating is essential. They will become granular if the heat is too sudden, scrambled if over-cooked. Stir them over the lowest possible direct heat, or in a bain-marie, with lukewarm water to start, raising the temperature of the water gradually to 'shivering'. Watch out! If you don't heat the water, the yolks won't thicken, but if you let it get *too* hot, the sauce will curdle.

★ If you've never made hollandaise before, and are wary of overheating the yolks, it pays to run some cold water into the sink before you begin, so that you can plunge the bottom of the pan into it at the slightest sign of curdling. This will cool the yolk instantly, even more so if you beat them as well. When recovered,

return pan to heat and carry on as before.
★ *The butter* is always added *gradually* to the yolks, otherwise they can't absorb it, and won't emulsify. Each addition should be completely incorporated before adding any more. If your recipe tells you to add cold butter to heated creamy yolks, the purpose is to cool the yolks immediately, and stop their cooking.
★ Melted butter, if called for, implies *melted*, not *hot* butter.

CURDLED HOLLANDAISE SAUCE. Can sometimes be rectified by beating in a tablespoon of cold water. Failing this, and using a small wire whisk, beat a tablespoon of the sauce with a teasp of lemon juice in a warmed basin until they thicken, then beat in remaining sauce, just one dessertspoon at a time.

LEFT-OVER HOLLANDAISE. Can be refrigerated for a short time, or you can pop it in the freezer if you like. To use again as hollandaise, beat a tablespoon or two of it in a pan standing in a bain-marie containing hottish water, then gradually beat in the remainder, a spoonful at a time. Alternatively, you can use it to enrich a béchamel or velouté sauce. Simply beat it into the sauce, a tablespoon at a time, aside from the heat, just before serving it. Avoid boiling the sauce because the butter will 'oil' and lose its flavour.

Mayonnaise

According to one theory, mayonnaise may take its name from the very old French word *moyeu*, meaning yolk of egg. According to another it comes from *mahonnaise*, celebrating the capture of Mahon, in Minorca, in 1756.

★ Mayonnaise, the 'Mother Sauce' of the 'Egg Yolk and Oil Sauces' (see page 133, Family Tree) is the best possible reason for having a liquidizer. A tricky and long operation by hand if you've never made it before, even an inexperienced cook can conjure up mayonnaise in the space of a few minutes with a model which will run at *low speed*.
★ Making mayonnaise by hand is more difficult and quite a different operation from making it in a liquidizer, but they have various things in common:

(1) *The oil.* Olive oil gives mayonnaise the best flavour, as long as one likes its fruitiness and doesn't mind its cost. Otherwise you can use a mixture of olive oil and good corn oil, or even corn oil alone. The latter is very flavourless though, and needs pepping up with extra lemon juice, to taste, when the mayonnaise is made. See also *Oil*, page 83. The emulsion may thin out and curdle if you try to add too *much* oil, because the binding properties of the yolks break down. 6 fluid ozs (about 160 ml) per large egg yolk is the ceiling.
(2) *The vinegar.* Use white wine vinegar or lemon juice, preferably the former, for the finest flavour and colour. Malt vinegar is too harsh *and* gives mayonnaise a bad colour, unless distilled. See also *Vinegar*, page 94.
(3) A tablespoon boiling water per egg yolk beaten into the made mayonnaise helps to make it lighter, and also acts as an insurance against curdling.
(4) If the mayonnaise is too thick, stir in a spoonful or two of cream just before you need it. This corrects the consistency, flavours and makes it creamy-smooth all at one stroke. On the other hand, if you'd rather cut *down* the richness, use soured cream or yoghourt instead of fresh cream.
(5) Curdled mayonnaise can be remedied by starting back at square one with a new yolk. Simply add the curdled mixture to the well-beaten yolk in the same way as you added the oil to the original yolk.
(6) Finely chopped herbs, if used, are added at the last minute, otherwise they lose their colour and will in due course turn sour. Alternatively, if you want to add them in advance, blanch them one minute, refresh, drain, squeeze dry and chop.
(7) It's important to *taste* mayonnaise before you serve it, to make sure it is both well seasoned and well flavoured.
(8) If mayonnaise thins out in the refrigerator, you can thicken it again by adding it very gradually to 1 teasp made mustard. First beat the mustard and 1 tablesp of the mayonnaise with a

wire whisk until they cream and thicken together, then beat in remaining mayonnaise, a teaspoonful at a time.

MADE BY HAND. *The egg yolks* should be large ones if to absorb all the oil. They should also be fresh, entirely free of egg white (including chalazae) and at room temperature, because the mixture is more likely to curdle if they're cold. It's easier to make up 2 or 3 egg yolks than 1, because there's a greater bulk of egg yolk to beat initially.

★ *The mixing bowl* is better for being warmed in hot water, to avoid chilling the yolks.

★ *A small wire whisk* is better than a wooden spoon to beat and break down the yolks – it takes a minute or two before they're thick and pale yellow, as they should be. Then they need beating again for another 30 seconds or so after you've added the vinegar and seasonings, to break them down even more. Only then are they ready to absorb the oil.

★ If you don't add the oil drop by drop to start with and if you don't beat the yolks and vinegar *constantly*, they won't emulsify – there's no time for a nap in the middle!

★ It's important to watch the *oil* rather than the mixture as you drop it in. The lip of the oil bottle (see *Oil dropper*) or a jug is easily steadied over the edge of the bowl, and you can tie a cloth round the bowl to steady it, see page 45. It's best to stop pouring about every 10 seconds, while continuing to beat, to make sure the oil is being absorbed.

★ Once the yolks and oil emulsify, the real danger of curdling is over and you can beat in the remaining oil a tablespoon at a time.

★ If the mayonnaise is too thick and difficult to beat before all the oil is added, thin it out with a few drops of vinegar or lemon juice, but if you've never made it before, it's probably safer not to *try* and add more than ¼ pt (generous 125 ml) oil per egg yolk.

MADE IN A LIQUIDIZER. Some people like to use whole egg, others prefer to use yolk, but whichever you do, it's easiest with a normal household-sized liquidizer to make up only one egg or one yolk at a time.

★ Mayonnaise made with *whole* egg lacks the richness, golden colour and 'body' of the real thing it seems to me, and thins out more readily in the refrigerator. I don't see any point in using it therefore when yolk alone produces an emulsion unmistakably like mayonnaise.

★ Success hangs upon the complete breaking down of the egg – or the yolk as the case may be – with the vinegar. Liquidize it together with the seasonings at maximum speed for 30 seconds. This makes it ready to absorb the oil, most easily poured in from a jug. Now turn on liquidizer at slowish speed, remove central cap (or lid, if no cap) and pour in the oil, in a thin steady stream – there's no need to worry about adding it drop by drop. Any worries you may have are over when the whirring noise of the liquidizer changes to a quieter one, which it does suddenly, when the egg and oil emulsify.

★ When using yolk only, you may find the emulsion is so thick that the blades will stick before you've added all the oil. If so, switch off, stir in a tablespoon of very hot water, and off you go again.

★ Whole egg will absorb about 3 tablesps more oil than egg yolk will, to reach a thick consistency, so if you add all that, you're bound to need a spot more vinegar and seasonings to counteract the extra oil's richness.

CURRY MAYONNAISE. This particular version is so good with chicken, fish or an egg salad that you may like to have the recipe. It serves 4. Sweat a finely chopped small onion in 1 oz (25 g) butter until soft and transparent, but not coloured. Stir in 3 or 4 rounded teasps curry powder and fry about 2 mins with the onion. Add a pinch of salt, 1 level tablesp honey and 2 level tablesps mango chutney sauce, stirring over low heat for 2 or 3 mins until thick. Sieve and cool it, then mix with ¼ pt (125 ml) home-made mayonnaise.

Mint Sauce

Can be varied by making it with brown

sugar instead of white, and/or lemon juice instead of vinegar. It's better made with wine vinegar than with malt, because wine cuts more effectively through the richness of a roast and its accompaniments.

★ Mint sauce has an extra-minty fresh flavour if you chop and then pound the leaves, rather than just chop them finely (see page 77).

★ Make the sauce at least an hour or two before the meal, to develop its full flavour, making it thick with mint, not watery.

Oil and Vinegar Sauces

See page 160.

Velouté Sauce

See page 139.

White Sauce

This sauce, made simply with butter or margarine, flour, milk and seasoning is *the* basic white sauce. So basic is it in fact to all cooking that for the sake of the non sauce-makers, here are precise details:

Coating consistency

---

1 oz. (25 g) butter or marg.
1 oz. (25 g) flour
½ pt. (250 ml) milk
salt and pepper

Pouring consistency

½ oz. (scant 15 g) butter or marg
½ oz. (scant 15 g) flour
½ pt. (250 ml) milk
salt and pepper

METHOD.

(1) Make roux:
 (a) Melt fat slowly, without really heating it, then set pan *aside* from heat. Stir in the flour and blend with a wooden spoon until absolutely smooth.
 (b) Return pan to low heat and cook roux 2 or 3 mins, stirring at intervals.

(2) Set pan *aside* from heat again and stir in the milk, very gradually at first, blending in each addition until smooth before adding more.

(3) Season with salt and pepper. (*If you want to, you can prepare as far as this earlier in the day.*)

(4) Heat and bring sauce to the boil, stirring constantly, then boil about a minute to thicken it properly and to make sure the flour is cooked.

(5) Taste, and correct consistency if necessary. (A coating sauce should coat smoothly the back of the wooden spoon.)

★ See also *Roux*, page 55, for other why's and how's.

★ You can now give this sauce flavour by enriching it with a nut of savoury butter (see page 131), or you can add a variety of flavourings such as grated cheese, chopped parsley, cooked chopped mushrooms or cooked sliced onion. *Whatever* you add though, nothing will make such a tasty sauce as that same flavouring stirred into Béchamel Sauce, see below, the 'superior' white sauce made in exactly the same way but with milk which has been previously flavoured. It's so little extra trouble, yet transforms the dull into the subtle.

★ Certain foods, crushed garlic or finely sliced shallot for instance, are sometimes cooked lightly in the *roux* because this way their flavour is more pronounced.

BÉCHAMEL SAUCE. This, and Velouté, see later, are the two 'Mother Sauces' of the White Sauces, the aristocratic relations of the simple white one above. The only difference between them and this basic white sauce is that for Béchamel you flavour the milk first, and for Velouté you use well flavoured stock *instead* of milk – usually the liquor in which the meat or fish has been cooked. These are the two, which with additions or slight alterations, can be made into any of the sauces in their group (see Family Tree, page 132).

★ With the addition of cream for instance, Béchamel becomes Cream Sauce (Sauce Crème), while Velouté with cream becomes Sauce Suprême. With the addition of cheese, an ordinary white sauce just becomes a Cheese Sauce, but a

Béchamel Sauce becomes Mornay Sauce.
★ Anyone with time on their hands may want to make Béchamel the perfect way, with carrot, onion, celery and leek etc but the rest of us must in these days probably settle for the lightning alternative, which for reference elsewhere in the book I'm going to call *Béchamel Milk*.

BÉCHAMEL MILK. All you need do to make $\frac{1}{2}$ pt (250 ml) sauce is put the following ingredients together in a small saucepan:

Ingredient	*Remarks*
$\frac{1}{2}$ pt. (250 ml) milk	Be generous with it, to allow for evaporation.
1 sliced shallot or small piece of onion, sliced 1 small bayleaf	Use dried onion if in a hurry
a few white peppercorns	Ground pepper may spoil the appearance of a sauce. (Salt is added later when you make the sauce.)
1 clove	Not official, but *I* think it's the making of the sauce.
pinch of celery seed	If available.

(1) Bring milk slowly to the boil – the slower the better, to extract all the flavours.
(2) Set pan aside from heat, cover with a lid and infuse 10–15 mins if you can spare the time – to draw out even more flavour.
(3) Strain, make up to $\frac{1}{2}$ pt (250 ml) again with extra milk if necessary, and use hot or cold, as ordinary milk.

★ A good roux is the foundation of a good sauce (use a white roux for a béchamel sauce), affecting flavour, colour and consistency for better or for worse (see *Roux*, page 55).
★ Having made the sauce as an ordinary white one, with the roux, milk (flavoured) and some salt (or the roux and *stock* if a velouté sauce), you can make it better still by enriching with butter, cream, or a cream and egg yolk liaison. (See *Butters, savoury*, if adding butter).
★ Sauces such as these are served with fish, chicken, veal, eggs or vegetables, and may also be the base for savoury soufflés, hot hors-d'oeuvres or cream soups.
★ White sauces containing wine or egg yolks tend to become discoloured if made in an aluminium pan; and a pan in which a starchy sauce has been made, is more easily washed if first soaked with cold water rather than hot.

VELOUTÉ SAUCE. Is like Béchamel (see above, and also *White Sauce*, page 138), but made with stock – chicken, veal or fish – instead of milk. The liquor in which food has been cooked and from which the sauce may be made, is often flavoured with wine, and the sauce may also include cream or milk. When enriched with a cream and egg yolk liaison, Velouté sauce must be one of the most delicious of any quickly made sauces.

Velouté used to be called *sauce blonde* because, ideally, it's a white sauce made with a blond roux (see *Roux*) instead of a white roux. If you have to use margarine instead of butter though, it's better to make a white roux than a blond, because margarine doesn't colour as butter does.

9
VEGETABLES, PASTA AND RICE

General Information

Vegetables grown in the British Isles are with some exceptions just as good as French – it's what we do with them, from the time we buy or pick to the time we serve them, that is so painfully different. In France vegetables are delicious enough to merit being served as a separate course; whereas here they are treated more as a nutritious necessity or as a main course filler-upper, than as one of the highlights of a meal.

★ Where the French shopper is discerning about her choice of vegetables, selecting and rejecting with meticulous care, we by and large will take what the greengrocer gives us. We'll even pick up the discoloured limp rubbish ourselves in *some* supermarkets, and pay full price for it too. Just as tender veal would become beef, or lamb become mutton, so tender beautifully flavoured young vegetables turn into something quite different. How crazy can we be to encourage people to think that the largest are the best at the village show, when in fact nothing about them makes them good eating? Some gardeners actually plan their vegetable digging or picking *round* their local show, allowing everything to grow huge in order, at the right time, to produce six perfectly shaped giants.

★ Vegetables are 'protective foods', protecting the body from illness, so of course they're best when eaten fresh and raw, nothing lost by cooking. Next best is to prepare and cook them perfectly. Most of us know the smell and flavour of a freshly picked tomato or grape, but many people don't seem to realize that the flavour of a freshly picked green vegetable is no less rewarding, although there's no glorious smell to advertise it.

★ You can't see vitamins disappearing any more than you can see an egg going bad, but this is just what begins to happen when you pick or dig up a vegetable, especially 'greens'. The longer they are stored, the greater the loss, and the sooner they are prepared before a meal and the more they're cut up, the faster that loss accelerates.

★ It's often easier said than done, but if you want the flavour of garden vegetables at its best, you should aim to cook 'greens' within an hour of picking. If prepare in advance you must – we all must sometimes, especially in winter – the important thing is to exclude light and air. Wrapped in foil or polythene, and refrigerated, deterioration is greatly slowed down.

★ While the English *mainly* simply boil most of their vegetables, the French are more imaginative. By blanching them first – either for just a few minutes or until nearly cooked, according to whatever you're going to do with them – you can vary their flavour and texture in all sorts of ways by sautéing, glazing, roasting, stuffing, or by making fritters or a purée (see later).

★ You *can* blanch and refresh a vegetable earlier in the day if necessary, and cook it in the same or another way later, when ready for it. See *Refreshing*, page 54.

DEEP-FREEZING VEGETABLES. Vegetables to be deep frozen are blanched in order to kill the enzymes which cause deterioration in colour, flavour, and to some extent, food value. An authority on the subject says the maximum acceptable storage time in the freezer for unblanched vegetables is – to take just 2 or 3 examples – 1 month for runner beans, 3 weeks for broad beans and 3 days for Brussels sprouts, compared with 12–14 months for blanched vegetables. The enzyme which breaks down Vitamin C is destroyed by blanching, so more 'C' is retained when vegetables are blanched than if stored unblanched for several months. (See *Refreshing*, page 54, and *Blanching*, page 31-2.) When you cook a frozen vegetable, allow less than half its normal cooking time after the water has returned to the boil. The longer you cook it, the poorer the flavour and texture.

BOILED VEGETABLES. They keep their goodness and cook best in a covered pan large enough for the vegetable to be in one layer, not piled up in a small pan. This way, if you choose vegetables of the same size – or cut them into equal-sized pieces – they'll cook quickly, and will all be ready at the same time. The fewer outer green leaves removed the better because that's where most of the goodness is.

★ Use shallow well-salted water to retain flavour and nutrients, because there's a heavy loss of mineral salts with deep water.

★ Put vegetables into fast-boiling water over maximum heat so that the water can come quickly back to the boil – when cooking time starts. Only then should you lower the heat, allowing a vegetable to boil slowly for its allotted time. The shorter the cooking time, the greater the food value and the better the flavour, colour and texture.

★ Many vegetables are fatless so if you're not worrying about waistlines or about eating too much 'animal' fat, do enrich and flavour them when you can by serving a sauce, or by tossing with chopped herbs and butter, cream or soured cream. It makes all the difference in the world.

SAUTÉD VEGETABLES. So tempting and so basically simple to prepare that they switch even the common spud, carrot, turnip, parsnip or swede into another class. Just as fried onions taste like a different vegetable from boiled, because the sugar in them caramelizes, so it does in lots of other vegetables, given the chance. An unpleasantly strong flavour is mellowed, a characterless texture becomes almost crunchy, and pale-coloured vegetables turn golden.

★ While some vegetables are sautéd in hot butter from start to finish, others – in particular root vegetables and potatoes – are previously blanched. Sliced or quartered as necessary, they are boiled until nearly but not quite cooked, and then sautéd in *hot* butter until turning golden. When tossed with flavourings such as freshly milled black pepper and chopped herbs just before dishing, it puts an edge on the dullest veg.

★ If you haven't sautéd vegetables in this way before, a few more guidelines may be helpful:

(1) Allow 1–1½ ozs (25–40 g) *butter* for 4 people, and rather more of a watery vegetable than usual, because it will shrink as the moisture is drawn out.
(2) Evaporate excess moisture from a hot blanched drained vegetable by returning it to the empty pan, and tossing over moderate heat for a minute or two – uncovered. If you don't do this, it will splutter and make the butter watery. Otherwise 'refresh' the vegetable after blanching, if for some reason you aren't going to sauté it straight away. If watery, like courgettes, cover in a colander with a weighted plate until required.
(3) Turn the whole mass of vegetables over occasionally, using a fish slice for potatoes, to prevent breaking up, or two wooden spoons for most other vegetables.
(4) Add salt when the vegetable is nearly cooked (about 10–20 mins according to type). Having been blanched in salted water, the vegetable won't lack flavour, but will stick to the sauté pan if you add salt to the butter.
(5) A minute or two before dishing, enrich and vary a vegetable's flavour by

stirring in and blending a pinch of a spice like nutmeg and 2 or 3 tablespoons of cream, soured cream or yoghourt. Herbs are added at the last second. There's no end to the permutations you can think up.

(6) As a change, mix with *another* vegetable: fried onions for instance go well with French or runner beans, or with potatoes. Tomatoes or mushrooms, lightly fried in butter, are other good 'mixers'.

MAKE FRITTERS. With flowerets of cauliflower or sprouting broccoli, with celery or with sliced aubergines, Jerusalem artichokes or courgettes etc. The important thing here is to blanch the cut-up or sliced vegetable first, just enough to partly tenderize, but not so long that it becomes soft and difficult to handle. Make sure too that the vegetable is compact – no stalks sticking out – otherwise the pieces are difficult to coat completely.

★ To give extra flavour, some vegetables are marinated, and others may be mixed with or coated in béchamel sauce before being dipped in the batter. The sauce should be thick enough to coat the back of a wooden spoon fairly thickly but smoothly, and used while just hot enough to set smoothly on the vegetable. Give the coated vegetables plenty of time to cool and set firmly, before dipping in the batter on a fork, otherwise you'll end up in a mess. Serve a savoury sauce with fritters when serving them as a separate course, e.g. mornay, mushroom or tomato etc.

PURÉES. Quickly reheated with butter or a little double cream, purées will be richer and twice as good as those served plain.

ROAST VEGETABLES. Such as potatoes, Jerusalem artichokes and parsnips, are blanched for a few mins first, to tenderize them partly, as well as to soften the outside and make them more fat absorbent.

GLAZED VEGETABLES. Such as carrot, turnip and onions make an attractive garnish, because they're so shiny, colourful and tasty. Rather a lot of butter and sugar are used in the *stock* in which they're cooked so that the liquid, during the long slow cooking, reduces to a syrupy glaze in the bottom of the pan.

★ Roll the vegetables about in the liquid to make them shiny, then sprinkle with finely chopped herbs for additional colour and flavour.

BOUGHT FROZEN VEGETABLES. These shouldn't, as a rule, come to too much harm before you get them home, because slight thawing won't spoil them, especially if they're still frosty.

★ Even if completely thawed, there's no health hazard, though both flavour and texture may suffer. The 'Do not re-freeze' instructions on packets protect manufacturers, who naturally and rightly want you to eat their produce while in tip-top condition. At the same time, it stops thoughtless people from thawing and re-freezing indiscriminately, which you can't do.

★ Vegetables fall into 7 main groups. Here are our most popular vegetables:

Roots	*Tubers*	*Bulbous*
Beetroot	Artichoke, (Jerusalem)	Garlic
Carrot	Potato	Leek
Parsnip		Onion
Radish		Shallot
Swede		
Turnip		

Green leaves	*Blanched stems*
Brussels sprouts	Asparagus
Cabbage	Celery
Chard, Swiss and Ruby	Chicory
Kale (Wintergreens)	
Lettuce	
Mustard and cress	
Spinach	
Watercress	

Flowers or heads	*Fruits and Seeds*
Artichoke, globe	Aubergine
Broccoli	Beans
Broccoli, sprouting	Courgette
Calabrese	Cucumber
Cauliflower	Peas
	Pepper, sweet
	Sweet corn
	Tomato
	Vegetable marrow

Artichokes, Globe

See page 115.

Artichokes, Jerusalem

Really the tubers of a species of sunflower, not artichokes at all. 'Jerusalem' is a corruption of *girasole*, Italian for sunflower.

★ Artichokes are beastly to peel, and such an irregular shape that they cook more evenly if *sliced* before blanching or boiling, unless of course you like them whole.
★ A tablespoon of lemon juice or vinegar, added to both steeping and cooking water, helps to prevent rapid discoloration.

Aubergines

Also known as egg plant or egg apple, these have been used for centuries, and are one of the great vegetables of the world, varying widely in shape, size and colour. Though fruits sold in England are generally pear-shaped, they may also be long and thin like a sausage, or round like a large ball. The colour ranges from ivory-white to yellow, and from the palest mauve to the deepest purple.

★ They've got to be fresh to be good; glossy, firm and of uniform colour, otherwise they're 'tired'. Sprinkling with salt, either when sliced or halved, and leaving them to stand for an hour or so, makes them less bitter and watery, see *Dégorger*.
★ The skin is full of flavour and prevents them breaking up when cooked, so aubergines aren't usually peeled except for a salad or purée.

Beans, Broad

Can be one of the horrors of the English table. It may seem extravagant to pick them when no longer than your small finger, and when the flower is just withered, but that's the gourmet's broad bean, eaten complete with pod. (Extravagance is when you waste a mountain of pods, to eat but a handful of their leathery contents.) Top, tail and wash them while tiny and tender, boil about 10 mins, and toss in butter with chopped savory or parsley.

★ The second stage for beans is when they're about as big as a good-sized pea. Boil them until tender, or blanch a few minutes before cooking in another way.
★ The third stage is the potentially grim one because so many people fail to blanch and skin them. How can anybody eat and *swallow* anything with such a flavour and texture? You can prepare them in advance of a meal if necessary, refrigerating them in a polythene bag: just a minute or two's blanching makes them firm and easy to handle, then after 'refreshing' for another minute or two, they'll pop out of their skins, like almonds.
★ Broad beans should be married to savory as peas are to mint; savory grown between the rows of beans keeping away the black-fly. Add a sprig to the cooking water, or chop the leaves finely to toss with the cooked beans and butter.

Beans, French

Also called *haricots verts,* these are heavenly when young and small enough to eat whole; not more than $\frac{1}{4}''$ (7 mm) thick, the seeds inside immature. If buying, be sure they're fresh and firm enough to snap crisply too.

★ However you're going to cook them, French beans are usually boiled first until tender, or nearly tender, according to need.
★ French beans take an even greater trouncing than most other vegetables, in flavour, colour and texture, if either overcooked or kept hot.

Beetroot

This and Sugar Beet are both members of the same family.

★ Beetroot 'bleed' and lose their flavour if you cut the roots, cut the stem too close to the top, or scrub them instead of just rubbing clean with your hands.

★ If you've never eaten tiny beetroot, boiled about an hour, and served hot (with butter or parsley butter and plenty of salt), you've missed something. (An unusual use is as a main breakfast dish in Sweden, but for the more conventional of us, they make an excellent hors-d'oeuvre.)

★ Have you ever had beetroot au gratin, made with mornay sauce? It's lovely with something like hot-pot or a stew.

Broccoli

The winter and early spring cauliflower.

Broccoli, Sprouting

Makes delicious fritters. Be sure to undercook the flowerets when blanching, otherwise they'll be too soft to handle. See pages 142 and 117.

Brussels Sprouts

A variety of cabbage brought to Britain from Belgium in the nineteenth century. How they're ill-treated – though I can't help feeling market gardeners and retailers (keener on size and weight than on flavour), may be just as much to blame as we cooks. If everyone asked their greengrocer for *small* sprouts (and insisted on having fresh ones), we might eventually get the best. Meanwhile nobody can stop those of us who have a garden from *growing* a 'small' variety. In view of all this, it's hardly surprising that these monsters taste, look and smell as foul as they often do by the time they're tender if you don't cut them in half, or cut a cross in the stalk of any smaller ones left whole. This way, the heat penetrates them faster, so they cook quickly. Allow small garden ones 6–8 mins, slightly larger 8–10, to keep them a brilliant green colour and slightly crunchy in texture. At all costs avoid overcooking or keeping them hot more than a few minutes – for I guarantee they'll be nasty to look at, smell and eat.

Cabbage

Grown for its leaves for so many centuries in so many lands, cabbage falls into two main classes, the smooth-leaved and curly-leaved, or Savoys. There are early and late varieties and although the majority we grow are green, you can have white or purple-red ones as well. You can eat cabbage cooked, pickled or raw.

★ Cabbage is a mine of mineral salts, one of which is sulphur – the cause of its nasty smell when cooking. If you prefer varieties which don't smell when cooked – because the sulphur is hybridized out of them – they are of course inferior dietetically.

★ Though notorious among British vegetables, it isn't the fault of the poor cabbage! When *properly* cooked, it's a lovely colour, has a slightly crunchy texture and is full of flavour.

★ Cabbage needs the minimum of water (because it contains plenty of that already), fine shredding, lots of salt and the shortest possible cooking time to make it *al dente*.

★ After draining and pressing hard with the back of a wooden spoon or vegetable press in the colander, toss it with butter and flavour with chopped herbs, grated nutmeg, caraway seeds, or whatever you like. You might even like it in a mornay sauce, au gratin?

★ If you're a good-health fan, serve red or white (Dutch) cabbage raw. Cole Slaw ranks amongst the best of salads, see page 159.

CHINESE CABBAGE. Has some good qualities, others not so good I think:

(1) It takes up less room in a small vegetable garden than most other varieties because it grows tall and thin, like a huge cos lettuce.

(2) Finely shredded, it boils in about 4 mins – half the time most varieties take – but despite this is insipid. (Use lots of salt and flavour it in the ways you would ordinary cabbage.)

(3) You can cook and eat the ribs like asparagus, and use the leaves raw in a salad if, unlike me, you enjoy its rather

strange texture and flavour when used in these ways.

RED CABBAGE. Flavourless if boiled, and loses its colour into the bargain. It may be an acquired taste, but red cabbage is usually considered best when braised with sour apples, or something acid, to flavour it and hold its colour. Long, slow cooking is essential to develop its full flavour, which some people find better still when reheated the next day, and yet again on following days.

★ Serve it with rich or strongly flavoured foods such as sausages, roast pork, venison, hare, roast goose or duck.

SPRING GREENS. Young Spring cabbages, before the heart is properly formed.

Calabrese

A type of sprouting broccoli, with an abundance of small *green* flowerets. Cook in any way like that or cauliflower. See also page 117.

Capsicum

See *Peppers, Sweet*, page 150.

Carrots

Contain precious vitamins and mineral salts. As so much of this goodness as well as flavour is in and close to the skin, it's much better just to well scrub young ones than to peel or even scrape them. You can peel old ones before or, more thinly, *after* cooking.

★ Carrots so often smell and taste almost nauseating, when they can (with a little know-how) just as easily be delicate and delicious, as for instance when sautéd (see page 141). A trick with old carrots is to slice them really thinly, or to cut them longways into six or eight pieces instead of four, to avoid that nasty strong flavour which develops during prolonged boiling.
★ 'Fines herbs' or chives buck them up as a change from the eternal parsley garnish, or cooked carrots are both tasty and cheerful when you mix them with finely sliced mushrooms (previously cooked a few minutes in butter) and sprinkle at the last moment with a chopped herb that you like.
★ Given time and patience (housewives can probably find neither, students may have to find both), you can make four small carrots from each of three or four large, to serve as a garnish, glazed: cut each one longways into quarters, then 'shape' each quarter into a realistic looking carrot with a potato peeler.

VICHY CARROTS. Carrots glazed in Vichy water in place of the usual stock. Carrots are supposed to be good for liverish people, the dish taking its name from Vichy, whose waters are considered particularly good for liver complaints.

Cauliflower

A variety of cabbage grown for its undeveloped flowers rather than for its leaves. Its name seems to derive from *Cole Flowers, cole* as you probably know being the generic term for the Brassica family. If you grow cauliflowers, you'll doubtless be aware that one picked with the morning dew still on it, has a finer flavour than one uprooted later in the day after the sun has dried it up.

★Cauliflower is at its best when cut into sprigs, because it cooks so quickly that both flavour and texture are perfect – boiled just 5–10 mins according to size.
★ If you *prefer* to cook it whole, cut a chunk out of the middle of the stalk, so that the heat penetrates the 'flower' quickly and speeds up cooking.
★ Blanched, refreshed cauliflower can be cooked in all sorts of ways, because it's bland enough to mix with other foods, yet has itself got lots of flavour and character. If likely to be short of time when actually cooking a meal, one *can* cook and refresh cauliflower earlier in the day, then reheat by steaming in a covered colander over boiling water for 2 or 3 minutes. It's not ideal, but *is* sometimes useful if you don't want to cut it into sprigs.

Celery

Served raw with cheese, celery should have the root left on because this is one of the best parts: remove the coarse outer stems, and the leaves of all but the smallest heart stems, and trim the root to a slight point. Now cut the 'head' into quarters, right down through the root.

★ However celery is to be cooked, most varieties need blanching about 10 mins first, to mellow the strong flavour.
★ Braised celery – especially good to serve with rich foods like pork or duck – needs long slow cooking to allow the flavours to blend perfectly together.
★ Celery loses its crispness when deep frozen, but still makes a useful flavouring for soups, sauces or casseroles.
★ See also page 158.

Chard, Swiss

Two vegetables in one. Grown essentially for its chards or mid-ribs, the outer green leaves you tear off can also be cooked, as spinach. Though I think you're unlikely to want it often, like say cauliflower, beans or peas, it makes (when young) an interesting change of vegetable for those with a garden, and space to grow it.

★ An easy and favourite way of mine to eat it is sautéd: first pull any 'strings' off the chards, just as off coarse celery, cut the ribs into $2\frac{1}{2}$–3″ (6–8 cm) lengths, and then blanch or steam them, to partly tenderize, before sautéing.
★ See also page 141.

Courgettes

A great vegetable to have in the garden, at their best when small and tender, as the flower fades. They grow as fast as weeds – almost as you watch them – can be cooked in lots of different ways and, though less easy to cook well afterwards, freeze satisfactorily sliced, halved or whole.

★ Their skins are colourful and full of flavour so leave them on unless coarse, when pare off the ridges in stripes with a potato peeler.
★ Sliced or halved courgettes are sprinkled with salt and left to drain for an hour or so in a colander, to make them less bitter and watery (see page 38). By the way, they're more attractive when sliced diagonally than cut straight across.
★ Despite their rather pronounced flavour, courgettes are amazingly versatile so for heaven's sake don't *just* boil them and coat with a white sauce! They make a lovely purée, are good au gratin, stuffed, sautéd or frittered, besides combining splendidly with other things like onions, tomatoes, herbs, spices, mushrooms, cream or nuts.

Egg Plant

The American name for *Aubergine*.

Fennel, Florence

A large bulbous root which looks like a monster head of celery, and is used similarly, though it tastes of anise. English grown fennel isn't always suitable to eat raw, due to its need for the right soil, as well as for sun and moisture.

Haricots Verts

See page 143, *French beans*.

Kale

Also from the generic name of the Brassica family, *Cole*, kale is believed to be the original form of the great cabbage family. It has sprouting, curled, finely dented leaves which never form a solid heart or head.

★ Of different varieties, mostly with a strong flavour, it is often sold as Winter Greens. Cook it like cabbage, or if you *like* it raw, you can wash it well and serve it as a dressed green salad, with or without lettuce etc.

Marrow, Vegetable

Best eaten when so young that the seeds have hardly formed and the skin is tender enough to eat. When *very* small you can use them as courgettes, and the more you pick them the more you'll get.

★ For speed, to cut the seeded centre out of a large marrow, use a plain scone cutter.

★ Like other vegetables, you can blanch and cook marrow in all sorts of ways, but if you're thinking of boiling it, think again: *steaming* is better because the marrow is less watery, firmer in texture and has more flavour.

Mushrooms

Cultured mushrooms should be white, firm, fresh and crisp enough to eat raw when finely sliced. *Don't* allow yourself to be fobbed off with limp and leathery ones, which neither fry nor grill well however long you cook them in an effort to make them tender. One trouble is that mushrooms fried more than a few minutes develop a nasty strong taste and smell. It pays to watch what you're buying, and if you don't like the look of them, ask for fresh. There are *often* better ones tucked away out of sight.

★ Mushrooms go through three stages of growth, at each of which they may be better for one purpose than another:

(1) *Buttons* haven't got much flavour, but are ideal for garnishing – because they're small – and best for sauces because they cause least discoloration.

(2) *Cups*, half open, are best for salads and for general use. Cut the stalks off level with the caps when frying or grilling, then they won't shrink as much as when stalkless.

(3) *Flats*, wide open, usually have the best flavour and are good for soup, casseroles and duxelles (a mixture used in stuffings, patties or a quick sauce).

★ Wipe rather than peel mushrooms unless very coarse, because the skins, like the stalks, contain lots of flavour. Slice the stalks finely before frying, sweating or stewing them with the mushrooms, or using them to flavour anything. Mushrooms are so watery that a few minutes cooking will reduce a pile of them, chopped, to 2 or 3 spoonfuls, so it's essential to get rid of some of this water *before* cooking them, when making something like a soufflé, duxelles, or stuffings: simply chop the mushrooms small, and *squeeze* the water out, by twisting them up tightly inside a clean piece of cloth.

★ Butter is the fat to give mushrooms a good flavour. They don't need much and, apart from bacon dripping, there's nothing to match it. Sautéd or sweated in butter, and flavoured with such things as shallots, herbs, spices, cream, or other vegetables, there are countless ways to serve mushrooms, not only as a vegetable or garnish, but as an important flavouring in innumerable dishes.

MUSHROOMS AS A GARNISH. Here are two easy ways to prepare them:

(1) If without button mushrooms, make mushrooms of different sizes the same by using a scone cutter the size of the smallest. (Use up the trimmings in the main dish if suitable, or to flavour something else.) Incidentally, a scone cutter is a good way to make *large* mushrooms uniform in size too, say to serve stuffed.

(2) Cut a large mushroom in half, through both cap and stalk, see fig 2, then slice each half finely from the centre outwards, to give several leaf-thin slices, as in fig 3. Use them raw on salads, or heat momentarily in butter to garnish something like a mushroom omelet or say fillets of fish.

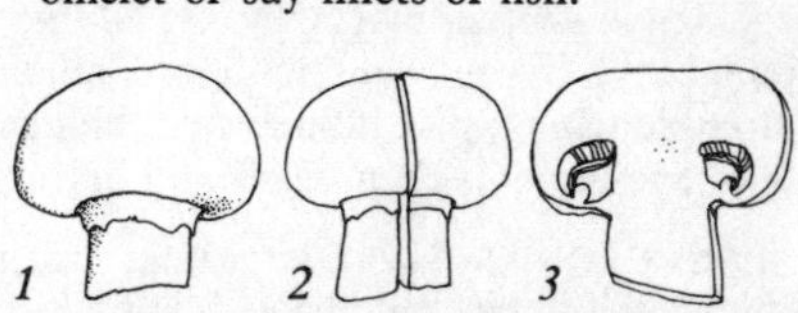

TO FREEZE MUSHROOMS. It is absolutely safe but not ideal because, being such watery things, they go mushy when thawed. Freezing concentrates their flavour however, so though much too soft and squashy to fry or grill, they make a tip-top soup or sauce, or are excellent for something like a casserole.

★ Wiped first, they'll freeze well for up to 6 months if blanched, only 3 months if not blanched.

★ If faced with a real glut of rather poor or very dirty field mushrooms, why not liquidize them and freeze the runny purée either in suitable quantities to make soup, or in ice trays? You can transfer the iced cubes to a polythene bag in the freezer and use them in the weeks ahead to flavour meat or fish dishes, sauces, vegetables etc, or to make soup. (They'll lose out slightly on flavour if you haven't time or can't face wiping them individually by the bucketful, but in this case break the rules and wash them under a cold tap before liquidizing.)

Onions

A native of Asia, and used the world over, onions are one of the basic aromatic vegetables of all European cookery. Anyone who doesn't like or can't eat them misses some of the greatest dishes there are. I think I'd give up cooking altogether if I couldn't eat onions.

★ Many English onions are so pungent that some people really *can't* digest them, so why not try a milder variety? I wonder why recommendations in gardening catalogues are usually about yield, size, shape, colour and storing qualities, but say so little about flavour? I'd put flavour and storing qualities first.

★ For anyone who finds onions indigestible, you can change their nature by boiling. Blanched just 3–5 mins before cooking in another way, they lose all their pungency. If you want to *fry* an onion after blanching, slice it finely first, blanch only one minute, then drain and dry.

SPANISH ONIONS. The large ones with a shiny golden skin, mild enough in flavour to eat raw in a salad and one of the best varieties to boil or braise. A *very* mild English onion can be used as a Spanish but you'll sometimes be better with shallots.

SHALLOTS. Famous in French cookery, shallots are another garden vegetable I'd hate to be without. Delicate in flavour, they grow abundantly, store splendidly and you can use them all year round for sauces, stuffings, salads and general cookery. Usually more easily digested than onions, they also go squashy when cooked, which makes them ideal for certain sauces, and in preparations like duxelles. If therefore it's the stringy *texture* of an onion that you don't like, why not try shallots instead? They're splendid in salads too because, unlike other onions, your palate doesn't retain the taste of raw shallots and spring onions.

★ If without shallots when a recipe calls for them, you can often use spring onions instead, or sometimes even a finely sliced onion – blanched one minute, refreshed and drained.

PICKLING OR BUTTON ONIONS. The best for garnishing because they're small. They are always served whole.

★ A speedy, tearless way to peel them is by blanching in fast-boiling water for 15 seconds, not too many at a time. Drain and refresh them, drain again, and then trim the ends sparingly so as not to loosen the layers when slipping off the skin.

★ If you want to tenderize them slightly, blanch 2 mins instead of 15 seconds.

CHOPPING ONION OR SHALLOT FINELY is quick and easy as long as you don't cut the root off – that's what holds body and soul together. In case you're not sure how to do it, this is the way:

(1) Remove skin, cut top off, and then cut onion in half from top to root, and put cut side down on a board, root end to your left.

(2) Slice it vertically, lengthwise, almost but not quite to the root, as illustrated:

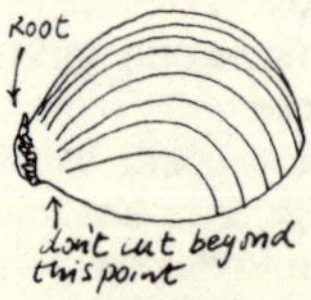

(3) Slice it horizontally, starting at the bottom and working up to the top – but still not through the root.

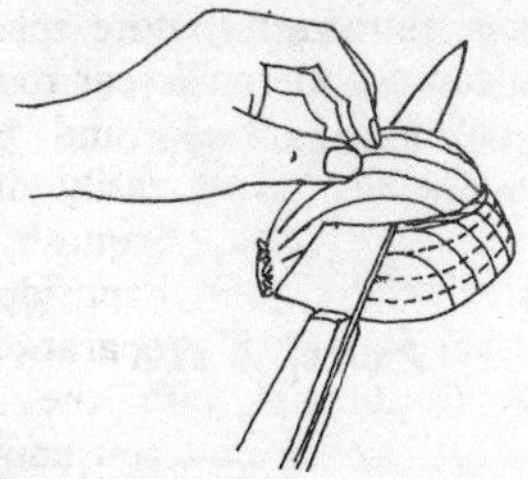

(4) Cut it *across*, downwards, into dice, starting at right hand end.

★ Sliced onions are often sweated (see page 59) to soften without colouring them before cooking with other ingredients which take a shorter time to cook.
★ The reason why fried onions are so delicious and turn golden is because the sugar in them caramelizes.
★ If you can't get rid of the smell of onion on your hands, wash them in cold water and rub with salt. Now rinse under cold water again and then wash in the ordinary way.
★ *Onion rings* need to be small for a garnish. If you haven't got a small onion, simply remove the outer layers of a larger.
★ *Dried sliced onions* are not to be scorned. They're a useful standby to flavour something like Béchamel milk for a white sauce when you're pressed for time, or if a dish only needs a hint of onion and it means cutting a whole one.
★ *Frozen sliced onions* are sometimes convenient too. You can either buy, or slice and freeze them yourself, raw or blanched. Store only 4–6 months if raw, and be sure to seal them in a thick polythene bag, to isolate.
★ *Tears* seem to go hand and glove with sliced onions, unless you have some pet solution like slicing them under cold water or out in the fresh air, or refrigerating the onion an hour or so before you cut it – to chill the juices which *cause* the tears. It's all apparently due to a chemical called *allyl isothiocyanate*. The eyes are particularly sensitive to it, so protect themselves by flooding with tears, to wash away the chemical.

Paprika

The Hungarian name for a sweet pepper. See also page 85.

Pasta

Pasta comes in all shapes and sizes. It is so bland that it calls out to be served with something savoury, many dishes taking their name from their accompanying sauce.

★ You need a large pan (without lid), just over half-filled with well salted, boiling water, to ensure the pasta has room to move around, without boiling over, as well as expand in volume. It's better to add pasta *gradually* to fast-boiling water, so that it never goes off the boil, then it dosen't get a chance to settle on the pan bottom. Long spaghetti isn't broken up: simply hold it upright in the boiling water – like a bunch of flowers in a jug – and coil it round the inside of the pan, as the lower ends soften in the water. 'Quick' macaroni, rings or shells are easily sprinkled in, a handful at a time. Keep pasta moving with a fork if *necessary*, until the boiling water itself keeps it moving.
★ Spaghetti (its name comes from the Italian word *spago*, string – 'fine strings') and macaroni only take about 10 mins to become tender and *al dente*; easily tested by biting a piece. Pastas become heavy and glutinous if overcooked.
★ An easy alternative way to cook spaghetti, macaroni or tagliatelle is to boil it fast for 2 mins, stirring continually, then set aside from the heat for 10 mins, covered by a tight-fitting lid.
★ A tablespoonful of oil in the cooking water works magic, preventing pasta either sticking to itself or to the pan. Pasta should be drained at once through a strainer, otherwise it goes soft, as if over-

cooked. Pouring scalding water through it now will take away any glueiness if you're slimming, otherwise it's better to melt a little butter in the hot pan and, with two forks, toss the pasta – say spaghetti – in it. Alternatively use olive oil. Seasoned with freshly milled black pepper, the spaghetti will be both tasty and 'separate'.

★ Noodles take less time to cook because they're so much thinner. Follow directions on packet for safety.

★ A large variety of pasta, like lasagne, is boiled about 10 mins until tender, before being baked in the oven. It pays to boil just a few pieces at a time, with oil, otherwise it sticks together. The cooked lasagne is easier to cope with too if, after draining, you spread the pieces out on a folded cloth, to cool. Handle with tongs.

★ See also page 85.

Peas, Green

They don't seem worth freezing unless from your garden. Bought by the sackful (time of picking usually unknown), their flavour after freezing may be indifferent, the economy is next to nothing compared with cost of a large bag of frozen peas, and it's certainly a time-consuming and wearying job. The professionals like Birds Eye, Findus and Bejam freeze their peas within 90 mins of picking. If not processed within this time, peas evidently lose their sweet taste and green colour. Few of *us* can in addition be expert enough to know, as they do, even to the hour, when peas are at their most perfect to harvest – and also do so.

★ Really fresh peas will be crisp, bright green and smooth, 2 lbs (say 1 kilo) yielding about 1 lb (say 500 g) of small tender peas, or $1\frac{1}{2}$ lbs (say 750 g) large.

★ Peas can be cooked in different ways according to their size and tenderness. Small garden peas cooked in the French way (sweated in butter with lettuce and spring onions), make a heavenly course on their own. Larger peas can be rejuvenated by blanching 5–10 mins before cooking in another way, say sautéd, or sweated in butter. Peas are lovely too when tossed in mint butter.

★ Be sure to refresh (page 54) peas you plan to serve cold, say in a rice salad, to retain their flavour, texture and brilliant green colour.

Peas, Sugar

Also known as *mangetout*, these are a wonderful vegetable to grow, and are as easy to freeze as other peas are troublesome, because they don't have to be podded.

★ Unlike other varieties which have a tough lining, this pea has a very tender pod so you can eat the whole thing, like asparagus, serving them as a separate course with melted butter. If you've never had them before, this is the technique:

(1) Pick them when *very* young, before the pigeons want them, when the peas have just formed in the pod. Wash.
(2) Boil them in heavily salted water for 10–12 mins until tender but still slightly firm – best to test one by eating.
(3) Eat them with your fingers, holding each by the stalk. Dip it into salt and melted butter and pop it into your mouth without leaving go of the stalk. Now close your mouth on it, pulling away the stalk, which will bring the two pod 'strings' with it.

Peppers, Sweet

Also called *Pimientos* or *Capsicum*. They should be glossy, firm and free of wrinkles. Be choosy – why pay the same price for poorer?

★ If you're lucky enough to have your own greenhouse as well as enough sun, peppers make most attractive pot-plants, especially when some of the fruits turn red. They're almost too beautiful to pick.

★ If you only want quarter or half a pepper for a dish, interleave the remaining quarters and pop them in the freezer. They freeze perfectly, even without blanching. Bought frozen sliced peppers are an excellent buy, and usually much better *value* than buying fresh peppers to freeze yourself.

★ People with an iron constitution seem

to be able to eat peppers raw without suffering, while others enjoy them so much that they think the suffering is worthwhile. The considerate cook however may 'temper the wind' by blanching them 2 or 3 minutes (and refreshing) before using as a garnish or in a salad, or before cooking them in another way. This not only makes them more digestible, but also takes the edge off their very strong flavour.

Potatoes

Take their name from the Spanish *patata*, that name originating from the native American word *batata*. They were first introduced to Ireland, and thence to England from America, in the late sixteenth century.

★ Potatoes can be one of the dreariest or one of the most exciting foods we eat, depending upon the variety of potato and upon the cook! How incredibly lucky we are that this staple part of our diet is so bland that it will go with meat, fish or poultry – however cooked – and that the potatoes themselves can be cooked in literally scores of different ways as well. It's because of their mild flavour that we don't tire of them, and that we can cook them in a rich way to go with a fatless dish; in a simple way to go with a rich; make them crisp to serve with soft foods; golden to go with colourless foods and flavourful to accompany bland ones. Practically anything you want to do with potatoes, you can do – but nothing is more boring than always boiling or mashing them.

★ Blanching often precedes cooking them in another way, just as with other vegetables. Potatoes can be blanched with their skins on, skins off, halved, sliced, or cut into balls with a baller. They should be tossed and dried off for a minute or so in the empty pan over very low heat if you're then going to put them into hot fat.

★ Lots of their flavour and food value is in and next to the skin, so you retain more of both if you blanch or boil potatoes *before* peeling. The skin you'll then pull away is much thinner than peel cut away with a knife or peeler. The main reason why jacket potatoes are so tasty, without even the addition of salt, is because nothing is lost, as into boiling water – which is usually thrown away – and because we eat the whole thing.

★ New potatoes are a great source of Vitamin C, so it's important not to prepare them hours before you need. What better or more delicious way anyhow than new potatoes dug, cooked and eaten within the hour? What worse potato than a variety such as Pentland Dales which, however good their yield to a farmer are really no good to a cook – not unless you'll put up with a flavourless sodden mush whatever you try to do with them? Two of my favourite varieties for all-round use are Lincolnshire Whites and the pink-skinned Desirée, though the latter don't seem so good for deep-frying.

★ Whether you're boiling old or new potatoes they're best put into boiling water, and the less you cut them up the better. This is to save them breaking up when cooked. You'll find a potato pan easier to wash up if you soak it first in cold water, rather than hot.

POTATOES FRIED IN DEEP FAT. Irresistible to lots of us, even if they do mean an extra inch round the waist – chipped, croquettes, dauphine, Dunkirk, game chips, gaufrettes, knots, matchsticks, ribbons, potato puffs or anything else you can think of. All of these are worth trying if you haven't come across them before.

★ Besides knowing how to fry in deep fat (page 41) potatoes themselves have some peculiarities:

(1) Raw cut-up potatoes need soaking in cold water at least $\frac{1}{2}$ hr to get rid of some of their starch, otherwise the pieces stick together when fried. If you can only spare about $\frac{1}{4}$ hr, stir them round with your hands in a large bowl of water, changing it 2 or 3 times. You'll see how starchy it is.

(2) Chips etc are dangerous to fry unless well dried, because the fat so easily foams up and bubbles over.

(3) Thick potatoes, like chips, are best fried twice, the fat reheated in between; first to soften without colouring them,

second time to make crisp and golden.

(4) Deep fried potatoes are salted *after* cooking, and of course, like other fried foods, go soft if you cover the serving dish.

ANNA POTATOES. A little tricky to prepare because the potatoes have to be sliced to just the right thickness; about that of a new penny. If too thin, they curl up and won't overlap evenly, but if too thick they may not be tender by the time the outside is golden.

★ Dry them very thoroughly too, otherwise they'll cook in their own steam rather than in the butter – and *do* use butter, not margarine, for a lovely golden finish and perfect flavour.

★ Be generous with the quantity of potatoes you use because they shrink a lot when cooked.

CROQUETTES. Made with Duchess potato, these are difficult to cope with if the purée is too soft: dry off the potatoes in the empty pan for a minute or so over minimum heat after boiling, and mix the purée with egg yolk rather than whole egg, which is too watery for croquettes.

★ Let the purée go cold before rolling it into cork shapes because it's too soft and difficult to shape when hot.

DAUPHINE POTATOES. A mixture of choux pastry and duchess potato, these are potatoes at their most scrumptious. They make a heavenly garnish and accompaniment to grills or steaks. In case you haven't got the recipe, here it is, briefly, to serve 5–6:

$\frac{3}{4}$ lb (375 g) Duchess potato (see next entry)

choux pastry, using 1 egg (page 101 if you need a recipe)

seasoning and deep fat

(1) Heat deep fat to 360°F, 185°C. (If too hot, the outsides will harden before the choux can expand, preventing them rising, as they should, to about the size of a large walnut.)

(2) Slide rounded teaspoonfuls of the mixture carefully into the hot fat, frying several at a time but taking care not to overfill pan. Fry about 6–8 mins, or until golden all over, turning them after a few minutes.

(3) Drain well on absorbent kitchen paper, serve very hot – and don't cover your vegetable dish with a lid.

DUCHESS POTATO. Must be firm enough to hold its shape when piped, so it's important to beat the hot mashed sieved potato with egg, preferably just the yolk, rather than with milk. In addition, the egg binds and flavours it. Pipe the potato as required while still hot, otherwise it goes solid.

★ These are the approximate proportions: 1 lb (say 500 g) potatoes, 1 egg or 2 yolks, $1\frac{1}{2}$ ozs. (40 g) butter or margarine, salt and pepper, pinch nutmeg.

DUNKIRK POTATOES. Taste rather like a sophisticated version of roast. To be sure they're tender inside by the time they're crisp and golden outside, choose smallish potatoes of even size, blanch about 10 mins, dry them off in the hot empty pan, and then deep fry about 20 mins.

GAME CHIPS. Have to be cut wafer thin, to curl up when fried. Slice them by machine if possible, or if by hand, make sure they are thin enough to see the knife blade through the slices.

★ Deep fat is used hotter than for ordinary chips, because game chips are so thin that by the time they're golden, the potato is cooked.

JACKET POTATOES. About the best of all healthwise, because there is no loss of goodness - or of flavour – into water thrown away. They are crisper than ever if you rub the skins with salt after washing them; or if you prefer them soft, rub the skins with oil before baking.

★ Jacket potatoes cook evenly and more quickly if impaled on a Spike Murphy, or with a couple of short metal skewers run through each. This is because metal conducts heat through the middle, cooking the potatoes from the inside as well as from the outside. See page 23.

★ If not served fairly soon when cooked, jacket potatoes develop a nasty strong smell and taste. If necessary to keep hot, cut a cross in each, to help to keep them 'sweet' longer.

NEW POTATOES. These contain lots of Vitamin C, as I've said earlier, so if you don't want to lose this, it's better to scrape them just before a meal than hours earlier. They are much easier to scrape when freshly dug – it's often this rather than the variety which makes new potatoes 'good scrapers'.

★ If the potatoes are tiny, it's quicker to skin them after boiling than to scrape before – some people enjoy eating them in their skins of course. Dried off in the empty pan and skinned when cool enough, they're lovely sautéd in butter, or make the best potato salad.

POTATO PUFFS. Made from smallish round potatoes sliced slightly thicker than a match-stick, and fried three times in deep fat. If either too thick or too thin, they won't 'blow up' the 3rd time they're fried, as they should. The fat should be about 380°F, 190°C, the potatoes fried 5–10 mins the first time, until tenderish but not coloured, and a few minutes the second time until light golden. The third time they should be puffy and golden.

★ See also page 151.

POTATO RIBBONS OR KNOTS. *Prepared* differently from game chips, but fried in the same way. To make *Ribbons*: slice a large peeled potato about ½″ (1¼ cm) thick (the slices of a small potato are too difficult to handle), trim off any projecting points, then peel very thinly round and round with a potato peeler, making the ribbons as long as possible. Make *Knots* the same way, but cut shorter ribbons, and tie a single knot in each. Dry them carefully, especially knots, otherwise they break easily. See also page 151.

ROAST POTATOES. Often seem to take a hammering, poor things. There's more to roasting them than just laying potatoes round a joint, basting now and then. In case yours aren't exactly Ritzy, here are some tips:

(1) Avoid using very small potatoes because roasting dries them out too much.
(2) Potatoes cook better if first blanched (boiled) 5 minutes in well salted water. Drain well in a colander, return to pan and dry them off for a minute or two over minimum heat, to make them floury, agitating pan two or three times meanwhile.
(3) Pierce all with a fork, in several places, to help them absorb a little of the fat and so keep them moist inside.
(4) Put them into *hot* fat, basting immediately. Baste and turn two or three times during cooking.
(5) If a joint is likely to be 'watery', especially a frozen one which hasn't thawed out completely, roast the potatoes separately. Though potatoes get much of their delicious flavour from the roast, they'll be soft rather than crisp outside if cooked in fatty *liquid* instead of fat containing limited meat juices.

SAUTÉ POTATOES. Aren't at all the same thing as fried, being cut up and cooked en masse in hot butter for 15–20 mins, the whole lot occasionally turned over with a fish slice.

★ New potatoes sauté best: boil them in their skins until *nearly* but not quite cooked, drain through a colander, return to pan and dry them off for a minute or two over minimum heat, then allow to cool before skinning. If you want to skin them while very hot, spear them with a fork or protect your hand by wearing a rubber glove. Whether skinned or not, avoid covering the potatoes before they're cold because any trapped steam will make them wet.

★ It's best not to sprinkle sauté potatoes with salt while cooking because this makes them stick to the pan. If previously boiled in well salted water, they won't lack flavour if you add a little more salt *after* sautéing.

★ Chopped herbs and freshly milled black pepper are also added at the last minute, their flavours being spoilt by cooking.

STORAGE. A sackful of potatoes will probably keep better in an outshed (if protected from frost) than in a cellar, where the higher temperature is likely to make them 'shoot' earlier and faster, so making them go soft before they should. It's essential to keep the shoots pulled off once they do start to grow – or the potatoes *will* go soft.

Rhubarb

Really a vegetable, though regarded and used as a fruit. The leaves contain a toxic element, making them unsafe to eat.

★ In some parts of the world, rhubarb has long been used medicinally for its purgative qualities, and only comparatively recently has it been used in Britain as a food.

Rice, Boiled

This is something many people say they can't cook, unless they use 'packet' rice, where you should follow the instructions. I make no claims to being as expert as anyone who has lived in a rice-growing country, but the grains *must* be separate so here are a few tips:

(1) *Ordinary long grain rice* (see page 87), needs washing thoroughly to remove the 'mill flour' which, if not washed out, makes the cooked rice gluey: hold it in a strainer for a minute or two under a fast-running cold tap.

(2) Use a large pan and deep, generously-salted water, so that the swollen rice has plenty of room to boil fast without boiling over.

(3) Put the rice into *fast-boiling* water, stirring it with a fork while water returns to boil if necessary: boil fast enough to keep the rice continually 'dancing'. Some people add a spoonful of lemon juice to the water, to help keep the rice white. (If you put a lid on the pan, the water will boil over.)

(4) Boil the rice 10 mins, until *al dente*. Test it if you like by eating a grain, or press one between thumb and finger.

(5) Drain thoroughly, then pour either boiling or cold water through, according to whether you want it hot or cold, to separate the grains.

(6) When rice needs stirring, use a two-pronged meat fork: you're sure to make it mushy with a spoon. See page 11.

(7) Dry it out if you like in a colander over a pan of simmering water, covered with a clean, dry, loosely folded cloth.

★ To freeze cold boiled rice, put in ice tray, without dividers, to quick-freeze in a shallow block. Remove from tray and seal in thick polythene bag before returning to freezer.

★ From a friend who has lived many years in Persia, I have learnt this easy and *lovely* way to serve rice:

(1) Boil it as above, but several hours or even several days before you need it, running *cold* water through it when boiled. Cover and refrigerate.

(2) Using a strong saucepan, melt – without heating – 2 ozs (50 g) *butter* for each $\frac{1}{2}$ lb (225 g) rice boiled.

(3) Aside from the heat, add rice and some extra salt. Stir with a two-pronged fork until every grain glistens, then cover and leave it until required.

(4) At *least* an hour before you want to serve it, stand pan over low heat, cover rice with only a loosely folded clean tea-towel and leave it, untouched, until time to serve. The crunchy golden rice on the bottom of the pan is the high-spot, while every grain is separate and delicious.

★ See also page 87.

BROWN RICE. Is cooked as boiled, above, but takes much longer to cook; about 40–45 mins. See also page 87.

PILAFF. Also known as *pilaf, pilau* and *pilaw*, this is of Middle Eastern origin, unlike *risotto*, which is of Italian.

RISOTTO. Takes its name from the Italian word for rice, *riso*. For the authentic dish, none other than Italian round grain rice is perfect. Its beauty is that during long slow cooking, and in a small amount of liquid, it manages to remain *al dente* while at the same time becoming creamy.

★ Rice for risotto is cooked in a totally different way from boiled rice. It isn't washed because there's no need to remove the mill flour, and because it must be dry, to fry in the hot butter or oil.

★ If you can't buy Italian rice, it is better to use short grain pudding rice than long grain, because it absorbs the stock better.

Spinach

Must be washed and re-washed until there's no sign of earth, the water clinging to its leaves being all it needs to cook in.

★ Spinach can be puréed in seconds with the coarsest cutter of a Moulin-légumes, which is much quicker than a liquidizer. If you find spinach too bitter, or don't care for it, have you tried adding a pinch of sugar? As for butter or margarine, it will absorb almost any amount you care to add; or is richer and creamier still with double cream – 'single' tending to be too watery.

★ Spinach purée goes twice as far, and is delicious, stirred into a creamy béchamel or mornay sauce.

Swede

A purée of swede is less watery and unpleasant with some potato purée and a little butter or margarine beaten into it. Swede is quite good sautéd too, this again making it less watery, besides giving a dull vegetable some character. See page 141.

Sweet Corn

Grown as a vegetable, sweet corn contains both sugar and starch, differing from field corn, which isn't sweet, and is more starchy. Nobody need explain the difference to you if you have ever tried eating field corn as sweet corn!

★ Grown in your garden, just turning yellow, and eaten within an hour of being picked, sweet corn is a magically different vegetable from the beautiful-*looking* golden, but over-ripe corn cobs we see lined up in the shops. Do try growing it, if you haven't already. The tiny end-of-season ones are sometimes the best of all – you may even be able to eat the whole thing, cob as well.

★ Frozen sweet corn-on-the-cob is one of the few vegetables which need thawing, completely, before being cooked.

Tomatoes

Tomatoes keep fresh longer, look more cheerful and are easier to eat for a picnic if you leave the stalks on. They really mostly need skinning though, and it's important just to loosen the skins without spoiling the flesh – which happens if blanched too long: cover with boiling water for only 10 seconds, before plunging into cold water and skinning.

★ Tomatoes are too watery, and the seeds too bitter, to use as they are for such things as an omelet, tomato purée or ratatouille. If a recipe calls for tomatoes to be 'juiced and seeded', therefore, cut them in half and squeeze gently, to leave only the flesh.

★ The bitterness of tomatoes can be counteracted easily in soups, sauces and sandwiches etc by adding a spot of sugar; and if you've never fried in butter, tomatoes sprinkled with sugar as well as with seasoning, you have a treat in store. The sugar caramelizes and gives them a completely different flavour, as well as sweetening.

★ Halved tomatoes are grilled round side up first, while still firm, and cooked long enough, altogether, to soften them without also losing their shape.

★ Skinned tomatoes freeze well for many purposes: either 'open freeze' them before sealing and freezing, or cut them up and freeze in an ice tray.

★ *As a garnish*, quartered tomatoes are usually better than sliced, because slices tend to disintegrate. If you cut the core out of each quarter with a sharp knife, it will take the seeds with it, and the tomato won't spoil the appearance of a dish by its wateriness.

★ You can make a *miniature tomato* from each seeded quarter if you put them, one at a time, round side down in a piece of butter muslin, then draw the tomato up into a ball, by twisting the muslin tightly around it. They look attractive in an hors-d'oeuvre, glazed with aspic, or for a tomato salad, sprinkled with French dressing. Heat lightly in butter if required hot, say to garnish a sweet pepper in place of the stalk, or in a potato nest.

Turnips

Traditionally served and at their best with fatty meat such as pork, sausages, ham, mutton, goose and duck, because when cooked in or with fat they can absorb large quantities of it. If turnips are simply boiled, it's the *lack* of fat which makes them so unappealing.

★ Except the small tender early ones, turnips are better blanched, before being cooked in another way. Sliced or quartered, this helps to tenderize them and gets rid of their very strong flavour at the same time.

★ Have you tried glazed turnips? They're delicious. See page 142.

Winter Greens

Another name for *Kale* (see page 146).

Zucchini

The Italian name for courgettes (also used by the Americans).

10

SALADS, SALAD COMPONENTS AND SALAD DRESSINGS

General Information

The great thing about salads is their freshness – their fresh flavour, crisp texture and their colourful appetizing appearance.

(1) *The flavour* depends upon using tender young vegetables (whether raw or cooked), salad plants or fruits, and tossing them in various piquant dressings. Some vegetables need to be marinated longer in the dressing than others to develop their full flavour, while certain *cooked* vegetables will have more flavour if turned over in the dressing while still hot – and left to cool in it.

(2) *The texture* of *cooked vegetable* salads depend upon the vegetables being perfectly cooked and, if not left to cool in the dressing, upon being 'refreshed' – plunged straight into cold water after being cooked and drained, as before deep freezing. *The texture* of *salad plants* depends upon them being well dried and 'unhandled' after washing (see *Salad basket*), upon being crisped in the refrigerator if appropriate, and upon being dressed at the last moment to avoid sliminess.

(3) *Colour* is no problem if cooked vegetables are refreshed, and as long as foods are not prepared too soon. Tomatoes especially go dull, and green vegetables lose their fresh colour when left too long in a dressing. Contrasting colours like those of beetroot, tomato, radish, carrot and red pepper should be used in moderation.

(4) *From a health point of view*, raw vegetables and salad plants are as good, if not better sources of Vitamin C than fresh fruit. Dressings make up for vegetables' deficiency in fat, as well as giving piquancy and helping the digestion of rich foods they may accompany.

★ It's surprising how many vegetables normally eaten cooked are unexpectedly good raw, when properly prepared and dressed. As in a fresh fruit salad, so many of their flavours mingle well together. Finely sliced mushrooms or green of leek, wafer-thin sliced courgettes, very young peas, tiny broad beans, finely sliced Brussels sprouts, or green or red cabbage are just a few examples.

★ Salads, besides their accustomed uses, may be the backbone of a mixed hors-d'oeuvre, or just the right thing to serve with a grill or roast. With hot fish, meat, poultry or game, a piquant salad not only clears the palate but enhances the flavour of the main dish too. Served individually and eaten direct from the salad plate, there's no chance of the hot meat plate spoiling the salad's crisp texture, nor of the salad dressing spoiling the main dish and its accompaniments.

★Vegetables 'à la Grecque' refer to highly flavoured cooked vegetables. They're sometimes combined with others in a mixed salad, or served in a mixed hors-d'oeuvre.

Beans, Broad

Delicious raw in a salad if they're really young and tender, marinated about ½ hr in a vinaigrette dressing. Alternatively, *cooked* beans are equally good as long as they're 'refreshed' straight away after boiling, then marinated as raw. See also page 143.

★ Chopped savory, added at the last minute, is a good partner for beans.

Beans, French and Runner

Keep their firm texture, lovely flavour and brilliant colour best if you 'refresh' them immediately after boiling, drain well, and then marinate them in a dressing for about ½ hr. I like them better this way than allowing them to go cold in the dressing, as some people recommend.

Beetroot

Needs to be marinated and turned over several times in dressing for *at least* 3 or 4 hours after it has been cooked, otherwise it tastes 'dead', just like cold beetroot in fact!

★ The way you *cut* beetroot has an extraordinary effect upon its flavour: served chilled, and either sliced wafer-thin, diced or cut into strips, it makes quite a different salad from thickly sliced, served at room temperature.

★ Beetroot makes a bad garnish because it discolours anything it touches. *For* beetroot, as a last-minute colour-giver, chopped chives, parsley, or finely sliced shallots or spring onions both relieve its redness and give extra flavour.

Cauliflower Salad

Just about uneatable if you allow a cooked cauliflower to *go* cold, but it's a totally different thing if you boil its *sprigs* for a few minutes until tender but still firm (see page 145), 'refresh' and drain them, then marinate an hour or two in the dressing.

★ 'Bouquets' of cauliflower make a change in a mixed hors-d'oeuvre: simply press 3 or 4 cooked refreshed flowerets lightly together to form a well-rounded surface, which you can then coat evenly and easily with mayonnaise.

Celeriac

Easier to peel sliced than whole, and there's less waste. Either grate or cut it into thin strips and eat raw, or blanch the strips momentarily if you prefer, to mellow the flavour. Celeriac is sometimes interchangeable with celery, and mayonnaise or vinaigrette dressing go well with it, watercress making a good garnish.

Celery

Gives a crunchy texture and lovely flavour to almost any salad, combining well with salad vegetables and many fruits, including nuts. With something like an oil and vinegar dressing, a cream or sour cream dressing, or mayonnaise thinned down with cream, the delicious sort of mixtures which come to mind are:

Cole Slaw (page 159);
Waldorf Salad (celery, dessert apple, walnuts, raisins);
Rice Salad (rice and, say, peas, sweet corn, celery, peppers etc);
Celery and Orange Salad;
Celery, tinned pineapple, sultanas (soaked 10 mins in hot water).

Chicory

The names endive and chicory are muddling because the French (and Americans) call our chicory 'endives', and our endive 'chicorée'. It's high time we sorted this out because a French menu may mislead some of us.

★ Avoid buying chicory heads which are beginning to turn green, because they're bitter. The plump white ones are best.

Chicory usually only needs wiping as it's seldom dirty inside, but do slice it with a stainless steel knife, otherwise you'll spoil its flavour.

★ Chicory is mild enough to mix well with lots of fruits and vegetables when you slice it finely or cut it into $\frac{1}{2}$ " ($1\frac{1}{4}$ cm) chunks and then separate them out. The larger leaves make good 'boats', filled with a dressed salad, say the remaining chicory, finely sliced and mixed with chopped apple and dates.

★ French dressing with a clove of garlic is the classic partner for chicory and endive, but you may prefer a cream dressing?

Cole Slaw

Sounds infinitely more tempting than *Cabbage Salad*, its meaning, *Cole* being the generic name for any plant of the Brassica family, and *Slaw* deriving from the Danish word for salad. This explains why it's never called Cole Slaw Salad. We have the Americans to thank for thinking up this scrumptious recipe which, with a little imagination, you can concoct in various ways with different fruits and dressings.

★ White Dutch cabbage or red cabbage make the best cole slaw, because of their nutty flavour, crispness, and because either is so solid that, with luck, they won't need washing. This is a big plus, because if you have to wash the cabbage, you've also got to dry it jolly well. Otherwise it dilutes the dressing, making the whole salad watery and tasteless.

★ You only need about 2 ozs (50 g) cabbage per person because, being uncooked, there's no shrinkage. Be sure to shred it finely, to make it delicate and to avoid the salad tasting too strongly of cabbage. It's a mistake to skimp on the other ingredients like apple (or well drained pineapple chunks), celery and walnuts etc because the salad's crunchy texture and lovely flavour depend on this sort of thing.

★ Be wise and make the dressing first, to prevent the chopped apple discolouring: a good cream dressing (page 160) subtly blends everything together, but don't for Cole Slaw substitute single cream, soured cream or yoghourt for the *double* cream because they all make it too watery. For quite a different result, you can toss and chill the vegetables in French dressing, then just before serving, turn them over in a mixture of equal quantities mayonnaise and double cream.

★ Taste Cole Slaw before you serve it, especially for sweetness. Then chill it for $\frac{1}{2}$ hr to help tenderize the cabbage.

Courgettes

If used raw in a salad, should be very young, sliced wafer thin and dégorgéd about $\frac{1}{2}$ hr before marinating in dressing, also for $\frac{1}{2}$ hr, to tenderize and flavour them. Leave the skin on, to give colour, and cut them diagonally to make them look nice.

Cucumber

A native of the East Indies and has been cultivated in China for 3,000 years.

★ Cucumber salad looks cooler and more colourful if you leave the skin on, or better still if you stripe it with a fruit decorator (page 12). Should you find the skin indigestible though, a potato peeler will take it off thinly and quickly.

★ All cucumbers are very watery and some varieties are bitter: cut paper-thin, as it should be, you'll find it has a much *better* flavour if you dégorgé it half an hour or so before covering with dressing (see page 38).

★ For the dressing, use lemon juice or white wine vinegar rather than 'red wine' or 'malt', either of which will spoil the colour of the cucumber. Alternatively you could use distilled (white) malt vinegar. It's better to make a slightly oily dressing like this one, than a sharp: stir 3 tablesps cream, one by one, into a dessertsp lemon juice mixed with salt, paprika and a good pinch of sugar.

★ Chopped chives, parsley, chervil, finely sliced spring onions or caraway seeds make a good garnish if you like any or all of these flavours.

Dressings

Make or mar salads, and there's no doubt about it that most of them are best freshly made. Besides sometimes binding together the ingredients of a salad (for example, rice salad) and making the whole thing more moist and tasty, they have another vital role: to make more digestible the rich sort of dishes which salads often accompany, like roast chicken, roast duck, or salmon.

★ Use two wooden spoons, wooden salad servers or your hands to toss and turn over salad plants and vegetables in a dressing, or vegetables in a marinade. They break up the food less than metal utensils and can't pass on a metal flavour. Marinating vegetables need turning over now and then to make sure the flavour penetrates throughout the food.

CREAM DRESSINGS. Really just a kind of oil and vinegar dressing, see below, using cream, soured cream or yoghourt instead of all or some of the oil, and lemon juice in place of the vinegar if you like. In case you'd like me to cross the t's and dot the i's, here's a delicious recipe: Mix a tablespoonful each of lemon juice and oil with seasoning and a pinch of sugar, then stir in 3 tablesps double cream, one at a time. Stir again just before using of course.

MAYONNAISE. See page 136.

OIL AND VINEGAR SAUCES or DRESSINGS. Also called Vinaigrette Sauces.

French Dressing (or Sauce Vinaigrette). This is the 'Mother Sauce'. It is also often used for a simple marinade.

★ The right ingredients for French Dressing are simple but important, though the proportion of oil to vinegar depends upon how sharp or bland you like it. This is the proportion most people like:

1 tablesp *wine* vinegar or lemon juice – or a mixture of both
3 tablesps olive oil or good salad oil
salt and pepper
$\frac{1}{8}$ teasp dry mustard, optional
1–2 dessertsps chopped green herbs in season, optional

★ Either shake the vinegar, oil and seasonings vigorously together in a screw-top jar, *or* mix the vinegar with the seasonings until the salt is dissolved and then add the oil. Either way, add herbs at the last minute, for perfect flavour and colour.

★ *The vinegar* is more important than lots of people realize. A dressing made with wine vinegar comes from a different world from one made with malt. Just as wine cuts through rich foods, so wine vinegar cuts through the oil in a dressing.

★ Herb vinegars are a good way of introducing other flavours to a salad.

★ See also *Vinegar*, page 94.

★ *The oil* ideal for dressings is 'olive', but it is expensive, and in addition some people dislike its sometimes strong fruity flavour, preferring to use a tasteless one such as a good corn oil. The degree of flavour varies considerably with olive oils according to their country and area of origin, see *Oil*, page 83. You may like sunflower oil better?

★ Heresy though the French consider it to add sugar, some people prefer it that way. Perhaps the French haven't met some of our bitter British lettuces!

★ For variations of French dressing, see page 133, the 'Family Tree' of sauces.

Endive

See *Chicory*.

'Fruit' Salads

Served with a hot or cold main dish, fruit salads really come into their own in winter when most salad plants are out of season. They also liven up a mixed hors-d'oeuvre, or make a cool, fresh starter for a summer lunch.

★ Fruits take on a new flavour when mixed together and dressed with a cream, or oil and vinegar dressing. They blend perfectly with raw winter vegetables like finely shredded cabbage, chopped celery or chicory, also with some cooked vegetables. You might for instance like orange segments and celery, banana and peach with raw grated beetroot and lettuce, or California Salad – lettuce, celery, cucumber, tomatoes, apple and banana?

★ Just as orange salad is good with roast duck, so are such combinations as apricot or pineapple salad with baked gammon or grilled gammon steaks; cherry salad with poultry or game; pear and grape salad with cold ham or roast chicken.

★ If you use tinned fruits, drain them well and use a rather sharper dressing than for fresh, to counteract the sweetness. On the other hand, you're almost sure to want to use a little sugar with some sour fresh fruits.

★ Lemon juice is sometimes better than vinegar in a dressing, a cream dressing going superbly with many salads (see page 160).

★ Experiments with fruit salads don't often go wrong: with lettuce or watercress, even the unlikely mixture of black grapes and sliced banana bound with mayonnaise is delicious with something like cold chicken.

Green Salad

Goes perfectly with such things as roast chicken, turkey or game, as well as with grills, omelets, some cheese dishes and many cold. It can consist of any green salad plant and herbs – nothing of another colour – and is dressed with a vinaigrette sauce.

★ Ideally, the torn-up coarsest lettuce leaves go at the bottom, the heart in the middle surrounded by the smaller leaves, so that the salad looks like a fresh head of lettuce – whether in individual bowls or in one large one. Arrange sprigs of watercress, endive, land cress or anything else green that you like amongst the lettuce, sprinkling it all lightly at the last minute with dressing.

★ Alternatively, simply toss the crisp green salad plants in dressing at the last moment.

Land Cress

American land cress is a good garden substitute for watercress. It's a hardy perennial plant which, in the South of England anyway, hardly gives up even in the winter. The tender young leaves are the best, used whole or chopped up with scissors, say together with chives, for a salad. A sprig also makes a cheery and tasty garnish for lots of savoury dishes.

Lettuce

One of the *most* rewarding things to grow if you have a garden, for with very little shelter, you can eat it nowadays almost every month of the year. With seeds sown at regular short intervals and the thinnings transplanted, to extend their maturing period, anyone with a vegetable patch can at *least* produce lettuces without a break, from spring to autumn.

★ This isn't a seedsman's catalogue, so I'm just going to suggest you look out for some of my different-season favourites:

Buttercrunch
Kloek
Kwiek
Premier
Tom Thumb
Valdor
Webb's Wonderful
Little Gem }
Sugar Cos } Cos
Winter Density }

MIXED LETTUCE. Somebody certainly had a brainwave here, to help the smaller household. Packets contain seeds for both cabbage and cos types, which mature at different times instead of bolting together. For good measure, there's a varied mixture of lettuces to eat. (Cos take their name from one of the Aegean Islands, once so called, from which they were introduced.)

★ Whether you buy or grow lettuce, wash and dry it thoroughly at least an hour before the meal, and put in bottom of refrigerator to make it crisp. (If without, store lettuce in a covered saucepan: with light and air excluded it will deteriorate less quickly than in a vegetable rack.)

★ It's important to dry lettuce properly. If you don't, the leaves won't become crisp, the dressing won't adhere to them, and in addition the dressing is diluted. See *Salad basket*, page 4.

★ A steel knife makes lettuce slimy, so tear up rather than cut any leaves too big to eat whole. If for something like a prawn cocktail you *have* to shred them, use a fine stainless steel saw-knife.

★ You can't *freeze* lettuce any more than you can hope to go on picking it in arctic conditions outside. As up to 97 per cent of it is water, there's no need to say why.

Mixed Salads

Also called Combination Salads or Salades Composées, they are of several categories. They may be based on mixed cooked vegetables, like Salade Niçoise and some rice salads, or they may consist of things like chicken, turkey, ham, tongue, fish or shellfish *with* salad plants and mixed vegetables. Into the latter group comes such a comparatively simple dish as cold beef salad, as well as the much more sophisticated ones such as salmon and lobster mayonnaise.

★ If a salad contains fish or poultry coated with aspic or chaud-froid sauce, then strictly speaking it's a cold entrée rather than a Mixed Salad.

Mushroom Salad

Good with cold chicken, cold meats, or in a mixed hors-d'oeuvre, but it has to be perfect to be good. The day before yesterday's mushrooms are unlikely to be crisp enough to eat raw, so this means making sure they're fresh and firm when you buy them. See page 147.

★ The mushroom caps need slicing paper-thin if they're to tenderize and develop flavour in ½–1 hr while marinating in a French dressing. In a shorter time, they'll taste of nothing, left longer they'll largely turn to water.

★ Red wine vinegar makes a good French dressing – which for this salad seems best slightly on the sharp side.

Salade Niçoise

Is of course a Mediterranean dish, with lots of variations. It's composed chiefly of Mediterranean foods which traditionally include cooked French beans, tomatoes, boiled potatoes, black olives, finely sliced green peppers, anchovy fillets, lettuce, hard-boiled eggs and perhaps tinned tuna fish.

★ Chopped fresh green herbs are added to the French dressing, which usually contains garlic, and needs lots of freshly ground black pepper. Serve this lovely dish as an hors-d'oeuvre or as a main course Mixed Salad, with the tuna.

★ Cut the beans in small diamonds before boiling and refreshing them, and dice the potatoes after they're boiled. Stone the olives of course, and quarter the tomatoes (juiced and seeded, otherwise they'll make the salad watery).

Orange Salad

Traditionally served with roast duck, but oranges make lovely salads to go with other dishes as well. When mixed with oil and vinegar, they don't taste the same as when fresh, and combine delightfully with sliced chicory or finely sliced shallots, spring onions or Spanish onions and black olives.

The orange segments must be absolutely free of pith as well as skin, otherwise will be bitter (see page 000).

Potato Salad

All the better for a little know-how, not to mention waxy *new* potatoes (not a dish to use up left-over or cold potatoes). If you mix the hot, *very slightly* under-cooked, diced potatoes in the dressing and allow them to cool in it, they'll absorb the flavour and acquire character they'd never otherwise have.

★ Main-crop potatoes break up less when steamed than boiled, and if you cook potatoes in their skins, they'll have lots more flavour than if peeled beforehand.

Toss them a few moments in the hot empty pan over low heat to dry them off, then skin and dress them.

★ Large quantities of thick mayonnaise give potato salad a cloying effect. It's much nicer made thinner, or with a well-seasoned French dressing, either of them flavoured with finely chopped shallots or spring onions, and chopped fresh green herbs.

Radishes

Make a decorative garnish and are no problem to digest if sliced wafer-thin, but if you like to serve them whole, leave on a tiny bit of the green tip, to hold them by.

★ A packet of mixed seeds scores over a single variety, because they mature at different dates, giving an extended harvest. The other bonuses are variety of flavour, size and shape, all from one sowing.

★ *Radish roses* are more successfully made with long thin ones than round, because they open up better. Cut about $\frac{3}{4}$ way down from root end to stem end – first one way, then the other, and perhaps twice more, like this ✳ – and leave to soak about $\frac{1}{2}$ hr in cold water.

Rice Salad

Splendidly colourful and easy for a winter party, or as the base of a Mixed Salad with left-over fish, shellfish, meat or poultry. It can be just as good as it looks, too, if the long grain rice itself is properly cooked (page 154) and allowed to cool in enough French dressing to glaze it. Stirred together with a two-pronged fork, the rice will absorb the flavour of the dressing as it cools, and the grains will remain separate instead of forming a stodgy mass.

★ All sorts of things besides the well-tried peas and pineapple chunks help to give rice salad flavour and colour:

(1) *Vegetables*, such as chopped red or green peppers (quickly blanched and refreshed), sweet corn, shredded celery, finely sliced shallots or spring onions. Cooked vegetables which have been *left* to go cold are second-rate. It's much better to cook, *refresh* and drain them, then they'll retain their fresh flavour, colour and texture.

(2) *Fruits*, such as tomatoes (juiced and seeded, see page 155), tinned mandarin segments, orange segments, chopped apple, sultanas or chopped browned nuts – added at the last minute, to make sure they don't go soft.

(3) *Herbs and flavourings*, such as chopped parsley, chives or dill, instant garlic powder or a pinch of cayenne.

(4) *Dressings* may consist of more French dressing or say a soured cream dressing (soured cream replacing oil in a French dressing) or a dressing made with equal quantities of mayonnaise and double cream.

Shallots

See page 148.

Spring Onions

If you serve them whole, they should have about $1\frac{1}{2}$–2 ″ (4–5 cm) of the top left on, to make them easy to pick up. Finely sliced spring onions can often take the place of shallot if necessary, either in a salad or in a cooked dish.

Summer Salad

A truly English salad and can include almost anything you can think of in the salad line – lettuce, chicory, endive, watercress, land cress, cucumber, tomatoes, radishes, spring onions, finely sliced shallot, chopped herbs, hard-boiled egg or cheese (grated, sliced or cubed).

★ As tomatoes and egg tend to disintegrate when sliced, it's nicer to quarter them, and salad plants should be tossed in an oil and vinegar dressing.

Tomato Salad

Much less watery if you quarter rather

than slice the fruits (serving them points upwards) and if you make and dress it more or less at the last minute.

★ Basil is wedded to tomatoes as mint is to peas, or you can garnish tomato salad with other finely chopped herbs such as parsley or chives, as well as with finely sliced shallot, spring onions or Spanish onion. See also page 148.

Watercress

Makes a lovely colourful, fresh-looking garnish for a hot dish like roast chicken or game, as well as for something cold, or in a salad.

★ Take off any white rootlets high on the stem, as well as discoloured leaves, but don't cut off all the stem – just the bottom coarse parts.

★ If you want to arrange watercress springs in tiny bouquets, you'll probably find it easiest to dip each bunch head-down in a well-emulsified oil and vinegar dressing, then shake gently to flick off any surplus.

11
FISH

General Information

Fish cookery is largely influenced by the flavour or lack of flavour of particular fish. While salmon for instance is naturally so succulent and delicious that it could almost cook itself, white fish by and large depend upon the cook enhancing their flavour, if not actually providing it.

★ Fish, like meat, takes flavour from the bones during cooking, hence fish on the bone tends to be more tasty than fillets. That is why fish like halibut are usually cut into steaks on the bone in preference to being filleted; it is the main reason why small fish, flat or round, have more flavour when cooked whole than when filleted; it is also why it is important, if possible, to *use* the head and bones when cooking fillets, to make good cooking liquor, or to make stock for a sauce.

★ Why leave the trimmings with the fishmonger when fish stock makes superb soups, even if you don't want it for the fish itself? If without *better* use for it, it makes tastier potato soup than does many a white stock. See *Stock, fish*, page 89.

★ From the cook's angle, fish are usually divided into three groups because each group has similar characteristics, requiring a similar approach:

OILY FISH. Those such as salmon, mackerel, sardines and the herring family are basically flavourful, rich (12–20 per cent fat) and not always easily digested, because most of their fat – oil – is distributed throughout their flesh. That's mainly why these fish are more nutritious and darker in colour than white fish, whose fat is largely stored in the liver, which we discard. It's also why cod liver oil and halibut liver oil can be produced, but not mackerel or herring liver oil.

★ You can poach, steam, grill or fry oily fish fairly successfully without much fuss, knowledge or extra flavouring, counteracting the richness with accompaniments such as a dressed salad or a piquant sauce, rather than accentuating it by rich methods of cookery or rich accompaniments.

★ Most oily fish make a good cold meal too, whether it's an elaborate dish like salmon in aspic, or a simple one like soused herring.

★ Brown bread and butter, which contains carbohydrates, is often served with oily fish so that the valuable protein in the fish isn't used up to give 'energy', instead of being used for 'body-building'.

WHITE FISH. They lack the richness and strong flavour of oily fish, but you can make up for these in the kitchen in almost dozens of different ways. Some fish are in fact so bland that, like potatoes, you can cook them in such varied ways that you need never tire of them. You can enrich or flavour them for instance by such simple means as frying, or by such sophisticated accompaniments as Béarnaise sauce.

★ Speaking generally, you can cook fillets of all such fish as dab, brill, flounder, plaice, sole, turbot, trout and whiting in similar ways, as you can most small whole flat fish and most large fish, whether whole, sliced or filleted. Due to the unique qualities of many fish however, there *are* methods of preparation and numerous dishes specific to certain types.

★ White fish is nourishing (17 per cent protein) without being fattening (.5 per cent fat) to those who worry, or ought to worry (!) about their weight. You can also cook it so lightly, and it's so digestible, that it makes one of the best foods you can think of for tiny children, old people or invalids.

SHELLFISH are divided into two groups, *crustaceans* and *molluscs*:

★ *Crustaceans* – eg crab, crayfish, lobster, prawn – take their name from the Latin word *crusta*, a crust or shell. Unlike other fish, and mammals, their skeleton is on the outside, their flesh inside.

★ *Molluscs* are themselves divided into two main groups:
Univalves (eg winkles, whelks, snails) and *Bivalves* (eg mussels, oysters, scallops, cockles).

★ In addition, there are the fish with tentacles, like the squid or octopus.

★ Even if you squirm at the thought of cooking it, you can't fault the fish in countries where they sell it live, tasting as it does of the sea. Freshness, important for all fish, is absolutely vital for shellfish, both for safety and flavour.

★ Some shellfish, like crab or lobster for instance, are as often served hot as cold because they can be just as good either way, yet taste quite different. To counteract their richness, generally, and to make shellfish more digestible, serve accompaniments like a piquant sauce, a dressed salad, lemon quarters and brown bread and butter.

★ It's hardly surprising that the French and English names of certain types of shellfish confuse some people. Anyone could be excused for thinking a Dublin Bay prawn was a kind of prawn, and some might be surprised to find that crayfish, crawfish and langouste are one and the same thing. If you're in a muddle, this collection of the more familiar fish may help you to unravel it:

PREPARATION OF FISH.

While many cookery books give instructions for choosing and cleaning fish as well as for cooking it, a few off-beat tips may be helpful:

(1) It's easiest to scrape the scales off fish with a sharp knife if you hold the fish upside down by the tail. You can then wash off any loose scales under running water.

English name	*French name*	*Comments*
crab	crabe	See also page 170
crayfish, sea-water	langouste	Also called crawfish
,, fresh-water	écrevisse	
Dublin Bay prawn	langoustine	Not in fact a prawn, but of the lobster family – sometimes up to 8″ (20 cm) in length. *Culinary* name 'scampi' comes from Italian word *scampo*. See also *Scampi*, page 176.
lobster	homard	See also page 173.
mussel	moule	See also page 174.
oyster	huître	See also page 174.
prawn	crevette rose	See also page 175.
scallop	coquille Saint-Jacques	Also commonly known as the *Pilgrim Shell*. Pilgrims finding empty shells on the shore used them as cup, spoon and dish. *Coquille* is French for shell, see also page 176.
shrimp	crevette grise	See also page 176.

(2) Dip your thumb and fingers in a small heap of salt so that you can grip fish firmly, and keep it under perfect control. Salt is useful too to rub off any black 'film' still remaining after cleaning, washing and drying a fish.

(3) Rolled or folded fillets of fish such as sole and plaice *must* be skinned because, quite simply, they are unpleasant to eat otherwise. The white skin's texture is no nicer than the black, so skinned fillets always score over unskinned, because you can eat the lot.

(4) Rolled fillets will look larger, will stand firmly and will not unfold if you lay each fillet skinned side upwards, and roll it from head to tail round a thick raw potato chip: the chip should be flush with the bottom of the fillet when the roll is standing up, and long enough to stick out at the top, to pull it out easily when the fish is cooked. The chip also makes a handle when coating the rolled fillet with egg and breadcrumbs.

(5) If you're cooking small flat fish whole, and dislike the constant battle on your plate with the tiny bones down the sides, then trim the fish to the edge of the flesh with scissors before you coat or cook it. It makes the fish look small, but it's easy and good to eat.

(6) Scoring, mostly of round fish, is only necessary when you cook fish whole: it prevents the skin from bursting, and it looks attractive. It also helps both the heat and the flavourings (from seasonings and sauces) to penetrate the fish.

METHODS OF FLAVOURING FISH. The most insipid of fish can swim into the luxury class as long as it's really fresh, for even these you can make distinctive in various ways.

(1) *Poaching*. Poach the fish in wine (or wine and water, or vermouth and water), fish stock, or a 'court bouillon'. Generally speaking, you need *just* enough liquid to cover the fish, but if you boil rather than poach it, it will break up and become watery: poach it in the oven or a frying pan, but be sure to grease whatever you cook it in, to prevent the fish sticking to it.

★ If you poach it in *wine*, flavour it with finely chopped shallots or spring onions as well as with seasoning, and use the strained wine afterwards to make a velouté sauce (page 139). This is a delicious way to cook fillets of white fish – and doesn't take much wine.

★*Fish stock* (page 89) may ideally contain wine, but you can also make it quite simply with the head, bones and trimmings of the fish you're cooking. 'Reduce' the fish stock after the fish is cooked, to concentrate the flavour, and then use it as wine above, to make a veloute sauce.

★ *Court bouillon* (page 37), a herby spicy liquid, is used *mostly* for whole fish or large pieces of fish.

★ If you poach fish in *milk*, the fish will have more flavour if fried first for a minute or two in a little butter.

(2) *Marinating*. Marinate the fish before you cook it. Even a simple marinade like lemon juice will give fish some zip if soaked in it for half an hour, first one side and then the other.

(3) *Using herbs*. Use parsley, thyme, bayleaf, dill or fennel to flavour poaching water, or in a sauce which will enhance the flavour of the fish. Alternatively use a herb butter or add a little parsley wine to the poaching water, or sprinkle chopped herbs on top of the cooked fish. You'll be able to think of other ways of introducing herbs too.

(4) *Stuffings*. You can stuff almost any kind of white fish, skewering the fish, or tying the stuffing in with thread if necessary.

(5) *Coating*. Coat the fish with egg and breadcrumbs, batter, seasoned oatmeal, or seasoned flour: egg and breadcrumbs will stick better, and the fish will have more flavour, if you dip it first in seasoned flour. Fine, dried white breadcrumbs give a better and more professional finish than fresh or golden breadcrumbs.

(6) *Frying*. If you fry fish, especially in deep fat or butter, it gives it a marvellous flavour. Deep frying is ideal for small whole fish, fillets and small pieces of larger fish. Shallow frying is good too, as well as for thicker slices (steaks) of fish which need longer cooking.

★ When you've fried fish in butter,

counteract the richness and make it really tasty by deglazing the pan with lemon juice, which you can then pour over the fish. See page 174, *Meunière*.

★ Alternatively fry some chopped nuts in the butter after the fish is cooked, and when nicely browned pour everything over the fish.

(7) *Grilling or baking*. Baste the fish with a savoury butter. If the fish is too large to grill whole, cut it into slices (steaks) 1–1½″ (2½–4 cm) thick, and cook them as whole fish: the smaller the fish the hotter the grill should be – larger fish need slower cooking so that the heat can penetrate the flesh gradually.

(8) *Steaming*. The fish can lie between two plates or in foil, with butter, to retain all the fish juices and flavour.

(9) *Serving with a sauce*. Make a fish velouté from the poaching liquid or from fish stock. Other suitable sauces include a Béchamel such as Mornay made with the *milk* in which you've poached the fish, and also sauces made independently of the fish such as Hollandaise, Tartare, savoury butters or hot butter sauces.

(10) *Serving fish 'au gratin'*. Either sprinkle the cooked fish with golden breadcrumbs before dotting it with melted butter and grilling it, *or* coat the fish with a sauce, say Mornay, then sprinkle it with grated cheese and breadcrumbs before grilling.

(11) *Garnishing*. Serve tasty and attractive garnishes such as lemon quarters, capers, fried parsley, chopped herbs, mushrooms fried in butter, shrimps, grapes or match-stick potatoes.

HINTS ABOUT COOKING FISH.

(1) A long flexible fish slice is essential because fish lacks the connective tissue of meat, so (for this and for other reasons) breaks up more readily when cooked.

(2) Place fish fillets boned side down first when you fry them in shallow fat: that way you only need to turn them once, reducing the risk of them breaking up. Another advantage is that the first side fried is usually the more golden: (butter for instance may brown before you fry the second side.)

(3) Fillets of fish or small whole flat fish fried in deep fat will *remain* flat if you fry them between two frying baskets – if you have them.

★ If frying fillets in shallow fat, they'll keep flat if, at the beginning, you hold them down with a pallet knife or a long fish slice. Otherwise they tend to curl up, so fry unevenly.

(4) Fillets of fish such as lemon sole, plaice and whiting, which tend to flake after poaching – unlike dover sole and brill which do not – are best cooked, sauced and served in the original poaching dish, to avoid their breaking up.

(5) Correct cooking times really matter. Under-cooked fish is uninviting, to put it mildly. Over-cooked fish loses flavour and also breaks up: fish is cooked when it is opaque, when the flesh has shrunk slightly from the bone, if any, and when the flakes – if flaked type of fish – are just beginning to separate.

★ Fish is usually cooked according to thickness rather than weight, but sometimes to both, especially in the case of large whole fish. Test fish always at the thickest part.

(6) When making such dishes as salmon mayonnaise or chaud-froid of halibut, and preparing the cooked fish, that's the time to remember that compact neat pieces help the general appearance of the finished dish: each piece will be easy to coat with sauce if you wrap it tightly in butter muslin while still hot. Pressed flat, the fish will firm up as it cools, making it easier to handle too. When quite cold, cover it with foil or damp greaseproof paper until ready to coat it.

SERVING FISH.

(1) Serve fried fish on a plain doyley, which helps to absorb excess fat not already absorbed by draining.

(2) Never keep fried fish hot in a *covered* dish, because the trapped steam makes it go soft.

Anchovies

To the ancient world they were what the

herring has been to ours. For all we know of the anchovy though, they might be *caught* in tins because, as they don't travel, we can never eat them fresh in England. Anyone who has once tasted them straight from the Mediterranean however, will know what an unrecognizably different fish the fresh anchovy is from the tinned.

★ Wash anchovy fillets in hot water and dry on absorbent kitchen paper if you dislike their saltiness or oiliness, or if for a particular purpose you want them fat-free.

★ If anchovies go hard, as they may if you don't use the whole tinful at once, you can soften them and at the same time get rid of their saltiness by soaking a few hours in milk.

★ If you have a freezer, you can pop any unwanted ones in there, for use another time, then they *won't* go dry.

★ Use them amongst other things to make:

(1) Anchovy butter (see page 131), to cook or serve with fish, or to add to a sauce served with fish.
(2) Anchovy Toast, see page 275.
(3) Anchovy Sauce, by adding anchovy essence, if you can obtain it, or anchovy paste to a white or béchamel sauce.

Bloaters

Are smoked ungutted herring, unlike kippers which are split, smoked and usually dyed.

★ Yarmouth bloaters became famous because of the herring being in prime condition when the shoals arrived off Yarmouth in the autumn, before they cast their roe. It's so essential to eat bloaters at once (they keep no longer than fresh fish) that in days gone by the epicure would go to Yarmouth – not allowing the fish to do the travelling – and even there, eating them before going to bed rather than waiting for breakfast!

★ Fry or grill them, or if you can be bothered with all the bones, make bloater spread.

Bream, Sea

Deserves more customers than it seems to have because, though it looks coarse, it has good flesh. You can just about *pull* the rough pink skin off the fillets before cooking as cod or haddock etc.

Brill

With light and delicate flesh, it is allied to the dab, plaice and sole, and belongs to the same family as the turbot. Cook fillets as sole, or a whole fish as turbot.

Brisling

Small sea-fish of the herring type, of North European waters, canned in oil like sardines, though quite unlike them in other ways.

Cockles

Small bivalve molluscs, which make a tasty fish soup and are good with Sauce Poulette (page 132 of Family Tree), or in fish sauces in place of oysters or mussels, when these aren't available. (Cockles are in fact often more difficult to get than oysters or mussels, depending on where you live.)

Cod

First introduced to Europe by the Basque mariners, who came upon it on their frequent whaling expeditions to Newfoundland.

★ Cod *steaks*, sometimes difficult to buy in these days when so many people want everything simplified, are twice as good as fillet. This is because, during cooking, so much flavour from the bone goes into the flesh. See also *General Information*.

COD FILLET, SMOKED. Isn't nearly so overpowering if soaked overnight in cold water before cooking.

Crabs

Known like lobsters as the cock and hen, crabs are quite tricky to select because the shell hides the meat – or lack of it. Medium-sized crabs, which are heavy in relation to their size, are usually best because they're both fleshy and 'sweet'. It's wiser to avoid:

(1) Crabs with missing limbs – you're losing good flesh.

(2) Very large crabs, which may be coarse.

(3) Those stuck with barnacles, which are probably old.

(4) Any which rattle when you shake them, because they'll be watery rather than fleshy.

(5) Tiny crabs, unless you're adept at preparing them, because the small amount of meat hardly justifies the fiddling work.

★ Lots of books tell you how to cope with a crab but here are a few tips:

(1) Use tongs to pick up live crabs if you're squeamish or not used to handling them.

(2) Lay a crab on its back to remove claws, first the big then the smaller ones, twisting them off inwards.

(3) Separate upper shell from lower by placing both thumbs under tail flap (the big part) and pushing up until body breaks from shell.

(4) Have one small basin for the white meat, another for the brown (mainly the liver and roe) and something else for the inedible parts: the spongy gills known as the dead men's fingers; the stomach, a little sac which lies near the head; and the twist of intestines with the greenish matter.

(5) To crack round the natural line on the underside of the shell, tap gently with a skewer and small hammer, when it will break off easily.

(6) The shell (and any claws used for garnish) will glisten and look lovely if you rub it over lightly with salad oil after scrubbing and drying.

Eel

The most nourishing of all fish, freshwater eel even more so than sea-eel (conger), salmon, mackerel or herring. It's so rich in fact that you may want to remove the layer of fat between the skin and flesh to make it more digestible.

★ Eel's blood may poison you if it gets into a wound, but cooking and the action of the gastric juices make it harmless.

SMOKED EEL. Delicious, and superior in many people's opinion, to smoked salmon. See also *Smoked fish*, page 121 and page 177.

Fish Cakes

Have more flavour when made with haddock than with cod and are delicious too using other fish like bream, halibut, salmon or even tinned mackerel.

★ You can't make fish cakes without egg, which coagulates when heated, binding everything together. Without, they'll disintegrate when fried: whole egg tends to make the mixture too soft, white of egg alone gives neither flavour nor colour, so it's better to use just the yolk which binds, flavours and makes the fish cakes golden at a stroke.

Fish Pie

Doesn't *have* to be made with parsley sauce, though people seldom make it with anything else. Whether you make cheese sauce, mushroom, mustard, anchovy or egg, the 'pie' will be more tasty if you use a béchamel sauce base (page 138), or if you include the liquid in which the fish was cooked, or use some stock made with its bones and trimmings (see *Fish stock*, page 89).

Haddock

One of the more aristocratic members of the cod family, but why must so many fishmongers only sell it filleted when it's so much better on the bone? Everything nowadays has to be made easy for us, though on balance we must often lose out.

★ Haddock excels when smoked, which explains why there's such a variety to choose from: golden cutlets, finnan haddock, smoked fillet and smokies. See also *Smoked fish*, page 177.

GOLDEN CUTLETS. Very small haddock filleted in a special way, dyed and cold smoked.

HADDOCK FILLET, SMOKED. Is often from a large fish, and too strong by far. Soaked overnight in cold water before cooking, its flavour is mellowed.

FINNAN HADDOCK. Undyed and cold-smoked, this has a finer flavour than golden cutlets, chiefly because the flesh takes flavour from the bone.

★ Finnan is a corruption of Findon, the name of a place near Aberdeen, famous for the finest smoked haddock.

SMOKIES. Small haddock smoked closed, instead of split, like finnan haddock.

Hake

Another close relation of the cod, with flesh which is tender, white, flaky and easy to digest. Cook similarly, remembering steaks will have more flavour than fillet. See also *General Information*.

Halibut

From *hali* and *butt*, means 'holy fish', supposedly because it used to be eaten on holy days. The largest of the world's flat fish, weighing anything from $1\frac{1}{2}$–400 lbs ($\frac{3}{4}$–180 kilos), the most enormous on record (landed at Grimsby in 1957) weighed 504 lbs and was thought to be over 60 years old.

CHICKEN HALIBUT. The very young fish weighing 2–4 lbs (say 1–2 kilos) have the finest flesh, larger halibut being coarser.

★ Cook halibut on the bone to know its real flavour, or cook fillets in almost any way you like (see page 167).

★ Halibut, like cod, is a wonderful source of Vitamin D – halibut liver oil – but we don't of course eat the liver when we eat the fish. See also *General Information*.

Herring

These fish move around Britain in a clockwise direction, which explains why at certain seasons of the year they are caught off different parts of our coast, and why those caught at some places are better than others, so much *depending* on that season.

★ Though the once 'penny herring' now costs a fortune by comparison, they're still as nutritious, tasty and bony as ever. In case you're not sure how to cope with them, here's the remedy for boniness:

TO CLEAN AND BONE.

(1) This is a slightly gory (though not too time-consuming or horrible) operation, so it's sensible to collect the gear you need before embarking on surgery: a sharp filleting (or similar shaped) knife, a pair of sharp, pointed scissors to cut off the fins, cooking salt to help you grip the fish firmly, a scrap of clean cloth or some absorbent kitchen paper to dry the fish and, on top of your chopping board, several layers of torn-up newspaper in which to wrap and get rid of the emerging mess.

(2) Hold herring upside down by its tail, head on board, and scrape off any loose scales with the sharp edge of your knife. Cut off all fins.

(3) Lay herring along board, head to your right, underside downward, and (at a slanting angle) *almost* cut off the head. Now *pull* it off where still attached by the uncut skin at the bottom. Hopefully, the innards should come away with it.

(4) Using knife or scissors, slit right down the underside and open fish out, taking care of any roe if still inside. Take out such roe, and remove any black 'film' by rubbing with salt.

(5) Remove backbone: open fish out as much as possible and lay it slit part downwards on chopping board. Now with the palm of your hand stretched right along it, press and flatten herring against the board. Turn fish over. Slip knife under backbone at head end and gently lever bone out, taking as many as possible of the small bones with it.

Pull out any other bones you see.
(6) Wash and dry fish well before cooking, eg dipping in seasoned flour or oatmeal to fry, or sousing etc.

HERRING, SOUSED. Are better if *cooked* the previous day because the liquid has a chance to gel slightly, and the fish firms up and absorbs more flavour from the liquid if allowed to cool and soak in it overnight. Vinegar not only counteracts the richness of oily fish like herring and mackerel but, combined with long slow cooking, softens and dissolves the smaller bones. That's why 'Roll Mops' are no problem to eat, even for children.

★ As soused herring tend often to receive rather unfair treatment, here's what to do:
(1) When cleaning and boning herring as above, leave on the back fin which, sticking up, acts as a herring's own garnish.
(2) Dip fish in liberally seasoned flour, and roll from head to tail, skin side outwards, then they won't unroll.
(3) Pack fish tightly in an ovenware dish, fins upwards, sprinkling over them a finely sliced shallot (or a little onion), salt, a few peppercorns, a clove and a cut-up bayleaf. *Just* cover with a mixture of equal quantities wine vinegar and water. (Wine vinegar gives a finer flavour and cuts through the richness of the fish better than malt.) If you *swamp* the herring with vinegar and water, there's no chance of the liquid gelling, and both fish and liquid will be insipid.
(4) Cover with lid or foil and bake in a slow oven, gas 2, 300°F, 150°C about $1\frac{1}{4}$ hrs. Allow to cool and 'set'.
(5) Serve with a little of the liquid over the fish, and with brown bread and butter, a wedge of lemon and a salad, all of which help to make it digestible as well as tasty.

Kedgeree

A corruption of the Hindustani name *khichri*, a favourite Indian dish, and one often served at Anglo-Indian breakfast tables. Though our English version is different from the Indian, it's one of the most savoury breakfast or supper dishes imaginable, when properly made. This involves:
(1) Using FISH and rice, not RICE with a dash of fish! You need *at least* 8 ozs (225 g) cooked flaked fish to half that quantity of long grain rice.
(2) Using really tasty fish: to me, no other fish compares with finnan haddock, but some people like to use a mixture of this and white fish, or smoked haddock fillet and white fish. Others use salmon.
(3) Boiling the rice properly (see page154), and stirring it (or the made kedgeree) always with a two-pronged fork, to make sure the grains are kept separate.
(4) Seasoning the kedgeree generously. Do be sure to taste it before serving, adding chopped parsley or chives at the very last moment, without cooking.

★ If you want to make it in advance, for convenience, try heating it like boiled rice, in the Persian way (see page 154): stir the cooked fish, hard-boiled egg and seasonings along with the rice into the melted butter, allowing a little *extra* butter. Cook 1 hr as directed for rice, sprinkling with chopped parsley or chives at the last minute. It's delicious, unusually crunchy and, in the refrigerator the night before, you can have it all ready for breakfast the next morning, if you put the pan over heat as soon as you get up.

Kippers

If properly smoked and well cooked, kippers are a delicacy – this you're sure to know if you've ever eaten either Craster or some of the finest small Scotch kippers. Some people prefer to grill them (brushed first with melted butter), others prefer to fry them, but either way if you cook them until dark brown and crisp, their smoky flavour is drawn out. You can also bake, poach or steam them.

VARIATIONS ON A KIPPER!
(1) Make kipper spread, if you have time to cope with the bones, to use as a sandwich filling, spread on canapés etc.

(2) Serve marinated (raw) kipper fillets as an hors-d'oeuvre, with brown bread and butter and lemon quarters. (Be sure to marinate them *several hours* to tenderize, flavour them and counteract their richness.)

(3) Make *Yarmouth Straws*: lay a tiny sliver of raw kipper between two uncooked, rather long cheese straws, pinch together the ends of the straws then twist each three-layer straw into a spiral before baking.

★ Kippers aren't only a breakfast dish: if you want to serve them for high tea or supper, they and malt whisky go hand in hand.

Lobsters

Around 2 lbs (say 1 kilo) in weight is the best size for eating, and should produce about 12 ozs (say 375 g) meat. The hen is thought to be more tender and delicate than the cock but there's less meat on it and it's not so firm when cooked.

★ Cooking or killing a live lobster always makes me shudder but, mercifully for anyone like me, there are others who don't seem to bat an eyelid. *Homard à l'Américaine* for instance calls for the lobster to be split alive, while for other hot dishes requiring uncooked meat, you can kill the lobster in a painless way first. It all depends what you're going to make as to what method you settle for:

FOR RECIPES USING COOKED LOBSTER. The lobster will have a finer flavour if you put it into *boiling* liquid (eg court bouillon, or court bouillon and sea-water) rather than cold because the former seals in the juices. If you bring it gradually to the boil in cold – *possibly* the more humane method – the flavouring juices in the lobster are drawn out into the liquid as it heats. (Be sparing with the vinegar in a court bouillon, otherwise you'll spoil the colour of the shell.) After simmering 10–15 mins to the lb (450 g), let the lobster cool in the liquid.

FOR HOT DISHES USING UNCOOKED LOBSTER. Just before cooking, either plunge the point of your knife into its head, between the eyes, or sever the spinal cord by making a small incision in the back of the shell at the juncture of the chest and tail.

★ When cutting a *boiled* lobster in half, there's less risk of breaking the shell when the tail is tucked underneath than when the lobster is stretched out.

★ The inedible parts of a lobster are: *The gills*, otherwise known as the dead men's fingers; *the stomach*, a hard sac or bag in the right side of the head; *the intestine*, a thin grey or black line running down through the tail meat. This can poison you if eaten.

★ Coral, the roe of the hen lobster, is greeny black when raw, bright red when cooked, while the green or creamy part of a lobster is the liver – and shouldn't be discarded. Should there be water inside, include it in the sauce if you're making one, to give it extra flavour.

★ Lobster and sherry have the same sort of affinity as say, duck and orange, or chicken and tarragon, so it's always safe to marinate cooked lobster for a short time in dry sherry before 'finishing' and serving. See also *Shellfish*, page 166.

Lump Fish

Eaten smoked, is also called *lumpsucker, henfish, sea-hen* or *paddle-cock*. If you've never heard of any of those names, you'll at least know the fish for its roe – salted, dyed black or red and sold as Mock Caviar.

Mackerel

These go off more quickly than almost any other fish, which explains why, at one time, it was the only fish allowed to be hawked in the streets in England on Sundays. With present-day freezing methods, of course, everything is different, but be sure the eyes are protruding, and the skin is iridiscent. Dull, limp fish with sunken eyes are indigestible, unpleasant to eat and may be poisonous.

★ Hot or cold, mackerel is one of *the* best fish. If you've never eaten it for instance *à la Meunière* (below) or soused, you've got a treat in store. Smoked mackerel is good too.

SOUSED MACKEREL. Clean and bone, prepare and cook as Soused Herring, (page 172), but cut each fish into two fillets (if large) before rolling up, and bake $1\frac{1}{2}$ hrs instead of $1\frac{1}{4}$ hrs.

★ See also *Oily Fish*, page 165.

Meunière, à la

Meaning 'as the miller's wife would cook it', this is a classic (and heavenly) way of cooking and serving small whole fish, fish steaks or fillets. Here, briefly, is the method:

(1) Dip fish in seasoned flour.

(2) Fry on both sides in a generous quantity of *hot butter* (saltless or clarified, ideally, which don't burn so readily) until cooked and golden. Transfer to warmed dish and keep hot.

(3) Lightly brown any remaining butter (if not already brown), 'deglaze' the pan with a dessertspoon or two of lemon juice, and pour this piping hot, lemon-flavoured butter over the fish before sprinkling it with chopped parsley.

Molluscs

See *Shellfish*, page 166.

Mussels

Full of protein and rich in Vitamin D, mussels aren't nowadays associated with danger the way they used to be, due to the scrupulous care taken in rearing. If you never buy them, do you really know what you are missing?

★ The chore of getting mussels to the table lies in their preparation:

(1) Make sure they're alive, discarding any that are open, broken, or remain open after tapping them sharply on the sink. Keep in cold water up to the last minute.

(2) Scrub and clean them meticulously, shaving off their beards (with which they cling to the rocks) and scraping off any barnacles. If you just give them 'a lick and a promise' kind of wash, the delicious juices, which pour out of the mussels as they open during cooking, will be fouled by the slime and dirt on the shells, almost certainly making the liquid unuseable.

(3) Soak mussels an hour or two in a pail or large bowl of fresh water, giving them time to disgorge some of their sand, and to make them less salty. Gritty mussels are as bad as gritty leeks.

(4) Lift carefully out of water, to avoid taking any sand with them.

★ You can *sometimes* substitute tinned mussels for fresh, using the liquid to make a sauce. Laced with a little white wine or vermouth in addition, your sauce will be superb.

★ The water inside the shells of live mussels plays a vital role in their flavour. *Lack* of this is the main reason why shelled mussels aren't much use except for something like garnishing, or to include in another dish. See also *Shellfish*.

Oysters

Were once plentiful enough to be amongst the cheapest foods in the nation's diet, records showing that 36 million of them were landed in 1898 on the coasts of England and Wales. At 4d a dozen they were eaten freely by the poorest families in Britain, only becoming a food of the rich later, when they grew scarce.

★ The *native* English oyster is too good to cook, which accounts for the English mostly eating them raw, just with lemon quarters, cayenne and brown bread and butter. Oysters must be *absolutely* fresh, shells tightly closed, and not opened until you have to, shortly before eating. To open, slide an oyster knife in at the hinge, snap the ligament which attaches the fish to the top, or flat shell and, embedded in crushed ice, serve the oysters each in their own tasty, salty liquor in the deep shell.

★ Today, to meet demand both here and

on the Continent, an industry practised by the Romans is passing from the hands of the fishermen to the culturists, from the natural oyster beds to artificial farms (such as on the Alderney coast), whence a fast-maturing Pacific type may reach the table 2 or 3 years earlier than our native oysters. See also *Shellfish*, page 166.

Plaice

The skin is coarse and clings very hard to the flesh, so it's easier to cut the skin off *fillets* individually, than to pull the skin off the whole fish. When skinning plaice to cook whole, pull the skin off from head to tail rather than from tail to head – it comes off more easily that way. See also earlier pages re methods of cookery.

Prawns

Those from the cold seas of the world are very different from those of the warm seas, which explains why they don't all look alike on a fishmonger's slab.

COLD-WATER PRAWNS. First choice for any cold prawn dish because they have a finer flavour and firmer texture than warm-water prawns. Blindfold, you'd *know* what you were eating, so although more expensive, they're worth it for something like melon and prawns, prawn cocktail (page 120) or prawns in aspic (page 129).

WARM-WATER PRAWNS. Grow much faster and are in far greater supply than cold-water prawns, and are the staff of life of Chinese restaurants. Use them in hot dishes where their poorer qualities aren't so obvious as in a cold dish, and where you can enhance their flavour with other tasty ingredients cooked with them.

★ 1 lb (450 g) fresh prawns yield about 6 ozs (150–175 g) peeled.

Roes

A marvel of nature for their delicacy and sometimes sheer beauty, roes are the eggs of fish in the breeding season, bringing to the table a novel range of flavours, textures and colours not usually found in other foods.

CAVIAR. The most famous of all roes comes from various members of the sturgeon family. 'Black' is the finest. Eat caviar well chilled, with hot toast, butter and lemon quarters.

MOCK CAVIAR. The roe of lump fish (see page 173) which when dyed black *looks* (but doesn't taste) like caviar. The same roe is sometimes dyed red.

COD'S ROE, SMOKED. This, mullet or tunny fish roe, is the main ingredient of the Greek dish *Taramasalata*.

CORAL. Greeny black when raw and going brilliant red when cooked, it is the roe of the hen lobster. Use to garnish, or sieve it finely to make lobster butter which you can use to flavour and colour a soup or sauce.

CRAB'S ROE. With the liver, this makes up the soft 'brown meat' of a crab, which explains its very different texture from the firm, fleshy 'white meat'.

THE ORANGE TONGUE OF A SCALLOP. Corresponds to the roe in fish, which accounts for it requiring shorter cooking than the white meat.

SOFT ROE. The sperm or milt of male fish. I've never tasted it, but carp is said to be the most delicate, then herring and mackerel. Wash them in cold water and strip off the tiny blood vessel that runs down one side. Use to garnish fish dishes, to make fritters, serve them in patties, in tartlets or on canapés, etc as well as on toast.

Salads, Fish

Best made with types of fish which have as much flavour hot as cold. These include the crustaceans, nearly all the oily fish, and white fish such as halibut and turbot. You may want to counteract their richness by a sharp dressing, or by sousing; or perhaps complement others with a rich sauce like mayonnaise. See *also Mixed salads*, page 162.

Salmon

One of few fish you can't really fault. Its glorious colour, delicate flavour, firm texture, suitability for cooking by almost any method, and its perfection when served hot or cold, smoked or potted, make it a magnificent fish for the table.

★ Whatever you plan to do with it, make sure your salmon is fresh, with bright silvery scales. Wipe rather than wash it, rubbing any bloody parts with salt.
★ *Boiled salmon* would be better described as *Poached salmon* because fish breaks up and becomes watery if, after putting it *into* boiling water, you allow the water to continue boiling. Cooking time depends partly on the thickness of the fish, but you won't go far wrong by allowing 10 mins to the lb (450 g) and 10 mins over, in plain, salted, 'shivering' water, 180°–190°F, 82°–88°C. Vinegar in the poaching liquid, whether water or court buillon, spoils the colour of salmon. If after cooking there's a thick creamy curd between the flakes, this is just because the salmon is river-fresh.
★ The difference between *tinned red* and *pink* salmon is simply one of species. Nearly all tinned salmon comes from the Pacific where there are five major species.

Sardines

The fry of the pilchard, taking their name from Sardinia, round whose coasts they abound.

★ In tins, sardines vary in flavour and quality according to the olive oil used, and to how long they are matured. Their bones are packed with calcium, so do eat rather than pick them out.

Scallops

Coquilles Saint-Jacques, they are at their very best in January and February when the roe is full and a bright orange colour. They're about the most delicious and nutritious of all shellfish. The roe is the 'bonne bouche', and so delicate that, when possible, it's cooked a shorter time than the white meat, even when you slice that through the middle.

★ If you buy *closed* scallops, you can be sure they're fresh. In addition they'll be moist, not desiccated as they tend to become when left about opened on the fishmonger's slab. If you prefer to buy them open, remember to ask for the other, deeper half of the shell should you want to serve the fish in it. There isn't enough room in the shallow half for fish, sauce and garnish.
★ When you've washed and scrubbed them, put scallops round side down in a warm place, say on a plate rack or in a very low oven, to open. (*Shallow* shell down, the messy water runs out.) Remove the black part and gristly fibre before you cook them.
★ If preparing scallops au gratin in the shells, support them in an ovenware dish to prevent them tilting, otherwise some of the sauce is almost bound to escape over the edge when grilled. See also page 166.

Scampi

The accepted culinary name for the tail-meat of what we call a Dublin Bay Prawn (see also page 166). The tail is the *only* part we eat.

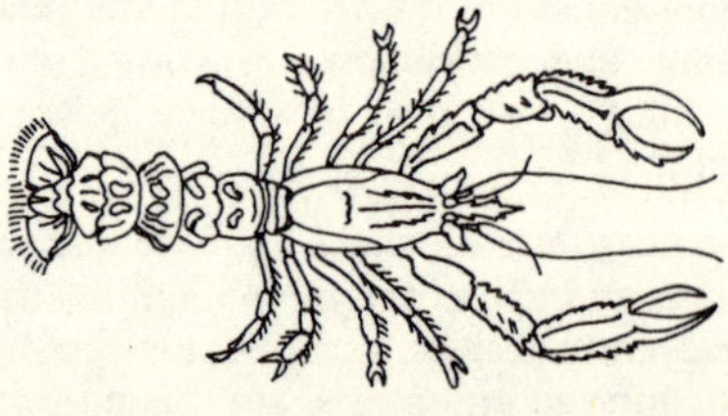

★ Unlike prawns and lobster, scampi don't change colour when cooked. The fish is naturally pink, darker red in parts.
★ Fresh, scampi have a sweeter taste and more delicate texture than lobster. Frozen? Well, blindfold, they might be difficult to recognize.

Shrimps

Either pink or brown when cooked. The tiny brown ones so much prized by the

Romans make much the best eating but, nearly 2,000 years later, they're still hell to peel!

★ Use shrimps to garnish fish or egg dishes, in a mixed hors-d'oeuvre, au gratin, on canapés, potted etc. See also page 121.

Skate

Such a weird looking fish that, if you're unfamiliar with it, it's worth asking your fishmonger if he can show you one. The only really fleshy parts are the fins which, understandably when you know what they look like, are called 'wings'.

★ On the delicate subject of how fresh to serve skate, Alexandre Dumas wrote 'Skate needs to mortify to be tender, and the transport from sea to Paris adds to its quality. As a matter of fact it is the only fish that can be kept for two or three days, even in thundery weather'.

Smoked Fish

Either cold-smoked like salmon, eel, kippers, bloaters, cod's roe and haddock (finnan, fillet, golden cutlets and smokies), *or* hot-smoked like mackerel, sprats and buckling.

★ All fish are brined before being smoked over oak or other hardwood shavings or sawdust, but while the cold-smoked fish are smoked to just a high enough temperature (86°F, 30°C) to impart flavour, the hot-smoked fish are, at about 200°F, 93°C, slightly cooked as well. Apart from smoked salmon, into which rock salt is rubbed, cold-smoked fish therefore keep less well than hot-smoked, and should be eaten soon after you buy them, like fresh fish.

★ See also *Smoked fish*, page 121.

Smokies

See *Haddock*, page 171.

Sole, Dover

Has an almost lacy-thin skin; so thin and so easily detached from the flesh that it is easier to pull it off the fish while it is whole than to cut it off when filleted. Unlike lemon sole and plaice with their tough skins almost glued to the fish, dover sole is skinned from *tail to head*, that being the easiest way to do it. (Lots of cookery books give the method.) Not only does the skin of the dover sole separate easily from the flesh, but also the bone from the flesh, after the fish is cooked. This is why it's essential to have dover sole, not 'lemon', for Sole Colbert – an egg and breadcrumb-coated, deep-fried whole fish, with its backbone removed after cooking and the cavity so formed filled with maître d'hôtel butter. Incidentally, it's easier to cut the bone at each end of the fish with scissors than with a knife.

SOLES, SLIP. Dover soles weighing less than $\frac{1}{2}$ lb (225 g). Though much cheaper than the larger fish, these small soles have an even better flavour and make a delicious meal, whole, for one person.

Sole, Lemon

See *General information.*

Sprats

Don't seem as popular as they ought to be, perhaps because they're so cheap, or because people don't know how to cook them? You can grill them and serve with mustard sauce, dry fry 5–10 mins, or dip in batter or seasoned flour and deep fry. (I like quickly to split and clean the larger ones.) Allow about $\frac{1}{4}$ lb (100 g) per person.

SMOKED SPRATS. Served with lemon quarters, freshly milled black pepper and brown bread and butter, they make a delicious hors-d'oeuvre. Allow 3 or 4 per person. See also *Oily fish*, page 165.

Trout

Have white, pinkish or 'salmon' flesh,

according to the waters in which they live. 'Salmon' trout differs from other types in that it (like the salmon) lives a greater part of its life in the sea. As a rule, treat this and the large trouts as salmon. The smaller river or lake trouts are excellent smoked, fried, grilled, poached or otherwise prepared in many different ways.

Turbot

These fish certainly assure their future – the female will lay up to 10,000,000 eggs in the spawning season!

★ This is one of our best white fish, its flesh white, firm and delicate in flavour. Avoid skinning or trimming turbot because its skin, fins and bones are all full of flavour. (Gastronomes prize the skin, also gelatinous matter in the fins.)
★ Turbot is often served with shrimp, lobster or anchovy sauce, whether poached (in plain salted water or in a court bouillon), baked or fried.

CHICKEN TURBOT. A small turbot weighing under 4 lbs ($1\frac{3}{4}$ kilos) – delicious cooked *à la Meunière* (see page 174).

Whitebait

See page 122.

Whiting

Belongs to the cod family but many of us fight shy of it without perhaps knowing what we're missing. Gastronomically, it is an important fish because its flesh, though tasteless, is also very light and easily digested. The fact that it is tasteless means you can cook it by almost any method you like (see *General information*) to make it *tasty*. It is often served with its tail between its teeth, in which position you can also stuff it.

★ Whiting was always cheap, and often fed to cats, because it was plentiful. The memory of that price is no reason to dismiss this silvery, fine-textured little fish.

12
MEAT

General Information

Meat is a major item in most family budgets so it's essential to know what you're looking for, to shop wisely and to buy where the standard is consistently high. There's often nowhere to beat the small 'family' butcher who rears his own beasts, feeds them on what he knows produces the best quality meat, kills them at the right age and understands the importance of proper hanging. If not careful, you can pay nearly as much, if not *just* as much, for second-quality meat as for first. It's for instance mainly because of the feeding that the best Scotch beef is famous for its flavour and texture, and that the best lamb is always so succulent and delicious. This explains why a prime *cut* is not necessarily a guarantee of prime quality, which depends on so many factors.

In addition to selling good meat, your butcher (even if in a supermarket) should know his stuff: a good one will actively enjoy advising you, and amongst other things will know how to cut meat for specialized dishes like beef olives or Wiener Schnitzel (and will be *able* to cut it), will sell you chops without bone splinters, and will without being asked trim away gristle and excess fat on meat.

The parts of an animal which do the least muscular work produce the prime cuts, while the 'working' parts – mostly from the forequarters of the animal – make up the cheaper cuts of meat. They are of similar quality to prime cuts from the same carcase, but usually have a high proportion of bone, fat and muscle fibre, which means they depend for their *tenderness* upon the cook.

Cheaper cuts of meat more often than not involve long slow cooking and should often include marinating the meat before you cook it, see page 48. (Besides a marinade giving meat extra flavour, the acids in it break down connective tissue and fibres.) As a general rule, the tougher the cut of meat, the slower and longer you should cook it: here a moist method of cookery such as braising or stewing is ideal. During the process, the meat tenderizes, and the goodness from all the connective tissue etc goes into the cooking liquor. Other ways to break down fibrous tissues are by beating the meat with a rolling pin, or of course by mincing it.

Meat is basically of two kinds, flesh and offal. The unusual textures and flavours of the latter give variety to our meals, most offal is easily digested, and some of it is of great nutritional importance.

The main reasons for cooking meat are to tenderize and make it digestible, to destroy bacteria, and – naturally – to make it taste and look good. Meat, like fish, takes flavour from the bone, so although you gain from the easy carving of a boned, rolled joint, you lose out on flavour and goodness. This, for instance, explains why something like best end of neck of lamb is so sweet and delicious and why a boned pork chop will have less flavour than say, spare ribs.

A good-sized frozen joint needs 36–48

hours to thaw out, slowly, in the refrigerator. If thawed faster, at room temperature, more juices will run out of it – and with those juices, a lot of flavour. Those people who, except in an emergency, roast small joints which are still frozen, can't know what they're missing in terms of goodness, but to cook a *rolled* joint in that condition is to risk salmonella poisoning. This is because the bacteria causing surface contamination of meat are normally destroyed by heat, but when meat is boned and rolled, the 'surface' is inside, and the heat may not penetrate enough to kill the bacteria.

Roasting a Joint

Roasting a joint isn't simply a case of sticking it in the oven with some dripping and basting it occasionally. If you want meat to be really succulent and tasty, and not to shrink out of sight, you need a little bit of know-how and must be prepared to go to a little bit of trouble as well. Here, in case you want them, are a few hints:

(1) CHOICE OF MEAT.

★ A large joint is in fact much more economical than a small because, pro rata, it shrinks much less. Even though you may only want to buy 2–3 lbs (say 1–1½ K), it will be cheaper in the long run to buy 4 or 5 lbs (say 1¾–2¼ K) and get the extra servings from it either as cold meat, or in made-up dishes. It's also labour-saving because you probably won't have to cook again for the next day or two – or will have cold meat to put in the freezer for another time.

★ For a joint *with* bone, allow 8–10 ozs (225–275 g) meat per person. Meat on the bone, as already said, has more flavour than meat without, and in addition it roasts better because the bone conducts heat through the centre of the meat.

★ For a joint *without* bone, like rolled ribs of beef, allow 6–8 ozs (say 175–225 g) meat per person.

★ Fat is an important part of a joint because any natural covering of it means the meat will be more tender and succulent. This is because a good top layer of fat bastes the joint automatically, and does away with 'spoon-basting', which by comparison dries the meat up and makes it shrink. Really lean meat doesn't roast well unless you lard it (page 46), bard it (page 31) or enclose it in a flour and water paste, page 185.

(2) STORAGE OF JOINT. Covered loosely with waxed paper or foil, and put at bottom of refrigerator, it will keep in near-perfect condition for 3–4 days – or you could marinade it for 24 hrs.

(3) PREPARATION.

★ Weigh meat and calculate cooking time, remembering that a thin joint needs less cooking than a thick one of the same weight. (See different kinds of meat for roasting times.)

★ A little seasoned flour rubbed into the surface of a joint makes the outside slice taste extra good, absorbs *surplus* fat and gives a lovely golden finish to the meat.

★ A few slivers of garlic here and there give subtle flavour. Do try it, even if you think you don't care for garlic.

★ Roasting (see also page 54) means 'all-round' heat, not standing a joint *in* hot fat, and as it were frying the bottom. With the thickest layer of fat on top so that it will baste itself, stand the joint either on a meat stand in the roasting tin, or perhaps better still on a bed of roasting vegetables, which are heavenly served with the joint. (Slice one or two large onions in two or three slices each, also a large carrot or two, and rest the meat on top. During cooking, the 'sugar' in them caramelizes, giving a lovely flavour to the gravy in the by-going.) If you stand the meat itself in the hot fat and baste with it as well, this draws out the juices, shrinking and drying the meat in the process. Although most people like to baste meat, I myself prefer to spread an *over-lean* joint (if not otherwise protected, as above) with a good layer of lard or dripping (whichever appropriate) *before* roasting, and then spread it again at ½ hr intervals with a little more, to keep the meat moist. (The juices in meat are essential to its flavour, moistness and non-shrinkage, so at all costs must be kept in, not allowed to escape.)

(4) THE OVEN. Have the oven hot before

you put the meat in, usually gas 7, 425°F, 220°C for the first ¼ hr, to seal the surfaces of the meat and prevent the juices escaping. Once again, everything you do is concerned with retaining the juices to keep the meat moist and full of flavour. See *Beef, Lamb, Mutton, Pork* and *Veal* for cooking times and oven temperatures.

★ Avoid using a fork to lift a roasting joint because juices will escape. It's better to use two spoons.

★ For consistently perfectly cooked meat, a meat thermometer removes the guesswork. If you haven't got one, make sure the meat feels springy when pressed with the back of a spoon, not spongy. Also press the meat with the back of a fork to see the colour of the emerging juices. If you like beef rare or medium done, the juices should be red or pink, whereas for 'well done' meat they should be clear. Pork and veal juices should never be pink because both must be well cooked to be palatable. Lamb you may like slightly underdone, in which case the juices will be just tinged with pink.

★ Allow the meat about ¼ hr to 'settle' after turning off oven, to make it easier to carve (see page 35).

(5) ACCOMPANIMENTS. Do serve the right ones, because they nearly all have a purpose: either to add richness, to counteract it, or to give complementary flavour or contrast of texture. Serve thick gravy with a stuffed joint, thin with others.

Cold Roast Meat

If you plan to serve roast meat cold for a particular occasion, you should for perfection cook it specially and let it go quite cold before carving: juices run out if you cut into a joint while it's hot, so the meat ends up dryer, with less flavour and a poorer colour.

TO CARVE COLD MEAT. An electric saw-knife will carve cold meat easily, thinly, economically and in good-sized slices which will have the maximum of flavour – different in every way from poorly carved meat.

★ To BOIL meat, see *Boiling*, page 32.

★ To BRAISE, see *Braising*, page 33.

★ To FRY meat, see *Shallow Frying*, page 42.

★ To GRILL meat, see *Grilling*, page 44.

★ To STEW meat, see *Stewing*, page 58, and *Brown stews*, page 196.

For the Freezer

I like buying the cuts and offal of my choice but if you plan to buy carcase meat and don't know what you're in for, it's worth thinking of the snags as well as the advantages. Here are some:

(1) If you can't cook or don't care for things like the head, heart or strong-tasting liver, you're paying the same price per lb. (say 500 g) for them as for the choice cuts which *seem* so cheap.

(2) Have you visualised the bulk of a cut-up animal, bones and all, and will it leave room for everything else you like to freeze?

(3) If the meat isn't already frozen, can your freezer cope with such a quantity quickly enough, before the meat suffers in quality?

(4) If the meat isn't labelled, will you know what's what? Will you be aware if anything is missing, and can you be sure you're getting the quality you wanted, and paid for? Some suppliers are excellent, others leave much to be desired. It's easy to be diddled unless you know your butcher.

★ Even in a freezer, meat will not keep indefinitely. According to the MEAT PROMOTION EXECUTIVE, their max. *recommended* storage times are

Beef 8 months
Lamb 6 months
Pork 6 months
Mince and offal 3 months
Sausage and cured
  green bacon 3 months
Smoked bacon 1 month

Meat in the Diet

You should try to include meat in at least

one meal each day as it is an essential part of a well-balanced diet. This is why:

(1) It has all the necessary mineral elements needed for good health.
(2) It contains phosphorus which combines with calcium to build and maintain strong bones, teeth and nails.
(3) It is rich in protein, the body-building material which is broken down into amino acids during the process of digestion. (10 amino acids are considered essential for children, 8 for adults, and all are present in meat.)
(4) Meat, *especially* liver, contains iron. As an essential ingredient in the formation of red blood corpuscles, this is a vital part of our diet. Iron helps carry oxygen round our bodies. Without, we become pale, breathless and lacking in energy.

Bacon

Bacon cuts come from the middle and forequarters of the pig, differing from gammon which is the hind leg. As for butcher-meat, it pays to shop where the quality doesn't vary. The quality depends on the breed, age and feeding of the pig, and the way in which it has been cured. It also varies according to the cut. Danish bacon for instance is specially cured to avoid over-saltiness, which explains why small cuts of this can be cooked without pre-soaking.

★ Whether you plan to boil, bake or braise bacon and gammon, allow about 20 mins per lb (450 g) and 20 mins over. Both lend themselves especially well to being boiled for half the cooking time (perhaps with cider in the water), then baked for the remainder, when you can finish off their cooking with various glazes or spicy toppings to give additional flavour. Should you want to bake a very lean joint throughout its cooking time, the old-fashioned way is still difficult to improve upon: enclose the meat in a flour and water paste (page185) to keep it moist, prevent it from shrinking and retain its glorious flavour.

★ To *store* bacon or gammon, replace the shop wrapping with a tight wrapping of kitchen foil, and put it in refrigerator. For larder storage of both cooked and uncooked meat, put it on a clean plate, cover loosely and keep it as cool as possible.

★ To *freeze* bacon, it should be vacuum packed and stored no longer than the stated time. The drying action of freezing is intensified by salt, used in curing, the meat becoming dehydrated and hard unless so protected.

GREEN BACON. Bacon which has been cured but not smoked, hence its much milder flavour.

BACON RASHERS. They won't curl up if you slash the fat before you grill or fry them; otherwise they do because the fat cooks and shrivels faster than the lean.

★ 'Back' rashers fry best overlapping each other like slates on a roof, the lean lying on top of the fat of the rasher under it. The fat becomes crisp and the lean keeps moist. Reverse the process for grilling, and have the fat on *top* of the lean, where it will baste and keep it moist. Whether grilling or frying therefore, the fat always protects the lean from the fiercest heat.

★ Unless you like the fat fried to a crisp, you can't leave the rinds on because their texture makes them inedible. Rather than fiddle around with a few rashers each time you want them for breakfast, it's quicker to cut them all off with scissors when you buy the bacon. Fry the rinds first, to make the pan greasy, then when frizzled you can crush them with a rolling pin and sprinkle over savoury things like scrambled egg, macaroni cheese, cooked vegetables etc, storing them in an air-tight jar.

★ In a covered container in the refrigerator, rashers store better unwrapped than wrapped.

BACON ROLLS. These cook faster and the rashers go further if you 'stretch' them before cutting into 2 or 3 pieces each, and rolling up: lay rashers on chopping board and elongate each with the blade of a knife, with firm stroking movements away from you.

Beef

Beef can be cooked in such dozens of different ways that, if you want to save expense and disappointment, it's worth knowing what all the cuts look like. Cut and quality determine the cooking method: if for instance you want to stew steak, it's quite pointless to buy a prime cut which not only costs more but also makes a poorer stew, because it lacks all the gelatinous matter that makes the liquor so good. If you want to roast, fry or grill beef, it's useless to buy anything *but* a prime cut, because only these will tenderize quickly enough in the greater heat required for these methods of cookery.

These are some of the signs of best quality beef:

(1) Lean meat is bright cherry red after it has been cut and is exposed to the air; flesh from old or poorly fed animals does not brighten after cutting. (Beef cuts which have been pickled ready for boiling will be grey in colour. The colour change is caused by the brine, and the meat will turn a nice pink during cooking.)

(2) Lean meat, particularly cuts intended for grilling or roasting, is best when marbled with fat. The flecks of fat melt into the lean, making it tender, succulent and full of flavour.

(3) The fat should be creamy white, *firm and dry*; yellow, oily fat comes from an old or poorly fed animal.

ROASTING. See also *Roasting a joint*, page 180 and *Roasting*, page 54.

(1) Allow 15 mins per lb (450 g) and 15 mins over for a nicely underdone joint on the bone, or 20 mins per lb and 20 mins over for a similarly cooked thick, boned and rolled joint. Allow *fillet* only 12–15 mins per lb making sure it is larded or barded, to protect the meat, keep it moist and give extra flavour. (Your butcher would supply and flatten the right 'barding fat'.)

(2) Roast beef in a preheated hot oven, gas 7, 425°F, 220°C for the first 15 mins to seal in the juices, then reduce heat to gas 5, 375°F, 190°C for remainder of cooking time. Roast *fillet* in a slightly hotter oven all the time, gas 8, 450°F, 230°C. (Preferably serve it slightly underdone.

★ Traditional accompaniments to roast beef are: Yorkshire Pudding (page 237); Roast potatoes; Horseradish Sauce; Thin gravy.

★ Accompaniments for roast *fillet* of beef are: Unthickened gravy, made basically with drippings from the meat and a *little* beef stock; Pont Neuf potatoes (potato chips, all of the same precise size – $2\frac{1}{2}''$ (6.5 cm) long and rather less than $\frac{1}{2}''$ (1.25 cm) thick; Dressed watercress to garnish.

The prime and better cuts are:

SIRLOIN. Roast either on the bone or boned and rolled – or bone and braise.

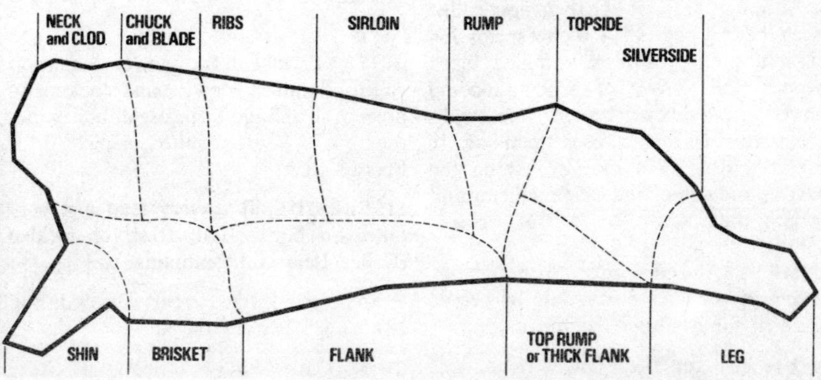

Beef carcase, showing 'what comes from where'. By courtesy of the Meat Promotion Executive.

SIRLOIN STEAKS. Grill.

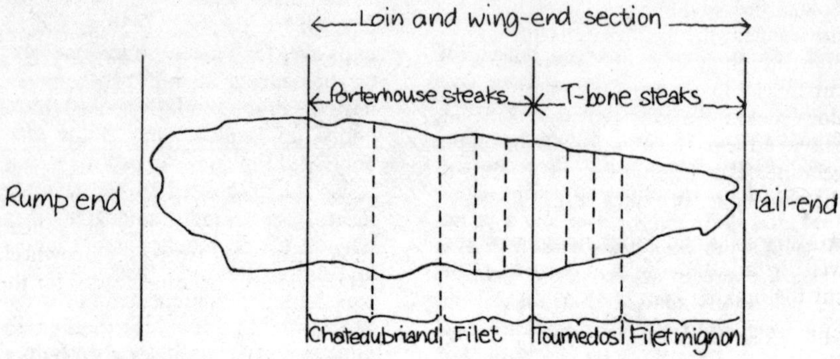

THE FILLET. (If separated from sirloin.) See drawing above.

On the inside of the sirloin bone, the fillet is the most tender of all cuts and, when roasted, one of the most choice of all beef dishes. See previous page.

★ *Fillet steaks* are enough to confuse any of us: different parts of the fillet are called by different names, according to whether they're cut from the rump end, the middle or the tail end. In some cases, a steak is called according to the thickness or portion of a particular cut. *Châteaubriand* for instance corresponds to the undercut or fillet portion of a porterhouse steak. It is 2″ (5 cm) thick, should weigh at least 1 lb (450 g) before trimming – and is always grilled. A thinner steak cut from this same portion is called a *filet*. What the French call *filets*, *tournedos* and *filet mignons*, *we* often refer to more generally as fillet steaks.
★ Although I myself like them *best* grilled (see *Grilling*, page 44) – with a sprinkling of salt, plenty of freshly milled black pepper, a sliced clove of garlic on top and served with a savoury butter – fillet steaks are more often sautéd: cook them quickly in hot butter to a nice brown on the outside and a juicy red inside, saucing and serving them according to your recipe.

RUMP STEAK. Grill or fry. Although not as *tender* as fillet steak, lots of people prefer it for its fuller flavour.

★ Use also for Beef Olives (lean, and thinly cut) and for Beef Strogonoff.

RIBS. Roast *fore ribs* and *wing ribs* either on the bone or boned and rolled. If preferred, bone and braise.

★ Grill (preferably) or fry *Entrecôte* Steaks. (The entrecôte, by definition, is the part of the meat between the bones of the ribs of beef. An *Entrecôte Minute Steak* is a very thin one which, as long as you like it rare, should cook in one minute on each side.)

Back Ribs and Top Ribs. Braise or pot-roast, or roast back ribs.

TOPSIDE. This is a lean cut usually sold rolled with a layer of fat tied round it. Better boiled or braised (or pot-roasted) than roasted.

★ Use thinly cut for Beef Olives.

The cheaper cuts are:

TOP RUMP. (Also called *thick flank*.) Fry or braise if *sliced*. Braise or pot-roast a *joint*.

BRISKET. Sold on the bone or boned and rolled. Requires slow, moist cooking to prevent shrinkage, so braise or boil rather than roast. Is often salted or pickled for Pressed Beef.

SILVERSIDE. It is very lean and contains no bone. Boil, fresh or pickled (Boiled Beef and Dumplings).

★ Some people like to roast silverside but *I* think it's better braised.

SHIN. (Called *hough* in Scotland.) Stew, casserole and use in dishes like hot-pot, beef steak and kidney pudding, a pie etc. Lots of people don't seem to realize what *superb* meat this is: there's hardly a scrap of waste on it, it is one of the cheapest cuts, has a lovely flavour and, given long slow cooking, makes the most delicious gravy – due to the muscle in it turning to gelatine. This is why, when cooked with the shin bone, it makes jellied stock.

★ Make soup and potted hough with it as well. In addition, shin is the traditional cut for making beef tea.

LEG. (Also called *hough* in Scotland.) Not always quite so good as shin I think, but you can use it in the same ways, see above. (How gelatinous it is varies according to an animal's muscle.)

NECK AND CLOD. Like shin, good for hot-pot and stews, but has less flavour and is less gelatinous.

FLANK. Boil (salted or pickled) for Pressed Beef. Braise or pot-roast on the bone. Stew.

CHUCK AND BLADE. (Sold as *shoulder* in Scotland.) Braise or stew. In my opinion *chuck steak* and *skirt* (which comes from inside the ribs and the flank), are inferior to shin for dishes where the meat is stewed.

★ *Beef Steak and Kidney Pudding* needs long slow cooking if to have its characteristic rich dark gravy and almost golden coloured suetcrust pastry. This isn't a dish for the pressure cooker, or for packet suet, if you want the real thing.
★ It's almost impossible to line a basin perfectly with a round of pastry: the easy way is to roll all the pastry into a round large enough to line and slightly overlap the basin, then cut out $\frac{1}{3}$ of it for the lid, see illustration.

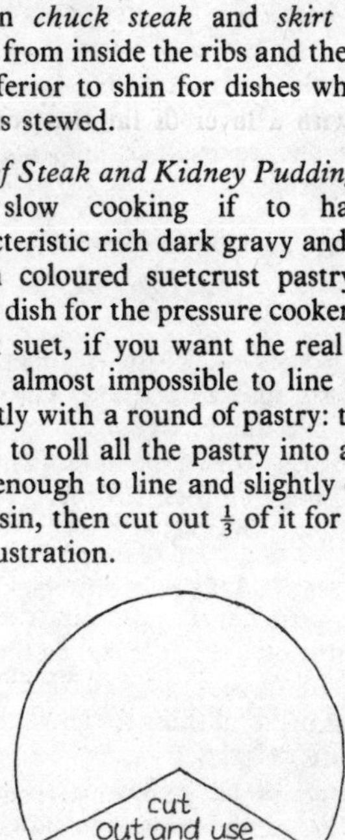

Form the larger piece into a kind of cone inside the basin, damping and overlapping the cut edges. Re-shape the cut-out piece to make the lid.

Brawn

Made from the trimmings of a pig after being killed, or from the pig's head together with either trotters or a cowheel, which provide the gelatine needed for the liquor to form a jelly when cold.

★ It is easier and the job is less macabre if you ask your butcher to *prepare* the head (or half-head) for brawn. Although there's lots of it, the meat (apart from the cheek) is rather tasteless, so be generous with seasonings and spices, subtle with herbs.
★ You'll need ingredients of this sort:

Half a fresh pig's head, *prepared*
1 or 2 pig's trotters, well washed
1 onion
20 peppercorns
1 blade mace
4 cloves
12 allspice
bouquet garni
cold water enough to just cover meat

★ The tongue is simmered a shorter time (2–3 hrs) than the other meat (3–4 hrs), which should be just falling from the bones when cooked.
★ Use brawn for hors-d'oeuvres, supper, sandwiches or as a main dish with salad in summer. Because it is served sliced, it is better to set brawn in a square or rectangular mould rather than round.

Flour and Water Paste

An old-fashioned method which is still just as good today for baking very lean joints of meat like gammon or venison. Sealed up inside and protected, the meat juices are retained so the meat shrinks very little, keeps nice and moist and is full of flavour. Gammon and bacon should first be soaked, a chicken should be brushed with oil, and venison is better if previously marinated (see page 222).
★ Here's briefly what to do:

(1) Make a dough just firm enough to roll out by stirring *approximately* ½ pt (250 ml) water into 1 lb (450 g) sieved flour. Turn dough onto a floured board and knead lightly, before rolling roughly to shape and size of joint, and large enough to enclose it. (For a very large joint, you may need 1½ lbs flour.)
(2) Lay joint *upside down* on dough before damping the edges and sealing in the meat, then the joins are sealed underneath the meat when you turn it the *right way up* to bake.
(3) Bake in a greased roasting tin for usual roasting time plus ¼ hr extra, to allow heat to penetrate the paste. There's no need for fat because the paste prevents any drying of the meat but if the crust looks like getting too brown, cover it with foil or oiled greaseproof paper.
(4) When meat is cooked, crack open and break away the crust. A joint is then usually returned to the oven for 10–15 mins without the crust, to glaze, brown, or otherwise finish off, according to recipe.

Gammon

Like ham, gammon comes from the hind leg of a pig, but is a smaller joint. The main difference between them is that gammon is cut from the carcase after the whole side has been brine cured, whereas ham is the whole hind leg removed from the carcase at the fresh pork stage, and cured individually, to ensure its special flavour. (See also *Bacon*, page 182).

Hams

A speciality of many countries. The wide differences between them depend on things like the breed of pig, the particular foods on which they may be fed, how the hams are cured and smoked, where and how long they are matured etc. The main types are:

AMERICAN HAMS. These include famous types like *Kentucky* and *Virginia*.

CONTINENTAL HAMS. *Parma*, *Bayonne*, *Westphalia* and the French country (locally cured) hams. If you have the opportunity, do try and compare them, and see which you like best.

IRISH HAMS. These are dry-salt cured and, after being boned, are peat-smoked.

ENGLISH HAMS. *Wiltshire* and *York* for instance. York ham is famous the world over because it is so consistently good in flavour, texture and appearance, due mainly to the cure. The meat is a lovely colour; firm and yet tender; mild without being in any way insipid.

Hamburger

Implies either a flat cake (or patty) made of minced meat, or the same thing served in a split roll with various garnishes such as a slice of tomato or fried onion, pickles, ketchup or indeed almost anything the roll will hold.

★ It's better to choose a lean cut of meat and have it minced than to buy fatty mince because your hamburgers will shrink less, taste better and won't be so indigestible. A little egg yolk or whole egg is essential to bind the mixture and prevent the cakes disintegrating when fried or grilled.

Kebab

The Turkish name for various dishes whose principal feature is skewered meat, traditionally lamb. Kebabs originated in the Caucasus where the mountain people impaled meat on their swords, roasting it outside over an open fire.

★ Kebabs are a splendid way of tickling a jaded appetite for they combine the best of everything on a single spike: an unlimited variety of flavour combinations, prime pieces of meat (nothing tough will cook in so short a time) and the natural succulence of all grilled or spit-roasted meat. It's worth telling your butcher you want the meat for kebabs, then he knows just what to give you.

★ If possible, you need proper kebab

skewers (see page 23). If you first run these through a piece of suet, everything will slip off more easily, or if you like garlic, why not run them through a clove of garlic instead?

MARINATED LAMB KEBABS. These are such a favourite of mine that I'm going to spell out the details. Give yourself a 24 hr start: *To serve 4*

1 lb. (450 g) fillet or boned shoulder of lamb

3 dessertsps. pineapple juice 2 dessertsps. soy sauce. 3 level dessertsps. clear honey	marinade, to flavour and tenderize meat

1 medium-sized can pineapple chunks – about 6 per person

About 12 spring onions or tiny shallots

Salt and black pepper

½ lb. (225 g) boiled long grain rice, see page 154.

Large tin baked beans in tomato sauce – plebeian, but easy and very good!

(1) *First day*. Trim excess fat and any skin from meat and cut it into largish bite-sized pieces. Put in a basin.

(2) Make the marinade: mix together pineapple juice, soy sauce and honey. Pour over the meat, mix well, cover with foil and refrigerate for 12–24 hrs, turning meat over occasionally to flavour it fully.

(3) *Second day*. Drain meat and reserve marinade, also drain pineapple chunks well. Thread meat, prepared spring onions and pineapple chunks onto 4 kebab skewers, alternating so that the onions flavour the meat. Season well with salt and freshly ground pepper. (Be sure to pierce the food through the middle, otherwise it won't cook evenly, and won't rotate evenly if on a spit.)

(4) Grill kebabs 1 minute on each side under preheated *red-hot* grill, at least 3″ (8 cm) from the heat. Now spoon over them a little of the retained marinade and grill under reduced, moderate heat for about 20 mins or until meat is cooked, turning kebabs every 3–5 mins and basting them each time with more of the marinade. (If uncertain whether meat is cooked, cut a piece to test it.)

(5) Serve the hot boiled rice in a 'wall' on a side-dish, put the heated beans in the centre and lay the kebabs on top. Scrape up all the juices and marinade in the bottom of grill pan and pour over rice, to flavour it. Serve piping hot.

Lamb

The meat of an animal under one year. Mutton, with its firmer flesh and stronger flavour, generally comes from an animal under two years. *Spring Lamb* is from a lamb 3–4 months old.

★ Some cuts are naturally expensive but make a glorious roast, while the more economical cuts make good stews. Whichever you're buying, look for fine-grained lean with a bright colour. The fat should be crisp and white, but not brittle. Leg and loin have a reasonable layer of fat covering the lean, which in turn is covered by a thin paper-like skin. This skin should be pliable to the touch, not hard and wrinkled: remove it from chops before cooking because, being on the side, it doesn't get cooked properly, but don't remove it from a roasting joint as it helps to retain the juices in the meat, and to cook it evenly.

★ Both lamb and mutton are more wasteful on the whole than beef because so much fat is embedded in the lean, as well as around the joints. It is the fat though which makes lamb so tasty and juicy – apart from stewing cuts – so if you cut *too* much off, you'll spoil your meat – just trim off any *excess*.

★ Use herbs to enhance the flavour of lamb roasts and casseroles: rosemary is a traditional herb for cooking with roast lamb, or, if you're stewing it, you may like rosemary, marjoram or basil added to a bouquet garni?

ROASTING. See also *Roasting a joint*, page 180, and *Roasting*, page 54.

(1) Seasoned flour rubbed into the surface of lamb helps to absorb surplus fat. Also, if you like the flavour of rosemary, make a few slits

in the covering skin of a joint, slipping a wee sprig of the herb into each.

(2) Lamb is best when *slow*-roasted so calculate cooking time (after stuffing) and allow 25 mins per lb (450 g) and 25 mins over. Allow a thick leg cut slightly longer.

(3) Given a joint with a moderate or good layer of fat on top, you shouldn't baste it: before you cook it, simply brush the joint with oil or melted lard or cooking fat, or *spread* the top with fat.

(4) Roast in a preheated hot oven, gas 6 400°F, 204°C for the first 15 mins to seal in the juices, then reduce heat to gas 4, 350°F, 175°C for remainder of cooking time.

(5) If you like lamb's sweetness accentuated, and the skin crisp and tasty, spread its fatty surface with redcurrant or mint jelly half an hour before end of cooking time. The sugar in the jelly caramelizes, making the lamb scrumptious.

★ Traditional accompaniments to lamb are: Stuffing, optional, to give extra flavour, to counteract richness and to make a joint go further; Mint Sauce, to counteract richness (Mint Jelly is delicious in addition, if you like its sweetness); Thick gravy if the roast is stuffed, otherwise 'thin'.

The prime and better cuts are:

LEG. (Known as gigot in Scotland.) Leg is often divided into fillet end and shank end. It is more economical and preferable, however, to buy the whole leg, basically because it cooks better: when roasting, it will lie where you put it (unlike the fillet end which is apt to tilt over) and, with its good covering of fat, is self-basting. Given these advantages, the meat shrinks less and is more juicy and tender than a smaller joint cut from it. Roast on the bone, or boned, stuffed and rolled. *Fillet end.* Roast. *Shank end.* Roast or casserole.

LOIN. Usually divided into *Loin end* and *Chump end*, unless you want a big joint. Roast in the piece, or boned, stuffed and rolled.

Loin Chops. Grill or fry.

Chump Chops. These are to lamb what rump steak is to beef – one of the finest cuts available for tenderness, meatiness and flavour. Grill or fry.

BEST END OF NECK. Roast, like loin, either on the bone, or boned stuffed and rolled. It has more flavour than loin but is much less meaty.

★ *A Crown Roast* is made with *two* best end necks but in my opinion never seems to taste as good as it looks, or *ought* to taste after so much work.

Cutlets. Grill or fry.

SADDLE. The whole back (*two* loin joints) left together – delicious, but too big for small families or small ovens.

The economy cuts are:

SHOULDER. (Not cut like this in Scotland.) Shoulder is sometimes divided

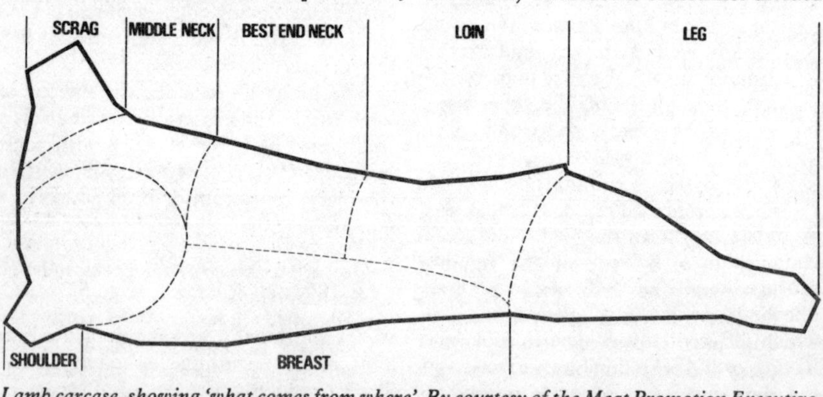

Lamb carcase, showing 'what comes from where'. By courtesy of the Meat Promotion Executive.

into *Blade end* and *Knuckle end*. Roast on the bone, or boned, stuffed and rolled.

★ Braise or casserole.

MIDDLE NECK. Usually cut into chops, then stewed, as in Hot-pot or Irish Stew.

SCRAG END. Nearly all bone, and better for soups than stews.

BREAST. A very fat cut which you can roast (boned, stuffed and rolled), braise or stew.

Mince

Isn't worth buying when as fatty as *some* butchers sell it: the fat in it melts when cooked so the meat both shrinks and is indigestible.

★ Mince should be lean, red and preferably finely ground: if your butcher hasn't got this on the counter, *ask* him for it, perhaps choosing the steak you'd like minced, even if slightly more costly – it depends what you want if for.
★ Use mince for things like galantine, meat loaf, meat balls, moussaka, lasagne, cottage pie, Cornish pasties, hamburgers, spaghetti Bolognese, mince on toast or steak tartare.
★ Butchers nowadays are mincing lamb, veal and even steak and kidney as money-savers, so it's worth experimenting with some of these for a change.

Mixed Grill

A dish complete in itself. It consists of grilled meats garnished with grilled fruits and vegetables such as tomatoes, banana and mushrooms, and served with maître d'hôtel butter, watercress, and chipped or other similar deep-fried potatoes. A grill does not include *fried* foods when you can't fit everything on the grill!

★ Meats may include fillet steak, lamb chop, lamb's kidney, fillet of veal, sausage, bacon rolls etc. The skill is in knowing the varying lengths of time which different things take to cook, and having everything done to perfection at the same time. Cooking times depend on the thickness and type of the meat, your personal taste for rare or well done meat, the distance from the grill and the intensity of the heat. Here's a rough guide for some of the more popular foods about 3″ (8 cm) from a red-hot grill: fillet steak 6–8 mins, lamb chop 10–12 mins, lamb's kidney 6–8 mins, sausages 10 mins, bacon rolls on skewer 5 mins, mushrooms 5 mins, halved tomatoes 3–4 mins. See also *Grilling*, page 44.

Mutton

Though mutton is eaten much less nowadays than lamb, it makes a better stew (such as Ragoût of Mutton or Irish Stew) because of its fuller flavour. When buying, the lean should be a dull red colour, of fine texture and firm to the touch; the fat creamy white, firm and hard.

ROASTING. See also *Roasting a joint*, page 180, and *Roasting*, page 54.

(1) Trim a joint of *excess* fat, rendering down the trimmings for dripping.
(2) A few sprigs of rosemary in the roasting tin help the flavour, as do thin spikes of garlic stuck into the fatty part of the joint and near the bone.
(3) Marinating (see page 48) an older and larger piece of mutton helps to tenderize it as well as giving extra flavour. If you then enclose the joint in a flour and water paste (page 185) before roasting, it is delicious: put on a meat stand in the roasting tin so that the crust won't absorb the dripping and, after cooking and breaking away the crust, return meat to hot oven, baste, then leave for about 15 mins to brown the surface.
(4) Cook mutton well: the juices should be clear when it is done. Allow 20 mins per lb (450 g) and 20 mins over.
(5) Roast in a preheated oven, gas 7, 425°F, 220°C for the first 15 mins to seal in the juices, then reduce heat to gas 5, 375°F, 190°C for remainder of cooking time.

★ Traditional accompaniments to mutton are: Stuffing, optional; Onion Sauce or onion purée (Soubise) is correct with shoulder; Redcurrant or other sharp-flavoured jelly such as mint, crab-apple, cranberry or gooseberry with leg, loin or neck; Thick gravy for a stuffed joint, otherwise thin; (slices of fried pineapple are also good with mutton).

★ The cuts of mutton are the same as lamb (see page 188).

★ Best for *roasting* are saddle (the prime joint), leg, shoulder, loin and best end of neck.

★ Joints suitable for *boiling* are leg and middle neck, and for *braising* leg, shoulder and stuffed breast.

★ For *stewing* and the making of ragoûts use breast, middle neck or head – scrag end as well if you think it's worth bothering with.

Offal

Derived from 'off' and 'fall' or 'waste parts', as the dictionary describes it. In fact offal is anything *but* this for it plays an invaluable part in our diet, besides giving us a welcome, occasional change from 'flesh'. Veal offal is the most delicate, delicious and digestible of all.

★ Offal, or 'variety meats' as the Americans more wisely describe everything, include all the extremities like head, tail, trotters and tongue, as well as the inner organs such as liver, kidneys, sweetbreads, heart, brains and tripe.

BRAINS. More delicate than sweetbreads, though similar in texture and flavour. Because they're so alike, both are prepared in virtually the same way to purify and whiten them (see page 192). When blanching is necessary, the *time* you blanch brains depends on the type of animal from which they come: calf, lamb, sheep, ox or pig. Calf's and lamb's brains are delicate and equally as good, but some people prefer sheep's, so it partly depends on preferences as well as on how you plan to cook them as to which type you should use. Whichever it is, it's essential to cook brains the day you buy them because they must be fresh. If impossible to do so within 24 hrs of purchase, at least soak and blanch them.

★ Various ways to cook brains include braised, sliced and sautéd, frittered, served in a cream sauce, or in a savoury sauce au gratin, eg mushroom.

KIDNEYS. Once reserved for chiefs and warriors as it was believed they gave both courage and strength to anybody eating them. Gout sufferers however can't eat kidneys *or* liver because either is liable to cause uric acid on digestion. This is because both are rich in proteins, which are different from the proteins of lean meat.

★ Here are a few tips on preparing kidneys:

(1) Kidneys can't be too fresh; they quickly lose their firmness, flavour and goodness, so it pays to buy them 'in their fat' when possible, then it's much easier to tell the fresh from the stale. With frozen kidneys, you must hope for the best.

(2) Soaking: *Lamb's and calf's kidney* tend to absorb water if washed or soaked, and there is nothing to be gained by doing so. *Pig's kidney* is less strong if soaked in milk (or even water) for about $\frac{1}{2}$–1 hr before cooking. *Ox kidney* is less strong if soaked, thinly sliced, in water with a little vinegar for an hour or so.

(3) After pulling off the fine skin and cutting a lamb's or pig's kidney in half longways (rounded side up, core side down), it's easiest to snip out the core with a smallish pair of pointed scissors.

★ Here are a few cooking tips:

(1) When cooked, kidneys should be tender and slightly pink near the centre.

(2) There are two main reasons why grilled, fried or sautéd kidneys easily go hard and dry: (a) Because a kidney is *surrounded* by fat, the meat itself is almost fatless. There is nothing to keep it moist therefore if you overcook it; (b) The juices pour out of a cut kidney (causing it to shrivel) unless, initially, your source of heat is very strong: if grilling, this means using a preheated red-hot grill and grilling the kidney for one minute on each side before cooking either side

fully. If frying or sautéing, the cooking fat or butter should be *hot* when you put the kidney in. As for grilling, cook it for one minute on each side before cooking either side fully.

★ *Ox and calf kidneys* are multi-lobed, the latter bought by weight and cut off the core by the butcher. Ox kidney is mostly only used in things like a stew, pie or beef steak and kidney pudding because, even when soaked, it is too strong alone. Unlike other kidneys, it needs long slow cooking. Kidneys play a vital role in these dishes because they both flavour and thicken the liquor.

LIVER. The most important of all offal, being rich in proteins (see *Kidneys* above) and itself the store-house in mammals of such essential nutrients as iron and vitamins. Because *so* valuable in the diet, and because many people dislike it on account of its unusual texture, it is important for most dishes to use liver which isn't too strong, like calf's (the finest of all) or lamb's; and to cook it properly. To start with, that means proper preparation, easing out the 'tubes' and core with a sharp-pointed vegetable knife in one hand, and with the thumb and fingers of your other; also pulling off the thin outside tissue.

★ Liver is quite versatile meat but be careful not to fry or grill it too long because, being almost fatless, it easily goes hard and dry. Although I personally like it best grilled (brushed with fat, well seasoned, scattered with a sliced clove of garlic and served topped with savoury butter), you can ring the changes in many ways like this:

(1) Cut in thin strips, coat with egg and breadcrumbs and fry.
(2) Make Liver Pudding – a light kind of steamed suet pudding in which the cut-up raw liver is mixed *with* the flour, breadcrumbs, suet and herbs etc. (You need a sauce with it.)
(3) Cook en brochette – pieces of liver threaded on a skewer alternately with similar-sized (but thinner) pieces of rather fat ham or bacon. (Don't forget to season and brush them with oil or melted fat before grilling.) Again, basted or served with a savoury butter, they're more tasty.
(4) Cut liver in smallish pieces, dip in batter and fry in deep fat.
(5) Make liver pâté, with calf's, lamb's or chicken's liver.
(6) Include pig's liver in pâtés.
(7) Use pig's liver to make stuffings.
(8) Serve liver casseroled. Here's a quick, simple recipe to serve 3: Dip 8–9 ozs (say 250 g) prepared, sliced calf's or lamb's liver in 1 tablesp seasoned flour, and lay slices in greased casserole. Mix together and then sprinkle over the liver 1½ ozs (40 g) fresh white breadcrumbs, 3 finely sliced mushrooms, 1 teasp each finely chopped onion and parsley, seasoning and a pinch of nutmeg. Lay two thinly spreadout rashers of bacon on top (each cut in half) and pour over ½ pt (250 ml) stock mixed with 1 dessertsp Worcester sauce. Cook in a slow to moderate oven, gas 3, 325°F, 165°C, for 1–1¼ hrs.

★ *Ox liver*, if used at all, is best in a spicy sort of dish which is cooked long enough to tenderize the meat, and where its strong flavour will be masked. To mellow it, first soak overnight in milk or salted water.

OXTAIL. A tasty 'end piece' which has been used for centuries to make one of the finest English soups and stews. Its excessive amount of fat – which gives the dish its character – means it must be cooked differently from other stews if not to be greasy, and so rich as to be indigestible. Make a two-day operation of it and you can't go far wrong. Here's a recipe, with some why's and wherefore's:

(1) Wash rather than wipe the jointed oxtail, to make sure the pieces are free of hairs etc.
(2) Using a fairly large saucepan, add enough cold water to barely cover the meat. (The less water you need, the more concentrated the final flavour, so the size of the pan has a bearing on the result.) Add some flavourings like a bouquet garni, a whole onion (stuck with a clove if you like), a blade of mace and *plenty* of seasoning before bringing to the boil, skimming and simmering gently about 2 hrs.

(3) Cool, then refrigerate the meat and strained liquor. (If you leave it overnight, the floating fat will set firmly enough on top to be able to *lift* it off next day.)

(4) Now continue as for other stews, briefly as below:

(a) Fry a finely sliced onion for a few mins in 1 oz (25 g) dripping, then add a sliced carrot and fry a minute or two more. Stir in a heaped tablesp flour to make a roux.

(b) Make a sauce in the usual way with the cooked roux and 1 pt (500 ml) of the (now jellied) liquor. Before bringing it to the boil, add 1 dessertsp vinegar or lemon juice to counteract richness, some more seasoning, a fresh bouquet garni, a spoonful of tomato purée if you like, and a few drops of gravy browning.

(c) Add pieces of half-cooked oxtail, and when the sauce returns to the boil, reduce heat and simmer very gently about $2\frac{1}{2}$ hrs or until the meat is just leaving the bones. (If preferred, you can just as easily cook it in an ovenware dish in a very slow oven.)

(5) Serve sprinkled with finely chopped parsley.

OX TONGUE. Expensive to buy cooked, so it's not only more economical but also much better to cook your own. In addition sliced as you need it, it doesn't go dry. Serve it hot with a savoury sauce, or boil, press and allow it to go cold.

★ *Pressed ox tongue*. It's ideal to have a tongue 'press' because it will cope best with varying sizes of tongue which, when cold and jellied, are also easily turned out. Otherwise you'll probably have to manage with a deep cake tin, 6″ (15 cm) in diameter for a largish tongue, and a heavily weighted, fitting plate or dish of some kind on top.

★ Soak a salted or pickled tongue about 24 hrs in cold water, changing the water once or twice, to get rid of the strongest flavour. Then after bringing the tongue to the boil in cold water, drain off that water as well, and re-cover with fresh. Put an onion (stuck with a couple of cloves) and a carrot or two in whole, and skim off the scum (impurities) from time to time during cooking. Allow tongue to simmer 40 mins per lb (450 g) and 40 mins over, topping up with extra boiling water if needed during cooking, to keep tongue covered.

★ To test when a tongue is cooked, pierce the tip with a pointed skewer or knife. If tender here, then the rest of the tongue is cooked and, when plunged at once into cold water, the skin will easily come off and you can readily remove the duct, gristle, fat and tiny bones from the 'root'. The tongue is now curled round and fitted *tightly* into the 'press' or cake tin, covered, weighted and left overnight to cool. There should be plenty of jelly to keep the tongue moist.

★ *Carving*. Slice cold, pressed tongue very thinly across the top of the round. As you cut off the first two or three slices, gently incline the knife, so that the top of the round has a slanting surface. This helps you to slice the whole tongue very thinly, without waste, down to the last small piece. If you are serving tongue *hot*, carve thicker slices, and against the grain of the meat. Carve *Glazed Slipper of Tongue* similarly, for each helping taking slices both from the centre and from the root end.

SWEETBREADS. These are glands – the pancreas and the thymus – of the calf, lamb or ox, and are only found fully developed in young animals. The thymus, or 'throat' sweetbreads, are elongated in form and neither so white nor so fat as the others, which are superior.

★ Calf and lamb sweetbreads are considered the most delicate of all the products of butchery, in flavour, texture and digestibility, but *must* be cooked the day you buy them to make sure they're fresh. Ox sweetbreads are coarser, stronger and bear no comparison with calf's and lamb's.

★ Sweetbreads, like brains, are dégorgéd (soaked in cold water to purify them) for 3–4 hrs before cooking. This is primarily to whiten them by drawing out the blood, though at the same time it softens their covering membrane which is then easier to pull off: leave them under a dripping tap if you aren't going to be around to keep changing the steeping water until it

is clear (no longer turning pink).
★ Sweetbreads and brains are blanched and then plunged into cold water if to be sliced or sautéd, to firm them up and make them easier to cut. They *aren't* blanched before braising because there's nothing to be gained, and quite a lot to be lost, in flavour and delicacy.

TRIPE. The stomach of ruminants, the best tripe coming from the ox. Depending on which stomach it comes from – which explains the differences in appearance and texture of tripe – it is of three kinds: Honeycomb, Blanket or Thick Seam. The *flavour* of all three is the same.

★ Tripe contains a large amount of connective tissue which is changed into gelatine during long slow cooking. It lacks flavour, hence the necessity to *provide* this in the way of onions, herbs and spices etc. Tripe is a valuable and easily digested food: in addition to protein, it contains an appreciable quantity of calcium from the lime used in its preparation. It shrinks a lot during cooking, so allow at least ½ lb (225 g) per person.
★ While in England the popular way of cooking it is Tripe and Onions, the classical way in France is 'Tripe à la mode de Caen', a time-taking and complicated dish on which to embark. The tripe (some of each type), cooked with cow heel or calves feet, leeks, carrots, onions, seasoning, cloves, thyme, bayleaf, garlic, cider and calvados is simmered very slowly in an earthenware (preferably) fireproof dish for at least 10 hours.

Ox

A fully grown, neutered male of domestic cattle. A young neutered ox is a bullock or steer.

★ Besides the flesh we eat, there's all the offal: kidney, heart, liver, 'tail', tongue, tripe, sweetbreads. (See under *Offal*.) In addition there are things like its suet – which is *best* for suetcrust pastry, Christmas Pudding, mincemeat etc – and bones, some of which particularly are invaluable for stock and for cold dishes like potted hough.

Pork

Takes its name from the Latin *porcus*, a pig, and is the fresh, uncured flesh. The meat would be darker in colour, and the flavour less good if the pig wasn't hung by the hind legs immediately after killing. The blood is drawn off and used to make black puddings.

★ When buying pork, look for firm, dry lean of a good pinkish colour. The fat should be firm and creamy white. Because pigs are killed young, every joint can be roasted and all the individual cuts from them are suitable for grilling or frying.
★ Bayleaf, basil, marjoram, parsley, thyme, sage and mixed herbs are all suitable for savoury stuffings and casseroles because they enhance the distinctive flavour of pork. Other good flavourings for pork dishes are cayenne, paprika, cloves, garlic, curry powder, mustard and chopped chives.

ROASTING. See also *Roasting a joint*, page 180, and *Roasting*, page 54.

(1) Make sure the joint has a good rind and that your butcher scores it for you, preferably deeply and evenly. If a *frozen* joint of pork is not scored, you'll be able to do it more easily while the meat is still frozen than when it is thawed – and soft.
(2) To make the crackling really brown and crisp, brush the scored rind with oil or melted lard before rubbing in a generous amount of salt. If you like, you can give the pork additional flavour by mixing a little pepper, dry mustard and dried sage *with* the salt. Alternatively (or as well), if you like the flavour of cloves, push a few into the scored rind, taking them out again just before you serve the pork.
(3) Avoid covering the rind with foil or anything, otherwise the crackling won't get crisp.
(4) Underdone pork is unpalatable: make sure it is properly cooked, using a meat thermometer if you have one. Weigh a joint after stuffing, allowing 30 mins per lb (450 g) and 30 mins over for a thinnish joint on the bone: 35 mins per lb (450 g) and 35 mins

over for a thick joint, especially when boned, stuffed and rolled.

(5) Place pork, rind uppermost, on a meat stand in a dry roasting tin. If without a meat stand, put the joint *in* the roasting tin, or straight onto an oven rack with a tin on the shelf below to catch the drippings – good but messy!

(6) Roast meat in a preheated hot oven for the first 20 mins to seal in the juices, gas 7, 425°F, 220°C, then reduce heat for remaining time to gas 5, 375°F, 190°C. If a joint is small and the crackling not quite crisp enough when the meat is almost cooked, raise the heat for the last 15 mins.

It is better *not to baste pork*: the thick layer of fat on top will automatically baste the lean below.

★ Traditional accompaniments to roast pork are: Sage and onion or other suitable stuffing, to counteract the richness of pork. (See also Savoury Pudding, page 196); Apple Sauce – unless you prefer, say, a sharp cranberry sauce; Thick gravy.

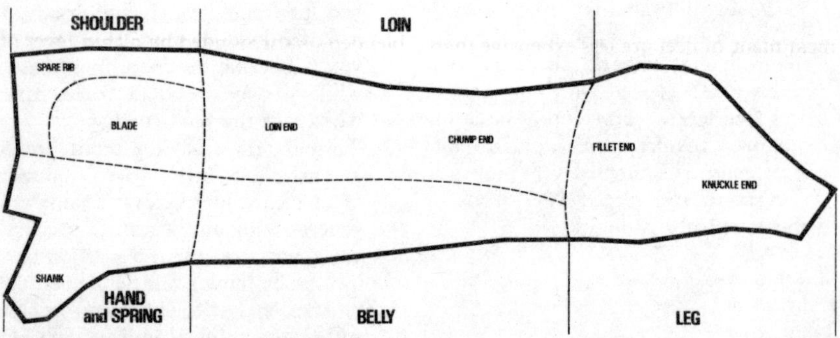

Pork carcase, showing 'what comes from where'. By courtesy of the Meat Promotion Executive.

The better cuts are:

LEG. Called gigot in Scotland, leg is the prime roasting joint but is often divided into fillet end and knuckle end because a whole leg is so huge – and expensive. The whole leg however roasts better and works out more economically than either joint cut *from* it because it stays where you put it during roasting, basted by its own fat, unlike the tender fillet end which so easily tilts over, the *lean* then on top.

★ *Fillet end* is a thick slice from the top of the leg. Roast, or slice into steaks for grilling or frying.

★ *Knuckle end.* Roast this. It's also excellent boned and stuffed.

LOIN. Roast on the bone, or boned, stuffed and rolled.

★ *Loin chops*, sometimes sold with the kidney in. Grill or fry.

★ *Chump chops* are large and meaty, coming from the chump end of the loin. Grill or fry.

★ *Chump end of loin.* Roast.

TENDERLOIN. Also known as the *pork fillet*, but don't confuse this with the fillet end of the leg, see above. Tenderloin is a lean, very tender cut on the inside of the loin bone. It's ideal for slicing and frying, especially if you coat the slices with egg and breadcrumbs and fry them in butter.

The less expensive cuts are:

SHOULDER. Roast. It's especially good boned and rolled.

★ Shoulder is often divided into *blade* and *spare rib*. *Blade* is good roasted, being excellent boned and stuffed. You can also braise or stew it. *Spare rib* can be roasted, or used for Raised Pork pies. *Spare rib chops* can be grilled, fried or braised.

HAND AND SPRING. Roast.

★ Often divided into *hand* and *shank*.

Hand can be boned and roasted, or can be boiled, fresh or pickled. *Shank* is good stewed.

BELLY. (Also called flank.) Roast thick end, stuffed. Braise, stew or boil, fresh or pickled.

★ *Sliced belly*. Grill (crisp) like bacon rashers, or fry it if you prefer.

HEAD AND TROTTERS. Make *Brawn*, page 185.

Sausages

A wonderfully convenient food for the cook because the variety is great, yet preparation may be almost nil. Made usually of pork, beef, veal or liver – or a mixture of some of these – you can buy them cooked or uncooked, spiced or unspiced, fresh or smoked. Many of the cooked continental sausages can be served with other cold meats and a salad, are delicious with crusty French bread or rolls for a quick snack, or make a tasty addition to an hors-d'oeuvre.

★ Here are some of the familiar kinds:

BEEF SAUSAGES. Sausages and sausage meat made of beef are less expensive than *pork* sausages and sausage meat mainly because they contain a smaller proportion of meat. Where 'pork' must by law contain a minimum of 65% meat, the minimum for 'beef' is 50%.

BIERWURST. A lightly smoked sausage of German origin as are many of the best sausages. Made from finely minced pork and flavoured with mustard seeds and a touch of garlic, it is cooked and ready to serve.

BLACK PUDDING. A rich, strong and to some people rather indigestible cooked sausage containing chopped pork fat and blood. You can eat it cold, or may prefer to slice and fry it to eat with bacon, or, to counteract its richness, with mashed potatoes and a vegetable.

'CHIPOLATA'. A corruption of the Italian word *cipollata*, a chive: as originally made, they were small chive-flavoured sausages.

FRANKFURTERS. Like *wienerwurst* (Vienna sausage) and *bologna*, frankfurters take their name from the city in which they were invented, so that strictly speaking, the genuine sausage only comes from that town or its immediate surroundings. The ancestor of the American hot dog, frankfurters are made basically from top quality lean pork, smoking giving them both flavour and colour. You can use them in lots of different ways, such as cut into slanting pieces for a mixed hors-d'oeuvres, with savoury spaghetti, in risotto – and of course to make hot dogs. Canned frankfurters must have a minimum of 70% meat, others not less than 75% meat.

GARLIC SAUSAGE, FRENCH. Cooked and smoked in the skin. It is made from coarse-cut ham and pork, with a *subtle* flavour of garlic.

LIVER SAUSAGE. This varies widely – there is liver sausage and liver sausage as anyone who has eaten the best of the continental and the worst of the British will know. Generally, the continental is a spreading sausage, containing minced pork and liver. The delicious Strasbourg liver sausage for instance is very smoothly blended, is surrounded by a thin layer of pork fat, and you can spread or slice it.

★ Serve liver sausage with freshly-made toast, melba toast (page 275) or black bread, on canapés, in buttered rolls or in really fresh, generously buttered sandwiches. Alternatively you can slice and include it in an hors-d'oeuvre or salad.

★ You can also make characterless and unspreadable (or nearly unspreadable) liver sausage spreadable, richer and infinitely more delicious by liquidizing 6 ozs (say 150 g) of it with 2 ozs (50 g) softish butter, 2 cloves of crushed garlic and plenty of freshly milled black pepper. (Cut sausage into thinnish slices and blend only a little to start with, gradually adding remainder.) Put in cold larder.

PORK SAUSAGES. See *Beef sausages*.

SALAMI. A highly seasoned and salted Italian sausage, differing from province to province, in the kind of meats used, in flavourings added, in shape and size, and in the salting and maturing.

★ Other countries make salami as well: *Danish salami* for instance is a smoked sausage made with finely minced pork and veal. Bright pink in colour, it has a hint of garlic and a distinctive salty flavour. *Hungarian salami* is a matured type made of finely minced pork.

Savoury Pudding

This can eke out a joint of roast lamb, mutton or pork besides counteracting the richness and being *very* tasty with any of them, or with sausages. Regard it as a stuffing and serve thick gravy. Here, briefly, is the recipe to serve 3–4: Sieve 2 ozs (50 g) self-raising flour with plenty of salt and pepper. Add 2 ozs each (50 g) of fine or medium oatmeal and grated suet (fresh or packet), 1 lightly rounded tablesp finely chopped onion or shallot, 1 heaped teasp chopped parsley and a pinch of mixed herbs if you like them. Mix all together, then stir in about 4 tablesps milk and water mixed, to make a stiff batter. Using a pallet knife, spread mixture evenly in a small shallow tin about 9″ × 6″ (23 cm × 15 cm) and bake approx $\frac{1}{2}$ hr in hot oven, gas 6, 400°F, 204°C or until crisp and brown both top and bottom. (If your joint is cooking in a slower oven, you'll probably have to cook the pudding about 10 mins longer at the lower temperature.) Serve cut into squares.

Stews, Thickened Brown

These need never be monotonous because you can ring the changes endlessly by using a different combination of ingredients. Here's a real opportunity to forget about recipes and use your own imagination, as long as you know the basic needs for a stew, like:

(1) Long slow cooking, to allow the cheaper cuts of meat such as *shin* to become tender and to make the sauce good. See *Shin*, page 184.)
(2) Using stock rather than water.
(3) Frying the onion, to bring out its flavour. Also fry things like sliced carrot or chopped mushrooms for a minute or two for the same reason.
(4) Dipping the meat in seasoned flour before frying, to flavour and brown it, also to help thicken the sauce.
(5) The subtle use of herbs.

★ Here are the sort of things to use:

(1)
FRESH VEGETABLES.
carrot
chopped celery or celeriac
sliced leek
chopped mushrooms
little sliced turnip or swede
chopped sweet peppers, fresh or frozen
pickling onions
whole shallots
sliced courgette
frozen sweetcorn
little chopped fennel

(2)
FRUITS.
skinned tomatoes, plus a teasp sugar
soaked prunes (beef or rabbit stew)
whole peeled chestnuts (beef stew)
canned pineapple

(3)
FLAVOURINGS.
bouquet garni, including herbs of choice and most suitable for type of meat
crushed garlic, or a clove or garlic in the bouquet garni
tomato purée
a twist of fresh orange peel
little wine, parsley wine, cider or beer, to replace some of the stock
a spoonful of vinegar or sour cream, stirred in at last
dry mustard, curry powder or chilli powder added to seasoned flour
a spoonful of chutney
good beef dripping (for a beef stew), to make the roux
freshly milled black pepper, stirred in at last

Tenderloin

The American name for the fillet – of beef, veal or pork.

Veal

Veal depends for its whiteness and flavour upon a calf being correctly fed, killed at the right age and properly slaughtered. It is lean and tender with a delicate pink colour, but the small amount of fat in the meat is the reason why many people prefer to braise it rather than roast, and why a joint for roasting should first be larded. Unlike beef, which so many of us prefer underdone, veal should be well cooked because it is immature meat.

ROASTING. See also *Roasting a joint*, page 180, and *Roasting*, page 54.

(1) Lard (page 46) or bard (page 31) leg or loin with pork fat before roasting so that the joint will cook without being basted.
(2) Give veal additional flavour either by stuffing or by rubbing seasonings etc into the joint, eg small spikes of garlic and tiny sprigs of fresh herbs slipped into the lean or fat; salt and pepper to which for variations you can add mixtures of: paprika, ground cloves, ginger, thyme, rosemary, tarragon, grated lemon rind. A typical mixture is salt and pepper with $\frac{1}{2}$ level teasp dried thyme and half a grated lemon rind.
(3) Allow 35 mins per lb (450 g) on the bone, 40 mins per lb (450 g) off the bone, stuffed weight.
(4) Roast in preheated hot oven, gas 8, 450°F, 230°C for the first 15-20 mins to seal in the juices, then reduce heat to gas 4, 350°F, 190°C for remainder of cooking time when the juices should be clear, not pink or red. Use a meat thermometer if you have one, to test.

★ Traditional accompaniments to veal are: Forcemeat stuffing or forcemeat balls, fried or baked in the oven; Bacon rolls; Lemon; Thick gravy.
★ The different cuts can be cooked in ways like this:

LEG. Roast or braise.

LOIN. Roast on the bone, or off; or braise.

★ Use as chops.

SHOULDER. Better boned, rolled and braised than roasted.

★ Use to make things like blanquette, fricassée or, minced, to include in pâtés.

BREAST. Bone, stuff and braise.

★ Stew. Use for galantine.

KNUCKLE. Braise or stew, eg Osso Buco, Blanquette. (This is, like shin of beef, superb meat for stewing because it is so gelatinous.) Cooked with the knuckle bone, it makes delicious and nourishing jellied stock.

CALF'S FEET. Used mainly for their gelatine, as knuckle. Use for calf's foot jelly and include in a braise such as Boeuf à la mode.

HEAD. Braise or boil. This joint includes tongue and brains, the latter often incorporated in the accompanying sauce. It's better to ask your butcher to *prepare* it, as with pig's head.

13
POULTRY AND GAME

General Information

Although poultry and winged game are often apparently so closely related, they may be poles apart when it comes to preparation for the table.

★ We can more or less take it for granted today that chickens, turkeys and ducks will be young and tender, but this isn't always so with game, many kinds of which depend for their tenderness and flavour upon being hung for the correct length of time. Where chicken, fish or butcher meat would be uneatable at such a stage, birds like pheasant, partridge and grouse only become perfect when they are 'gamy', 'high', or by some people's standards slightly 'off', perhaps with a greenish tinge on the thin skin of the abdomen. When hanging game therefore, and deciding how long to give it, it is essential to take into account personal taste as well as the type of bird and the weather – cold, hot or possibly thundery. Also older birds, which you can usually tell amongst other things by their hard scaly feet, need to hang longer than young. For most people's tastes, game birds are mature enough when you can pluck the tail or breast feathers *easily*.

★ Where chicken has such a bland flavour that you can cook it in scores of ways with all kinds of flavourings, each game bird has its own distinctive flavour. This is a flavour to be *complemented*, not altered or lost. A wild bird's flavour will to some extent depend on what it feeds on, the *quality* of its flavour also reflecting the quality of the food on which it has fed. Why else the fame of, say, Scotch grouse?

★ Where chickens are plucked immediately after killing – because it is easiest to do this while the bird is still warm, and makes no difference to the flavour – game birds are hung with their feathers on. Where chickens are plucked head hanging downwards and hung by the feet so that the blood will drain into the neck-skin and keep the flesh white, game birds are hung by the neck, tied tightly to prevent air entering by the mouth. So it goes on.

★ Both poultry and game are simply wiped inside, *washing* taking away their flavour. Some types of bird are so dry that they may need larding or barding to make them moist and juicy (see page 46 and 31), while others are better still for a piece of butter slipped inside.

★ Young game is nearly always roasted, for the simple reason that this is the way it tastes and eats best, especially when cooked in butter. Old game on the other hand usually ends up better used for soup or pâté, potted, or in something like salmi, a raised pie or a casserole. Venison, or an old hare, rabbit or game bird is improved by marinating, which not only flavours but also tenderizes tough meat (see page 48).

★ The other principal way to flavour is by serving the right accompaniments and, for poultry, with stuffings. The classic accompaniments nearly always complement the flavour and may have some additional purpose like counteracting richness, *providing* richness, giving moisture, colour or perhaps contrast of texture.

★ After hanging, you can freeze game with fur or feathers on, or off, as you like, but you can't safely hang it *after* freezing because it deteriorates too rapidly when thawed. The important thing is to use a *thick* polythene bag – or strong foil and then polythene – to prevent freezer burn (page 000) which destroys flavour besides making the flesh dry. Feathered game particularly should be thawed gradually in a cool place, otherwise it is difficult to pluck without tearing the skin. Oven-ready game and poultry will also lose less of its juiciness and flavour if thawed slowly, about 36–48 hrs in refrigerator.

★ It's unwise to cook a *frozen* bird. Salmonella, a common cause of food poisoning, can lurk in the intestines of all animals, birds and fish. It is usually destroyed quickly by heat but when you roast a bird, the body cavity – where bacteria can linger – is slightly insulated by all the surrounding flesh, so if this is frozen, the heat may never penetrate enough to destroy the bacteria.

ROASTING A BIRD. This is a different proposition from roasting a joint of meat because a bird is complete in itself, not a cut from something larger, usually with areas of unprotected flesh. The flesh of a bird is completely covered by and protected by skin (unless unhappily this is torn), usually with a layer of fat underneath. During roasting – providing you don't enclose the bird in a roasting bag or *wrap* in foil where it will, as it were, steam-roast – the flesh becomes firm and remains nicely moist while the skin, thanks to basting (which tends to dry and spoil *meat*) becomes crisp and golden. If *before* roasting, you brush a bird with oil or melted butter, results are even better.

★ Unlike meat, which is cooked throughout its cooking time in the same position, fat uppermost, most kinds of bird are best placed first on one side, then the other and finally, for the longest time, breast upwards. Thus any juices dripping into the cavity flavour and keep moist alternating parts of the flesh, instead of collecting in bottom of carcase. Turkey

SEASONS FOR GAME

Species	*Season*	*Comment*
MAMMALS		
Deer, red	1st Aug.–30th April	Males, England and Wales
Deer, red	1st Nov.–28th Feb.	Females, England and Wales
Deer, red	1st July–20th Oct.	Males, Scotland
Deer, red	21st Oct.–15th Feb.	Females, Scotland
Roebuck	All year	England and Wales
Roebuck	1st May–2nd Oct.	Scotland
Roedeer	1st Nov.–28th Feb.	England and Wales
Roedeer	21st Oct.–28th Feb.	Scotland
Hare, brown and blue mountain	All year	No close season but must not be sold between March and July
BIRDS		
Grouse	12th Aug.–10th Dec.	
Partridge	1st Sept.–1st Feb.	
Pheasant	1st Oct.–1st Feb.	
Ptarmigan	12th Aug.–10th Dec.	
Snipe, common and jack	12th Aug.–31st Jan.	
Wildfowl		
Mallard, Teal, Widgeon, Wild goose	1st Sept.–31st Jan.	Inland
	1st Sept.–20th Feb.	Foreshore

(if not too large to manipulate), chicken, pheasant, grouse and other game birds nearly all benefit from such treatment. To avoid damaging a bird's skin, use two wooden spoons to turn it – or, for a small bird, you could use tongs. (*Continual* rotation is one reason why a spit-roasted bird is so succulent and delicious.)

★ 'Frothing' the breast makes a bird look and taste delicious. About 10 mins before it is cooked, remove fat (if any) used to bard it, baste the bird with the hot dripping, dredge it with flour and baste again. Return the bird to the oven until it is a good brown colour and frothy.

★ Use a small roasting tin for a small bird, then you won't need as much fat, there's less surface from which the tasty juices can evaporate, and less likelihood of butter (if roasting in butter) burning.

TO DRAW A CHICKEN, OR OTHER FOWL. Collect your tackle before getting into a mess: chopping board, trussing needle, a clean damp cloth, two good lengths of strong thin string, some newspaper for the unwanted parts, and a sharp, pointed knife, preferably a French cook's knife.

(1) Singe carcase (after plucking) over low gas or other clear flame, when possible, in preference to singeing with a taper or long match, either of which can cause charring.

(2) Draw sinews in legs – one of the great advantages of drawing a bird yourself, because it makes such a difference to the tenderness and enjoyment of the drumsticks: (a) About 1″ ($2\frac{1}{2}$ cm) below hock joint, cut through to bone at the front of leg, but only through the yellow surface skin at the back, where the sinews lie. (b) With bird breast side up on the chopping board, its feet dangling over front of table, *break* each leg off where you have already cut them: hold bird down with one hand, knock its foot sharply down with the other. (c) Twist the foot well, then pull it away from the leg, hopefully bringing all the sinews with it – one for each toe. Use damp dish cloth to grip foot if easier, or, with a skewer, to pull out any straggling sinews. (If a bird is old and the sinews tough, you may have to pull them out one by one in this way with a skewer.)

(3) Trim extreme end of wings and cut off 'thumbs' with knife or scissors.

(4) Cut off head, leaving as much of the neck as possible, to have plenty of loose skin to tuck under bird later.

(5) Place bird on chopping board, breast down, neck towards you. With one hand, pinch up a portion of the skin along the back of the neck; with other hand, slip point of knife under the skin down to bottom of neck and slit skin full length of neck to expose neck *bone*. Sever this at shoulders.

(6) Still at neck end, ease out crop, windpipe and gullet. Insert your long finger into body cavity along the backbone, loosening the lungs and any other organs you can reach and loosen. (If all the internal organs are *loosened*, first from the neck end then from the other, almost everything should come away together later, without breaking, and therefore with the minimum of smell and unpleasantness.)

(7) Stand bird on its shoulders, breast towards you, grasp the parson's nose and make an incision between vent and tail, taking care not to cut into the intestines. Hook up the last portion of these with your first finger, and, inserting knife into body, between the intestines and the uncut skin, cut out vent.

(8) Place bird on its back, tail more or less towards you. Leave vent attached to intestine, but move it temporarily away from aperture. With your longest finger, now loosen everything possible from inner 'walls' of carcase before gripping gizzard and easing it out, with all the other organs following it.

(9) Make sure pink spongy lungs are out – they're near the ribs.

(10) Wipe bird inside with clean damp cloth. Don't *wash* it because you'll spoil its flavour among other things.

(11) Cut giblets away from organs, and use to make stock for gravy or a

sauce. (a) *The liver*. Cut gall-bladder away from it, carefully, without breaking. (This is a longish, narrow, dark-coloured sac.) (b) *The heart*. Cut off the fat and tubes. (c) *The gizzard*. Cut up the centre, through outer part only, so that you can then pull it away from its horny lining without spilling lining's messy contents. Wash well. (d) *The neck*.

TO TRUSS A CHICKEN OR TURKEY FOR ROASTING.

(1) Fold loose neck skin down over the opening and tuck it underneath the bird. Double the wings back to hold it in position.
(2) Thread trussing needle with string, knotting other end.
(3) Lay bird on its back, tail to the left. Take both legs in the left hand and draw them back over the breast as far as possible. Pass the needle through the body between the body and the thigh, catching in a tip of the wing when pulling string through. Turn the bird onto its breast. Stick the needle through the folded wings from the outside of the elbow to the tip of the wing as it lies on the shoulder. Pass the string over the back. Reverse the stitch down the other wing, and tie the ends tightly under the elbow. This completes front part of bird.
(4) Thread needle with other piece of string. To secure legs in correct position, hold the skin tightly over the tip of the breast-bone, passing the needle through. Unthread needle.
(5) Using your first finger as a hook (palm upwards), put it inside the bird, feel for the string under the breastbone and pull string out. Loop it over your finger, turn your hand over (palm downwards) and put the now twisted loop over the parson's nose. Pull both ends of the string to close up the hole, pass the ends round the hock end of the 'drumsticks' and tie tightly so that the legs are pulled down over the opening, and the breast muscles pushed up to give a plump finish. Bird should, if properly trussed now lie quite steadily on the table – and in due course for carving.

TO JOINT A CHICKEN. This is easier when you have a fresh than a thawed frozen bird because the latter is more slippery and difficult to handle. All you need is a chopping board and a very sharp knife – preferably a French cook's knife – to cut the bird into 8 good-sized joints: 2 pieces breast, 2 wings each with a piece of breast, 2 thighs and 2 drumsticks.

★ Here's one way to set about it:

(1) Lay bird first on one side then on the other to cut off each leg – drumstick and thigh – pulling thigh bone back at bottom to expose joint, and cutting off 'oyster' in one piece *with* the thigh. (The oyster is a small delicate piece of meat on each side of the back: almost scoop it out with the point of the knife.) Cut each leg at joint, to separate drumstick from thigh.
(2) Turn chicken, breast towards you, and carefully cut down one side of the breastbone. Lifting chicken flesh away, continue cutting and scraping with the knife to remove flesh from bone, taking wing with it. Lay this on chopping board and cut diagonally into two pieces – it looks nicer that way – so that the wing has a section of breast with it. Repeat operation on other side of breast.

★ Use carcase to make stock, the bones from limbs as well if cooking chicken off the bone.

★ Many dishes call for chicken joints to be skinned: if too slippery to hold easily, a damp clean dish-cloth will give you a better grip.

TO BONE A CHICKEN OR OTHER FOWL. This isn't easy to follow from a book and, even with understanding, is a time-taking and fiddling job without experience. If you don't feel like tackling it yourself, some butchers will bone a bird *for* you, but you reap in the dining room what you sowed in the kitchen because there's nothing simpler to carve than a boned stuffed bird.

★ The aim is to remove the flesh with the skin from the carcase bones without piercing the skin except where you *have* to cut it. The skin (with flesh) then acts as a container for the stuffing called for in a recipe.

★ It's unnecessary work and makes boning more difficult if you 'draw' the bird first. You need a small sharp knife, eg a vegetable knife, to work close to the bone, mostly scraping rather than cutting the flesh away. To avoid tearing the skin – so easily done at the ridge of the breastbone where skin and bone meet – the cutting edge of your knife must always face the bone, never the flesh.

The method of boning depends on what you're making:

★ *To bone, for stuffing and reshaping, as a bird*:

(1) Draw the leg sinews. Cut off the end joints of the wings and remove head, neck and crop, all as described on page 200. Cut legs off at hock joint.
(2) Pull loose neck skin well back and scrape the flesh off the wishbone. Place the knife at the back of the wishbone and force it out.
(3) Place the bird on its tail end and cut between shoulder bones. Scrape the flesh off the wing bone to the first joint and remove the bone. This is the only bone removed from the wings.
(4) Skin down the back very carefully about half way down, removing the 'oysters' from the hollows.
(5) Cut away the two cutlets from the breastbone and remove the flesh from the trunk right down to the leg joints, rolling it back as you work.
(6) Push up and bend back the leg, to make it easier to cut between the joints, and remove the bones. Alternatively, leave *in* the drumstick bones. They make the bird easier to stuff and give it a more realistic shape, but the drumsticks will have to be set aside (for family!) when carving.
(7) Pull the flesh well down, taking care not to puncture the skin. Cut from the end of the breastbone right through the vent.
(8) When all the flesh is off the carcase, turn everything right side out and stuff according to your recipe (see one suggestion below). Position the breast cutlets, and shape the 'creature' as far as possible to resemble a chicken. Truss it with wings and neck skin underneath, legs close to body, so that it later presents an easy surface to coat evenly with chaud-froid sauce and aspic.
(9) If you tear the skin while boning, stitch it up with a needle and thread.

★ *A suitable stuffing for a boned chicken*:

(1) Half a small tinned tongue, turned round side up, to form the breast – with the breast cutlets on top of it.
(2) 8–12 ozs (225–350 g) sausage meat, to pack round tongue, fill drumsticks, pack at tail and neck end.
(3) 1 or 2 hard-boiled eggs, sliced, also to place round tongue
(4) Seasoning.

★ *To bone, when the flesh is to be rolled, as for a galantine*:

(1) Draw the leg sinews, also remove head, neck and crop all as described on page 200.
(2) Cut a deep slit down back of bird from neck to tail, to expose the backbone. With your small sharp knife, its edge always cutting against the bone, scrape and cut the flesh from the carcase bones down one side of the bird, pulling flesh away from carcase with fingers as you cut.
(3) When you reach the ball joints connecting the wings and the second joints to the carcase, sever them and continue down the carcase just until you reach the ridge of the breast where skin and bone meet. Take care here – and again when you reach the same place on the opposite side of the breast – because the skin is thin and easily slit.
(4) Repeat same operation on the other side of the bird.
(5) Lift carcase frame and cut very closely against the ridge of the breastbone to free the carcase, but not to slit the thin skin covering the breastbone.
(6) Chop off the wings at the elbows, to leave just the upper wing bones attached.
(7) Arrange this frog-like creature on a board, flesh side up. Scrape the meat from all the bones not yet removed and pull out the bones.
(8) Remove any bits of fat attached to the flesh and the bird is ready to stuff.

Chicken

Chicken's popularity must stem largely from its mild but lovely flavour – mild enough to blend wonderfully with a huge variety of foods – and from its own versatility. Providing it is properly cooked, you can make a feast of an old bird or a young, serve chicken just as deliciously cold as hot, cook it fresh or 'use it up', cook it whole, boned and stuffed, in individual joints or cut into pieces. Almost anything you want to do with chicken, you can do.

★ Tarragon is its classic flavouring.

ROASTING A CHICKEN. See also *Roasting a bird* page 199, and *Roasting*, page 54.

(1) Veal forcemeat stuffing is traditional but many people prefer chicken without because forcemeat dominates and alters the flavour of the meat. Use 2–3 ozs (50–75 g) forcemeat or a mixture of forcemeat and sausage meat.

★ Use a different kind of stuffing if preferred, or to give variety.

(2) Allow 20 mins per lb (450 g) and 20 mins over in a preheated moderate-to-hot oven, gas 5, 375°F, 190°C. (As chicken is a delicately flavoured and rather dry meat, a hot oven such as is required for some types of meat tends to dry up a chicken's natural juices.)

(3) Roast chicken for 15 mins first on one side, then on the other, basting when you turn it, before placing breast upwards for remainder of time. (The legs take longest to cook so should be uppermost for the longest time.)

(4) Brushing a chicken with oil or melted butter before roasting helps to protect the flesh and makes the skin crisp and golden. Also it is best to protect the breast *initially* with a rasher of bacon or buttered paper, tucked in. Remove it later to let the breast brown.

(5) A chicken roasted in butter has the best flavour. Other suitable fats are oil, white cooking fat or lard. Dripping, other than bacon dripping, in my view spoils a chicken's true flavour. Baste regularly to cook a bird properly.

(6) If you haven't got a meat thermometer, a chicken is cooked when: (a) The meat tends to shrink from the end of the drumsticks. (b) A sharp fork runs easily into the thigh joint. If the escaping juice is pink, cook the bird a little longer.

(7) Traditional accompaniments to Roast Chicken are: Stuffing (optional, see point 1 above); Bread Sauce; Bacon rolls; Sausages (preferably chipolata, as they're intended as a garnish, not a meal); Thin gravy, unless bird is stuffed, when it should be 'thick'; Game chips or boiled new potatoes (the modern substitute for chips is, alas, often warmed potato crisps); A dressed green salad. (You may prefer instead to serve a comparatively mild-flavoured vegetable such as peas, green beans, new carrots – or even cole slaw.)

(8) A dished chicken is better for being allowed to stand at room temperature for 5–10 minutes before you carve it, so that the juices will retreat back into the tissues. Providing you don't cut into it, it won't lose much heat.

(9) *To carve*: (a) Press thighs down outwards, away from the body, so that you can see the joint and cut the legs off. Separate drumsticks from thighs, unless the bird is *very* small. (b) To cut off the wings, take a line from the top of the wishbone right down through the joint, to include a good portion of breast meat. (c) Cut breast in two or three slices either side of the breastbone. If a bird is very small, cut off each side of the breast in one piece.

★ Game shears or saw-edged scissors are a great help at the joints.

ROASTING A CHICKEN IN BUTTER. This is a French way and is a rich but positively sumptuous method of cooking chicken:

(1) Make and put this stuffing into body cavity. Mix together 2 ozs (50 g) softish butter, a little chopped fresh or dried tarragon (essential to this recipe), a good pinch of salt and plenty of freshly ground black pepper.

(2) Brush bird all over with melted butter – or you could use oil.

(3) Put about 2 ozs (50 g) butter in roast-

ing tin and roast bird as described for *Roasting a chicken* above, points 2, 3 and 6. Baste as usual.

(4) Accompaniments to this type of roast chicken are: Game chips – or, if you must, warmed potato crisps; A dressed green salad, essential to counteract the richness; The gravy (juices) and butter from the roasting tin (served in a 'gras-maigre' gravy boat – one with a hole near the bottom of one side – you can pour the tasty gravy out through the hole while *most* of the butter floats on top).

COLD ROAST CHICKEN. If you plan to serve roast chicken cold, roast it in oil, which doesn't congeal when cold. The bird will remain moister and will taste better if not cut into until cold because fewer juices will escape.

TO BOIL A CHICKEN. See page 207.

TO STEAM A CHICKEN. See page 207 for cooking time.

There are an almost infinite number of ways in which to serve a roasting chicken. Here are *some* of the popular dishes to be found in many recipe books:

COLD DISHES.
Boned Chicken. Stuffed, and coated with chaud-froid sauce.

★ To bone, see page 201.
Chaud-froid of Chicken. Cooked boneless portions of chicken, preferably breast, coated with chaud-froid sauce.
Chicken Calcutta. Cold chicken portions – boneless – coated with curry mayonnaise (page 137).
Chicken Mayonnaise. Cooked, boneless portions of chicken coated with mayonnaise mixed with aspic jelly, with a final coating of aspic.
Galantine. See page 209.
Potted Chicken. See page 216.
Chicken sandwiches or rolls. Be generous with the butter and serve *very* fresh.
Chicken liver pâté. You can often buy chicken livers at a supermarket.

HOT DISHES.
Blanquette of chicken. Similar to fricassée, the main difference being that the cooking liquor is thickened (to make a sauce) *after* the chicken (or veal) is cooked. Finished with a liaison of cream and egg yolks, this is a delicious way to serve chicken. You can make a plainer, simpler version by omitting the liaison.
Bouchées or Patties. Use frozen 'cases' if you like. They come in different sizes. Fill with a tasty chicken mixture. (You could use filling for Chicken vol-au-vent.)
Casserole-roasted Chicken, eg Poulet Poêle à l'Estragon.
Chicken casseroles. Classic dishes such as Coq au Vin, Poulet sauté Marengo, Poulet sauté Chasseur.
Chicken in a cream sauce such as Chicken Normande or Chicken à l'allemande.
Fricassée of chicken. Made with raw chicken, not cooked chicken in a dull white sauce, as so many people seem to think it is. Basically, the meat is sautéd in butter before using the butter to make a white sauce with chicken stock, in which the chicken is then cooked. Lastly, it is enriched with an egg yolk and cream liaison.
Chicken and ham croquettes. Minced cooked chicken and ham bound with a panada, coated with egg and breadcrumbs, formed into croquettes and fried in deep fat.
Chicken kromeskies. Balls or rolls of croquette mixture or farce, rolled in a thin slice of bacon, dipped in batter (preferably a delicious yeast batter), and fried in deep fat.
Chicken pancakes. Pancakes containing a savoury chicken mixture (such as used for croquettes for instance), lined up in a dish, coated with a tasty sauce and served au gratin.
Chicken pie. Usually made with a boiling fowl. Be sure to make stock with the carcase before making the pie, unless you already have chicken stock on hand.
Chicken rissoles. Similar to croquettes but enclosed in thin pastry before coating with egg and breadcrumbs and frying in deep fat.
Chicken risotto or Pilaff. See *Risotto*, page 154.
Chicken risotto-stuffed green peppers.
Curried chicken. Delicious if you include pineapple chunks in the curry. Serve *at least* six accompaniments, eg *Boiled rice*

(page 154); Fried almonds or cashew nuts (page 274); Browned coconut (cook in low oven or under grill, turning coconut over once or twice with a fork); Sliced cucumber, sliced banana (sprinkled with lemon juice to prevent discoloration, melon balls and/or tomato salad (page 163); Chopped hard-boiled egg; Rings of fried onion, dipped first in seasoned flour, then fried in oil; Mango chutney; Poppadoms (see page 274 for how to cook but not to make).

Chicken vol-au-vent. For a short cut, use a large packet of frozen puff pastry, eg Jusrol. If without oval vol-au-vent cutters (one large to cut it out, the other smaller to cut the 'lid'), roll pastry to a rectangle about 8″ × 6″ (20 cm × 15 cm), trim all edges cleanly with a sharp knife, and then cut a 'lid' in the pastry with the knife. Glaze with egg before baking but be sure not to brush any cut edges, otherwise the pastry won't rise there. After baking, while still hot, carefully lift out lid and remove any doughy centre.

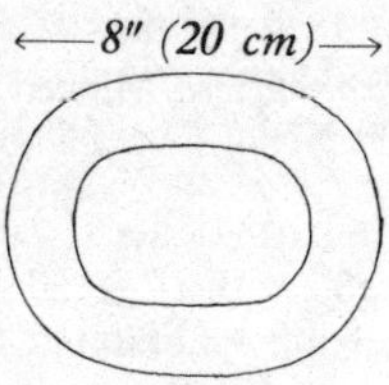

Vol-au-vent case before baking, using cutters.

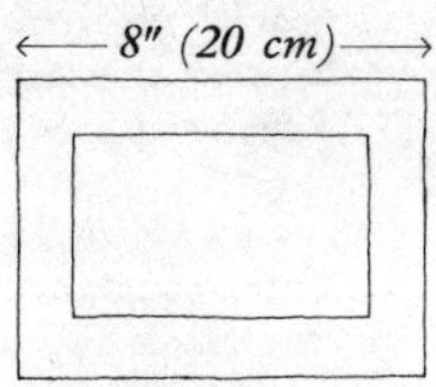

Vol-au-vent case before baking, cut with a knife.

★ *For filling*, make $\frac{3}{4}$ pt (generous 375 ml) béchamel coating sauce (page 138), to which add cut-up cooked chicken and say, some sliced mushrooms previously fried in butter with a little seasoning.

CHICKEN STOCK. Use as a base for many white soups and sauces, see page 89. If you have a freezer, you need never be without stock, storing it in the form of ice cubes.

POUSSINS. Baby chickens 4–8 weeks old, usually less than a lb (450 g) in weight and enough for one or, at a stretch, two portions, depending partly on how they're cooked.

★ Because *all* their flesh is so tender, they're ideal for grilling or frying – as well as roasting – but it's up to the cook to give them flavour. This explains why if roasted they're often stuffed, if grilled they're improved by marinating and, if fried, are best fried in butter – mixed with a little oil, to prevent burning.

★ *To fry or grill*, they must be opened out and *flattened*, otherwise they won't cook evenly, but if you take the flesh off the bone you'll lose flavour: use a sharp knife to cut along one side of the backbone, from the inside. To divide in half, use scissors or game shears to cut at breastbone.

★ Grilling, after marinating, is one of *my* favourite ways to eat poussin: cook them 18–20 mins about 3″ ($7\frac{1}{2}$ cm) from the heat under a preheated red-hot grill for just one minute on each side, thereafter under moderate heat for 8–9 mins on each side.

★ *Suggested marinade*: well-seasoned French dressing made with lemon juice rather than vinegar, and flavoured with tarragon.

★ *Suggested accompaniments*: Grilled rashers of bacon, cooked alongside the chicken for the last few minutes; Tarragon butter (pages 78 and 131); Game chips; Dressed green salad.

SPRING CHICKENS OR BROILERS. From 2–4 months old, therefore at $1\frac{1}{2}$–2 lbs (675–900 g) will serve three people at a stretch. You can roast (or spit-roast), or split, flatten and fry or grill them, like poussins.

★ Here are two ways to fry:

(1) Dip the skinless cut-up chicken pieces in seasoned flour, coat with egg and fresh white breadcrumbs, chill about an hour to firm up the coating, then fry in a frying basket in deep fat, 340°F, 170°C for about 8–10 mins. (If you use raspings instead of fresh white crumbs, they will burn; if the fat is too cool the chicken will be greasy and indigestible; if too hot the crumbs will brown and burn before the chicken is cooked.)

★ If necessary, see *Deep fat frying*, page 41.

(2) Dip flattened chicken halves (see *Poussins*) in seasoned flour, to protect and give them flavour before frying skin side down in a large strong frying

pan in hot butter and oil over moderate heat. (Use 1 dessertsp oil to 2 ozs (50 g) butter.) When browned, turn chicken skin side up, cover pan now, to tenderize them, add a pinch of dried or chopped fresh tarragon and cook gently about 15 mins, basting now and then. When cooked (the juices clear, not pink), deglaze pan with a tablespoonful or two of dry vermouth and pour all this tasty liquor over the chicken.

CAPON. A roaster, 7–10 months old, which has been neutered. Fat and full of flavour, capons weigh from 6–10 lbs ($2\frac{3}{4}$ – $4\frac{1}{2}$ K) undrawn.

★ The capon owes its existence to a curious Roman law passed when the city was at its height of glory and extravagance, the gluttony of the wealthy extreme. It was feared that the enormous consumption of hens would lead to their extinction, so by law it became forbidden to fatten and eat them. There was however no mention of the cock so, concerned to try and fatten *them* for the table, a surgeon experimented with gelding. Thus it was by chance found that the flesh was more succulent and tender than that of the forbidden hen, and that birds could be almost doubled in size. There's more flesh on a capon than on any other bird, the fat being marbled and worked through the lean tissue, rather than pocketed as with other fowl. (Today's cock is neutered by a pill or by injection.)

★ Cook and serve in any way as a chicken or turkey.

POULARDE. A *hen* which has been neutered, to increase its size – a roaster weighing 4 lbs (say 2 K) or over. See *Chicken*.

BOILING FOWL. A hen over 10 months old. Due to present-day mass production and to deep freezing, this old bird is much less in evidence than it used to be.

★ *For serving whole, coated with sauce*, a boiler is 'drawn' in the same way as a roasting chicken but trussed slightly differently: to make the legs tender and to present a flat even surface for coating the legs are 'pocketed' – put under the skin – and the parson's nose is tucked inside.

★ To pocket the legs:

(1) Place bird on its back, tail towards you. Starting just above the vent, separate the skin from the flesh until you can get two of your fingers between the skin and the flesh. Work these fingers under the skin towards the leg.
(2) Loosen the skin round the drumstick, keeping your fingers between the skin and the flesh. Bend back the hock joint of the leg and cut through the skin and the tendon just below the joint.
(3) Remove the shank and the wide tendon at the joint, leaving the round bone clear.
(4) Put two of your fingers inside the skin above the vent and gather the loose skin into folds. Press your thumb on the end of the hock bone, pushing the drumstick towards the wing and close to the body. Then push the hock bone towards the end of the breastbone nearest the vent until it is pocketed between the skin and flesh.
(5) Repeat with second leg.

TO TRUSS A FOWL FOR BOILING.

(1) Thread trussing needle with a 2 ft (60 cm) length of thin string, and knot at other end.
(2) Lay bird on its back, neck end nearest to you, holding the thighs close to the body. Pass needle through thigh, just behind the joint, through the carcase and out through the other thigh.
(3) Turn bird over. Pass needle through the 'elbow' of the wing, over the back to hold down the loose neck skin, and out through the other wing 'elbow'. Unthread needle, pull ends of string tightly and tie a double knot between the wing and the thigh.
(4) Press the 'parson's nose' inside the body cavity, and tuck in the loose skin from the drumsticks.
(5) Smooth the skin from the breastbone over the vent, and pull to the back of the bird.
(6) Thread needle with a slightly shorter length of string this time and pass the needle through the flesh under the tip of the breastbone.

(7) Cross the string under the bird and, holding the ends of the drumsticks as close to the body as possible, bring the string to the top of the bird and tie securely.
(8) Tuck in any surplus skin under the drumsticks and smooth the skin all over the bird, making sure that the flap of skin under the body is held firmly in place by the string.

TO BOIL A FOWL.
(1) Tying slices of lemon over the breast (or rubbing it with a cut lemon) and wrapping a bird in a clean cloth, is an old-fashioned but good way to keep the flesh white. If you don't do this, be sure to skim the water from time to time, otherwise both skin and flesh will go a nasty colour.
(2) To make sure you put the bird into the right amount of *boiling* water, put fowl in the pan first, cover it with cold water and then take bird out again while boiling the water. (If you put the bird into cold water and bring it to the boil, flavouring juices will be drawn out of it into the liquor.) If necessary, top up with boiling water during cooking.
(3) To give the cooking liquor and the fowl flavour, you need plenty of salt in the water besides the prepared giblets, an onion stuck with 3 or 4 cloves, a bouquet garni and a chunk of carrot.
(4) Boil fowl for 5 mins then reduce the heat and *simmer* 2–3 hrs according to age of bird. (If you boil rather than simmer it, the flesh will harden.) Test with a fork near the thigh to see when it is tender.
If boiling a moderate sized *roasting chicken*, allow $\frac{3}{4}$–1 hr, a large one 1–1$\frac{1}{4}$ hrs, or a very large one 1$\frac{1}{4}$–1$\frac{1}{2}$ hrs.

★ Accompaniments to boiling fowl are: Coating sauce to cover fowl, made with equal quantities milk and strained cooking liquor; Sieved yolk of egg and finely chopped parsley, to garnish; Creamed potatoes or boiled rice; A colourful but mildish vegetable such as Brussels sprouts, green peas or beans, courgettes or new carrots.

★ Should you want to *steam* a fowl, cook half as long again as for boiling, wrapping it in a clean cloth as for boiling.

Duck

Duck, which has much more carcase and far less flesh than a like-sized chicken, is drawn and trussed in much the same way, but with these differences:
(1) Cut legs off at hock joint – unless you prefer to leave *on* the scalded, scraped feet.
(2) Cut wings off at elbow, because the lower part is mostly bone.
(3) Cut out the wishbone, to make the breast easier to carve.
(4) Minimize the richness by:
(a) Removing oil sacs at base of tail – if still there.
(b) Removing any loose fat from cavity and around the neck.
(c) Pricking the skin with a fork at $\frac{1}{2}''$ (1$\frac{1}{4}$ cm) intervals along the thighs, the back and the lower part of the breast, to help let the layer of subcutaneous fat escape during cooking.
(5) After stuffing or seasoning the cavity, sew or skewer the legs, wings and neck skin to the body to make the bird compact and plump-looking.
(6) Sew or skewer a *stuffed* bird at vent, to keep the stuffing in.

ROASTING A DUCK. See also *Roasting a bird*, page 199.
(1) You need a young one. Only a duckling under 6 months is really perfect for roasting. (They tend to grow thinner as well as tougher after 8 months.)
(2) *Stuffing* counteracts the richness of a duck and, because it keeps the flesh moister, also makes it more tender. If you're not a sage-and-onion fan, try another stuffing such as Apple and Walnut: sweat a finely sliced onion in $\frac{1}{2}$ oz (15 g) butter until nearly soft. Mix it with 2 ozs (50 g) each of breadcrumbs and sausage meat, $\frac{1}{2}$ level teasp herbs, a few chopped walnuts, a chopped sour apple, seasoning and egg yolk (or half a

small whole egg) to bind.

★ As a quick alternative to the more time-taking stuffings here are three easy ways to give flavour:

Either (a) Slip a peeled cored cooking apple into the cavity.

(b) Season the cavity with salt, pepper, a pinch of thyme or sage and a small sliced onion or shallot.

Or (c) Mix the chopped duck liver with a finely sliced shallot, a clove of crushed garlic, 1 tablesp chopped parsley, seasoning and a little mixed-up egg to bind.

(3) *The roasting tin.* Choose one just large enough to hold a duck easily, then you won't need any dripping, just 2 tablesps water or stock: the duck itself provides the fat, *some* of which at intervals it is better to pour off – or draw off with a bulb baster. Although some people swear by basting a duck, there's no *need* to: with so much of its own fat beneath the skin, a duck is self-basting, which keeps its flesh moist and makes its skin crisp.

★ A duck roasts best however if you keep turning it: place it breast up for the first 15 mins, then *approx.* 30 mins on each side, then the last 15 mins breast up again.

★ If you lay the bird on a thickly sliced carrot and onion, these will give extra flavour to the gravy.

(4) *Roasting time* – in the centre of a moderate oven, gas 4, 350°F, 175°C – depends of course on a duck's weight and whether it is stuffed or not. Here's a guide, in case you want it:

★ To test when cooked, prick duck at fattest part of thigh or drumstick. If the juices that run out from there, and from the vent (when you lift and drain duck) look pinkish, the duck is medium rare – the way the French like it. If the juices run pale yellow, the duck is well done.

★ If you want to have it ready in advance, a roast duck won't spoil if left for ½ hr in a turned-off hot oven, door ajar.

(5) Traditional accompaniments to roast duck are: Sage and onion stuffing (but not *too* heavy-handed with the sage!); Apple sauce; Thick gravy if stuffed, otherwise thin; New or Duchess potatoes, to minimize richness; Green peas – or other vegetable such as braised celery. turnips or Brussels sprouts.

(6) *Carving* a duck is different from carving a chicken, naturally, because its anatomy is different: cut the crackling skin with the point of a sharp knife, and cut the meat from the breast in long, rather thin slices – in slivers. One way to do this is to turn the dismembered bird first on one side and then on the other, its tail towards you, cutting diagonally. You may find it easier to cut the wing joints with game shears rather than with a knife.

OTHER GOOD WAYS TO COOK OR USE DUCK INCLUDE:

★ Roasting in various other ways, including the famous Duck à l'orange.

★ Spit-roasting.

★ Braising or casseroling, perhaps after marinating the duck in a red wine marinade.

Weight of bird when drawn	*No. it will serve*	*Cooking time for medium rare*	*Cooking time for 'well done'*	*If stuffed, add on:*
3½ lbs (say 1½ K)	3 or 4	65–70 mins	75–85 mins	20–30 mins
4½ lbs (say 2K)	4	75–80 mins	85–95 mins	20–30 mins
5½ lbs (say 2½ K)	5 or 6	85–90 mins	95–100 mins	20–30 mins

★ Make salmi.
★ Serve it cold, or make it into cold dishes the same as many chicken dishes, eg Chaud-froid of duckling, galantine, pâté, pâté en croûte (boned, stuffed duck baked in a crust).
★ Make soup.

DUCK FAT, RENDERED makes good dripping toast: spread it on hot toast, sprinkle lightly with salt and put back under grill again for a few moments, to help the fat melt and the toast to absorb it.

DUCK, WILD. These (Mallard, Widgeon, Teal) shouldn't hang longer than a day, the flavour becoming rancid rather than gamy, like that of a well-hung grouse or pheasant. In addition, it is *safer* to eat wild duck without delay. You need two birds for four people or, at a stretch, two mallards for five.

★ Because of their sometimes rather strong fishy flavour, depending on what they feed on, it's wise to take precautions before you roast them – mallard and teal especially:

(1) Remove oil-sacs near tail – their contents keep the feathers oiled.
(2) *Blanch* the birds: put them in a roasting tin with a sliced onion and enough boiling salted water to baste thoroughly. Spend several minutes at the kitchen table just spooning the onion-flavoured water over them. (Alternatively, you can marinate them in a well-flavoured marinade or, less effective I think, stuff each bird's cavity either with a small peeled orange or two, or with a raw potato and an onion or an apple.)
(3) Pour water away, drain birds well, wipe dry, rub skin all over with salt, and then smear liberally with either softened butter or olive oil.
(4) Bard or lard the breast. (Unlike the fattiness of a domestic duck, wild duck is by comparison dry.)

★ *Roasting* or spit-roasting are the best ways to cook wild duck, which should be underdone, and served hot. Roast teal or widgeon about 25 mins, mallard about 30 mins – preferably in butter – in the middle of a preheated hot oven, gas 7, 425°F, 220°C, basting 2 or 3 times to prevent the flesh drying out.
★ Accompaniments for roast wild duck are: Orange salad; Bigarade sauce – an orange flavoured brown sauce; Game chips or creamed potatoes; Watercress, to garnish.
★ *Other suggestions for wild duck*, should you tire of eating it roast: marinate it (eg in a liquid containing red wine and port) and then braise, pot-roast or casserole it, or you can make it into salmi, page 218. You can use up *cooked* wild duck in things like risotto, savoury pancakes, patties, or just in a tasty béchamel sauce, served with croûtes of fried bread.

Galantine

Originally referred to a boned, stuffed and pressed chicken served in its own jelly, its name deriving from the Latin word *gallus*, a cock. Towards the end of the seventeenth century, however, other birds, also meat and fish, began to figure in this dish, but the term galantine, by itself, still implies galantine of poultry. When made with something different, the main ingredient is always named, as in Galantine of Veal, or Galantine of Partridge or Grouse.

★ The meat itself may be stuffed, or may be minced and combined with other meats and flavourings. It is very like pâté, the difference between them being in the cooking: if the meaty mixture is baked in a fat-lined terrine it is a terrine or pâté; if baked in a pastry crust it is a pâté en croûte; if *steamed*, it is a galantine.
★ A few hints:

(1) The meats should be finely minced, preferably together, preferably twice, to blend perfectly.
(2) Be generous with seasoning, a cold mixture of this sort tends to lack flavour.
(3) To blend the mixture thoroughly and to give the galantine a light texture, beat the ingredients vigorously together with a wooden spoon.
(4) A galantine needs very gentle cooking, tied in a clean cloth. If

cooked too fast, the meat will harden and some galantines will crack on the surface.

(5) For the right texture, a galantine should be weighted and left overnight to cool.

(6) *If* when cold a galantine's surface is greasy rather than jellied, wring a clean cloth out in very hot water, fold it and place over the galantine for a few minutes.

(7) If the meat hasn't jellied when cold, meat glaze or aspic help to keep the meat moist at the same time as garnishing it.

Game

PLUCKING GAME. It would be easier to pluck game if we didn't afterwards have to chase after the feathers. In the kitchen, you only have to sigh or sneeze for the 'downy' ones to take off, so it's easiest to work on several layers of spread-out newspaper and from time to time clear the decks. Game is ready for cooking when the tail feathers come out quite readily when pulled – unless you like it very 'high'.

★ In case you're flummoxed by the prospect of a feathered bird, here are some tips:

(1) All the skin is tender, especially the breast and neck-skin. To minimize the risk of tearing it – because a damaged bird roasts less well than a perfect – grip the skin tightly between thumb and fingers of one hand while close beside them carefully pulling out the feathers with the other.

(2) To have some sort of organization and to be able to see what you're doing, pluck in this order:
(a) Underside of wings.
(b) The tail. (Keep the best 6 tail-feathers of a *pheasant* to stick in the vent, giving the bird a festive look on the serving dish.)
(c) From neck to tail on breast side of bird, then from neck to tail on back.
(d) Legs.
(e) Upper side of wings, cutting off the wing tips.

(3) Singe bird over a low gas flame, or other clear flame, to make less 'whiskery'.

DRAWING GAME. Draw as for *Chicken* (see page 200), apart from some minor differences:

(1) The leg sinews aren't pulled out, for it's a game bird's *wings* that are the hard-worked part. The feet are in fact left on, so *scald* the legs and cut off the claws.

(2) Snipe is roasted *without* being drawn or decapitated, see page 219.

TRUSSING GAME. Truss game as *Chicken* (page 201), apart from:

(1) The wings: fold these up at the sides of the body instead of underneath.

(2) Truss the legs so that the feet lean well back towards the breast. (To help 'set' them in this position, lay a bird's feet against the roasting tin when you *roast* it, first on one side, then the other.)

ROASTING GAME. See *Roasting a bird*, page 199, for general information, and individual birds for details specific to each.

FRIED BREADCRUMBS. These are so often a disappointment that is seems a pity not to spell out the simple details. This quantity serves 6:

1 oz (25 g) butter (preferably but not necessarily saltless or clarified, which burn less easily)
2 ozs (50 g) golden breadcrumbs (raspings) which, unlike white breadcrumbs, give a delicious nutty flavour

(1) Heat butter in strong frying pan over moderate heat until it foams. Wait until foam almost subsides but *not* until the butter begins to go brown.

(2) Stir in crumbs, reduce heat to low and stir frequently if not continually – to brown them evenly – for a few minutes until a darker golden colour. (If not cooked slowly and for long enough they will lack flavour, but if cooked too fast or too long the butter will burn.)

(3) Serve hot in a warmed sauceboat with roast game – pheasant, partridge, grouse etc.

Goose

Goose is drawn and trussed as a duck, and in much the same way as a chicken (page 200), but with these differences:

(1) Cut legs off at hock joint.

(2) Cut wings off at elbow – because the lower part is mostly bone. (Even then, the remaining part makes poor eating.)

(3) Cut out the wishbone, to make the breast easier to carve.

(4) Minimize the richness by:

(a) Removing any loose fat from cavity and around the neck. (See *Goose fat*, next page, for what to do with it.)

(b) Pricking the skin with a fork at ½″ (1¼ cm) intervals along the thighs, the back and lower part of the breast, to help let the layer of subcutaneous fat escape during cooking.

(5) After stuffing or seasoning the cavity, sew or skewer the legs, wings and neck skin to the body, to make the bird compact and plump looking.

(6) Sew or skewer a stuffed bird at vent, otherwise some of the stuffing will escape during cooking into the fat in the roasting tin.

ROASTING A GOOSE. See also *Roasting a bird*, page 199.

(1) A bird under 6 months old and from 9–11 lbs (4–5 K) is best: smaller are largely bone, while larger tend to be tough, because usually older.

(2) *Stuffing* counteracts richness and, because it keeps flesh moister, makes it more tender.

★ Goose and prunes have an affinity with each other, so a prune and apple stuffing (or even a chestnut stuffing) is to many people a welcome change from sage and onions.

★ The goose's liver is often included in the stuffing because it gives so much flavour, but if you want something really quick and simple just to cut down its richness, try stuffing the bird with peeled and cored sour apples.

★ Although you can have the stuffing prepared, ready to put in, it's better actually not to stuff the goose until just before you cook it, otherwise it can spoil both bird and stuffing.

(3) If before roasting you rub over the skin with flour, it helps absorb some of the surface grease as well as making the skin crisp.

(4) Goose isn't basted because with so much fat of its own, beneath its skin, it is self-basting. To protect it during the rather long cooking, cover the breast with a piece of foil or a sheet of greased greaseproof paper for the first 45 minutes. (Some people baste a goose with *boiling water* to help in the dissolution of all subcutaneous fat.) There is so *much* fat that you may at intervals need to ladle some of it out of the roasting tin – or better still, draw it off with a bulb baster.

(5) *Roasting time* – Goose should be 'done to a T' – 180°F, 82°C, on a meat thermometer, the meat juices running pale yellow: if overcooked, the breast meat especially will be dry; if undercooked, goose is indigestible and unpalatable.

★ Cooking time of course depends on the weight of the goose and whether it is stuffed or not. Roast it in the centre of a preheated hot oven for the first 15 mins, gas 7, 425°F, 220°C, then reduce the heat to gas 4, 350°F, 175°C, for remainder of cooking time. If you're unsure how long to give it, here's a rough guide. As you'll see, the larger the goose, the less time per lb (450 g) it takes to cook:

Weight of bird (drawn)	*No. it will serve*	*Approx. cooking time, unstuffed*	*If stuffed, add on:*
9 lbs (say 4 K)	6–8	about 2 hrs	20–40 mins
9½ lbs (say 4¼ K)	8–9	about 2¼ hrs	20–40 mins
10½ lbs (say 4¾ K)	9–10	about 2 hrs, 20 mins	20–40 mins
11½ lbs (say 5¼ K)	10–12	about 2½ hrs	20–40 mins

(6) Traditional accompaniments to goose are: Sage and onion stuffing; Apple sauce (pineapple isn't traditional, but fried 'rings' make a good variation); Thick gravy, if stuffed, otherwise thin; Watercress, to garnish.
(7) *Carve goose* as duck, see page 208.

BRAISED GOOSE. Some people prefer this to roast, finding it more tender and flavourful, but less rich. Cook it at gas 3, 325°F, 165°C, a lower temperature than for roasting, but for a similar length of time. See (5) above.

GOOSE FAT. Rendered down from the loose fat *inside* the bird, goose fat is much too good to waste, being excellent for sautéing or basting. Once rendered, it will keep for weeks in the refrigerator. To prepare:
(1) Cut fat into ½″ (1¼ cm) pieces and simmer about 20 mins in a covered saucepan with ½ pt (250 ml) water, to draw the fat out of the tissues.
(2) Remove pan lid and boil liquid slowly to evaporate the water. (The fat will splutter as the moisture in it evaporates. When it *stops* spluttering, the fat is pure, ready for use.)
(3) Strain the pale yellow liquid through butter muslin.

★ Goose fat is also a delicacy smeared on soft fresh bread, sprinkled with salt and freshly milled pepper.

GOOSE LIVER. A valuable part of a goose, both for its goodness and its flavour. The liver of other birds is just as good but the goose's is larger, and when the bird is grossly overfed and deprived of exercise, the liver may grow to as much as five times its normal size. This explains why geese in some countries, France particularly, have been bred and fattened for centuries especially to make Pâté de foie gras, and why the *flesh* of these birds is inferior to the flesh of a bird reared specifically for roasting.

GOOSE STOCK. Makes an excellent brown sauce: make it as chicken stock (page 89), using the gizzard, neck, heart and wing tips – the liver as well if you haven't used it in the stuffing or to make goose liver pâté, like chicken liver pâté. Simmer the stock about 2 hrs.

GREEN GOOSE. A gosling under 3 months old. As its flavour is easily overpowered by a stuffing, you're better *not* to stuff it – or anyway not with sage and onions.

MICHAELMAS GOOSE. A young goose; tender, delicious and less rich than a mature bird because it hasn't had time to develop so much fat.

★ The tradition dating back to the sixteenth century of the English eating goose on Michaelmas Day appears almost to have died out. The custom originated with Queen Elizabeth who was at table when the news of the sinking of the Spanish Armada was brought to her. Because the principal dish that day was roast goose, and because it was a favourite dish of hers, she decreed that the glorious occasion should be commemorated by serving roast goose on Michaelmas Day (29th September) every year.

WILD GOOSE. A bird which I confess I've never either eaten or cooked, but it is said not to compare in flavour with a domesticated. Because it is so much leaner, one good way to cook it is evidently in a flour and water paste (page 185) in a slower oven and for a longer time than a farmyard goose – probably about 3 hrs. Remove the crust and froth the bird's breast (page 200) about 20–30 mins before you expect it to be ready.

Grouse

At their best young, and between mid-August and mid-October. This is probably the finest of all game birds and is, in the culinary sense, unique to the British Isles. The best come from Scotland, parts of Northern England, Wales and the West of Ireland. Whether you eat it hot or cold, grouse is equally good.

★ Young birds are best roasted, old birds marinated and casseroled, or made into tasty dishes like grouse pudding (beefsteak and grouse actually), raised pie, pâté or potted grouse. They also make a good salmi.
★ Grouse should be well hung to develop

its true flavour. Allow young birds about a week in warm weather – unless badly shot or moist *thundery* weather – or up to a fortnight if cold, and if you like them 'high'. (Use the tail feathers as a guide, see page 198.

TO ROAST GROUSE. See also *Roasting a bird*, page 199.

(1) As the flesh is inclined to be dry, it's best to bard the breast and put a nut of seasoned butter inside the bird, as well as roasting it in butter.
(2) The liver is almost too good to use in the stock: fry lightly, mash and spread it on an oval slice of bread, all ready to slip underneath the bird when you froth the breast about 15 mins before the bird is cooked.
(3) Make the giblet stock in advance – you'll need it to make thin gravy with the drippings in the roasting tin.
(4) Allow *about* 35 mins in the centre of a preheated hot oven, gas 6, 400°F, 204°C. If a bird is very high, be sure to cook it well.
(5) Accompaniments to roast grouse are: Fried breadcrumbs (page 210); Bread sauce; Thin (giblet) gravy; Game chips (page 152); A dressed green salad; Watercress, to garnish.
(6) *To carve*. Young grouse are usually cut in half, allowing half a bird per person.

Guinea Fowl

Though related to the pheasant, guinea fowl isn't as succulent and good to eat because it never runs to fat and the flesh is naturally dry. The bird takes its name from its homeland, the West African coast of Guinea, from where it was originally brought to Europe by the Greeks. Although in England it has been domesticated since the fifteenth century, in its native haunt it is wild.

★ The flavour isn't too unlike that of either a chicken or pheasant, and you can *cook* it as either, in almost any way – but it's *better* cooked according to pheasant recipes because of its fatlessness.
★ A few facts may help:

(1) Hang guinea fowl at least 2 days in warm weather, longer in cold. Pluck just before you cook (or freeze) it.
(2) Stuff it or not as you like. A lump of butter in the cavity for instance will help to make the flesh moist, as will any stuffing containing fat.
(3) Truss like game.
(4) Bard the bird well, to protect, make moist and give the flesh flavour.
(5) Roast as pheasant (page 215), allowing *about* 1 hour.
(6) Accompaniments for roast guinea fowl are: Bread sauce; Redcurrant jelly; Thin gravy; Game chips; Watercress, to garnish.

Hare

At its best in late December. Young hares are best for roasting or jugging – the two most usual methods of cooking hare – while the older are usually best marinated (to tenderize and flavour them) before braising, casseroling or stewing. In addition, you can make many tasty dishes like raised pie or potted hare; hare soup, pâté, pudding or brawn.

★ A hare is never eaten 'high'. Hung head downwards, with a bowl to catch the blood, and without skinning or paunching (drawing), allow a fully grown hare up to 10 days in very cold weather, about 6–7 days when warm. A good-sized hare will serve 9–10 people, a leveret 6–8.

TO SKIN AND DRAW A HARE:

(1) Cut off the legs at the first joint.
(2) Slit the skin along the belly and loosen it from the body.
(3) Draw it over the hind legs by pulling away inside out. Pull towards the tail.
(4) Pull the skin towards the head and off the front legs.
(5) Draw the skin towards the neck, then, with a sharp knife, remove it from the head. (You may want to cut off the head while you're about it.)
(6) Slit the belly and pull out the internal organs, reserving the liver if you want it, to stuff a hare before roasting. Collect in a basin all the blood if you're roasting or jugging the hare. (It collects under a piece of membrane

in the ribs, so take care when breaking this.)

(7) Apart from the tail end, wipe rather than wash a skinned hare, to avoid it losing flavour.

JUGGED HARE. When it is properly made, jugged hare is one of the best English dishes. The essential points are:

(1) Long slow cooking, until the meat is completely tender – ready to leave the bones. Young or old, a hare must always be well cooked. (It's better *over*cooked than undercooked.)

(2) Port – a large glassful – to give flavour. Alternatively, use a glass of the red wine marinade if the hare was first marinated.

(5) The use of the hare's blood as a liaison, to thicken the liquor after the hare is cooked: add 2 or 3 tablesps of the hot liquor very gradually to the blood (as you would add it to a cream and egg yolk liaison), then stir this back carefully into the sauce. Reheat the sauce gently, to thicken it without boiling, otherwise it will be curdled by the blood.

★ Accompaniments for jugged hare are: Fried forcemeat balls; Redcurrant jelly.

Partridge

Young birds, which are best roasted (or can be split and grilled), are at their plumpest and best in October. Because of their delicate and perfect *natural* flavour, young partridge shouldn't be hung until 'high' – give them just three or four days. In cold weather, older birds may hang up to a fortnight. These are better marinated and then braised or stewed rather than roasted, or you can make them into dishes like salmi, raised pie, galantine, pâté or potted partridge. *Cold* roast partridge, and bacon, makes a breakfast fit for Lucullus.

TO ROAST PARTRIDGE. See also *Roasting a bird*, page 199.

(1) To help keep the flesh moist and to give flavour, cover the breast with a rasher or two of fat bacon and put a nut of butter (mixed with seasoning and a few drops of lemon juice) inside the bird, as well as cooking it in butter.

(2) Make the giblet stock in advance – to make thin gravy with the drippings in the roasting tin.

(3) Roast about 10 mins in the centre of a preheated very hot oven, gas 7, 425°F, 220°C. then reduce heat to gas 6, 400°F, 204°C, for remainder of cooking time – *about* 30 mins altogether. (Baste and turn bird every 10 mins to make sure it cooks perfectly.)

(4) If liked, slip a slice of bread under a bird about 15 mins before it's cooked, to catch the juices and become crisp. Accompaniments to roast partridge are: Fried breadcrumbs (page 210); Bread sauce; Thin (giblet) gravy; Game chips (page 152) or potato straws; A dressed green salad (avoid any 'overpowering' vegetable, particularly one of the cabbage family); Watercress, to garnish.

(5) *To carve.* Cut in half, allowing half a bird per person.

Pâté (Terrine)

Made from the game or poultry of your choice, together usually with veal and pork, the proportions of these depending on the richness or dryness of the bird or animal in question. To make pheasant pâté for instance, you may want about 1 lb (450 g) each of lean veal and pork belly to the meat of one plump bird, but for duck pâté you'd need correspondingly less *fat* meat and rather more *lean* meat.

★ The ideal way to make these pâtés is with an uncooked bird, but as it's so much easier and quicker to strip the flesh of a partly cooked bird (say roasted about 20 mins) than an uncooked, this is the way it's often done. A bird's liver, raw, is sometimes minced along with the flesh and the other meats.

★ See also *Pâté*, page 119.

Pheasant

The most beautiful of all our game birds, pheasant was in ancient times known as the bird of Phasis. Its name originates from the river Phasis, between the Black and Caspian Seas where the *bird* originated.

★ Young birds are of course best – and *at* their best from November to January – but must be hung long enough to *taste* of pheasant: in a cool place, preferably one with lots of fresh cold air, this means at least five days in normal weather, or up to about 12 days when very cold – unless they're badly shot. The hen is normally plumper, more tender and more succulent than the cock, but the cock is larger, even if not *quite* so good. This is why birds are usually sold by the brace and why, if the purse allows, it is better to cook a 'pair' rather than a single bird.

★ As with most other game birds, young pheasants are *best* roasted; older birds marinated before stewing, casseroling etc, or making into all the traditional things like galantine, pâté, raised pie, salmi, potted pheasant or soup.

TO ROAST PHEASANT. See also *Roasting a bird*, page 199.

(1) To help keep the flesh moist and to give flavour, bard the breast. Some seasoning and a few strips of juicy steak inside the bird will give it even more flavour.
(2) Roast about 10 mins in the centre of a preheated very hot oven, gas 7, 425°F, 220°C, then reduce heat to gas 6, 400°F, 204°C for remainder of cooking time – about 40–60 mins altogether according to the size and age of the bird. (Baste it at least each time you turn it.)
(3) A slice of white bread slipped underneath the bird about 15 mins before it's cooked is unorthodox but delicious. Saturated by the bird's juices, and made crisp by the hot fat, this is what makes my mouth water when I think of pheasant.
(4) If you *want* to stuff a pheasant, here's one very simple suggestion: 1 oz (25 g) butter mixed with salt, pepper, a pinch of cayenne and a few wiped, chopped-up mushrooms.
(5) To make chirpy, serve with six of the best tail feathers coming out of the vent.
(6) Accompaniments to roast pheasant are: Fried breadcrumbs (page 210); Bread sauce; Thin (giblet) gravy; Game chips or potato straws; A dressed green salad; Watercress to garnish.
(7) *Carve* as chicken. A pheasant's legs are quite a lot darker and more highly flavoured than the breast and wings, so some people *prefer* the dark meat to the white.

TO SERVE A ROAST PHEASANT COLD. An old country custom which is still just as good today: the moment the roast pheasant leaves the oven, wrap it up closely in a cloth wrung out in cold water or cider. Cover it then with a clean sack or an old piece of blanket or rug and leave to cool. (Because the steam is kept in, the breast is moist and succulent, instead of rather dry, as cold pheasant tends to be.)

TO SAUTÉ PHEASANT. Bone and flatten (but don't skin) the joints; coat each piece with egg and seasoned breadcrumbs, and sauté in hot butter (or butter and a little oil) over lowish heat until cooked, *about* 30 mins. Turn joints about every 5 mins.

Pigeons

The pigeon has been kept for centuries in semi-domestication in many parts of the world. Better known in biblical terms as a dove, it has for thousands of years had religious connotations. It was because of its prized flesh that this was the bird chosen for sacrifice – yet in Britain today pigeons are classed as vermin.

★ Until the eighteenth century, before turnips and swedes were introduced to British agriculture, and we could keep cattle and sheep alive through the winter, non-breeding animals had to be slaughtered and preserved in salt. Pigeons in those days therefore supplied the wealthy with fresh meat during the months when little other *fresh* was available. In castle, monastery and manor-house, the 'table' was the chief concern, so that by the middle of the seventeenth century, every house of importance had its own dovecote in which hundreds or even thousands of these prolific birds could be, and were, accommodated.

★ The dovecote originated in Rome. Some Romans were so impatient to fatten the squab as soon as they were covered with down that they separated them from the parent birds and fed them on white bread already half-chewed by men specially hired for the work.

★ Pigeons are at their best from March to September, a young bird being recognizable by its small pink legs, fat breast, flexible beak and thick neck. Properly cooked, they make as good a meal as almost any game bird. See also Squab.

HANGING, PLUCKING AND DRAWING.

(1) You can hang a pigeon a day or two or not at all, as you like but, to keep the flesh a better colour, it should be hung head downwards for at least an hour immediately after shooting. Otherwise, the meat is very dark.

(2) If you can pluck a pigeon while it's still warm, the feathers will almost fly off. It's the easiest of all birds to do. (Scalding with boiling water may be a *quick* way to de-feather a pigeon, but it toughens both the skin and the outer layer of the flesh.)

(3) Draw a pigeon when you pluck it. The liver contains no gall so you can either leave it in the bird for extra flavour, use it in a stuffing if you're roasting the bird or, if you have many birds, make pâté.

★ It's because cooks had to be imaginative if people weren't to tire of pigeon that old cookery books abound with pigeon recipes. Young birds are *best* roasted (see below) or grilled – in the same way as poussins (see page 205). Old birds are usually improved by marinating and can be braised, casseroled, stewed, curried, made into a pie, a pudding (with steak), a raised pie, salmi, pâté, soup or potted poussins (see page 205). Old birds are of pigeon if prepared to spend the time.

TO ROAST PIGEON. See also *Roasting a bird*, page 199.

(1) Allow one plump young bird per person.

(2) To protect the flesh and give extra flavour, either bard the breast with a fat bacon rasher or brush the bird with melted butter and dust lightly with flour. Best of all is to brush it with butter *and* bard it.

(3) Stuffing – at the neck end, as a chicken – is optional. Here's one suggestion: sauté the pigeon's liver and a chopped mushroom in a walnut-sized piece of butter. Mash them when cooked and mix with 2 rounded teasps fresh white breadcrumbs, seasoning and any remaining butter in the pan. If liked, add a touch of sherry or brandy.

(4) Roast 25–35 mins according to size in a preheated hot oven, gas 6, 400°F, 204°C, basting frequently.

(5) A small slice of bread slipped under the bird about 15 mins before it's cooked will absorb the juices, become crisp in the fat and is *delicious* with the bird.

(6) Accompaniments to roast pigeon are: Fried breadcrumbs – if no bread under the bird; Thin gravy; Bacon rasher used to bard bird – with a *pigeon* this is served; Watercress, dressed, to garnish.

(7) *To carve.* Cut in half down the centre.

★ However you cook pigeon, the fat you use shouldn't be too intensely hot, otherwise it will spoil the delicate flavour of the flesh.

Potted Meat

Cooked, finely minced meat preserved in pots or jars, Potted Meat is so concentrated, compact and well preserved that in days gone by it was an ideal food for seamen and travellers to take on their journeys. Covered with a thick layer of butter to exclude air, and refrigerated, any meat's keeping time is greatly extended.

★ Potted meats are more or less the

English equivalent of a French pâté or terrine. Their basic difference is that for potted meat, the meat is cooked before being preserved, whereas for pâté the meat is cooked in the dish in which it is to be stored and served.

★ Here's one tasty recipe, to serve 5 or 6:

$\frac{1}{2}$ lb (225 g) cooked, boneless chicken or game
2 ozs (50 g) cooked ham or streaky bacon rashers
2 ozs (50 g) softish *butter*
salt and cayenne pepper
pinch ground nutmeg
pinch ground mace
1 clove garlic, optional
saltless or clarified butter, as required to cover surface

(1) Mince 'meat' and ham together.
(2) Liquidize together – adding meat to liquidizer a little at a time, to prevent machine sticking – the meats, cut-up butter, salt, spices and crushed garlic.
(3) Press into pots and cover with a $\frac{1}{4}''$ (7 mm) layer of *barely* melted cool butter. Tilt pot carefully in all directions to seal in the contents. Leave butter to harden.
(4) Cover with foil or cellophane to store and refrigerate.
(5) Serve with hot toast or crusty French bread or rolls.

★ A few tips:

(1) Old game is better marinated before being cooked, to tenderize and flavour it. It won't then need quite such long cooking, so the flavour benefits in two ways.
(2) A touch of garlic gives a subtle flavour. It's worth trying, even if you think you don't like garlic.
(3) If without a liquidizer, or one strong enough to cope with meat, *pound* everything together, then pass the mixture through a sieve.
(4) If you overheat the butter to pour over the top, it will 'oil' and separate: melt it over minimum heat. If it's too hot when you pour it over the meat, it will tend to penetrate rather than lie on top of the meat.
(5) Saltless butter gives a better flavour and preserves the meat better than salted.

Rabbits

Best from October to February. Wild ones are paunched (drawn) immediately they are killed and shouldn't be hung longer than for a day if to be really fresh and good.

★ A good-sized rabbit weighs approximately $2\frac{1}{2}$ lbs (a generous kilo) and will feed 5–6 people. A tame rabbit may weigh twice as much but is unlikely to have the lovely flavour of a wild one which may have been tucking into corn or your best garden lettuces. The doe is generally larger and has a better flavour than the buck.

★ It isn't always easy to choose a rabbit, but above all it must *smell* fresh: if the ear tears fairly easily, a rabbit is young, and if the kidneys are buried in fat, it is certain to be good.

★ To whiten and improve the flavour of a rabbit's flesh, also to make it more digestible, soak rabbit overnight in some vinegar and water – 1 dessertsp vinegar to 1 qt (1 L) water. Unless planning to roast it, joint it before soaking, then if you want to – or if the rabbit is old and needs it – you can marinate it afterwards.

TO SKIN A RABBIT. See *Hare*, page 213.

TO JOINT A RABBIT.

(1) Cut off all legs at joint and cut 'wings' away from the ribs.
(2) Cut the back into three or four pieces according to size of rabbit.
(3) Use the head (split, and minus eyes) to make stock while the rest of the rabbit is soaking.

★ There are many better ways of cooking a rabbit than roasting it – because roasting tends to make the flesh dry. If you *do* roast it, stuff and baste frequently in order to keep it all as moist as possible. You can grill or devil rabbit, stew, casserole or curry it; make it into galantine, a pie or soup – or you can substitute rabbit for veal in a recipe like fricassée or blanquette. As long as you have soaked it to remove its strong flavour, you can even in some recipes use rabbit instead of chicken.

Raised Pie

A pie moulded entirely from pastry – top crust, walls and bottom. Made basically with meats such as veal and ham, pork, gammon and hard-boiled egg, pigeon or any game meat (or perhaps a mixture of game meats) and served with a salad, it makes a delicious supper or light luncheon dish, or is ideal for picnics. You *can* serve it hot but *I* prefer it cold, freshly made, when the crust is crisp.

★ Though lots of people fight shy of hot water crust pastry (see page 103), it is easy to make. The other thing that puts people off can be the mould, but if without the right kind of hinged raised pie type, you can make your own individual 'mould' (page 17), use a loose-bottom oval mould, or even a loose-bottom cake tin.
★ Here are a few tips:
(1) Small pies are easier to make than large.
(2) Have everything ready for the filling before making the pastry so that you can then get on quickly before it cools and becomes difficult to handle.
(3) Cut the meat *small* so that it will cook in the same time as the crust. A tough bird should be marinated, and a bird may even be partly cooked.
(4) Use enough stock just to moisten the filling without also making pastry base soggy, ie about 1 tablesp stock to meat for 4 ozs (100 g) pastry.
(5) Fit pastry into mould carefully, without holes, otherwise there'll be an escape-hatch for the stock/gelatine liquor added *after* cooking, especially if too liquid when you pour it in.
(6) After rolling out and moulding the pastry (to come marginally above top of mould), adding the filling (traditionally mounded towards the middle), covering with pastry lid and sealing edges, it is easier to trim the edges with scissors than with a knife. Use the trimmings to make small pastry leaves, each to span from pie centre to side.
(7) Egg yolk makes the best glaze because it gives the pie a shiny golden finish.
(8) A tiny funnel (made of card, and held in shape with a paper clip) stuck into the central hole in lid of pie, ensures steam can escape from within and that the nearly-setting stock can, after pie is baked, be poured in.
(9) Hot water crust pastry needs a pre-heated very hot oven for the first 10–15 mins, gas 8, 450°F, 230°C, reduced then to gas 4, 350°F, 175°C for remaining time, approx. $\frac{3}{4}$–1 hr *altogether*. About half way through cooking time, when the pastry is set, carefully take pie out of its mould and brush the sides now with glaze, to make them golden too.

Salmi (or Salmis)

An abbreviation of the French word *salmisgondis,* meaning a hotchpotch – and though time-taking, this is one of the very greatest hotchpotches, mainly because of its lovely sauce.

★ The word *salmi* indicates a mixture of two processes: roasting (lightly, so that the flesh is slightly underdone), then casseroling, when the bird's cooking is completed in the sauce. The *amount* of sauce you need depends on a bird's size.
★ You can make salmi with any game bird, young or old, or with duck, goose or pigeon.
★ Here's one recipe:

	Comments
1 lightly roasted pheasant (page 215)	Could use partridge or grouse etc, first macerated if an old bird
1 oz (25 g) raw lean ham or bacon	
1 oz (25 g) saltless or clarified butter	Margarine or salted butter would burn. You *could* use 3 dessertsps oil
1 small onion or 2 shallots	
$\frac{1}{2}$ small carrot, thinly sliced	
1 oz (25g) flour	

cont.

	Comments
1 teasp. tomato purée	
$\frac{3}{4}$ pt (375 ml) good *brown* stock	
salt and pepper	
bouquet garni	
4 tablesps port	Use red wine if you like
1 dessertsp redcurrant jelly	
a few button mushrooms	
a nut of butter	
a few glacé cherries	Use stuffed olives if you prefer
fleurons of pastry (page 40)	Baked fleurons, of course
a little finely chopped parsley, to garnish	

SALMI *method.*

(1) In a strong saucepan over low heat, lightly fry the diced ham or bacon (rind as well) in the butter.
(2) Add finely sliced onion and fry it just 2 or 3 mins before adding carrot, frying it also a few mins. Set pan aside from heat.
(3) Stir in the flour, return pan to heat and cook roux over minimum heat for 15–20 mins or until a good brown colour, stirring at frequent intervals. (This long slow cooking of the roux gives the sauce extra flavour.)
(4) Set pan aside from heat again and stir in the tomato purée, then the stock, gradually at first, as for any sauce. Season.
(5) Bring sauce to the boil, stirring constantly, add bouquet garni, reduce heat, cover pan and simmer sauce very gently about 20 mins, skimming occasionally if necessary.
(6) Meanwhile joint the pheasant and lay the skinned (and preferably boned) pieces in a casserole.
(7) Add port and redcurrant jelly to the *strained* sauce, simmer it about 10 mins and then pour over the pheasant.
(8) Cook in slow oven until bird is tender, probably about $\frac{1}{2}$ hr after it starts to cook, depending of course on how old a bird is and how long you roasted it. (Alternatively, you *could* simmer it in the saucepan on top of cooker.)
(9) Serve garnished with the mushrooms fried lightly in the nut of butter, the glacé cherries heated in boiling water, fleurons of pastry and parsley.

Snipe

At its best in October and November, and should be eaten when fresh, some people thinking it most delicious when cooked straight after being shot. Its rather distinctive flavour is due to the snails and worms on which, mainly, it feeds.

★ Although you can cook snipe in other ways – for instance grill, casserole or make salmi – they are best roasted, or spit-roasted.

TO PLUCK AND TRUSS FOR ROASTING.

(1) Don't, as for most other game birds, go and cut off a snipe's head: the beak is needed as a skewer, so simply pluck the head and remove the eyes.
(2) When plucking, handle snipe with 'kid gloves' – their flesh is very delicate.
(3) Don't draw snipe either. Their entrails (or 'trail' as the internals are sometimes called) play an important part in a bird's flavour and, minus the gizzard, are to gourmets one of the most succulent morsels.
(4) Truss as other game birds, but instead of using trussing needle and string, twist the head round and pass the *beak* through the legs and body.

TO ROAST SNIPE. See also *Roasting a bird*, page 199.

(1) Allow one bird per person. (Snipe weigh between 2 and 10 ozs – 50 g and 250 g.)
(2) Brush with melted butter, and bard it with a fat bacon rasher to protect the flesh during cooking. For the best flavour, also *roast* in butter.

(3) Put a slice of bread under the bird before roasting, to catch the drippings from the trail. Serve the bird *on* the bread, then crisp and tasty.
(4) Roast in preheated hot oven, gas 6, 400°F, 204°C for 12–20 mins depending on whether you like snipe very underdone or just slightly underdone. Avoid over-roasting anyway, and baste several times.
(5) Accompaniments to roast snipe are: Fried breadcrumbs (page 210); Clear gravy; Game chips; Orange or green salad; Watercress, to garnish.

Squab

A young pigeon not more than 4 weeks old. At 28 days it is at its peak – a plump, tender and delicious meal for one.

★ Split and fry them in butter with a spoonful of oil, or in good olive oil, or grill, roast or cook as young pigeon (page 216).

Turkeys

First introduced by the Spaniards to Europe from Mexico (where turkeys had long been domesticated) in the earlier part of the sixteenth century. Until then, the name 'Turkey' applied to the bird we now call a guinea fowl – which is thought to have been introduced to England from Turkey, although originating in West Africa. One reminder we have of this is that when Shakespeare wrote of a turkey, he in fact meant a guinea fowl.

★ The turkey-hen is a better buy than the cock because, weight for weight, the hen is the fleshy one while the cock has the heavier bones. As a rule, the hen is also more tender than the cock, so if you're buying an oven-ready bird and can't tell which is which, it's wise to ask. Allow ¾–1 lb (say 350–450 g) per person if a small bird (say under 10 lbs or 4½ K); ½–¾ lb (225–350 g) per person if a medium-sized bird; ½ lb (225 g) per person if a large bird, say 20 lbs (9 K) and over.

TO DRAW A TURKEY. See page 200.

TO TRUSS A TURKEY. See page 201.

TO BONE A TURKEY. See page 201.

TO ROAST A TURKEY IN THE ENGLISH WAY. See also *Roasting a bird* (page 199) and *Roasting* (page 54).

(1) Your chosen size of bird must obviously to some extent depend on the number of people you want it to serve, see above, but a medium-sized turkey is *easier* to cook than a very large, and fits better in the average oven. A very small bird, especially a cock, is uneconomical.
(2) A frozen turkey will take at least 48 hrs to thaw *slowly and completely* in its vacuum-sealed bag – possibly even longer, especially if the bird is very large or the weather very cold. If you thaw it quickly, say in a hot room or by putting in a bowl of cold water, an excessive amount of juices will drip into the bag, instead of remaining in, and flavouring, the bird.
(3) *Stuffing* gives extra flavour, helps to keep the flesh moist and 'stretches' the number of servings. Veal forcemeat in the neck cavity is enclosed by the loose neck-skin, folded and stitched under the bird when you truss it. Chestnut and sausage-meat stuffing goes into the *body* cavity, to be spooned out when the turkey is carved.
(4) Because of the long time in the oven and the fact that a bird's breast cooks more quickly than the other parts, it's essential to protect the breast during the earlier stages of cooking: better than bacon rashers, a loose covering of foil or anything else, I like best to bard it (page 31) with a 'sheet' of pork fat – which a butcher will provide and flatten for you if you tell him what you want it for. Tied on, this bastes the breast continually. First brush the whole turkey with oil or melted butter, to help keep the flesh moist.
(5) The roasting tin should be large enough to baste and turn the turkey easily, and should contain enough fat, when melted, to cover well the bottom of the tin.

(6) Roasting in a *hot* oven tends to dry out and make a turkey rather stringy, particularly a very large bird. Slower cooking seems to keep the flesh moister: in a preheated oven gas 3, 325°F, 165°C, allow approximately: 3–3½ hrs for a 10–12 lb (say 4½–5½ K) bird, stuffed weight; 3½–4 hrs for a 13–16 lb (say 6–7¼ K) bird, stuffed weight; 4½–5 hrs for a 17–20 lb (say 7¾–9 K) bird, stuffed weight.
★ About 20–30 mins before turkey should be cooked, remove the barding fat, froth the breast (page 200) and raise the oven to gas 5, 375°F, 190°C to make the breast crisp and golden.

(7) If without a meat thermometer, guides to when a turkey is cooked are:
(a) When the meat tends to shrink from the end of the drumsticks.
(b) When a sharp fork runs easily into the thigh joint. If the escaping juice is pink, cook the bird longer.

(8) Accompaniments to roast turkey are: Veal and/or chestnut stuffing; Bread sauce; Bacon rolls; Thick gravy – 'thin' if the bird isn't stuffed; Cranberry sauce; Chipolata, to garnish; Watercress, to garnish.

(9) *To carve* a turkey is a different proposition from carving a chicken because the limbs are too big to serve

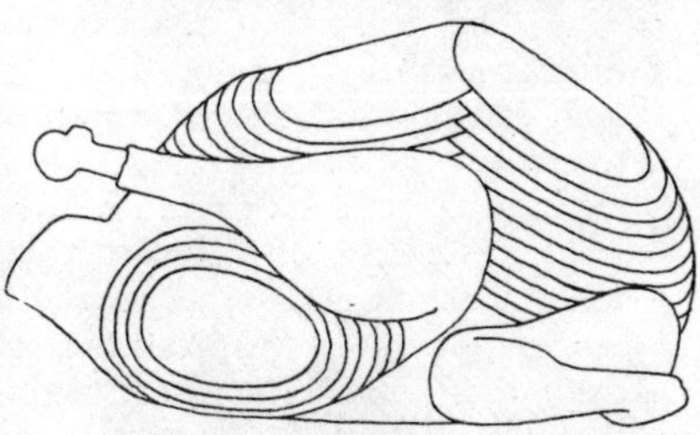

in one piece: cut off the drumstick, *slicing* it and the thigh, and serving some of this dark meat with each portion of breast. For a small bird carve the breast in single slices as for chicken, but carve a large bird in alternate ¼″ (7 mm) slices as illustrated.

COLD ROAST TURKEY. Can be used up in almost any way as cold chicken, often with the tasty stock made from its carcase. Here are a few recipes you'll probably be able to find in one of your own cookery books, under *Chicken* if not under *Turkey*: croquettes, kromeskies, savoury pancakes, patties, rissoles, risotto, vol-au-vent, turkey hash or potted turkey. Turkey is of course good too added to a béchamel sauce and served with croûtes of fried bread; served cold with curry mayonnaise, or as a filling for fresh baps when you want an easy snack round the fire.

★ Alternatively you can *freeze* some of the turkey and finish it up when you like, not when you're sick of the sight of it. Once off the carcase, it doesn't take up too much space: interleave with foil or thick polythene the limbs and sliced breast meat, then whatever quantity you eventually want *from* the freezer, you can without difficulty take out.

TURKEY BREAST OR JOINTS. Now sold throughout the year, breast or joints will make all sorts of dishes. Try coating the breasts in egg and seasoned fresh white breadcrumbs before frying in butter with a little oil. Off the bone, and cut into smaller pieces, you can make things like curry, fricassée or blanquette, or any kind of casserole for which you'd use a jointed chicken.

Venison

The name comes from the Latin word *venari*, to hunt, and is the meat of any kind of deer. The flesh of the male, or buck, has a better flavour than that of the doe, but no venison has much fat and all is by nature dry and inclined to be tough: you can counteract the dryness by larding or barding a roasting joint, or alternatively by enclosing and protecting it inside a flour and water paste. You can make the meat *tender* by correct hanging and by marinating it well before you cook it. The custom of dredging venison with black pepper and ground ginger before hanging it in muslin is to help preserve the meat during its necessarily long hanging/tenderizing time. In cold weather allow about 12–20 days in a cool airy place. To test from time to time, run a skewer into it near the bone. When it smells slightly gamy, the meat is ready for marinating and then cooking.

★ The haunch, loin, saddle and fillet are the best parts so these are the most suitable for the faster methods of cookery like roasting, grilling, frying or sautéing. You can, if you prefer, *braise* the haunch or loin – or shoulder – casseroling or stewing the cheaper cuts. Venison also makes a good galantine or raised pie, or – with minced *cooked* meat – a tasty cottage pie.

TO ROAST A LARGE JOINT OF VENISON.

(1) It's better to weigh the joint before rather than after marinating, then you can calculate the cooking time and will know 'where you are': according to the thickness of a joint, allow 20–25 mins per lb (450 g) and 20–25 mins, over.

(2) Marinating venison for 24–48 hrs (or longer in cold weather) is an important step in its successful cooking. A marinade not only helps to tenderize the meat by breaking down the tough fibres, but also flavours and makes it less dry. The roasting tin in which you're going to cook it may also be the best in which to marinate and occasionally turn it over. You need a good quantity of marinade – at least 1 pt (500 ml) – to make sure the meat is well soaked, and to have plenty with which to baste the meat from time to time.

(3) It's important to dry the marinated meat before roasting it, otherwise the fat in the roasting tin is going to get very watery and the meat will as a result cook in steam rather than in dry heat.

(4) Some of the strained marinade can be used for Venison Sauce, the remainder saved for future use. (You can store marinade as ice cubes in the freezer.)

(5) Before roasting, venison must be larded, barded or enclosed in a flour and water paste as it is too dry and fatless to roast without. Your butcher would supply the fat, and flatten barding fat if told what it's for.

(6) Roast in preheated oven, gas 7, 425°F, 220°C for the first 15 mins to seal in the juices, then reduce heat to gas 5, 375°F, 190°C for remainder of cooking time.

(7) Accompaniments to roast venison are: Redcurrant or rowan jelly, or cranberry sauce; Clear brown gravy, or better still if you can be bothered to make it, Venison Sauce (Poivrade Sauce plus redcurrant jelly and cream); Roast or creamed potatoes; French beans.

14

SWEETS AND PUDDINGS

General Information

Sweets and puddings are our forté. This is one course where, by and large, I think we can knock spots off the French, if they will forgive me. Most English people consider it an important part of any main meal, our repertoire is enormous, and we both expect and have high standards when we are entertained or are entertaining.

★ Like savoury sauces, dozens of sweets and puddings are simply varieties of a few basic recipes, hence if you know how to make one, you can make any other version. To be successful however, it's a good thing to understand the changing characteristics of *Eggs* (page 106) and *Cream* (page 70), the unusual qualities of *Gelatine* (page 74) and the importance of *Consistencies* (page 36). The latter especially play a vital role in the texture and volume of most light and airy sweets. When making such dishes as a cold soufflé, a cream or a mousse, whipped cream and any mixture to which it is added should be of similar consistencies, so that the two will blend perfectly together to give the dish its characteristic texture (see *Whipping cream*). This is one reason why recipes frequently direct that a mixture should be left until cool and beginning to set before adding cream and/or whisked egg white – because it will by then be thicker. Another reason is that if whisked whites and whipped cream are added to a warm mixture, they will lose their stiffness and thin out, spoiling the texture and reducing the volume of the sweet. Egg whites should not in fact be whisked before a mixture shows signs of setting, unless the bowl has been standing on ice, when the mixture is therefore likely to set quickly.

★ Because intense cold tends to thicken a liquid, gelatine-based sweets which were perfect at room temperature will become (and remain) rubbery if long refrigerated. If for instance you refrigerate a soufflé overnight, it will become stiffer than if you chill it for just an hour or two, or not at all. According to Davis Gelatine, recipes which actually call for the use of a refrigerator have their gelatine content adjusted accordingly.

★ In addition, overchilling masks and therefore spoils many flavours, chocolate particularly. Unlike a spoilt texture however, a flavour will recover at room temperature. See also *Unmoulding*.

Apples, Baked

These need a little know-how if to be delicate and not dreary. It's all up to your choice of apple and what you do – or don't do – with them:

(1) Choose the *right* type of *cooking* apple, not a dessert apple: large sour varieties such as Bramley's Seedling, Howgate Wonder, Grenadier or Lord Derby all bake beautifully because they're juicy as well as acid.

(2) Choose even-sized apples so that, to become tender and cook perfectly,

one apple doesn't need five minutes longer than another.

(3) After washing and coring, run a skin-deep cut round the middle of each apple, the ends of the cut to meet. The apples will then puff up like soufflés, instead of *bursting* – and looking a mess.

(4) Stand apples in a greased baking tin or ovenware dish before sweetening: with a rounded tablespoonful of sugar (mixed with a little ground cinnamon if you like) in each hole, a nut of *butter* on top, and a dessertsp of water per apple round about, they'll form a lovely, buttery, caramelized syrup – providing you don't cook them in too hot an oven.

(5) Bake apples in the middle of a moderate oven, gas 4, 350°F, 175°C for about 40–60 mins according to size, or until tender when tested down the inside with a skewer. (The outside becomes soft before the middle.) If overcooked, your apple 'soufflés' will flop, which explains the reason for using fruit all of a similar size.

(6) Fluffy, liquidized custard and, if you can rise to it, some whipped cream as well, combine deliciously with the apples and their toffee-like syrup.

Apple Strudel

This seems like a conjuring trick because the dough (made from only 4 ozs (100 g) strong flour, ½ level teasp salt, 1 *small* egg, 1–1½ tablesps warm water and 2 teasps oil), is transformed into a lacy-thin, tea-towel-sized sheet of paste. You really have to make this to believe it – then eat it hot or cold, with ice cream, Crème Chantilly or even single cream. If you've no need to slim, it's delicious also for elevenses or at tea-time. It's something I enjoy making even more than eating, and that's saying something.

★ To help solve the problems with the dough:

(1) It must be soft but not sticky, otherwise it will be impossible to manipulate after kneading and resting. The *kneading* is to make it smooth and elastic. *Resting* the dough for ½ hr – in a small basin, covered with a cloth – is to strengthen the gluten in the flour and increase the dough's elasticity so that it will stretch, as far as possible without tearing, to an enormous size.

(2) The rolled-out rectangular-shaped dough is manipulated on a large clean tea-towel to which, unlike a pastry board or table top, it doesn't stick. In addition, lacy-thin as the pastry becomes, the tea-towel later facilitates the pastry's rolling up.

(3) Using initially the floured backs of your hands and your knuckles, and working from the underside, you can pull and stretch the pastry in all directions providing you keep it spread out. (If it forms folds, the surfaces will stick obstinately together.) Work from the middle outwards because once the outer edges are very thin, it is more difficult to get at and stretch the middle.

(4) When fully stretched, that original tiny lump of dough should be nearly the size of the tea-towel and lacy enough to see its pattern through.

★ The rest, with a recipe, is plain sailing but the strudel should be cooked soon if not at once after it is made, before the apple juice starts to run, and spoil the pastry.

Battenburg Cake

Bought Battenburg makes a quick, easy and delicious sweet – to serve in individual dishes:

(1) *Bottom layer*. A slice of Battenburg, soaked with a dessertsp. each of fruit syrup and sherry, madeira, rum or whatever you like best with the fruit you're using.

(2) *Middle layer*. Prepared fresh, or well drained canned fruit, eg strawberries, peaches, sliced banana, fresh raspberries, apricots, lychees.

Top layer. Crème Chantilly (see page 240) or (though not so good) if you're dieting, the arrowroot-thickened fruit syrup (page 63).

Beignets

French for fritters, in a wide sense.

Beignets Soufflés

A type of fritter, made with choux pastry. The temperature of the fat is the tricky part: if too hot initially, the outsides harden before the choux can expand, so they don't rise. The fat should be hot but not smoking – 320°–340°F, 160°–171°C – the heat being raised slightly while the beignets are frying.

★ Avoid using a frying basket because the choux will stick to it.

★ After the beignets are cooked, it's quicker and more efficient to toss them in caster sugar in a paper bag than on a sheet of paper.

Bread and Butter Pudding

Should be made with *egg* and milk, not custard powder, and soaked long enough – about $\frac{1}{2}$ hr – before baking to allow the bread to absorb most of the liquid. (Made with 'powder', the custard sets on top of the bread instead of being absorbed, so the top layer of bread doesn't go crisp and brown and the pudding ends up quite different.)

★ Unorthodox though it is, bread and butter pudding assumes a delightfully different character when made with mincemeat in the middle, instead of dried fruit and a flavouring of nutmeg: lay the cut-up buttered bread in the bottom of the dish, spread it lightly with mincemeat, cover with remaining pieces of bread and strain the warm egg/sugar/milk mixture over.

★ In case you've never tried it, vanilla ice cream served with bread and butter pudding makes it twice as good.

Charlottes

Probably take their name from Charlotte, wife of George III. The original Charlottes were made of fruit, in a mould lined with thin slices of buttered bread – and served hot, The only thing these charlottes have in common with Charlotte Russe is their outward appearance.

CHARLOTTE RUSSE. Prepared with Bavarian cream which is set in a plain round mould, lined sides and bottom with sponge fingers, this dish was invented by Carême, regarded even today as the founder of classic French cookery. Here are just a few tips:

(1) To decorate the bottom of the mould with jelly, see page 45.
(2) Line up the Savoy fingers on a board to make them all the same length, trimming their edges to make them fit each other closely. As the mould is narrower at the bottom than the top, taper the fingers slightly, if necessary, to make them fit. (Bought Savoy fingers are usually of a more regular shape than home-made.)
(3) The Bavarian cream, or Bavarois as it's sometimes called, (basically an egg custard mixed with whipped cream, and set with gelatine) must be just on the point of setting when poured into the mould; otherwise it will ooze out between the Savoy fingers. If on the other hand too 'set', it won't pour into and fill the mould evenly.
(4) An unmoulded Charlotte Russe is very fragile. Handle it with care.

FRUIT CHARLOTTES. These are crisper and better when made in a charlotte mould (page 16) or tin pie-dish than in a glass or ovenware dish because metal is a better conductor of heat.

★ If the fruit is too watery, it will make the bread soggy and the charlotte will collapse when unmoulded. It may also disintegrate if you don't allow it to 'set' for a few minutes before turning out.

Christmas Pudding

Should be made well ahead of Christmas because, with maturity, the flavour improves. Generally speaking, the more sugar, fruit and alcohol a pudding contains, the longer and better it will keep. I *have* kept one from year to year, though after a few months, I tend nowadays to pop one in the freezer where it's less in the way.

★ A Christmas pudding cooked in a pressure cooker doesn't compare with one gently steamed: the traditional, naturally dark colour and lovely flavour of a properly made pudding are acquired during hours of slow cooking, not by the addition of gravy browning, very dark sugar, carrot or anything else.
★ If serving 'alight', see page 40, *Flambé*.

'Creams'

Made, basically, with whipped cream and an equal quantity of either rich creamy egg custard or fruit purée. A custard is flavoured with such things as chocolate (melted in the milk), coffee essence or diced ginger, to give chocolate, coffee or ginger cream respectively. A fruit purée can be made from fresh, frozen or canned fruit. (A fruit purée freezes perfectly if you have surplus fruit: I like to liquidize about 3 ozs (75 g) sugar with ½ lb (225 g) of, say, strawberries or raspberries before freezing. This makes ½ pt (250 ml) purée.)

★ Use egg yolks in preference to whole eggs for a custard. They make it thicker, smoother and richer: allow 4 yolks to ½ pt (250 ml) milk for this sweet (see page 240).
★ See also *Gelatine*, and introduction to this chapter re cream and consistencies.
★ You can dress up a cream and at the same time make it go further by decorating the bottom of the mould first, with jelly, and by chopping up more jelly to serve round it (see page 45).

Custards

Are richer, smoother, have a finer flavour and colour, and are less likely to curdle if made entirely with egg yolks; two yolks replacing each whole egg given in any recipe. If this seems too extravagant or too rich, or if you prefer to use whole eggs, do at least increase the proportion of yolk to white by adding an *extra* yolk. This will lessen the risk of a custard curdling and at the same time improves its texture.

★ After lightly mixing the warmed milk with the eggs, they're always *strained* into the cooking dish. This is to hold back the chalazae, one of the main causes of curdling (see page 107).
★ If you boil or even nearly boil a custard, it will become full of holes, leathery and rather indigestible. This is because it has curdled, and explains why custards are always cooked at a low temperature; either very gently in a steamer or, if in the oven, in a bain-marie or roasting tin containing cold water to come about half way up the dish. To avoid curdling, these custards are *never* cooked in 'direct' heat.
★ All custards are better covered during cooking – with foil, a lid or oiled greaseproof paper – to prevent the surface becoming dry and brown.
★ When cooked, a custard should be firm but slightly shaky. To test, stick the point of a small vegetable knife in the middle – always the last place to set – and press back a little of the custard. If cooked, there'll be no sign of *liquid*.

CUSTARD, BAKED. See above.

CRÈME BRÛLÉE. The richest and most heavenly form of baked custard, made with cream instead of milk, and with a caramelled top, for which I, personally, like Demerara sugar most. Serve it well chilled, with chilled stewed fruit, or just by itself, if to enjoy its full flavour.

★ Use 1 pint (500 ml) single cream, 8 large egg yolks, 2 ozs (50 g) granulated sugar and a small teasp vanilla essence for the custard itself, and another 2–3 ozs (50–75 g) Demerara or caster sugar later, for the top.
★ If you *beat* the yolks and sugar together until fluffy and pale yellow before stirring in the hot cream, the custard will be lovely and light.
★ Bake as *Custards* (above), using something like a shallow soufflé dish, but at all costs, don't let it boil. Allow *about* ¾–1 hr according to depth, in a slowish oven, gas 3, 325°F, 165°C, the covered dish stand-

ing in a roasting tin of water of course.
★ It's important to cool and then chill the custard for several hours before covering the top with a thinnish layer of sugar, and caramelizing it under a hot grill. (If still warm, it may boil under the intense heat, ruining its texture.)
★ Two last thoughts:

(1) It's safer to protect the rim of the dish with a strip of foil before putting it under the hot grill.
(2) It's often easier to make the custard 24 hrs before required, Covered, this allows plenty of time to chill it *before*, and for at least 2 hrs *after*, caramelizing.

CRÈME CARAMEL. Another variation of a baked custard, but can equally well be *very* gently steamed, see *Custards*. I like best of all to make it entirely with egg yolks, which make it creamy and delicious. One can always use up the whites in meringues – what better partner for this sweet anyway?

★ If serving Crème Caramel hot, allow the custard to cool and 'set' a few minutes before unmoulding it, otherwise it may collapse. If serving it cold, allow it to cool in its tin. Hot *or* cold, Crème Chantilly served with it makes this a redhot favourite, especially with the menfolk.
★ *A metal mould or tin* such as a charlotte mould or moule à manqué tin (or darioles) is the best thing to make it in because the heat can't break it, and the caramel will run freely and thinly on tin, coating it evenly and easily, especially if you've warmed it first. On the other hand, caramel is apt to set quickly, thickly and unevenly on ovenware china, so although a French soufflé dish will usually stand up to the heat, it isn't as successful. Whatever you use though, there's no time for day-dreaming once the caramel is ready. Have the warmed tin standing on a thick wodge of newspaper, to protect your table top from the intense heat, and use an ovencloth to cover your hands. (Caramel burns, like sealing wax, are real torture.) Pour the caramel all at once into the tin, tilting and circulating it quickly to cover all surfaces, then leave it to cool at room temperature. If you either refrigerate or pour hot custard into it now, the caramel will crack, not that this seems to alter its final appearance.
★ Don't wash the caramel pan! If you heat the milk for the custard in it, the caramel flavour will permeate the whole sweet – like deglazing a pan in which you have *sautéd* food.
★ *The caramel* itself is quite easy if you know how, but can be tricky if you don't. Here are a few tips:

(1) It's unwise to use a non-stick pan, which may be scratched by the grittiness of so much sugar, or damaged by the great heat. Some people like to use a frying pan, but I find a small strong saucepan is better because the sugar seems less apt to crystallize when deep than when shallow. (You *can* buy a special pan, called a Sugar Boiler.)
(2) The proportion of water to sugar doesn't really matter. You can make caramel with a small amount of sugar and a panful of water if you boil it long enough, or with no water at all, because sugar caramelizes when all the water evaporates. It's *easier* with water than without however, so for a pt (500 ml) of custard, you won't go far wrong with 4 ozs (100 g) sugar and 4 tablesps water. Many old recipes call for 'loaf' sugar because at one time this was the purest, and therefore least likely to crystallize. Nowadays icing, granulated, caster and cube are all equally pure so why not use granulated, the cheapest?
(3) Follow the guidelines for making a strong syrup (page 275). The vital thing is to be sure the sugar is dissolved *before* the syrup boils and never to stir it *after*. Once the sugar is dissolved, boil the syrup rapidly until light caramel in colour, at which point the sugar now starts cooking quickly because the water is evaporated. All you need do now is keep an eye on it, not letting it get *too* dark because it will very quickly burn and go bitter, the sugar having lost its sweetening power. Even slightly agitating the pan at any time may cause the sugar to crystallize. When brown, at once line the tin with it, as explained earlier.

★ Make the custard exactly as for a baked custard – 1 pt (generous 500 ml) very hot milk poured onto 8 yolks (or 4 eggs plus 1 or 2 yolks) mixed with 1 oz (25 g) granulated sugar and about ½ teasp vanilla essence. Strain it into the caramelled tin, cover and cook as *Custards*, until set – not forgetting to stand it in water if you bake it, and using the middle of a slowish oven, gas 3, 325°F, 165°C. (They're easier to bake perfectly than to steam because most ovens can be controlled at a given temperature.)

Flans

Can be made with French Flan pastry (pâte sucrée) or flan pastry, the latter being simply a rich shortcrust pastry made with egg yolk and butter or margarine – no lard. See *Pastry*, pages 103 and 102.

★ Traditionally, a *fluted* flan ring is used for a sweet flan. Both it and the baking sheet should be greased for French flan pastry because with its high sugar content, it may otherwise stick.

★ It's important for flan pastry to be the right consistency if it's to be crisp and light. If too wet, the pastry will be heavy. If too dry, the dough cracks and is difficult to manipulate without breaking.

★ Roll flan pastry about 1½–2″ (4–5 cm) larger than flan ring's diameter, to allow for the sides, and for shrinkage while it's relaxing after rolling. Otherwise the pastry will shrink during baking, and may be too shallow in places to hold semi-liquid fillings. (There's no need to make allowance for French flan pastry shrinking.)

★ If you lift the pastry up over the rolling pin and centre it above the flan ring, you're less likely to tear it than if lifting it with your fingers. Slide the rolling pin out, fit the pastry close to lower edges of ring, and use your small finger to press the pastry carefully but firmly into each flute.

★ Cut off the untidy bits of pastry at the top, with your rolling pin, not a knife: simply bend any surplus pastry over the sharp top of the flan ring and roll from middle to far side, then from middle to near side, and pull the trimmings away.

★ Prick flan pastry with a fork before baking it blind, otherwise the bottom may rise. See *Baking blind*, page 30.

FILLINGS FOR FLANS. These can be of many kinds, somc cooked together with the pastry, others used in a flan case previously baked blind. Here are a few:

(1) Coat attractively arranged, fresh or well drained canned fruit, with an arrowroot-thickened syrup. This, unlike cornflour, is the perfect finish, because it gives a clear, tasteless glaze (see *Arrowroot*, page 63). If decorating with cream, allow the glaze to cool completely first, otherwise the cream will slide about.

(2) Lemon curd and Cream filling – delicious and very quick (see page 266).

(3) Pour hot Crème Patissière (page 264) into the cold, baked flan case, and allow it to cool and set. Arrange fruit such as sliced banana on top, brushed with hot sieved jam, to glaze as well as to prevent the fruit discolouring.

(4) Stir things such as desiccated coconut into hot Crème Patissière, used as above. Alternatively, flavour the Crème Patissière, in various ways if you like. Topped with meringue and baked about ½ hr in a preheated cool oven, gas 1, 275°F, 135°C (or until crisp and golden), you can serve it hot or cold – nicer cold I think.

(5) Half fill an uncooked flan case made of French flan pastry, with fruit such as stoned cherries or thinly sliced apple. Now cover the fruit evenly with 'Frangipane', using 1 egg quantity for a 7″ (18 cm) flan. (The frangipane is sweet, so apple won't need sugar.) Bake 30–40 mins, or until firm and golden, then brush and glaze the top while still hot, with thin icing made of icing sugar and stock syrup, to make it shiny.

Fools

Probably got their name from the French

word *fouler*, to press or crush. In culinary terms, *fouler* means to press through a sieve.

★ Ideally, fools are made with equal quantities fruit purée and cream, not purée and custard. Whipping cream is almost better than double, because if to blend perfectly with the purée, cream should only be half-whipped. See *Cream*, page 70.

★ If dessert gooseberries are sweet, ripe and soft enough to use raw, like raspberries or strawberries, there's every reason to do so. Liquidized with sugar to taste, then sieved and blended with a similar quantity of cream, this is a fool you'll never forget.

★ Here are a few more assorted tips:

(1) Unless you use a liquidizer – which *I* wouldn't be without for worlds – icing sugar dissolves more easily than caster with raw fruits.

(2) The purée and the half-whipped cream should be about the same consistency if to blend properly, so stewed or canned fruits must be well drained. Watery raw fruits such as raspberries and strawberries naturally make a watery purée, the fool *sometimes* being more a drink than a sweet. I like to thicken such purées very slightly with arrowroot, using 1½ level teasps to ½ pt (250 ml) purée (see *Arrowroot*). To avoid cooking *all* the purée and so spoiling its lovely fresh flavour, heat and thicken only half the purée, then thin it down with the remainder.

(3) If you use a proportion of cream and custard, liquidize the cold custard with the purée before blending with the cream. Custard made with custard powder is creamier and lighter if it *is* liquidized, but make it thicker than required because it thins when liquidized.

(4) You can fold a stiffly whisked egg white into a fool at the last minute if you like. Though not traditional, it makes the fool go further and is a good way to use up a spare white.

(5) A few drops of lemon juice, or a spoonful or two of liqueur give a lovely flavour; and a drop or two of colouring may do wonders for the appearance.

(6) Serve fool ice-cold, preferably in individual dishes. It's far nicer, and easier to eat than a helping from a large bowl.

(7) Serve Savoy fingers, tuiles or something like meringue fingers, for contrast of texture.

Frangipane

Said to take its name from its inventor, an Italian called Frangipani, who lived in Paris at the time of Louis XIII. It is used as a filling, with pastry of some kind, often in tartlets or a flan – heavenly it is too. Frangipane is basically just a sandwich cake mixture using ground almonds instead of flour. A level dessertsp flour (to 1 egg) in addition to the ground almonds, slightly stiffens the mixture, and a few drops of almond essence help to accentuate the almond flavour.

Fritters, Fruit

Best made with fruits which are ripe enough to have plenty of flavour but firm enough to handle.

★ Fruits taste super when macerated because this both sweetens and flavours them (see *Macerating*). Bananas and strawberries need only ¼ hr, most other fruits about ½ hr. If soaked longer, they'll be too soft. Do be sure to drain and dry them before dipping in fritter batter, otherwise they'll make it watery and will splutter madly in the hot fat.

★ If not macerating, nearly all fruits (except things like bananas, dessert apples or canned pineapple rings) will at least need sweetening. Put them on a tray, sprinkle with caster sugar, leave ½ hr and then dry them. Who can forget the bitterness of a sour 'cooker' inside that eagerly awaited and perhaps expensive apple fritter?

THE BATTER. This is easier to cope with if it's deep, so use a smallish basin in which you can submerge and coat the fruit completely.

★ Air, beaten into the whisked egg whites, is the only raising agent, unless the mixture also contains yeast, so the batter is therefore always made with plain rather than self-raising flour. A *yeast* batter, by the way, makes about the best fritters ever, I think – light, crisp and dangerous for the waistline.
★ Another way to make them crisp is to mix 1 dessertsp oil with each 2 ozs (50 g) flour – though I'm not quite sure why it does so.
★ Leave a batter to rest for ½–¾ hr before adding the whisked egg white if you can. This gives it time to thicken, so it will coat the food better. (You can't achieve the same results by *making* a thicker batter because that means raising the proportion of flour, which of course produces heavy fritters.)
★ The stiffly whisked egg white will blend more evenly with the batter if you fold one tablespoonful in first, and then fold in the remainder. For perfect results the batter should just coat the back of a wooden spoon without running off. If the white isn't whisked stiffly enough, the batter may be thick enough to coat the first lot of fritters, but may thin out by the time you can fry the second.
★ Some people like to dip each piece of fruit into the batter in the curves of a fork, but I personally find it easier to hold each in my fingers. Either way, you can easily slip the battered fruit into the hot fat – but beware of burning yourself.

THE DEEP FAT. This should be about 360°F, 182°C. If much cooler, the fritters won't float and will absorb the fat. If much hotter, the outside of the fritters will be burnt by the time the inside is cooked. There's also a danger in trying to fry too many at once, because the temperature of the fat will drop too low.
★ It's better not to use a frying basket because the batter tends to stick to the wire, the surface of the fruit becoming exposed to the intense heat. Turn them over when golden underneath, to brown evenly. If overcooked they'll burst. For further information, see *Frying, deep fat*.
★ Fritters are usually tossed in caster or icing sugar, but 1 level teasp ground cinnamon sieved with 2 ozs (50 g) sugar gives a spicy flavour to fruits such as apple, banana and peach.
★ Serve fritters on a fancy doyley (to absorb any excess fat) in an *uncovered* dish – if covered at any stage, they'd lose their crispness.

Fritto Misto of Fruits

The Italian name for a *variety* of fritters. This is just as easy to make as fritters of one kind, except that you may need to macerate some of them separately.

Fruits, Stewed

Stewed fruits such as apple quarters or unripe pear halves taste sweeter and don't break up so readily when put into a boiling *syrup*, as they do if simply brought to the boil with sugar and water. The larger the pan the better too, the fruit cooking evenly when in one layer, but apt to become mushy if piled up.

★ Use a metal spoon to make the syrup, but two wooden ones to turn fruit over. They don't break it up so easily.
★ *Ripe* peach and pear halves don't usually need *cooking*: simply lay them in the boiling syrup, turn them over straight away to prevent discolouration, bring syrup back to the boil and set the covered pan aside from the heat. After a few mins, turn the fruit over to soften the other side, then leave it to cool.
★ Soft fruits like raspberries and strawberries don't usually need cooking either, and are easier still: cover them in a basin with a small quantity of strong, boiling syrup, and leave to cool.
★ Use a syrup with a smaller proportion of water to sugar for watery fruits such as rhubarb or apple, than for hard fruits such as quinces or unripe pears.
★ Lemon juice may be used for two reasons: to give flavour, and to prevent fruit breaking up. *Avoid* using it of course if you want a purée.
★ Stewed fruit can be made more substantial by thickening the hot syrup with arrowroot, potato flour or cornflour (see page 63).

Jelly, Lemon

Home-made lemon jelly, cleared with egg white and egg-shell, certainly has a splendid flavour, but so it should after such a long-winded process.

★ A few points need special care to make sure that nothing will make cloudy a sweet which should be crystal-clear:

(1) Pan, bowl and jelly bag should be scrupulously clean, the bag never washed in soapy water. It pays to scald it just before using, to help the jelly run through more quickly.

(2) Wash and peel the lemons with a potato peeler rather than use grated rind, which includes bitter pith.

(3) Wipe the eggs before 'separating', and crushing the shells. All the impurities in the liquid will cling to the shells, like metal to a magnet, when the whisked mixture is hot enough for the egg whites to coagulate. It's important to stop whisking *just* before it reaches boiling point though, otherwise the impurities will be released back into the liquid.

(4) Let the liquid run through the jelly bag by itself; resisting all temptation to squeeze, press, or help it; otherwise you'll make it cloudy again.

★ The liquid should be about $\frac{1}{3}$ lemon juice, $\frac{2}{3}$ water, and a larger proportion of gelatine is used than for something like a soufflé or cream, because it loses some of its strength by being almost boiled.

★ The jelly acquires a stronger lemon flavour by being 'infused' for about 10 mins in a *warm* place before being cleard. Don't skip that soaking period.

Jelly, Milk

Quite easy as long as you don't try to dissolve the gelatine in milk, because it gives a curdled appearance. It is not a true curdle however, because the milk is perfectly sweet.

★ The milk should be used cold. Flavouring and sugar are added, and the gelatine is dissolved in a little hot water and added when cool; and always the gelatine is added to the milk.

★ If the milk is chilled, stand it in warm water for a few moments, otherwise the gelatine won't mix with the intensely cold liquid, but will set in globules or will string. Should that happen, strain out most of the milk and stand the container in a basin of warm water. As the milk warms, the gelatine will dissolve, so you can then stir in the rest of the milk.

Jelly, Packet

This will set quickly on hot days or when you're in a hurry if you dissolve it in about half of the required quantity of nearly-boiling water, then top up with ice cubes, stirring until they melt.

Junket

A junket won't set if the milk is warmer than blood heat (see *Rennet*, page 86), or if you disturb the milk after adding the rennet to it. This explains why junket is more likely to set if you add the rennet at the very last second – after the serving dish or sundae glasses are placed where you intend to leave them while the junket is setting, and after you've stirred sugar and colouring (if any) into the milk. You can only safely move it when *set*.

★ If you like to flavour junket with ground nutmeg – heaven knows, it needs *some* flavour if served by itself – sieve it onto the set junket from a height. This way, you can sprinkle it on sparsely and evenly. Alternatively serve junket with cream, a fruit salad or stewed fruit.

★ You can also dress up junket and make it a bit more appealing by decorating it with angelica leaves (see page 62) and cherry. Make them light and dainty, though, or they'll sink, and leave a liquid.

★ Junket is often given to invalids because it's so easy to digest, the rennet having already got to work on the milk.

Meringue

There are 3 principal types of meringue:

(1) MERINGUE SUISSE. The kind we make with whisked egg whites and sugar, for meringues and toppings for sweets and puddings, see Meringues below.

(2) MERINGUE CUITE. Made with egg white and icing (or sometimes caster) sugar beaten over low heat until thick enough: to stand in peaks, and used for things like piping, petits fours or smallish cakes, or as a cake filling. It doesn't collapse like Swiss meringue would for a cake filling, because of course the egg white has been coagulated and 'set' by the heat.

(3) MERINGUE ITALIENNE. Made by pouring a sugar syrup (boiled to 260°F, 127°C) onto stiffly whisked egg whites, and whisking until thick. This can be used when cold for things like Baked Alaska, certain pastries, cake fillings, or to replace whipped cream. As above, the heat coagulates and 'sets' the egg whites. You'll need to follow a recipe.

MERINGUES. Such a popular and easily made sweet, whether for the family, a dinner party or for a crowd, that they're worth some concentration if you're not already a dab hand? If you can't make good meringues, it's probably because you trip up over one or more of these four things:

(1) The eggs themselves may not be fresh enough: if old, or if they've been badly stored, the whites will be too watery to whisk properly.

(2) You may not be whisking the whites to the correct consistency at each stage:
(a) They should look like cotton wool before you add the first lot of sugar – about quarter of the total. The reason for adding this sugar now is to strengthen the whites so that they can then support the larger amount following.
(b) They should be 'rocky', shiny like satin, before you fold in the remaining sugar. (For *details*, see *Whisking*, page 61.)

★ Beware of *over*-whisking too. This breaks down the structure of the egg white, which changes and collapses. Only when perfectly whisked, can meringue be piped in sharp shapes which will *hold* that shape.

(3) The sugar may not be properly folded and 'cut' into the whisked whites (see *Folding*, page 000). (I prefer granulated to caster for meringues, or you *can* use icing or even Demerara. Allow 2 ozs or 50 g per egg white.)

(4) The oven may be too low when you put the meringues into it, or, because you may not beforehand have set the shelves where you need them – in the coolest part – there's excessive heat loss at a crucial time while you do so. The oven should be preheated as well as prepared, gas $\frac{1}{4}$–$\frac{1}{2}$, 200°F, 93°C. While most people know that meringues cook best in a very low oven, many seem not to be aware that it must be *hot enough initially* to coagulate and 'set' the egg white before it melts and 'weeps'. If you've *forgotten* to preheat the oven, it's much better to leave the piped meringues on the kitchen table than to put them into too cool an oven.

(5) Once the meringues have had time to set throughout, say after 15–20 mins, the slower you cook them, the whiter and firmer they'll be. Good meringues will dry out in 3–4 hrs: they should be firm when pressed underneath, but may need turning later on, depending mostly on their position in the oven. Those in the coolest part may not need turning. This is where a fan-assisted oven comes into its own because a whole batch of meringues will cook perfectly in the same time, in the same, constant temperature.

★ Some further tips:

(1) Prepare the baking sheet/sheets before you heat the oven or start the meringues. There doesn't seem anything as good as a sheet of *oiled* greaseproof paper on an oiled baking sheet: it's easier to lift the cooked meringues off this than off foil or waxed paper. In days gone by, the technique was to use a thick wooden board because on wood, which is a bad conductor of heat, meringues don't turn brown underneath. Modern baking sheets, however, are thick, just as

good and readily available in any home where there's a serious cook.

(2) To fill the piping bag easily, see page 53. If without a piping bag, shape the meringues with two wetted dessertspoons.

(3) After piping meringues onto prepared baking sheet/sheets, sprinkle with caster sugar to improve their texture, then pop them into the heated oven.

(4) Cool the cooked meringues on a wire tray, then put *at once* into an airtight container. If left out, they absorb moisture from the atmosphere, quickly losing their crispness.

(5) If you like eating them really crisp, avoid filling meringues before you must, because now they will absorb moisture from the cream as well as from the atmosphere.

(6) Double cream is best, 'whipping' being too watery.

(7) To set them off well and help them to stand steadily, serve with the cream-filling upwards, in coloured paper cake cases. Use a fancy doyley underneath, and a dish which looks too large for them, to act as a picture frame.

(8) Meringue halves will store at *least* a week or two if properly made and in an air-tight container. Some people store them in their freezer, thinking they don't become so dry, but I find that makes no difference.

MERINGUE TOPPINGS. Toppings for sweets and puddings only need about half as much sugar per egg white as meringues, say 1–1½ ozs (25–40 g). The meringue is *made* in the same way but cooked slightly faster, for a shorter time.

★ Cook hot things like Queen of Puddings in the cooler half of a slow oven, gas 1, 275°F, 135°C for about 30–45 mins or until crisp, the peaks lightly browned – the 'centre' still soft. If you cook the meringue faster, its flavour is less good.

★ Sweets such as flans or Fruit Crust – say canned peaches, with meringue on top – which are to be served cold, need longer slower cooking to firm up the centre, otherwise they'll flop as they cool. Allow about ¾–1¼ hrs at gas ¾, 250°F, 120°C.

PAVLOVA CAKE. A lovely variety of meringue which owes its soft marshmallowy centre to the teaspoonful or so of vinegar or lemon juice added after folding in the sugar.

★ Cornflour – about 1 level tablesp to 3 egg whites – prevents the sugar weeping and helps to dry out the meringue, which is cooked for a shorter time in a hotter oven than meringues. Fold it in at the last minute, with a little of the sugar. The more cornflour you use, the drier the meringue.

★ This is a recipe worth digging out, and excellent for a dinner party because you can keep the meringue at *least* a week in an airtight container.

Milk Puddings

These do seem often to deserve the drab name they've got, yet I can't think of many puddings I like better than creamy 'rice', with stewed apple and softly whipped cream to crown things.

To make milk puddings like rice creamy:

(1) Be sure to use the right proportions of grain to milk. The creamier the milk the better of course, but dried milk does just as well, if you double up on the margarine or butter.

(2) Soak whole grain puddings such as rice or tapioca at least ½ hr before cooking. This softens the grain, helping it later to absorb the milk.

(3) Use a slow oven – no higher than gas 2, 300°F, 150°C.

(4) Stir the pudding at least once, preferably twice, when a thin skin forms on top, after about ½ hr and again after about 15–30 mins if you can remember, before the skin goes brown. Stirring prevents the grains sticking together in little heaps, consequently all can fully absorb the milk.

CHOCOLATE CORNFLOUR PUDDING. This changes magically from stodge to fluff if you liquidize it, skin and all, when cold. The consistency thins though, so it won't *set* again.

★ The skin on top of a cold blancmange is

due to evaporation from the surface, so if you aren't going to liquidize later, sprinkle the top lightly with sugar to prevent a skin forming – unless you like it, of course.

RICE PUDDING. This is made with short grain pudding rice because it's absorbent, very white, and goes creamy when cooked, unlike long grain which is much less absorbent and doesn't go creamy. See also *Milk puddings*, above.

★ One way of eating up *cold rice pudding* is to remove the skin, dredge the top with Demerara sugar and grill it to a caramel. Eat soon when cool, before the caramel melts. (Before grilling, protect the rim of the dish with a strip of foil.)

Mince Pies

These freeze perfectly, the mincemeat usually being moister when they're frozen uncooked.

★ Freeze in their bun tins until stiff enough to pack in a covered container, which gives better protection against damage than a polythene bag.
★ Small mince pies are often made with either shortcrust or a flaky type of pastry, but a large pie is best made with flaky or rough pastry – not with frozen puff pastry.

Pancakes

Still traditional on Shrove Tuesday, even though we don't nowadays have to use up the milk, fat and eggs once forbidden during the Lenten fast.

★ They are just as light, if not lighter, when made with equal quantities of milk and water instead of all milk; and one egg to 2 ozs (50 g) flour makes much better pancakes than one egg to *4* ozs flour, as called for in many recipes. Pancakes will be lighter too if the batter is chilled for a while, because cold air trapped in it will expand more than warm.
★ Fat is used only to grease the pan well before making each pancake, to ensure each slides out easily; never actually to fry them in. They should be lacy-thin, and are lighter when turned over with a pallet knife than when tossed – sorry to be a spoil-sport!
★ Lemon Butter pats make pancakes sumptuous (see page 241). Make up to $\frac{1}{4}$ or $\frac{1}{2}$ lb (say 100–200 g) butter while you're about it, if you have a freezer. Alternatively, have you tried eating them with a lump of ordinary butter inside, along with the traditional lemon juice and sugar? This is a scrumptious North Country custom.
★ If you want to freeze pancakes – I don't, because nobody can persuade me they're as good – they'll be lighter with about a tablespoon oil or melted butter stirred into 4 ozs (100 g) batter. Cool the pancakes quickly too, on a wire tray, to let the steam escape.
★ For *Pan*, see page 18.

Peaches

Are easily skinned if first covered with boiling water for just half to one minute.

Pie, Fruit

Lovely made with a melt-in-the-mouth *rich* shortcrust pastry (see page 105). 1 level teasp ground cinnamon sieved with 8 ozs (225 g) flour, gives a nice spicy flavour to pastry for an apple pie or mince pies etc – or you may like it in a pear flan?

★ It's better to put the sugar in the middle of the fruit than on top, then it won't make the pastry soggy underneath.
★ A little cornflour or semolina mixed with the sugar (2 rounded teasps to 4 ozs (100 g) sugar) makes the juice of fruits like apples, blackberries or rhubarb deliciously syrupy instead of watery.
★ There's no need to use a pie funnel in a fruit pie because there should be enough fruit to come above the level of the rim of the pie-dish, to *support* the pastry. By the time the fruit softens and shrinks, the pastry will have 'set', so shouldn't collapse into the middle.
★ Put the strip of pastry round the rim of the pie-dish with its *cut* edge outwards,

because this edge is open, not sealed, and can rise perfectly when baked.
★ Raise the pastry slightly at one corner of a fruit pie, for steam to escape, otherwise the underside of the pastry will be soggy.

PLATE PIE. Will be crisp underneath as well as on top if you make it on an aluminium or old-fashioned enamel plate – because metal is a better conductor of heat than ovenware glass or china.

★ If you freeze an uncooked plate pie, it's wise to brush the inner surfaces of the pastry with egg white. This seals the pastry, preventing seepage of fruit juice, which would make it soggy.

Sabayon

The French name for *Zabaglione*, but uses white wine instead of Marsala. See page 237.

Soufflés

Cold soufflés such as Milanaise (lemon) or Chocolate are *best* the day they're made because then the texture is perfect, especially if you can use really *fresh* eggs (see *Whisking*).

★ It's always tricky to try and advise anybody about the size of soufflé dish required, because so much depends on other things besides quantities; how fresh and large the eggs are; how well you beat the yolks and sugar; how skilfully you whisk the whites etc.
★ A large doubled strip of foil to stand 2″ (5 cm) above the top of the dish allows for 1″ ($2\frac{1}{2}$ cm) of soufflé above it, is easy to fix on, and *far* easier to take off, without spoiling the edge, than greaseproof paper. Grip ends together, first with a paper clip, then tie it on tightly with string to prevent mixture escaping down the side, because this is difficult to wipe off when set.
★ Ideally you need a large mixing bowl each for the yolks/sugar mixture, the cream, and the egg whites, because in none of these ingredients could you entangle enough air if using *small basins*. A soufflé *depends* on air.
★ The yolks/sugar bowl should be big enough to sit steadily on top of a pan of hot water without the water touching it. If it does touch, or if the water is actually boiling, you'll end up with cooked yolks instead of whisked. They need *gentle, indirect heat* to become light and fluffy.
★ You can't go wrong with the temperature of the water if, when it boils, you stand the pan in the sink and beat the yolks and sugar over it, there. It's a comfortable height at which to beat, and you can't easily scald yourself either. Beat the yolks and sugar 'to the ribbon', to give the mixture enough body to support the other ingredients when added. If not beaten enough, it will thin out.
★ If the mixture refuses to thicken – perhaps because the eggs aren't very fresh – try adding an extra yolk.
★ I prefer 'whipping' cream to double cream (see page 70) because for a soufflé cream is only half-whipped. To blend perfectly with the beaten yolks and sugar, you should whip it to their consistency. See also page 223.

Sponge Puddings

These can be varied in innumerable ways, baked or steamed. You're bound to know lots of the following, but some you may not have thought of, or recognized their simple base:

EVE'S PUDDING. Bake the sponge mixture on top of the prepared fresh, or canned fruit. With a name like this, the fruit is of course officially apple, very finely sliced – with sugar in the middle rather than on top.

CASTLE PUDDINGS. Bake in darioles and serve with jam sauce, or if chocolate, serve with chocolate sauce or a sweet white sauce.

SYRUP SPONGE. Put golden syrup (or jam for a jam sponge) at the bottom of a pudding basin or darioles. Steam. For variety, add a few chopped glacé cherries and a little chopped angelica to the mixture.

LEMON, CHOCOLATE, SPICE,

GINGER, FRUIT, DATE, PINEAPPLE PUDDING etc. Add the necessary flavouring to the mixture – respectively lemon rind, cocoa, mixed spice, ground ginger, dried fruits, chopped dates and a spice, chopped canned pineapple. Steam. Serve a complementary sauce, such as egg custard, an appropriately flavoured sweet white sauce or a hard sauce (see page 241).

UPSIDE DOWN PUDDING. Use a shallow tin like a moule à manqué or sandwich cake tin, spreading its inner surfaces with creamed soft brown sugar and margarine – about 1 oz (25 g) of each for a 1-egg pudding. Decorate the bottom with pineapple and glacé cherries, spread sponge mixture on top and bake about ¾ hr in a slow to moderate oven, gas 3, 325°F, 165°C. It tastes every bit as good as it looks when turned out, and served with cream, custard or better still, both.

WEST RIDING PUDDING. Bake sponge mixture in a pie-dish, first lining its sides with a thin strip of shortcrust pastry, and spreading jam or lemon curd in the bottom.

PLAIN STEAMED SPONGE PUDDING. Serve a well flavoured sauce such as sweet 'white', lemon, lemon butter, strawberry butter, arrowroot or cornflour-thickened fruit syrup, or differently flavoured custards made in the English or French way.(Vanilla-flavoured pudding.)

Syllabub

That fattening, delicious old-English sweet made with ½ pt (250 ml) *double* cream, a large lemon, 3 ozs (75 g) sugar and 2 or 3 tablesps sherry (or sherry and brandy), syllabub is better made with lemon zest than lemon rind. Alternatively, if you use rind, soak it for 2–3 hrs in the juice, to give the juice extra flavour before you strain and use it.

★ Much depends upon the freshness of the cream – you can't make syllabub if it's 'buttery'. Whip it to light peaks before stirring in gradually the other mixed-together ingredients, and then whip the whole lot until thick.

★ If made much in advance of the meal, the sherry may separate out, especially if you don't refrigerate it at once.

★ Serve it well chilled in individual glasses – the cream can be chilled in advance – decorated with finely chopped pistachio nuts. You'll want something with a contrasting crisp texture to serve with it – like tuiles or Savoy fingers.

Tarts

Pastry 'shells' with a sweet filling, sometimes decorated with lattice. Unlike a pie, the filling is never completely enclosed.

Trifle

Trifle is well named – there's no knowing what one is going to find under many an inviting creamy top. It's not a sweet you can make in 10 minutes.

★ For the basics you can't beat good home-made sponge cake soaked at least 2 or 3 hours – to make it firm enough to support the cream – in plenty of *cooled* custard made with egg yolks. You need about a pint (500 ml) for 6 people, bearing in mind that if you use it while still warm, it won't have thickened fully as it should. (Custard made with custard powder is incorrect because it will set on top of the sponge cake, rather than soak into it.)

★ Sherry, rum or liqueur, not to mention jam, fruit and ratafia biscuits, are all traditional ingredients of the real thing.

Yoghourt

This calls for just a little skill if always to be successful, but it's well worth making your own because home-made is so much less expensive than bought. A machine is not necessary.

★ Here are the chief causes of failure:

(1) Using a 'starter' ('made' yoghourt) which isn't fresh. Refrigerated, yoghourt can be used up to about a fortnight old. It doesn't freeze satisfactorily.

(2) Wrong temperatures:
(a) If the milk is too hot when you add the starter to it, yoghourt bacteria will be killed.
(b) If the milk isn't kept warm enough during incubation, the bacteria won't multiply.

(3) Wrong ingredients:
(a) A sterilized or pasteurized yoghourt can't be used as a starter.
(b) Sweetened condensed milk is 'out' because so much sugar stops the bacteria growing.
(c) Fresh milk is unsuitable unless first sterilized, because of bacteria other than those needed for the yoghourt: heat milk to just below boiling point (for milk, this is 196°F, 91°C), maintain at that temperature about 10 mins, let it cool to 104°–113°F, 40°–45°C, strain and then use as other milks in recipe given below.

(4) Adding a flavouring before incubation. If nothing worse anything like crushed fruit is likely to sink to the bottom. Add *afterwards*.

PLAIN OR NATURAL YOGHOURT (to serve 4)

1 pt (500 ml) Long Life or (diluted) evaporated milk
2 dessertsps plain yoghourt (room temp.)

(1) Heat milk to 104°–113°F, 40°–45°C (just above blood heat, in case you haven't got a thermometer) in a saucepan which has a close-fitting lid.
(2) Stir in the yoghourt and mix well.
(3) Cover with lid, wrap saucepan in a towel and put in a warm place until set, 12–24 hrs (eg airing cupboard or somewhere about 70°F, 21°C). Alternatively, you could put it in a wide-necked vacuum flask. Refrigerate.
★ Generally speaking, the longer the yoghourt incubates, the thicker and more acid it becomes. If it *fails* to set, reheat gently, add more starter and leave another 24 hrs.
(4) Keep back a few teaspoonfuls to start your next batch. (You can't go on for ever using starter from your last batch because eventually it becomes too weak. At that point you need some *new* yoghourt.)

Yorkshire Pudding

This is lighter when made with half milk and half water instead of all milk. The batter, contrary to many an old recipe, is much better for being chilled than beaten, because trapped cold air (caught when sieving the flour) expands more than room-temperature air when heated, so it rises better.

★ The right-sized tin has a real bearing on results (see page 27) and a tin gives a crisper 'Yorkshire' than an ovenproof dish, because metal is a better conductor of heat.

★ Heat is essential for success. You need a hot oven, hot lard (or cooking fat) in a hot tin, and a quick hand to *keep* things hot. The oven must be hot enough initially to make the batter rise and then holds its shape. Use the hottest part of it and have it preheated at gas 7, 425°F, 220°C for the first ¼ hr, then lower to gas 5, 375°F, 190°C for *about* another ¾ hr.

★ If you have a large family and a restricted purse, one large farm-fresh egg *will* raise 6 ozs (150 g) flour – plain of course. Use a tin about 12″ × 9½″ (30 cm × 24 cm).

★ If you cut off the thick edges of any left-overs, so that the remaining piece is flat and will cook evenly, Yorkshire pudding is lovely fried 2 or 3 minutes on each side. Serve it with the cold beef, or as a pudding (fried in butter or oil) with golden syrup – or deep freeze it along with the sliced cold beef.

Zabaglione

Can be served by itself in glasses either warm or cold, or as a sauce poured over or accompanying certain hot puddings and sweets, such as Christmas Pudding, sponge puddings or stewed fruits. The Italians use Marsala, while the French use white wine and call it Sabayon.

★ It's a little tricky to make. You need:

(1) The right-sized basin for the quantity you're making. It's difficult for instance to beat 2 egg yolks and sugar properly if the basin is too big, while

on the other hand it is difficult to entangle enough air as they thicken if the basin is much too small.

(2) *Shivering*, *shallow* water in the pan under the basin. If the yolks are overheated because the water is too hot or too deep, they'll cook before you can beat air into them.

(3) An electric hand-beater if you've got one, otherwise something like a small balloon whisk, to beat enough air into the mixture to get the volume.

(4) To beat the mixture at intervals while it's cooling, if serving it cold. It's never better though than when just made – thick, warm and full of flavour. (Cold zabaglione really calls for a different recipe.)

15
DESSERT SAUCES

General Information

Sauces can make or mar sweets and puddings, perhaps by their absence even more than by their presence. They can enrich and give flavour to the simplest pudding; by their sharpness counteract the richness of others; provide moisture with dry dishes, a soft creamy texture to partner a hard, or a dash of colour to cheer a dull. In addition, a hot sauce can make a contrast for ice cream, or a chilled sauce may be the perfect choice for something hot.

★ With a sauce, you can dress up, vary and disguise the plainest sponge, or you can 'crown' the most sophisticated sweet. Some of them require skill, few are very time-taking, nearly always they are a bonus.

Chocolate Sauce

To serve over vanilla ice cream, canned pears or sliced banana etc, chocolate sauce makes a handy store in the refrigerator. I never make less than ½ pt (250 ml) because, providing you keep it chilled and covered, it lasts for weeks. This recipe uses stock syrup, which helps to make the sauce shiny:

2½ ozs (say 65 g) plain dessert chocolate, eg Bournville
½ pt (250 ml) *warm* stock syrup (page (page 275)
½ teasp vanilla essence
1 dessertsp–1 tablesp rum, optional

(1) Melt shredded or grated chocolate in basin over pan of shallow, very hot but not boiling water (see page 68 if necessary).
(2) Set basin aside from heat and stir syrup into chocolate, a little at a time to start with. Flavour with vanilla, and if liked also with rum. Taste.
(3) Allow to go quite cold, to thicken properly.
(4) Cover with foil and refrigerate until required.

Note. If the stock syrup is too hot it will turn the chocolate to rock. If cold, it's *difficult* (but not impossible) to mix it evenly with the chocolate before the chocolate cools and hardens.

Cream, Slightly Sour

Double or whipping cream is *delicious* if you whip about 1 level tablesp vanilla sugar (or icing sugar plus a few drops vanilla essence) and *about* 1 teasp lemon juice with ¼ pt (125 ml) of the slightly sour cream. Taste, and adjust as you like it.

★ Surprisingly perhaps, an unpleasant acidity is transformed into a most likeable sharp flavour.

Cream, Whipped

As an accompaniment, whipped cream goes further and isn't quite so rich if you fold a stiffly whisked egg white into ½ pt

(250 ml) whipped *double* cream.

★ I wouldn't use it for piping because it soon collapses – *best* made just before you need it too.

Crème Anglaise

A sophisticated version of our English boiled custard or custard sauce – the way we *ought* to make it! It is made with *yolks* rather than *whole* eggs and contains just enough cornflour or potato flour not to thicken it but to prevent the custard scrambling if marginally overheated. (Approximately 1 level teasp 'starch' to $\frac{3}{4}$ pt (375 ml) milk.)

★ Vanilla is the basic flavouring: in addition you may like to stir into the finished sauce a spoonful or two of your favourite liqueur, add a spoonful of coffee essence, or, while heating the milk, melt a little shredded chocolate in it?
★ The sauce is served either warmed or chilled, depending on what it accompanies, eg fruit salad, a pudding or wherever it could take the place of cream.
★ With additional egg yolks and with double cream it becomes the custard used for ice creams. Also with more egg yolks, plus whipped cream, gelatine and flavouring, it is ready to be a Bavarian cream.
★ See also *Custard, Boiled,* following.

Crème Chantilly

More subtle and much more delicious than ordinary whipped cream and *no* extra bother for anyone who has a jar of vanilla sugar in their larder (see page 93). The term *Chantilly* indicates a slightly sweetened vanilla-flavoured whipped cream.

★ You can use double or whipping cream; lightly whipped to accompany a hot or cold sweet, or more stiffly whipped *double* cream if to pipe or use in meringues, a gâteau or with pastries etc.
★ Precise quantities aren't necessary: just whip *about* a rounded teasp vanilla sugar (preferably icing sugar) with $\frac{1}{4}$ pt (125 ml) cream, or more to taste.

Custard, Boiled (Custard Sauce)

When made with whole eggs this is as unattractive as it sounds, besides having the most idiotic name imaginable for a sauce which at all costs must *not* be boiled. The French name 'Crème à la Vanille' sounds so much more enticing, and so is the sauce if, despite a recipe stating '1 egg', you instead use '2 yolks'. The sauce will have a finer flavour, is much less likely to curdle and will be richer, smoother, yellower and thicker – and thicker still when it's cold. (Use 3 large yolks to $\frac{1}{2}$ pt (250 ml) milk.)

★ It's because of the conflicting temperatures at which an egg white and egg yolk set that whole eggs curdle or at best make a wretched sauce: you can't win because the white coagulates (begins to solidify) at a lower temperature than the yolk, so if you heat the milky liquid enough for the yolk to thicken it, that's *too* hot for the white.
★ As yolks themselves coagulate well below boiling point, this explains why there's no *need* to boil a custard, and why it will be worse rather than better if heated above 165°F, 74°C.
★ A few more tips:

(1) It's better to stir the heated milk in a thin stream onto the whisked egg and sugar than to tip it in all at once, especially if you've rather *over*heated the milk. This way the yolks are warmed gradually instead of being suddenly cooked.
(2) Rinse pan with cold water after heating the milk and before straining back in the milk, eggs and sugar. Otherwise, if a pan is very hot, the eggs may start to solidify before you have a free hand with which to stir.
(3) Hot custard *left* in a hot pan may, due to the heat of the pan, scramble. If serving it cold, therefore, pour the custard straight into a cold basin, stirring it from time to time as it cools. If serving it hot, cool slightly first by beating for a minute or two aside from the heat. If necessary to *keep* it

hot, use a bain-marie containing warm water.

(4) If your luck is out and custard curdles, try liquidizing it.

Custard Sauce 2

When made with custard powder, custard sauce can be creamy, fluffy and delicious, or thick, skin-covered and abhorrent, depending on the cook.

★ Homogenized or Long Life milk make extra creamy custard because with these milks the cream and milk are emulsified. Liquidizing (skin and all) when cold or nearly cold makes custard smooth and light – but it needs to be *made* slightly thicker, to allow for thinning.

★ If without a liquidizer, you can stop skin *forming* either by covering the hot custard straight away with a disc of foil, or by sprinkling the surface with sugar. (Either method prevents evaporation from the surface.)

Fruit Sauce

A fruit sauce to serve with ice cream or a light dessert should be made with very ripe fruit so that you can liquidize or sieve it easily to make a purée. Though the fruit needn't be perfect, it must of course be good.

★ If you're without a liquidizer, icing sugar dissolves more readily than caster or granulated, when you're making a sauce with something like fresh raspberries or strawberries. If you *have* a liquidizer, the sweetened purée will thicken slightly if you whizz it at high speed for 2–3 minutes.

★ Lemon juice perks up a fruit sauce. Cognac or Kirsch, in addition, will pep it up.

Fruit Syrups

Usually better when thickened with arrowroot than with cornflour. Arrowroot is both tasteless and clear – the correct glaze to show up the painstakingly arranged fruit in a flan, or the cherries in tartlets etc.

★ 2 level teasps arrowroot thicken $\frac{1}{4}$ pt (125 ml) fruit syrup, the sauce (or glaze) being cooked and ready to use the moment it thickens and clears. By contrast, cornflour must be cooked several minutes after it has boiled if not to have a raw taste.

Hard Sauces

Those such as rum, lemon or strawberry 'butter' give a fillip to certain sweets and many steamed puddings. They may have a similar or a contrasting flavour to whatever they are accompanying, but whichever it is, they make a pleasant change from the more conventional kinds of sauce most people serve.

★ Here are some ideas to start you off. Be imaginative and experiment with different combinations of butters and puddings:

Butter	*Kind of pudding*
Brandy	Traditional with Christmas Pudding and mince pies.
Chocolate	Castle puddings, vanilla-flavoured plain sponge, chocolate, ginger.
Coffee	Castle puddings, vanilla-flavoured plain sponge, chocolate, walnut.
Lemon	Castle puddings, lemon sponge (Canary), pancakes.
Orange	Vanilla-flavoured plain sponge, marmalade, pineapple sponge.
Raspberry	Plain sponge, jam roly-poly, rice pudding.
Rum	Baked apples, apple dumplings, grilled bananas, rich fruit pudding, mince pies, spiced jelly.
Spice	'Fruit' sponge, Christmas pudding (if you don't want a spirit), mince pies, apple (plate)pie, Spotted Dick.
Strawberry	As raspberry.

★ These hard sauces are as good after freezing as before but they don't keep for ever, despite the sugar to preserve the butter. With a freezer it's worth making up this sort of quantity at a time, otherwise I'd make less:

HARD SAUCES (to scrvc about 8).
4 ozs (100 g) softish butter
4 ozs (100 g) sieved icing sugar, caster sugar or soft brown sugar, see 'tips', point 4.
Flavouring, eg
brandy – 2 tablesps brandy, or to taste
chocolate – 2 ozs, (50 g) melted plain dessert chocolate, eg Bournville, added quickly (before it hardens) to full quantity creamed butter and sugar.
coffee – 2 teasps coffee essence, eg Camp.
lemon – zest of 1 large lemon and 1 tablesp strained juice
orange – zest of 1 large orange and 1 tablesp strained juice.
raspberry – 2 tablesps purée fresh rasps.
rum – 2 tablesps rum, or to taste.
spice – 1 level teasp (or more, to taste) ground mixed spice, sieved, preferably with the sugar.
strawberry – 2 tablesps purée of fresh strawberries.

METHOD.
(1) Cream butter until soft, then gradually add about three quarters of the sugar, beating until soft as whipped cream.
(2) Beat in flavouring: if a liquid, add a little at a time and blend in each addition thoroughly before adding any more.
(3) Add and beat in remaining sugar.
(4) Pile up in a dish and leave to harden, or make it into 'pats', pipe in stars, or chill and cut into blocks or shapes, using a cutter dipped in boiling water.

★ And here are just a few tips:
(1) In order to harden, these sauces *must* be made in advance – so there's no last minute rush as with a sauce.
(2) The fruit flavoured butters taste best when made with saltless butter.
(3) If the butter is fairly soft, it's much easier to cream it with the sugar. If not then beaten until soft as whipped cream, the mixture won't 'accept' and blend with a liquid flavouring, which anyway must be added gradually for the same reason.
(4) Choice of sugar depends on whether you like a smooth or gritty texture, or the flavour of brown sugar. As a general rule, I find icing sugar best.
(5) Zest or *very* finely grated rind of a citrus fruit is much better than more coarsely grated rind. Zest has no bitter pith, just lovely flavouring oils.

Jam Sauce

More economical if you simmer ¼ pt (125 ml) fruit juice or water for a few minutes with 3 large tablesps jam, and then thicken this with 2 level teasps arrowroot or cornflour, slaked and added in usual way. A few drops of lemon juice, added at the last moment, counteract the sweetness.

Sabayon

This is a lovely sauce to serve with such things as fresh fruit salad, apple charlotte, Christmas or a steamed sponge pudding.

★ There are recipes for using it warm or cold, depending on what you're serving it with. To serve it warm, you can use your ordinary recipe for Sabayon (*Zabaglione*, page 237). One way of using the same recipe cold is to add an extra yolk – say 4 yolks instead of 3 – beating the sabayon frequently (over ice) as it cools. If just *left* to cool, the wine separates out.

White Sauce, Sweet

See *White Sauce*, page 138, and make the following adjustments:
(1) Omit pepper.
(2) Add 1 dessertsp granulated sugar to ½ pt (250 ml) sauce just before dishing.
(3) Add the flavouring of your choice. Essences are volatile, evaporating easily if a sauce re-boils, so they too should be added at the last minute. Shredded or grated chocolate can be dissolved in the milk.

16

BREADS, CONTINENTAL BREADS AND SCONES

General Information

Bread, rolls and scones you make yourself are totally different from anything one can usually buy, once you've learnt the ropes.

★ Two essential skills are knowing how to knead effectively and knowing the correct consistency of a dough, particularly a bread and an oven-scone dough. Bread *isn't* time-taking – it's just that the minutes you do spend on it are spread out over a longer period. If you have a home to look after, it shouldn't be too difficult to fit this kind of baking into your daily routine now and then, though it's bound to be more complicated for anyone who has to keep one eye on the clock, like a mother continually ferrying children to and from school.

★ Most home-made bread keeps better and longer than bought, and if you have a freezer, it's almost just as easy to make up a large amount of flour as a small. Apart from crusty loaves, which tend to part company with their crust, most breads freeze excellently. So do oven scones, especially if while still frozen you pop them into a slow oven, see page 248.

Bread

Bread is wonderful stuff really. Using just a morsel of yeast, a bag of flour with some salt and water changes into golden crusty loaves.

THE INGREDIENTS.

Strong flour is *best* for white bread, if you really want the perfect loaf – crisp surface, firm texture and a good shape – but plain household flour is cheaper and makes good bread too. I believe *most* people couldn't tell one bread from the other.

★ A dough made with a strong flour will absorb marginally more water than one made with soft household flour, because it contains more gluten. You'll also have to knead this dough slightly longer than the other, to reach the same condition. See also *Flour*, page 72.

Yeast. See page 96.

Salt, besides giving flavour, plays an important part in a bread dough: too little makes a dough sticky and more difficult to manipulate, while too much inhibits growth of the yeast and delays fermentation – so your bread will take longer to rise. Use 2 level teasps per lb (450 g) flour.

Lard isn't a basic ingredient of bread, but helps to make it lighter and keep longer. For best results, I prefer lard to a white cooking fat – about a scant oz (25 g) per lb (450 g) flour, rubbed in.

The liquid – water for ordinary bread of course – should be lukewarm. At this temperature it is warm enough for the yeast to grow, but not hot enough to kill it. You won't go far wrong if you mix $\frac{1}{3}$ boiling water with $\frac{2}{3}$ cold, unless you plan to let the dough rise overnight, when it's *cold* water you want.

★ It is best to take your courage in both hands and add the liquid in one fell swoop to the flour. If you make the dough a bit too wet, it's easy to add a little extra flour, but if you hold back some of the liquid and make a 'tight' (stiff) dough, you *cannot* then add more liquid, because the outer surfaces of the dough simply become a paste.

★ The consistency of the dough may be the making or marring of your bread, because if too tight, it can't expand during fermentation and will make a close-textured, heavy loaf. The dough should be soft without being *sticky*; the bowl and your fingers clean by the time kneading is finished. Incidentally, bread made with water has a crisper crust than when made with milk, or milk and water.

★ A few tips about bread-making:

(1) I find the kitchen sink a good working height for kneading a dough in its mixing bowl. Much depends on one's height.

(2) The dough must be properly kneaded, whether by hand or with a dough hook, for bread to be a good texture. Kneading strengthens the dough, and spreads the yeast evenly through it: carry on until the dough looks smooth and slightly shiny, and feels firm and elastic. It will probably take 5–10 mins, but depends on the type of flour used, and upon your skill in kneading.

(3) Dough rises perfectly in its bowl if enclosed in a huge polythene bag, to keep it soft and moist. These are ideal 'greenhouse' conditions for fermentation, and much more effective than the old damp tea-towel idea. If without a bag large enough to enclose the bowl, put the dough direct into a smaller bag – oiled and loosely tied, to allow room for it to rise. (If the bag isn't oiled, the dough will stick to it, or if the dough isn't covered, to exclude air, a crusty skin will form on top).

(4) Make the first 'rising' fit in with *you*, whether you're cooking, doing housework or want to sleep – then leaving dough in a cold larder overnight. It's immaterial how much the dough rises at this stage, providing the bowl is big enough, because the next stage is 'knocking back' – unless you're using the quick method, with just one rising. When fully risen a dough should, however, be at least doubled in size, shapeless in appearance and springy to the touch.

(5) A warm dough will rise perfectly in a warm kitchen, but should you want to speed things up:

(a) Slightly increase the proportion of yeast to flour, eg use 1½ ozs (40 g) yeast to 3 lbs (1.35 K) instead of 1 oz (25 g).

(b) Stand the polythene-covered bowl in 2 or 3 ins (5–8 cm) of water as hot as your hand can bear – say in your washing-up bowl. (Avoid raising dough in a metal bowl because the heat of the water would penetrate it and kill the yeast).

(6) Unless a risen dough is sticky, which it shouldn't be, avoid using any extra flour on the table when kneading it, otherwise you'll change the dough's character, making it difficult to manipulate. This second kneading, known as 'knocking back', is to give the bread a good even texture, and to knock out any air bubbles which would burst and leave holes in the baked bread.

(7) If you brush bread tins with melted lard or white cooking fat, which are both *pure* fats, the bread won't stick to the tins.

(8) To prevent a proving dough, in bread tins, sticking to the polythene bag in which they're enclosed, brush the top of each loaf with melted lard or cooking fat.

THE OVEN. This must be very hot initially, to kill the yeast and so stop the bread rising: bake 10–15 mins in the hottest part of the oven (allowing room for it to rise), gas 8, 450°F, 230°C, then lower to gas 5, 375°F, 190°C for remaining time.

★ If feasible, give bread the oven to itself. If you have to adapt the heat to suit other foods or work out a jig-saw to fit them in, bread is seldom so successful.

★ To make especially crusty loaves, create steam by putting a roasting tin of boiling water on the floor of the oven. (The reason *why* the crust is so different from the crumb is because the moisture is dried out of the surfaces of the dough by the heat.)

★ Cool bread on a wire cake tray. If left in its tins, the crust will be tough and the crumb soggy, due to trapped steam.

★ See also *Bread*, page 243.

Bread, Brown

Made with 100% stoneground wholemeal or wholewheat flour it is, healthwise, the best of all breads, see page 00. Though many people use brown flour entirely, the bread isn't quite as solid when a *little* of it is replaced with some white flour; say $\frac{1}{6}$ or $\frac{1}{8}$ of the total. With a little lard rubbed in, it's lighter still.

★ See also *Bread*, page 243.

Bread, Garlic

Gives a meal character, whether a plate of homely soup, a light lunch, a buffet supper or a barbecue.

★ I prefer to use a Vienna loaf or milk twist, because the inside stays soft, while the outside goes beautifully crisp, without becoming as crusty as a French stick.

★ When cutting the loaf diagonally into thick slices, beware of cutting through the bottom crust, because this holds body and soul together after you've buttered both sides of each slice, and pressed the loaf back into shape again.

★ You'll need 1 clove crushed garlic mixed with *about* 3 ozs (75 g) butter, the butter being easier to spread if first creamed with a dessertsp hot water.

★ Bake the foil-wrapped loaf 15–20 mins in a hot oven, gas 7, 425°F, 220°C. If not served hot, preferably in a folded napkin to *keep* it hot, garlic bread is as unpleasant as it is indigestible.

Bread, Milk

Is just a rich form of white bread. Where ordinary bread is made with water and very little fat (if any), milk bread is made with milk and quite a lot of fat. In addition, some recipes call for egg and the making of a slightly sticky dough which, because it's too soft to knead, has to be beaten. I prefer the drier *consistency* of an ordinary bread dough which I think makes lighter bread.

★ I use these quantities:

	Brief comments
3 lbs (1.35 K) strong or plain white flour	Mix together
3 rounded teasps salt	
1 rounded tablesp gran. sugar	Add to flour
4 ozs (100 g) butter or margarine	Rub into flour
1 oz (25 g) fresh or $\frac{1}{2}$ oz (15 g) dried yeast	See yeast, p. 96. Mix in usual way before adding to flour etc.
about $1\frac{1}{4}$ pts (700 ml) tepid milk	
egg, to glaze	

★ Recipes containing dried fruit, egg and extra sugar require a little extra yeast – the amount given above, but to 2 lbs (900 g) flour – because these ingredients slow down fermentation. The greater the proportion of these ingredients, the slower the fermentation.

★ Milk bread has a softer crust but a richer and more even golden colour than bread made with water.

★ See also *Bread*, page 243.

BAPS. These (12 per lb or 450 g of flour) are made from a dough which is a *cross* between a bread dough and the milk bread dough above. Alter those quantities as follows:

(1) Use more fat – 2 ozs (50 g) per *lb* (450 g) of flour.

(2) Use equal quantities of milk and water, instead of all milk.

MILK TWISTS. Made with a milk bread dough, these keep well in a freezer, so I usually make up that full quantity of flour, dividing the dough between small loaves of bread, milk twists and/or dinner rolls, according to need. $\frac{1}{2}$ lb (225 g) flour makes one 'twist'.

★ Providing you can plait – and of course make a good dough – a milk twist is plain sailing, despite *looking* complicated.

Here's the method, from the stage when the dough has risen and been 'knocked back':

(1) Form dough into a huge 'sausage', then roll it out flat, smooth side uppermost, with a rolling pin, see Fig. 1.
(2) Cut *almost* from end to end into three equal strips, see Fig. 2.
(3) Open out the strips (Fig. 3), plait them fairly tightly and press the ends together where they meet, see Fig. 4. Lay bread on greased baking sheet.

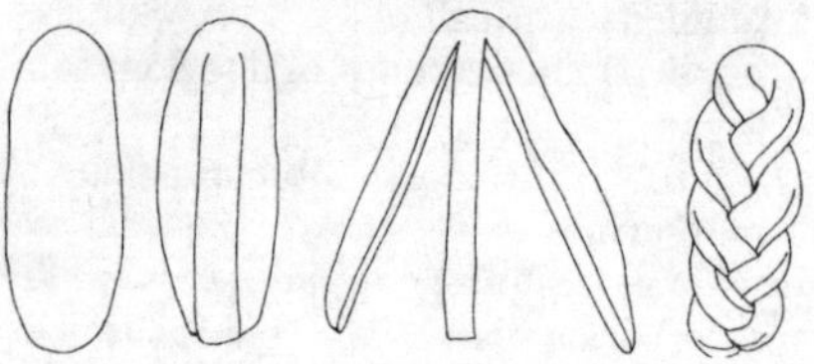

1. 2. 3. 4.

(4) Cover with a clean tea-towel, prove (put to rise) and when about doubled in size, glaze with egg and sprinkle top lightly with poppy seed, to decorate.
(5) Bake in hottest part of preheated hot oven, gas 7, 425°F, 220°C for 10 mins to kill the yeast, then reduce heat to gas 5, 375°F, 190°C until golden all over and hollow-sounding when tapped underneath – about 25–30 mins altogether. If getting too brown, cover bread with a butter wrapper for the last few minutes.
(6) Cool on wire cake tray.

ROLLS, BRIDGE. Also made with a milk bread dough, these are small elongated dinner rolls with a soft crust. $\frac{1}{2}$ lb (225 g) flour makes 16.

★ Some tips about their making:

(1) Lay the cigar-shaped pieces of dough a finger's width apart from each other on a greased baking sheet. When risen, they'll join up into a strip.
(2) When baked, instead of putting the rolls on a cake cooling tray, wrap and leave them in a slightly damp tea-towel for the first few minutes. The trapped steam makes them soft.
(3) To fill quickly, leave them in a strip: make one operation each of splitting, buttering and filling, *then* separate them.

ROLLS, DINNER. Home-made dinner rolls please almost everyone. $\frac{1}{2}$ lb (225 g) flour will make 8 large, 12 medium or 16 dainty dinner-size rolls.

★ The professionals shape dinner rolls two at a time in a matter of seconds, one under the lightly floured palm of each hand, on an unfloured board. This is a knack, needing a circular movement of each hand, not to mention just the right amount of pressure. It's worth asking someone who knows how, to show you.

★ For a perfect finish, sprinkle the glazed rolls lightly with poppy seed just before you bake them.

Bunwash

A syrupy glaze brushed over certain buns and breads *after* baking. Sometimes two coats are needed, to give a good glaze.

★ It's very simple: dissolve 2 ozs (50 g) granulated sugar in 4 tablesps water (or sometimes 2 milk and 2 water) and simmer for 2 mins.

★ Be sure to have both the glaze and whatever you're coating very hot, to give a really shiny finish.

Croissant

Comes from the French word, *crescent* – of the moon. Croissants are said to have originated in Budapest in 1686. In besieging the city, the Turks had dug underground passages in an attempt to reach the centre of the town. Budapest bakers working during the night, heard the noise, raised the alarm, and the Turks were repulsed. As a reward, the bakers were granted the privilege of making a special pastry in the form of a crescent; the emblem of the Ottoman flag.

★ Croissants need *butter*, for its flavour, and strong flour for its extra gluten. Only these will make the real thing – the traditional thin layers of characteristically flavoured pastry that won't collapse in the oven. They aren't worth making otherwise.

★ Croissants are a combination of a pastry and a yeast dough. This explains why the dough is kept cool during the early stages, is relaxed and chilled between rollings, but is finally left to rise at room temperature. If however 'proved' in *too* warm a place, such as you might choose for a bread dough, the butter will melt.

★ It is generally quicker and easier in the long run to roll the pastry to a given sized square or rectangle, than to roll it at random, and then cut it vaguely into squares: well-shaped croissants start as well-shaped triangles, but you *may* need to elongate the base of each slightly, to make a good crescent.

★ A hot oven is essential, to kill the yeast, and to prevent the butter melting and running out before the starch grains in the flour can burst and absorb it.

Danish Pastries

Aren't exactly a slimming cure but are worth every minute of the time they take to make. Serve them for elevenses, a buffet lunch, a teenage buffet supper, or as part of a simple lunch.

★ A cross between a yeast mixture and puff pastry, everything must be kept cold because of the high proportion of butter. In fact once you're past the first stage, the dough is *treated* as puff pastry.

★ The dough is soft, like a scone dough, but is rolled and 'relaxed' as pastry, keeping it square at the corners, and avoiding rolling and sealing it at the ends.

★ After making the dough into various shapes, and enriching them with almond paste etc, treat again as a yeast mixture and leave to rise at room temperature until puffy. If in *too* warm a place though, the butter will melt and spoil their texture.

★ Like yeast mixtures and any rich pastry, they need a preheated hot oven, gas 7, 425°F, 220°C. Bake about 10–15 mins until golden and crisp, yet at the same time soft!

Oatcakes

More tricky to make than bread or scones because oatmeal and water, unlike flour and water, don't form a paste and make an elastic dough. This is because oats, unlike wheat, contain no gluten.

★Here are a few tips:

(1) *The ingredients.*

(a) *Oatmeal.* Fine oatmeal cooks more quickly than medium or coarse, so is the most suitable when making oatcakes on a girdle. The coarser grains are fine for oven-baked oatcakes which have both top and bottom heat simultaneously.

(b) *Salt* – 1 level teasp per 8 ozs (225 g) oatmeal – is as important to oatcakes as to porridge.

(c) *Fat.* Bacon fat, lard or dripping are *traditional* because in the past these were the fats always available. You can also make oatcakes with butter, margarine or white cooking fat.

To make thin oatcakes, the fat is added melted and hot, with very hot water, to help the oatmeal swell, bind and make the dough pliable enough to roll out thinly. To make thick oatcakes, the fat can equally well be rubbed in.

(d) Bicarbonate of soda has an advantage over baking powder: it improves the brown colour of the oatcakes.

(2) You need a softish dough because if too dry, it will crumble and be difficult to roll out: to make rolling easy, have plenty of oatmeal on your board and sprinkle more on top of the dough while kneading it, or if it sticks to the rolling pin. (You can do with oatcakes things you *can't* do when rolling pastry.)

(3) Quick kneading and handling are essential when using hot melted fat and hot water because once the dough cools it is difficult to manipulate and more easily falls apart.

(4) For cooking in the traditional way, on one side only on a greased girdle, the dough must be rolled very thinly. If too thick, the oatcakes won't cook properly, neither will they curl up at the corners. In cottage style, the second side was toasted in front of the fire but you can equally well finish them off in the oven.

Rolls etc, Reheated

Rolls, baps, buns, scones, tea-cakes etc., can be reheated and made almost as good as fresh ones, direct from freezer to oven: put them on a baking sheet in a slow oven, gas 2, 300°F, 150°C for *about* 10 mins. Cool on a wire cake tray.

Sandwiches

These earned their name from the fourth Earl of Sandwich. The story goes that he would gamble for days on end, without even stopping for a meal. In order not to interrupt play, he had his meat served to him between two pieces of bread.

★ Generously buttered sandwiches, made preferably with thinly sliced, crustless new bread, have many advantages over meanly buttered: quite apart from their flavour, they will keep soft longer, won't absorb moisture from the filling, and will dry out less if you freeze them. If you have many to make, it's easier to spread the butter – *and* it goes further – if you first beat a little hot water with it. Allow 1 dessertsp water to 4 ozs (100 g) butter.
★ Savoury sandwiches are usually made in brown bread and are served on a plain doyley, to distinguish them from 'sweet' which are mostly made in white bread and are served on a fancy doyley.
★ Frozen sandwiches, wrapped first in heavy-duty foil and then in a polythene bag, will keep best if you put a crust or slice of plain bread at the end of each small pile.

Scones, Drop

Always popular but alas seldom well made. They should be light as a feather, generously buttered and only hours old. The fresher the better.

★ If it's because you haven't got a good recipe that you don't make them (or perhaps aren't very successful when you do), here's a lovely one, to make about 12 scones:

3 ozs (75 g) plain flour
1 level teasp cream of tartar
½ level teasp bicarbonate of soda
good pinch of salt
1 level tablesp gran sugar
1 *large* egg
about 3 tablesps milk

★ Briefly, here's how:
(1) Sieve flour, cream of tartar, bicarbonate of soda and salt into a basin. Add sugar.
(2) Mix to a thick batter with the lightly mixed egg and the milk, see point (a) below.
(3) Cook spoonfuls of the mixture until golden on both sides on a well greased hot girdle over moderate heat, turning them over with a pallet knife when biggish bubbles begin to form over the surface.
(4) Put the scones straight from girdle into the folds of a clean tea-towel on a wire cake tray. Leave there to cool.

THE WHY'S AND HOW'S.
(a) The correct consistency of the batter is essential. It should be thick enough for a trail dropped from the spoon gradually to disappear. If too thin, the scones won't rise properly; if too thick, there'll be an uncooked layer in the centre.
★ If you leave the batter for a while before cooking the scones, it will thicken. In that event, add a little extra milk before you *do* cook them, to correct the consistency.
(b) I usually start heating the girdle when collecting the ingredients, then it's about the right heat when I'm ready for it. If it's too hot, the scones will be hard and too dark a brown. If too cool, they'll be leathery.
★ When in doubt, cook *one* scone to test.
(c) It's better not to cook too many scones at a time. Even if you've got the knack of turning them – the pallet knife flat underneath, and a quick flick of your wrist – one's aim isn't always perfect. The fuller the girdle, the more difficult to turn one without spoiling another.
(d) Cooling drop scones in a cloth is essential to their texture. This traps the steam, keeping them soft and springy.
(e) You can freeze drop scones if you like, but I'd never *recommend* it. Their light

texture doesn't recover.

Scones, Girdle

These *can* be made from the same mixture as oven scones, but with a slightly stiffer dough. As they cook with only bottom heat, roll them to only half the thickness. If too thick, they'll burn outside before being cooked inside. Use a preheated girdle over lowish heat.

Griddle Cake

The Scottish name for a drop scone. See previous page.

Scones, Oven

White oven scones aren't difficult to make, but it's not often one meets the best because so many people seem to slip up over one or more of these things:

(1) *By using the wrong flour*. Self-raising flour makes heavy, poor scones because it doesn't contain enough raising agent. It's much better to use plain flour with cream of tartar and bicarbonate of soda. Do sieve the dry ingredients too, to trap air and to break up any tiny lumps of bicarbonate, which can't unite with the acid.

(2) *The consistency of the dough*. A scone dough is soft and moist, without being sticky – wetter than shortcrust pastry for instance.

(3) *The thickness of the scones*. They should be *thick* – ½″ (1¼ cm). You should only get about 12 × 2″ (5 cm) scones from ½ lb (225 g) flour.

(4) *The oven*, which needs to be preheated and *very* hot, gas 8, 450°F, 230°C. Use the top (or hottest part) of it, to raise the scones fast, and to cook them until crisp and golden.

★ The cutter is a detail: a fluted one is normally used for sweet scones; plain for savoury, to avoid confusion. Dip it in flour and cut the scones without twisting it, to make them a perfect shape.

★ Just in case you aren't happy with your own recipe, these quantities make good scones:

½ lb (225 g) plain flour
1 level teasp salt
1 level teasp cream of tartar
½ level teasp bicarbonate of soda
2 level tablesps gran sugar
2 ozs (50 g) margarine (lard gives no flavour, and quite a different texture).
scant ¼ pt (about 125 ml) milk
egg, beaten, to glaze (for perfection)

★ You can vary this basic mixture in all sorts of ways, like this:

CHEESE SCONES. Lovely hot. Omit the sugar. Add 2 ozs (50 g) finely grated cheese after rubbing fat into flour. Use extra milk.

FRUIT SCONES. Add 1–2 ozs (25–50 g) currants and/or sultanas with the sugar.

GINGER SCONES. Heavenly fried, and served hot. Sieve 2 level teasps ground ginger with the dry ingredients. Roll the dough thin (¼″, or just over ½ cm) and fry over lowish heat in hot lard for a few minutes on each side. Split, butter, sprinkle with caster sugar and eat at once.

SPICE SCONES. Sieve 2 level teasps ground mixed spice with the dry ingredients, and add 1–2 ozs (25–50 g) sultanas with the sugar.

SYRUP SCONES. Use 1 level teasp bicarbonate of soda instead of ½ level teasp, and add 1 dessertsp warmed golden syrup to the milk. (These are good hot as well as cold).

WHOLEMEAL SCONES. Lovely for breakfast with butter, marmalade and clotted cream – and not out of the question for anyone with a freezer. See previous page. Use ¾ brown flour, ¼ white. Omit sugar.

17
CAKES

General Information

The right choice of ingredients probably affects cakes as much as, if not more than, most other things. For consistently perfect results, one also needs to weigh rather than guess because whether a cake is light or heavy, depends upon the right *balance* of dry and liquid ingredients, as well as upon skill in making. How otherwise could twelve or more people all using the same recipe for a competition end up with such incredibly varied results?

★ To know more about the chief ingredients, see *Chapter 111*, but here briefly are the main points:

INGREDIENTS.
Eggs which are farm-fresh make the lightest, biggest and best cakes, because the fresher they are, the more air they will trap when beaten, creamed or whisked (see also pages 106 and 107).

Butter, because of its lovely flavour, is the ideal fat for most cakes, those made with it usually keeping fresh best as well. If I could always afford it, then butter I would generally use, though for something like a sandwich cake a mixture of butter and soft margarine is almost preferable, the former for its flavour, and the latter for its lightness. Butter is difficult to *cream* thoroughly if too cold, so it always pays, for creamed mixtures, to have it at warm-room temperature.

Margarine creams well, particularly the soft brands with which it's easy to make a fairly good cake; whether by the traditional creaming method, or the modern all-in-one cake mix when all the ingredients are simply beaten together.

White flour is always sieved, to entangle air, however fine the flour. Sieving also ensures that dry ingredients are completely blended, and that there are no lumps in anything. Generally speaking, plain household flour is streets ahead of self-raising. It can be used for almost anything and everything, with a given amount of any raising agent; or with none, when 'air' is the raising agent. Self-raising flour on the other hand has a stable quantity of one type of raising agent, whether a recipe calls for it, or not.

Sugar is more important than some may realize. Caster is best for creamed mixtures because, being so fine, it blends perfectly with butter. Granulated is good for 'rubbed in' mixtures, or when sugar is to be melted, when its coarser crystals don't matter.

Salt figures in many recipes. Without it, many cakes would be entirely flavourless. It also makes the gluten in the flour more elastic, so helps a mixture to rise well.

★ A 'plain' or 'rich' cake is determined by the proportion of fat and sugar to flour, not by a high or low proportion of dried fruit etc. A plain cake has half, or *less* than half, fat to flour; while a rich cake has half, or *more* than half fat to flour. It's because plain cakes contain less fat that they go dry more quickly, and don't keep as well as rich.

★ *Sponge Cake* (like Swiss Roll) belongs to a separate group because, technically, it contains no fat.

★ The way in which the fat and sugar are incorporated with the flour usually distinguishes the type of cake: the fat is generally rubbed into the flour for plain cakes, or creamed with the sugar for rich. The *melted* fat and sugar are added to the flour for the gingerbread 'family'.

PREPARATION. It's usually wisest to prepare the cake tin, arrange the oven shelves as you want them and turn the oven on before you start a cake. A pre-heated oven is generally essential because some raising agents begin to act as soon as moisture is added. In addition, air, beaten into, say, a sponge mixture, will be lost if the cake isn't cooked immediately. Once in a hot oven, the trapped air will expand, the egg will coagulate and *hold* the air.

★ As a general rule, small cakes are cooked at the top (or hottest part) of a hot oven, large cakes lower down, in a cooler oven. Some cakes, particularly fruit cakes, are cooked in falling heat, the oven temperature gradually lowered.

★ The choice of tin will often affect results. For instance, a cake cooked in a shallow tin such as a sandwich or moule à manqué tin, usually has a better texture than the same mixture in a deep tin, because the heat penetrates the mixture faster.

★ To be sure a cake won't stick to its tin, I like best to brush it with a *pure* fat such as melted lard or white cooking fat before dusting it out with flour. If you use butter or margarine, the salt in these tends to make a baked cake stick. Keep these wrappers to grease baking sheets, pie-dishes and so on rather than for cake tins. For cakes requiring long cooking or with a high fat and/or sugar content, the tin ought to be lined, see *Lining a cake tin*.

WHEN COOKED. Most cakes will shrink slightly from the sides of the tin when cooked. In addition, creamed mixtures will spring back if you press the top lightly with your finger tips.

★ A cake tends to stick, and sometimes even to break, if you turn it out of the tin as soon as it's cooked. Given 2 or 3 minutes – or up to 5 minutes for a rich cake – to contract and firm up, there isn't the same risk. (There are exceptions.)

★ Certain cakes, such as shortbread, flapjacks and those with a high proportion of fruit like a wedding or Christmas cake, are *not* cooled on a cake cooling tray as this spoils such textures: most other cakes however *must* be, because trapped steam makes them heavy.

★ To turn a cake out of a loose-bottomed tin without having a burning-hot bracelet round your wrist, use something like a storage jar or large can of fruit: stand it on a surface you can't damage, rest the cake tin on top and slide the tin off.

FLAVOURINGS AND COLOURINGS. These require careful use. If you can add a flavouring essence with a liquid, it blends more evenly than if added by itself.

★ As colourings last for years, it's worth buying the best. Coloured cakes such as Battenburg or Neapolitan tend to lighten rather than darken when baked, but for most purposes, use colourings sparingly.

CREAMED MIXTURES. These may curdle if the butter and sugar aren't beaten together until light and fluffy, if the eggs are very cold when added to the creamed fat and sugar, or if they're added too fast. Curdling is due to the fat, cooled by the cold egg liquid, separating out from the sugar and eggs – and of course a curdled mixture tends to make a heavy cake because it doesn't hold as much air. You can sometimes put it right by beating in a tablespoonful of the sieved flour, which will absorb the excessive moisture in the eggs or fat. Another way to restore the creamy consistency may be to warm the bowl in warm water. Ideally, the eggs should be about the same temperature as the creamed fat and sugar, so if you *do* have to take them direct from the refrigerator or from a cold larder, whisk them for a minute or two in a warmed basin, standing it in a bowl of fairly hot water.

★ Although electric mixer instructions may tell you to add an egg whole, it still pays to whisk it first in order to trap more air.

★ Fold the flour and other dry ingredients into creamed mixtures with a metal rather than a wooden spoon, to make a beautifully light cake. See *Folding*.
★ Make a shallow hollow in the middle of the mixture to prevent a large cake 'peaking' there. If despite this a cake does rise to a peak, it's generally because the oven was a bit too hot, or because you had the cake too high up in it. Creamed mixtures are cooked at a slightly lower temperature than 'rubbed-in'.

ALL-IN-ONE-MIXTURES. The quick and easy one-stage way of making cakes, these are best made with a soft margarine which, unlike a harder fat like butter, blends immediately with the dry ingredients and eggs. For perfect blending, they should all be at room temperature.

★ If you're good at and like making cakes in the traditional way, you may feel cheated by the comparatively small cake which identical ingredients (apart from extra raising agent) will sometimes make in *this* way. The difference is accounted for by the additional amount of air trapped in a traditionally made mixture.

SERVING AND STORING CAKES.

(1) If icing a cake which has risen too much in the middle, level it off, turn upside down and ice the bottom.
(2) Small cakes such as Genoese Fancies, cherry tartlets or butterfly cakes look more professional when served in white or coloured paper cake cases, and even the simplest cake looks more attractive on a fancy doyley, on a plate large enough to 'frame' it.
(3) Store cakes in separate airtight containers, or if share a tin they must, in separate polythene bags. At all costs avoid mixing cake and biscuits: the biscuits will absorb moisture from the cake and will be soft almost before you can say Jack Robinson. (A quick way to open any paper-wrapped packet of biscuits is to cut the packet in half with a sharp knife.).
(4) Many cakes, but not all, store well in a freezer. As water in an icing is readily absorbed into the cake, especially if the cake isn't first glazed (see page 262), it is nearly always better, because of this and for the appearance, to ice cakes *after* freezing.

Battenburg Cake

Simply a variation of Genoese Pastry surrounded by almond paste. It needs a special tin, with divider, so that the coloured half of the mixture can't spread into, and mix with the other, uncoloured half.

Brandy Snaps

So called because, for the real thing, the cream is flavoured with brandy.

★ The ingredients need *precise* weighing, because if the mixture is the tiniest bit too stiff, it doesn't spread properly when baked; or if too soft, the snaps are so thin that they break easily when shaped. The recipe *I* like uses 1 oz (25 g) each of *butter*, sugar and flour, 2 ozs (50 g) golden syrup, $\frac{1}{2}$ level teasp ground ginger and a pinch of cream of tartar. (The cream of tartar makes them set harder, and keeps them crisp longer.)
★ It's better not to try and bake more than four at a time, on a well greased baking sheet. They cool so quickly when cooked that it's difficult to manipulate more before they harden, in a matter of almost seconds.
★ If without cream cornet moulds, make pipe-shaped snaps instead, wrapping them round the greased handle of a thick wooden spoon. Lard is the best fat to grease cornets or spoon.
★ Put brandy snaps in an airtight container the moment they cool, unless filling and eating them right away. They soon go soft in the atmosphere, and should be eaten the same day unless *sealed* in a small tin.
★ Brandy snaps are only tip-top when crisp enough to earn their name, and to contrast with the soft cream inside, so fill at the last minute. It's easiest to *pipe* in the cream – $\frac{1}{4}$ pt (125 ml) for 12 snaps, as above.

Butterfly Cakes

One of the simplest examples of a 'creamed' mixture (see page 251). When the weight of an egg is used in butter, sugar and flour with raising agent, you don't need any extra liquid. Using these proportions, cakes are lighter and stay fresh longer than when made with a larger quantity of flour, and milk in addition.

★ These little cakes, like Queen Cakes, are moister and have a soft outside when baked in paper cake cases – and much nicer I think than baked direct in the bun tins, whether non-stick or otherwise.
★ To be feathery-light, cook them at the top (or hottest part) of a hot oven, gas 6, 400°F, 204°C until golden and firm to the touch.
★ You can make all kinds of butterflies for a children's party, using the halved crest of each cake as the two wings, and with differently flavoured and coloured butter icings and decorations. See *Butter icing*, page 262.

Cherry Cake

If the cherries are weighed down with syrup they can't *help* sinking: wash them in hot water, dry in a cloth, chop and then toss lightly in about a tablespoon of the sieved, weighed flour.

Coconut Buns

Just a variety of rock bun, using desiccated coconut instead of the dried fruit and mixed peel. Allow 1½ ozs (about 40 g) to ½ lb (225 g) flour.

Coffee Kisses

The variety of rock bun I like best – although it might be difficult to spot this dull base. Omit the dried fruit and mixed peel, replace the tablespoonful of milk with 3 dessertspoons coffee essence, and roll the mixture into about 30 large marbles instead of piling it up in 12 heaps. Bake 10–15 mins in a moderate oven (cooler than for rock buns) until firm, light golden and a good brown colour underneath. Put together in pairs with coffee butter icing and top with coffee glacé icing.

Éclairs

Not as difficult and time-taking to make as they may appear, the home-made variety killing any future appetite for bought. The important thing is to make good choux, see page 101.

★ Using a ½″ (1¼ cm) plain pipe, be sure to press out with a pallet knife any pockets of air which may be trapped in the mixture in the piping bag, otherwise it's difficult to force the éclairs without the 'chain' occasionally breaking.
★ Allow the choux to cool completely before actually baking the éclairs, because they'll rise better if the mixture is cold.
★ If the choux is properly made and baked, the éclairs will be hollow. To make sure they're dried out inside, it pays to make a tiny slit in the side of each with the sharp point of a vegetable knife, after about 20 minutes cooking. If even after this the inside is still soggy, scoop it out carefully with the handle of a teaspoon, or it will spoil the éclair's texture.
★ It's usually quickest and neatest to *pipe* in the whipped cream, especially if you have many to fill. They're also easier to ice neatly if you tilt them lengthwise. Held like this over the icing basin, the chocolate glacé icing forms a straight strip down the middle, without dripping down the sides.

Flapjacks

One of the same group of cakes as gingerbread, when the fat is incorporated by melting it. The principal difference between them is that gingerbread is made with flour, flapjacks with porridge oats.

★ Brown sugar gives flapjacks more flavour and a richer, darker colour than granulated, and butter or margarine give more flavour than lard or cooking fat.

★ Flapjacks aren't difficult to make as long as you just *warm* the fat, sugar and syrup. If overheated, the mixture becomes toffee-like.

★ Although these are not true flapjacks – because it's not traditional to replace half of the porridge oats with cornflakes – this recipe (making 16) is the best I've ever come across:

3 ozs (75 g) butter or margarine
3 ozs (75 g) soft brown sugar
2 ozs (50 g) golden syrup
2 ozs (50 g) porridge oats
2 ozs (50 g) cornflakes, fresh and crisp
good pinch of salt
1 oz (25 g) chopped walnuts

(1) Melt butter over low heat, stir in and dissolve the sugar and syrup, then mix in porridge oats, cornflakes, salt and nuts.
(2) Spread evenly in greased Yorkshire pudding tin (page 27) and bake at top of preheated slow/moderate oven, gas 3, 325°F, 165°C for about 15–20 mins or until a rich golden colour.
(3) Cut into squares or fingers while very hot and leave in tin to cool.
(4) Divide up when cold and store at once in an air-tight tin.

Fruit Cakes

Those with a high proportion of fat and sugar, brown and burn more readily than plain mixtures. This explains why it pays to use a good quality tin and, when necessary, to line it with two or even three layers of greaseproof paper to come 2″ (5 cm) above the top (see page 46). I'm afraid you can't skimp on your care either, because a perfectly shaped cake doesn't turn out of a badly lined tin.

WEDDING CAKE. The original bride's cake was made from aromatic ingredients, crowned with an icing made from sweet sugar and bitter almonds, emblematic of the sweetness and pain in every marriage. When *making* a three-tier cake, if easier to make all the mixture at once, you can if necessary keep the two smaller uncooked cakes in a cold larder overnight, baking them the following day.

FRUIT CAKES IN GENERAL. Here are some tips about a few of the ingredients:

(1) Use plain flour, with raising agent if required, for cakes with a high egg content. Self-raising flour contains too *much* raising agent, giving a cake a dry, crumbly texture. As the proportion of egg increases, the amount of raising agent decreases, so that in a very rich mixture such as a wedding cake, there may be no raising agent whatever.
(2) Soft brown sugar is often used in a fruit cake. Creamed with butter, it blends just as smoothly and well as caster sugar, and in addition gives a cake more flavour and a richer, darker colour.
(3) Bicarbonate of soda used with vinegar may be the raising agent for a simple fruit cake. The bicarbonate helps to brown the cake, vinegar combining with it in the same way as does cream of tartar in scones etc.
(4) Ground almonds figure in many recipes. They help to keep a cake moist as well as giving flavour.
(5) Brandy also makes a cake moist and gives flavour. In addition, it helps a cake to keep better and longer than it otherwise would.

★ To bake a Christmas or wedding cake containing a lot of dried fruit and requiring long cooking, protect it with newspaper. It is a bad conductor of heat, so reduces the penetration of heat to the cake. It also prevents a thick crust forming on the sides and bottom of a cake:

(1) Tie several layers of newspaper round the outside of the tin.
(2) Stand cake on a thick pad of newspaper on a baking sheet.
(3) Rest a square of foil or thin card on top of cake, to protect and keep the top soft as well.
(4) Rich fruit cakes are usually baked in the coolest part of the oven, see page 251.

TO TEST WHEN COOKED. Fruit cakes are some of the most difficult to test because, with a paper-lined tin, it isn't easy to judge when the cake starts to shrink from the sides. The safest method is to stick a warmed, fine metal skewer into the centre of the cake. If it comes out quite clean, the cake is cooked. If not, cook the cake a further 10–15 mins, then test again.

★ *To cool* a cake with a high proportion of fruit, leave it in its tin. This keeps the cake moist and helps to keep the crust soft – quite a different result from the same cake cooled on a wire cooling tray. (The paper should be left on until you want to ice or eat the cake.)

★See also *Creamed mixtures*, page 251, and *Royal icing*, page 267.

Gâteau

French for *cake.* Implies in this country quite a different kind of cake from such essentially English ones as say, gingerbread, cherry, Madeira or fruit cake. Gâteaux in England, and large gâteaux on the Continent, usually describe huge feather-weight sponges with soft rich fillings and delectable icings, *or* equally irresistible works of art with a sweet-pastry base. (See *Genoese pastry*, *French flan pastry* and *Crème au beurre fillings.*) These gâteaux are classics, bearing classic names such as Gâteau Moka aux Amandes, Caravelle, Alcazar, St Honoré, usually according to their flavouring, filling and particular form of decoration.

★ A very large moule à manqué tin (page 26) is ideal for a sponge-based gâteau. Such a shape is easy to decorate artistically and will cut into a number of large servings, whether for a buffet lunch or supper, a dinner party, or for tea.

Genoese Pastry

The basic cake of the French cuisine. It is simply sponge cake – which technically is fatless – with butter added. Butter helps a sponge to keep better, giving it a moister and slightly closer texture which will crumble less when cut. This explains why Genoese is used in preference to a fatless sponge for gâteaux, petits fours and innumerable small fancy cakes collectively known as Genoese Fancies.

★ Your choice of cake tin will depend on what you want the Genoese for: a greased, lined Swiss roll tin for Genoese Fancies for instance, or something like a moule à manqué (greased, and the bottom lined) for a decorated cake or gâteau.

Genoise Commune

'Common' Genoese makes an excellent gâteau, and is also the sponge used for Genoese Fancies and Petits Fours. It has a firmer texture than the richer Genoise Fine, so for these small cakes is the easier to manipulate. Here is the recipe:

4 ozs (100 g) plain flour
pinch of salt
2 ozs (50 g) *butter*
4 large eggs, as fresh as possible
4 ozs (100 g) caster sugar

(1) Prepare tin: grease and line a Swiss roll tin, or grease and line the bottom of a moule à manqué (or other suitable) tin. Brush with melted lard and dust out with flour.
(2) Sieve the flour and salt twice, then return them to strainer, ready to sieve a third time.
(3) Melt butter over minimum heat and set aside to cool.
(4) Beat eggs and sugar 'to the ribbon' (page 54) in a mixing bowl over very hot but not boiling water.
(5) Beat for a further 2 or 3 mins aside from the heat, to cool mixture.
(6) Sift flour all over top of mixture, then very gently pour the cooled butter over this 'carpet' of flour. Using a tablespoon, fold and cut in the flour and butter together as quickly as possible, ensuring there are no pockets of flour either in bowl of spoon or at bottom of bowl.
(7) Pour at once into prepared tin, continuing to fold even while pouring, and quickly spread mixture flat.
(8) Bake a flat Genoese (in Swiss roll tin) at top, or a moule à manqué tin in middle of preheated moderate hot oven, gas 5, 375°F, 190°C until golden and cooked. For cooking times, see 'tips', point 6.
(9) Turn out, remove paper and cool on a wire tray.

★ Some tips, in case you want them:

(1) *The ingredients.*
(a) The flour should be slightly warmed, to make a light sponge. If cold, it will chill the eggs which will release some of the air just beaten in. (As air is the only raising agent in a Genoese, everything you do is directed towards incorporating and retaining as much of it as possible.)
(b) Butter, essential for flavour and to help the cake keep well, should be approximately the same temperature as the egg mixture to which it is added. If you heat rather than just melt it, it will 'oil' and separate, then won't blend properly with the other ingredients. The proportions of butter to flour may range between half and equal quantities, as in Genoise Fine. The more butter there is, the more skill required to incorporate it.
(c) Caster sugar is essential for a smooth even texture. Granulated doesn't dissolve so readily and gives the cake a speckly surface.

(2) The water in pan mustn't be deep enough to touch bottom of mixing bowl. If it does, or if it's actually boiling over heat when you beat the eggs over it, they'll cook and coagulate before you can beat air into them. The eggs need *gentle, indirect* heat if to become light and fluffy. I find it safest and easiest to take the pan of boiling water to the sink, and beat there.

(3) If you fail to spread the mixture flat in the tin, it will bake unevenly, the shallow part being overcooked before the deeper is cooked. In addition, it will spoil the shape of a gâteau, or would vary the thickness of small cakes cut from it. Some cakes find their own level, this doesn't.

(4) To cut cold Genoese with a (sharp) cutter, it's better – unlike other pastry – to twist the cutter slightly to right and left as you cut. A straight cut makes the edges ragged, crumbly and difficult to coat and decorate.

(5) *The oven* should be quite ready: preheated, with shelf in correct place, then there's no serious loss of heat when you put the cake in.

(6) *Approximate cooking times*:
3 egg mixture in a Swiss roll tin, about 12–15 mins at top of oven
3 egg mixture in an 8″ (20 cm) *top* diameter moule à manqué tin, *about* 30–40 mins, in middle of oven
4 egg mixture in a Swiss roll tin, about 15–20 mins at top of oven
4 egg mixture in a 9″ (23 cm) *top* diameter moule à manqué tin, *about* 30–40 mins in middle of oven.

(7) *Flavourings* such as lemon juice aren't used because a liquid makes the mixture heavy. Dried fruit, glacé cherries etc are never used because the mixture is too light to support them – they'd sink. You'll find in fact that flavourings such as chocolate, orange, lemon or coffee are usually added in the form of icings and fillings.

Gingerbread

One of the most popular kinds of 'melted fat' mixtures – when the melted fat, sugar and syrup are added in liquid form to the sieved flour and other ingredients.

SOME OF THE INGREDIENTS.

★ *Plain flour* is essential because the raising agent in 'self-raising' would conflict with bicarbonate of soda, which is necessary for a gingerbread's dark colour (see page 63).

★ *Golden syrup and black treacle mixed* are a good combination for flavour and colour. Black treacle by itself tends to give rather a strong bitter taste, while golden syrup alone makes an anaemic cake. It's always better to *weigh* the syrup. If gingerbread is doughy or sunken in the middle, you probably used too much.

★ *Moist brown or Demerara sugar* make a richer, better flavoured, darker coloured cake than white sugar.

★ *A pure fat* like lard, or white cooking fat such as Spry, Trex or Cookeen, makes a better gingerbread than a fat which contains water, like butter or margarine. Some people prefer good clarified dripping.

A few tips:

(1) Line the tin, otherwise with so much sugar and syrup the cake will stick to it.
(2) Just melt and warm the fat, sugar and syrup. If over-heated, the mixture may be slightly toffee-like.
(3) If you take ages to blend the syrupy liquid with the flour, the cake will have a tough shiny crust. A sharp-edged tablespoon is quicker for this job than a thick-edged wooden spoon.
(4) Avoid the natural temptation to beat the mixture like a batter. Beating frees the gluten in the flour, and the gluten – being a sticky substance – prevents the mixture from rising properly, making the cake close in texture and shiny on top.
(5) Gingerbreads – plain, rich, with fruit, nuts or spices – need a slow-to-moderate oven. In a hot oven, with such a high percentage of sugar and syrup, these would burn easily.
(6) A gingerbread *should* be 24 hours old before you cut it. When first cold, the outside is crisp and rather hard – the way *I* love it, I must admit. During storage, this crispness disappears, the cake becoming soft and slightly moist.
(7) Gingerbread deep freezes perfectly.

Madeira Cake

So called because in the nineteenth century, it was often served with a glass of Madeira, being a suitably plain version of a 'rich' cake.

★ Citron peel (slightly different from lemon peel, see page 69) is correct if available, to decorate the top, otherwise you may have to use orange or lemon. If not thinly sliced, free of sugar and put on top of the cake after the mixture has 'set', the peel will sink.
★ It is characteristic of Madeira cake to rise and crack in the centre.

Petits Fours

Little oven cakes, 'four' being French for an oven. This is why, strictly speaking, things like glacé or marzipan fruits and stuffed dates aren't actually petits fours, although they often appear in an assortment. Petits fours are therefore, correctly, only of two groups: rich and dry. The former are mainly tiny filled and/or iced cakes, usually based on choux, Genoese or French flan pastry; the latter tiny biscuit-type cakes such as tuiles, macaroons or shortbreads.

★ However you make them and whatever their shape, they should all be to a similar scale, fitting into the same-sized paper sweet cases. They are the perfect ending to a sophisticated dinner.
★See also *Genoese pastry*, page 255.

Rock Cakes

So called because of their rock-like appearance when you put them in the oven, not because of their texture when cooked! Much depends on the quantity of milk used, too much making them solid.

★ As rock cakes are the simplest example of a 'rubbed in' mixture and therefore – with varying minor alterations – the foundation of many other small cakes, you may like to have the recipe spelt out:

8 ozs (say 200 g) plain flour } or S.R. flour
1 level teasp baking powder }
1 level teasp salt
4 ozs (100 g) butter or margarine
3 ozs (75 g) granulated sugar
1 oz (25 g) mixed peel
2 ozs (50 g) currants, sultanas or seedless raisins
1 large egg
1 tablesp milk

(1) Sieve flour, baking powder and salt into mixing bowl, then rub in the fat.
(2) Add and mix in the sugar, finely chopped mixed peel and dried fruit.
(3) Using a fork, mix to a stiff dough with the mixed egg and milk, using your hand if necessary to bind the mixture together.
(4) Divide mixture into 12 equal-sized pieces and pile on a greased baking sheet in rocky heaps, roughening the

top of each with a fork.

(5) Bake *about* 15 mins at top (or hottest part) of a hot oven, gas 6, 400°F, 204°C until golden and firm. Cool on a wire tray.

★ Though unconventional, a sprinkling of Demerara sugar over the uncooked rock cakes makes them deliciously crunchy.

Sandwich Cake, Victoria

A cake dedicated to Queen Victoria, this isn't easy to make perfectly, probably because people don't cream the butter and sugar enough, aren't careful enough with the eggs (see *Creamed mixtures*), or use too hot an oven. You may find the top of a slowish oven, gas 3, 325°F, 165°C, gives more even rising and a larger, lighter cake.

★ If you have a freezer, why not make two cakes while you're about it, halving the mixture and adding two different flavourings? (See also pages 250 and 251.)

Shortbread

Not worth bothering to make unless you use butter, no other fat giving this lovely cake its characteristic flavour. Caster sugar is also necessary because granulated tends to caramelize and make a speckled cake.

★ Rice flour or ground rice helps to prevent shortbread rising, as does pricking it all over with a fork before baking.
★ With such a high proportion of sugar, shortbread needs a greased baking sheet – and it's difficult to make a *good* one without a flan ring. Uncontrolled, it tends to spread and go thin at the edges, which may get over-baked if not burnt by the time the middle is cooked.
★ To be crisp and biscuity, shortbread needs a slow oven, gas 2, 300°F, 150°C, until light golden colour. It is cooled on the baking sheet, acquiring an uncharacteristic cake-like texture if you transfer it to a wire tray.
★ Have you ever added chopped walnuts to shortbread? As long as you like walnuts, you'll like this.

Sponge Cake

Technically, a fatless sponge, used of course to make various cold sweets as well as Swiss Roll, Sponge Cakes, Fingers and Drops. With butter added, it becomes Genoese Pastry.

★ Traditionally, sponge cake has a sugary crust: simply dredge your prepared cake tin with equal quantities caster sugar and rice flour sieved together.
★ If your recipe gives a tablespoonful of hot water to a 3 egg sponge, this is thought to make a light cake.
★ See also *Genoese pastry*, page 255.

Swiss Roll

Often made with butter, though a true *sponge* is made without. If however you aren't going to eat it all the first day, butter helps it to keep both moister and longer. See *Genoese pastry*.

★ Without butter, you need a hotter oven for a shorter time than for Genoese – gas 7, 425°F, 220°C, for about 7 or 8 mins, or until golden and softly firm.
★ Waste no time once the sponge is cooked, otherwise you won't be able to roll it up. You'll find it easier to roll if you turn it upside down onto a sheet of sugared paper laid on top of a hot, wet, squeezed out tea-towel: slip off the paper quickly and carefully, cutting off the cake's edges with a sharp knife before spreading the sponge with jam and rolling it up. If you're slow, the edges will go crisp as they cool, making the sponge crack when you roll it.
★ With the 'end' tucked underneath, leave the hot tightly-rolled sponge in paper on the cake cooling tray for a minute or two, to 'set' slightly and prevent it unrolling, *then* unwrap it and leave to cool.

Swiss Roll, Chocolate

Better not attempted before mastering a

plain roll. It needs butter because, if fatless, it is difficult to roll and unroll without splitting.

★ As butter icing obviously can't be spread on the hot sponge, the sponge must be pliable enough to unroll and fill when cold: one way to do this is to roll it rather loosely the first time, leaving it in the paper like a plain Swiss Roll for a minute or two. Now unroll and roll it up again (without the paper), doing this once or twice more, as it cools.

★ If you like nuts, fold in 1 oz (25 g) of chopped walnuts after the flour; or if you like Arctic Roll, spread the sponge with ice cream instead of butter icing, wrapping it first in foil and then in polythene, to freeze. Thaw at least 10–15 mins before required.

CHOCOLATE LOG. Simply a chocolate Swiss Roll piped lengthwise with butter icing or chocolate crème au beurre. A tablespoon of sherry perks up the icing and it's easier to pipe if you start at the bottom of one side, not on the top.

Tartlets

CHERRY and other fruit tartlets should be made with flan or French flan pastry because both of these stay crisp and short, unlike shortcrust which is toughened by liquid from the fruit.

★ The fruit syrup makes a bright, clear and tasteless glaze when thickened with arrowroot; unlike cornflour, which has its own rather distinctive flavour, and makes a cloudy glaze.

JAM TARTLETS. End up about the same size as the bun tins if you use a fluted cutter one size larger, to allow for the pastry shrinking slightly.

★ Each needs very little jam, otherwise it boils up over the edges when they're baked. Be mean with it.

Tuiles

French for tiles, these biscuity cakes are shaped like curved tiles, over a rolling pin. Serve them at tea-time, with morning coffee, or better still as contrasting texture with a soft cold sweet like zabaglione, syllabub, fool, or apple snow.

★ I wouldn't try to put more than four at a time on a well greased baking sheet because, like brandy snaps, you have to catch them at the right moment for shaping because they quickly cool and go brittle. Watch them like a hawk when nearly cooked: one moment they're perfect, the next, overdone. They should be just brown round the edges, still dark-straw-coloured in the middle. Incidentally, if you spread them too thick on the baking sheet, you won't be *able* to shape them.

★ Lift each carefully but quickly on a pallet knife, and shape them one by one over a rolling pin, pressing the 'tile' round it with a cloth, rather than with your hand, to shape it. Pop them at once into an airtight tin when cold because they *must* be crisp. (It's usually for their texture that they're served.)

★ Shape tiny tuiles for petits fours over the handle of a wooden spoon.

Vanilla Slices

An enjoyable way to grow fat. The way *I* like them best is spread with royal icing *before* you bake them. This means rolling the pastry very thin, otherwise the icing will burn before the pastry is cooked.

★ A small packet of thawed frozen puff pastry ($7\frac{1}{2}$ ozs – say 200 g) will make about a dozen. Here's what to do:

(1) Cut the very thinly rolled pastry into equal-sized rectangles.

(2) *Spread* each almost to the edges with a quickly made, thick royal icing – sieved icing sugar, softened with egg white. (If too thin, it will run off and seal the edges, preventing pastry from rising perfectly.)

(3) Bake about 7–12 mins on a wetted baking sheet in a hot oven, gas 7, 425°F, 220°C, or until the pastry is golden and the icing caramelled.

(4) Cool. Split, spread lower half with apricot or raspberry jam, and whipped cream or Crème Chantilly. Put body and soul together again.

18

CAKE ICINGS AND FILLINGS

General Information

Fillings and icings can transform the plainest cake. What for instance is simpler than a Genoese sponge, yet what more elaborate than the rich gâteau it can become? Time taking? Yes, but for anyone with a freezer and a mixer, it's seldom much extra work to step up the quantities and prepare enough fillings and trimmings for three or four cakes while you're about it.

★ With one or two Genoese or sandwich cakes in the freezer as well, even producing quite a sophisticated gâteau becomes more a matter of assembly than of labour. It just doesn't make sense – to *my* mind – to toil so much for one filling when you can equally well make and freeze more.
★ A few tips may be of help:

(1) Try to make fillings and icings harmonise or contrast with the flavour and texture of the cake.

(2) Cakes made in a moule à manqué tin are easy to ice professionally. The icing will flow smoothly and gradually down the outward sloping sides, instead of dropping down as over the edge of a precipice, leaving gaps.

(3) If a cake is over-baked or a bad shape, doctor it:
(a) Where too brown, rub carefully with a very fine grater.
(b) If 'peaked', level the top and turn the cake upside down to ice.
(c) If one side is deeper than the other, be generous with a filling and reassemble the cake so that it's flat, the thick part of the top over the thin of the bottom.

(4) Before splitting a cake to fill, cut a tiny vertical wedge somewhere up the side, then it's easy to reassemble as it was.

(5) A turntable helps you to give wedding or Christmas cakes etc a professional finish.

(6) It's usually easier, except with fondant, to ice a cake on an inverted large plate than on a cake tray.

(7) Sieve icing sugar, however fine. The tiniest lumps make an icing look rough, and the most microscopic will obstruct an icing tube. The longest way round is the shortest way home.

(8) If you can be bothered, brush a sandwich or sponge cake over with apricot glaze (page 262) before covering with glacé or fondant icing.

(9) Use colourings sparingly. They tend to darken when icing sets, and it's easy to add an extra drop but quite a performance to tone down a colour. You won't go far wrong if you dip the point of a hat pin or fine skewer into the bottle of colouring, then shake the drop off into the icing.

(10) Keep covered with a piece of damp cloth any icing you aren't using straight away. Once exposed to air, the surface soon dries out, then when you stir it, lumps get into the icing.

(11) Prick any air bubbles with a hat pin as soon as they form.

★ See also *Paper icing bags*, page 1, and *Icing tubes*, page 27.

Almond Paste (Marzipan)

Can be made with yolks, whites, or whole egg, depending on what you want it for. Yolk for instance is ideal for marzipan on a Christmas or wedding cake to be coated with royal icing, giving a lovely flavour and a rich golden colour. Egg white gives no flavour but a sharper, clearer colour than yolk if you're making *coloured* marzipan. It's a matter of primary colours, as with paints.

★ A few hints may be of help:

(1) A *mixture* of caster and icing sugar is essential to give almond paste its correct texture and to make it easy to manipulate. For icing a cake, it should be firm enough to roll and handle, but not so dry that it will crack.

(2) In uncooked almond paste, be sure to use the full amount of sugar, to preserve the raw egg.

(3) Almond or ratafia essence helps to bring out the full flavour of the ground almonds.

(4) Orange flower water gives fragrance.

(5) If you 'over-work' marzipan, the ground almonds will release too much oil, making the mixture sticky and difficult to roll out. A little extra sugar may correct it.

(6) Use caster sugar on pastry board and rolling pin. Flour spoils marzipan.

(7) Keep the marzipan covered with foil, polythene or an upturned basin if you're working with only *some* of it. Uncovered, it soon dries out.

(8) To colour almond paste is sometimes easier said than done – successfully. The tricky part is to blend the colour perfectly with the paste so that it will neither look streaky from under-working, nor be oily from over-working. Here's one way to do it:
(a) Add as many – or as few – drops of colouring to the paste as you think necessary.
(b) Roll the paste into a long sausage, knot the ends together, then squash it a little.
(c) Roll again into a sausage, knot and squash. Continue in this way until the colour is completely blended.

(9) If not covering almond paste with royal icing, give it a professional finish by brushing with gum arabic solution (see page 266).

(10) Brush a fruit cake over with egg white or apricot glaze before covering with almond paste, to control any loose crumbs and to make the icing stick to the cake.

American Frosted Icing

Can be used on almost any type of cake from a light sponge to a Christmas cake. Firm and crisp outside, it is soft underneath, and bland enough to team up with almost any flavour of cake – splendid for a child's birthday.

★ Some tips:

(1) Prepare cake decorations in advance, ready to place without delay.

(2) A thermometer saves guesswork: if the syrup doesn't reach a high enough temperature, the icing won't set. If *over-heated* it will set too hard.

(3) Timing is important: aim to have the egg whites whisked very stiffly just as the syrup reaches 238°–240°F, 115°–116°C, then there's no delay in using it.

(4) Pour the syrup from a *height* onto the whisked egg whites (whisking as you do so), to cool the syrup as it falls. If you hold the pan too close, the boiling syrup will cook and coagulate the whites, which will go lumpy instead of meringue-like.

(5) Whisking takes several minutes, until the icing is a light spreading consistency. You can tell when it's ready to use because it changes in texture and appearance from a shiny soft mixture to a dull very light texture, not unlike cotton wool. If you don't whisk it enough, you'll find yourself *pouring* it over the cake, or if you

whisk it too long, the icing will harden before you can coat the cake.

(6) Use quick bold strokes to spread the frosting before it sets. If coating a Christmas cake, swirl it in peaks.

(7) Allow to cool and set before eating, otherwise it won't have its characteristic texture.

BROWN SUGAR FROSTING. Similar to American Frosted Icing, but use Demerara instead of granulated sugar, and boil the syrup slightly higher, to 248°F, 120°C.

Apricot Glaze

Useful to brush over sponge cakes of all kinds before coating with glacé or fondant icing. You can also use it on a Christmas cake to make almond paste stick, or to seal the inside of a baked pastry case before putting in a damp filling which would otherwise spoil the pastry.

★ Brushed over cakes, it prevents any cake crumbs finding their way into the icing, helps icing to run smoothly over a cake, and prevents icing from going dull – because the cake doesn't so readily absorb moisture from the icing.

★ Use it hot so that you can brush it on evenly, but be sure to let it cool and set before *icing* a cake, otherwise it will melt the icing.

★ Store any unused glaze in a covered container, reheating it to use when required.

Butter Cream Fillings

See *Crème au beurre*, next page.

Butter Icing

Has the best flavour when made with saltless butter. You can use as little as half butter to sugar, or as much as equal quantities of each, depending on how rich you like or want it, but of course if you don't use *icing* sugar, the icing won't have its characteristic smooth texture.

★ If you beat the butter until soft and light before adding the icing sugar, a spoonful at a time, the sugar is less likely to fly everywhere. The bonus of creaming them until your arm aches, if you've no electric mixer, is a larger amount of icing – because of all the air beaten in – and a light fluffy mixture which will spread or pipe easily.

★ The colour generally indicates the flavour of a butter icing, and certain decorations tend to team up with that flavour, see below:

Colour of Icing	*Usual flavour*	*Sort of decoration*
pink	vanilla	glacé cherries
white	vanilla, or almond and/ or ratafia essence	glacé cherries, or almonds
green	almond and/or ratafia essence, or peppermint	almonds chocolate
orange	orange juice and finely grated rind	angelica, mimosa or chocolate vermicelli etc.
pale yellow	lemon juice and finely grated rind	mimosa, angelica etc.
coffee	coffee essence	nuts – browned almonds or walnuts etc.
chocolate	melted chocolate, or cocoa and vanilla ess.	nuts or chocolate of some kind

Coffee Icing

Best and most easily made with coffee essence. Allow about 1 teasp 'Camp' coffee and 2–3 teasps warm water to 4 ozs (100 g) sieved icing sugar.

Crème au Beurre

An icing, a filling, or both, which you can vary with all kinds of flavourings to make the sort of sponge gâteau one dreams about. Rich and ruthless for the figure, these Butter Creams are really neither very extravagant nor too difficult to make and usually emerge from a freezer as well as they go in, as long as you don't add nuts, which go soft. Use crème au beurre also to decorate Genoese Fancies, petits fours or butterfly cakes, to fill meringues, to fill *and* ice a sandwich cake, or to ice a chocolate log etc. There's no end to the times you can use them, and they are icings which by and large pipe or spread superbly because of their smooth, almost mayonnaise-like texture.

★ Two variations are made with egg yolks, another with egg whites, or there's a different, less good version made with Crème Anglaise. Their basic ingredients are butter, sugar, eggs and a flavouring.

BUTTER. Saltless is best, for its flavour. Have it at warm-room temperature, otherwise you may find it is difficult to blend but very ready to curdle.

ICING SUGAR. Gives this filling its characteristic smooth texture, but granulated is used when making the version with sugar dissolved in water.

EGGS. Should be fresh enough to whisk well, otherwise you can't trap enough air to make the icing fluffy and light.

FLAVOURING. Rather depends on the *type* of crème au beurre because some will accept more liquid than others. When using lemon or orange, zest is better than rind because it contains no bitter pith, won't spoil the smooth texture of the icing, and won't block an icing tube so easily.

★ If a butter cream is too soft to use when first made, chill it in a cold larder until of spreading or piping consistency.
★ These are my three favourite kinds:

(1) CRÈME AU BEURRE MÉNAGÈRE or HOUSEHOLD BUTTER CREAM. Richer and I think not *so* light or quite so good as the other two, but is child's play to make if you have a mixer. It's so easy in fact, I will jot down the recipe: Beat together at moderate speed for about 5 mins or until smooth and light 6 ozs (150 g) cut-up soft butter, 3 ozs (75 g) sieved icing sugar and 2 egg yolks. Then *gradually* beat in your chosen flavouring, eg
2 tablesps Grand Marnier (*my* favourite)
2 tablesps rum or kirsch
2 teasps coffee essence
1½ tablesps lemon juice and zest of ½ lemon
2 ozs (50 g) melted plain dessert chocolate (stir this all in at once, before it sets).

(2) CRÈME AU BEURRE À LA MERINGUE. Most easily made with an electric hand-whisk. Be careful not to rest the basin over a pan of water which is either boiling or too deep, otherwise the heat will cook and coagulate the whites before you can whisk air into them.

★ If you don't whisk the meringue long enough, until it stands in peaks, or if you don't then whisk it aside from the heat until it's *cold*, it won't thicken properly when you beat in the butter bit by bit.
★ Flavour it with zest of orange or lemon, melted chocolate, coffee essence or browned nuts.

(3) CRÈME AU BEURRE MOUSSELINE. A truly heavenly filling but not easy to make without a thermometer because the syrup has to be boiled exactly to 216°–218°F, 102°–103°C.

★ Many recipes tell you to add the butter to the 'mousse', but it's much less likely to curdle if you do it the other way round and add the mousse, spoonful by spoonful, to the soft, well-beaten butter.
★ Hold the pan high above the *well-beaten* yolks as you slowly pour and whisk the hot syrup onto them, because if it's too hot when it lands on them, the yolks will cook and coagulate before you can beat

air into them. Another pitfall is that if you don't whisk the mixture thick enough at this stage – to the ribbon – you'll end up with something more like a liquid than a 'mousse'.

★ You can use all sorts of flavourings with Mousseline, usually adding the one of your choice to the made mousse. These are the quantities I use:

2½ ozs (say 70 g) granulated sugar
3 tablesps water
2 large egg yolks
5 ozs (say 140 g) *butter*
flavouring of choice

Zest of 1 lemon or orange and about 1 tablesp juice, to taste
Zest of 1 orange and about 2 tablesps Grand Marnier
Rum, kirsch or cassis to taste
2 ozs (50 g) melted plain dessert chocolate
2–4 ozs (50–100 g) praline, pounded
2–4 ozs (50–100 g) browned almonds or hazel-nuts
about 2 tablesps sieved fresh strawberries or raspberries.

★You can't pipe very successfully with nuts of course!

Crème Patissière

Also known as *Pastry Cream* or *Confectioner's Custard.* As its name suggests, a good filling for something like a flan, a fruit vol-au-vent or éclairs. It's useful because you can flavour it in various ways, it will refrigerate several days, or deep freezes perfectly. It also makes a creamy pouring custard if liquidized.

★ Be sure to pour the milk gradually onto the well-beaten yolks, sugar and flour, so that the yolks are gently warmed rather than suddenly cooked.

★ The starch in the flour, cornflour, potato flour or whatever you use, prevents the custard from curdling when boiled, as it must be, to *cook* the starch.

★ If you want to use pastry cream cold, dot the top with a little softened butter to stop a skin forming – caused by evaporation from the surface. Alternatively, cover with a disc of foil, or stir the custard frequently as it cools.

★ Add a spoonful or two of cream when the custard is cold, if you can spare it. It's worth it, to give richness, flavour and a silky-smooth texture.

Crème St Honoré

Although used also in tarts, cream puffs and as a dessert cream, this was first made as a custard cream filling for Gâteau St Honoré. That commemorates a one-time Bishop of Amiens, considered to be the patron saint of pastrycooks and bakers.

★ You'll need a recipe, but it is just an elaborate version of Crème Patissière, with stiffly whisked egg whites added to the cooked mixture. This won't thin out and collapse as you might fear because the egg whites coagulate with the heat, then holding their firm texture like cooked meringue.

★ If you can't spare as many egg whites as this recipe calls for, use fewer. (If nothing else, a smaller number will make Crème Patissière go further.) Flavour Crème St Honoré with a liqueur, orange zest, chocolate, praline or whatever your recipe calls for. If serving it cold, it should be well chilled.

Fondant Icing

The perfect icing for a light sponge, for example gâteaux, petits fours or Genoese fancies. The icing cuts easily because it remains soft – important when the cake underneath is feathery-light. Before icing a sponge, for best results, first brush the top with apricot glaze (see page 262).

★ A few tips:

(1) Make more icing than you need, allowing 1 lb (450 g) sugar for the average-size cake. Stored in a plastic bowl with lid, any surplus icing will keep perfectly for future use on small cakes. Made at least a day or two before you need it, the icing will mature and improve.

(2) If you're lucky enough to have a marble slab, this – well damped – is the ideal thing on which to make

fondant: it is better than anything else because it cools the syrup quickly, is steady as a rock to work on, and makes manipulation of the syrup easy. Using a wetted mixing bowl is more time-taking because the syrup takes longer both to cool and to 'work'.

(3) Make the syrup in the usual way (see page 275), boiling it to 238°–240°F, 115°–116°C, then plunge bottom of pan into cold water to halt cooking. Liquid glucose or cream of tartar in it is used as a deterrent to the crystallization of the sugar.

(4) When the syrup stops bubbling, pour it in a steady stream onto your marble slab, butcher's tray or whatever, leaving any final scrapings in the pan as these are liable to crystallize.

(5) The syrup must be at the right temperature when you start 'working' it. If too hot, the fondant will be rough and sugary. If too cold, you won't be able to manipulate it.

(6) The aim is to make the syrup opaque and firm: on a flat surface, work it from the sides to the centre with a pallet knife or wooden spatula. In a bowl, mix it intensively with a wooden spoon in a repeated figure-of-eight movement.

(7) When the syrup has 'turned', knead it (press with your fingertips) until smooth, small lumps at a time, keeping the remainder covered with a damp cloth to prevent drying out. (If it goes hard, cover with a damp cloth, leave ½ hr and then knead.) When you've got it all soft, in one lump now, cover with a damp cloth or put in an airtight container until required.

(8) *Warming* the icing ready for use can be tricky. If you over-heat it, it will be hard and will lose its gloss: if not made warm enough it won't set well. It's quicker but more risky to warm it over direct heat, slow but sure to melt it over hot (not boiling) water, taking it *off* the water at intervals to prevent it getting too hot. Resist the temptation to *beat* it, as this traps air which will make your icing full of bubbles.

(9) The correct consistency is essential. If too thick, the icing will set on the sides of a cake before you can coat them properly. It should be thick enough to coat a wooden spoon smoothly, and when trailed back into the bowl, the trail should disappear quite quickly. Thin it down, if necessary, with warm stock syrup. (You *can* use warm water, but the icing won't be so smooth and glossy.)

(10) Colour and flavour fondant as you like (see page 262 for combinations).

(11) If you ice a cake, or small cakes, on a cake cooling tray over a large mixing bowl, you can save and re-use the drippings another time.

(12) Pour fondant all at once over top of a cake, if necessary tilting or tapping briskly the cake tray to make the icing flow evenly down the sides.

Frosting and Icing

Words used interchangeably in America, although in England we always talk of icing a cake.

Glacé Icing

Takes its name from the French *glacer*, in cookery meaning 'to ice' or 'glaze'. If you want glacé icing to *stay* glossy, first brush a sandwich cake with apricot glaze (page 262).

★ Some people mix their icing with stock syrup to make it smooth and glossy, while others mix a few drops of oil with the liquid. Whatever you use, if the liquid is warm, it will help to melt the icing sugar.

★ I like a sweet-sour icing, if I may call it that, on something simple like a sandwich or coconut cake – icing sugar mixed with lemon juice. Unlike water, this gives some flavour and 'bite', even if it doesn't stay glossy long.

★ As far as possible, colourings and flavourings should match (see page 262).

CHOCOLATE GLACÉ ICING. Better

made with cooking chocolate than 'dessert' because it's softer when set and doesn't go so dull (see page 67). If however you do use 'dessert', add a peanut sized piece of butter or a few drops of salad oil to give the icing a smoother, more glossy finish.

★ If because of its flavour you prefer to use dessert chocolate, I'd choose a recipe calling for a good-sized piece of butter. This not only helps to keep the icing soft but in addition makes it deliciously fudgy.
★ Should you like the flavour of peppermint, why not sometimes add a few drops of oil of peppermint to your icing?

Gum Arabic

Excellent amongst other things for glazing almond paste. This is intriguing stuff – crystals which will dissolve in water and form a solution.

★ $\frac{1}{2}$ oz (15 g) crystals will be enough to glaze the coloured almond paste on a Christmas cake, or lots of sweets or cake decorations *modelled* in almond paste.
★ To use it:

(1) Wash the crystals in a fine strainer, to prevent them making the solution dirty, then crush with a rolling pin to make dissolve more quickly.
(2) Put crystals in something like a Colman's glass mustard jar which is small and not too thick, then cover with 3–4 dessertsps very hot but not boiling water. Stand this in a basin of hot water and stir frequently, replacing water in basin as it cools.
(3) In about an hour, or when the crystals form a sticky solution, strain it through butter muslin and use. (If making a larger quantity, use a double saucepan over minimum heat.)
(4) Colour solution now, if you like, before painting on the almond paste like varnish, preferably with a top-quality paint brush. (Use it colourless for coloured almond paste.)
(5) Covered, in something like a chemist's tiny pill bottle, any surplus will keep for weeks. See also page 75.

FROST. Looks attractive sprinkled over the top of a red Christmas cake for instance.

★ To make: Using a paint brush, spread the gum arabic solution thin as a film over a shiny-surfaced dish, leaving it to dry gradually. When it looks 'crazed', scrape off with a pallet knife and store in a small sealed container until required. (If you spread the solution too thickly, it forms a plastic-like sheet, or if you use a rough surfaced dish, it won't form a film.)

Lemon Curd Filling

Delicious for a sandwich cake, sponge gâteau, flan, tartlets or meringues, especially if the lemon curd is home-made: simply stir 4 tablesps lemon curd into $\frac{1}{4}$ pt (125 ml) softly whipped cream.

Marbling or Feather Icing

An attractive but very economical way to decorate an iced cake or biscuits: make a little more icing than needed to coat the cake, then put the extra in a small basin. Colour this, and with a little icing sugar added, make it very slightly stiffer before putting in a paper icing bag with its tip cut off. Ice the cake in the usual way, but quickly, before the icing sets, pipe the *coloured* icing in straight lines across it, at regular intervals apart, see Fig. 1. Now run a hat pin or fine skewer *across* these lines at similar intervals, first in one direction, then the other. Where the lines cross each other, they'll be 'pulled', making a sort of zig-zag pattern, see Figs. 2 and 3.

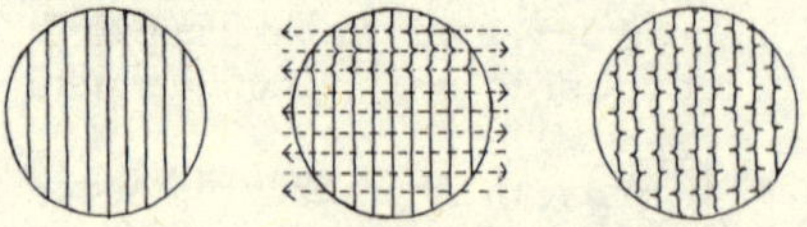

1 *2* *3*

Marzipan

From the French *massepain*, a mixture thought to have been made originally by an order of nuns. See *Almond paste*, page 261.

Pastry Cream

See *Crème patissière*, page 264.

Royal Icing

Needs to be harder for a wedding cake than for a Christmas or birthday cake, both to support the weight of other tiers and to preserve the cake. A similar hard icing, made entirely with egg whites, is also the only one you can use successfully for elaborate piping such as trellis-work.

★ A few general tips may be helpful:

(1) Avoid using an aluminium mixing bowl because it gives icing a greyish cast.

(2) 1 teasp glycerine or pure honey per lb (450 g) of icing sugar, prevents the icing from becoming rock-hard.

(3) Add a drop or two of blue colouring to give an illusion of whiteness. Alternatively, use a few drops of 'laundry blue', or a few grains scraped from it.

(4) Beat a 'hard' icing until it will stand up in *straight* peaks when you lift a wooden spoon sharply out of it.

(5) It is quicker and less strenuous to use an electric mixer than to beat by hand, providing you don't let the icing get full of bubbles. To avoid these, beat the whites with just *half* the icing sugar at *slow* speed for only 5–7 mins until light and fluffy, then stir in remaining icing sugar by hand.

(6) If too stiff, thin down royal icing with egg white, not with water.

(7) Even while you're working with it, keep closely covered with a thick damp cloth any icing still in the basin – to prevent contact with air, which will make it set. Icing will in fact keep like this for weeks, as long as the cloth is kept damp. You can then use this icing as it is, or thin it down whenever you want to with more egg white. For example, any surplus from the first coating on a cake, can be thinned down a week later as part of the second coating.

(8) Using a hat pin, prick at once any air bubbles which form in the icing.

(9) If possible, leave an iced cake to dry in a warm airy room. The faster it dries, the whiter it will be.

(10) You can model royal icing like almond paste, providing it's stiff enough, to make things like Christmas roses, lilies of the valley or a bow of ribbon.

Sugar, Coloured

Not a real icing of course, but a quick and colourful substitute, if you first brush the top of a cake with egg white, to make the sugar stick.

★ Use 2 or 3 drops of colouring per rounded tablesp sugar: put the sugar on a piece of waxed paper (say a piece from a cornflake box) and, with your fingertips, work the colouring evenly into it.

Sugar, Icing

Can be sprinkled evenly over things like pastries or cakes from a tea-strainer if you're without a sugar sifter.

★ To make an attractive pattern on the top of a cake with icing sugar, lay a doyley on it then dredge with sugar and lift doyley carefully off. The icing will gradually dissolve, so don't prepare *too* soon.

19
BEVERAGES

Beverages – only three included here – play a great part in our lives. Besides replacing water lost by the body in various ways, they are a central part of hospitality, warm us up when we are cold, refresh us when we are hot. Some help to rouse us in the morning, others to sleep or keep us awake when we're tired, even to calm us down when suffering from shock. We cannot *live* without drink.

Cocoa

In the tropical regions of America, the cocoa tree was cultivated even in prehistoric times. The Aztecs of Mexico and the Incas of Peru dried the beans in the sun, roasted them in pots, crushed and kneaded them into cakes. Using carved wooden beaters, the cakes were mixed together with water, vanilla and spices to make a cold drink. The beans were at one time even used as money, a hundred being enough to buy a slave.

★ Cortez, after conquering Mexico, brought back cocoa beans to Spain, and with them the secret of making a drink. Not until over a century later however, in 1650, did the English learn to make it.

★ Cocoa and Drinking Chocolate are less stimulating but more nourishing than tea or coffee. In addition, from the health angle, they conceal the flavour of milk, even making it tempting as a hot drink or an iced chocolate milk shake to the child who doesn't want food or *dislikes* milk.

★ Because of the starch in it, some cookery books recommend quickly boiling cocoa after making, to give it more body and improve its flavour. Rowntree Mackintosh, the experts, disagree with this, saying that as the amount of starch is comparatively low, it in fact makes virtually no difference to the drink's thickness, and spoils rather than improves the flavour of the milk.

★ See also *Chocolate*, page 67.

Coffee

Legend has it, according to Twinings, that 'Coffee would never have been discovered at all if the superior of an Abyssinian monastery had not remarked upon the extreme liveliness of his goats when they had browsed upon the leaves of a certain plant which grew nearby. His monks were far less lively; indeed, they tended all too often to fall asleep over their devotions. So the abbot tried on them a decoction of the plant's berries: with the happiest results because the monks became models of wide-awake piety, and their fame – and that of the coffee berry – spread far and wide'.

★ The coffee berry has no rivals but the secret of course is that coffee and tea contain caffeine, a drug just strong enough to give a fillip, yet mild enough that we can drink it daily throughout our lives without any ill effect. Coffee and tea divide the world between them and, say some people, national drinks and national characteristics seem to go together, so strong are the effects of wine which sends one to sleep, coffee which wakens one up, or tea with its sense of well-being.

★ Coffee drinking began in England in 1637, the first coffee house being opened in Oxford a few years later. Coffee houses then soon opened up in London, becoming centres of social, cultural and political activity. It was from one of these two thousand, in Tower Street, started by Edward Lloyd around 1688, that Lloyd's the underwriters originated. The word 'tip' is also said to have originated in the coffee houses: boxes nailed on the wall bore the words 'To Insure Promptness' so that those wanting quick service could, by payment *into* the box, receive it.

★ The English may excel at making puddings, if not at making coffee. Many retailers, housewives and consumers are alas so uninformed that, even using better quality coffee, we make a drink inferior to that of coffee-drinking countries using poorer beans. To get the full benefit out of the coffee berry it *must* be skilfully roasted, so it pays to buy your coffee from a coffee specialist.

★ Here are some tips from an expert:

(1) Buy in small quantities and store in an airtight container. If not fresh, coffee is a different drink.

(2) Coffee should be crystal clear: if the water actually boils, the coffee will be cloudy and its flavour spoilt. This explains why percolators make comparatively poor coffee, since they can't 'perk' *without* boiling. The Melitta system, using filters, may make much better coffee in a fraction of the time and at lower fuel cost.

(3) Keep the inside of your coffee jug or percolator clean. A 'build-up' makes coffee bitter.

(4) Use a measured quantity of coffee to water, according to your own personal taste: a good proportion is 2 heaped tablesps to 1 pt (500 ml) water.

(5) Avoid making coffee in anything aluminium. This spoils both flavour and colour.

(6) Be careful never to boil hot milk. It changes in flavour and spoils the coffee. You can add cream or a little cold or hot milk, but don't use too much or you will lose the fine flavour of the coffee.

(7) Expensive equipment isn't necessary to make good coffee. For perfect results:
(a) Measure coffee into a *warmed* earthenware or china jug or coffee pot.
(b) Pour on the freshly boiled water, stir well and stand it for 5 mins in a warm place.
(c) Draw a spoon across the surface to skim the coffee grounds, then leave a further minute to develop full flavour.
(d) Strain into cups or a warmed coffee pot, pouring gently, stirring the coffee just before serving if a large quantity. (It tends to settle, the thin on top, thick on bottom.)
(e) Add milk, cream or sugar to taste.
(f) Never reheat coffee. The flavour completely changes – for the worse.

SPICED ICED COFFEE. Cool, creamy and delicious, this is how you make it:

(1) Make 2 pts (say 1 L) double or treble strength coffee and flavour with the pared rind of ½ orange. (Soak it in the very hot coffee, stirring coffee occasionally as it cools.)

(2) Strain and chill coffee.

(3) Stir, pour into long glasses, add a ball of vanilla ice cream and top with whipped cream and a hint of grated nutmeg.

(4) Serve with a cinnamon stick, to stir.

GAELIC COFFEE. May light up your evening!

(1) Warm a stemmed whisky goblet and pour in one measure of Irish whiskey. Add 3 cubes sugar.

(2) Fill goblet with strong black coffee to within 1″ (2½ cm) of the brim, stirring to dissolve sugar.

(3) Top off to brim with double cream poured carefully over the back of a spoon, so that it floats on top of the coffee. (Don't stir, as the best flavour is obtained by drinking the coffee and whiskey through the cream.)

HIGHLAND COFFEE. Similar to Gaelic, but uses Scotch whisky.

COFFEE NAPOLEON. Brandy instead of whisky.

COFFEE BALALAIKA. Vodka instead of whisky.

Tea

Tscha, Ch'a, Tcha – Chinese names for tea from which our word 'char' derives.

★ Introduced to the Western world barely three centuries ago by the Dutch – who in the East had learnt the habit of tea-drinking from the Chinese – tea is thought to have had a practical origin: the Chinese for centuries had had to boil their drinking water, so to mask its unpleasant taste, they started flavouring it with herbs. Extraordinary it is that this one particular leaf, also found to have strong medicinal qualities, should have completely overshadowed all others, to become one of the two daily beverages of the majority of mankind.

★ When first brought to England, tea was so heavily taxed that only the rich could afford it, so when Twinings started serving it in their first coffee house in 1706, it was more as a sideline and a gimmick than as anything else. Not until the duty was removed in 1784 did the British people really begin to drink tea, so that by the early 1900's the 'cuppa' was part of life and a panacea in any time of stress.

★ When tea was at its most costly, tea-caddies – the word derives from the Malayan work 'kati', a measure of weight – were designed to store it under lock and key. Often divided into two sections, one for 'green' tea and one for 'black', the châtelaine herself kept the key, she it was who made the tea, and so it was that afternoon tea parties became the fashion.

★ What most of us classify as Indian tea includes tea from India, Africa, Indonesia, Malaya etc, whose teas are

Blend	*Origin*	*Characteristics*
EARL GREY A blend of fine Oriental teas with flavouring	A secret blend of Indian and Chinese teas with flavouring, passed to Earl Grey by a Chinese Mandarin over 125 years ago	Delicately scented, producing a pale clear liquor
DARJEELING A blend of Darjeeling and other fine teas	Darjeeling teas are grown in the Himalayan foothills of India	Muscatel flavour
LAPSANG SOUCHONG A blend of Lapsang Souchong and other fine teas	A blend from the Province of Fukien, in China	Large leaf, pale liquor, slightly smoky flavour ar aroma
KEEMUN A blend of Keemun and other fine teas	The tea of Old Imperial China	Produces a light liquor – delicately flavoured – fre tannin
ASSAM A blend of Assam and other fine teas	Assam teas are grown in the Assam region of Northern India	Produces a full coloured – the traditional British tea at its best

grown from Assam seed. China teas include Keemuns and Lapsang Souchongs and other various exotic teas which are grown from China seed. Ceylon and Darjeeling teas were grown originally with China seed. Indian teas contain more tannin than China. Green teas, unfermented teas from China, contain none.

★ Tea varies not only from country to country, soil to soil and plantation to plantation, but also literally from one day to another on the same plantation, according to the rain. In low lying districts, plucking takes place about once every seven days – sometimes every 4 days – so any week's picking may be different from either the previous or the next. Yet *we* always expect to buy the same tea under a particular label! It is because a tea-taster will know precisely which leaves will blend with which, in never ending different combinations and in precisely the right proportions, that we can do so. The speed at which he tests scores of teas a day, his acute palate, his memory and infinite knowledge about tea together enable us to buy any specified tea with consistent qualities.

★ Just as you'd choose a wine for its flavour, bouquet, colour, the food with which it is to be served, the time of day, or your preferences, so it should be with tea. There are different teas for all occasions: a delicately flavoured tea, so lovely and cooling on a hot summer's day, isn't the one to make you sit up at breakfast; a stimulating strong Indian tea which *is* just right for breakfast, is certainly not the one to go to sleep on. I find the different characteristics of tea so absorbing that you *also* may enjoy knowing what Britain's oldest tea merchant says about some kinds you'll know well.

★ Considering that we make tea countless times a week for years and years on end, you'd think we'd all be specialists. Many people are of course, but one doesn't have to be a connoisseur to know that a great

How to Serve	*When to Serve* *As a Drink*	*Special Dishes*
Hot with a drop of milk, or a slice of fresh lemon. Sugar optional	As afternoon tea	Good with shortbread and dainty sandwiches
Hot, with milk or lemon and sugar to your liking. Iced, just with a slice of fresh lemon	Mid-morning break In summer	Excellent after a curry
Hot – without milk or sugar Iced – with a slice of fresh lemon	During the day, when you've time to enjoy the special flavour. In summer, in the garden	At its best with Chinese or Japanese food – drunk throughout the meal and with spicy foods For any special occasion
Hot – with a dash of milk but no sugar	Afternoon tea	Accompanying Chinese food
Hot, with milk and sugar	Early morning, and for breakfast	Family tea

By courtesy of Twinings of London

many aren't! Here's hoping that you experts will forgive me for passing on a specialist's tips for the benefit of those less well informed:

TEA. Will keep fresh for 18 months – 2 years if in an airtight container and kept dry. It goes without saying that a good cup of tea starts with good *quality* tea. Use the quantity *you* like – one teasp per person and one for the pot may be too little for some, or too much for others. Why not try blending your own, say 1 part Earl Grey and 3 parts Darjeeling, to have the flavour and aroma of the former, with the stimulation and darker colour of the latter?

THE TEAPOT. Should be as clean inside as out, otherwise a 'layer' builds up, making all teas taste bitter.

★ A china teapot makes the best tea. It scores too over silver or stainless steel because you can tell at a glance if the inside is clean. China takes more warming than metal though, which perhaps explains why people who forget to warm it well first, think china teapots make *poor* tea.

★ Aluminium turns tea blue, and if an enamel pot is chipped, the iron will react on the tea.

SUGAR. Spoils the flavour of a good tea – but gives extra energy if that's what you need. A leading authority once said 'It would be almost as rational to add cream and sugar to wine as to fine and delicately flavoured tea.'

MILK. Should be poured into the cup first if to blend properly with the tea. Though this may not be the way you like it, it's said to be the correct way to drink tea with milk.

A TEA-COSY. Brings out the worst in tea, extracting its tannin, the bitterness of which spoils any flavour. It is better to serve weaker cooler tea, and perhaps relegate your cosy to keeping the boiled eggs warm at breakfast.

BREWING.

(a) Discard any stale water in the kettle, as well as any thought of using water from the hot tap – or for that matter any other kind of water which isn't drawn freshly from a well run *cold* tap. Otherwise the tea will be flat.

(b) Warm the teapot. Using a cold pot, you at once lose the value of the boiling water, essential to draw the flavour out of the tea.

(c) Put teapot beside kettle, to pour water onto tea the instant it boils. If you walk across the kitchen to the teapot, the water will lose its oxygen – and once again will make flat tea.

(d) Stir tea, put on lid and infuse just long enough to extract the flavour: small leaf teas, due to their strength and pungency, need only about 2–3 minutes. Large leaf teas need 5–6 mins. If infused longer, the tannin is also extracted. If a big teapotful, stir again just before serving because tea tends to settle, the thin on top, thick on bottom.

TEA-BAGS. Account for about half of the total tea market and are a recognized alternative to loose tea. If you have a complex about them, have you contemplated the advantages?

(1) Many of the best kinds of tea are now available, so with a Jack Sprat situation in your family, you can each have the tea of your choice.
(2) They're a saving both of fuel and time. You need only enough boiling water to fill the cup/cups.
(3) The tea infuses in seconds because it is so fine – ideal for that quick 'cuppa', especially in the early morning, either in kitchen or at bedside.
(4) Depending on how many cups you drink, tea bags may be more economical than loose tea for the one, or two-person household.
(5) No teapot to wash up, no leaves to dispose of.

ICED TEA. Starts off like ordinary, but you need four times as much tea as usual. When infused, *strain* the tea into an equal quantity of cold water. Pour cold tea onto ice cubes in large glasses, adding a little fresh lemon juice, sugar, or a leaf of mint if you like. See *Darjeeling* and *Lapsang Souchong*, page 270.

20
MISCELLANEOUS

The Cheeseboard

Often seems an afterthought in English homes and restaurants because so *little* thought may be given to it. This is quite different in France, where cheese is served before the sweet and is an integral part of a meal. Fresh crusty French bread, crisp biscuits, butter and celery hearts when in season should all help to make the cheese course as tempting as any other.

★ If you can manage to serve three or four different *types* of cheese, then your selection will be more inspired. This is the sort of variety to think about:
One hard or semi-hard, eg Stilton, Gorgonzola, Roquefort, Caerphilly, Canadian or a mature Cheddar, Lancashire, Leicester, Wensleydale, Cheshire.
One soft, eg Brie, Camembert, Dolcelatte, Pont l'Evêque, Bel Paese.
One reasonably mild in flavour, eg Gruyère, Jarlsberg, ordinary English Cheddar, Edam, Gouda, Double Gloucester.
One unusual, eg Gourmandise, Esrom, Tôme au raisin, Caboc, a goat's cheese or a smoked or garlic cheese.
★ Serve the cheese on fresh vine leaves if you're lucky enough to have any, keeping it covered and moist with foil until the moment you serve it.
★ It's usually better to buy cheese in smallish quantities and eat while perfect, especially some of the softer varieties like Brie. Such a cheese, at the peak of perfection, may be over-ripe and indigestible two days later.
★ See also *Cheese*, page 66.

Cream, Mock

Has only limited use in my opinion, for soups, sauces and 'pouring'. It's easily made with 4 ozs (100 g) saltless butter melted over low heat in $\frac{1}{4}$–$\frac{1}{2}$ pt (125–250 ml) milk, according to thickness required. Then liquidize this fatty milk for 30 seconds at maximum speed when at blood heat. Chill. It looks extraordinary when cold, but a quick stir rectifies it.

★ Though mock cream has scant resemblance to fresh, because it doesn't hold air in the same way, you *can* whip it: use only $\frac{1}{4}$ (125 ml) milk and, while warming it, sprinkle over a level teasp gelatine.

Croustades

'Cases' made of pastry, hollowed-out bread rolls, or fried or baked bread filled with some tasty preparation such as duxelles, a creamy vegetable mixture, or the sort of filling you'd use for a vol-au-vent.

★ The quickest and easiest to make from bread, simply involve dipping large rounds of fairly thinly sliced bread on both sides in melted *butter*, pressing them into bun tins, and baking in a moderate oven for 20–25 mins until crisp and golden. They're delicious, either for a homely or a sophisticated meal.

Garlic Powder

Make or buy it. It's an excellent way to preserve garlic should you have a surplus, or like to have some 'instant' at hand for an omelet, a stew or anything else.

★ The one snag about making it is its pungency. Do it while alone in the house, and with wide-open windows! Slice the peeled garlic cloves *fairly* thinly, then dry them out, first one side and then the other, in a slow oven until crisp but barely coloured. Pound in a mortar or with the end of a rolling pin, then sieve and store in an airtight jar or bottle.

Meat Glaze

Used to glaze meats such as galantine, slipper of tongue or brawn, to flavour soups and sauces, or you can use it in place of stock. It is made from best meat, veal or poultry stock, 'reduced' to a syrupy consistency and becomes a stiff jelly when cold. (*Poor* stock will evaporate without going syrupy.) Any salt added becomes concentrated as well of course, so it's important to undersalt the stock when you make it.

★ The reducing is a long though trouble-free process, perhaps taking 3 or 4 hours, so it's not worth bothering with a small quantity. 5 pts (say $2\frac{1}{2}$–3 L) stock makes only $\frac{1}{2}$–$\frac{3}{4}$ pt (250–375 ml) meat glaze. This is how to make it:

(1) Boil the strained fat-free stock slowly in an uncovered pan until reduced to about $1\frac{1}{2}$ pts (say 750 ml) – *exact* quantities are immaterial.
(2) Strain through butter muslin or a very fine sieve into a small saucepan, and now boil again to reduce it until syrupy enough to coat a wooden spoon lightly. (If you fail to strain and transfer the stock to a clean pan, the sediment will burn more easily in the final stages, when it needs watching carefully anyway.)
(3) Strain. Freeze any surplus to your needs as ice cubes, or refrigerate it in a covered jar. If the top develops a few spots of mould, when refrigerated, it's said not to be harmful and is easily washed off under warm water, but I never feel too enthusiastic about this: after washing it, simmer in a saucepan over low heat with a spoonful of water until again reduced to a thick syrup.

Nuts, Devilled

Salted nuts, with cayenne added to the salt.

Nuts, Salted

Such as almonds and cashews are ten times better 'home-fried' than bought. (Our word 'cashew' comes from the Portuguese *Caju*.)

(1) Fry the blanched nuts in preheated oil over low heat, the oil well covering the bottom of the frying pan. Turn nuts constantly, to make sure they brown evenly. If cooked too fast, they'll burn before being crisp through.
(2) Drain thoroughly, first in the draining spoon used to stir them, and then on absorbent kitchen paper, to avoid greasiness.
(3) While still hot, toss in table salt.

Poppadoms

Can be bought in tins or packets ready to cook. To be crisp and delicious, don't fry them before you must:

(1) In a deep frying pan, heat oil about 1″ ($2\frac{1}{2}$ cm) deep to about 340°F, 170°C (use a deep-fat pan if preferred).
(2) Cook poppadoms one at a time until crisp, turning them over with tongs when fully spread out, and curled. Drain on absorbent kitchen paper.
(3) Stand them up against each other on a baking sheet – like a child's house of cards – and dry off for several minutes in a slow oven. (Otherwise they'll be greasy.)

(4) Serve in a basket or on a plain doyley on a very large plate.

Syrup

Made with a metal spoon, because a wooden one may pass on the flavour of other strong foods for which it has been used.

★ Many *old* recipes call for loaf sugar. At one time this was the purest form of sugar, and therefore less likely to crystallize than granulated or caster. Nowadays icing, caster, granulated and cube (replacing loaf) are all absolutely pure – and granulated is cheapest.
★ It's unwise to use a non-stick pan to make a syrup. Some non-stick surfaces are damaged by the grittiness of the sugar, and the syrup will be adulterated.
★ The main thing to remember about a syrup is that the sugar *must* be dissolved before the water boils, because a syrup with a high proportion of sugar will crystallize if stirred *after*. In fact, there is often so little liquid that the sugar is being melted and not dissolved. Stir it over low heat as much as you like therefore to dissolve it, then get rid of the spoon. Simply bring the syrup to the boil, and leave it alone.
★ A thermometer is invaluable for a strong syrup which has to be boiled to a high temperature for specific purposes. Liquid glucose or cream of tartar is sometimes stirred into such a syrup as soon as the sugar is dissolved, acting as a deterrent to the crystallization of the sugar. Now cover the pan for a few moments so that the trapped steam can wash down any crystals which may have formed on its sides. If crystals form again later, brush down the pan sides with a pastry brush dipped in boiling water, but don't, whatever you do, agitate the pan to try and dissolve them because that just makes things worse.
★ If a syrup has to be boiled to say 240°F, 116°C, it's safer to stop at 238°F, 115°C, because the heat of the pan will still cause the temperature to rise. If on the other hand you leave it to reach the exact temperature called for, plunge the bottom of the pan momentarily into cold water, to halt cooking.

SYRUP FOR STEWED FRUIT. Is boiled in an uncovered pan, usually for 5–7 mins. As the water evaporates, the syrup becomes more concentrated, so sweetens without being too watery.

Syrup, Stock

The sweetest of sweet syrups, with various uses. You may just as well make a quantity at a time because it keeps well in a refrigerator, especially if you add a spoonful of liquid glucose to prevent the sugar graining. Quantities are 2 lbs (900 g) sugar to 1 pt (generous 500 ml) water.

★ Make it like a strong syrup, above, boiling to 215°–220°F, 102°–104°C, then cool slightly and strain.
★ Use it full strength or diluted, according to need and recipe – for sorbets, to preserve soft fruits in the freezer, to make glacé or fondant icing, to make an excellent chocolate sauce for ice creams (page 239) etc, or simply to stew fruit.

Toasts

ANCHOVY TOAST. Good if you like anchovies! Fry sliced bread in butter (or *toast* it if too rich), spread with anchovy butter (page 131) and top with anchovy fillets.

CINNAMON TOAST. Tasty at tea-time, so if you make a quantity of the mixture at a time, it's there when you want it: sieve together 3 parts caster sugar with 1 of ground cinnamon. Sift generously over hot-buttered toast. Alternatively, use cinnamon sugar (page 93).

FRENCH TOAST. Bread soaked in seasoned, mixed-up egg – with a little milk to make the egg go further if you like – then lightly fried on both sides in hot fat. Some people like it best served with bacon for breakfast, others like it under a poached egg or fried sardines etc.

MELBA TOAST. Toast split through the

middle and toasted on the inside, made originally for Dame Nellie Melba, the famous Australian singer.

(1) To keep the toast flat, toast the bread until dry but not coloured on each side before toasting either side golden.

(2) While very hot, cut off the crusts, lay your hand flat on top, split the toast and pop it back under the grill to brown the bready side.

(3) Serve very fresh on a plain doyley on a plate (with plenty of butter pats), to accompany things with a soft texture like pâté, soup, fish etc. (Rich with butter and spread with marmalade, it's delicious even for breakfast.)

Bibliography

SIMONE BECK, LOUISETTE BERTHOLLE, JULIA CHILD: *Mastering the Art of French Cooking*
MRS BEETON: *Poultry and Game*
MICHAEL BRANDER (EDITOR): *International Encyclopedia of Shooting*
A.G.CAMERON: *Food and its Functions*
THE CHAMBERLAINS: *The Flavour of France*
A.O.COOKE: *A Book of Dovecotes*
ELIZABETH DAVID: *French Provincial Cooking, Italian Food*
LEN DEIGHTON: *Où est le Garlic, Action Cook Book*
MURIEL DOWNES: *Cake Making in Pictures*
LILLI GORE: *Game Cooking*
GOOD HOUSEKEEPING: *Home Freezer Cook Book*
DOROTHY HARTLEY: *Food in England*
E.M.HILDRETH: *Science of Food*
HELEN JEROME: *The Fine Art of Cooking, Concerning Cake Making*
KENWOOD: *Kenwood Recipe Book*
AILEEN KING: *Better Cookery*
HELEN McCULLY: *Nobody Ever Tells You These Things*
JILL McWILLIAM: *Book of Freezing*
PROSPER MONTAGNE: *Larousse Gastronomique*
NATIONAL FEDERATION OF WOMEN'S INSTITUTES: *Poultry and Game*
DORA SETON: *Essentials of Modern Cookery, Advanced Cookery*
ANDRÉ L. SIMON: *A Concise Encyclopedia of Gastronomy*
ANDRÉ L. SIMON, ROBIN HOWE: *A Dictionary of Gastronomy*
MICHAEL SMITH: *The Best of British Cookware*
CONSTANCE SPRY, ROSEMARY HUME: *The Constance Spry Cookery Book*
KATIE STEWART: *The Times Cookery Book, Katie Stewart Cooks* (also many articles in *The Times*)
KATHLEEN THOMAS: *The Sporting Wife*
FLORENCE WHITE: *Good Things in England*

Other sources of information

MANUFACTURERS AND INFORMATION SERVICES, IN ALPHABETICAL ORDER

Alcan Polyfoil Limited, Associated Health Foods Limited, Bejam News, British Egg Information Service, Cadbury Typhoo Food Advisory Service, Cannon Industries Ltd, CPC (United Kingdom) Ltd, Brown & Polson Division, Elizabeth David Catalogue, Davis Gelatine Ltd, Metal Box Ltd, Pasta Information Service, Princes Foods Ltd, Quaker Oats Ltd, Meat Promotion Executive, David Mellor's *Kitchen Guide*, Rowntree Mackintosh Limited, Suttons Seeds, Tate & Lyle Refineries Ltd, R.Twining & Company Limited, Van den Berghs, The Young Group of Companies

INDEX

Agar Agar, 62
Agitating, 30
Aïoli, Family Tree, 133
Air, a raising agent, 62
how it acts as, 251
Al dente, 30
Almonds, to skin, flake or shred, 82
devilled and salted, 274
Almond essence, 62
Paste, 261
American Frosted Icing, 261
Anchovies, 168
Anchovy Toast, 275
Angelica, 76
candied, 62
Antipasto, 30
Apple, to vandyke, 60
Baked, 223
Pie, 234
Pie (plate), 235
Stewed, 230
Strudel, 224
Apricot Glaze, why, how to use, 262
Apricots, Macerated, 47, 48
Arctic Roll, *see* Swiss Roll, Chocolate, 259
Arrowroot, origin of, 63
qualities of and how to use, 63
Artichoke, Globe, 115
Jerusalem, 143
Asparagus, to prepare and cook, 116
to serve cold, 116
Rolls, 116
Aspic Jelly, bought, 63
general information, 116
to chop, 45
as garnish, 43
Mayonnaise, proportions for, 117
Aubergines, 143
Avocado pears, 117
Bacon, general information, 182
rashers, to store and to fry, 182
rinds, to cook, use and store, 182
Green, definition of, 182
Rolls, to make, 182
Bags, paper icing, to make and fill, 1
piping, nylon, 2
polythene, 2
Bain-marie, 2
Baked Alaska, type of meringue for, 232
Baking, general information, 30
Baking blind, 30
powder, 63
sheets, 3
Baller (ball-scoop), types and technique, 3
Bananas, Macerated, 47, 48
Baps, 245
Barding, 31
Barquettes, to cut out, 31
Basil, 76
Basin, pudding, *see* Bowls, 5
Basket, blanching, 4
chip or frying, 18, 42
garlic, 4
salad, 4
Batter, general information, 31
for fruit fritters, 229
Bavarian Cream, *see* Crème Anglaise, 240
Bay, 76
Bean slicer, Zipp, 4
Beans, broad, 143
for a salad, 158
French, 143
for a salad, 158
runner, for a salad, 158
to take the 'strings' off, *see* Potato peeler
soya, 88
Béarnaise Sauce, Family Tree, 133
Béchamel milk, to make, 139
Sauce, to make, *see* Family Tree, 138, 132
Beef, *see also* Meat, 183–5
general information, 183
to carve, 35
all the cuts of, 183–185
to roast, 183
Olives, steak required for, 184
Steak and Kidney Pudding, 185
Strogonoff, meat required for, 184
Beef Tea, meat required for, 185
Beetroot, general information, 143
for salad, 158
Beignets, meaning of, 225
Beignets Soufflés, 225
Beurre Bercy (white wine), *see also* Family Tree, 131
Blanc, *see* Family Tree, 133
au Citron, *see* Family Tree, 133
Manié, to make and use, 31
Marchand de Vins (red wine), *see also* Family Tree, 131
Noir or Noisette, general information, 134
Beverages, *see also* Cocoa, Coffee and Tea, 268–272
Bicarbonate of soda, general information, 63
Bierwurst, 195
Bin, pedal, 4
Bind, general information, 31
Biscuits, quickly to open a pkt. of, 252
Bisque, main ingredients of, 126
Black Pudding, 195
Blanching, why, what and how, 31
Blanching basket, 4
Blancmange, Chocolate, 233
Blender, *see* Liquidizer, 15
Blending, general information, 32
dry ingredients, 32
a liquid with dry ingredients, 32
Blind, Baking, 30
Bloaters, 169
Board, melamine, 5
wooden chopping, 5
pastry, 5
Boiling, general information, 32
Bone, a fowl, general information, 201
to stuff and reshape as a bird, 202

to stuff and roll, 202
Boning, general information, 32
Bonne femme (à la), 49
Borage, 76
Bouchées, origin of name, 117
Chicken, 204
Bouillabaisse, origin, main ingredients, 126
Bouillon, 33
Bouquet garni, to make and use, 33
Bourgignonne (à la), 49
Bowls, aluminium, disadvantage of, 5
copper, 5
mixing, 5
plastic washing up, 5
wooden salad, 5
Brains, 190
Braising, definition of, 33
the why's and how's of, 33
Brandy, for cooking, *see* Wine, 96
Butter, 241, 242
Snaps, origin of name, recipe and tips, 252
Brawn, 185
Brazil nuts, 82
Breads and Continental Breads, 243–8
Bread, general information, 243–5
frozen, to heat, 63
the ingredients for, 243
the oven, 244
storage of, 63
tins, 26, 244
tips about making, 244
Brown, 245
Garlic, 245
Milk, 245
Milk Twist, 245
Breadcrumbs, dried white, 64
fresh white, 64
refrigeration of, 20
golden (raspings), 64
fried, for game, 210
Breakfast, meaning of and need for, 33
Bream, Sea, 169
Bridge Rolls, 246
Brill, 169
Brisling, 169
Broccoli, 144
Broccoli, Sprouting, 117, 144
Brochette, *see* Skewers, 23
en, 49
Broiler, 205
Broiling, 34
Brown Sugar Frosting, 262
Brushes, pastry, 6
Brussels sprouts, 144
Bulb baster, use of, *see* Duck or Goose, 208, 211
Bunwash, 246
Butter, cooking with, general information, 64
Anchovy, *see also* Family Tree, 131
Bercy (white wine), Family Tree, 131
Brandy, 241, 242
Chocolate, 241, 242
clarified, 36
Coffee, 241, 242
Colbert, Family Tree, 133
Cream fillings, *see* Crème au Beurre, 263
Egg yolk, Family Tree, 133
Garlic, *see also* Family Tree, 131
Herb, Family Tree, 133
Horseradish, Family Tree, 133
Icing, general information, 262
colour and flavour combinations, 262
Lemon, 241, 242
Lobster, general information, 131
see also Coral, 175
Maître d'hôtel, *see also* Family Tree, 131
Marchand de Vins (red wine), *see also* Family Tree, 131
Melted, *see* Butter Sauces, hot, 134
Mustard, general information, 131
see also Mustard, 82
Orange, 241, 242
Paprika, Family Tree, 133
Raspberry, 241, 242
Rum, 241, 242
Sauces, hot (savoury), 134
(sweet), *see* Sauces, Hard, 241
Savoury, general information, 131
for grilled food, 131
to enrich sauces and soups, 131
to garnish cold dishes, 131
as a spread or filling, 134
with boiled vegetables, 131
Shallot, *see also* Family Tree, 131
Shellfish, *see also* Family Tree, 131
Spice, 241, 242
Strawberry, 241, 242
Tarragon, *see also* Family Tree, 131
some details about, 78
Tomato, *see also* Family Tree, 131
Wine, red, *see* Marchand de Vins, 131
white, *see* Bercy, 131
Buttermilk, definition of, 65
Button onions, *see* Onions, 148
Cabbage, general information, 144
Chinese, 144
Dutch white, for Cole Slaw, 144
red, braised, 145
for Cole Slaw, 144
Caffeine, *see* Coffee, 268
Cake Icings and fillings, 260–67
general information and tips about, 260
Almond Paste, to colour, 261
a few hints about, 261
with egg yolk or white?, 261
American Frosted Icing, 261
brown sugar, 262
Butter Cream fillings, *see* 263
Icing, general information, 262
colour & flavour combinations, 262
Chocolate Glacé Icing, 265
Coffee Icing, 263
Crème au Beurre, general information, 263
uses of, 263
Ménagère, 263
à la Meringue, 263
Mousseline, 263
Crème Patissière, 264
Crème St Honoré, 264
Fondant Icing, tips about, 264
uses of, 264

Frost, to make, 266
Frosting, meaning of, 265
Glacé Icing, general information, 265
Lemon Curd filling, 266
Marbling (or Feather Icing), technique, 266
Marzipan, *see* Almond Paste, 261
origin of name, 266
Pastry Cream, 264
Royal Icing, uses of and tips about, 267
to model, 267
Cake tins, 26
tray, 6
Cakes, *see also* under individual names, 250–59
general information, 250
all-in-one mixtures, 252
choice of ingredients for, 250
choice and preparation of tins, 251
creamed mixtures, 251
flavourings and colourings for, 251
plain or rich mixtures, 250
serving and storing, 252
Battenburg, type of tin required, 252
bought, for a sweet, 224
Butterfly, 253
Cherry, 253
Christmas, general information, *see* Fruit Cakes, 254
Fruit, general information, 254
to bake, 254
to cool, 255
best ingredients for, 254
to test when cooked, 254
Madeira, 257
Pavlova, 233
Rock, 257
Sponge, 258
Victoria Sandwich, 258
Wedding, origin of, 254
general information, *see also* Fruit Cakes, 254
Calabrese, 145
Calorie, general information, 34
count of certain foods, 34
Canapé, 34
Canned foods, general information, 65
storage life of certain, 65
Capers, 66
Capon, origin of and general information, 206
Capsicum, 150
Caramel, to make and line a tin with, 227
Custard, *see* Crème Caramel, 227
Caraway, 76
Carmine, origin of, 66
Carrots, 145
Vichy, 145
Carte (à la), 49
Carving, general information, *see also* individual birds, 35
cold meat, 35, 181
Cashews, devilled and salted, 274
Caster, sugar, *see* Dredgers, 9
Catering equipment shops, to find, *see* Balloon whisks, 28
Cauliflower, general information, 145
cold, for salad, 158
Caviar, 175
Mock, 175
Cayenne pepper, 66
Celeriac, 158
Celery, general information, 146
in salads, 158
Celsius, 52
Centigrade, 52
Cereals, general information, 66
Chalazae, 35
Chambré, 35
Chard, Swiss, 146
Charlotte, Fruit, 225
Russe, 225
Chasseur, 49
Cheese, general information, 66
best kinds for cooking, 67
tips about cooking, 67
food value of, 66
mouldy, to use, 67
refrigeration of, 20
storage and freezing of, 67
Cheeseboard, to make interesting, 273
Cherries, Glacé, general information, 67
to decorate with, *see* Hatpins, 14
as a *hot* garnish, *see* Salmi, 219
Macerated, 47, 48
Cherry stoner, 6
Chervil, 76
Chicken, general information, 200–207
to boil, *see* Fowl, Boiling, 206
to bone, general information, 201
to carve, 203
dishes, cold and hot, 204, 205
to draw, 200
to fry, general information, 42
to grill, general information, 44
to joint, 201
to roast, *see also* Chicken Roast, 200, 203
to steam, *see* Fowl, Boiling, 207
to truss for boiling, 206
to truss for roasting, 201
Croquettes, 204
Curried, accompaniments for, 204
Fricassée of, 204
Galantine, 209
Kromeskies, 204
Pancakes, 204
Pie, 204
Potted, 216
Rissoles, 204
Roast, 203
to serve cold, 204
in butter, 203
Vol-au-vent, 205
Chickens, specific names of, according to age
boiling fowl, 206
capon, origin of and how to cook, 206
poularde, definition of, 206
poussins, 205
spring or broiler, 205
Chicory for salad, 158
Chip basket, *see* Frying basket, 18, 42
Chipolata, origin of name, 195

with roast chicken, 203
Chives, general information, 76
to chop, 35
Chocolate, general information, 67
the fat present in, 67
to grate easily, 68
hardening or scrambling of, 68
to melt without liquid, 68
Butter, 241, 242
Cooking, 67
Cornflour Pudding, 233
dessert, milk, 68
plain, 68
drinking, 68
Glacé Icing, 265
Log, 259
Sauce, cold, 239
Cholesterol, *see* Fats, Saturated, 39
Chopping, general information, 35
chives, mint and parsley, technique, 35
Chowder, origin of name and definition of, 126
Cider, 68
Cinnamon, 68
Sugar, to make, 93
Toast, 275
Citric acid, 69
Citron, 69
Clarifying, of fats, 36
Cloths, dish, 6
oven, 6
Cloves, 69
Coating foods for deep fat frying, 42
shallow frying, 42
with sauce, 36
Cob-nuts, *see* Hazel-nuts, 82
Cockie-Leekie, origin of name, 126
Cockles, 169
Cocoa, general information, 268
butter, the fat in cocoa beans, 67
Coconut, desiccated, to brown or colour, 69
Buns, 253
Cocotte, 6
Cod, 169
fillet, smoked, 169
roe, smoked, 175
Coffee, general information, 268
history of, 268
tips about making, 269
Balalaika, 270
Butter, 241, 242
essence, for cooking, 69
Gaelic, 269
Highland, 269
Iced Spiced, 269
instant, for cooking, 69
Icing, 263
Kisses, 253
Napoleon, 270
Cognac, for cooking, *see also* Wine and Rum, 87, 96
Colander, 7
Cole Slaw, 159
Colourings, food, general information, 73
in cakes, 251
Concasser, 36
Condiments, *see* Seasoning, 57
Consistencies, general information, 36
esp. for sweets, 223
Consistency, coating, 36
dropping, 36
Consommé, 126
Cooker, Pressure, 7
Cookers, choice of, facts to consider, 7
advantages of a fan-assisted, 7
Cooking fats, white, general information, 69
advantages over lard, 69
origin and qualities of, 69
Coquille Saint-Jacques, general information, 17(
alternative names, 166
Coral, *see* Roes, 175
Cornflour, general information, 70
in a fruit pie, 234
Pudding, Chocolate, 233
Cos lettuce, origin of name, 161
Courgettes, general information, 146
for a salad, 159
Court bouillon, 37
Crabs, 170
roe of, 175
Crawfish, alternative names, 166
Crayfish, alternative names, 166
Cream, general information, 70
half-whipped, 70
refrigeration of, 20
slightly sour, as accompaniment, 239
whipped, 70, 232, 239
double, 70
frozen, 70
Long Life, 71
Mock, to make, 273
Orange-flavoured, to make, 85
single, 70
soured, uses for, 71
in mayonnaise, 136
'whipping', 70
Cream, to (butter and sugar), 37
Cream of tartar, origin of and to use, 71
unusual functions of, 71
Creamed mixtures, general information, 251
'Creams', Fruit or Custard, 226
Crème Anglaise, 240
au Beurre, general information, 263
uses of, 263
Ménagère, 263
à la Meringue, 263
Mousseline, 263
Brûlée, 226
Caramel, 227
Chantilly, 240
Patissière, 264
St Honoré, 264
Crescents, to cut, 37
Crevette, *see* Shellfish chart, 166
Croissant, 246
Croquettes, Chicken and Ham, 204
Croustades, 273
Croûtons, to make and serve, 126
fried in garlic butter, 126, 131
Crown Roast, meat required for, 188
Crustaceans, 166

Cucumber, to 'stripe' with fruit decorator, 12
  history of, 159
  Salad, general information, 159
    dressing for, 159
Cups, American measuring, 8
Curdled 'creamed' mixture, cause of and to rectify, 251
  Custard Sauce, cause of and to rectify, 240
  Hollandaise Sauce, to rectify, 136
  Mayonnaise, to rectify, 136
Currants, origin of name, 71
Curry, Chicken, accompaniments for, 204
Curry powder, 71
Custard powder, origin of, 71
Custards, general information, 226
  Baked, 226
  Boiled (Sauce), 240
  Confectioner's, 264
  Crème Brûlée, 226
  Crème Caramel, 227
  Sauce, egg, *see* Boiled,
    made with powder, 241
Cut, egg whites into a mixture, *see* Folding, 40
Cutters, parsley, 8
  pastry or scone, 8
Danish Pastries, 247
Dariol moulds, 17
Darne, meaning of, 49
Dates, 71
Daube (en), meaning of, 49
Decorating, *see* Garnishing, general information, 43
  examples and purpose of, 43, 44
Deep freeze, *see* Freezer, 11
Deer, season for, 199
  See also Venison, 221
Dégorger, 38
Degrease, 38
Diable (à la), 49
Dicing, vegetables, 57
Dill, 77
Dinner Rolls, 246
  to reheat from freezer, 248
Dishes, casserole, 8
  fluted gratin or baking, 8
  soufflé, 9
Dough hook, 9
Dovecote, *see* Pigeon, 216
Doyleys, purpose of, 9
Dredger, flour, 9
  sugar, 9
Dredging, 38
Dressing, Cream, 160
  French, 160
Dressings, Oil and vinegar, 160
    see also Family Tree, 133
  Salad, general information, 160
Dried Fruits, 71
Dripping, general information, 71
  reason for clarifying, 36
  Toast, *see* Duck fat, rendered, 209
Dublin Bay prawns, general information, alternative names, 166
  See also Scampi, 176
Duck, 207–9
  fat, rendered, 209
  Wild, 209
Dusting, 38
Duxelles, *see* Mushrooms, 147
  (à la), 49
  Family Tree, 132
Éclairs, Chocolate, 253
Écrevisse, *see* Shellfish chart, 166
Eel, 107
  Smoked, *how* smoked, 177
  Nutritional value of, 170
  to serve, 121
Egg plant, *see also* Aubergines, 146
Eggs, general information, 106–108
    cooking temperature of, 107
    to freeze, 108
    refrigerated, cooking with, 107
    refrigeration of, 20
    shells, uses of in cookery, 108
    storage of, 106
    structure of, 106, 107
    whites, general information, 40, 60, 107
    yolks, general information, 107, 108
  Boiled, 108
  en Cocotte, 108
  Coddled, 109
  coddler, 10
  Easter, 109
  Fried, 109
  Fried in deep fat, 109
  Hard-boiled, 109
  Mayonnaise, 117
  Mollets, 110
  Poached, 110
  poacher, 10
  poaching ring, 10
  pricker, 10
  Scotch, 112
  Scrambled, 111
  separator, 10
  stand, 10
Endive, *see* Chicory, 158
Entrecôte steaks, definition of, 184
Entrée, 38
Equipment, kitchen, *see* individual items of, 1–29
Faggot of herbs, 38
Family Tree – of Savoury Sauces, 132, 133
Farce, 38
Fat, rendered, 54
    duck, 209
    goose, 212
  to rub into flour, 99
Fats, cooking (white) general information, 69
  saturated and polyunsaturated, 39
    foods high in, 39
  refrigeration of, 21
  vegetable, 94
Fatigue, to avoid, *see* Sitting down to cook, 57
  see also Kitchen sink, 23
Feather Icing, technique, 266
Fécule, *see also* potato flour, 40
Fennel, Florence, used as vegetable, 146
  as herb, 77
Figs, Macerated, 47,48
Filberts, *see* Hazel-nuts, 82

Fillings, Cake, *see* Cake Icings and Fillings, 260–267
Fines herbes, 49
Finnan haddock, 171
Fish, *see also* individual fish, 165–78
  general information, 165
  to bake, 168
  to braise, general information, 33
  canned, storage life of, 65
  cooking of, various hints, 168
  ways of flavouring, 167
  fried, to serve, 168
    coatings for, 167, 42
  to fry in deep fat, general information, 41, 42
  shallow fat, general information, 42, 167, 168
  to grill, general information, 44, 168
  'oily', general information, 165
  to poach, general information, 53
    in a court bouillon, 167, 37
    in fish stock, milk or wine, 167
  preparation of, 166
  refrigeration of, 21
  shellfish, general information, 166
    English and French names chart, 166
  smoked, general information, *see also* 177
  to steam, general information, 58, 168
  'white', 165
Fish Cakes, 170
  Pie, 170
  Salads, 175
  Slices, good and bad, 10
  Smoked, to serve, 121
Flan rings and frames, metal, 10
Flambé, 40
Flans, sweet, 228
  meringue topping for, 233
Flapjacks, 253
Flavouring essences, how to incorporate, 251
Fleurons, 40
Florentine (à la), 49
Flour, general information, 72
    brown or wheatmeal, 73
    household soft, 72
    plain, white, 72
    self-raising, brown or white, 72
    strong, 72, 243
    wholemeal, roller milled, 73
    wholemeal or wholewheat, 100% stoneground, 72
  to measure in spoonfuls, kitchen and 'standard', 24
  seasoned, 40
Flour and Water Paste, 185
Foil, 11
Folding, 40
Fondant Icing, 264
Food colourings, general information, 73
  in cakes, 251
Fools, Fruit, 228
Forestière (à la), 49
Fork, two-pronged meat, 11
Fowl, to bone, 201
  to draw, 200
  Boiling, 206
Frangipane, 229
Frankfurters, 195
Freezer burn, 41
Freezer, Food, blessings of a, 11
    choosing a, 12
    foil for use in, 11
    polythene bags for use in, 2
    ways of using, 11
Freezing, as a method of preservation, 41
  why necessary to fast-freeze, 41
  Open, 41
French Toast, 275
Fricassée, Chicken, 204
Fritters, Fruit, 229
  Vegetable, 142
Fritto Misto of Fruits, 230
Frosting, meaning of, 265
  Brown Sugar, 262
Frothing – a bird's breast, 200
Fruit, general information, *see also* under individual fruits
    canned, storage life of, 65
    juices, refrigeration of, 21
    purée, to freeze, see 'Creams', 226
    'soft', to freeze in sugar, *see* Sugar, 91
    'soft', to freeze in syrup, *see* Sugar, 91
    syrup, to stew fruits, 275
  Cakes, 254
  'Creams', 226
  Crust, meringue topping for, 233
  decorator, how and when to use, 12
  Flans, 228
  Fools, 228
  Fritters, 229
  Pie, 234
  Pie, plate, 235
  Sauce, 241
  Stewed, 230
  Syrups, for glaze or sauce, 241
Frying, deep fat, 41–2
  coating foods for, 42
  the fat, care of, 42
    choice of, 41
    to cool quickly, 42
    dangers of, 41
    temperatures for, 42
  frying basket, 18, 42
  shallow fat, 42
Fumet, 43
Funnel, metal jam, 12
  pie, 12
Galantine, 209
Galettière, 18
Gall bladder, bird's, to recognize, 201
Game and Poultry, *see also* individual kinds of, 198–222
  general information, 198
    to bone, 201
    to braise, general information, 33
    to draw, 200, 210
    to freeze (game), 199
    to fry, general information, 42
    to grill, general information, 44
    to marinate, general information, 48
    to pluck (game), and *when* to, 210
    to roast, general information, *see also*

individual kinds of, 199–200
seasons for (game), 199
to truss, 201, 210
Chips, 152
Galantine of, 209
Pâté, 214
Potted, 216
Salmi of, 218
shears, see Chicken, to carve, 203
Gammon, 186
Garlic, general information, 73
to crush, 73
basket, 4
Bread, 245
Butter, *see* Savoury Butters, 131
powder, to make, 274
press, 13
Sausage, French, 195
Garnishing, general information, 43, 44
Gas flames, 44
Gâteaux, general information, 255
Gazpacho, 127
Gelatine, general information, 73, 74
to dissolve and use, 74
history of, 73
in ice cream, 74
nutritional value of, 74
used with milk, 74
quantity required, 74
with raw pineapple, 74
soaking of, 74
based sweets, 223
to freeze, 74
Genoese Fancies, Genoese pastry required for, 255
Genoese Pastry, general information, 255
Genoise Commune, recipe for, 255
tips about, 255
Fine, *see* Genoise Commune
Giblets, bird's, what and how to prepare, 200
Ginger, root, origin and use of, 74
to bruise, 74
stem, 75
Gingerbread, 256
Girdles, 13
to prove, 53
Gizzard, bird's, to empty, 201
Glaće Icing, 265
Glaze, Apricot, 262
egg, for pastry, rolls etc., 44
Fruit Syrup, 241
Meat, 274
Glucose, liquid, 75
Gluten, general information, 75
to isolate and see it, 75
Golden cutlets, 171
Goose, general information, 211
fat, to render, store and use, 212
liver, 212
stock, 212
Green, 212
Michaelmas, 212
Wild, general information, 212
Gooseberry Fool, 229
Goulash, type of stew, 44
Grapefruit, general information, 118
to cut into segments, 85
to freeze, 118
knife, 14
to prepare, 118
to vandyke, 59
Grapes, different types of, 75
Gras-maigre gravy boat, *see* Accompaniments, 204
Grater, Mouli, 13
nutmeg, 14
Graters, general information, 13
Gratiner, 44
Gravy, 134
boat, gras-maigre, 204
browning, general information, 75
Parisian essence, 85
Grecque (à la), 50
Grenadine, 75
Griddle, *see* Girdle, 13
Grilling, general information, 44
Grouse, general information, 212
season for, 199
Guinea fowl, 213
Gum arabic, general information, 75
to make and use solution, 266
Haddock, 170
Finnan, 171
Golden cutlets, 171
Smoked, how smoked, 177
Smoked fillet, 171
Smokies, 171
Hake, 171
Halibut, 171
Halibut, Chicken, 171
Ham, pasteurised canned, storage life of, 65
Hams, 186
Hamburger, 186
Hands! – an extra one, 45
Hard sauces (flavoured butters, sweet), 241, 242
Hare, general information, 213
to skin and draw, 213
Jugged, 214
see also Seasons for game, 199
Haricots Verts, *see* French beans, 143
Hatpins, uses of, 14
Hazel-nuts, 82
Herbs, 76–78
general information, 76
to freeze, 76
refrigeration of, 21
Angelica, *see also* Angelica, candied, 76
Basil, 76
Bay, 76
Borage, 76
Caraway, 76
Chervil, 76
Chives, general information, 76
to chop, 35
Dill, 77
Fennel, Florence, 77
Marjoram, Sweet, 77
Mint, general information, 77
to chop, 35
chopped, to release extra flavour, 77
Peppermint and Spearmint, *see* Mint, 77

Oregano, 77
Parsley, general information, 77
to chop, 35
to garnish with, 77
Fried, in deep fat, 77
Wine, 77, 96
Rosemary, with lamb, 187
Savory, 78
Tarragon, general information, 78
Butter, 78 & 131
Stuffing, for chicken, 203
Vinegar, 78 & 95
Thyme, 78
Herb Vinegars, 95
Herring, general information, 171
to clean and bone, 171
Soused, 172
Hollandaise Sauce, *see* Sauces, Savoury
Hollandaise (à la), 50
Homard, *see* Lobster, 173
Honey, 78
Hongroise (à la), 50
Hors-d'oeuvres, *see also under* individual dishes, 115–122
general information, 115
Mixed, 119
Horseradish, 78
Huître, *see* Oyster, 174
Ice cubes, uses of, 45
cube tray, to freeze various foods, 45
Icings and fillings, *see* Cake Icings, 260
Icing bags, paper, 1
tubes, 27
Ignition temperature – of fats, 45
Indienne (à la), 50
Ingredients, *see under* each kind of, 62–97
Irish Stew, meat required for, *see* 'middle neck', *and* Mutton, 189
Italienne (à la), 50
Jardiniere (à la), 50
Jam Sauce, 242
Jars, storage, 25
Jelly, to chop, 45
to decorate a mould with, 45
Lemon, 231
Milk, 231
packet, to set quickly, 231
Julienne (à la), 50
Junket, 231
Kale, 146
Kebab, general information, 186
skewers, *see* Shish, 23
Kebabs, Marinated Lamb, recipe for, 187
Kedgeree, 172
Kettles, 14
Kidneys, general information, 190
calf's, 190, 191
lamb's, 190
ox, 191
pig's, 190
Kippers, general information, 172
how they're smoked, 177
Fillets, Marinated, 173
Straws, *see* Yarmouth Straws, 173
Kirsch, 78
Kneading, bread dough, advice about, 46
purpose of, 244
fondant icing, 265
shortcrust pastry, 105
Knife sharpening, 46
Knives, general information, 14
electric, to cut bread thinly, 115
to carve cold meat, 181
filleting, 14
French cook's, 14
grapefruit, 14
pallet, 14
saw, small fine, 15
vegetable, 15
Knocking back – a bread dough, 244
Knocking up – pastry, 46
Kromeskies, Chicken and Ham, 204
Lamb, *see also* Meat, 187–189
general information, 187
to carve, 35
all the cuts of, 188
to roast, 187
Spring, 187
Kebabs, Marinated, 187
Land cress, American, 161
Langouste, alternative names, 166
Langoustine, alternative names, 166
Lard, general information, 78
Larding, 46
Larding needle, 15
Lardoons, 46
Lasagne, *see also* Pasta, 150
Lemons, general information,
to freeze, 80
juice of, 79
refrigeration of, 21
rind, grated, 79
pared, 79
zest of, 61
to 'stripe' with fruit decorator, 12
Lemon Butter, 241, 242
Butterflies, general information, 46
to make, 79
Curd filling, 266
Lentils, *see* Pulses, 86
Lettuce, 161
Cos, origin of, 161
refrigeration of, 21
Leveret, *see* Hare, 213
Liaison, definition and purpose of, 46
Beurre Manié, *see also* Fécule and Roux, 31
cream and egg yolk, 123
Lime juice, 80
Limes, 80
Lining, cake tins, square or rectangular, 46
round, bottom only, 47
quickly, 47
fully, 47
Liqueurs, for cooking, 96
Liquidizer, 15
Liver, general information, ways of using, 191
calf's, 191
Casserole, 191
goose, 212
lamb's, 191

ox, 191
pig's, 191
pigeon, oddity of, 216
Sausage, 195
Spread, 195
Lobsters, 173
roe of, *see* Coral, 175
Lump fish, 173
Lyonnaise (à la), 50
Macaroni, *see* Pasta, 149
Mace, 80
Macerating, general information, 47
fruit/liqueur combinations, 48
Mackerel, general information, 173
Smoked, to serve, 121
how smoked, 177
Soused, 174
Magic Spoon, 28
Mallard, general information, 209
season for, 199
Marbling, technique, 266
Margarine, general information, 80
clarifying, 36
Marinade, 48
Marinated Lamb Kebabs, 187
Marinating, 48
Marinière (à la), 50
Marjoram, sweet, 77
Marrow, Vegetable, 147
Marzipan, origin of name, 266
see also Almond Paste, 261
Mayonnaise, *see* Sauces, Savoury,
Measures, liquid, 15
Measuring cups, American, 8
spoons, 24
Meat, *see also* different kinds of, 179–197
general information, 179
to boil, general information, 32
to braise, general information, 33
in the diet, 181
for the freezer, 181
to fry, general information, 42
to grill, general information, 44
refrigeration (storage) of, 21
to roast a joint, *see also* Beef, etc., 180
for serving cold, 181
roast, to test when cooked, 181
roasting, general information, 54
to stew, general information *see also* Meat Stews, below, 58
Meat Glaze, 274
Potted, 216
Stews, thickened brown, 196
Melba Toast, 275
Melons, general information, 118
to freeze, 119
ways to serve, 118
Ménagère (à la), 50
Menu, general information, 48
names of classic dishes, *see* table, 49–51
planning, 51
Meringue cuite, 232
Italienne, 232
Suisse, 232
Meringue toppings, 233
tubes, 28
Meringues, common causes of failure, 232
further tips about, 232
Metric quantities and measurements, 52
Meunière (à la), 'table' of classic dishes, 50
method of preparation, 174
Milanaise (à la), 50
Milk, general information, 81
boiling point of, 81
to colour, for children, 73
to heat, without skin, 81
hot, in coffee, 269
storage of, 21
in tea, 272
Béchamel, to make, 139
dried, 81
homogenised, 81
pasteurised, 81
sterilised, 81
Ultra-heat-treated (U.H.T – Long Life), 81
Milk bread, 245
Jelly, 231
Puddings, 233
Twist, 245
Mill, pepper, 16
vegetable, 16
Mince, general information, 189
uses of, 189
Mince pies, 234
Mincer, 16
Minestrone, origin of name, 127
in the Italian way, 127
Mint, general information, 77
to chop, 35
chopped, to release extra flavour, 77
Minute steak, entrecóte, 184
Mirepoix, 52
Mixed Grill, 189
Mixer, electric fixed, general information, 16
to whisk egg whites, 28
hand, uses of, 16, 28
Mocha (or Moka), 52
Molasses, 82
Molluscs, 166
Moulds, charlotte, 16
dariol, 17
jelly, 17
raised pie, hinged, 17
individual, to make, 17
Moule à manqué tins, general information, 26
Moules, *see* Mussels, 174
Moulin-legumes, *see* Vegetable mill, 16
Mushrooms, general information, 147
to extract water from, 147
to freeze, 147
to fry or grill, preparation, 147
as garnish, 147
refrigeration of, 21
Salad, 162
Mussels, 174
Mustard, 82
Butter, 131
seed, 82
Mutton, general information, *see also* Meat, 189
to carve, 35

Nantua (à la), 50
Nectarines, Macerated, 47, 48
Nicoise (à la), *see also* Salads, 51
Noodles, 150
Normande (à la), 51
Nutmeg, 82
Nutrients, the, 52
Nuts, general information, 82
  almonds, to blanch, flake or shred, 82
    ground, 82
    nibs, 82
    salted, 274
  brazils, origin of name, 82
  cashews, salted, 274
  cob, *see* Hazel-nuts, 82
  devilled, 274
  filbert, *see* Hazel-nuts, 82
  hazel-nuts, 82
  peanuts, 83
  pistachio, 83
  salted, 274
Oatcakes, 247
Oatmeal, 83
Oeufs Mollets, 110
Offal, *see also* individual kinds of, 190–193
  general information, 179, 190
Oil, general information, 83
  corn, 83
  groundnut, 83
  olive, 84
  soya, 84
  sunflower, 84
  vegetable, 84
Oil dropper, to improvise, 17
Olives, 84
Olive stoner, *see* Cherry stoner, 6
Omelet, French, 111
    variations of, 112
  Spanish, 112
Onions, general information, 148
    to chop finely, 148
    to make digestible, 148
    rings, for garnish, 149
      batter-dipped, 43
      floured, fried, 205
    tears, when slicing!, 149
  dried sliced, 149
  frozen sliced, 149
  pickling or button, general information, 148
    as garnish, 43
  shallots, 148
  Spanish, 148
  spring, 163
Oranges, general information, 85
    to cut into segments, 85
    to freeze, *see* lemons, 80
    refrigeration of, 21
    to slice without pith, 85
    zest of, 61
  Macerated, 47, 48
Orange Butter, 241, 242
    flavoured cream, 85
    flower water, 84
Oregano, 77
Oven, position of foods in, *see* Baking, 30
  temperatures, comparing gas and
    electricity, 52
  temperatures, general information, *see*
    Baking, 30
Ox, 193
Oxtail, 191
Ox tongue, pressed, 192
Oysters, 174
'Oysters', of a fowl, *see* Joint a chicken, 201
Panada, 52
Pancakes, Chicken, 204
  sweet, 234
Pans, baking, 17
  deep fat, 17
  egg poaching, 10
  frying, 18
  omelet, 18
    to prove, 53
  pancake, 18
  preserving, 18
  sauce, 18
  sauté, 19
Paprika, 85
Parboil, 52
Pare, 53
Parisian essence, 85
Parsley, *see* herbs, 76
Partridge, general information, 214
  season for, 199
Pasta, general information, 85
  to cook, 149
Pastries, Danish, 247
Pastry, 98–105
  general information, 98–100
    to cut, 100
    escape of steam from, 100
    to glaze, 100
    handling of, 99
    choice of ingredients for, 98
    oven temperatures, 100
    to relax, 100
    to roll, technique, 55
    to roll a circle of, *see* Shortcrust, 105
    to roll and fold, 99
    rolled out, to lift up easily, 100
  board, 5
  brushes, 6
  Cheese, 100
  Choux, recipe for, 101
    tips about, 101, 102
  Flaky, 102
  Flan, 102
  French flan, 103
  frozen, bought and home-made, 103
  Genoese, 255
  Hot water crust, 103
  Pate Sucrée, *see* French flan above, 103
  Puff, 104
  Rough puff, 104
  Shortcrust, 105
    rich, *see* Shortcrust, 105
  Suet, 105
Pastry Cream, 264
Pâté, general information, 119
  de foie gras, *see* Goose liver, 212

Game or Poultry, 214
Maison, 119
Patties, *see* Bouchées, 117
Paupiettes, 51
Pavlova cake, 233
Peaches, to skin, 234
Macerated, 47, 48
in syrup, *see* Stewed Fruits, 230
Peanuts, 83
Pears, to stew, 230
Macerated, 47, 48
Peas, green, 150
split, *see* Pulses, 86
'sugar', 150
Pepper, 85
Peppercorns, black, 85
white, 86
Peppermint, *see* Mint, 77
Peppers, sweet, 150
Petits Fours, general information, 257
Genoese pastry required for, 255
Pheasant, general information, 215
season for, 199
Pickling onions, 148
Pie, Chicken, 204
Fruit, 234
Fruit plate, 235
uncooked, to freeze, 235
funnel, 12
Raised, 218
Pigeon, 215, *see also* Squab, 220
Pilaff, 154
Pilgrim shell, *see* Scallop, Shellfish chart, 166
Pimientos, *see* Peppers, sweet, 150
Pinch – of salt etc., 53
Pineapple, Macerated, 47, 48
Piperade, 112
Piping, to acquire skill, 53
bags, 2
bags to fill, 53
Pistachio nuts, 83
Plaice, 175
Plums, Macerated, 47, 48
Poaching, 53
Point – of garlic or cayenne, 53
Polonaise (à la), 51
Polythene bags, 2
Poppadoms, to cook, 274
Poppy seed, 86
Pork, *see also* Meat, 193–195
general information, 193
to carve, 35
all the cuts of, 194
to roast, 193
Porridge oats, 86
Pot-roasting, *see* Roasting, 55
Potato flour, 86
mashers, 19
peeler, 19
Potatoes, 151–154
general information, 151
deep fried, general information, 151
to store, 153
Anna, 152
Chips, to cut, *see* Slicing and dicing, 57
to prepare and fry, 151
Croquettes, 152
Dauphine, 152
Duchess, 152
Dunkirk, 152
Game Chips, 152
Jacket, 152
Knots, 153
New, 153
Pont Neuf, 183
Puffs, 153
Ribbons, 153
Roast, 153
Salad, 162
Sauté , 153
Potted Meat, 216
Poularde, definition of, 206
Poultry and Game, *see* Game. *See also* individual kinds of each, 198–222
Poussins, 205
Prawns, general information, 175
in Aspic, 120
Cocktail, 120
Dublin Bay, *see* Shellfish chart, 166
Provençale (à la), 51
Proving a bread dough, 53
a girdle or omelet pan, 53
Prunes, origin of, 71
Ptarmigan, season for, 199
Puddings and Sweets, *see also* under individual names, 223–238
Bread and Butter, 225
Castle, *see* Sponge, 235
Chocolate Cornflour (Blancmange), 233
Christmas, 225
Eve's, *see* Sponge, 235
Milk, general information, 233
Queen of, meringue topping for, 233
Rice, 233, 234
Sponge, various flavours, 235
Upside Down, 236
West Riding, 236
Yorkshire, 237
Pulses, 86
Purées, to make quickly, 53
Fruit, to freeze, *see* 'Creams', 226
choice of sugar for, *see* Icing sugar, 92
Quenelles, *see* Choux pastry, 101
Quince, to stew, 230
Rabbit, general information, 217
to joint, 217
to skin, *see* Hare, 213
Radishes, 163
roses, 163
Ragoût, 51
Raised Pie, 218
Raising agents, list of, 53
Raisins, 71
Ramekins, *see* Cocotte, 6
Raspberry Butter, 241, 242
Fool, 228
purée, to freeze, *see* 'Creams', 226
Raspberries, Macerated, 47, 48
in syrup, 230
Raspings, 86

Ratafia, 86
Ratatouille, 121
Rechauffés, 54
Recipes, on filing cards, 19
  magazine etc., 20
Reducing – liquids, 54
Refreshing – why, when and how, 54
Refrigerator, special advantages of, 20
  how to store foods in, 20, 21
Rendered fat, 54
Rennet, general information, 86
  see also Junket, 231
Rhubarb, general information, 154
  to stew, 230
Ribbon, to the 54
Rice, general information, 87
  brown, general information, 87
    to boil, 154
  Italian, 87
  long grain (Patna type), general information, 87
    to boil, 154
    to freeze, 154
    to serve in Persian way, 154
    Uncle Ben's type, 87
  short grain, general information, 87
Rice flour, 87
  ground, *see* Rice flour, 87
  paper, 87
  Pudding, 233, 234
    cold, to eat up, 234
  Salad, 163
Risotto, 154
Rissoles, Chicken, 204
Roasting, general information, 54
  a bird, general information. *See also* individual birds, 199
  a joint, general information, *see also* beef, lamb etc., 180
Roasting bags, *see* Roasting, 55
Roebuck and Roedeer, seasons for, 199
Roes, fish, 175
Roll mops, *see* Herring, Soused, 172
Rolling pastry, technique, 55
  and folding, technique, 99
  pin, 21
Rolls, to reheat from freezer, 248
  Bridge, 246
  Dinner, 246
Rosemary, *see* Lamb, 187
Rotisserie, 21
Roux, general information, 55
  white, blond and brown, 55
Rubbing – fat into flour, 99
Rum, for cooking, 87
  Butter, 241, 242
Sabayon, 235
  Sauce, 242
Saffron, 88
Sago, 88
Saint Germain, 51
Salads & components, *see also under* individual names, 157–164
  general information, 157
  Beetroot, 158
  Cauliflower, 158
  Cucumber, 159
  Fish, 175
  Fruit, 160
  Green, 161
  Lettuce, 161
  Mixed (Salades Composées), 162
  Mushroom, 162
  Niçoise, 162
  Orange, 162
  Potato, 162
  Rice, 163
  Summer, 163
  Tomato, 163
Salad basket, 4
  dressings, *see* Dressings
  plants, refrigeration of, 21
Salami, 195
Salmi of Game, general information, also recipe, 218
Salmon, 176
  smoked, *see* Smoked fish, 177
  tinned, pink and red, 176
Salmonella poisoning, to avoid, 180, 199
Salpicon, 56
Salt, general information, 88
    origin of word, 88
    with boiling vegetables, 88
    in a bread dough, 243
    in many cakes, 250
  cooking, 88
  rock, 88
  sea, 88
  table, 88
Sandwiches, origin of name, 248
  to make well, 248
  to serve – or freeze, 248
Sardines, 176
Sauces, Dessert, 239–242
  general information, 239
  Chocolate (cold), 239
  Cream, slightly sour, 239
    whipped, as accompaniment, 239
  Crème Anglaise, 240
    Chantilly, 240
  Custard, Egg (Boiled), 240
    using custard powder, 241
  Fruit, 241
    Syrups, 241
  Hard (flavoured butters), 241, 242
  Jam, 242
  Sabayon, 242
  White, Sweet, 242
Sauces, Savoury, 129–139
  General information, 129
    to correct consistency of, 129
    ways of giving flavour to, 129
    functions of, 129
    lumpy, to correct, 129
    skin on top of, 129
  Family Tree of, 132, 133
  Aïoli, Family tree, 133
  Allemande, Family tree, 132
  Anchovy (two bases), Family tree, 132, 133
    Butter, *see* Savoury butters, 131

Family tree, 133
Andalouse, Family tree, 133
Apple, 130
Aurore (three bases), Family tree, 132, 133
Béarnaise, Family tree, 133
Béchamel, to make, 138
Family tree, 132
Bercy (two bases), Family tree, 132
Bercy Butter, *see* Savoury butters, 131, 133
Beurre Blanc, Family tree, 133
au Citron, Family tree, 133
Noir or Noisette, general information, 134, Family tree, 133
Bigarade, Family tree, 132
Bourgignonne, Family tree, 132
Bread, 130
Brown, general information, 130
Family tree, 132
Butter, hot, general information, 134
Family tree, 133
Butters, Savoury, general information, 131, 134
Family tree, 133
Caper, Family tree, 132
Cardinal (two bases), Family tree, 132, 133
Chantilly, Family tree, 133
Chasseur, Family tree, 132
Chaud-froid (two bases), Family tree, 132
Choron, Family tree, 133
Colbert, Family tree, 133
Colbert Butter, Family tree, 133
see also Savoury butters, 131
Collioure, Family tree, 133
Cream Dressing, to make, 160
Family tree, 133
Crème, Family tree, 132
Curry (two bases), Family tree, 132, 133
Deglazing, Brown, to make, 134
Diable, Family tree, 132
Duxelles, Family tree, 132
Egg, Family tree, 132
Egg yolk Butter, Family tree, 133
see also Savoury butters, 131
Egg yolk *and* butter, list of, Family tree, 133
Egg yolk and oil, list of, Family tree, 133
Fennel, Family tree, 132
Fines Herbes, Family tree, 133
French Dressing, to make, 160
Family tree, 133
Garlic Butter, *see* Savoury butters, 131
Family tree, 133
Gravy, general information 134
Herb Butter, *see* Savoury butters, 131
Family tree, 133
Hollandaise, general information, 135
curdled, to rectify, 136
left over, 136
made by hand, 135
made in liquidizer, 135
see also Family tree, 133
Hongroise, Family tree, 132
Horseradish Butter, Family tree, 133
see also Savoury butters, 131
Indienne, Family tree, 133
Italienne, Family tree, 132
Lyonnaise, Family tree, 132
Madeira, Family tree, 132
Maître d'hôtel Butter, Family tree, 133
see also Savoury butters, 131
Maltaise, Family tree, 133
Marchand de vins Butter, Family tree, 133
see also Savoury butters, 131
Marseillaise, Family tree, 133
Mayonnaise, general information, 136
curdled, to rectify, 136
made by hand, 137
made in liquidizer, 137
oil and vinegar for, 136
see also Family tree, 133
Mayonnaise, Curry, to make, 137
Mint, general information, 137
Family tree, 133
Mornay, Family tree, 132
Mousseline, Family tree, 133
Mustard (two bases), Family tree, 132, 133
Mustard Butter, *see* Savoury butters, 131
Family tree, 133
Normande, Family tree, 132
Oil and vinegar, general information, 160
Family tree, 133
Orange, Family tree, 132
Paloise, Family tree, 133
Paprika Butter, Family tree, 133
see also Savoury butters, 131
Parisienne, Family tree, 132
Piquant, Family tree, 132
Poivrade, Family tree, 132
Poulette (two bases), Family tree, 132
Ravigote (three bases), Family tree, 132, 133
Remoulade, Family tree, 133
Robert, Family tree, 132
Shallot Butter, *see* Savoury butters, 131
Family tree, 133
Shellfish Butter, *see* Savoury Butters, 131
Family tree, 133
Soubise, Family tree, 132
Suprême, Family tree, 132
Tarragon (three bases), Family tree, 132
Tarragon Butter, Family tree, 133
see also Savoury butters, 131
ingredients for, 78
Tartare, Family tree, 133
Tomato Butter, *see* Savoury butters, 131
Family tree, 133
Velouté, to make, 139
see also Family tree, 132
Venison, Family tree, 132
Verte, Family tree, 133
Vin blanc (two bases), Family tree, 132, 133
Vinaigrette, *see* French Dressing, 160
White (basic), to make, 138
see also Family tree, 132
Sausages, general information, 195
beef & pork, meat content of, 195
Bierwurst, 195
black pudding, 195
chipolata, origin of name, 195
Frankfurters, 195
French garlic, 195
liver, 195
salami, 195

Sauté, 56
Savory, 78
Savoury, purpose of a, 56
Savoury Pudding, to serve with meat, 196
Scalding, 56
Scales, general information, 22
coins used as weights for, 22
Scallop, general information, 176
alternative names of, 166
roe of, 175
Scampi, general information, 176
origin of name – and alternatives, 166
Scissors, 22
Scones, general information, 243
to reheat from freezer, 248
Cheese, 249
Drop, recipe and tips, 248
Fruit, 249
Ginger, 249
Girdle, 249
Oven, common causes of disappointment, 249
quantities for, 249
Spice, 249
Syrup, 249
Wholemeal, 249
Score (fish), how and why, 44, 167
Scraping food off chopping board, 56
Searing, 57
Seasoning, 57
Semolina, 88
Shallots, 148
Shellfish, 166
Shish, *see* Skewers, 23
Shivering, 57
Shortbread, 258
Shrimps, general information, 176
Potted, 121
Sieves, 22
Simmering, 57
Sink, kitchen, extra uses for, 23
Skate, 177
Skewers, uses for, 23
brochette, 23
shish, 23
Skin forming on top of sauces, cause of and to prevent, 129, 241
Slaking, 57
Slicing and dicing, technique, 57
Smoke point, of fats, 58
Smokies, 171
Snipe, general information, 219
season for, 199
Sole Colbert, 177
Sole, Dover and lemon, 177
slip, 177
Soubise, definition of, *see also* Family Tree, 51
Soufflé, origin of word, 58
dishes, 9
Soufflés, Savoury, general information, 113
baked, 113
steamed, 114
Dessert, cold, 235
Soups, 123–128
general information, 123–125
croûtons for, 126
ways of giving flavour to, 123
tips about making, 124
Artichoke, 125
Asparagus, 125
Beetroot, 126
Bisque, 126
Borscht, *see* Beetroot soup, 126
Bouillabaisse, 126
Cauliflower, 126
Chowder, 126
Cockie Leekie, 126
Consommé, 126
cream, general information, 125
Fish, 127
Garlic, 127
Gazpacho, 127
Lentil, 127
Minestrone, 127
Mulligatawny, 127
Mushroom, 128
Onion, French, 128
Pea, 128
Potato, 128
purée, basic recipe and tips, 124
Vichyssoise, recipe for, 128
Watercress, 128
Soya beans, 88
oil, 84
Spaghetti, to cook (*see also* Pasta), 149
Spanish onions, 148
Spatula, flexible metal, 23
plastic or rubber, 23
wooden, 23
Spices, general information, 89
Spice Butter, 241, 242
Spike Murphy, 23
Spinach, 155
Spirits, for cooking 96
Spit roaster, *see* Rôtisserie, 21
Spoonfuls – of dry ingredients, to measure, 58
liquids, to measure, 58
Spoons, kitchen, as used in this book, 24
measuring, sets of, 24
table, uses for, 24
Sprats, fresh and smoked, 177
how smoked, *see* Smoked fish, 177
Spring chicken, 205
greens, *see* Cabbage, 145
onions, 163
Squab, general information, 220
fattening of, *see* Pigeon, 216
Steak, *see* Beef, cuts of, 184
Steaks, entrecôte and entrecôte minute, 184
fillet and sirloin, 184
Steamer, 24
Steaming, 58
Stewing, 58
Stews, thickened brown, 196
Stock, general information, 89
brown, 89
cubes, 90
fish, 89
goose, 212
white, 90
Stock syrup, 275

Storage jars, 25
Strainers, 25
Strawberries, in syrup, *see* Stewed Fruits, 230
  Macerated, 47, 48
Strawberry butter, 241, 242
  Fool, 228
  purée, to freeze, *see* 'Creams', 226
Stuffings, *see* Farce, 38
Suet, 90
Sugar, 90–93
  general information
    to colour, 267
    to freeze soft fruits in, *see* pt. 6, 91
    hints for using, 93
    history of, 90
    lumpy brown, 92
    qualities and uses of, 90
    in tea, 272
  caster, 92
  Cinnamon, to make, 93
  coffee crystals, 92
  cube, 92
  demerara, 91
    London, 91
  granulated, 92
  icing, 92
  loaf, brown, 92
  moist – or soft, 91
    in marmalade, 91
    a substitute for, 91
  preserving, 93
  Vanilla, to make, 93
Sultanas, 71
Sunflower oil, 84
Suprême, 51
Sweating, 59
Swede, 155
Sweet corn, 155
Sweetbreads, 192
Sweets & Puddings, *see under* individual names, also under Puddings, 223–238
  general information, 223
Swiss Roll, 258
  Chocolate, 258
Syllabub, to make, 236
Syrup, Fruit (as glaze), 241
  golden, 93
  stock, 275
  sugar, to freeze soft fruits in, *see* pt.6, 91
    to make, 275
    for stewed fruit, 275
Tabasco Sauce, 94
Table d'hôte, 49
Tablespoons, uses in cookery, 24
Talmouse, 59
Tannin, *see also* Tea-cosy page 272, 271
Tapioca, 94
Taramasalata, to stuff tomatoes, 122
  roe for, 175
Tarragon, *see* Herbs
Tart, definition of, 236
Tartlets, Cherry, 259
  Jam, 259
Tasting, 59
Tea, general information, 270
    blending your own, 272
    choice of, *see* chart, 270, 271
    hints about making, 272
    history of, 270
    how long to infuse, *see* Brewing, 272
    how to serve, *see* chart, 271
  Assam, 270, 271
  China, *see also* chart, 271
  Darjeeling, 270, 271
  Earl Grey, 270, 272
  'green', definition of, 271
  Iced, 271, 272
  Indian, 270
  Keemun, 270, 271
  Lapsang Souchong, 270, 271
Tea-bags, 272
  caddies, 270
  cosy, disadvantage of, 272
Teapot, choice and care of, 272
Teal, general information, 209
  season for, 199
Temperatures, for deep fat frying, 42
  oven, general information, *see* Baking, 30
    comparing gas and electricity, 52
Tenderloin, definition of, 196
  of pork, 194
Terms and techniques, 30–61
Terrine, *see* Pâté, 119
  choice of dish, 25
Thermometer, meat, 25
  sugar and deep fat, 26
Thyme, 78
Tin opener, 26
Tins, bread, general information, 26
    to grease, *see* pt. 7, 244
  cake, general information, 26
    choice of, 251
    to grease, 79, 251
    to line, 46
  moule à manqué, 26
  roasting, choice of size for game and poultry, 200
  tart, with removable base, 27
  Yorkshire pudding, 27
Toast, Anchovy, 275
  Cinnamon, 275
  Dripping, *see* Duck fat, rendered, 209
  French, 275
  Melba, 275
Toasting – thinly or frozen sliced bread, 59
Tomatoes, general information, 155
    to freeze, 155
    as garnish, 155
    to juice and seed, 155
    miniature, to make from large, 155
    to skin, 155
    to vandyke, 60
  Salad, 163
  Stuffed, 121
Tonic water, refrigeration of, 21
Treacle, 94
Trifle, 236
Tripe, 193
Trout, general information, 177
  Smoked, to serve, 121

Trussing needle, 27
Tubes, icing, 27
  meringue, 28
Tuiles, 259
Turbot, 178
  chicken, 178
Turkey, general information, 220
  to bone, 201
  breasts or joints, 221
  cold roast, to use up, 221
    to freeze 221
  to draw, 200
  to roast, 220
  to truss, 201
Turnips, 156
Tweezers, uses for in cookery, 28
Unmoulding – creams and jellies etc., 59
Vandyking, general information, 59
  apples, 60
  grapefruit, 59
  tomatoes, 60
Vanilla essence, 94
  pods, 94
  Slices, 259
  Sugar, to make, 93
Variety meats, *see* Offal
Veal, *see also* Meat, 197
  general information
    to carve, 35
    some cuts of, 197
  Blanquette of, *see* Blanquette of Chicken, 204
Vegetable fats, 94
  Marrow, 147
  mill, 16
Vegetables, *see also* individual names, 140–156
  general information, 140
    to blanch, 31
    to boil, 141
    canned, storage life of, 66
    to freeze, 141, *see also* Blanching and Refreshing, 32(7), 54
    fritters, 142
    frozen, bought, general information, 142
    frozen, to cook, 141
    glazed, 142
    purées, 142
    to refresh, 54
    refrigeration of prepared 'green', 21
    roast, 142
    sautéd, 141
    seven groups of, table, 142
    to sweat, 59
Velouté Sauce, to make, *see* Family Tree, 139
Venison, general information, 221
  to carve, 35
  seasons for deer, 199
Vichyssoise, recipe for, 128
Vinegar, general information, 94
  for mayonnaise, 136
  for oil and vinegar dressings, 160
  Garlic, to make, 95
  Herb, to make, 95
  malt, 95
    distilled, 95
  wine, red and white, 95
Vol-au-vent, Chicken, 205
Water, present in foods, 95
  ice-cold, for pastry and batters, 96
  salt, boiling temperature of, 96
Watercress, for garnish or salad, 164
Weights, substitute for, 22
Whisking – egg whites, 60
Whisks, general information, 28
  balloon, 28
  coil-rim, Sky-line, 28
  electric, fixed, 28
    hand, 28
  magic spoon, 28
  rotary, 29
  whipper (or batter whip), 29
  wire, 29
Whitebait, 122
Whiting, 178
Widgeon, general information, 209
  season for, 199
Wildfowl, seasons for, 199
Wines, for cooking, 96
  fortified, for cooking, 96
  home-made, for cooking, 96
  Parsley, quantities for, 96
Winter greens, 156
Yarmouth Straws, 173
Yeast, dried active, to store and use, 97
  fresh, general information, 96
    to incorporate in a dough, 97
    to freeze, 96
    proportions of, to flour, 97
    to test if fresh, 96
Yoghourt, chief causes of failure, 236
  to make, 237
  uses of in cooking, 97
Yorkshire Pudding, 237
  left-over, to use up, 237
Zabaglione, 237
Zest, 61
Zester, 29
Zipp bean slicer, 4
Zucchini, 156